THE MEDIA TRILOGY

Robert Harris was born in 1957. After graduating from Cambridge University he joined the BBC in 1978, working as a reporter on *Newsnight* and *Panorama*. In 1987 he became Political Editor of the *Observer*, moving to the *Sunday Times* two years later as a columnist.

He is the author of six books. *Selling Hitler*, which is included in this volume, was made into a television serial for ITV in 1991. His first novel, *Fatherland*, published in 1992, was translated into twenty-three languages and has sold 3 million copies.

by the same author

THE MAKING OF NEIL KINNOCK
A HIGHER FORM OF KILLING
(*with Jeremy Paxman*)

THE MEDIA TRILOGY

Robert Harris

faber and faber

LONDON · BOSTON

First published in this edition in 1994
by Faber and Faber Limited
3 Queen Square London WC1N 3AU

Gotcha! first published in 1983
© Robert Harris, 1983
Selling Hitler first published in 1986
© Robert Harris, 1986
Good and Faithful Servant first published in 1990
© Robert Harris, 1990, 1991

Photoset in Sabon by Parker Typesetting Service, Leicester
Printed in England by Clays Ltd, St Ives plc

A CIP record for this book is
available from the British Library

ISBN 0-571-17231-8

2 4 6 8 10 9 7 5 3 1

CONTENTS

INTRODUCTION

The three books contained in this volume were published over a period of almost eight years, from 1983 to 1990, and I should confess at once that at no point during their composition did I dream I was writing a 'media trilogy'. The word *trilogy* suggests a rather grand conception, demanding, at the very least, a degree of prior intention on the part of the author. A novelist or a playwright embarking on a cycle of three works would surely attempt to link them in some way. Characters would recur. Common themes would be expounded. There would be a unity of treatment and style.

No such long-term scheme was in my mind when I sat down to write about the media's coverage of the Falklands War. And *Selling Hitler*, published four years after *Gotcha!*, had no connection with its predecessor whatsoever (unless you count the fact that Gerd Heidemann spent his honeymoon in Argentina, looking for Martin Bormann). Four years after *Selling Hitler*, *Good and Faithful Servant* took me off in yet another different direction. True, Bernard Ingham had also appeared in *Gotcha!*, but even the most rabid conspiracy theorist has never detected his hand behind the Hitler diaries. The three books which follow are therefore self-contained and separate. They are not even about the same subjects. One is about a war, one a fraud, and the third is a biography. In a bookshop you might find them classified under 'Military', 'True Crime' and 'Politics'.

And yet, and yet . . . Curiously enough, despite the lack of a long-term plan on my part, and for all the obvious differences, these books do now seem to hang together as well as separately. If unity of treatment and style and the recurrence of theme and character really are the criteria that define a trilogy – well, somehow I seem to have written one by accident.

First and foremost, all three books tell stories. They follow a cast of characters – or, in the case of the Ingham biography, a single character – through a series of adventures. Their structures are chronological. They contain (I hope) jokes. They were written (as opposed to researched) at speed – *Gotcha!* in four weeks, *Selling Hitler* in twelve and *Good and Faithful Servant* in ten. Each subject was chosen because it interested me, because I had some slight involvement in it to begin with, and because I wanted to find out more about it.

I can remember to the day, almost to the hour, the moment at which each book was born. In the case of *Gotcha!* it was the morning of Friday 7 May 1982 when I walked into my office and saw the *Sun*'s editorial 'Dare Call It Treason' lumping the BBC, the *Guardian* and the *Daily Mirror* together as 'traitors in our midst'. At the time I worked for the BBC. This was at the end of a week which had seen the same paper print its notorious 'Gotcha!' headline and Margaret Thatcher denounce my colleagues for not 'fully and effectively' putting over the British 'case'. Reading the *Sun*'s ineffable prose ('a British citizen is either on his country's side – or he is its enemy'), it suddenly struck me that this was one of those rare, defining moments, when the world around you suddenly snaps into sharper focus. I had never as a reader seen anything like the tabloid coverage of that war, nor experienced as a journalist such overt official bullying, nor felt as a 'British citizen' so ill-informed about what was happening. By the end of the day I had drawn up an outline for *Gotcha!*, complete with the title, from which I barely deviated when I came to write the book a few weeks later.

The initial impetus for *Selling Hitler* came shortly before

Christmas that same year, when I met the ultra-right-wing historian David Irving at a party. He was holding a glass of beer (German, appropriately enough) and crying into it that he had just wasted several days in Munich chasing so-called 'Hitler diaries' that had turned out to be forgeries. When, four months later, on 23 April 1983, *The Times* announced that Rupert Murdoch had bought the serial rights in exactly such documents ('Hitler's secret diaries to be published') I knew – *knew* – that this was going to turn into one of the funniest media stories for years.

Good and Faithful Servant was conceived over a longer timescale. I had first interviewed Bernard Ingham in 1982 while writing *Gotcha!*. In 1987 I became the *Observer*'s lobby correspondent and was able to watch him in action at first hand. By then he had achieved a quite legendary status in Whitehall. Cabinet ministers lived in fear of him. He had come to epitomize Margaret Thatcher's style of government. I toyed with the idea of writing about this phenomenon, but couldn't come up with a suitable form. Then, on 24 July 1989, he briefed the media to devastating effect about the 'meaningless' title of Deputy Prime Minister bestowed upon Sir Geoffrey Howe. As with the *Sun* editorial seven years before, this one event seemed to crystallize all my vague ideas. If Ingham was so powerful that even Deputy Prime Ministers were but chaff beneath his flail, why not treat him as such? Why not subject him to the sort of instant biography usually reserved for party leaders?

The genesis of each of these three books, then, lay in a headline. That is appropriate, for each of them is about my profession, journalism. They are concerned, overwhelmingly, with reporters – war reporters, investigative reporters, political reporters, local reporters – and the people who try to control them: proprietors and editors and press officers. The individuals and their nationalities may change from book to book but the species remains the same, be the specimens under examination British, German or American.

The careful reader will find that each of these books contains a quotation from Evelyn Waugh's *Scoop*. These were small and conscious acts of homage on my part, a recognition that Waugh had captured the essence of modern journalism as long ago as 1938 with a satirical precision never bettered. Journalists (and I include myself here) are intrinsically comic figures, none more so than those who are most jealous of their status: war correspondents (*Gotcha!*), investigative reporters (*Selling Hitler*) and lobby editors (*Good and Faithful Servant*). All three books are about the business of reporting, and the *Scoop*-like antics and absurdities it entails – talking your way on to a battleship and sponsoring a missile, hiding behind a bale of wool to escape being thrown out of a war zone, collecting suitcases full of cash to buy secret diaries, attempting to strangle a more successful rival, hunting for elderly Nazis in the jungles of Brazil, trudging round the rain-sodden villages of Yorkshire reporting on whist drives and talking dogs, climbing the back stairs of Westminster to attend Lobby briefings that don't officially exist.

And herein lies the common theme that binds these books together: how, in the process of being gathered and transmitted, information is fought over, distorted, buried, managed, mangled, stamped on, twisted, spun, slanted, fabricated and forged. This does not happen all the time, or even most of the time, but usually when the stakes are high you can detect a whiff of it: during a war, at election time, when big money is involved. These books are about what happens in that gap between the occurrence of the event and the appearance of the headline, between what journalism claims to be about and what it often is.

* * *

When I wrote *Gotcha!* my television set had three channels; now it has thirty-nine. Much of the news and current affairs coverage of the BBC was at the time shot on film; reporters had to wait around while it was processed. There was no cable television in the UK, no satellite channels. Nobody had ever heard of CNN. There were no cellular phones (or if there were, I had never seen one), few laptop computers (*Gotcha!* had to be written on a typewriter) and no handy video cameras. The Falklands War may have happened a mere twelve years ago, but in terms of the media technology then available it happened in a different world.

It is not only technology that has changed. So have the relative power and scale of the world's media. Imagine any government now daring to exclude reporters or to slow up transmission of pictures. Our expectations have changed. The 'Desert Storm' operation against Iraq in 1991 pointed the way to how our wars will be fought in future: on television, as round-the-clock, round-the-world entertainment.

In the original introduction to *Gotcha!* I made a rather sweeping claim. My book, I said, was about 'the power of information and the struggle to control it': a fight whose implications might yet 'prove more important than those of the real war in whose shadow it was fought'. For this piece of authorial conceit I was roundly attacked by one of the journalists who had sailed with the Task Force. But twelve years later I think I was right. The Falklands adventure did not change much in terms of warfare or diplomacy, let alone reverse Britain's long-term decline as a world power, but it did signal the start of a new phase in the evolution of the media.

In 1982 'media studies' was still a fairly rare option in higher education. Now, you cannot move for media courses, media professors, media centres, media analysts, media books, media pages. Rupert Murdoch's media empire alone now claims to touch 'more than two-thirds of the planet' and it is predicted that the media generally, by the end of the century, will be equivalent in value to one-sixth of the entire world economy. In *Selling Hitler* I wrote of Murdoch:

> The Hitler diaries deal was exactly what he was looking for: he would publish the book, serialize it in three continents ... he might even make the movie which he could eventually show on Channel Ten, his television station in Sydney. The Hitler diaries potentially were a model for the internationally integrated media package.

To this list, one could now add far more. Murdoch has since launched or acquired Sky television, a national American TV network and the film studios of Twentieth Century-Fox. 'We are in the entertainment business,' was his famous comment on the Hitler diaries fiasco. The US entertainment business is now, globally, a bigger dollar-earner than the American automobile industry.

I could have tried to bring the texts of these three books up to date, to take account of these and other changes. I could have doubled the length of *Gotcha!* by adding details from the score or more of subsequent academic analyses of the media's coverage of the Falklands war. I could have described the latest conspiracy theories about the origins of the Hitler diaries (no more plausible, I might add, than the original set). I could have inserted quotations from Bernard Ingham's self-serving memoirs in which he claims, for example, that he never meant to undermine ministers – he only meant to *help* them ...

But once one starts to tamper with books in this way, they can start to fall to pieces in one's hands. Besides, what is the point in republishing them now if not partly to be able to view the past without hindsight? The whole point about *Gotcha!* is that it is not balanced and academic but passionate and immediate. When *Selling Hitler* was written, Germany was still divided and the Berlin Wall seemed a permanent fixture: facts which were integral to the development of the fraud. Parts of the original edition of *Good and Faithful Servant* were dictated over the telephone to the printers on the morning Margaret Thatcher announced her retirement.

So I have made no revisions. What follows are three books very much of their time, which describe three quite different aspects of the media in the 1980s. They were planned separately but can, I hope, be read together. They may be approached in any order. They form, albeit by accident and somewhat to their author's surprise, a media trilogy.

Robert Harris
Kintbury, March 1994

GOTCHA!

*The Media, the Government
and the Falklands Crisis*

CONTENTS

ACKNOWLEDGEMENTS

I would like to record my thanks to Douglas Millar, Clerk to the House of Commons Defence Committee; Kenneth Derbyshire, Director of the Audit Bureau of Circulations; the Institute of Practitioners in Advertising (for permission to quote from the National Readership Survey); Simon Jenkins of the *Economist*; Pat Kavanagh of A. D. Peters. Laurence Rees gave me great help and support. Willa Hancock showed me loyalty and kindness above and beyond the call of duty.

I would also like to thank Christopher Capron for granting me permission to start writing this book; and my editor, David Lloyd, who was generous in giving me the leave which enabled me to complete it.

My greatest debt is to those, both in government and in the media, who talked to me about their roles in the crisis. Most asked me not to name them. I respect their wishes and give them my thanks.

R.H.
December 1982

DRAMATIS PERSONAE

ON BOARD *INVINCIBLE*

Alfred McIlroy	Reporter, *Daily Telegraph*
Gareth Parry	Reporter, *Guardian*
Michael Seamark	Reporter, *Daily Star*
Tony Snow	Reporter, *Sun*
John Witherow	Reporter, *The Times*
Roger Goodwin	Ministry of Defence Press Officer

ON BOARD *HERMES*

Brian Hanrahan	Reporter, BBC Television
Michael Nicholson	Reporter, ITN
Bernard Hesketh	BBC cameraman
John Jockell	BBC sound recordist
Peter Heaps	ITN engineer
Peter Archer	Reporter, Press Association (later replaced by Richard Savill)
Martin Cleaver	Photographer, Press Association
Robin Barratt	Ministry of Defence Press Officer (later replaced by Graham Hammond)

ON BOARD *CANBERRA*

Patrick Bishop	Reporter, *Observer*
Ian Bruce	Reporter, *Glasagow Herald*
Leslie Dowd	Reporter, Reuters

Robert Fox	Reporter, BBC Radio
Max Hastings	Reporter, London *Standard*
Charles Lawrence	Reporter, *Sunday Telegraph*
Martin Lowe	Reporter, Wolverhampton *Express and Star* (later replaced by Derek Hudson of the *Yorkshire Post*)
Robert McGowan	Reporter, *Daily Express* (joined at Ascension Island)
Alastair McQueen	Reporter, *Daily Mirror*
David Norris	Reporter, *Daily Mail* (joined at Ascension Island)
Kim Sabido	Reporter, Independent Radio News
John Shirley	Reporter, *Sunday Times*
Tom Smith	Photographer, *Daily Express* (joined at Ascension Island)
Jeremy Hands	Reporter, ITN
Robin Hammond	ITN cameraman
John Martin	ITN sound recordist
Alan George	Ministry of Defence Press Officer
Martin Helm	Senior Ministry of Defence Press Officer
Alan Percival	Ministry of Defence Press Officer

INTRODUCTION

The *Sun* prints all of its 4 million copies in London and as a result is the first national newspaper in Britain to go to press. On the night of 3 May 1982, with most of its journalists on strike, the paper was produced by its management aided by a handful of non-union staff.

These are the two reasons advanced by the editorial director of Rupert Murdoch's News Group Newspapers to excuse what was probably the most famous headline of the Falklands war: 'Gotcha!', used to describe the sinking of the Argentine cruiser, the *General Belgrano*. 'I agree that headline was a shame,' he says. 'But it wasn't meant in a blood-curdling way. We just felt excited and euphoric. Only when we began to hear reports of how many men had died did we begin to have second thoughts.'

A few minutes after eight o'clock that evening, the first copies began coming off the presses. By the time Kelvin Mac-Kenzie, the paper's editor, had remade the front page, the whole of the first edition – upwards of 1,500,000 copies – was already on its way to the north of England, Scotland and Northern Ireland, bearing witness to the *Sun*'s initial 'excitement and euphoria'. In subsequent editions, a more subdued headline, which the *Sun* apparently believed better in keeping with the sombre news, was used: 'Did 1200 Argies Drown?'

Such was the brief life and abrupt death of a headline which has nevertheless secured its own place in the history of the Falklands war.

'Gotcha!' both epitomized and, as it turned out, marked the

high point of the tide of jingoism whipped up by Fleet Street. The day the headline appeared Britain suffered her first major loss when HMS *Sheffield* was destroyed. The darker side of jingoism is a paranoid tendency to blame defeats on subversion at home. The BBC, the *Daily Mirror* and the *Guardian* were accused of 'treason' by the *Sun*, taking its cue from the Prime Minister, who deplored the BBC's failure to identify itself more closely with 'our boys' on the task force. It was the start of an uncomfortable week for the Corporation, which culminated in its Chairman and present Director-General being howled down by half the Conservative Party in the House of Commons.

A reaction set in. The attack on the broadcasters was followed in the latter half of May and the first half of June by a ferocious counter-attack in which Fleet Street joined, aimed principally at the Ministry of Defence. Six weeks of anger and frustration in London over the lack of information and television pictures were compounded by growing evidence of wholesale bungling by the Ministry of Defence with regard to the task force correspondents. The charge was led by the BBC's Assistant Director-General: 'The miscalculations of the handling of the information war are, I suggest, a better target for back-bench wrath than the BBC,' he wrote on 3 June. A week later the House of Commons Defence Committee obliged by announcing its intention of holding an inquiry into how Whitehall handled the coverage of the conflict.

This book is based on the written and oral evidence collected by the Committee and on interviews with the leading protagonists in the 'information war'. Whereas the Committee confined itself specifically to the record of the Ministry of Defence, I have added two other aspects: the coverage of the war by Fleet Street, particularly the tabloids, and the political row surrounding television output.

What follows is an account of the power of information

and the struggle to control it which took place in April, May and June 1982. The implications of *this* fight may yet prove more important than those of the real war in whose shadow it was fought.

ONE

Pens and Bayonets

The night-duty press office at the Ministry of Defence is a claustrophobic room on the ground floor, furnished with four telephones, a television, a shabby wooden cupboard and a small bed. Its lightly dozing occupant in the early hours of Friday, 2 April, was a public relations officer of many years' standing called Roger Goodwin.

For more than six hours he had been answering calls about a rumoured invasion of the Falkland Islands and telling news agencies and night editors that London had heard nothing. At 2 a.m. the telephone rang again. Pulling on a pair of trousers and still wearing his pyjama jacket, Goodwin made his way to the fifth-floor naval operations room to be briefed by Admiral Sir Henry Leach, the First Sea Lord. Leach, just returned from Downing Street and dressed in a dinner jacket, announced that it now looked certain that an invasion would take place that day. Six hours later, just after 8 a.m. London time, Argentine troops went ashore on the Falklands.

Goodwin and his colleagues in the Ministry press office spent the day that followed in a state of siege. Ten public relations officers manned thirteen telephones and dealt with what one called 'a tidal wave' of inquiries from Britain and abroad.

We could tell what time the world was waking up. The first

wave of calls came from Britain and Europe early in the morning. Then, at lunchtime, Canada and America – first the east coast, then the west. By the end of the day it was Japan, Australia and New Zealand . . .

Almost all were requests for places on board the naval expedition being mobilized in Portsmouth. 'We got requests from people who wanted to sail with the task force from Dallas and San Francisco. I remember one man demanding to go who worked on the *Rocky Mountain News*.' All the requests were added to a central list, which by the time the fleet sailed contained hundreds of names submitted by over 160 separate organizations. According to another press officer, there were 'around twenty requests for accreditation from the BBC alone' – from individual programmes, from the World Service, from the Pebble Mill Studios in Birmingham, 'from some people who said they worked for the unit that made *Sailor* and who wanted to make a documentary about life aboard the task force . . .' Some requests were bizarre, including one from Roddy Llewellyn, the former escort of Princess Margaret.

The Ministry of Defence's problems were made worse by the fact that they had little idea of what was going on. Demands for confirmation of the rumoured invasion could only be met with the blanket statement that there was 'no information available'. Two hundred yards away across Whitehall, the Foreign Office was still undecided about whether or not an invasion had taken place.

In the House of Commons, MPs were clustered round news agency tape machines which were quoting claims from Buenos Aires that Port Stanley had been seized. But at 11 a.m. in the Chamber, the deputy Foreign Secretary, Humphrey Atkins, assured MPs that no invasion had taken place. 'The report on the tapes comes from an Argentine newspaper. We were in touch with the Governor half an hour ago and he said that no landing had taken place at that time.' At 2.30 p.m., the Leader of the House of Commons, Francis Pym, rose to tell MPs once again that the situation was unchanged. It was not to be until six o'clock in the evening, ten hours after the landings on the Falklands, that the Government finally confirmed that the islands had been seized. For anyone seeking information it was a day of frustration and confusion – a foretaste of the chaos that was to come.

It is an axiom of military planning that in time of war the interests of the armed forces and those of the media are fundamentally irreconcilable. The regulations later issued to the task force correspondents put it succinctly: 'The essence of successful warfare is secrecy. The essence of successful journalism is publicity.' Of the three services, the Royal Navy is traditionally the most wary in its dealings with the press. Life on board ship is an enclosed, secretive world. Unlike the Army in Northern Ireland, the Navy has had little experience in handling the modern media. The fact that the Falklands war had to take the form of an 8,000-mile naval operation with a limited land battle at the end of it meant that from the media's point of view, there were bound to be problems from the outset.

Preparations to send a task force to liberate the islands in the event of an invasion had begun on Wednesday, 31 March, supervised by Sir Henry Leach in consultation with the Fleet's Commander-in-Chief, Sir John Fieldhouse. Significantly, the more politically attuned Chief of the Defence Staff, Admiral Sir Terence Lewin, was at that time in New Zealand. On Friday morning, an hour after the invasion, when the Ministry of Defence asked how many journalists would be allowed to sail with the task force, the answer which came back from Fleet Headquarters at Northwood was: none. When the

Ministry insisted that to exclude the press totally was unthinkable, the figure was grudgingly changed to six, and then increased to ten, including a television team. The Navy's attitude was summed up by Leach, who wanted to know whether he was expected to load his ships with 'pens or bayonets'.

The man in charge of dealing with the media in the Ministry of Defence at this time was not a PR specialist but a career civil servant. Ian McDonald was later to achieve fleeting international stardom as the Ministry's official spokesman, but his natural habitat is Whitehall's undergrowth of committees and non-attributable briefings, hidden from view. McDonald was completing an attachment as Deputy Chief of Public Relations; previously he had been concerned with the Ministry's recruitment and salaries. When the Falklands were invaded, McDonald was acting head of the department. Not until 13 April did the new Chief, Neville Taylor, arrive, and the gulf in responsibility and personality between the two men was to become an important element in the Ministry's handling of press relations during the war.

McDonald's initial plan – one which would, in retrospect, have avoided many of the major problems which were to follow – was to have the correspondents fly out to Ascension Island and join the task force there, midway through its voyage to the South Atlantic. This would have given the media and the armed forces two precious weeks in which to organize and to reach agreement as to how any military action should be reported. But again, the Navy proved uncooperative.

Despite the fact that reporters could have been landed in total darkness and escorted off the island immediately, despite the fact that the Navy would have had total control over communications, there was, said one MoD man, 'a total, total ban on any movement into Ascension' on the part of the press. Sir John Fieldhouse explained later:

What I was concerned about was that people should get out of the aircraft and see that there was no air defence at Ascension. There were no missiles protecting that airfield at that time. There was no reason why a frogman could not have got out of a rubber boat on the coast and walked straight in amongst all these aircraft and planted demolition charges without any difficulty at all, such was the enormous activity around.

With this option ruled out, there was no alternative but to get the correspondents on board before the fleet sailed – and by Sunday morning, after a weekend spent arguing with the Navy, McDonald had less than twenty-four hours left.

'Had anyone deliberately set out to confuse the issue,' Brian Hitchen, the London editor of the *Daily Star*, later wrote, 'they could hardly have been expected to do a better job than the Press Office at the Ministry of Defence on 4 April 1982.' To the *Guardian*, the arrangements for the accreditation of correspondents to the task force were 'rushed and confused'; to the *News of the World* 'complete chaos'; to *The Times* 'peremptory and short-sighted'; to Max Hastings of the London *Standard* 'dogged from the outset by the resolute opposition of some parties in the Royal Navy and the Ministry of Defence to taking correspondents to the South Atlantic at all'.

McDonald convened a meeting at the Reform Club in Pall Mall, of which he is a member, attended by the editors of BBC Television News and ITN, and by an assortment of technical experts. It was agreed that the two organizations would each be allowed to send one correspondent; that they would share the same cameraman and sound recordist; and that an engineer would sail with the fleet to test the possibilities of transmitting pictures back to London. With television taking up five places, this left a further five to be divided up among the press.

The Director of the Newspaper Publishers' Association (NPA), John Le Page, was just settling down to Sunday lunch at his home in Essex when the telephone rang.

> I thought it was probably someone ringing to tell me about some industrial dispute, but it turned out to be a press officer from the Ministry of Defence telling me that the task force was going to sail early the next day and it was essential that any correspondents wanting to sail with it arrived at Portsmouth by midnight that evening. They wanted the NPA to nominate the names of who was to go. In order to arrange accreditation the Ministry said they would have to receive the names within the next four hours.

Abandoning his lunch, Le Page spent the next ninety minutes telephoning almost every newspaper in Fleet Street: all insisted that their correspondents should be allowed to go. 'The only thing I could do was put all the names in a hat and let my wife draw the winners. It sounds incredible, but what else could I do?' Mrs Le Page picked the *Daily Mirror*, the *Daily Express*, the *Daily Telegraph* and the *Daily Mail*. Le Page had already agreed with the Ministry of Defence that the fifth place should go to the Press Association.

This was the beginning of what Le Page describes as 'hell: the worst day I've ever had'. With the lines almost constantly engaged, it took him almost an hour to get through to the Ministry of Defence and give them the result. Once it became known among the remaining four national daily and eight national Sunday newspapers that they were to be given no facilities aboard the task force, Le Page's telephone began ringing, and for the remainder of the day he fielded calls from company chairmen, managing directors and editors.

The disappointed newspapers launched a violent lobby to get their own reporters accredited to the task force. Sir Frank Cooper, the Permanent Under-Secretary at the Ministry of

Defence, was rung up at home by, among others, the news editor of the *News of the World*. 'We stressed that we wanted to go and were promised that someone would call the news editor back at home. He received no calls ... He found the MoD unhelpful and, we suspect, obstructive.' Pressure was brought to bear upon the Defence Secretary, John Nott; the Scottish newspapers – totally excluded, along with the foreign and provincial press, from the NPA draw – lobbied the Secretary of State for Scotland. As one senior MoD official put it: 'Whoever had strings to pull was pulling them.'

The decisive intervention came from 10 Downing Street. Bernard Ingham, the chief press secretary to the Prime Minister, had already spent most of Friday and Saturday nights talking to editors. On Sunday, the whole weight of the press's disappointment and frustration was brought to bear on Downing Street. The *Daily Star* was one of a number of papers which wrote directly to the Prime Minister:

> I believe you will be horrified to learn that the *Daily Star* and three other national daily newspapers, *The Times*, the *Guardian* and the *Sun*, have been excluded from sailing with the naval Task Force on the ludicrous grounds that there is not enough room aboard the ships.
>
> Please help us to be there when Britain's pride is restored by the armed might which you promised the nation.
>
> Only you can give the order to have the name of our writer, Michael Seamark, included on the Ministry of Defence sailing list of accredited correspondents which is being closed tonight.

It has now entered the mythology of Fleet Street that, in the words of the *Star*, 'had it not been for the direct intervention of the Prime Minister ... half the British Press would have been waving the Task Force goodbye from the quayside.' In fact, Bernard Ingham intercepted all letters and messages before they reached Mrs Thatcher, who was preoccupied with other matters, and without consulting her he instructed the Ministry of Defence to ensure not only that more reporters went but also that they comprised a more representative group. The mere flourishing of Mrs Thatcher's name was enough. The Royal Navy gave in.

There were now approximately six hours left before midnight, the deadline by which correspondents had to report to Portsmouth, and reporters had already begun converging on the naval base.

'I was told', recalls the BBC's Brian Hanrahan, 'about one o'clock on Sunday to be down in Portsmouth by eight o'clock that night.' Michael Nicholson of ITN was on a walking holiday in the Lake District when his office caught up with him at 2 p.m. on Sunday afternoon and told him to go straight to Carlisle, where a light aircraft was waiting to fly him south; he was in Portsmouth by 7 p.m. Tony Snow was told that evening by his paper, the *Sun*, 'that I should "head towards Portsmouth" and telephone when I got near'. At 8 p.m., Michael Seamark of the *Star* was still at the Ministry of Defence, fruitlessly trying to obtain accreditation; at 10 p.m. he finally received permission to join the task force and drove south furiously, abandoning his car in Portsmouth. Gareth Parry of the *Guardian* was at home when his office rang at 9.30 to tell him to be in Portsmouth by midnight, leaving him forty-five minutes to catch the last train. 'He just happened to be there,' said his editor, 'and he leapt on to a train carrying a sweater and a paperback.' *The Times* only heard that their reporter, John Witherow, had a place at 10.15 that night.

Little more notice was accorded to the press officers selected to accompany the journalists on the task force. Two MoD public relations men were told at lunchtime on Sunday that they would be sailing the next day: Roger Goodwin, whose normal job is dealing with press matters for the Navy, and Alan Percival, formerly the PR officer for the Ulster Defence

Regiment. The third and most senior member of the trio who originally sailed with the task force was the Navy's deputy head of public relations at Fleet Headquarters at Northwood, Robin Barratt.

The allocation of press officers and journalists to particular ships was decided by the Navy at Northwood, and the slowly expanding list of correspondents showed the extent of the ground it had been forced to concede. Originally no places had been set aside for journalists, then on Friday there were six, on Saturday ten, and now, after pressure from Ingham – and also from Nott, who told the Navy it was a political, not a military matter – the total had reached fifteen, comprising two photographers, a BBC cameraman and sound recordist, an ITN engineer and ten reporters.

Gradually word about who had been given places spread among the journalists crowded in Portsmouth's Holiday Inn. The BBC's Robert Fox, hoping to cover the war for radio news and the World Service, was told that he wouldn't be going; so too was Kim Sabido of Independent Radio News, who discovered that his place had gone to the ITN engineer Peter Heaps (Fox and Sabido were both given berths, later in the week, on the *Canberra*). Of the few who were to sail the next day, Gareth Parry (*Guardian*), John Witherow (*Times*), Mick Seamark (*Daily Star*), Tony Snow (*Sun*) and Alfred McIlroy (*Daily Telegraph*) found themselves assigned berths on board HMS *Invincible* with Roger Goodwin. The television team – Hanrahan and Nicholson, together with cameraman Bernard Hesketh, soundman John Jockell and engineer Heaps – were put aboard the flagship, HMS *Hermes*, along with the Press Association (PA) reporter Peter Archer and the PA photographer Martin Cleaver; the accompanying PRO was Robin Barratt. David Norris of the *Daily Mail* was placed alone, and unattended by anyone from the MoD, on the Royal Fleet Auxiliary *Stromness*.

The most aggrieved pair were Robert McGowan and Tom Smith, respectively reporter and photographer for the *Daily Express*. To their disgust they found themselves confined to a logistics landing ship, the *Sir Lancelot*, due to slip away quietly twenty-four hours after the rest of the fleet. McGowan complained both to the *Express* office and to Alan Percival, the PR man assigned to travel with them; it was hopeless. 'There was no appeal,' he wrote bitterly afterwards. 'We were told to take it or leave it.'

Early the next morning, the correspondents were given a last chance to call their families before the warships moved off, *Invincible* leading the way, at 10.15. Many were still exhausted by what the *Daily Mail* later called the 'mad scramble to secure places' of the previous forty-eight hours. Behind them lay a weekend of chaotic last-minute phone calls, interrupted plans and desperate journeys. Ahead of them lay – what? None could have anticipated that they would spend more than six weeks at sea, a large part of that time under air attack; or that they would become part of Britain's first major amphibious assault since D-Day; or that they would be expected to dig their own trenches, cook their own rations and generally survive on their own a gruelling three-week campaign: none of this was foreseen. The general attitude was summed up by the editor of BBC Television News, who dispatched Brian Hanrahan to the South Atlantic with the words, 'You've just had a sailing holiday. How about another one?'

Gareth Parry was one of the reporters who was to have a particularly grim campaign. He is a veteran war correspondent, with twenty years' experience covering conflicts in Africa, the Middle East, Cyprus and Vietnam (where he lived for a year); yet he had never encountered anything like this.

> I genuinely thought we'd be sailing for a couple of days around
> the Isle of Wight; maybe if we were very lucky we'd get to the

tropics. I couldn't conceive of the idea that we were going to war in such an old-fashioned way. It's extraordinary that even today nothing can apparently be settled without hurling large amounts of explosive at one another.

Parry's attitude was typical. 'See you in a week' had been another editor's parting remark to his task force correspondent. Patrick Bishop of the *Observer* recalled how one group of journalists – who were to sail with the second contingent of the task force later that week – 'held a sweepstake on the date when the ship would turn to come home. My bet was it would be within a week. The longest was 27 May.' In the same spirit Robert McGowan bet Alan Percival £5 that they wouldn't see a shot fired in anger.

The armed forces are prepared for war; journalists are not. Most were too young even to have remembered, let alone endured, National Service. Yet arguably the Falklands was to require greater physical and mental readiness than any war covered by the media in recent times. The haphazard way in which journalists were selected and sent on their way, in most cases without even the most rudimentary equipment, could easily have proved fatal. As it was, three reporters returned home before the fighting was over, and at least one appeared to be visibly distressed when recalling his experiences.

The military sent a psychologist with the task force to study the reactions of men under the stress of war. He stated at the outset to one Ministry official that in his view the press would prove a 'weak link'. Perhaps the same thing would have happened if the reporters had joined the fleet at Ascension, as McDonald had originally proposed. But the reporters would then have had a clearer idea that it was no 'sailing holiday' that they were letting themselves in for.

The journalists on *Hermes* and *Invincible* were followed four days later by a further thirteen aboard the requisitioned liner-turned-troopship, *Canberra*. This brought the total to twenty-eight and represented a crushing victory by Whitehall over Northwood. Indeed, there is today a general belief in the Ministry of Defence that although initially too few journalists were to be allowed to join the task force, in the end there were too many. As Sir Frank Cooper told MPs four months later: 'There is no doubt in our minds – and this may surprise you, but I am going to say it now – we had more people with the task force than we could properly cope with in the light of the conditions on the ships and on land.' And one senior official recalls: 'We were pressing the Navy to take the largest possible number of reporters without any real idea of what we were getting into.'

The four extra days given to prepare the *Canberra* did little to ease the confusion which had marked the departure of the carriers. Securing a place was still a matter for string-pulling and special pleading, frequently spiced with a little discreet blackmail. Ian Bruce of the *Glasgow Herald* was there thanks to 'pressure from MPs favourable to the cause of Scottish press coverage' (i.e., one suspects, Scottish MPs in the Glasgow area). Max Hastings of the London *Standard* relied upon everybody he knew 'in political circles who might have any influence whatsoever upon the Minister of Defence or the Ministry of Defence'. Leslie Dowd of Reuters owed his inclusion to the 'considerable pressure' applied by his agency to Sir Frank Cooper. It took 'impassioned pleas' from the BBC and ITN, together with the personal intervention of John Nott, to get a three-man television team aboard *Canberra*. They were finally granted their places less than six hours before the ship sailed.

What, meanwhile, of the foreign press, whose calls had swamped the MoD's press office on the day of the invasion? No provision was made for them at all. Sir Frank Cooper now admits, 'With hindsight, we probably ought to have had one or more representatives of the foreign press,' but he adds, 'They were singularly disinterested right at the start.' Like most journalists, claims one Ministry official, 'they simply couldn't believe that the whole business wouldn't be sorted out by Al Haig and the UN.' This is unfair. What really happened was that, lacking the necessary domestic political influence, the foreign press were unable to follow up their initial requests with calls to the MoD from MPs, Cabinet Ministers and ennobled newspaper proprietors. As a result, they failed to secure a single place, leaving Reuters as the only 'international' organization on board the task force. 'The addition of just one other organization,' claimed Michael Reupke, their editor-in-chief, 'would have made this a genuine news operation rather than appearing a British propaganda exercise.' It was a short-sighted error on the part of the Ministry of Defence, one which could have been avoided and which did considerable damage. The Foreign Press Association called the MoD 'indifferent' to the world's media, and claimed that 'the negative image which the Falklands conflict elicited in some foreign newspapers must to some extent be ascribed to that indifference.'

Yet, given the hostile reception at that time being accorded to the *British* reporters by the Royal Navy, it was perhaps fortunate that there were no foreign papers on board. Relations froze even before the *Canberra* set sail. On the night before she left, Alastair McQueen of the *Daily Mirror* was having dinner with a senior Ministry of Defence press officer at Southampton's Post House Hotel, when a Royal Navy commander icily told him: 'There is no room for you. We do not have the proper accommodation for you and you would be much better staying back here in the UK. You are only taking up space we could put to much better use.' McQueen felt that 'he seemed to have the impression that journalists were demanding officer-standard accommodation. Our only aim was to accompany the forces.'

Strict, security-conscious, conservative and facing the prospect of a dangerous operation which would leave very little margin for error, most naval officers viewed the imminent arrival on board of a mob of undisciplined, unfit, metropolitan civilians with something approaching disgust. 'The Navy's idea of PR', says one MoD man, 'is to get the mayor and the local newspaper editor on board and give them pink gins in the wardroom.'

Captain Chris Burne, the senior naval officer on *Canberra*, initially refused point-blank to have the media on his ship and had to be ordered to his face to do so by Captain Tony Collins, dispatched to Southampton by the Ministry of Defence to oversee the embarkation of the journalists. Burne retaliated by assigning the reporters to the worst accommodation on the ship – the Goanese crew quarters – and there they would have remained, at least according to some MoD press officers, had it not been for the intercession of the chief public relations officer accompanying the task force, Martin Helm. (Two weeks later Burne is said to have tried to have Helm removed for constantly badgering him with requests on behalf of the press.) After this inauspicious start, the ship sailed on Good Friday, 9 April.

As *Canberra*, *Invincible*, *Hermes* and the rest of the force headed towards the Falklands, they already had stowed on board all the problems which would later dog the coverage of the war. The Navy was hostile and aggrieved at being overridden. Some of the reporters, in the rush to get places, were not physically or psychologically prepared for what lay ahead. The media representatives as a whole, correctly suspecting that they were with the fleet only on sufferance, were ready for a fight. As for the Ministry of Defence, it had twenty-eight representatives of the press at sea with no clear idea of how their copy could be vetted, what disruption its transmission would cause to the Navy or what political problems lay in store at home ... Only later in the crisis, when successive diplomatic initiatives had failed to find the expected solution and the fighting began, did the strains inherent in this fragile situation really show.

TWO

All at Sea

Before embarking, the task force correspondents filled in accreditation papers so old that they contained passages in Arabic, relics of the Suez adventure twenty-six years before. The correspondents promised 'to submit for censorship all books, articles, or other material concerning the task force during the period of operations and to abide by the decision of the censorship authorities concerned'. The grounds for censorship were to be strictly military ones. Before *Canberra* left, Captain Tony Collins gave a lecture to the journalists. 'He told us', recalls Kim Sabido, 'that there would be no way our material would be censored for things like style or taste. If a marine got into a fight with a para, and even if one of them was killed – well, fine, we could report it.'

Strict guidelines governing what the press could report were laid down by Sir Frank Cooper at a meeting held on 7 April with the editors of the national media. These stressed the need 'to maintain strict security' and were sent to the task force commanders:

> Officers and crews of ships with embarked correspondents should be reminded of the standard rules for dealing with the press and are to be specifically briefed to avoid discussing with them or in their hearing the following:-
> a. Speculation about possible future action.

   b. Plans for operations.
   c. Readiness state and details about individual units' opera-
       tional capability, movements and deployment.
   d. Details about military techniques and tactics.
   e. Logistic details.
   f. Intelligence about Argentine forces.
   g. Equipment capabilities and defects.
   h. Communications.

All such details were to be removed from correspondents'
reports.

Journalists rarely submit easily to censorship, but the rows
which followed the issuing of the MoD's guidelines went far
beyond the sort of disagreements which might have been
expected.

The men charged with the main burden of imposing censorship were the Ministry of Defence press officers accompanying the task force, the 'minders' as they became known.
Upon these luckless civil servants the press later vented ten
weeks of pent-up grievances and bitterness.

In Michael Nicholson's view,

> these men were not only unqualified, they were unwilling to
> help. They were afraid: they were looking over their
> shoulders: they were constantly worried about London.

> I found the MoD PRs lazy [wrote Tony Snow], loath to agree
> to do anything that involved them having to do any work;
> obstructive ... and dishonest – I was lied to by them on a
> number of occasions.

To Alastair McQueen they seemed

> unable to drag themselves away from the cosseted environ-
> ment in which they normally deal with defence correspon-
> dents. They were totally unequipped for a wartime role. They

did not understand the requirements of newspapers, radio or television organizations. They had absolutely no sense of urgency or news sense. They had absolutely no idea of deadlines or how to project a story to obtain the maximum impact. In my opinion they were completely out of their depth.

Even before the task force sailed, their presence aroused violent impulses. Gareth Parry recalls how, a couple of minutes before *Invincible* left Portsmouth, he and some other journalists on board saw their minder, Roger Goodwin, making a last-minute call from a telephone box on the quayside:

> There was a coil of rope lying nearby, and the ship was literally about to sail. We all looked at one another. Have you ever imprisoned anyone in a phone box with a length of rope? You should, it's very effective. In retrospect we would have saved ourselves an awful lot of bother.

It is scarcely surprising that three months after the end of the war, the minders still had about them a furtive, hunted air, like minor criminals on the run.

Their position was an invidious one, sandwiched as they were between a set of newspaper journalists instinctively hostile to interference and naval officers who – with a few honourable exceptions – appear to have regarded the media as little better than an Argentine fifth column. 'Our role in the end was as whipping boys between the press and the Navy,' says one minder. 'We helped get rid of the worst excesses of both sides.' To Sir Frank Cooper, they were 'the hinge on which the door was going to grate however much oil was put on it'.

There were five minders with the fleet, their day-to-day task being to take the reporters' copy, check it to ensure that it did not breach any of the guidelines laid down by the Ministry, have it cleared by an officer on board ship and then arrange for its transmission back to London. In addition to Roger Goodwin, Alan Percival and Robin Barratt, there were a further two PROs, Martin Helm and Alan George, on board the *Canberra*.

Roger Goodwin, a heavily built man, married, with a long record in public relations in Cyprus, Hong Kong and Germany, was to become a particular butt of press criticism. 'It was felt,' wrote one editor, 'that his knowledge of Fleet Street deadlines was somewhat inadequate – possibly explained, I understand, by the fact that before joining the MoD he was an Agricultural Correspondent for a Midlands newspaper.' (Nicholson later claimed: 'They would say, "We understand your problems: we are ex-journalists ourselves," and we discovered they were night-subs on the *Mid-Somerset Chronicle* or something: they were mostly failed journalists rather than ex-journalists.')

Although *Invincible*'s captain, Jeremy Black, was initially well-disposed towards the press, the carrier was a nest of problems. Not the least of Goodwin's worries was the presence of Prince Andrew, a helicopter pilot on the same ship as reporters from the *Sun* and the *Daily Star*. From the moment Goodwin stepped on board, unaware of his escape from incarceration at the hands of Gareth Parry, he was besieged with requests to interview the Prince. Like most officers, Andrew first learned there were to be reporters on board when he rounded a corner and saw a group of them. His first reaction was to ring Buckingham Palace and complain. He also sought out Goodwin, who had to advise him that having the press on board was something that the Prince, like everyone else, would have to accept. Tony Snow and Mick Seamark of the *Sun* and the *Daily Star* were told that it was 'not MoD policy' to give members of the Royal Family serving with the armed forces undue publicity. Undeterred, one of Snow's first dispatches, printed on the following Saturday (10 April) began:

'I Hunt the Enemy with Andy'
SUN MAN JOINS THE PRINCE ON
SOUTH ATLANTIC COPTER PATROL
I flew on a helicopter mission
with Prince Andrew yesterday . . .
to hunt down enemy ships.

Not until the fourth paragraph did the *Sun*'s readers learn that the Prince was actually flying a long way from Snow in 'a second helicopter covering a nearby section of the ocean'. The journalists were forbidden to approach Andrew, and it was the Prince himself who later broke the silence by coming over to the five *Invincible* reporters in the bar one evening and offering to buy them a drink.

As far as the tabloids were concerned, Prince Andrew was one of the major stories of the war. This made the lot of Robert McGowan, the *Daily Express* man confined to *Sir Lancelot*, all the harder to bear. He was unable to get near the Prince, and soon he had even more troubles. *Hermes* and *Invincible* had been seen leaving port; *Sir Lancelot* had not, and London therefore directed that its presence with the task force be kept secret. McGowan overcame this problem in finest Fleet Street tradition, telling *Express* readers mysteriously that he was on board 'HMS *Cinderella* – the Ship that Can't be Named'. Unfortunately, three days out at sea radio silence was imposed on the fleet. The carriers had secure communications enabling their reporters to carry on filing stories; *Sir Lancelot* had not and the ship that couldn't be named now also couldn't transmit. 'We were blacked out by radio silence,' moaned McGowan. 'No words or pictures could be sent by us for eight days on the way to Ascension Island.' He was later to say that he received more help from the Russians when he was covering the invasion of Afghanistan at the end of 1979 than he did from the British in 1982.

There were to be so many quarrels between media, minders and Navy during the empty week before the task force entered into actual operations that it is impossible to do more than pick out the key incidents. Initially, on *Invincible* at least, things did not go too badly. Captain Jeremy Black is something of a showman. 'A large, slightly balding man,' noted John Witherow of *The Times*, 'he had an American-style baseball cap with J. J. Black emblazoned across the back which he sometimes wore on top of his white anti-flash hood, and drank tea from a mug with "Boss" on the side.' Black is also one of those rare individuals, beloved by the media, with a natural ability to speak in headlines: he answered one question about whether the task force had passed the point of no return by telling reporters: 'There are no Rubicons in the South Atlantic.' Black told Goodwin that he believed it was right that the media should be accompanying the task force and promised to do everything he could to help them. He instituted regular daily briefings for the five *Invincible* correspondents. For the first two days these were on the record. But as Black was the only commander who was talking to the press in this way, he soon discovered he was dominating the coverage in London in a manner that was likely to annoy his naval peers. From 7 April the briefings became off the record; Black's words had to be attributed to 'a senior naval source'.

The *Invincible* journalists were lucky with their captain; the *Hermes* reporters were not. Michael Nicholson, the ITN reporter, said later:

> Captain Middleton did not like the press. He said to us from the very start that we were an embarrassment to him. He said, I remember, that it was not the first time he had been to war because he was at Suez but it was the first time he had been to

war with the press and he was not looking forward to the journey. ... He gave briefings for the first two or three days and that was the end of it. I got very friendly with a number of senior officers at commander-level and on one evening they confessed to me that they were outraged by a briefing they had had from the Captain in the few days after Portsmouth on our way out, in which they were told to be wary of us and that the information flow throughout the ship would be restricted because of our presence. They said it was the most disgraceful briefing they had ever encountered.

This briefing of Lyn Middleton's would appear to have been based on the signal received from the Ministry of Defence on 7 April directing task-force commanders to remind their officers of the 'standard rules for dealing with the press' and 'to avoid discussing with them or in their hearing' the classes of information regarded as unfit for publication. Later Nicholson believed that this determination not to reveal anything to the media on board – even though their dispatches were vetted anyway – led to the censoring of the ship's own daily broadcast of information to its company, the 'pipe':

> these pipes became less and less frequent and less and less informative and we were told by members of the wardroom that this was because we were aboard and that it was becoming embarrassing for information to be broadcast on the pipe because we were able to listen to it.

Officers and crew began to complain to the *Hermes* journalists 'that the ship was suffering from a lack of information because of our presence'. Hanrahan, Nicholson and the Press Association reporter Peter Archer were driven to rely increasingly on sympathetic 'deep throats' among the ship's officers. Eight days out at sea, Robin Barratt, the minder on board

Hermes, flew over to Roger Goodwin and arranged that his contingent of journalists should fly over to *Invincible* to do some filming and to record an interview with the more amenable Black.

Wednesday, 14 April, was a bad day for Goodwin. One of the features of the so-called 'information war' was that everyone fought everyone else: Whitehall fought the Navy, the Government fought Whitehall, all three fought the media, and the media, as 14 April demonstrates, fought among themselves. The *Invincible* journalists had survived for a week on a diet of unattributable briefings; now Black gave Hanrahan and Nicholson a television interview, something which is, by its nature, on the record. Archer of the PA witnessed the interview, wrote a story based upon it quoting Black by name and dispatched it to London, thus scooping his competitors. When the *Invincible* journalists discovered this, there was, one eyewitness recalls, 'a blazing row in the wardroom'. This became still more heated when Nicholson discovered that a task-force helicopter had flown to Dacca in West Africa three days before to pick up an engineer from the garden of the British embassy to help repair a damaged gearbox on *Invincible*. So far no television pictures had been able to leave the fleet, and this would have been a perfect opportunity to send them back to London. Black had actually signalled Northwood that he wanted permission to use the helicopter to fly back TV pictures but had received no reply. There were more complaints, more arguments, the outcome of which was that Black began privately referring to the press as 'the fourth form' and instructed Goodwin to ensure that Nicholson never came on board again.

Two days later, on 16 April, Black asked that all journalists' copy leaving *Invincible* should henceforth be cleared through his secretary, Richard Acland.

It was less than two weeks into the voyage and already the

strain was beginning to show. The five *Invincible* journalists all slept in the admiral's unoccupied offices filled with filing cabinets. It was, recalled John Witherow of *The Times,* in *The Winter War,* 'rather like sleeping in a canning factory during an earth tremor':

> as the ship vibrated the files reverberated, as in an outlandish and off-key tintinnabulation. I tried sleeping with ear defenders and then with cottonwool earplugs. Neither was effective. We tried to locate the root of the noises, sticking sheets of paper between the cabinets – also with no success. Gareth Parry of the *Guardian* struggled naked over desk tops in the middle of the night, tapping the ceiling in a futile attempt to pinpoint a particularly irritating rattle. He retired to his camp bed muttering, 'Sleep is release. The nightmare starts when we wake up.'

On *Hermes* the press slept in the NAAFI's quarters; on *Canberra* conditions varied. Robert Fox and Kim Sabido shared a cabin – 'right in the bowels of the ship,' remembers Sabido, 'filthy and full of cockroaches. The loo kept flooding and the floor was awash with water. Mind you, Burne would've had us in the bilges if he could.'

'Emotionally', says Nicholson, who has covered fourteen wars, 'it was the worst thing I've ever done.'

For the broadcasters the problems were much greater than those encountered by the print journalists. Reporters on *Invincible* could at least stay on board ship, their copy transmitted via the carrier's communications centre. For Hanrahan and Nicholson, sending even a short voice dispatch to London posed enormous physical difficulties. Three days out from Portsmouth, when radio silence was imposed on the task force, dispatches had to be sent using a commercial telephone system known as MARISAT, carried on the Royal Fleet Auxiliary *Olmeda*. Hanrahan and Nicholson would have to wait

wait around on the deck of *Hermes*, sometimes for hours, until a helicopter could be found to fly them to the MARISAT ship. Often the journey would be made in heavy mist; at the end of it the reporter would be winched down, in heavy seas, on to the deck. There would generally follow another long wait before the satellite relaying the transmission could be contacted and a link established with London. Then, once the piece was read, the whole process of waiting, winching and flying would have to be repeated. 'Often you just went to your bunk hoping you'd never have to get out of it. You tended to get very tense, explode, say and do things which in normal times you wouldn't have done.'

The frustrations were compounded for Nicholson and Hanrahan by their belief that the Navy could have done something to ease the problem. Hanrahan heard that instead of their having to fly over to a MARISAT ship, voice communications were possible on a 'secure' line between the carriers and London; calls were even being routed along MoD telephone extensions. At first he was told by the Navy that this was impossible, 'but I later learned the link was used regularly, offered acceptable quality, and that voices could be recognized over it. To have recorded over that link would have saved much time (and wear and tear) for all personnel – and the helicopters.' Another method which would have cut out the waiting and the journeys would have been to use the ship-to-ship radio to speak from *Hermes*, through the MARISAT ship, and on direct to London. Yet, according to Nicholson:

> this was refused by Captain Middleton of *Hermes* on the grounds that the transmission would give away our position. Yet twice he gave us information this way because he wanted good news to get to London quickly. One instance of this was his telling us of the sinking of the *General Belgrano*.

With these frustrations and discomforts, personal relations inevitably became ragged. Nicholson, an impressively experienced and highly paid reporter, whom even his best friends would not describe as self-effacing, is said to have announced in the wardroom that he would be unable to live on the salary of a Rear-Admiral, a remark which was not well received. The BBC cameraman, Bernard Hesketh, accused (along with the other *Hermes* journalists) by one senior commander of being tantamount to an Argentine intelligence officer, 'pulled up his trouser legs and showed his wounds that he had got in France in the Second World War saying, "How dare you call me a spy? These are the wounds I got from the Nazis."'

For one man it all became too much. When *Hermes* reached Ascension Island, Robin Barratt, the senior PRO responsible for trying to keep the peace between the media and the Navy, was clearly suffering from something akin to nervous exhaustion. The head of public relations at Northwood flew out, saw him and immediately ordered him home – an indication of the state things were reaching. Barratt was the first but not the last victim of what Nicholson later confessed to be 'the overwhelming feeling which comes over one after a period at sea confined on a ship – irrationality, hostility, almost paranoia'. A short while later the MoD sent out a replacement PRO, Graham Hammond.

For some, however, the conditions served only to reveal hidden strengths. Brian Hanrahan emerged as one of the best-known reporters of the war, transformed, William Boot-like, from a man whom his BBC colleagues describe as a 'quiet, shy and unassuming' former stills clerk with a passion for amateur dramatics. 'Brian was extraordinary,' says one task-force colleague. 'The tougher it got, the cooler he became. A remarkable man.' Hanrahan knew virtually nothing about military matters; his ignorance was the key to his success. 'The advantage of being an innocent in these circumstances', he mused later, 'is that you tend to ask the questions the people back home would ask – "Why are they doing that? What effect will it have?"' It was Hanrahan's 'sense of wonder' at the power of modern weapons that helped him to convey the feel of the war to the general public.

Jeremy Black was becoming increasingly disenchanted with the press on his ship. Due to her engine trouble, *Invincible* arrived at Ascension after *Hermes* on 16 April. The ship's company was promptly informed over the pipe that its members would qualify for a Local Overseas Allowance of £4, but an hour or so later the Ministry of Defence decided against giving the men the extra money. There was, one official noted in his diary, 'extreme anger and upset' on board. Servicemen formed queues to complain to the journalists, who duly wrote dispatches about ill-will aboard the task force. The stories which resulted exasperated Black. He was unable, under the MoD guidelines, to stop the reports and did not attempt to do so, but he 'felt hurt and irritated'. Nor were the press feeling particularly amenable as, to their astonishment, London had refused to allow correspondents even to mention the fact that they were at Ascension. This was apparently done to avoid offending the Americans, 'although', as the BBC pointed out, 'the use of Ascension was common knowledge internationally, having been published in the USA'. It was also being discussed regularly in news bulletins in Britain, as the task-force reporters discovered to their chagrin a few days later, when newspapers and cassettes of TV programmes reached them.

Black's mood was not improved by growing complaints from *Invincible*'s communication officers that they were being swamped by press copy. Between them the five journalists were transmitting around 4,000 words of copy every day, with A. J. McIlroy of the *Daily Telegraph* writing particularly copiously (at one point he sent back four 1,000-word pieces in thirty-six hours). Already under orders from Northwood to keep its transmissions to a minimum, this meant that something like 30 per cent of the daily workload of the ship's communication centre was devoted to press reports. Goodwin soon began receiving written complaints from the officers involved.

Invincible's signals were processed through four visual display units, two devoted to incoming messages, two to outgoing. It was not, the main communications office informed Goodwin, simply a matter of telexing the stories and forgetting them. To send one press report would first take an operator an average of thirty minutes to transfer it to tape; it would then take time to link up with a satellite; frequently the message would be garbled in transmission, and London would ask for a repeat. In all, a single story could take between ninety minutes and three hours to reach London. At one time, *Invincible* had a backlog of 1,000 signals awaiting transmission.

Among these, on 19 April, were three which Black regarded as vital: one dealt with a piece of electronic warfare equipment that he urgently needed; the second was a request for a spare part for one of the ship's two missile radar systems, designed to alert the carrier to air attack; the third concerned a malfunction in the computer which guided the ship's Harrier jets into land. 'Passing out of the ship on that day,' claimed Black subsequently, 'and taking 30 per cent of my out-going traffic, as they did every day, was the [press] copy – some 3,500 words.' He quoted from one article:

> The Page Three Girls are going to war. Fifty outsize pin-up pictures, each one 2 foot by 6 inches, were airlifted to the task force and are now on their way to the Falkland Islands. They were flown into Ascension Island, 4,000 miles from Britain,

and then dropped by helicopter on to the *Invincible*. They were featured on a television show on the ship's closed-circuit television and then distributed so that there is at least one in every mess in the ship.

Black picked out another passage:

Skinhead Ian 'Walter' Mitty would put the frighteners on anyone. With his close-shaved head, tattoo-covered body and heavy bovver boots, he looks every inch what he is – a hard man. But Walter, 20, from Richmond, Yorkshire, was near to tears yesterday when he learnt that his dearest wish – to get at the Argies with his bare hands – had been denied.

('The youngest guys in the signals centre – I'm talking about kids of 19 or so – used to come and ask me why I kept giving them all this "dross and tripe" to transmit,' remembers one minder – an experience shared by most of his colleagues, both at sea and, later, on the Falklands.)

Black eventually insisted that press copy should be filed during the night, the slackest period for signals traffic. This meant that an average story would not appear until two days after it was written. A report compiled on a Monday morning, for example, would be likely to be transmitted in the early hours of Tuesday, missing the deadline for that day's paper and not, therefore, being printed until Wednesday. It was the press's turn to feel aggrieved, all the more so a few days later when Goodwin, on his own initiative and authority, limited each correspondent to a maximum of 700 words per day.

With tempers on board frayed, *Invincible* moved out from Ascension on the second leg of the voyage to the Falklands. The day she left, Alexander Haig's attempts to find a peaceful solution collapsed, and Gareth Parry's anticipated cruise around the Isle of Wight suddenly seemed a much more serious affair. Jeremy Black called a meeting of the journalists and told them that if any of them had any doubts or fears about their capacity to take what lay ahead, they should leave now, and he would arrange a flight from Ascension back to London. No one took up his offer. 'It suddenly seemed we had passed the point of no return,' wrote John Witherow, and he found that many of the crewmen were surprised they had remained. Almost everyone seemed to have believed that the press would abandon ship before things became dangerous. When the average sailor discovered the reporters had elected to stay of their own volition, 'they treated us either as deranged madmen or as warmongers. The next question would be along the lines of "I suppose you blokes are being paid a fucking fortune to be out here?" To deny it merely provoked disbelief.' On board *Hermes*, Brian Hanrahan found that the decision to stay broke down some of the reserve with which they had been treated. 'There was a great fear that we were going to go as far as Ascension, leave with a parcel of secrets and blab them out. Once it became clear that that was not the case, things improved a lot.'

Behind the carrier group came the amphibious landing force, centred on the troopship *Canberra*. Alan Percival, Robert McGowan and Tom Smith left *Sir Lancelot* and joined the main force on board the converted liner. So too did David Norris, who up to this time had been relatively free from interference. He wrote acidly afterwards: 'I was transferred, under protest, from *Stromness* to *Canberra* and into a morass of bureaucracy and acrimony.' Like their colleagues on *Hermes* and *Invincible*, all the pressmen chose to stay, with the exception of Martin Lowe, the reporter representing the regional press. Having seen the ship's doctors, he was evacuated to Ascension's Wideawake Airfield and flown home. 'When he went,' recalls Kim Sabido, 'we all said he was the sanest man among us.'

Depleted, aggrieved, frustrated, and in some trepidation, the minders and the media were borne south by the Navy to war.

THREE

Bingo/Jingo

Meanwhile back in London the Falklands war had enabled Fleet Street to indulge in emotions and language which has been denied to British newspapers for a generation. This was no shady adventure like Suez, no messy, drawn-out conflict like Ulster. 'The fleet sails now in restitution,' proclaimed the *Guardian* on 5 April. 'The cause this time is a just one.' On the morning that *Invincible* and *Hermes* left Portsmouth, *The Times* carried a massive leader entitled 'We are All Falklanders Now': 68 column inches, more than 5 and a half feet, of authoritative prose rolling inexorably to its majestic conclusion:

> The national will to defend itself has to be cherished and replenished if it is to mean something in a dangerous and unpredictable world....
>
> We are an island race, and the focus of attack is one of our islands, inhabited by our islanders. At this point of decision the words of John Donne could not be more appropriate for every man and woman anywhere in a world menaced by the forces of tyranny: 'No man is an island, entire of itself. Any man's death diminishes me, because I am involved in mankind; and therefore never send to know for whom the bell tolls; it tolls for thee.' It tolls for us; it tolls for them.

The *Daily Mail* spoke of the resurgence of national will in terms of 'the spring sun shining and the daffodils in full bloom' and warned:

> Forcing Argentina to disgorge the Falklands is a bloody, haz-ardous and formidable enterprise. It can be done. It must be done. And Mrs Thatcher is the only person who can do it. But she will have to show ruthless determination and shut her ears to the siren voices.
>
> If she flinches, if this bold venture fizzles out in vainglorious bathos, Margaret Thatcher, her Government, and the Tory Party will be sunk.

Like the *Mail*, the *Guardian*'s leader writer also sought inspir-ation in nature:

> The time scale will stretch and stretch as fleets form and churn throughout April across 8,000 miles of the Atlantic. Easter, digging gardens, picking daffodils, will come and go. . . .

Having pronounced the task force 'just', the *Guardian* called in Churchillian terms on 'the ranks of Parliament' to 'contain their wrath and relish through the interminable weeks of impending conflict'.

Echoes of the war and of Munich were everywhere. In the *Daily Express* Lord Carrington and John Nott were 'Thatcher's guilty men. . . . They have misled themselves, the Cabinet, Parliament and the country. They have deceived everybody but the Argentinians.' 'If he has not the grace to resign,' said the *Mail* of Carrington, 'she should sack him.' 'Sack him and his whole rotten gang!' was the view of Andrew Alexander, the *Mail*'s political commentator: 'The plain fact is that the Foreign Office is rotten to the core, rotten with appeasement, rotten with real scorn for British interests ("nar-row nationalism" they call them), rotten with duplicity. . . .'

Amid all these tolling bells, blooming daffodils and churning seas it was at first easy to miss the distinctively shrill note being struck by Britain's biggest-selling tabloid, the *Sun*. On 5 April, Carrington was caricatured as a mouse alongside Churchill as a bulldog. 'We'll Smash 'Em!' was the banner headline on 6 April: 'Cheers as Navy sails for revenge'. Lord Carrington was the 'super-smoothie who became a scapegoat':

> HMS Carrington was finally sunk yesterday ... torpedoed by over-confidence and wrecked by the humiliation of the Falklands disaster.
>
> And for Peter Alexander Rupert Carrington, 6th Baron and Foreign Secretary, his resignation was the inglorious end of more than thirty years in politics . . . .
>
> One of his scornful colleagues once told me: 'Carrington is okay. But when the chips are down, when difficult decisions have to be taken, he's either in Australia or chatting up some African chief.'

On the same day, the *Sun*'s editorial ('Show your iron, Maggie') took up a full page devoted largely to an attack on the Foreign Office:

> Since the days of Chamberlain, it has been a safe haven for the appeasers.
>
> ITS CODE has been that of the old Etonians and playing the game.
>
> ITS PHILOSOPHY has been: Never rock the boat. Never offend foreigners . . . .
>
> For ourselves, we do not care where it finds its recruits ... provided they have fire in their bellies and a determination in their heart that no one is going to push Britain around.
>
> And that NOTHING comes ahead of the people of Britain, their lives, their prosperity, their future.
>
> The Iron Lady must be surrounded by men of iron!

Whereas the rest of the press generally abandoned much of its early rhetoric and concentrated over the next three or four weeks on the merits of the various peace proposals, the *Sun* sustained the same level of patriotic fervour. Indeed, it went much further. Although there had been violently patriotic papers in Britain before, this was the first time old-fashioned jingoism had been allied in wartime to a modern, mass-circulation British tabloid. All the new techniques of popular journalism – the massive, sloganizing headlines, the provocative comment, the presentation of news stories to buttress editorial comment – the whole box of tricks that was first perfected in the 1950s by the *Daily Mirror*, was employed by the *Sun* during the Falklands crisis. The results were among the most spectacular side-effects of the war.

Every weekday in Britain it is estimated that 31.3 million people read a national newspaper; on Sundays that figure rises to more than 33 million. Almost 80 per cent of British households see a national newspaper each day. One of the myths of the Falklands war is that the sales of newspapers rose dramatically during the conflict. In fact, there was little change. The market is already saturated and is thought to be incapable of further expansion. It is this salutary fact which has led to the present cut-throat circulation war, in which scarcely any of Britain's eight national daily and eight national Sunday papers are making a profit and in which each can hope to survive and prosper only at the expense of luring readers from a rival.

Of all the Fleet Street papers, the *Sun* over the past decade has proved the toughest competitor. Bought by Rupert Murdoch in 1969 from the Mirror Group, printed on his *News of the World* presses and pioneering the 'page three' picture of a topless model each day, the *Sun* has become a publishing phenomenon. Within eighteen months of taking over, Murdoch had doubled its sales. It outstripped the once unassailable *Daily Mirror* and by the mid-1970s was the largest-selling daily paper in Britain. Today, over 4 million people buy the *Sun*. Its readership is estimated to be 12.2 million; they are predominantly young (3.2 million are aged between 15 and 24) and lower-working class (9.3 million are in Britain's three lowest social classes, C2, D and E). It is a commercial success which underpins the Murdoch empire and which, in 1981, enabled him to buy Times Newspapers. (*The Times*, incidentally, is read – not bought – by 0.9 million people, of whom just *4,000* are in social classes C2, D and E.)

Only in the last two years has the *Sun* had any reason to worry. A precipitate price increase in the summer of 1980 caused sales to dip badly. The whole formula of the paper began to seem tired and stale. By the spring of 1981, the *Mirror* had caught up – and indeed for a few heady weeks may actually have overtaken its rival. The *Sun*'s problems were made more serious by the fact that its readership was being undermined by a new, brash tabloid, the *Daily Star*. The *Star*'s gimmick, playing on the British obsession with bingo, was each day to print a series of numbers which its readers could check off on special scorecards distributed throughout the country. Each week, the lucky readers with the right sequence of numbers won large cash prizes. 'It's a much better way of getting readers than advertising on TV,' says the *Star*'s London editor, Brian Hitchen. 'If you run a £500,000 advertising campaign on TV, you're very lucky if 2 per cent of the new readers stick with you. With bingo we were getting a sticking rate of 37 per cent.'

Murdoch moved swiftly to staunch the *Sun*'s loss of readers. 'We'd had a bad patch for about nine months,' says Peter Stephens, the Editorial Director of News Group Newspapers. 'We got off our backsides in the spring of 1981.' The *Sun* introduced its own bingo game, on a much bigger scale than that of the *Star*. Through the Post Office every home in the country received a supply of score cards. Massive prizes of

£50,000 a week were offered. A national television advertising campaign was launched. The price of the paper was cut by twopence for ten weeks. The *Sun* put on 160,000 readers overnight, and within three months the paper had increased its circulation by 500,000 copies a day.

Having tempted the readers to buy the paper, it was now necessary to keep them hooked: to revitalize the flagging editorial content Murdoch decided to bring in a new editor. His choice was Kelvin Mackenzie, a ruthless 35-year-old with a generally acknowledged genius for Murdoch's brand of journalism.

MacKenzie had begun his rise as one of the *Sun*'s 'back bench' – the five senior sub-editors who decide the make-up of each night's paper. From this position he moved with Murdoch to New York to help in the restyling of the Australian tycoon's latest acquisition, the *New York Post*, a paper which was promptly driven relentlessly down-market in a vicious battle with the rival *Daily News*. He was lured back to London by a tempting offer to work on Lord Matthews's *Daily Express*, but after six months, says Stephens, 'we pinched him back.'

'Driving, youthful, modern-minded, brash' is Stephens's description of his younger colleague. 'A bit noisy, but the staff respond to this.' To a fellow Murdoch editor, Derek Jameson of the *News of the World*, MacKenzie is 'hardworking, almost a workaholic – he's in the office before everyone else, and often he won't leave until eleven at night. He's abrasive, ferocious. . . . His idea of relaxation is playing a few violent games of squash.' When the Queen asked Fleet Street editors to go to Buckingham Palace and discuss with her their coverage of the Princess of Wales, MacKenzie refused on the grounds that he was 'too busy'. He almost invariably refuses to give interviews; his reluctance is said to follow one broadcast in which, to the horror of News Group executives, he cheerfully admitted to being prepared to do anything to sell newspapers. ('I regret to say,' he wrote in July, 'neither myself nor any of our staff wish to talk about the way we reported the [Falklands] conflict.')

MacKenzie was successful in beating off the *Mirror*'s challenge. Whereas in April 1981 the *Sun* was selling 3,546,000 copies a day, in April 1982 the paper sold an average of 4,121,000; in the same period the *Mirror*'s circulation slipped back by 200,000. 'It's not a newspaper,' insists Mike Molloy, the editor of the *Mirror*, whose face seems to clench at any mention of the *Sun*.

> It has no tradition or concept of itself. It's run by a proprietor who spends half his life on jumbo jets, and by a brilliant committee of marketing men. It's a technician's paper, a device for making money, with no pretensions to being anything other than ... [he breaks off, searching for a description] ... Christmas-cracker wrapping.

In order to keep up with the *Sun* and fend off the *Star*, the *Mirror* also introduced bingo; so did the *Daily Mail*. Not since the 1930s, when the *Daily Herald*, the *Express*, the *Mail* and the *News Chronicle* flooded the country with every imaginable free gift, from insurance to complete sets of Dickens, has the circulation war been fought more keenly or at greater expense. The *Sun*'s bingo promotion is said to have cost £3 million; the Mirror Group's £2.3 million. 'A massive poker game is going on in Fleet Street,' says Molloy, 'with bigger and bigger stakes. Sooner or later, something's got to give.'

The key to the struggle of selling newspapers, in the opinion of Derek Jameson, is to 'persuade the reader to break his habits':

> Staying with a paper is an emotional commitment. He gets used to it. A paper strikes a chord in him. It's very rare in life that

something comes along and persuades him to change it. One way might be bingo. Readers were changing papers at the rate of 100,000 a week thanks to bingo. Then along comes the war. War is an emotional business – blood, courage, guts, valour – it's something big enough to persuade people to change their paper. War and bingo.

It was against this background, in April 1982, that Fleet Street approached the Falklands crisis.

The *Daily Mirror* has been a supporter of the Labour Party since the war. In recent years, four of its senior executives have been given life peerages. Many of its editorial staff are Labour Party members. Like Michael Foot and the Parliamentary Party, the *Mirror* found itself caught between its dislike for Mrs Thatcher and its detestation of General Galtieri. The task force was a gamble, a venture so closely tied to the Prime Minister that on its success or failure depended her political future. What was the *Mirror* to do? On 5 April, it came out against using force in an editorial headed 'Might isn't right':

> the main purpose of British policy now should be to get the best possible settlement for the islanders.
>
> We could probably throw the Argentines out of the Falklands. But for how long?
>
> Is Britain willing to spend hundreds of millions of pounds to keep in the area an army, navy and air force strong enough to repel any future invasion?
>
> If it is, where is the money coming from? If it isn't, what happens to the islanders when we leave? . . .
>
> The islands don't matter. The people do. We should offer each of them the chance to settle here or anywhere else they choose and we should pay for it.
>
> What we must not do is promise to eject the invader and

then desert them at some later date. The Argentine occupation has humiliated the Government. But military revenge is not the way to wipe it out.

Similar leaders followed, their titles alone conveying the consistency of the paper's line: 'A time for truth' (7 April), 'Time to stay calm' (8 April), 'Point of no return' (15 April), 'If all else fails ...' (20 April), 'The dangerous hours' (23 April), 'Bleak outlook' (26 April), 'Keep on talking' (27 April). 'We wanted the whole thing sorted out by negotiations,' says Molloy. 'We were very cool about the task force.'

The *Mirror* was embarked on a dangerous path. When three national newspapers opposed the Government's handling of the Suez crisis in 1956, they lost readers heavily. The *Guardian* lost 30,000 in a matter of days, though it later recouped them. The *Observer* lost 30,000 in a week, fell behind the *Sunday Times* for the first time and never caught up again. It was the *Daily Mirror* itself which fared worst, losing 70,000 readers. The lesson appeared clear. Supported by Rupert Murdoch, who remained in daily contact with MacKenzie throughout the conflict, the *Sun* moved swiftly to corner the market in patriotism and to label its rival firmly as a disloyal defeatist.

The *Sun* had already attacked 'the sinking *Daily Mirror*' as a 'paper warrior' on 2 April, the day of the invasion. On 6 April it struck again. 'At home the worms are already coming out of the woodwork,' taunted the *Sun*.

The ailing *Daily Mirror*, which tried to pretend that there was no threat to the Falklands until the invaders had actually landed, now whines that we should give in to force and obligingly settle the islanders. But our whole experience with dictators has taught us that if you appease them, in the end you have to pay a far greater price.

'Once the war started, we were 100 per cent for it,' says Peter Stephens, himself a former deputy editor of the *Sun*. 'We had a black-and-white view of this war. It was us or the Argentinians. We had no dilemma about this.'

Other tabloid journalists were equally committed. 'Most people would've been pig-sick if there hadn't been a fight' is Brian Hitchen's analysis of the mood of the country. 'They wanted to get down there and beat the hell out of someone.' But even the London editor of the *Daily Star* was to find the *Sun*'s coverage 'over the top'.

'Youths demonstrated outside the Argentinian Embassy in London last night,' reported the *Sun* on 3 April. 'They sang "Rule Britannia", ending with "Don't Cry for me, Argentina, We're going to Nuke you".' 'Sack the guilty men!' ran the paper's editorial on the same day. 'What the hell is going on at Britain's Foreign Office and Ministry of Defence?' To oppose sending the task force was to be 'running scared'; on 7 April 'The Sun Says' fired this salvo:

> Out of the woodwork, like the political termite he is, crawls No. 1 Left-winger Tony Benn to demand the evacuation of the Falkland islanders. . . .
>
> And of course, he immediately wins backing from the whining namby-pamby ultra-Left, who always run scared at the first sign of a crisis.

The following day, the *Sun* printed a two-page spread of photographs of British marines surrendering on the Falklands. 'LEST WE FORGET' was the headline. 'This is why our lads are going to war.'

> These were the first moments of humiliating defeat for our brave Falklands few. It was a black moment in our history . . . a wound we cannot forget. But now our troops are on their way . . . to wipe out the memory and free our loyal friends.

The *Sun*'s attitude to a negotiated settlement was summed up in a five-word headline on 20 April: 'Stick it up your Junta'. 'We urge every housewife *not* to buy corned beef produced in the Argentine' was the theme of an early campaign. Two days later the *Sun* reported that 'all over the country, families blacked the "bully" beef to show the South American bully boys what they thought.' 'Angry Sonia Lewis of Hockliffe, Beds.' was reported as saying: 'Refusing to buy corned beef is one way we Brits can show the flag.'

The average Argentinian – 'Johnny Gaucho' – was reported as 'getting the jitters'. 'Several have stopped me', claimed the *Sun*'s David Graves in Buenos Aires on 7 April, 'and queried in trembling voices: "Will the British bomb Buenos Aires?"' Argentinians were 'Argies', a good target for humour. A daily series of 'Argy-Bargie' jokes was instituted, and soon the *Sun* was able to tell its readers, 'Your very own gags have been pouring in': 'They are so funny that we have decided to give £5 for every reader's Argy-Bargie joke published. Plus a can of Fray Bentos "non Argentinian" corn beef. Today's joke was told to us by Titus Rowlandson, 9, from Brighton. . . .' (Titus earned £5 for a joke about two British soldiers wiping out hundreds of 'Argy' soldiers.)

The *Sun*'s promotions department was equally busy. On 7 April, 'to give the lads a big morale-booster', the paper began distributing free badges bearing the legend: 'The Sun says Good Luck Lads'. (Derek Jameson was later seen wearing one at the Savoy for the British Press Awards.) By 30 April, this side of the *Sun*'s activities had expanded further:

Are you feeling shirty with the enemy? Want to give those damn Argies a whole lot of bargie?

Course you do! Well, here's your chance to put your feelings up front.

Our 'Stick it up your Junta' T-shirt is a Sunsational

reminder of the most popular headline to come out of the Falkland Islands fight.

And it's on offer at the super-low price of only £2. . . .

'The Sun Says Knickers to Argentina!' was the banner headline on 16 April. 'Britain's secret weapon in the Falklands dispute was revealed last night . . . it's undie-cover warfare.' The article revealed that 'thousands of women' were 'sporting specially made underwear embroidered across the front with the proud name of the ship on which a husband or boyfriend is serving.' Even Prince Andrew had 'bought several pairs of battle-briefs. . . . But Palace officials are keeping mum about who will get them as a Royal gift.' Alongside the story was the inevitable picture of 'delightful Debbie Boyland . . . all ship-shape and Bristol fashion' in her 'nautical naughties' embroidered with the name of HMS *Invincible*. (It was Tony Snow's report on reaction to this story, dispatched from the carrier three days later, which so aggravated Captain Black.) Within two weeks the *Sun* had returned to the same theme under the headline 'Garters to the Tartars', this time with 'Karen Clarke, 19' modelling an *Invincible* garter.

When the *Sun* tackled the actual news of the war it was often wildly wrong. On 7 April the front page was dominated by a picture of a jet airliner and the headline 'Off to War by Jumbo!' reporting that four British Airways jumbo jets were to fly '4,000 battle-ready troops to the Ascension Islands [*sic*]'. 'From there,' the report went on, 'it is just a seven-hour flight to the occupied islands.' In reality, not only were there no such plans but it would have been physically impossible to use jumbo jets in this way. 'Navy Storms South Georgia' was the banner headline days before any attack was mounted. Similarly, also on the front page, on 28 April, the *Sun* proclaimed 'In We Go!' Three weeks before the landings the article reported that 'Britain's crack troops were moving in last night for the Battle of the Falklands ... waiting for the invasion that could be only hours away.'

The 'In We Go!' headline came shortly after the start of an eleven-day strike by members of the National Union of Journalists (NUJ) belonging to the *Sun* chapel. The entire paper was being produced by thirteen editorial staff, including MacKenzie and Stephens. 'We hardly got any sleep,' says Stephens. 'We all became totally exhausted. Everyone ate at the office – it was a bit like being in a bunker. Looking back on it, it's amazing that we kept the paper going.' It was in this period that the *Sun* produced some of the best-remembered features of its war coverage, including the 'Gotcha!' headline, and a story on 1 May which became a *cause célèbre*:

Stick this up your Junta!

A Sun missile for Galtieri's gauchos

The first missile to hit Galtieri's gauchos will come with love from the *Sun*.

And just in case he doesn't get the message, the weapon will have painted on the side 'Up Yours, Galtieri' and will be signed by Tony Snow – our man aboard HMS *Invincible*.

The *Sun* – on behalf of all our millions of patriotic readers – has sponsored the missile by paying towards HMS *Invincible*'s victory party once the war is over.

The article was accompanied by a picture of a missile with the caption 'Here it comes, Señors. . . .'

Three days later Tony Snow reported, 'The *Sun* has scored another first ... by downing an Argentine bomber.' According to Snow, the '*Sun*'s sidewinder' hit one of three Argentine Canberras intercepted by British war planes. He quoted the pilot who carried the *Sun*'s missile: 'Another Harrier and I came up and they did not see us. We got behind them and I fired the missile from fairly close range. A little while later the Canberra blew up.'

The strongest reaction to the missile-sponsoring story came not in London but from the men with the task force. 'A lot of people were very upset,' remembers Gareth Parry. 'There was a general feeling that it was a sick thing to do.' There were letters complaining about it in *Invincible*'s newsletter. Other crewmen complained to Roger Goodwin. On *Canberra* the journalists felt strongly enough to send a joint message to the *Sun* in London. 'Look,' says Peter Stephens, 'we were tired. We just didn't have the time to sit around and have a sage discussion about the rights or wrongs of it.'

Earlier in the crisis, on 10 April, the *Sun* had featured a new video game called 'Obliterate', in which the player commanded a British submarine trying to torpedo Argentine ships. The *Sun* was now presenting the whole war as a video game come to life. First 'with guns blazing a massive Argentinian invasion force grabbed the tiny Falkland Islands in a chilling dawn raid.' Now Britain threatened, in the *Sun*'s words, 'to shoot Argies out of the skies' while 'Navy helicopters blasted two gunboats to smithereens.' The jubilant 'Gotcha!' which greeted the sinking of the *Belgrano* on 4 May was no aberration. It was the logical culmination of the *Sun*'s coverage. It was the equivalent of Zap! or Pow! or – a headline which the *Sun* actually used later in the war – Wallop! They were comic-book exclamations used by the *Sun* to describe a fantasy war which bore no resemblance to reality. No other paper, not even the *News of the World*, which printed a scorecard:

Britain 6
(South Georgia, two airstrips, three warplanes)
Argentina 0

came as close to portraying the war as a colourful game.

The danger was that the *Sun*, like its counterparts in Argentina with their repeated reports of the sinking of *Invincible*, did nothing to prepare its readers for setbacks. They echoed Mrs Thatcher's famous comment at the outset of the crisis: 'Defeat? The possibility does not exist.' The shock was all the greater, then, when on Tuesday, 4 May, the cowardly, bean-eating, risible gauchos somehow managed to destroy HMS *Sheffield*.

'I shall never forget the horror of the loss of the *Sheffield*,' recalls Stephens. 'It was as though we'd all been kicked in the stomach. There were only thirteen of us. Somehow we had to pick ourselves up off the floor and produce a paper. We had to shovel that story in fast.'

The paper's front page was given over almost entirely to a massive headline: 'British Warship Sunk by Argies'. Inside, a blank space was substituted for the daily cartoon, dropped 'because it is now considered inappropriate'. In the editorial column the *Sun* reported 'a grievous blow.... *Yet this tragedy, shocking as it is, can in no way affect Britain's resolve.*'

Meanwhile the *Daily Mirror* called the sinking 'Too High a Price':

> Calculating and miscalculating politicians started this conflict. Now it is up to them to end it. Quickly. . . .
>
> Now it is time for the politicians to risk their reputations and find peace. Their biographies should not be written in the blood of others. . . .
>
> It is time to prove that peace through diplomacy is the only policy that pays – and we must do it before there is yet another tragedy at sea.

'The killing has got to stop,' repeated the *Mirror* on 6 May, and produced a startling front page: a long, narrow picture of a grim Mrs Thatcher which ran from top to bottom of the page, with a caption, headline-sized, running down the side of it, a word to a line: 'Outside No 10 where last week she was saying "Rejoice" Mrs Thatcher shows the strain of the desperate days of May.'

Other papers caught the same mood, in particularly the *Guardian*, whose cartoonist, Leslie Gibbard, reproduced the famous Donald Zec cartoon of a shipwrecked sailor clinging to a wave-tossed raft, first published in the *Daily Mirror* in 1942. Then the caption had read ' "The price of petrol has been increased by one penny" – Official' and had almost led to the *Mirror*'s being closed down under wartime regulations. Now Gibbard changed the caption to read ' "The price of *sovereignty* has been increased" – Official.'

Both papers reflected a feeling in the wake of the loss of the *Sheffield* that the recovery of the islands might not be worth the sacrifice, that the Royal Navy might be heading for disaster. There was, as will be described below, some panic in Parliament, especially among Conservatives. This found an outlet in attacks upon the BBC, in which Mrs Thatcher joined on 6 May.

The combination of all these events was too much for the *Sun*. A characteristic reaction of ultra-patriotic papers in times of crisis is to turn on 'enemies within'. In the First World War, for example, Horatio Bottomley's *John Bull* attacked Keir Hardie and Ramsay MacDonald, opponents of the war, as 'two traitors within our gates' who should be court-martialled for high treason. The *Sun* lies firmly in the *John Bull* tradition. Critics of the task force before the fleet suffered losses were cowards; sceptics now were traitors. 'Dare call it treason' was the title of the *Sun*'s editorial on Friday, 7 May. Its author was 53-year-old leader writer Ronald Spark, formerly a journalist of the Daily Express.

> There are traitors in our midst.
>
> Margaret Thatcher talked about them in the House of Commons yesterday.

She referred to those newspapers and commentators on radio and TV who are not properly conveying Britain's case over the Falklands, and who are treating this country as if she and the Argentines had an equal claim to justice, consideration and loyalty.

The Prime Minister did not speak of treason. The *Sun* does not hesitate to use the word. . . .

What is it but treason to talk on TV, as Peter Snow talked, questioning whether the Government's version of the sea battles was to be believed?

We are caught up in a shooting war, not a game of croquet. There are no neutral referees above the sound of the guns. A British citizen is either on his country's side – or he is its enemy.

What is it but treason for the *Guardian* to print a cartoon, showing a British seaman clinging to a raft, above the caption: ' "The price of sovereignty has been increased" – official'?

Isn't that exactly calculated to weaken Britain's resolve at a time when lives have been lost, whatever the justice of her cause?

Imagine a cartoonist who produced a drawing like that in Buenos Aires. Before he could mutter: 'Forgive me, Señors' he would be put up in front of a wall and shot.

The *Guardian*, with its pigmy circulation and absurd posturing, is perhaps not worth attention.

The *Daily Mirror*, however, has pretensions as a mass-sale newspaper.

What is it but treason for this timorous, whining publication to plead day after day for appeasing the Argentine dictators because they do not believe the British people have the stomach for a fight, and are instead prepared to trade peace for honour?

We are truly sorry for the *Daily Mirror*'s readers.

They are buying a newspaper which again and again

57

demonstrates it has no faith in its country and no respect for her people.

'Kelvin felt very strongly,' explains Peter Stephens, who chaired the editorial conference at which the leader was agreed. 'I personally thought "treachery" was a bit too much when applied to individuals.'

Reaction was instantaneous. Ken Ashton, the general secretary of the National Union of Journalists, issued a statement calling it 'odious and hysterical'. To Peter Preston, editor of the *Guardian*, it was 'sad and despicable'. Michael English, a Labour MP, urged the Attorney General to prosecute the *Sun* for criminal libel. The strongest reaction came from the *Daily Mirror*.

When Mike Molloy saw the *Sun* on Friday morning his first instinct was to speak to the paper's legal department, which advised him that the *Mirror* could almost certainly win an action for libel. Instead, he decided to publish a reply. The *Mirror*'s leader writer is Joe Haines, a former press secretary to Harold Wilson. That Friday happened to be his day off, but Molloy called him at home and asked him to come in. The two men discussed the subject briefly. Haines retired to his office, inserted a sheet of paper into his typewriter, and started work. The resulting article took him exactly one hour and ten minutes: 'They're best written that way, when you're angry.' Molloy substituted the word 'harlot' for 'whore' and deleted three lines. ('I can't remember what they were,' says Haines. 'I think they were about Nazi Germany.') Otherwise the editorial ran exactly as Haines had written it, taking up an entire page, illustrated with *Sun* headlines, and captioned 'The Harlot of Fleet Street'. 'A coarse and demented newspaper' was the *Mirror*'s description of its rival.

There have been lying newspapers before. But in the past month it has broken all records.

It has long been a tawdry newspaper. But since the Falklands crisis began it has fallen from the gutter to the sewer. . . .

It has been seen on American TV as an example of how British newspapers cover the crisis. Far from helping our cause, it shames it.

From behind the safety of its typewriters it has called for battle to commence to satisfy its bloodlust. The *Sun* today is to journalism what Dr Josef Goebbels was to truth. Even *Pravda* would blush to be bracketed with it.

The *Daily Mirror* does not believe that patriotism has to be proved in blood. Especially someone else's blood. . . .

We do not want to report that brave men have died so that the *Sun*'s circulation might flourish.

Though such is the temper of the British people that they are as likely to be repelled by the *Sun*'s treatment of the fighting as is every decent British journalist. . . .

A Labour MP yesterday called for the *Sun* to be prosecuted for criminal libel. There is no point in that. It has the perfect defence: Guilty but insane.

What would be more useful would be if the *Sun* was compelled to carry an official Government announcement on each copy: 'Warning: reading this newspaper may damage your mind.'

Reactions to the *Mirror*'s attack varied. Haines was inundated with letters and phone calls of congratulation, mainly from other journalists, including the leader writer of the *Daily Star*. Michael Foot (who himself later condemned the 'hysterical bloodlust' of the *Sun* in the House of Commons) wrote to Molloy praising the article. So, too, did Lord Cudlipp, the editor who took the *Daily Mirror* to its peak circulation of over 5 million in the 1960s. Some, though, thought it too violent and detected behind it the *Mirror*'s years of frustration at being unable to recapture its old position as Britain's

59

largest-selling daily paper. 'The spectacle of the *Sun* and the *Mirror* at each other's throats has not been a pleasant one,' wrote the advertising trade newspaper *Campaign* on 13 May:

> It was absurd of the *Sun* to make its accusations of treason; but it was certainly undignified of the *Mirror*, which until then had been pursuing a moderate line with admirable objectivity, to respond with a full page and a headline shrieking about 'The harlot of Fleet Street'.

'It was hysterical, silly and misguided to give so much space to criticism,' says Peter Stephens. 'A foolish piece of journalism, ludicrously overstated.'

The *Sun* itself claimed, 'Hundreds of readers have phoned us, firmly supporting our views. . . . True Brit John Platt – a boiler attendant who was in the Navy in World War Two – wept with emotion as he called in to support our condemnation of traitors. . . .' Disarmingly entitled 'Why all the fuss?' the *Sun*'s editorial presented the issue as a threat to press freedom:

> Our message to Mr English, the National Union of Journalists and anyone else who is interested is this:
>
> We shall not be gagged on any matter of deep public interest.
>
> We shall treat crude threats with the contempt they deserve.
>
> As for the BBC, the *Guardian* and the *Daily Mirror* (whose editorial line is now endorsed by the Communist *Morning Star*), we know they are happy when they are dishing it out.
>
> It remains to be seen whether they can take it.

The following Wednesday, 12 May, the *Sun*'s NUJ chapel met to consider a motion condemning Kelvin MacKenzie for publishing the 'treason' editorial. It was defeated. The views expressed in the *Sun*, claimed the reporters, 'have never been necessarily those of all or even part of the journalists on the newspaper'. Ronald Spark, author of 'Dare call it treason', remained unrepentant. A move to expel him from the NUJ for breaches of the union's code of conduct led to a disciplinary hearing which Spark refused to attend. 'You ask if your committee's session will be convenient for me,' he wrote to the NUJ's Assistant Secretary.

> As far as I am concerned you can meet at midnight on a raft in the middle of the Thames or at any other time or in any other place. I have not the slightest intention of attending, and no one will have any authority to represent me. I shall correspond with you no further. I shall ignore any so-called findings. Had I the common touch of, say, a *Guardian* leader writer, my attitude to your committee could be summed up in two words. Get stuffed.
> Yours truly,
> Ronald Spark

(Spark was finally expelled six months later for a leader described by the NUJ as 'vituperative, callous and clearly designed to inflame public opinion' and which cited 'the law of treason as a weapon with which to prevent others from exercising their rights of free speech'. The NUJ's decision was widely attacked in Fleet Street as an over-reaction, and after an appeal Spark was reinstated.)

For its part, the *Sun* used the publicity to identify itself even more closely with the task force. From 11 May every front page bore the slogan 'The Paper that Supports our Boys'. A 'Task Force Action Line' was established, down which the *Sun* poured everything from chocolate biscuits to love poems, from page three pictures to cassettes of the Cup Final, presided over by reporter Muriel Burden, 'Darling of the Fleet'. The comic-strip headlines continued. Argy Jets Shot Down (13 May), Our Planes Blitz Argy Ships, How our Tough Guys Hit Pebble Island (17 May), Argies Blown out of the Sky (24 May), Panicky Argies Flee Barefoot (3 June), Hero Bayonet Troops Kill Fifty (14 June). Following their peace initiative, the 'contemptible, treacherous Irish' joined the *Sun*'s gallery of hate-figures: 'Don't buy Irish golden butter. . . . Don't holiday there this summer. It's not much but it's better than giving succour to our new enemy.' The names of all thirty-three Labour MPs who voted against the Government on 20 May were printed as a 'Roll of Shame'. 'Enemy quail at the touch of cold steel,' reported the *Sun* on 14 June. 'The Argies had no stomach for close-quarters combat and crumbled before the Task Force's full-blooded assaults.' The level of abuse was kept up to the end, even spilling over on to the sports pages during the coverage of the World Cup. 'Argies Smashed. . . . They strutted, they cheated and afterwards they bleated. That was the arrogant Argentines last night. They swaggered on as world champions, and crawled off, humiliated by little Belgium. . . .'

Yet if the *Sun* hoped by such coverage to improve circulation, there was no evidence of that by the end of the war. Throughout the country as a whole there was only a tiny rise in the total circulation of all Fleet Street papers: from 14.9 million per day in March to 15.2 million in May (when fighting was at its height), falling back to 15 million in June – an overall increase of less than 1 per cent. In the same period, the *Sun* actually *lost* sales of 40,000 a day, while the *Mirror* added 95,000. 'We put on 100,000 thanks to a promotional campaign just before the war started,' says Molloy, 'and we managed to keep most of them.' Peter Stephens agrees: 'I don't think anyone prospered or suffered as a result of the war.'

Bearing in mind the precedent of Suez, this was, from the *Mirror*'s point of view, an impressive performance. Why was this? The Falklands war was, after all, a much more popular venture than Suez. If papers opposed to military action lost readers in 1956, surely they should have done even worse in 1982?

In advance of detailed academic research one can only speculate, but it seems almost certain that the explanation lies in the expansion of television over the past twenty-five years. At the time of Suez there were less than 6 million television licence holders in the United Kingdom; today there are around 18 million. By 1971, a BBC Audience Research Unit report found that 86 per cent of the population found television a 'trustworthy' source of news; only 30 per cent 'trusted' newspapers.

The Falklands crisis rammed home the lesson of how powerful a means of communication television has become. When the Ministry of Defence spokesman appeared 'live' on television to announce the latest news from the South Atlantic, the night editor in Fleet Street was receiving the information no more swiftly and in no different a manner from his readers sitting at home. Voice reports from the television correspondents with the task force were arriving back hours, sometimes days, ahead of written dispatches. Throughout the war, as the *Daily Mail* pointed out in its evidence to the Commons Defence Committee, 'most of Britain's national newspapers were largely dependent on taking notes from Brian Hanrahan and Michael Nicholson.'

Given this immediacy, fewer people care any more what the *Sun* or the *Mirror* says. With bingo, the mass-circulation papers of Fleet Street are ceasing to be 'newspapers' in the traditional sense. As bingo can apparently lead half a million readers to change their newspaper in a matter of weeks, it is scarcely surprising that the editorial pages are fast turning into wrapping paper for that day's lucky numbers. Add to this the fact that in recent weeks the *Sun* has sometimes had seven pages of sport and a further five of advertising in a twenty-eight-page paper, and the reason why the Falklands war hardly touched circulation may well stand explained.

FOUR

Nott the Nine o'Clock News

The Falklands campaign came to be called 'the worst reported war since the Crimea'. Newspaper correspondents' dispatches from the task force often arrived in London too late to be used; some never arrived at all. The first still picture from the South Atlantic did not come through until 18 May, over three weeks late, and even then it turned out to be an embarrassingly naked propagandist photograph of the Union Jack being unfurled over South Georgia. Newspapers were forced to rely on artists' impressions of what was happening. Pen-and-ink illustrators were called out of retirement. A vigorous, heroic depiction of fighting, normally confined to the pages of *Victor*, found its way on to the news stands and added to the unreality of the war.

For television the situation was, on occasion, marginally *worse* than it had been during the Crimea. In 1854 the Charge of the Light Brigade was graphically described in *The Times* twenty days after it took place. In 1982 some TV film took as long as twenty-three days to get back to London, and the average delay for the whole of the war, from filming to transmission, was seventeen days. 'They almost became the Dead Sea scrolls by the time we got them in,' complained David Nicholas, the editor of ITN. For most of the war, television had to rely for news from the task force on voice reports alone, illustrated by a caption showing a picture of the correspondent who was speaking.

For many broadcasters this 'radiovision' was hard to accept. During the 1960s and 1970s, news reporting changed out of all recognition; nowhere was this revolution greater than in the coverage of wars. From Vietnam onwards, through the struggles in Africa, the middle East and latterly El Salvador, television has depicted the violence of war from the heart of the fighting. Lightweight, hand-held cameras first enabled television to get to the front line; now electronic newsgathering (ENG) equipment has ensured that such pictures can be transmitted via satellite and studio into millions of homes in the space of a couple of hours. Television gives everyone a ringside seat. In May 1980 British viewers were able to watch the SAS storming the Iranian Embassy as if it were a Cup Final: live, with commentary, at peak time, simultaneously on both main channels. The implications of this access were widely expected to be profound in the event of any future British conflict. Yet for the bulk of the Falklands war, the camera might as well not have been invented. The crisis lasted for seventy-four days, and for the first fifty-four there were no British pictures of any action.

The reason for the lack of pictures was primarily a technical one. Transmitting TV pictures via satellite from on board a fast-moving warship is a vastly more difficult process than transmission from on land. Both the BBC and ITN have their own satellite ground stations, but there was no way in which these could have been properly stabilized to transmit from the deck of a ship; nor did they have the sophisticated auto-tracking equipment necessary to keep the ground station pointing along the critical narrow path of the satellite as the ship changed course. This meant that any picture transmitted from the task force would have to be sent through the Navy's own satellite communications. The BBC and ITN did everything they could to prise such facilities out of the Ministry of

Defence. At a meeting before the aircraft carriers left Portsmouth, Ian McDonald was persuaded to allow an ITN engineer, Peter Heaps, to sail on board *Hermes* and to test her SCOT military satellite terminals to see whether they could be used to broadcast television pictures. The technical problems posed were immense. Television pictures require at least 1,000 times the frequency range used by the normal voice and signal traffic which military satellites are designed to handle.

Nevertheless, according to David Nicholas, things at first looked 'pretty promising'. On 8 April, the BBC and ITN – who acted in concert throughout – had further talks with McDonald, and on 11 April two television engineers were given access to an operational satellite earth station at the Royal Air Force base at Oakhanger. Equipment was modified by ITN and flown out to *Hermes*. But when the ship reached Ascension, Heaps was ordered home by ITN. Nicholas claimed:

> We were told at that stage that in order to get the pictures back we would have to use the SCOT satellite. . . . It was explained to us that in order to do that they would have to close down the satellite as far as military traffic was concerned for some twenty minutes or half an hour, and they did not wish to do that. . . . That is when we pulled the engineer out. We later learned that there were moments, for one reason and another, and certain phases of the day when the SCOT satellite was closed down anyway. . . . That is something we were never able to establish.

'After this,' wrote the BBC in its evidence to the Commons Defence Committee, 'no real progress was made' until, on 14 May, a technical conference was held at the Royal Signals and Radar Establishment, Defford. Two possible solutions to the impasse were discussed. One was to use the British military satellite SKYNET II, the other to use the American military satellite DISCUS. Extensive tests using simulated transmissions were carried out at Defford on 19 May. To the engineers' delight, black-and-white pictures of reasonable quality were produced; a cassette of the results was shown to the Ministry of Defence.

But once again there were problems. The SKYNET satellite was not in the right position to pick up signals from the task force's area of operations. In order to send pictures back one ship would have had to detach herself from the carrier group and sail to the South Georgia region, which lay just within the area covered by SKYNET. This option was ruled out, leaving the American DISCUS which, according to the BBC's Assistant Director-General, Alan Protheroe, posed even more difficulties:

> to have used the DISCUS satellite would have meant asking the Americans to tilt that satellite very slightly so that its reflection would cover the area which we required. The three American television networks made an approach to the Pentagon to discover what the possibilities were of that satellite being tilted. They were not rejected, if I can put it that way. The request, the suggestion, was not rejected out of hand. The Pentagon, I understand, made it clear that they would require a formal approach from the Ministry of Defence or the British Government. I have no knowledge that such a request was made.

The MoD later admitted that indeed no such formal request *was* made. Instead an 'informal' approach was made at 'desk [*i.e. low*] level'. According to Commander P. H. Longhurst, an MoD communications expert, the response was 'very negative'.

Without satellite facilities, film from the task force simply had to be put on the next ship heading back to Ascension. In an age of supposedly instant communications, what were perhaps the most eagerly awaited television pictures in the world travelled homewards at a steady 25 knots. Other ingenious solutions, such as attaching cassettes of ENG material to balloons and allowing them to drift until picked up by a Nimrod aircraft, were discussed in a desultory way, and dismissed.

Although ITN and the BBC later went out of their way to pay tribute to the enthusiasm of individual officers, there was a general feeling among the broadcasters that the MoD was not particularly anxious to ensure a regular flow of television pictures. ITN was 'convinced that satellite pictures could have been transmitted from *Hermes*. But there was an absence of will by high authority to try it.' Alan Protheroe also spoke of a 'lack of will': 'A crusty RN officer said to me: "You're the chappie who wanted to put that satellite thing in the middle of the flight deck. Would've stopped us flying, y'know. . . ." There are moments when a long, slow pull at a stiff Scotch is the only possible response.'

Although the MoD is insistent that the lack of pictures was solely due to technical problems, other evidence suggests that the broadcasters' suspicions may have some foundation. Ministers, military chiefs and civil servants freely admit in private their relief that there were no television pictures to worry about. Sir Frank Cooper said in July:

> To be quite frank about it, if we had had transmission of television throughout, the problems of what could or could not be released would have been very severe indeed. We have been criticized in many quarters, and we will no doubt go on being criticized in many quarters, but the criticism we have had is a small drop in the ocean compared to the problems we would have had in dealing with television coverage.

With 'very severe' problems envisaged in the higher reaches of the Government, it is scarcely surprising that the broadcasters detected a 'lack of will' when it came to facilitating regular television coverage. Sir Frank Cooper was airing a general anxiety, known to have been shared by, among others, John Nott.

When the collected coverage of the campaign *was* eventually broadcast, after the Argentine surrender, it included some harrowing shots of badly burned faces and blown-off limbs. But the worst material was never shown. It was weeded out by the television companies themselves. Major-General Sir Jeremy Moore, the commander of the British land forces, afterwards wanted 'to pay tribute to the good taste of our journalists that they did not show anything as unpleasant as could have been available'. Imagine the nightmare which would have faced the Ministry of Defence in London if pictures of air attacks and casualties, of men suffering from strain and fear, had been coming back every day at the height of the fighting. What pictures would have been censored? And on what grounds? As Neville Taylor, the present chief of public relations at the MoD, later put it:

> I know a lot of film was taken which they [the TV editors] decided . . . was of such a nature that they did not wish to put it on the screen. Had there been live television, I do not think one can simply say, 'Well, of course, it would be censored.' We would be entering into the realms of style and content and taste, *which I am sure we have got to do* [author's emphasis], but at the moment I cannot see a way of establishing criteria that establish that deletion of that film clip is OK and that bit is all right, if one is talking about sensitivities on taste and not operational security.

The Ministry would have been caught in a political minefield. Too much censorship and there would have been accusations that the Government was attempting to 'sanitize' the war; too little and there would have been outrage from the military and from distressed relatives.

Even with the trickle of pictures that did come back there were problems. Whenever material from the task force arrived at the BBC, the MoD was immediately informed, and senior army and naval officers would hasten to Television Centre in west London for a viewing. But, complained the BBC, the officers 'appeared not to be fully briefed and differed in their attitudes to their task'. Enraged editors found censorship going far beyond security and straying into questions of 'taste' and 'tone'. The BBC was told not to use a picture of a body in a bag, not to use the phrase 'horribly burned', not to show a pilot confessing, jokingly, that he had been 'scared fartless' on one mission. 'Clearance', rather than emotive words like 'censorship' or 'vetting', was the Ministry's euphemism for this extraordinary process.

In the face of unacceptable material, the bureaucrats always had their traditional stand-by: procrastination. Two voice dispatches (without pictures) came in simultaneously describing the disaster at Bluff Cove in which fifty British servicemen were killed. Michael Nicholson's was 'up-beat', speaking of 'a day of extraordinary heroism'. Brian Hanrahan's was more sombre, talking of a 'setback' for the British and including a line which the censors in London found offensive: 'Other survivors came off unhurt but badly shaken after hearing the cries of men trapped below.' Nicholson's piece was passed. Hanrahan's was temporarily blocked. By the time it was released, with the distasteful line cut, the news bulletins were over and both ITN and the BBC had been forced to use the Nicholson version.

Similarly, when film material reached Ascension after its long sea voyage from the Falklands, or even when it finally arrived in Britain, it was, according to the BBC, often 'deliberately delayed'. Several consignments were considered sensitive and were held up, without further explanation, for

GOTCHA!

'security reasons'. Small wonder that the BBC's evidence to
MPs after the war was unusually uncompromising and outspoken: 'In this area it is the BBC's deep concern that the
Ministry of Defence has come very close to the "management" or "manipulation" of news, an idea that is alien to the
concept of communication within a free society.' It was not
that the broadcasters objected to the argument that some
pictures were too shocking to be shown, especially when
families of the men concerned might be watching. Indeed, the
evidence of what occurred after the war, when the worst
pictures were discarded and the military expressed their gratitude, shows that television was ready to censor itself and to
abide by the rules of 'good taste'. *The objection was to the
Ministry of Defence's deciding how the war would be
presented.* The special circumstances of the Falklands campaign ensured that the Government had unique control over
how the war appeared on television. Because there were no
satellite facilities, the MoD could regulate the flow of pictures
and deodorize the war in a way that few other democratic
Governments – especially recent Administrations in the USA
– have been able to get away with.

The American experience in Vietnam did as much as anything
to shape the way in which the British Government handled
television during the Falklands crisis. To ITN it seemed that
'the Vietnam analogy was a spectre constantly stalking the
Falklands decision-makers and was invoked privately by the
military as an object lesson in how not to deal with the
media.' To the American-born defence correspondent of the
Economist, Jim Meacham – who actually served as an officer
in Vietnam – civil servants and soldiers often observed: 'This
is why you Americans lost the Vietnam war, because you had
a free press.' General Moore described how the possibility of
'gory pictures' being shown on TV 'brought forcefully home

to me the problem that the Americans had during the Vietnam conflict'. The theme recurs repeatedly in off-the-record conversations with the men who shaped official policy with regard to the handling of the media. As it was clearly such a vital factor in conditioning attitudes, it is perhaps worth considering briefly how valid it is to draw an analogy between the two wars.

On the face of it, they were totally dissimilar. One lasted two and a half months; the other lasted the best part of a decade. One involved a relatively small professional force; the other was fought by hundreds of thousands of conscripts. One was fought on British territory; the other was a war of intervention in a foreign country. One was essentially a maritime expedition; in the other the fighting covered several countries. In virtually every respect the two had nothing in common. One of the few things they did share, however, was that they were both fought in the age of television; and because America's first major military defeat coincided with the advent of TV, there was a tendency, especially among the armed forces, to connect the two. This may be a convenient excuse for the Pentagon. It is scarcely borne out by the facts.

Jim Meacham told the Commons Defence Committee:

> I speak as a person who fought as a serving officer of medium grade, so I suppose I bore some responsibility for the loss of the war. We lost because we fought it wrong, not because the free press reported it right. I do not accept this for a minute. At the end of the day the American public and the American Congress forced the Administration to give up this war because it was not going to win. The body politic does not have any sharp instruments; it has only blunt-edged instruments. The Government had five years with almost unlimited expenditure to fight this war and failed to win it and I think gradually the body politic, the electorate, Congress, came to

realize it was not going to win. Through the medium of the free press, which had by and large reported the war fairly accurately (although obviously mistakes were made), the American public got a picture of that war and ended it. If there is an argument for a free press in a democratic country, this surely is it, that imperfectly they did come to the conclusion that they had to end this war and did end it.

If you work from the assumption that the Vietnam war was something worth going on with, that the Americans could have won it, that it would have been better had they stayed, anything that worked against that, including television, was harmful. Television showed the brutality of what was a particularly bloody war, and it emphasized, by the constant repetition of pictures each night, how long it was dragging on and how little was being achieved. If, on the other hand, you work from the assumption – as most Americans now do – that the Vietnam war was a mistake in the first place, how can you blame television? The reverses were purely military ones. The costs, human and economic, proved too great to be borne. Television merely reflected this state of affairs. It did not create it. The Tet offensive was mounted by the Vietcong, not CBS. To reason that because Vietnam was televised and was also lost, *ipso facto* any war extensively televised can never be won is a logical absurdity.

Nor is it true that exposure to television pictures of blood and gore prompted people to become more pacific. American viewers saw vastly more horrific images of war than did British viewers of the Falklands conflict. They saw, to pick merely the most famous examples, a man being executed by being shot in the head, a girl plastered with burning napalm, and Morley Safer's 1965 film of American soldiers methodically destroying the village of Cam Ne. Yet evidence suggests that prolonged TV coverage actually encouraged the

American public to *support* the war. A survey conducted by *Newsweek* in 1967 found that 64 per cent of viewers felt *more* like 'backing up the boys in Vietnam' as a result of watching TV; only 26 per cent said it made them feel more hostile to the war. By 1972 a further *Newsweek* survey revealed that people were becoming progressively more indifferent to the horrors being repeated nightly on their TV screens. The war had become unreal. Television, wrote Michael J. Arlen, the TV critic of the *New Yorker*, 'for all the industry's advances, still shows one a picture of men three inches tall shooting at other men three inches tall'. As Philip Knightley later put it in his book on war correspondents, *The First Casualty*: 'when seen on a small screen, in the enveloping and cosy atmosphere of the household, some time between the afternoon soap-box drama and the late-night war movie, the television version of the war in Vietnam could appear as just another drama.' A prominent American psychiatrist, Fredric Wertham, found that TV had the effect of conditioning viewers to accept war. Some might argue that this dulling of the senses and confusion of reality with fantasy is potentially much more dangerous than any sapping of the appetite for war by nightly exposure to its agonies.

The MoD, naturally, did not see it that way. As early as 1970, at a Royal United Services Institute seminar, the then Director of Defence Operations, Plans and Supplies at the Ministry of Defence, Brigadier F. G. Caldwell, told his audience that after Vietnam, if Britain were to go to war again, 'we would have to start saying to ourselves, are we going to let television cameras loose on the battlefield?'

Twelve years later, the evidence of the military commanders in the Falklands to the House of Commons Defence Committee shows how much the Caldwell interpretation of Vietnam still held sway. 'Thank heavens we did not have unpleasant scenes shown,' said Brigadier Tony Wilson, the commanding officer of 5 Brigade. 'It would have been singularly debilitating to our wives and our families.' Wilson, Moore, Captains Black and Middleton and the task force commander, Admiral Woodward, all believed that their men would have preferred their families at home not to see precisely what they were involved in. To Wilson it was a 'merciful relief' that between the landing on the Falklands and the ceasefire 'we got no letters, therefore we were totally unaware of the effect that the war was having on our own wives and the like.' General Moore spoke of the 'very great strain' felt by his 11-year-old son 'because he was very conscious that our pictures were on radio and television every day. . . . He felt a very heavy responsibility, almost as if he was commanding the land forces, poor chap.'

There is a great danger here that subjective reasons, like General Moore's understandable concern about his son, based on a partial view of the American experience in Vietnam, may combine to prevent television coverage of war on the dubious grounds of its possible effects on morale rather than for clearly understood reasons of operational security. The military are always going to insist on the maximum amount of secrecy: 'I wouldn't tell the people anything until the war is over,' an American military censor is reported to have remarked, 'and then I'd tell them who won.' But if we allow censors to stray from straightforward matters of security and enter into questions of taste and tone and 'national morale', we are in a different area. In a war in which the homeland is threatened with invasion and the whole of the native system of government is at stake, clearly the morale of the ordinary citizen is a vital consideration. In such circumstances some freedoms may have temporarily to be suspended, as they were in the Second World War. But in relatively limited operations like the Falklands, can the same criteria be applied? Is it legitimate for the Government to deny its people the right to see such things as bodies in bags or to hear phrases such as 'horribly burned'?

The Falklands war went on long enough to raise such questions, but not long enough to answer them. A few more weeks' fighting, a few more television pictures, and we might indeed have learned how far the Government and the military have taken the so-called 'lessons of Vietnam' to heart.

Some idea of the complexity of the relationship between politicians, civil servants, military commanders and television can be seen in the way all four reacted to the first and most shocking of Britain's reverses in the Falklands campaign: the loss of HMS *Sheffield* on 4 May.

Sheffield, a Type 42 destroyer with a crew of 270, was on picket duty 20 miles ahead of the main British carrier group when shortly after 2 p.m. she was hit by a single, air-launched Exocet missile. On board *Hermes* Brian Hanrahan saw 'a pillar of white smoke on the horizon, which continued to climb until dark and the decision was made to abandon her'. Two frigates, *Arrow* and *Yarmouth*, were sent to help fight the fire, but their efforts were in vain and at seven o'clock that evening the ship was finally abandoned.

Confused signals of what had happened began arriving in London towards the end of the afternoon. By 6 p.m. Mrs Thatcher had been told, and an emergency meeting of Ministers and service chiefs was convened at her room in the House of Commons. The mood, according to one of those present, was 'very grim'. Clearly, a statement would have to be issued soon: already, by 7.40, the BBC had heard through 'political sources' that *Sheffield* had been hit and was pressing for further news. Throughout the war, the British were anxious not to give extra credence to Argentine statements by allowing them to be first with the news of British losses. Accordingly, Ian McDonald, the Ministry of Defence's official spokesman and at this point in the war still the official in charge of the MoD's public relations department, hastened to the House of Commons. He waited outside Mrs Thatcher's room until, shortly before 9 p.m., John Nott emerged briefly to tell him that the meeting had agreed to announce the attack on *Sheffield*. McDonald raced back to the MoD Press Centre, set up two days before and housed in one of the MoD's large 'historic' rooms. He is said to have drafted the details of the short statement on the journey back from Parliament.

The BBC's main television bulletin, the *Nine o'Clock News*, was actually on the air when McDonald burst into the Press Centre. The BBC's political editor, John Cole, was talking about the day's events at Westminster. He was suddenly told through his earpiece to wind up his report, and the BBC switched through live to the MoD. McDonald, seated like a newsreader behind a desk, was given a cue by the BBC cameraman and began to read.

> In the course of its duties within the total exclusion zone around the Falkland Islands, HMS *Sheffield*, a Type 42 destroyer, was attacked and hit late this afternoon by an Argentine missile. The ship caught fire which spread out of control.
>
> When there was no longer any hope of saving the ship, the ship's company abandoned ship.
>
> All who abandoned her were picked up. It is feared there have been a number of casualties, but we have no details of them yet.
>
> Next of kin will be informed as soon as details are received.

McDonald was so nervous during the reading of this statement that at one point he thought he would never be able to reach the end.

For anyone who saw it, it was a dramatic piece of television: the news bulletin proceeding in its usual way, a momentary confusion, and then the dramatic appearance of the sombre, dark-suited McDonald with his funeral parody of an announcer's voice. It was a shock deeply resented by many of the professional broadcasters, who had no opportunity to soften its impact and who felt they were being forced into a position of treating McDonald almost as if he were one of their own correspondents. Richard Francis, a former director of News and Current Affairs at the BBC, spoke of McDonald's 'eerie style' as he delivered the news 'in a way that hit at the stomachs of the country'. There were 12 million viewers of the *Nine o'Clock News* that night, the largest audience reached by the programme in the whole course of the war. 'We had no opportunity to condition this mass audience to what was to follow,' claimed Francis. The news was heard simultaneously all over the country: by wives and families of men who had been on board *Sheffield*, by fellow naval officers in the wardroom at Devonport, where McDonald's statement was greeted by a stunned silence followed by swearwords, and by MPs at the Palace of Westminster.

The House of Commons is the kind of institution that is easily swept by panic and rumour. John Nott had already told the Leader of the House, John Biffen, that he was not prepared to make a statement that night, but now the Conservative Whips began to come under intense pressure from nervous back-benchers. In the Chamber, a debate on Scottish local government was in progress when the news broke. MPs of all parties rose one after the other to demand a statement on the loss of the *Sheffield*, and finally, much against his will, Nott came into the Chamber a few moments before 11 p.m. Some indication of the confusion within the Ministry of Defence can be gathered from the fact that Nott began by saying that twelve men were missing, and a few minutes later a note was seen being passed along the benches from his Civil

Service advisers forcing him to revise his estimate of casualties in the light of fresh news to thirty.

While all this was going on in London, 8,000 miles away Brian Hanrahan and Michael Nicholson were filming survivors coming on board *Hermes*. By listening to conversations on the bridge, by talking to men rescued from *Sheffield* and from snippets of information picked up from friendly officers, the two men had arrived at a 'rough order of magnitude' of casualties, which led them to believe, said Hanrahan, that it was 'something below fifty'. 'Certainly by six o'clock in the evening,' claimed Nicholson, 'we knew that most of the survivors had been rescued, that *Sheffield* was still afloat.' But to Nicholson's chagrin, he was prevented from sending a dispatch stating, '*Sheffield* has been hit. She is still afloat. Most of the crew has been saved.' Nor was Bernard Hesketh, the TV cameraman, allowed to hitch a lift in one of the helicopters travelling between the carriers and *Sheffield* to film what was happening. 'There were a lot of people to get to and fro,' explained Admiral Woodward later, 'fire-fighting equipment and all the rest, so on the afternoon of the strike there was no question of getting press there, and the premium on weight per helicopter was a matter of lifesaving, not of photographing chaps drowning.'

A day of frustration for the reporters was capped when the BBC World Service, picked up on board ship, broadcast McDonald's statement, and later reported Nott as telling the House of Commons that *Sheffield* had been sunk and it was not known how many survivors there were. Later Nicholson supplied the Commons Defence Committee with a bowdlerized version of his diary entry for 4 May. The full entry was more outspoken:

Action stations piped 1310 hours, enemy planes detected on 118 degrees: 1420 hours HMS *Sheffield* hit by single Exocet from Etendard fired from six miles. Survivors came aboard. RAF Vulcan bomber makes 2nd attack on Stanley airfield ... also our Harriers have another go. One of our planes is missing ... Nick Taylor's. We are not allowed to report any of this. *I stick my neck out all day on this island sweating every time I hear a red air alert and at the end of the day I hear some fart who goes to bed every night in London* [i.e. McDonald announcing the news]. We are suffering heroic redundancy.

The frustrations continued throughout the days which followed. On 5 May, the day after the attack on *Sheffield*, her captain, Sam Salt, and some of his men, were found by Nicholson 'in the dark on the floor of the hangar deck'. 'Extraordinary man,' noted Nicholson. 'Agrees to be interviewed but MoD PR intervenes and Salt is taken away for a briefing. He returns two hours later, a different and much-subdued man.' It was Nicholson's belief that Salt 'had been told about certain areas he should not talk about and was a totally different man ... they were censoring before the camera was switched on.'

Another incident which suggests that the Navy was concerned with censoring as much on the grounds of taste and tone as on strictly military criteria occurred two days later, when the body of a *Sheffield* casualty was buried at sea from the quarter-deck of *Hermes*. The television reporters were told to keep away: 'It wouldn't be decent to film it.' In a later argument with the MoD minder on *Hermes*, Graham Hammond, Nicholson recorded Hammond as telling him: 'You must have been told you couldn't report bad news before you left. You knew when you came you were expected to do a 1940 propaganda job.'

The Navy naturally did not want bad publicity – and as it controlled every facet of the environment in which the journalists worked, it was well placed to get its own way. For several days after the attack on *Sheffield*, repeated requests to be allowed to send Bernard Hesketh to film the still-burning ship were refused. 'We were interested in hiding the fact that *Sheffield* was still afloat from the Argentinians,' says Woodward, 'because that might have encouraged them to attack again.' This seems an odd excuse, given the fact that there was no way the television pictures (which would anyway be subject to censorship) could be got back quickly to London. Eventually, after three days, Woodward relented – but only because he needed the pictures for his own use. 'It became necessary for me to have rather more direct information, if I could, of the state of the ship.' Hesketh was accordingly sent off in a helicopter and flew over the burning hulk. The Admiral was pleased with the result: 'They took some jolly good photographs which were of immense use to me.' Only after the cassette of ENG material had been fully analysed on a video machine by Woodward and his advisers was it released to the broadcasters. The following day HMS *Sheffield* sank.

The announcement of *Sheffield*'s sinking, when it was made back in London, revealed another way in which the authorities subtly 'cleaned up' the image of the war for television. Sir Henry Leach, the First Sea Lord, instructed Ian McDonald not to announce the final loss of *Sheffield* in a televised statement. 'The discreet black and white of newsprint was considered more dignified than the glare of television,' was how one insider described the reasoning behind this decision. Each day McDonald would read a statement to the media. He would then pause, order the cameras and lights to be switched off, and then answer questions. Television was allowed to record only the statement, never the question-and-answer sessions. It was in one of these non-televised exchanges that McDonald let slip the fact that *Sheffield* had sunk. (The refusal to allow, after the statement, the televising of any further comments – which were attributable and not off the record – was justified on the grounds that a 'code' had sprung up between McDonald and the press, in which he would hedge, fence and often joke, behaviour which was considered likely to 'confuse' a mass audience and which would have robbed McDonald of his aura of omnipotence.)

When the public did finally see the television pictures of the events surrounding the loss of *Sheffield*, they were three weeks old. The pictures of the survivors and the interview with Captain Salt were filmed on 4 and 5 May and transmitted on the night of 26 May. The pictures of *Sheffield* taken for Admiral Woodward on 7 May were finally shown in London on 28 May. By then the landings had taken place at San Carlos Bay, fighting on the Falklands had been going on for a week, and the war had moved into a completely different phase.

Television's presentation of the loss of *Sheffield* showed the extent of the authorities' control over the media: the terse official statement in London, the restrictions on filming and reporting imposed by the Navy, the use of non-televised question-and-answer sessions to minimize the impact of bad news, the painfully slow progress home of pictures, so that they were of little more than historical interest by the time they arrived. 'There has been confusion,' insisted the BBC at the end of the war. 'There have been failures. ... Above all, there has been a failure of perception of the role of the media in a free society at a time of conflict. Even within the identifiable parameters of security, there have been attempts to "manage" or "manipulate" the news.' Subsequently questioned about these allegations by the Labour MP John Gilbert, Sir Frank Cooper was unrepentant:

> We did not produce the full truth and the full story and you, as a politician, know as well as anyone else that on many occasions the news is handled by everybody in politics in a

way which rebounds to their advantage. I regard that as something for politicians to decide but where lives are at stake, as they were in this case, I believe it was right to do as we did and I have never lost a moment's sleep on it.

Television journalists, like newspaper reporters, expect that in the normal course of events politicians and civil servants will try to manipulate them. But the situation during the Falklands crisis was not normal. The unique circumstances of the campaign gave the authorities virtually complete control over news of the fighting. Information, especially pictures, came out in a thin trickle.

This had some exotic side-effects. Current affairs programmes came to resemble a strange hybrid between children's television and sport. Tasteful watercolours had to represent what was happening in two of the areas to which cameras had no access: Parliament and the South Atlantic. Toy models of ships and aircraft moved endlessly across giant maps (or 'sandpits' in TV jargon). Around these clustered retired military commanders, passing their professional comments on the match in progress, on likely tactics and possible results. Clips from promotional films for planes, ships and missiles became scratched through repeated showings. . . .

To the increasing annoyance of officials and some politicians, the networks turned for news to Argentina. For the first time in history, television could freely report the enemy's view of the war. There were interviews with ordinary Argentinians and even with military officers. Film of the war taken by Argentine TV was shown in Britain. And, perhaps inevitably, some slight credence began to be given to the Argentine version of events as a result.

One of the most disturbing elements in the 'information war' [claimed the BBC] was the change in approach of the Argentines. Initially, the Argentine claims were patently hysterical, self-evidently propagandist, and unerringly identified as such by the broadcasters . . . but to our intense dismay, it began to emerge that some of the Argentine claims were possibly true and accurate. Journalists realized (with considerable difficulty, and with alarm, let it be said) that increasingly Argentine claims merited close examination, and should not, as hitherto, be rejected out of hand. The in-built delays in the MoD system, which prevented swift rejection or confirmation of such claims, was a self-inflicted wound. It gave the Argentines, internationally, a credibility they did not deserve. The MoD's information was, too often, the 'runner-up'.

And that, perhaps, was the greatest damage of all.

By the beginning of May, BBC executives in Portland Place and White City were feeling thoroughly frustrated. They had no pictures. They had a strong suspicion that they were being used and that the MoD was not telling the whole truth. They had programmes to fill and precious little information to go on. For news they were having to rely increasingly on statements from Buenos Aires and leaks from intelligence sources in Washington. . . . The effect on the BBC's coverage began to be noticed, especially within the Conservative Party.

Newsnight was reckoned by the BBC to be having 'a good war'. Its speciality – explaining in detail the background to daily events – was ideally suited to the fast-moving Falklands story. The programme was extended from five to seven nights a week; on some evenings its normal audience was quad-rupled. On Sunday, 2 May, the programme's defence expert, Peter Snow, was trying to analyse precisely what was going on in the South Atlantic, using information from Britain, the United States and Argentina. 'Until the British are demon-strated either to be deceiving us or to be concealing losses from us,' he concluded, 'we can only tend to give a lot more credence to their version of events.'

The programme had only just come off the air when a complaint came in from the Conservative MP for Harrow, John Page. *Newsnight*, he said, was 'totally offensive and almost treasonable'. Page's anger was provoked by what he called the BBC's 'unacceptably evenhanded' approach to the war in balancing reports from the MoD against those of Argentina. Page, a 62-year-old former Royal Artillery officer, was not the only angry viewer. In his sixth-floor office in the Ministry of Defence, Frank Cooper – though an old admirer of Snow's – was watching *Newsnight* with increasing exasperation ('Peter was behaving as if he were a disinterested referee,' commented Cooper).

The following day the BBC moved in swiftly to try to quell the beginning of the controversy:

> In times of hostility, as at all other times [ran an official statement], the BBC has to guard its reputation for telling the truth. In its coverage of the situation in the South Atlantic, BBC Television and Radio has reported British, American and Argentine statements and reactions while stressing the unreliability of Argentine claims.

The storm might have blown over. But then, on Tuesday, came the news of the loss of *Sheffield*. A mood close to panic gripped the Conservative Party. 'It was a terrible night,' recalled Julian Critchley, a back-bench Conservative MP. 'For the first time there was a realization that what we had started might end badly – not just for the Tory Party, but for the nation and for everyone involved in the task force.' In this emotional state many Conservative MPs were in no mood to listen to the BBC's Reithian pronouncements about guarding a reputation for truth. Until now the BBC had been reporting the war. From this point on it was part of it.

FIVE

The Enemy Within

The BBC is rarely popular with Prime Ministers, especially Prime Ministers in time of war. As long ago as the Second World War, Winston Churchill, according to Lord Reith, described the Corporation as 'an enemy within the gates, doing more harm than good'.

At the time of the Suez crisis, Anthony Eden was incensed by what he saw as the BBC's unpatriotic behaviour: he found it 'insulting' that the Australian premier, Robert Menzies, was initially denied the opportunity to give a television broadcast in support of the British Government on the grounds that this would be unfair to the Opposition. He was equally furious to discover that BBC World Service programmes were quoting British newspapers antipathetic to his policies over the Canal, and that the Labour leader, Hugh Gaitskell, was to be given the right of reply to his prime ministerial broadcast. Relations deteriorated to a point at which, in October 1956, the Prime Minister ordered the Lord Chancellor, Lord Kilmuir, 'to prepare an instrument which would take over the BBC altogether and subject it wholly to the will of the Government'. 'The next I heard,' wrote Harman Grisewood, at that time chief assistant to the BBC's Director-General, 'was that Eden had found Kilmuir's draft inadequate and he had been asked to prepare something stronger.' No wonder that on 28 November the writer and broadcaster Harold Nicolson

noted: 'The BBC are very fussy about not making any controversial remarks about Suez.' Illness and defeat intervened
before Eden could take his schemes any further.

Given this record, it is not surprising that the BBC braced
itself for trouble from the outset of the Falklands crisis. The
young BBC journalist who produced the Menzies broadcast
when it eventually took place after pressure from Eden was
Alasdair Milne. Twenty-six years later, he was the BBC's
Director-General-designate. 'I always thought the Government would turn on us,' he remarked. 'Once there were losses
and the Government came under pressure, they would be
likely to turn on the media and the BBC in particular. But it
happened several days later than I expected.'

Such an attack was all the more likely given the personality
of Mrs Thatcher. Within six months of taking office in 1979
she had attacked the BBC in Parliament and called on it to
'put its own house in order' following some filming of the
IRA. Repeated bouts of anger, both privately and publicly
expressed, punctuated the following two years. Generally ill
at ease on television, Mrs Thatcher is inclined to tick off the
media in much the same way as she is said to hector her
colleagues.

A good example of this tendency during the Falklands
conflict – the memory of which still causes her staff to wince –
came after the recapture of South Georgia on 25 April, when
she emerged from 10 Downing Street and strode in front of
the television cameras with John Nott and a retinue of
advisers in tow. 'Ladies and gentlemen, the Secretary of State
for Defence has just come over to give me some very good
news, and I think you'd like to have it at once.' Mrs Thatcher
nodded to Nott. 'The, er, message we've got . . .' he began,
and went on to read out Admiral Woodward's signal: 'The
white ensign flies alongside the Union Jack in South Georgia.
God save the Queen.' An immediate chorus of 'What happens

next?' arose from the assembled reporters. 'Just rejoice at that news,' instructed the Prime Minister, firmly, 'and congratulate our forces and the marines. Good night, gentlemen.' Mrs Thatcher walked back to No. 10 pursued by questions: 'Are we going to declare war on Argentina?' 'Rejoice!' came the parting injunction from the retreating Prime Minister before the door was slammed, literally in the media's face.

The Prime Minister herself did not see *Newsnight* on 2 May but her advisers did, and when, on 6 May, John Page rose to ask her about the media during Questions to the Prime Minister, she was well prepared. Would she, asked Page, in the course of her 'extremely busy and responsible day',

> try to find a few moments to listen to the radio and watch television, and judge for herself whether she feels that the British case on the Falkland Islands is being presented in a way that is likely to give due confidence to friends overseas and support and encouragement to our Service men and their devoted families?

The Prime Minister replied:

> Judging by many of the comments that I have heard from those who watch and listen more than I do, many people are very concerned indeed that the case for our British forces is not being put over fully and effectively. I understand that there are times when it seems that we and the Argentines are being treated almost as equals and almost on a neutral basis. I understand that there are occasions when some commentators will say that the Argentines did something and then 'the British' did something. I can only say that if this is so it gives offence and causes great emotion among many people.

Other Conservative MPs followed the Prime Minister's lead. Speaking on the same day to a London conference on terrorism and the media, Winston Churchill, a Conservative defence spokesman, attacked broadcasters for 'reporting live propaganda out of Buenos Aires', and added, without any apparent sense of irony: 'I believe it to be a travesty of the role of the journalist to swallow hand-outs, and report what is provided at face value ... I believe one must exercise one's judgement and not allow oneself to become a vehicle for propaganda and misleading information.' Robert Adley, MP for Christchurch and Lymington, accused the BBC of being 'General Galtieri's fifth column in Britain'. Conservative papers in Fleet Street joined in. The *Sun* denounced Peter Snow as being among the 'traitors in our midst' (see chapter 3). The *Daily Mail* felt that 'Mrs Thatcher was quite right when she criticized some of the Falklands news coverage on radio and television.'

A few hours after the Prime Minister's comments, the BBC's Chairman, George Howard, had an opportunity to reply in an after-dinner speech at the Hilton Hotel. The Corporation, he insisted, 'is not, and could not be, neutral as between our own country and the aggressor'.

> Coupled with that is a determination that in war, truth shall not be the first casualty. .... The public is very rightly anxious about the future, and deserves in this democracy to be given as much information as possible. Our reports are believed around the world precisely because of our reputation for telling the truth.

The BBC did not change its policy. Despite complaints, news-readers continued to refer to 'the British' rather than to 'our' forces – a decision based on precedents established in 1939 and reaffirmed in 1956. 'If you start talking about "our troops" and "our ships",' explained Milne, 'then it is natural to speak of "our policy" when you mean the present Government's policy, and then our objectivity would no longer be credible.' This restriction was not applied to the task-force correspondents who came to identify very closely with the men they were with and who spoke of 'we' and 'our'.

On the following Saturday night (8 May) the evening news reported on the funeral of Argentine seamen killed in British attacks, included film of a Buenos Aires press conference, 'and – to add insult to injury –' complained Robert Adley, 'we had a film of the Argentine-Bulgaria football match with a great show of national fervour.' It was the start of a busy period for BBC telephonists as callers rang in to complain about 'disgusting' even-handedness and 'undue reverence' for Argentine casualties. These skirmishes were but a curtain-raiser for the open warfare that was to come.

That weekend, a few hundred yards from Television Centre, in the crumbling old studios in Lime Grove which once housed British Gaumont, *Panorama* finished the first rough assembly of a film about opposition to the war. For more than a week, reporter Michael Cockerell and producer Tim Shawcross had been interviewing opponents of the Government's policy. The rough-cut was viewed by the head of BBC Television current affairs programmes, by *Panorama*'s editor, and by the programme's recently arrived presenter, Robert Kee. Kee, in particular, violently disliked the film, and a long list of changes was agreed; twenty alterations were made to the script, and there were a further eighteen cuts in the film itself. One entire sequence, an interview with a dissenting Conservative MP, Robert Hicks, was dropped. Four anti-war voices remained: those of two Labour MPs, George Foulkes and Tam Dalyell, and two Conservatives, David Crouch and Sir Anthony Meyer. Eduardo Crawley, a journalist, analysed the war as it appeared from Buenos Aires. Such a film was likely to be controversial at any time. Following a week in which television's treatment of the war had already been attacked in Parliament by the Prime Minister, the programme was destined from the outset to provoke uproar.

The film was due to be transmitted on Monday 10 May. That morning, a meeting of Mrs Thatcher's inner circle of Ministers, the 'War Cabinet', discussed the whole question of the media and the Falklands campaign. One of the prime objectives of the Government was to keep public support for the war at a high level, especially following the loss of the *Sheffield*. There was concern at the way in which the war was coming across on television and a considerable amount of criticism of the MoD for the lack of television pictures: the task force had now been at sea for more than five weeks, and still nothing had come back to London. (Significantly, two days later the MoD once more got in touch with the broadcasting organizations to have another try at getting pictures back by satellite.) Fresh from this discussion, the Foreign Secretary, Francis Pym, went straight to a meeting of the House of Commons Foreign Affairs Select Committee. Once again the question of television was raised, this time by yet another Conservative back-bencher, Peter Mills, the MP for Devon West. 'All of us are aware of the criticisms of the presentation, particularly by the BBC,' Pym told the committee. 'The Government are very concerned about it indeed.' He urged anyone in the country who disapproved of the BBC to write to the Corporation direct. It had not been a good day for the broadcasters, and it was by no means over yet.

'Good evening,' began Robert Kee at the start of that night's *Panorama*. 'The Government, the country, perhaps the world itself, is precariously balanced this evening. . . .' The first item in the programme was an interview in New York with Jorge Herera Vegas, the Argentine Minister to the United Nations. After five inconclusive minutes of this, Kee appeared once more in order to present a long and in parts tortuous introduction to Michael Cockerell's film. Instead of labelling it, simply and clearly, as a film about the minority view of the Falklands, Kee devoted about three minutes to a restatement of various points of view, including those of Argentina, Mrs Thatcher and the Archbishop of Canterbury. The fact that what followed was not meant to be a representative report on the general state of opinion in Britain was rather buried.

Seen in retrospect, the film hardly appears the 'subversive travesty' it was subsequently accused of being. But the timing could scarcely have been worse, and this time, in her flat in 10 Downing Street, Mrs Thatcher *was* watching. She saw George Foulkes labelling the sending of the task force 'a crazy reaction' and Tam Dalyell asking why, if the Argentines were as 'unpleasant' as she claimed, Britain had, in the last twenty years, 'traded with them, welcomed many of their most senior people from the Junta in this country and sold them arms all the time'; she saw one of her own MPs, David Crouch, warning that 'if the war goes on ... we may be judged to be standing on our dignity for a colonial ideal', while another Tory back-bencher, Sir Anthony Meyer, his voice breaking, made an appeal for peace:

> Once you get into a war situation, anybody who says 'For God's sake, let's stop it' is labelled as a defeatist. This is a label that you ... you have to face up to it. My experience in the war was no worse than anybody else's, except that all my friends were killed. ... I saw the effect that it had on their families, and it left me with a horror of war which goes very, very deep. I just ... if our national survival is at stake, yes, clearly, we have to fight. If we're faced with the Russians – I'm not a disarmer or a unilateralist – if we're faced with the Russian threat, of course we fight. But anything short of that – I don't believe that killing can ever be the right answer.

'I think the principles involved are quite clear,' commented Eduardo Crawley:

> Let me put it like this. Principle number one is that one cannot

tolerate the occupation of part of one's territory by a foreign power, and it is perfectly legitimate to try to expel the intruder; principle number two is that one cannot negotiate sovereignty under duress, namely while somebody else is occupying part of one's territory; principle number three, it is wrong to flout a resolution by the United Nations Security Council; this puts one out of international law, so to speak.

Now, odd as it may seem to the British public, these are precisely Argentina's arguments. . . .

Finally, the Prime Minister – 'transfixed' is how one source described her – heard Cockerell describe how one of her 'former Cabinet Ministers with excellent Ministry of Defence contacts told me that there had been reservations from the start about the Falklands mission by the Chiefs of Staff', specifically Sir Michael Beetham, Chief of the Air Staff.

Following the film there was a studio interview lasting about ten minutes with Cecil Parkinson, the Conservative Party Chairman. It was noticeable that Parkinson made no reference to the film despite the fact that he had been sitting watching it. 'And that is all from *Panorama* for this evening,' said Kee at the conclusion of the programme. 'Until next week, when we will again probably be discussing the Falklands crisis in, we hope, a different mood, good night and' – he added with prophetic finality – 'goodbye.'

Reactions to the programme were immediate and almost unanimously hostile. About four hundred callers rang to register complaints, but these represented perhaps only half of the total, as hundreds more found the lines to the BBC's duty office jammed. Those who did get through had to wait on average twenty minutes to register their views; some waited almost an hour. The BBC's Manchester newsroom alone took over forty calls. The complaints began within a couple of minutes of the programme's going on the air (these were objections to the interview with the Argentine Minister), and the last were still being logged in the early hours of the following morning. Other complainants turned to Fleet Street. *The Times* reported 'a number of people' who rang it to complain. The *Sun* remade its front page: 'Outrage over the Beeb!' proclaimed the banner headline: 'Storm at Panorama's "despicable" Argie bias'. The paper reported 'dozens of patriots' who rang and 'branded *Panorama* a "bloody disgrace" .... former Cabinet Minister Geoffrey Rippon called it "one of the most despicable programmes it has ever been my misfortune to witness".'

Mary Whitehouse issued a statement calling the programme 'arrogant and disloyal': 'It prostituted the power their profession gives as broadcasters. To spread alarm and despondency was a treasonable offence in the last war. One wonders what succour this sort of broadcasting gives the people of Argentina.'

At the House of Commons, a group of Conservative MPs led by Eldon Griffiths, Anthony Grant and Peter Mills tabled a motion entitled 'Anti-British Broadcasting by the BBC':

> This House, having provided that the BBC shall enjoy all the benefits of broadcasting on the basis of a compulsory levy on the public and in the context of a democratic society whose freedoms require to be defended if they are to endure, records its dismay that some BBC programmes on the Falklands give the impression of being pro-Argentine and anti-Britain, while others appear to suggest that the invasion of these British islands is a matter in which the BBC is entitled to remain loftily neutral: and calls on the Corporation, if it cannot speak up for Britain, at least not to speak against it.

'I told you this would happen. See what you've done,' said Kee to Cockerell and Shawcross the following day.

That morning in *The Times* John Page returned to the

attack on *Newsnight*, referring to Peter Snow's 'superior tone of super-neutrality which so many of us find objectionable and unacceptable'. Perhaps, he wondered, it might be possible to set up some kind of independent complaints board to monitor the BBC?

Prime Minister's questions were due to be taken at 3.15 that afternoon. Any hopes the BBC may have entertained that *Panorama* would not be brought up were swiftly dashed. Mrs Sally Oppenheim, a former Minister in Mrs Thatcher's Government, rose to denounce the previous night's *Panorama* as 'an odious, subversive travesty in which Michael Cockerell and other BBC reporters dishonoured the right to freedom of speech in this country', and to ask: 'Is it not time that such people accepted the fact that if they have these rights, they also have responsibilities?' Having seen the programme and anticipated the question, Mrs Thatcher had carefully rehearsed her remarks:

THE PRIME MINISTER: I share the deep concern that has been expressed on many sides, particularly about the content of yesterday evening's *Panorama* programme. I know how strongly many people feel that the case for our country is not being put with sufficient vigour on certain – I do not say all – BBC programmes. The chairman of the BBC has assured us, and has said in vigorous terms, that the BBC is not neutral on this point, and I hope his words will be heeded by the many who have responsibilities for standing up for our task force, our boys, our people and the cause of democracy.

MR WINNICK (Labour MP for Walsall North): Does not the Prime Minister agree that one of the virtues of a political democracy is that radio and television should be independent from constant Government control and interference? Would it not be useful if some of her right hon. and hon. Friends stopped their constant intimidation of the BBC? Perhaps the

Prime Minister would take the hint as well?

THE PRIME MINISTER: It is our great pride that the British media are free. We ask them, when the lives of some of our people may be at stake through information or through discussions that can be of use to the enemy – (*Interruption*) – to take that into account on the programmes. It is our pride that we have no censorship. That is the essence of a free country. But we expect the case for freedom to be put by those who are responsible for doing so.

The ultra-patriotic Sir Bernard Braine ('Braine of Britain', as he is known), who had earlier said that the Argentine occupation was enough 'to make any normal Englishman's blood boil', was quickly on his feet. Has the Prime Minister, he thundered over a swelling chorus of cheers and boos, 'been made aware of the rising tide of anger among our constituents at the media treatment and presentation of enemy propaganda and the defeatist views of an unrepresentative minority? Is she aware that an increasing number of people are telling us that this amounts to a sort of treachery?' At the word 'treachery' there was a minor eruption, with Conservative MPs waving their arms and pointing at Tam Dalyell and Tony Benn sitting on the Labour benches. 'Our people,' said the Prime Minister, when the din had subsided, 'are very robust and the heart of Britain is sound. I hope that individually they will make their views directly known to the BBC, by their letters and telephone calls.' The Labour leader, Michael Foot, entered the fray. The Prime Minister's remarks, he said, were 'concerned with the important matter of how freedom of discussion is to be conducted in this country'. 'Some of us', he added to loud Labour cheers, 'are determined to defend it.' He went on:

Before the right hon. Lady pursues further her strictures of the BBC, where I am sure people are seeking to do their duty in difficult circumstances, will she take some steps to reprove the attitude of some newspapers that support her – the hysterical bloodlust of the *Sun* and the *Daily Mail*, which bring such disgrace on the journalism of this country?

THE PRIME MINISTER: ... The media are totally free to discuss and publish what they wish. Equally, as the right hon. Gentleman has demonstrated, we are free to say what we think about them.

Before the exchanges could progress any further, Tam Dalyell rose to make a point of order which brought the afternoon to its noisy climax. Sir Bernard Braine, he said, had referred to himself and the other Labour MP who took part in *Panorama*, George Foulkes, as traitors, while Mrs Oppenheim had referred to 'dishonour': 'Some of us who have been in the 7th Armoured Division, who have been gunner operators on tanks and many of whose contemporaries in training were shot up with the King's Royal Irish Hussars in Korea, take it ill to be accused of treachery and dishonour.' Uproar ensued as MP after MP rose to try to make points of order. The Speaker suggested that 'it would be in the interests of the House if, during these difficult days when there is severe tension both here and in the country, we tried to avoid the words "treachery" and "treason", and such things, because they advance nobody's argument.' Refusing to take any further points of order, he brought Prime Minister's Question Time to an abrupt end. Later that same day a group of furious Conservative MPs surrounded Sir Anthony Meyer in a corridor. 'You are a disgrace', said one of them, 'to your school, your regiment and your country.'

The row was given extensive coverage in the press. In the absence of any pictures or much news from the South Atlantic, here was a fight in which everyone could take part. It was a gift to Fleet Street cartoonists. The *Daily Mail* showed

Mrs Thatcher as a television newsreader: 'Here is the news. There has been a shake-up at the BBC.' The *Daily Express* depicted a studio set labelled 'Traitorama' and a discussion between the Kaiser, Admiral Tirpitz and Generals Hindenberg and Ludendorff: 'If Britain admits German sovereignty over the "British" Isles,' says one, 'we'll stop the war.' In the *Mirror* a family watches as its television blows up with the caption 'Her Majesty's Government regrets the necessary destruction of your set, but points out you were tuned to the BBC.' In the *Sun* the BBC newsreader is an Argentinian, complete with sombrero and Zapata moustache: ''Ello! 'Ere's ze latest unbiased news on ze Falklands crisis.'

John Stokes, Conservative MP for Halesowen and Stourbridge, writing to *The Times* about the BBC, lamented 'the apparent inability of its management to *supervise* producers properly'. Sir Angus Maude, a former Cabinet Minister in charge of overseeing the Government's media 'image', complained that the BBC 'seemed to be deliberately combing the world to find people who could be persuaded to say that almost everything the British Government did was either militarily dangerous or diplomatically inept'. 'Whatever happened to the BBC Voice of Britain?' asked an article in the *Daily Mail*, suggesting that the Corporation was politically biased and run by 'lightweight liberal intellectuals'.

Most newspapers picked up a remark made by the Managing Director of BBC Radio, Richard Francis, who told the International Press Institute in Madrid:

> feelings of humanity apart, to report the resilient reaction of the Argentine people to the losses among their armed forces provides an important element of the picture for the British people. The widow of Portsmouth is no different from the widow of Buenos Aires. The BBC needs no lesson in patriotism.

The *Sun* suggested that 'smug Mr Francis should be down on his plump knees, giving thanks' that he wasn't living in Argentina, where journalists were 'kidnapped, terrorized and beaten and then dumped practically naked'.

Yet despite all the abuse, the BBC refused to yield. This surprised some. In the past it has not always been so deaf to political criticism. But Sir Ian Trethowan, the Director-General, was away at that time, and in his absence his designated successor, Alasdair Milne, remained firm. 'We might increase our popularity by appearing jingoistic,' he said in an interview with the London *Standard* on 12 May, 'but then no one would believe what we were saying. I do not intend to trade our reputation to please such critics.' The BBC, he claimed, is 'the British Voice of Truth':

> The notion that we are traitors is outrageous. There is no one in the BBC who does not agree that the Argentines committed aggression. But this is not total war. One day we will be negotiating with the enemy so we must try to understand them. We at the BBC have re-examined our broad policy and will not change it. We have no sense of guilt or failure.

A few hours after the article appeared, Milne's resolve was to be given a severe testing in the last set-piece battle between the BBC and the Conservative Party during the Falklands war.

The Tory Media Committee normally attracts only a handful of MPs to its meetings, but on the night of Wednesday, 12 May, more than a hundred crowded into Committee Room 13 at the House of Commons to what was advertised as an opportunity to 'exchange views' with George Howard and Alasdair Milne but turned into what one blood-spattered participant later described as 'an ox-roast'. 'You have to understand', says one 'wet' Tory backbencher, 'that as far as most Conservatives are concerned, the BBC is at best a collection of Hampstead liberals. At worst, it's a Marxist conspiracy.'

The two BBC men were, at first sight, totally dissimilar. Milne, a professional broadcaster all his life and still only in his early fifties, is a product of Winchester and New College, Oxford, a man renowned for a forensic intellect and a cutting tongue. Howard, 62, ex-Eton, ex-Balliol, is a wealthy land-owner, a former officer in the Green Howards (the family regiment) and owner of Castle Howard. There was an unspoken arrogance in both men which provoked additional anger within some sections of the Tory Party.

From the outset it was accusations rather than questions that were hurled at the two men from a violently hostile meeting. Milne tried to answer:

> The first time I spoke [he recalled later], they barked, 'Can't hear you!', so I said I'd speak up. Then they shouted, 'Still can't hear you. Stand up!' It was like being in the Star Chamber. When they got really angry, they started waving their order papers and growling like dogs.

Milne was not cowed – he was furious. After the first few minutes he took no further part in the proceedings. 'He sat there,' says one MP who was at the meeting, 'a small figure, hunched and saturnine, with an expression of mixed incredulity, contempt and anger.'

The main job of tackling the criticisms fell to the bulky figure of George Howard, 'who stood like an eighteenth-century Whig grandee – which in many ways is what he is – confronted by a group of angry tradesmen and looking as though he'd like to set the dogs on them'. Normally Howard has a reputation for wearing shirts with the pattern and texture of sofa covers, but in honour of this occasion he was soberly dressed in dark suit and tie.

The first part of the meeting was devoted fairly specifically to attacks on the *Panorama* programme. The denunciations then moved into the broader area of the BBC's coverage, with furious attacks from such figures as Winston Churchill, Alan Clark and John Biggs-Davison. Churchill in particular attacked the remarks of Richard Francis, claiming that 'at least the widow of Portsmouth pays a licence fee.' Howard tried to quote the precedent of the Second World War. To roars of 'Hear hear!' and the banging of desk tops, Churchill mocked that at least then the BBC hadn't given equal time to Dr Goebbels: 'I suggested he should have the courage to sack those responsible for *Panorama* or offer his resignation. He ducked that one.' 'He was kicked all round the room,' said one MP of Howard. 'It was the most appalling, lamentable and disgraceful performance. There was no apology or contrition.'

At the end of an hour, MPs streamed out of one door, while Milne, white with rage, and Howard, his face dripping with sweat, slipped out of another, heading, it was widely believed, for the more congenial atmosphere of William Whitelaw's office.

The descriptions of the private meeting given out that night by MPs read like the type of one-line reviews normally found outside cinemas showing horror films: 'Blood and entrails all over the place', 'They were roasted alive', 'They went for their throats'. 'We have seen the whites of each other's eyes,' commented Geoffrey Johnson Smith, the chairman of the meeting. To Sir Hector Monroe, former Sports Minister, it was 'the ugliest meeting I have ever attended in my years as an MP'.

It was a tribal ritual of a sort which only the English ruling-class male, with his experience of public-school raggings, could have mounted; in retrospect it can be seen to have exposed and destroyed the Conservative right's witch-hunt against the BBC virtually overnight. Neither Milne nor Howard had shifted their ground, yet from this point onwards there was to be little more criticism of the BBC. It was as if someone had thrown a switch. The MPs drifted away and seemed purged of their anger. Milne and Howard were left to lick their wounds. Milne, according to Geoffrey Johnson Smith, 'simply seemed profoundly unimpressed with the intellectual calibre of the arguments put up against him'. Howard told reporters afterwards: 'I am not prepared to apologize for the programme.' According to the *Observer*, the main injury was to his dignity. He objected to newspaper reports of him mopping his brow as if in terror: 'It was very, very hot in that room.' The extent to which the poison had been drawn can be gathered from the fact that the following week, Sir Ian Trethowan, now back at the BBC, paid a visit himself to the Commons and was heard in respectful silence by an all-party meeting of MPs.

A week which had begun badly for the BBC ended remarkably well. *The Times*, the *Guardian* and the *Daily Mirror* all carried editorials supporting the corporation. So too did a number of regional papers, including the *Yorkshire Post* and the *Glasgow Herald*. A clear signal to the militant right of his Party to calm down came on Friday from the Leader of the House of Commons, John Biffen. He told Conservatives in Scotland that, 'like the freedom of dissent and debate in Parliament, free speech is a bulwark of the national liberty which the Conservative Party has always defended.' The most unexpected statement, but perhaps the most significant, came from the Prince of Wales. On 14 May, in a speech given at the Open University before an audience which included George Howard, he praised the British media for being made up of 'independent personalities' and 'not servants of the state machine'. He admitted they might 'get it wrong from time to time', but added, 'My goodness, you certainly can't please everybody.'

The only fly in this soothing ointment, as far as the BBC was concerned, was Robert Kee. On the day that John Biffen and Prince Charles made their contributions to the debate, Kee made his in a letter to *The Times* attacking *Panorama*:

> I am naturally grateful to the Chairman and Director-General-designate of the BBC [he wrote] for loyally defending me among other colleagues against criticism of the film section in that programme, but wish to release them from the obligation in my own case since I must dissociate myself from the defence.

Kee revealed that he had been so unhappy with the 'poor objective journalism' of the film that he had actually considered disowning it live on air, 'but in the interests of immediate programme solidarity decided not to'.

Kee had taken over as presenter of *Panorama* at a salary of around £1,000 per programme the previous January. It had not proved an especially happy arrangement from the beginning, and the 62-year-old presenter had made a shaky start to the Falklands war, first in a carping and much criticized interview with Lord Carrington immediately after the latter's resignation on 5 April, and then, in the edition before the controversial 'anti-war' programme, in an interview with the Prime Minister considered by many to be excessively obsequious. After his letter to *The Times*, which breached the agreement under which he was employed, the BBC decided to suspend Kee for a month, pending a decision about his future. To his colleagues on *Panorama* it seemed a maliciously ill-timed moment to attack them, just as the argument about Monday's programme appeared to be over. They made it clear that they would be unhappy at having to work with him again, and Kee, under contract anyway to the new breakfast programme *TV-AM*, resigned. He never presented *Panorama* again. It was a bitter end to an association with the BBC spanning almost a quarter of a century, which had included a highly praised series on the history of Ireland.

The noisiest attacks on the BBC may have come from the right, but the broadcasters were also under continual fire from the left. On 9 May the Ad Hoc Falkland Islands Peace Committee (a pressure group composed of nineteen organizations, including the Campaign for Nuclear Disarmament and the United Nations Association) wrote to the BBC setting out its belief that 'the coverage of the Falklands Islands conflict has been biased towards the military viewpoint to the detriment of the minority view, which calls for an immediate truce, negotiations and a stop to this war.' Tony Benn repeatedly insisted that the media were deliberately ignoring 'the people in this country who want the war to end'. The Glasgow Media Group, persistent left-wing critics of television news coverage, claimed to show that the peace groups were given a disproportionately small amount of publicity by comparison with their size and importance.

The BBC found its supporters in the centre of the political spectrum. The Liberal leader, David Steel, and the SDP MP William Rodgers tabled a Commons motion on 11 May regretting the 'intemperate attacks' made on the BBC: 'These attacks are deeply distasteful to many of those members who have hitherto given the Government steady support.' Even within the Conservative Party it was noticeable that certain senior figures appeared to be distancing themselves from the Prime Minister: William Whitelaw, as Home Secretary the Minister ultimately responsible for the BBC, was eloquent in his complete silence on the subject; John Biffen went out of his way to defend the principle of free speech; and Francis Pym, while suggesting that members of the public should write to the BBC if they had any complaints, pointedly remarked: 'It is not for me to express a view, even if I had one.' Add Prince Charles and the editorial support of *The Times* and the *Sunday Times*, and it is clear that the Establishment moved swiftly to protect one of its own kind.

This appeal to the centre goes beyond mere sympathy for the BBC as an organization. Television, as William S. Paley, the man who created CBS, has remarked, is itself a *consensus* medium. In its news coverage it reflects and consolidates accepted beliefs. It does little to help foster new ways of thinking. Hence its persistent critics are generally to be found on the radical fringes of politics. If the BBC has had a rougher time than usual over the last few years, that is mainly because of the arrival on the scene of a Prime Minister very much *not* in the consensus mould, along with the general ascendency of militants in both major parties. The reaction of these groups to the television coverage of the Falklands war was symptomatic of a much more deeply rooted hostility.

If politicians tended to respond according to type, what did the average viewer make of television's coverage and the row which surrounded it? Undoubtedly the argument made an appeal to a certain type of right-wing nationalism lurking behind many a suburban lace curtain. 'You snide bastard,' ran one typical letter to Michael Cockerell. 'We're sick and tired of you lefties sitting in your cushy jobs and not having the decency to remember your duty as an Englishman. . . . We want and expect loyalty and patriotism from our reporters in emergencies like this. You'd better watch it, you overbearing prejudiced creep.' But every reporter and producer occasionally receives such letters (for some reason often in green ink on lined paper). The BBC switchboard had been jammed often enough before the Falklands war, possibly from the same people, following programmes on subjects like immigration.

It is impossible to estimate how many letters and phone calls came as a direct result of the Foreign Secretary's and the Prime Minister's call to the public to make its views known to the BBC. Anger is a much stronger feeling than satisfaction, and because of the effort required to register a view, the number of complaints is inevitably in excess of the number of compliments. Even so, in an interview with Chris Dunkley published in the *Financial Times* on 15 May, Alasdair Milne claimed: 'On the night after the Media Committee row we had 251 against us but 200 ringing in support. That's most unusual.' The claims made by some Conservative MPs about the number of letters they were receiving from constituents who were hostile to the BBC may also have been exaggerated. 'Because I'm a former chairman of the Media Committee,' says Julian Critchley, the Conservative MP for Aldershot, 'I reckon to get more letters about this sort of thing than most MPs. During the whole of the war I received just one letter complaining about the BBC.'

Further support for the theory that the attacks on the BBC were unrepresentative of the mood of the country as a whole can be seen in two opinion polls commissioned at the time. An independent survey carried out for the BBC by the Audience Selection company found that 81 per cent of 1,049 viewers and listeners questioned thought that the BBC had behaved 'in a responsible manner in its coverage of the Falklands crisis'; only 14 per cent thought it had not been 'responsible'. The same proportion, 81 per cent, thought the BBC should 'pursue its traditional policy of reflecting the full range of opinions'; 10 per cent thought it should not. The poll was conducted on Thursday, 13 May, after the controversial *Panorama* and *Newsnight* programmes and the attacks in the Commons.

The following week, a poll conducted by Gallup for the *Daily Telegraph* was slightly less favourable but still broadly reinforced the earlier findings. Sixty-two per cent thought the Corporation was reporting the crisis fairly; 22 per cent thought it was not. When broken down according to political affiliation, the poll showed clearly that the closer to the centre of the political spectrum, the greater the support for the BBC.

Question: The BBC in particular have been criticized for not fairly representing the British point of view. Do you think this criticism is or is not justified?

	Con. %	Lab. %	Lib. %	SDP %
Is	32	25	26	12
Is not	57	61	64	71

One of the justifications for the attack on television was that it gave aid and comfort to the enemy not merely by reporting his point of view, but also by the amount of harmful speculation about military options it fuelled. Both networks had a stage army of retired military officers who appeared regularly to give their views of the significance of events in the South Atlantic. 'We had a smallish band of people,' said the editor of ITN, 'who, like World Cup commentators, we had as part of the essential team.' On 29 April Mrs Thatcher expressed her unhappiness with this stream of semi-informed comment. 'Everything they say', she told Parliament, 'may put someone's life in jeopardy.'

The notion that Argentina might pick up useful ideas from these discussions was flatly rejected by the broadcasters. 'Argentine intelligence just isn't that defective,' claimed Milne. That is also the private view of senior officials inside the Ministry of Defence now that the war is over. An enormous amount of technical data about British weapon systems is available from unclassified sources such as Jane's books on ships and aircraft. At one point ITN set out to do a story showing how much information was available simply in the trade press of the international arms industry. 'In the event the story was squeezed,' lamented David Nicholas after the war. 'I regret that we did not do that. I think the public would have understood how much more readily accessible this information was.'

The Argentines certainly should have been aware of our fighting capability. Not only did we sell them a large amount of our military hardware, but we also laid on demonstrations of specific items, such as the Harrier jet, in an effort to persuade them to buy. Nor were retired officers likely to think up many strategic ideas which would not have already occurred to the Argentines themselves. As Sir Frank Cooper pointed out:

> Anyone who looked at the map would see it is not as though there are vast numbers of population centres or vast numbers of roads. I think there are 60 miles of paved roads in all the Falkland Islands – no, less than that. You do not need to be a genius to start speculating: the range of military options was indeed a fairly narrow one.

It would have greatly suited the Government if the media had confined themselves to straight reporting of the very limited amount of hard news which was available about the Falklands campaign, completely ignored what was going on in Argentina, and left it at that. But such an idea seemed preposterous to the broadcasters. At a time of enormous world interest they would have had to cut back their news and current affairs output: they could not have filled the programmes with what was officially available. But beyond that, the networks understandably felt a *duty* to inform the public.

The attack on television, which started and ended so abruptly, coincided with a period of doubt about the wisdom of sending the task force – doubt which some programmes reflected. This nervous atmosphere, coupled with a long-standing antipathy towards the BBC among certain Conservative back-benchers, produced a week-long crisis in relations between the Corporation and the Government. The BBC was singled out for attack rather than ITN because it has more resources for reporting foreign news and because it produces, in programmes like *Newsnight* and *Panorama*, many more hours of news and current affairs. It is also a British institution, publicly owned, with a unique history and reputation.

The BBC was caught in a pincer attack: the Ministry of Defence and the lack of news and pictures of the task force on one flank; the Conservative Party with a demand for more 'helpful' coverage on the other. The Falklands crisis reinforced the lesson of 1940 and 1956: that in time of war a conflict of interests inevitably exists between the Government and the BBC.

SIX

The Ministry of Truth

The battle between the BBC and the Government was given extensive coverage in the rest of the world's media. The *Guardian*'s Harold Jackson reported from Washington:

> The recent parliamentary row about the BBC's handling of the crisis was reported by American television in much the way it might have reported the tribal rites of Borneo headhunters – as a weird quirk, surviving unsuspected in the modern world. ....
> This American view of war reporting stems not only from the First Amendment guarantee of a fair press, but from a simple democratic conviction that the taxpayer has a right to know how his money is being spent and to express his opinion about it.

Sir Bernard Braine startled American audiences when he appeared on US network television to denounce *Panorama* as 'the pathway to anarchy'.

The BBC row illustrated the contrast between the position of the media in this country and the constitutionally safe-guarded role of the press in the United States. Paul Scott Mowrer, editor of the *Chicago Daily News*, defined the duty of the press as it is seen in American eyes in a speech made during the Second World War: 'The final political decision rests with the people. And the people, so that they may make up their minds, must be given the facts, even in war time, or, perhaps, *especially* in war time.' It is clear that in many respects the British people were *not* given the facts during the Falklands war. Information was handed out slowly and often reluctantly by the Ministry of Defence; rumours were allowed to circulate unchecked; and the British authorities frequently used the media as an instrument with which to confuse the enemy.

The military commanders were quite open about their intention of making use of the press. According to John Witherow, Captain Jeremy Black told the *Invincible* journalists that they were 'one of the weapons systems in the fight against Argentina'. When *Hermes* left Ascension, Brian Hanrahan recalled:

> We had a chat with the Admiral, Admiral Woodward, who said it was his intention to try and cause as much confusion to the enemy as possible; he intended to keep them guessing about what he intended, where he intended to do it and what means he intended to deploy and if there was any way in which he could use us as part of that attempt to confuse the enemy, he intended to do so.

Woodward happily confirmed the conversation:

> As I remember it, I probably said words to the effect that all is fair in love and war, and a military man for military reasons should be prepared to use misinformation, as we call it; but I think I probably qualified it by saying, perhaps as a result of conversation with Mr Hanrahan and Mr Nicholson, that I quite recognized this might be politically unacceptable.

Newsmen, said the Chief of the Defence Staff, Sir Terence Lewin, after the war, were 'most helpful with our deception plans'.

'Deception' and 'misinformation' are recognized military techniques in which the British have long experience. 'In wartime,' Churchill told Stalin in his famous comment at Teheran in 1943, 'truth is so precious that she should always be attended by a bodyguard of lies.' During the Second World War there were many examples of official concealment or outright lying to the press. The British Air Ministry exaggerated the known number of enemy planes shot down during the Battle of Britain by one-third. During the 'Crusader' tank battle in North Africa, the British claimed to have destroyed more tanks than Rommel actually possessed. German claims that we were deliberately bombing their civilians rather than their military installations were true but were dismissed as 'propaganda'. The extent of our military defeats in France in 1940, in Greece and at Dieppe were all concealed. When correspondents described the situation at Anzio in 1944 as 'desperate', Churchill told the Commons that 'such words as "desperate" ought not to be used about the position in a battle of this kind where they are false. Still less should they be used if they were true.'

A generation later, in 1982, this was still the official view. But the difference was that this was not Total War, in which the morale of a munitions worker had to be nurtured as much as a commando's. This was a limited action. The two sides never even declared war. Yet the military reacted as if national survival were at stake. When Sir Terence Lewin was asked whether 'deceiving the press or deceiving the public through the press is reasonable . . . on grounds of operational security or morale', he replied:

> I do not see it as deceiving the press or the public; I see it as deceiving the enemy. What I am trying to do is to win. Anything I can do to help me win is fair as far as I am concerned, and I would have thought that that was what the Government and the public and the media would want too, provided the outcome was the one we were all after.

The omission of certain crucial pieces of information, the decision to restrict press briefings to a minimum, the censorship on grounds of taste as well as on grounds of security – all created an image of the war in the British media which often bore little relation to the truth. 'I looked in the newspapers,' said Max Hastings on his return from the Falklands, 'and was simply staggered to see what a load of complete misinformation was being transmitted.' This policy, combined with the fact that only British reporters were allowed to sail with the task force, had ramifications that extended beyond Britain itself. The Vice-President of one American network news organization told ITN:

> The British press was discounted here as a reliable source of news all during the Falklands engagement. It was understood, although not really mentioned, that there were a lot more things going on than the press reported and that therefore there was a form of lying going on. Not necessarily the lying of telling false facts but saying misleading things for devious purposes. What was reported would have been believed here if there were Americans present.
>
> I mention this in part because to us news executives one of the annoying parts of it all was to rely so heavily on so few people who had no connection with our news operations. But that is a parochial concern which is not necessarily a problem for any Parliament. What should be a problem for those in Parliament is that the Government always wants to be believed but in circumstances like that, it won't be. A prescription for disbelief is easy to write: don't let any nation in; be obvious in your manipulation of what the reporters there say; protest that you are the home of the free and the land of the brave.
>
> Basically, I think it is any nation's right to run its war any way it likes. What it ought not to expect is that others will believe its protestations when it does so in a foolish way.

Britain, said Alan Protheroe towards the end of the Falklands conflict, 'lost the information war'.

It was the Ministry of Defence in London which was held to be chiefly responsible for the poor quality of the coverage and for several incidents which either bordered on, or manifestly were, the result of 'misinformation'.

The official in charge of the MoD's public relations department when the Falklands crisis began was, by a fluke of timing, a man with no formal training in handling the press. Ian McDonald, 46 years old, is a career civil servant who has spent his entire working life in the MoD, having joined it after graduating with a degree in English and Greek from Glasgow University. After years of steady promotion he had become, by 1979, the assistant secretary in charge of Division 14, the Ministry's recruitment and pay section. Although not a post renowned for requiring a detailed knowledge of the world's media, three years ago McDonald abruptly moved across to become the Ministry of Defence's deputy chief of public relations (DCPR).

Public relations officers in Whitehall belong to a structure that is separate from the department in which they happen to work, administered by the Central Office of Information. The post of DCPR at the MoD was an historical aberration outside this system, created after the Labour Defence Secretary, Fred Mulley, was photographed asleep at an RAF ceremony attended by the Queen. The job of DCPR was created specifically in order that an able professional civil servant could act as a personal PR shield for Mulley. But when Mulley left, the post was not abolished. Instead a classic case of bureaucratic evolution ensued. The position of DCPR was enhanced by the presence of a weak chief of public relations and by the fact that its occupant had constant access to the main source of power, the Secretary of State. Additional duties were added. By the time McDonald took over, DCPR was responsible for handling the media in all matters relating to nuclear weapons. 'It was a crazy situation,' says one senior Whitehall information officer. 'I don't know how any professional PR man worth his salt could put up with it.'

When the post of chief of public relations fell vacant at the end of 1981, McDonald applied for it. He was considered to have a good chance, if only because he was one of the few MoD civil servants to enjoy a close personal association with the prickly John Nott. But McDonald was passed over. The job went instead to Neville Taylor, the favoured candidate of the Prime Minister's press secretary, Bernard Ingham. Because of illness and a backlog of work at his old job as head of PR at the Department of Health and Social Security, Taylor was unable to take up his new post immediately. It was agreed that McDonald should continue as acting head of PR at the MoD until June 1982. It was in this state of bureaucratic confusion that the Ministry of Defence public relations department suddenly found itself caught up in the most hectic crisis in its history.

To deal with the world's media, McDonald had working to him three service directors of public relations – military officers principally responsible for liaising with service PR men scattered among the British forces around the world – a further four servicemen and eighteen civilian press officers. In the initial rush to arrange accreditation, McDonald also had to try to lash together some sort of information policy to present to Nott. 'I can remember very distinctly', he said later, 'that there was a time at which I closed the door of my office and locked it and sat trying to think it out for five minutes.'

The plan McDonald emerged with was a novel one. Most journalists were expecting the Ministry of Defence to provide extra facilities. McDonald decided to *cut back* drastically on the MoD's contacts with the media. Hitherto, defence correspondents had been kept informed of the general direction of the Ministry's policy by means of regular off-the-record briefings with the Permanent Under-Secretary, Sir Frank Cooper: these were to be stopped. Information was to be rationed strictly to official statements, which would be issued each day at noon by McDonald. Apart from this, no information was to be communicated to the media. There were three central reasons for this clamp-down, as McDonald later explained:

> First of all, we ourselves, and the Chiefs of Staff, were working out what to do; there was no absolute plan at that stage; it was being formulated. . . . Secondly, at that time the main initiative was with the Foreign Office and with diplomacy. The task force was seen very much as an adjunct to that diplomacy. The Foreign Office was having its regular briefings, and therefore it seemed to me that the MoD . . . could restrict itself to on-the-record briefings. The third thing was the security aspect. There was a very strong feeling that in fact to talk about where the Fleet, the task force, was, how it was being split up as it sailed to the Falkland Islands, would be to give information to the Argentinians about possible intentions. I did not see how, talking unattributably off the record, we would be able to avoid trespassing on those kinds of areas.

McDonald simply stopped speaking privately to the press, and he instructed everyone else in his department to do the same.

The press took the cancellation of background briefings badly. It laid the foundation, wrote the Press Association, for 'the loss of credibility from which [the] MoD never recovered'. Some defence correspondents, dependent on being spoon-fed information in non-attributable briefings, were left with nothing to say. Even many conscientious journalists were wrong-footed. Over recent years the only battles spoken of in the Ministry of Defence have been those fought over budgets and Treasury forecasts. The last thing many *defence* correspondents expected to have to write about was a *war*. 'Today we have a new breed of defence correspondent,' says one official, 'who is much more adept at writing about things like cash limits than warfare. The Falklands hit this type of journalist amidships.'

Tony Smith, the defence correspondent of the *Daily Star*, wrote that the press was 'enraged that normal practice was not carried out. . . . we were given no more information than the man from *Pravda*.' The blackout extended to the most respected correspondents. 'In normal times,' claimed Jim Meacham of the *Economist*, 'I could call up the Chief of Public Relations and ask how many tanks are in Germany and he would tell me, within reasonable tolerance. During the Falkland Islands war they would not tell me if there were any tanks in Germany or even if there was a Germany.' Members of the Foreign Press Association attacked 'the high-handed or indifferent attitude' of the MoD and claimed that the 'inadequacy' of the briefings led 'to Argentine sources exercising undue influence in the foreign press'.

The refusal of the MoD to give the media guidance did nothing to stop speculation. Indeed, as David Fairhall, the defence correspondent of the *Guardian*, pointed out, 'it was sometimes the lack of real information that led, rightly or wrongly, to speculation about tactics.' McDonald's policy – which was approved by Sir Frank Cooper and John Nott – fostered a climate in which rumour festered and the press became highly suggestible.

When the crisis began, newspapers reported that HMS *Superb*, one of Britain's nuclear-powered hunter-killer submarines, was on her way to the Falklands. Where did this story originate? No one seems able to remember. It was suggested that the submarine was seen leaving Gibraltar, and then that a Conservative MP, following a briefing by the junior Foreign Minister, Richard Luce, told the press that *a* submarine was on her way south. It somehow became accepted as fact and illustrates how, in the absence of hard news, the press feeds off itself. Jon Connell, defence correspondent of the *Sunday Times*, describes the process:

> Because information was so thin one was picking it up sometimes from one's colleagues, sometimes from reading other newspapers and getting what were not really confirmations but probably talking to somebody in the House or somebody in the MoD who might indicate, yes, there was a submarine on the way, or something to that effect. I cannot precisely remember in that instance what it was that made us print it.

It later emerged that *Superb* was undergoing repairs at her base in Scotland. Yet whenever the journalists asked McDonald to confirm that *Superb* was in the South Atlantic, he refused to comment. The MoD's defence was that it never reveals the positions of its submarines. But to the press it looked as if they had been misled deliberately: it was, after all, useful for the British to have the Argentine navy believe there was a submarine lurking closely by to deter it from venturing out of harbour. 'We were positively and unquestionably encouraged', claimed Jim Meacham, 'to think (and write) that this nuclear submarine had gone south.' The result, as Connell observed, was to make the defence correspondents look 'pretty silly . . . because obviously our sources were not good'.

For hard news of what was happening the media had to rely on McDonald's attributable noon briefings. At their inception he made two promises to the journalists: he would not tell them 'an untruth', but neither would he say anything which might prejudice the success of the task force or jeopardize the lives of the men aboard it. In the interests of keeping the second promise, he came perilously close to breaking the first.

On the way to Ascension, *Invincible* developed severe problems with her engines. Rumours reached London, by way of American intelligence, that one of the carriers was in trouble. McDonald knew he would be asked questions and knew also that a 'no comment' would provoke a flurry of damaging speculation. But by an extraordinary stroke of luck the press had become convinced that it was the aged *Hermes* rather than the modern *Invincible* which was in difficulties. They asked: 'Is *Hermes* suffering from mechanical problems?' McDonald was able to deny it firmly and to bring the briefing swiftly to a close. It was not always so easy.

On Wednesday, 21 April, men of the Special Air Service (SAS) were landed on a glacier on the remote island of South Georgia. By the following morning they were in severe difficulties and three helicopters set off to rescue them. In blizzard conditions, with winds of up to 100 miles an hour, two of the helicopters crashed. No one was injured, but thirteen SAS men and four helicopter crewmen would have died in the freezing conditions had it not been for the skill of a single Wessex helicopter pilot in rescuing them.

In London, when the news first came through, it was thought that there were no survivors. 'You can imagine how we felt,' says one senior MoD official. 'This was the first real action of the war, and it was a terrible reversal. It provoked hideous memories of the American helicopter disaster when they tried to rescue the hostages in Iran.' The accident was so sensitive that it was agreed not even to raise it at the morning meeting of the Chiefs of Staff committee. With negotiations with Argentina still in progress, it was thought that the news of the disaster might change the mood in the country and the House of Commons. It might even lead to the recall of the task force.

It was in the full knowledge of what had happened on South Georgia that Ian McDonald faced the press on 24 April and told them: 'The task force has not landed anywhere.' Newspapers had already begun claiming that operations to recover South Georgia were under way. Sceptical reporters began to press McDonald. He refused to go any further or to define what he meant by 'the task force' or a 'landing'. Technically, McDonald insisted afterwards, he had not broken his pledge never to tell 'an untruth'. The SAS patrol, he argued, was not 'the task force'. The loss of the two helicopters emerged only by accident three weeks later, when a serviceman wrote home telling what had happened.

When South Georgia *was* captured on 25 April, the British public were given the morale-boosting but completely false impression that it had been an effortless victory. The defence correspondents were treated, said Meacham, to 'a fairly comprehensive briefing, we thought, by a Marine Corps officer at the Ministry of Defence with a great big map about how this went ... it certainly led us all to believe that the South Georgia operation had been a great success.'

In Downing Street that night Mrs Thatcher instructed the press to 'Rejoice!' In Parliament the next day she praised the 'professional skill' of what was portrayed as an operation of surgical precision. On board *Hermes* Admiral Woodward gave an interview in which he jubilantly described the near-fiasco on South Georgia as 'a walkover'.

The press reflected the official line. The *Daily Telegraph* called the British forces 'cockleshell heroes'. 'Victory: Quick-Fire Marines Grab Penguin Isle' was the headline in the *Daily Star*. 'Victory!' proclaimed the *Sun*, reprinting in large type Woodward's grandiloquent signal which began 'Be pleased to inform Her Majesty. . . .' The Government's triumph over the media was almost as great as the victory over Argentina. When Max Hastings on board *Canberra* read the newspapers a few days later he could hardly believe it:

> Reports published in the newspapers in London of the way in
> which South Georgia had been retaken were complete and
> absolute rubbish from beginning to end . . . they did nothing to
> help our credibility on the spot when members of the task
> force were reading them. One wondered who had been feeding
> them all this stuff. . . .

Meacham considered it 'one of the major disinformation
operations of this campaign'.

With the onset of fighting, the pressures on the Ministry of
Defence to provide information became far greater. The Falklands crisis was now the dominant news story in the world.
Hundreds of British and foreign journalists had been assigned
to cover it. Clearly, it was no longer possible to limit facilities
to a single noon statement followed by a question-and-answer
session, briefings from which television and radio were completely excluded. Accordingly, a week after the retaking of
South Georgia, on Sunday, 2 May, the MoD opened an
Emergency Press Centre – known as 'the concourse' – which
had as its focus a large ground-floor room, appropriately
decorated with a portrait of Horatio Nelson.

The Centre opened at 10 a.m. and closed at 10 p.m.,
although occasionally it remained in use throughout the
night. Inside were a battery of telephones, including eight
direct lines to the largest media organizations. Radio and
television studios were housed inside the MoD and outside in
temporary huts in the car park. Visual display units were
installed, eventually capable of calling upon 1,250 pages of
computerized information: journalists could summon up all
previous official statements and answers to questions, par-
ticulars of task-force ships, biographies of senior officers –
every detail, down to how many Chinese cooks were sailing
with the fleet. Reporters had everything they needed except

the one thing they wanted most: news.

Over it all presided the urbane and evasive McDonald. By the time he emerged on to the floor of the concourse at noon he had already been at work for more than four hours, and the short statement he would read was the collective product of more than a dozen hands.

It had its genesis at 7.30 a.m., when McDonald arrived at the Ministry of Defence to read through the morning newspapers and to prepare a short summary of their contents. At about 8.30 he would meet Sir Frank Cooper to discuss information policy and listen in while Cooper was briefed on the overnight situation by the MoD's night-duty staff. The first broad outline of what might be released to the media would begin to take shape.

From the MoD McDonald would walk across to 10 Downing Street for the daily meeting of the Information Co-ordination Group, chaired by Bernard Ingham. Here the British Government's overall public relations strategy was decided between a variety of interested officials, including Nicholas Fenn, head of PR at the Foreign Office, a representative from the Central Office of Information ('responsible', in the words of the MoD, 'for maintaining the information effort abroad'), an official from the Cabinet Office, and the private secretary to Cecil Parkinson, who, as the one member of the War Cabinet without a department to run, had become the Government's chief ministerial spokesman. Sir Frank Cooper delicately described the activities of this group as 'a touching hands exercise'.

Back to the MoD again, where McDonald would attend the daily meeting of the Chiefs of Staff committee. 'The higher you get,' declared Sir Terence Lewin, 'the more aware you are of the great importance of public support and the part that the media play in providing you with public support and parliamentary support.' The extent of that awareness was reflected in the prominence given to PR on the Chiefs of Staff Committee's agenda: it was always considered as the third item, after discussion of the relative military situations of Britain and Argentina. The Committee's members – the three service chiefs, Lewin, Cooper, Nott (or, more often, his private secretary), and representatives from the intelligence services and the Foreign Office – would listen while McDonald read out his summary of the editorial policies being adopted by each of the Fleet Street papers, devoting special attention to those critical of any aspects of the war. Drawing on the views of the Downing Street meeting, and having heard the latest information from the South Atlantic, McDonald would then outline what he thought should be released to the media. Almost every day, said Lewin, the committee would take a view on the content of the statement to be made at noon that day to the press and decide whether or not to release certain pieces of information.

McDonald would then personally clear his draft statement with Cooper and Nott. At about 11.45 it would be sent off for typing, while McDonald snatched a few moments to brief the senior members of his own PR department. Finally, at 12 o'clock McDonald would make his way to the Press Centre, read out the statement, and invite twenty minutes of questions, nearly all of which he would neatly sidestep. The journalists called these daily rituals 'The 12 o'clock Follies'.

McDonald sweetened these generally futile exchanges with an unexpected display of showmanship. He had mild eccentricities of pronunciation: like a good classicist, he insisted on calling *Hermes* 'Hermays'. He was always ready to deflect questions with a suitable quotation. When asked to comment on the reliability of Argentine claims, he referred the media to Act III, scene iv, lines 52–4 of *Hamlet*. A frantic search for a copy of the play revealed the information:

Look
Here, upon this picture, and on this,
The counterfeit presentment of two brothers.

When the press corps had a special information centre tie made
– a pattern of red question marks on a dark background –
McDonald took to wearing one. The atmosphere of camar-
aderie and frustration, with anything up to 250 journalists
milling around waiting for news, reminded McDonald of a
prisoner-of-war camp.

Little of the flavour of this was conveyed on television, for
which McDonald adopted an attitude of great solemnity. Most
of his statements were recorded and shown on news bulletins.
Occasionally he was cued in 'live'. McDonald had never
appeared on camera before. The only advice he was given
beforehand was to hold his hands still, to look straight ahead
and to speak very slowly. The result was so far removed from
the normally slick performance of television personalities as to
make McDonald an overnight sensation. His slow and mechanical delivery earned him the nickname 'McDalek' from the
press. To Keith Waterhouse he was 'the only man in the world
who speaks in Braille'. Richard Ingrams wrote: 'He looks and
sounds like some especially gloomy dean reading the second
lesson at Evensong in a huge and draughty cathedral.'

Television transformed McDonald from an unknown
bureaucrat into a national celebrity. Taxi drivers refused to
take his fare. When it became known that he was a bachelor,
several offers of marriage arrived at the MoD. Throughout the
war, McDonald appeared to be most popular with women
viewers. One letter he still treasures reads simply:

Ian McDonald MP,
Defence Minister.

Dear sir,
    I would like to thank you for the calm, soothing way you

handled every announcement during the Falklands conflict.

As a mother of a marine who had serious burns out there, I can say with confidence that YOU helped me and my family, so don't let the stupid newspapers jibe you.

And please stay in office. We need gentlemen like you.

Fleet Street printed every piece of information about him they could find. He was the son of a Glasgow fish merchant. He lived in Belsize Park. He was shy. He wore washable suits. He collected exotic Indian art. He enjoyed Shostakovitch and Emily Dickinson. He had a snowy-haired, 73-year-old mother. ('I've never known what he did at the Ministry of Defence,' she told Jean Rook of the *Daily Express*, 'until he suddenly appeared on the telly. He's a wonderful son to me. . . .') A picture of McDonald aged six months was published, captioned 'The Naked Civil Servant'.

After the war, ITN attacked McDonald and recommended that 'In the event of a similar conflict, the chief defence spokesman should be a major military figure of the status of general or equivalent.' McDonald always argued strongly the other way: that by having all military information delivered by a civilian, Britain underlined that she was a democracy and 'scored a trick' over military dictatorships like Argentina. Besides, as he freely admitted, he was enjoying every moment of it.

But even as Ian McDonald was rising to prominence in newspaper articles and on television, his position behind the scenes was being undermined. Unknown to the media, a struggle was developing inside the MoD over who should control the Ministry's information policy.

Neville Taylor, the MoD's designated chief of public relations, had decided, in the light of the Falklands crisis, to leave the Department of Health and Social Security two months ahead of the originally agreed date in order to take up his new job at the Defence Ministry. He arrived on 13 April and immediately received an unpleasant surprise. When he opened his letter of appointment on his first morning he was informed that he was to take charge at once of all areas relating to the Ministry's public relations, *except the Falklands*. 'It merely said, in effect,' he recalled, ' "You are chief of public relations. These are your responsibilities but for the time being you will not be responsible for the Falklands public relations activities." ' He confessed to feeling 'some personal disappointment'.

This was scarcely surprising. Taylor, highly regarded by other senior Whitehall PR men, was a professional public relations expert. Until 1970 he had worked full-time at the MoD. He knew some of the service chiefs from the 1960s, when he had handled the media during the fighting in Indonesia. He chafed at his restricted responsibilities. 'I wanted to get stuck in the day I arrived,' he said. Instead he had to stand aside and watch a career civil servant doing the most important part of his job.

Given the natural antipathy that was likely to exist between two men who had competed for the same job only a few weeks before and the tremendous strain under which everyone at the senior levels in the MoD was working, a conflict between Taylor and McDonald became inevitable. Taylor came to represent all the grievances of the Ministry's professional public relations men who felt they had been by-passed by the administrator McDonald, who had centralized power in his own hands to a remarkable extent. All his staff had been forbidden to maintain their normal relations with the press. Only he was privy to the details of task-force operations through his attendance of the Chiefs of Staff Committee and his meetings with Cooper and Nott. He personally drafted the Ministry's public statements. Apart from rare occasions when a military expert was called in to provide additional information, only McDonald briefed the media.

The most frustrated group were the serving officers, the military directors of public relations whose normal task of looking after the 'image' of their particular services was completely suspended. Later Sir Terence Lewin was to express his sympathy with their predicament. 'I would have seen them playing a larger part earlier on,' he told the Commons Defence Committee, and went even further in his criticism:

> I believe not only could we have made more use of the Directors of Public Relations, Army, Navy and Air Force, who have built up a range of contacts with the media but also I believe we could have made more use of the public information officers, the public relations officers in each unit. Each unit in all the three services, down to ship, battalion, squadron level, has a nominated officer who as a part-time job is a public relations man . . . I do not think we made enough use of those chaps.

In retrospect, it was clearly one of the MoD's greatest failures. ITN 'repeatedly asked for facilities to record some of the efforts being carried out in industry, among the services and in the dockyards' but was turned down. 'To a public deprived of hard information about their own side and obliged to see and hear the uninhibited coverage of Argentine determination, such positive news would have come as water to a thirsty Bedouin.' As it was, 'great opportunities were missed for the positive projection of single-minded energy and determination by the British people in their support of the task force.' As David Nicholas shrewdly pointed out, the weeks during which there were no television pictures 'corresponded with the period when the Prime Minister was moved to ask why was nobody giving news about our boys'.

Another result of the concentration of power in the hands

of McDonald was that the service PR directors – the DPRs – would often not learn what had been happening in the South Atlantic until fifteen minutes before McDonald gave out the information to the media gathered in the Press Centre. The nearest they came to any significant role was during the slack periods in the afternoon, when, in the early days, McDonald would leave the MoD to snatch a few hours' rest. Then they each took a turn as acting chief of public relations on a rota basis.

To add insult to injury, the DPR also had to face the anger of journalists demanding to know why no one in the MoD was any longer prepared to speak to them.

> Correspondents [wrote ITN] became aware of the tension between the press office machine and the military directors of public relations. The impression was that the DPRs were not privy to the fuller background enjoyed by the deputy chief press officer who had been briefed by the Permanent Under-Secretary.
>
> Tensions built up between the civil servants who were controlling the information, the military PR men, who thought they should be controlling it, and the poor 'desk officers', who knew little, said little, and received flak from the press corps.

'The information service was actually told less than the press were,' said Bob Hutchinson of PA. 'On many occasions we told the information service what was going on.' The BBC's Alan Protheroe, who maintains close contacts with the military PR men in the MoD, reflected their frustrations in an article in the *Listener*, describing how they had been 'discounted and virtually eliminated from full and proper participation by the "administrative" civil servants'; he added, in another dig at McDonald: 'This practised machine was shunted into a siding by the mandarins.'

Slowly at first, but with increasing determination, Taylor

began to dismantle McDonald's control. His first direct involvement with the Falklands war came towards the end of April, when he was put in overall charge of the arrangements for the establishment of the Emergency Press Centre. He also lobbied Sir Frank Cooper to restart the off-the-record briefings that had been stoped by McDonald at the beginning of the crisis.

Cooper had been surprised at the extent of the media's hostility, and later he came to believe that McDonald's plan had been a mistake. 'I think,' he told the House of Commons Defence Committee after the war, 'with hindsight, that was probably an unwise decision – that we should have gone on with them or restarted them rather more quickly than we did. I think, given one's time over again, I would not have done it that way, quite frankly.' He refused to accept that the cancellation of background briefings had added to the amount of speculation in the media, but conceded it had done nothing to stop it.

On 11 May Cooper held the first off-the-record briefing since McDonald imposed his ban. For the remainder of the war these were held twice a week, chaired by Cooper, usually accompanied by a senior military officer or civil servant.

As May wore on and the fighting in the South Atlantic escalated, the disagreements between McDonald and Taylor became more bitter. Taylor criticized what he felt was the rigidity of the arrangements by which McDonald handled the media. He also opposed the installation of permanent camera positions in the Press Centre on the grounds that the moment McDonald walked in, the lights were switched on and the most insignificant news was given an artificial sense of drama. For his part, McDonald wanted to increase the involvement of television. Often the noon statement was not read out but simply distributed as a printed press release. McDonald thought he should make a televised announcement every evening. There was, according to one witness, 'violent dis-agreement' over this, with Taylor insisting that it would make the Ministry of Defence totally synonymous in the public's mind with McDonald.

The most serious argument between the two men arose over censorship. Until the early part of May the only control over the dispatches of the task-force correspondents was exer-cised in the South Atlantic. But as the fleet moved further south and fighting began, this expedient came to be regarded as inadequate. Two incidents in particular provoked trouble in London. On 1 May, the Fleet's Commander-in-Chief, Admiral Sir John Fieldhouse, who was directing operations from the naval headquarters at Northwood, learned that the task force had shot down two Argentine Mirage fighters through watching the news on television. He promptly sent off an angry signal to *Hermes* demanding to know why he had not been informed first.

Two days later, a British submarine torpedoed the *General Belgrano*. Michael Nicholson, on board the MARISAT ship *Olmeda*, happened to overhear on the bridge the name of the nuclear submarine responsible, HMS *Conqueror*. This was confirmed to him by what he calls 'a senior naval source'. Nicholson promptly broadcast the information in a dispatch to ITN's *News at One*. As far as Fieldhouse was concerned, this was the final straw. Not only are the whereabouts of individual British submarines regarded as top secret, but the death toll inflicted by the *Conqueror* was so great that it was believed that the officers and crew should be shielded from adverse publicity. Fieldhouse fired off such a stinging rebuke to Captain Middleton on *Hermes* that Middleton, in order, as he put it, 'to make known to him my displeasure', never spoke to Nicholson again.

Fieldhouse demanded the setting up of a second screen of censorship in London to vet all copy dispatched from the task force. Individual captains were no longer to be trusted. 'It was my opinion that it should be taken out of their hands,' said the admiral, 'and that the overall control of information should be handled by the Ministry of Defence.'

The dispute between McDonald and Taylor was over the form which that censorship should take. McDonald thought that the media, as far as possible, should censor itself. He wanted to build on the D-Notice system of voluntary restraints by editors. It would, in his view, be courting disaster for the Ministry of Defence PR department to become involved in the vetting of copy. Once they started along such a path, it would lead inexorably to the accusation that they were censoring on the grounds of taste as much as for operational reasons. Taylor derided the ramshackle D-Notice system and put forward the view that if any group were going to operate a second tier of censorship, it would be better if it were PR experts who understood the demands of the media. Taylor won, and McDonald found himself adroitly outmanoeuvred and at odds with his own department's official policy.

It was at this point that Sir Frank Cooper intervened. His personal opinion was that McDonald had done a better job than his predecessor, but that Taylor would do a better job than McDonald. Having made a decision, Cooper, a formidable administrator, was not the kind of man to delay his implementation of it. ('He looks like a cuddly teddy bear,' says one of his colleagues, 'but he's deadly.') Towards the end of the second week in May, Cooper told McDonald that he thought he was in danger of overdoing it. He was looking tired and strained. He should take a holiday. McDonald demurred. Cooper insisted. On 14 May McDonald told reporters in the Press Centre that he was taking the weekend off to spend at home with his mother in Glasgow. When he returned to London three days later, he found that Neville

Taylor was in complete control of the Ministry's PR depart-ment – including the Falklands. From 18 May onwards, McDonald was simply the Ministry's official spokesman.

By the middle of May, Sir Frank Cooper was conducting two regular sets of background briefings, one for editors, the other for defence correspondents. Neither was considered very useful.

The editors' meetings were concerned largely with com-plaints about facilities: it was soon apparent that they had nothing to do with information. On one occasion, 6 May, Sir Frank Cooper kept silent about the loss of two Harriers in a mid-air collision, while downstairs in the Press Centre it had become common knowledge and was shortly afterwards announced by Ian McDonald. Brian Hitchen of the *Daily Star* described the meetings as 'farcical':

> I was originally under the impression that the reason for the briefings was to establish mutual trust and understanding between the MoD and the press so that certain information which the Chiefs of Staff may not have wanted held up to public eye could be discussed and explained. This was a naive dream on the part of myself and most editors.

The *Observer* described them as 'mostly unproductive'. Occa-sionally they degenerated into noisy squabbles; Derek Jameson in particular was vociferous in his attacks on Sir Frank. 'Whenever it got a bit hot,' says Jameson, 'he'd drag up "the national interest". Here are you screaming, "Where's my bloody pictures?" and he says "It's my job to safeguard lives." There's not much of an answer to that.' At one meeting a television executive told Cooper that the MoD's organiza-tion of press coverage 'isn't a cock-up. It's an effing cock-up.' Jameson joined in asking: 'Next time, why don't you borrow the Israeli army's director of public relations?' 'Cooper', says

Hitchen, 'slammed down his glass of water, gathered up his papers and said, "I don't have to take this." We were all left looking at one another.' It was at one of these sessions that William Deedes, editor of the *Daily Telegraph* and an old friend of Cooper's, presented the Permanent Under-Secretary with a copy of *Scoop* and referred him to the passage in which the foreign correspondents – 'all, in their various tongues, voluble with indignation' – confront the Minister of Propaganda.

The defence correspondents proved to be much better behaved. Only 'accredited' journalists – that is, reporters recognized by the MoD as established defence writers, representing 'reputable' publications – were admitted to Cooper's meetings. When the *Sunday People*, which doesn't have a defence correspondent, hastily appointed one, he wasn't considered to be in the 'front line' and received less access to briefings than his colleagues. Second-class treatment was also given to the Scottish, foreign and provincial press. The men at Cooper's briefings were all journalists well known to the MoD, reporters used to Whitehall's 'lobby' system, in which politicians and civil servants give briefings attributable only to a 'senior source'. The dangers of the lobby, its tendency to corrupt journalists and to leave them vulnerable to manipulation, have often been pointed out. As David Leigh wrote in his book on the press and government, *The Frontiers of Secrecy*: 'Having had their hands tied, journalists in Britain are then made to dance.' When the MoD's non-attributable briefings were stopped by Ian McDonald at the beginning of the war, many reporters were left gasping for information, like patients whose life-support systems had been switched off. Now that 'background' material was flowing again, the journalists were grateful – and ripe targets for misinformation.

The most dangerous moment of the war, as far as the

British were concerned, was the landing on the Falklands. 'I think getting people ashore,' said Cooper later, 'and even more important, getting the supplies that go with the people ashore so that they can survive ... was perhaps the most sensitive part of the whole operation.' The key to the task force's strategy was to take the Argentines by surprise, make an unopposed landing, and consolidate as rapidly as possible. An amphibious assault is one of the most hazardous of military ventures, in which all the advantages lie with the defender. When the Allies landed in France in June 1944, the real operation, 'Overlord', was covered by a deception plan ('Fortitude') designed to convince the Germans that the main attack would not be in Normandy. No 'Fortitude'-style deception was planned for the Falklands. But anything which might confuse the Argentines would help to ensure the success of the British landings.

At the morning meeting of the Chiefs of Staff on Thursday, 20 May, the committee held a final discussion on the task force's plan to put 3,000 men ashore at San Carlos Bay. Although it was agreed that Admiral Woodward could alter the timing of the assault at his discretion, it was provisionally fixed for 4 a.m. on Friday morning.

Twelve hours before the landings, at 4 p.m. on Thursday afternoon, Cooper met the defence correspondents. 'I have looked up my notes that I made at that briefing,' Jim Meacham told MPs in July.

> We were told that there were all sorts of things going on all over the islands – I think that is the correct quote – which we took to mean various little raids. We were told that we could expect to see more of these small raids along the lines of Pebble Island [which had occurred a week earlier, when eleven Argentine aircraft were destroyed] but not to expect a D-Day landing. . . .

The briefing only lasted fifteen minutes, and at the end of it the correspondents dutifully filed out to report what they had been told.

The Fleet Street press the following morning was unanimous in its descriptions of Britain's next military move. Both the *Daily Mirror* and the *Daily Express* had the same front page headline: 'Smash and Grab'. According to the *Mirror*:

> There will be no bloody D-Day style landings. Instead the 5,000 troops who have been prepared for action for days will begin a series of attacks by air and sea.

The *Express* claimed:

> There will be no mass landing, D-Day style. It will be a series of smash-and-grab operations by the back door, knocking out the Argentinian occupation bit by bit. . . .The defence source said: 'There will *not* be a single punch.'

The *Daily Telegraph* reported:

> a single D-Day type frontal assault has been ruled out. . . . 'Attrition is the name of the game,' said a senior Whitehall source . . . 'there [will] be no set-piece battle.'

The *Guardian* quoted 'highly placed Whitehall sources':

> Rear Admiral Sandy Woodward is about to begin a series of landings and hit-and-run raids against Argentine positions on the islands. . . . There [will] not be a D-Day type invasion.

The Times wrote:

> Sources were not expecting to see a repeat performance of D-Day.

And the *Sun* declared:

> It means a series of hit-and-run raids, not a massive invasion.

> Whitehall chiefs predicted a war of attrition . . . they ruled out
> a huge single operation like D-Day. . . .

In the early hours of Friday morning, as Fleet Street papers bearing this unanimous message were distributed around the country, 3,000 troops were going ashore on the Falklands in Britain's biggest amphibious assault since D-Day. The briefing had been totally misleading, but Cooper was unrepentant. He told the Commons Defence Committee:

> When I saw the press on the evening before, I certainly did not tell them the whole story. I make no bones about that whatsoever. I certainly said I did not expect a D-Day type of invasion, and I did not expect a D-Day type of invasion because the whole aim of the operation was to get the forces ashore on an unopposed landing. A D-Day type invasion in my mind is actually an opposed landing – and, if I may say so, I knew what I was talking about because I have been on one – but I certainly did not tell people that we were going ashore with the forces that we were. I am quite ready to accept that I did not unveil the whole picture, and I am delighted there was a good deal of speculation, and it was very helpful to us, quite frankly. . . . We did not tell a lie – but we did not tell the whole truth.

Cooper's suggestion that in ruling out a D-Day landing he was actually only ruling out an opposed landing is a flimsy excuse. 'I personally reject this disingenuous explanation. Every journalist in that room had the same impression I did at that briefing,' says Meacham. 'It certainly gave me the impression that we were not going to see a main landing and we did see one. There is no question in my mind whatsoever that that was done on purpose.' The unanimity of the press coverage, the use even of the same phrases, suggests that Cooper's message to the journalists was quite clear: there would be no single, large-scale assault, opposed or unopposed; there would instead be a war of attrition.

If Cooper did deliberately mislead the press – and his defence is more a matter of nuance than outright denial – was he justified? Immediately before the briefing he spoke to Ian McDonald about what he intended to say and told him: 'You really don't understand how vulnerable we are.' Later he described the British military situation as critical: 'We were really right at the end of the string.' When the task force commanders returned to London and met Cooper after the recapture of the Falklands, they all shared one reaction: immense relief that they had been able to carry out an unopposed landing. Cooper had reason to believe that British newspapers were closely monitored in Argentina. If the deliberate planting of false stories could mislead the enemy for a crucial twenty-four hours while the bridgehead was established, why not do it?

The implications of a policy of misinformation for a democracy reliant on a free press are immense. But even putting those issues to one side for the moment, there is the obvious, practical danger that the long-term damage of such a policy will far outweigh any short-term benefits. By the end of the Falklands war, the Ministry of Defence was fast losing credibility, even among journalists normally sympathetic to it. 'I still find myself now,' says Bob Hutchinson, defence correspondent of the Press Association, 'months after the Falklands, speaking to the Ministry of Defence over quite trivial things and not actually believing what they say, because the seven weeks inside the Ministry of Defence taught me not to believe what they say.' Incidents of misinformation like those concerning HMS *Superb*, the recapture of South Georgia and the San Carlos landings did lasting damage to press relations and to the image of Britain abroad. 'Those briefings may have had the effect of misleading the Argentine forces,' wrote the editor-in-chief of Reuters. 'They certainly had the effect of reducing the credibility in many countries of British Government statements we reported thereafter.' Michael Evans, defence correspondent of the *Daily Express*, found that after 20 May MoD statements were 'treated with considerably more scepticism'. The *Oberver* wrote that 'the net result of such misinformation was greatly to erode our confidence in the reliability of MoD briefings as a useful source of information.' Politicians, civil servants, and military commanders will hardly be in a position to complain in the future if the media reports enemy claims as well as our own and refuses to accept at face value everything issued by the British authorities: the Falklands war undermined the assumption that it is the other side which always lies and never the British.

Five days after Cooper's briefing, on Tuesday, 25 May, the MoD's information policy came under attack once more. At 8.30 p.m. that evening, ITN were setting up their equipment in John Nott's office to record an interview for that night's *News at Ten*. Nott arrived on time, but just as he was about to sit down, a sheaf of signals was thrust into his hand. He thumbed through them with increasing dismay. They informed him (erroneously, as it later turned out) that a number of ships had been hit during Argentine air attacks and that the situation was serious. Nott told the ITN team that he would have to pull out of the interview. The journalists could see that something was wrong. Nott blurted out that the MoD 'had some news' and that he would try to give them a live interview at 10 p.m.

A short while later, Fleet Headquarters at Northwood received a signal from the South Atlantic stating that HMS *Coventry*, a Type 42 destroyer, had been hit, and that she had capsized and sunk within twenty minutes. It was, says one senior MoD official, 'a hideous evening'. The First Sea Lord told Nott that as the ship had sunk so quickly, she might well have taken most of her 280 crew with her.

The immediate reaction of the Navy was to keep the whole episode secret. As Sir Henry Leach explained, *Coventry* had been fitted with the Sea Dart missile system. 'The Argentinians had Sea Dart and there is no doubt that the nature of their air attacks was constrained by their knowledge of Sea Dart.' The news that, after *Sheffield*, a second ship fitted with the system had also been knocked out, 'could have affected their immediate operations'.

From Northwood, Sir John Fieldhouse rang Sir Terence Lewin and asked him to ensure that the media heard nothing: he wanted to avoid letting Argentina know about the loss of the ship, and also to have time to contact the next of kin of the men killed. Lewin was forced to tell him that such a policy was impossible: Nott had already hinted at bad news to ITN, and rumours were by now spreading downstairs through the Press Centre.

Nott intended to appear on *News at Ten* and wanted to announce that *Coventry* had been hit. The senior naval men were horrified. Lewin and Leach, with Fieldhouse joining in by telephone, strongly urged Nott to say nothing. Lewin said later: 'We were unanimous and said, "Don't announce it." The Secretary of State wanted to announce the name of the ship but accepted our military advice.' The compromise agreed was that Nott should announce that one ship had been hit, but that he would not name her.

Nott had to leave immediately for the ITN studios in Wells Street, near Oxford Circus. As he walked out of the Ministry of Defence, he told Ian McDonald to make an announcement in the Press Centre simultaneously with his interview on ITN. Nott said he would work out the form of words he would use while being driven to the studio in his car. His private secretary would ring McDonald when they arrived at ITN and dictate to him the statement he should read.

The audience which watched Nott that night was later estimated to be 10.2 million. He said that 'bad news' had been received: 'One of our ships has been badly damaged and she's in difficulties. I can't give any further details at the moment – the news is still coming in about her. Clearly, from what we know at the moment it is bad news, and I should say that right away.'

It was a serious misjudgement. In the remoteness of the television studio, Nott had no idea of the effect his words were having. In the crowded atmosphere of the Press Centre, Ian McDonald knew at once that they had made a mistake in not announcing *Coventry*'s name. The mood of the journalists was so sombre that having read the statement, McDonald, on his own initiative, told the reporters that the ship 'in difficulties' was not one of the aircraft carriers. When the journalists began pressing him, and asked whether it was the *Canberra*, he turned on his heel and walked out of the room.

In their anxiety to preserve security, the naval commanders caused widespread anxiety throughout the country. Leach said that relatives of 'the entire task force range up that night' to ask for news. Fleet Street newspapers described themselves as 'besieged' with calls and Mike Molloy attacked Nott's method of breaking the news while at the same time leaving the country in suspense as 'deplorable and heavy-handed'. 'If after last night's news I had had a relative with the task force,' said the BBC's Richard Francis, 'I would have had a most terrible night. I am very worried that this whole thing has not been thought through.'

'It was quite obvious by next morning we were wrong,' admitted Lewin, 'but it was a decision that was made in a very short time and under great pressure.'

The *Coventry* affair added fresh voices to the chorus of complaints against the MoD. Peter Viggers, the Conservative

MP for Gosport, had been watching *News at Ten* with some servicemen's wives. 'They have been worried all night,' he said on 26 May. 'All they heard yesterday was that a ship had been damaged, but they didn't know which ship it was.' That afternoon in the House of Commons John Nott agreed with MPs that 'in retrospect' withholding *Coventry*'s name 'may have been the wrong judgement'. Privately he was angry at having allowed his instincts to be overruled by the military, and he pointedly told MPs that he had been 'relying very much on the advice of the Chief of the Defence Staff and the Chief of the Naval Staff, and, through them, the Commander-in-Chief'.

One of the most persistent critics of the MoD's handling of press and public relations was the chief press secretary at 10 Downing Street, Bernard Ingham. At the beginning of the war he had been astonished at Ian McDonald's decision to suspend normal relations with the media. 'I certainly took the view that when you are in a crisis of this kind, the last thing you do is withdraw the service to the media,' he said later. 'I think that is not the time to withdraw your service to your clientele.' Ingham expressed his views bluntly to McDonald and lobbied hard to have Neville Taylor installed as chief of public relations.

'We got the distinct impression,' said Bob Hutchinson, 'that Number 10 was more than unhappy at the way the MoD were handling the war – *more* than unhappy – and there were times when Number 10 were briefing on subjects which the MoD refused to talk about.'

Downing Street was more alert than the Ministry to the need to maintain good relations with the press – 'to keep them sweet and on our side', as McDonald put it. Just as the MoD used the media to confuse the enemy, so Ingham and the rest of the Government sought to use them to sustain support for the war.

In the week that *Coventry* was lost, the press were encouraged by political sources to believe that the British forces were about to move out from their bridgehead at San Carlos Bay. 'We are planning to move and to move fast,' Cecil Parkinson assured radio listeners on Sunday, 23 May. 'It is not our intention to be drawn into a long and bloody war.' That afternoon, Ingham briefed journalists in similar terms, and Fleet Street the following day painted a morale-boosting picture of the British land forces poised to strike. 'We're not going to fiddle around,' Ingham – disguised as 'a senior source' – was quoted as saying.

As Sir Frank Cooper later pointed out, there were few strategic options open to the British land forces. Assured all week by official statements that an attack was imminent, journalists studied their maps of the Falklands and concluded that the British were about to move south from the bridgehead to attack Darwin and Goose Green. Speculation was further encouraged by a forty-eight-hour blackout on news from the Falklands. The *Daily Express*, which had predicted an attack following Ingham's briefing at the beginning of the week, gave over its front page on 27 May to a wildly inaccurate story actually headlined 'Goose Green is Taken'. Speculation was boosted by Mrs Thatcher during Prime Minister's Questions. 'Our forces on the ground,' she told MPs amid murmurs of approval, 'are now moving forward from the bridgehead.' On the same day, John Nott told a private meeting of backbenchers to 'expect good news'.

Unaware of this excitement in London, 8,000 miles away on the Falklands men of the 2nd Parachute Regiment were moving in to position for their assault on 27 May when they heard a BBC defence correspondent broadcast over the World Service that they were about to attack Goose Green. In Bush House, after five days of officially inspired anticipation, the report seemed harmless enough. But to many of the soldiers it looked as if their plans had been leaked behind their backs in London. 'How many enemies are we supposed to be fighting?' asked one man. Max Hastings reported: 'The colonel commanding the positions attacked by Skyhawks last night told me furiously that if a BBC correspondent arrived in his area, he would be sent immediately to the prisoner-of-war cage.' Colonel 'H' Jones, commander of the paratroops, muttered savage threats of suing 'John Nott, the Ministry, the Prime Minister, if anyone's killed'.

In the event, eighteen men, including Jones himself, died in the attack, and there was a controversy in London. The World Service held its own inquest into the affair, and the BBC issued a statement insisting that it had broadcast 'no information which has not been readily available to other broadcasters and other journalistic organizations from official sources in London, *including the MoD*'. Stung by this, and by Jones's widely reported intention of suing him, John Nott ordered a detailed investigation within the Ministry of Defence. An internal report blamed general speculation and failed to trace any specific leak within the Ministry. But coming so soon after the public relations blunder over HMS *Coventry*, the incident did the MoD damage. Its credibility was not enhanced by the fact that, following a misinterpreted telephone call from the Falklands, it had announced the recapture of Darwin and Goose Green at 9.40 p.m. on Friday, 28 May – eighteen hours before the Argentine garrison surrendered.

Reporters who detected a division between the MoD and Number 10 had their suspicions confirmed eleven days later. On 8 June, enemy aircraft attacked the landing ships *Sir Galahad* and *Sir Tristram* at Bluff Cove. Fifty men were killed. 'We wished to conceal the extent of the casualties,' said Sir Terence Lewin, 'because we knew from intelligence that the Argentines thought they were very much higher.'

For three days, on the orders of John Nott and the Chiefs of Staff, the Ministry of Defence refused to release the number of casualties. 'There were deliberate attempts to get the media to exaggerate the numbers of dead and wounded,' claimed the Press Association. 'Reports of 220 dead and more than 400 wounded emanated from a radio ham in the Falklands, doubtless briefed by the military, and picked up in Bristol.'

On 10 June, Nott refused to disclose the extent of British losses to the House of Commons. Later that same day he had a meeting with journalists who pressed him for guidance on the number of casualties. He told them: 'Speculate as you wish.' 'The Bluff Cove incident,' admitted Lewin, 'when we deliberately concealed the casualty figures, was an example of using the press, the media, to further our military operations.'

By Friday, 11 June, Ingham thought the speculation had been allowed to go on long enough. The *Sun* appeared that morning with a banner headline stating '70 DEAD'. Ingham told correspondents that he believed the number of casualties was less than that figure. The MoD was furious: the Downing Street briefing, said Neville Taylor, 'became the subject of pretty heated discussion between Bernard Ingham and myself'.

By the end of the war, the Ministry of Defence's reputation for telling the truth had fallen so low in the estimation of the media that rumours began circulating that 'psyops' – military jargon for psychological warfare operations – were being conducted against the press.

It was known that one psyops unit was operating within the MoD. This was the team which ran the British propaganda station, Radio Atlantico del Sur, designed to lower the morale of Argentine troops on the Falklands. A BBC transmitter was requisitioned, and from 19 May onwards it broadcast a stream of pro-British news stories, sentimental music, appeals for peace and lists of Argentine wounded. Interrogation reports from captured troops were used to enable 'record requests' to be played for individual Argentinians on the islands, such as Captain Malinotti, 'all the boys from Santa Fé' and Colonel de Rega. . . .

The Press Association was told that psyops were also used to misinform the British media. 'Apparently two lieutenant-colonels and a wing-commander from the Latimer Defence College were brought to the Ministry to develop psyops themes. Initially there was, we reliably understand, an attempt to mix this input with information coming out of the Ministry.' A senior MoD official privately cites two stories he claims were planted by psyops personnel. One was a graphic but fictitious account of the activities of the Special Boat Section in the recapture of South Georgia, which found its way into at least one newspaper. The second – which the MoD information department refused to release – came from one of the ships with the task force, and reported that after his plane had been hit, an Argentinian pilot had baled out and landed *astride* one of their guns.

Psyops was added to the catalogue of complaints against the MoD: a list of grievances so long, loudly expressed and detailed that four days before the end of the war, the House of Commons Defence Committee announced its intention of investigating the Ministry's handling of press and public information during the Falklands crisis. Their inquiries were to cover not merely the allegations against the MoD in London, but also the growing volume of criticism filtering back from the South Atlantic.

SEVEN

From Our Own Correspondent

As *Canberra* neared the Falklands, the journalists on board underwent an intensive series of briefings to prepare them for the land campaign ahead. There were demonstrations in first aid and lectures on such minutiae of survival as how to catch and eat sea birds. Patrick Bishop of the *Observer* wrote:

> We were taught how to build stone sangars out of rocks and peat to protect ourselves from shell splinters and enemy bombs; how to dig slit trenches and shell scrapes to increase our chances of coming through a bombardment alive; and the importance of having 18 inches of dirt above your head to stop the shrapnel from airburst bombs.

The *Canberra* journalists consoled themselves with the knowledge that they were at last about to get ahead of their rivals on *Hermes* and *Invincible*. For more than a month they had been complaining to the Ministry of Defence minders that the reporters with the carrier group were stealing all the glory: they had been able to file first-hand reports of the Harrier attack on Port Stanley, the loss of *Sheffield*, the sea and air bombardment of the Falklands, the attack on Pebble Island, as well as on numerous sorties and air raids. The *Canberra* journalists had been under some pressure from their offices for equally good stories. Kim Sabido had actually been asked by Independent Radio News to read out a report on the recapture of South Georgia implying that *Canberra* was involved in it, even though he was hundreds of miles away from the island and had only heard about it on the World Service.

As a result of the *Canberra* press corps' complaints, the task force commanders had decided, shortly after leaving Ascension Island, to give them an advantage in the land campaign by allowing them to go ashore on the Falklands first. 'They had not had anything to report at that time,' said General Moore. 'I believe there was a feeling . . . that it was their turn and they should be allowed to go and get their bit of coverage, whereas the other people who had been reporting on what had been going on at sea had had their show for the moment. . . .'

Each *Canberra* journalist was attached to a unit. Bishop, for example, was assigned to cover 42 Commando; Robert Fox and David Norris to 2 Para; Alastair McQueen, Max Hastings and Jeremy Hands to 40 Commando. Robert McGowan of the *Daily Express* joined 3 Para: 'I spent a lot of time with them. They briefed me on how to survive, the sort of clothing I would need which they supplied, the sort of terrain, the weather, the kind of food I would be eating and the kind of opposition they thought we would be up against.' A couple of days before the landings, most of the journalists transferred with their units to the landing ships *Intrepid* and *Fearless* and prepared to go ashore.

Meanwhile on the aircraft carriers things were not running so smoothly. On *Hermes* Captain Middleton had by now been refusing to speak to Michael Nicholson for two and a half weeks. The tensions on the flagship which had existed on the voyage to Ascension had worsened. On 11 May, Admiral Woodward was told by the MoD that a Nicholson dispatch had alerted the Argentines to the fact that the carrier group was moving inshore to carry out a naval bombardment. 'I said nothing of the sort,' complained Nicholson in his diary, 'but Woodward says he has asked for a transcript ex London and I'll be "sacked" if it's true. Transcript confirms I said nothing of the kind. No apology.'

> It was at this time [wrote Nicholson] we decided, because of the continuing hassle, that we should prefix our reports 'Censored'. But we were told by MoD PR Graham Hammond and the Navy that this wouldn't be allowed. Peter Archer of the Press Association sent a service telex to his London boss saying his reports were censored. The word 'censored' was censored.
>
> I find it extraordinary that when BBC/ITN men in Poland sent censored reports out of that country in the days post-martial law, Polish censorship was made public. When I sent back censored reports years ago from Israel and Pakistan again I said so. We aboard *Hermes* were not allowed to make British censorship public.

On 15 May Nicholson witnessed the attack on Pebble Island from HMS *Glamorgan* but was unable to get off in time to file a story that night. 'I confronted [the] lieutenant in charge of helicopter assets. I was told, "You bastards are the lowest-priority rating, at the bottom of the list, and that's where you'll remain." ' Peter Archer wrote:

> Early one evening I handed copy to the *Hermes* MOD man who was sitting in the wardroom drinking a glass of port. I told him the story was urgent and asked if it could be dealt with immediately. I returned half an hour later to find the unvetted copy soaking up port and other spilt liquors on a wardroom table.

The constant air attacks, worry about his family and the frustrations of trying to report what was happening eventually proved too much for Archer. He wanted to leave. It was arranged between the Ministry of Defence and the Press Association editor in London that he should return home, and Archer was on his way back within twenty-four hours. His replacement, Richard Savill, was flown to Ascension and joined HMS *Bristol*. He was preceded by a characteristic signal sent by Sir John Fieldhouse warning the task force to be careful of him:

> HMS *Bristol* personnel to avoid discussion of any operational matters with Savill, who can be expected to take full advantage of his environment to glean newsworthy information. Speculation on possible courses of action, operational capability of task force/individual units and state of readiness must also be avoided. Names of ships and individual units should not be specified. . . .

The tensions on the other aircraft carrier, HMS *Invincible*, had been building up ever since the carrier had left Ascension. 'Anxiety was running very high,' recalls Gareth Parry. 'We were spending up to fourteen hours a day at defence stations, sweating out air alerts in anti-flash suits. In a situation like that you get tired and irritable.'

The physical discomfort heightened the feeling of professional frustration. Although, as the *Canberra* journalists had pointed out, the reporters on *Hermes* and *Invincible* were in the thick of the action, they were generally not allowed to report on anything that had happened until after it had been announced in London. The journalists on the two carriers would be told that a news blackout had been imposed on such incidents as the Vulcan bomber attack on Port Stanley, the destruction of HMS *Sheffield*, the loss of two Harriers in a mid-air collision – only to hear the same news announced over the BBC World Service a few hours later. By the time the *Invincible* journalists filed their reports, they were out of date. 'All our major news stories arrived too late for publication,' claimed Tony Snow. 'The common feeling among journalists with the task force was that we were risking our lives for nothing.'

Captain Jeremy Black was sympathetic to the newsmen's feelings, and on 7 May he signalled London with a proposal that journalists' copy should be transmitted from the task force as quickly as possible and then held in London for simultaneous release with the Ministry of Defence's official announcement. He never received a reply.

Although he tried to be helpful, Black was in fact losing patience with the five journalists on *Invincible*. A series of incidents, trivial in themselves but cumulative in their effects, gradually transformed him from one of the few naval officers who were happy to talk to the press to a man who couldn't wait to get them off his ship.

On 6 May, Mick Seamark wrote a story beginning 'Day Thirty-Two: Death Stares Us in the Face', which prompted Black to call the correspondents together and lecture them on the need to avoid damaging the morale of families at home. The next day, following the mid-air collision of two Harriers, Black had to deal with a complaint from the squadron's commanding officer, 'Sharky' Ward, that he had been 'doorstepped' that morning outside his cabin by Snow and Seamark demanding an interview about the missing pilots.

An indication of Black's shortening temper came on 13 May, when he learned that Michael Nicholson had come on board to interview survivors from the Argentine fishing vessel *Narval*. He gave Roger Goodwin, the MoD minder, a 'very uncomfortable five minutes', demanding to know how Nicholson had got on *Invincible* despite the fact that he had issued orders a month ago that he was never to set foot on board again.

On 15 May he once more called Goodwin in to see him, this time to tell him that the press's dispatches on the Pebble

Island raid, submitted that evening, were much too long and detailed to be transmitted. Goodwin decided to wake Alfred McIlroy of the *Daily Telegraph* at 1.30 a.m., and between them the two men set about drastically cutting the entire press's copy. The atmosphere the next day when this was discovered was described by Goodwin as 'frosty'.

Three days later there was more trouble when one journalist used the MARISAT link on *Olmeda* to call his girlfriend, causing great resentment among crewmen, all of whom had been forbidden to make personal calls.

The crisis in relations between Black and the press came to a head on 19 May, when Black went on the ship's closed-circuit television to announce that the landings were to take place at San Carlos Bay the day after next. Several journalists took notes from the briefing, which were immediately confiscated by one of Black's naval secretaries. Then Alfred McIlroy tried to send a message to his office: 'Please close my New York bank account as there is only a dollar left' – which Black suspected of being a coded reference to the landings. Black was now keen to get rid of the press. For their part, the journalists were anxious to escape from the claustrophobic atmosphere of the ship and to cover the imminent landings.

They had no suitable clothing. They had no equipment. They had no rations. They had not been given any training. They had no units to join when they did get on shore. Nevertheless, Black and Goodwin decided that the reporters should leave *Invincible* – which was not going inshore – and that Goodwin would then attempt to persuade the army to accept them on land.

On 20 May, a grey day with high winds lashing the ships with rain, *Invincible* rendezvoused with the Royal Fleet Auxiliary *Resource*. The *Invincible* journalists, together with Goodwin, left the carrier by helicopter and were winched down onto the deck of the *Resource*. To the correspondents' dismay, they discovered that they were on an ammunition ship, heavily laden with bullets, shells, grenades and anti-aircraft missiles, and that they would not be moving into San Carlos Bay until at least two days after the landings. In addition, the reporters were told that the ship's MARISAT system had broken down. For the next two days the *Resource* stayed out at sea with the carrier group. When the MARISAT was repaired, the five journalists filed stories on the landings based on what they heard over the World Service and any scraps of information they could pick up on board.

On 23 May, the *Resource* moved to join *Canberra*, and Goodwin journeyed over to the liner to discuss the predicament of the 'Invincible Five', as they had become known, with the chief Ministry of Defence press officer, Martin Helm. He was told that the plan was for them to wait and join 5 Brigade, at that moment heading southwards on board the *Queen Elizabeth II*. When Goodwin returned to *Resource* and told the reporters the arrangement, he met with a barrage of abuse and complaints. As if to emphasize their lack of preparation, the 'Invincible Five' were joined by three *Canberra* reporters, Kim Sabido, Patrick Bishop and John Shirley, who had just filed stories on the landings and were returning to shore. 'They were all dressed up like action men,' says Parry. 'They'd got morphine jabs and field dressings, proper boots, waterproofs, helmets and sleeping bags. We felt pretty sick.'

That night, under cover of darkness, *Resource* moved into San Carlos Bay. At dawn on 24 May, the reporters woke up to find themselves a few hundred yards from shore. It was the *Invincible* journalists' first glimpse of the Falklands.

The Argentine air attacks began at midday. Parry innocently inquired why no one was wearing anti-flash gear. 'Because,' came the reply, 'if we get hit, what you'll need is a fucking parachute.' Parry was told that *Resource* was carrying explosives equivalent to half the force of the Hiroshima atom bomb. When the air raids began, Sabido was down below. 'I ran up on to the deck. I looked around, and there, coming in at head-height, was an Argentine plane. I could literally see the pilot's face as he flashed past.' A photograph taken from on board *Resource* that day shows the *Stromness* less than 100 yards away and between the two ships a massive fountain of water where a bomb has just exploded. Some journalists took shelter in the bowels of the ship. Parry stayed on deck: 'At least you can see what's going on out in the open. It's considered bad for morale to sound an air-raid warning on an ammunition ship, so the only way you could tell when they were coming in again was to catch the noise of alerts drifting across the bay from other ships.'

That afternoon, the 'Invincible Five' suffered the anguish of watching the three fully equipped journalists from *Canberra* clambering on board a helicopter and being flown the quarter of a mile to rejoin their units on land.

Some sort of solution was clearly becoming urgent. Goodwin – who had spent the air raids pressed face-down on the deck – had received a message from Brigade Headquarters on shore telling him that the five reporters would be offered a 'facility ashore once situation stabilized'. That could take days. Goodwin went across to *Fearless* and made contact with a naval lieutenant who promised to try to arrange for the journalists to be taken ashore. The next morning – now four days after the landings – Goodwin took a unilateral decision to get his press contingent off *Resource*, whether the land forces were ready for them or not.

It was a decision warmly welcomed by the press. As Gareth Parry later told the Commons Defence Committee: 'Four days on a fully laden ammunition ship under air attack almost by the hour is enough to prompt you into a good idea of where you should be and where you should not be and – I am not being facetious – it really is the wrong place to be.'

Goodwin's reasoning was that the marines would simply have to accept the presence of the reporters as a *fait accompli*. He ushered four of them – Gareth Parry, Tony Snow, Mick Seamark and John Witherow – into a helicopter and watched, with a feeling of great relief, as they disappeared towards the shore. (McIlroy stayed at sea for a few more hours that afternoon and left in the early evening.)

'It felt marvellous to be ashore,' remembers Parry. 'Especially the silence. All we'd had for seven weeks was noise. The peace was beautiful. You could drink it. And the natural colours, the greens, something completely absent at sea.' The tranquillity lasted only a short time. The helicopter pilot had deposited them in a muddy field full of sheep, miles away from Brigade Headquarters where they were supposed to be. There was nothing to do but walk. Parry recalled:

> The day ended with a march in total darkness along what appeared to be a succession of country lanes. It was pitch-black. The hedges along either side were filled with snipers. Every so often as you went along you'd hear a bush rattle its bolt. We were terrified. We could have been shot at any moment. Added to which, we soon realized we were following an escort who didn't know where Brigade HQ actually was.

Alan Percival, an MoD minder from *Canberra*, was sitting in a potting shed close to Brigade HQ checking reporters' copy, when, shortly after 7 p.m., the door opened and Alfred McIlroy appeared. McIlroy had been dropped by helicopter in the *right* location. He had no sleeping bag and was wearing an ordinary pair of shoes. He asked Percival for some kit. Percival told him there wasn't any: any spare equipment had been given to the medical teams and crews manning the Rapier missile batteries. Brigadier Julian Thompson had informed Percival that he hadn't so much as a single pair of windproof trousers to give to the journalists. Percival told McIlroy he would have to leave. Even fully equipped marines and paratroopers were being evacuated, suffering from exposure. McIlroy left under protest, telling Percival he would write a story announcing that he'd been thrown off the Falklands by the British Army.

Finally, at midnight, the potting shed door opened again to admit Parry, Witherow, Seamark and Snow. They, too, had expected to find extra equipment and at first refused to believe that there were no spare sets of clothing in the entire task force. All Parry had managed to cobble together before leaving *Invincible* were 'bits and pieces, webbing that did not fit and a pack with no handle which was next to useless'. They had lightweight navy boots, but these were little protection in the freezing weather and thick mud. Percival told them they would not be accepted by any unit and they would have to leave at first light.

The four journalists spent the night in a nearby house, huddled for warmth between the sleeping bags of some arctic warfare troops, and agreed the following morning between themselves to try to avoid being sent back – especially if it meant going back on an ammunition ship. They went and hid among some bales of wool.

An hour or so later, they were spotted by Kim Sabido.

John Shirley, Patrick Bishop and myself were walking by when we saw the four *Invincible* journalists all hiding, wearing Navy boiler suits and carrying what looked like a suitcase. It was pathetic. The only rations they had was a packet of cheese sandwiches they'd been given by the ship's cook on *Resource*. We asked them what they were doing. They said they were hiding and begged us not to give them away.

'We were actually under air attack at the time,' says Parry. 'I was sheltering in a crevice. One of the *Canberra* journalists said, "My God, am I pissed off to see you. You guys have got no right to be here." I thought: what a welcome. We would have been delighted to have shared the Exocet attacks with them.' To this day, Parry believes they were 'betrayed' by one of the *Canberra* reporters. The four *Invincible* men were rounded up by Alan Percival, together with a Royal Marine public relations officer, Captain David Nicholls, and put on board the landing ship, *Sir Geraint*, where they were joined by Alfred McIlroy. The empty ship, which had no MARISAT link, sailed back out into the Total Exclusion Zone which the reporters had left six days before. There it patrolled endlessly up and down in front of the carriers. At first the journalists were unable to work out what was happening. Then they realized that they were on board an Exocet decoy, designed to draw off a missile attack from the big ships.

The representatives of all three British 'quality' daily newspapers, together with reporters from two mass-circulation tabloids, spent the next eight days stranded out at sea, filing occasional stories based on reports heard over the World Service. On 31 May, the fifth day in this captivity, Gareth Parry recorded laconically in his diary: 'Still waiting in the Total Exclusion Zone. Bright clear day. Perfect missile-attack weather. Yesterday we learned two missiles were launched against us. But apparently they missed.' It was about this time that Parry began receiving signals from the Ministry of Defence addressed to 'Paul Keel', a *Guardian* reporter working in London: 'Presumably if I'd been killed they would have contacted Keel's next of kin.'

Neville Taylor subsequently defended the action of his department in keeping the journalists off the Falklands: '[they] were not trained, were not equipped, were not familiarized, and we refused in London to issue instructions that they should be put ashore. We felt that that was a matter for the operational commanders on the spot to judge the moment when it was right.'

The 'Invincible Five' might well have stayed out at sea had they not, on 28 May, written a combined plea for help to their editors in London, which was eventually transmitted from *Invincible* three days later:

PRIORITY/PRIORITY 311548Z MAY 82
FROM HMS INVINCIBLE
TO MODUK
INFO CINCFLEET
RESTRICTED

Defence Press Office pse pass to editors named. Times, Guardian, Telegraph, the Sun and Daily Star. May 28 this is our situation since we went ashore two days ago with MoD approval. We were removed from the Falkland Islands by MoD and army press officers. . . . We are now on a supply ship in the Total Exclusion Zone, devoid of communications and have received through the captain a signal from MoD saying we must transfer to ships that are no longer in the area. The security aspects prevent further details other than to say we are effectively off the islands for at least the next ten days. . . . Our recommendation is that all pressure should be applied for equal treatment your correspondents and earliest return San Carlos Bay in interests our newspapers.

The message produced an immediate reaction in London. 'The level of thoughtlessness by your embarked press officers reaches a fresh zenith daily,' wrote Brian Hitchen of the *Daily Star* to Sir Frank Cooper on 1 June. 'I consider, Sir Frank, that the treatment of the press during the Falklands crisis has been shameful and have no doubt whatsoever that a full explanation will be called for at the appropriate time in the future.'

Cooper met Hitchen and the other editors at 6 p.m. that evening and promised to intervene on the reporters' behalf.

The following day, Wednesday, 2 June, the 'Invincible Five' transferred to *Stromness*, which that night moved back inshore, and on 3 June the reporters finally landed. It was exactly two weeks since they had left *Invincible* to go ashore.

By contrast with their last brief visit, Port San Carlos was practically deserted, its only function now to act as a supply depot moving up stores for the final offensive. 'There was an awful feeling,' says Parry, 'of having missed the story.' That night the reporters slept in a sheep shed.

Even now they were still not properly equipped. Parry had some socks and boots and a sleeping bag which was not designed for Antarctic conditions. His main protection was an extremely uncomfortable waterproof suit. Moving around during the day caused a heavy sweat, and the moment the sun went down, 'there was the most terrible chill as the perspiration froze inside the suit.' Seamark, also poorly equipped, recalls nights spent shaking from head to foot with cold.

The following day, the 'Invincible Five' split up. McIlroy and Snow went south with the Guards, while Parry, Seamark and Witherow, joined by Richard Savill of the Press Association, made for Fitzroy, spending the night huddled in a garage. Parry's war was now very nearly over. Dispirited, exhausted, lacking the proper kit, he stayed on land for a few more days and then sought refuge on *Hermes*. He was given a place on a ship going back to Ascension and left before the Argentine surrender – the third journalist to drop out of the war before the end. 'It was the first campaign I had ever covered where my own kith and kin were fighting,' he reflected afterwards. 'And it was a complete disaster.'

It wasn't only the *Invincible* journalists who were kept off the Falklands.

'Cooped up on ship since landing,' Richard Savill signalled

the Press Association in London. 'No access to shore. Slowly overcoming problem. *Canberra* press had it all. Hope for bite of cherry soonest.' Not until two weeks after the landings were Savill and PA photographer Martin Cleaver allowed permanently on shore.

A similar ban extended to the television journalists on *Hermes*. Brian Hanrahan said:

> My particular team, which was one of two television cameras there, were forbidden to leave the ship for about ten days or so after the landings had taken place. The argument was that they had too many people ashore and they did not want any more, and even to go ashore for a day and look around, we were told we could not do that.

The reason advanced by General Moore was that the television crew 'had not been training with our men on the way down, and with its heavy equipment and so on, moving about in the mountains, would probably have been a liability to itself and to my men to look after them'.

Covering the campaign on the Falkland Islands, as the *Canberra* journalists quickly discovered, was a gruelling experience. In other wars, correspondents can at least normally return after a few days at the front to a comfortable hotel. On the Falklands the journalists had to share many of the discomforts of the men twenty-four hours a day, seven days a week. Robert McGowan of the *Daily Express* was with 3 Para: 'I had to dig my own trench, cook all my own food, carry some of their mortar bombs for them – and lost 2 stone in weight doing so.' There were no cars, no beds, no canteens. Even a simple matter like having a cup of tea often involved breaking some ice off the top of a pond, melting it, adding water-purifying tablets, getting a small fire going and boiling it. Robert Fox called it 'the rat-pack war':

When I say 'rat pack', I am borrowing the military abbreviation for 'rations pack', which we lived on solidly (the *mot juste* in the case of biscuits AB and AB fruit and compo paste) for days and weeks in the field. There was a small choice. First, you either had 'rats Arctic' or 'rats GS (General Service)', with a further variation between menu 'A' and menu 'B', which meant either dehydrated chicken supreme or curry. According to the gourmets, the Arctic rats were better, but needed much more water, fine for Arctic snows, not so good in the Falklands, where the perils of liver fluke lurked in many of the streams.

Journalists went without such luxuries as a bath for weeks. The day before the Argentine surrender, a group of journalists on the side of Mount Kent were putting on delousing powder. Kim Sabido recalled their experiences:

> If you were going to the front line, you had to walk and sleep in atrocious conditions. You had to be very fit. Your feet were just raw with walking. Several of us had to go back for treatment. Charles Lawrence of the *Sunday Telegraph* was taken back twice suffering from trench foot and exposure. Some people just withdrew into themselves and didn't even bother to push up to the front line.

'If you think you are getting frostbite,' an ex-SAS survival expert told Robert Fox, 'stick your toes in your oppo's crotch. It's the warmest part of his body, and that's your best chance.'

There were two basic forms of transport: by helicopter or on foot. Getting dispatches back to London in such conditions was often a matter of luck. Reports could be transmitted back to London only through the MARISAT ships inshore or through a Satellite Communications Centre capable of sending written copy, set up on land in a tent in Ajax Bay. This SATCOM facility was manned by Alan Percival – one of the few MoD minders for whom the journalists had a good word – who lived in some squalor in a tent alongside it. On one memorable occasion the entire SATCOM centre was blown away when a Chinook helicopter landed too close to it; it took several hours to restore it to working order.

The problem for the journalists, scattered with their units across hundreds of square miles of countryside, was to get their copy sent back to the transmission points. Robert McGowan explained:

> This particular war was unlike any other, in so far as you were with your unit. You could not just pop back to the local Intercontinental Hotel and file the copy; you lived in the trenches. Literally, you had to flag down a helicopter, put your copy into an envelope and ask that helicopter pilot if there was any way he could get it to HMS *Fearless*, the central point for vetting all press and TV copy. The pilots did a magnificent job in that direction, but they had other priorities, so sometimes that copy took a very long time to get to *Fearless*. . . .

Once cleared by the MoD PR officer on *Fearless*, reports then had to be sent for transmission to MARISAT ships or to the SATCOM centre in Ajax Bay. Frequently copy was lost. 'The first four dispatches I attempted to file from the beachhead simply vanished without trace,' claimed Ian Bruce of the *Glasgow Herald*. Richard Savill listed five reports he'd written which never reached London: a survivor's account of the Exocet attack on *Atlantic Conveyor*; copy on the moonlit run by the requisitioned fishing boat *Monsoonan*; Brigadier Wilson's account of the dash to occupy Bluff Cove; an account of the battle for Mount Harriet; and a pooled piece from Port Stanley, sent on the Monday night after the surrender.

When copy did manage to get through, it was invariably late. Patrick Bishop wrote that 'the weight of military traffic on the only land-based communications satellite meant that copy took a very low priority and was taking up to twenty-four hours to transmit.' 'We received some dispatches three or four days late,' said Michael Reupke, Reuters' editor-in-chief. 'Sometimes the delay made the reports unusable.'

Having been vetted once on the Falkands, copy was then censored again in London. It was in the operation of this second filter, as Ian McDonald had predicted, that the Ministry of Defence was accused of making alterations on grounds of taste. The censors were military officers working within the Ministry's Defence public relations staff. 'From 21 May onwards at least one of the military staff officers in DPRS saw the embarked press's copy before it was passed to editors,' stated the MoD. 'This vetting process within the MoD was carried out as quickly as possible, and the average time taken to clear and prepare dispatches for collection was under one hour.'

The censors mainly removed names of officers and men, descriptions of the units involved in attacks and other military details. But on some occasions they strayed into other areas. They asked for the deletion of this section of a story on a field hospital filed by Richard Savill:

> Surgeons working round the clock in the makeshift field hospital today carried out their hundredth major operation since the fighting started. A total of 220 casualties have now been brought to the centre where four surgical teams are working in appalling conditions. As I toured the hospital – a disused refrigeration plant – the wounded were stretchered in from the battle front after arriving by helicopter. Many were wrapped in blood-soaked bandages. One bare-topped fatality was placed outside the building beneath a blue blanket. The casualties I saw were all Argentinians. Surgeon-Commander Rick Jolly, who is in charge, praised his team of surgeons working in dust and poor light. 'Despite the horrors of modern

warfare, it is our proud boast here that everyone who has come in alive has gone out alive to the hospital.'

The censor, Wing-Commander Monks, gave his reasons for demanding the deletion of this passage in a note to the PA editor:

We are concerned that this story will cause a great deal of worry in the families of British servicemen. They are likely to believe that hospital treatment is inadequate. Whereas we believe that Richard Saville [*sic*] was commenting on Argentine wounded neglected by their own people and recovered under difficult battlefield conditions.

We would be grateful if your treatment of this story could bear in mind our genuine wish to avoid unnecessary worry and suffering in families here at home.

Another example, which occurred later in the campaign, concerned some derogatory remarks made by John Shirley of the *Sunday Times* about the Guards of 5 Infantry Brigade:

Unlike the marines and paras, the Guards, it seems, have not been taking daily exercise. They have complained about the food and grumbled about their cabins. One man is rumoured to have suffered a heart attack running up stairs. They are not liked. Nor, for that matter, is the captain of the *QE2*. Despite the fact that he had forty-two days' rations on board, the story is that he would not release any stores before sailing back to Ascension Island.

Lt.-Colonel Stephenson at the Ministry of Defence ordered that the whole paragraph be omitted on the grounds that this information 'would be very useful to the enemy'. Another section of the same dispatch, referring to the 'chagrin' of troops on the Falklands that the bodies of men killed might not be sent home, was to be omitted, 'as it could rekindle the worries of the bereaved'.

Patrick Bishop suspected that Ministry of Defence officials, both in London and in the Falklands, 'stifled any suggestion that the campaign was doing anything but rolling inexorably towards victory'. He later gave some examples to the House of Commons Defence Committee:

> On Thursday, 27 May, I wrote an article saying that the British advance was in danger of being bogged down and quoted senior officers to this effect. By the time this was released in London the references had been removed and the piece began about halfway through on a more optimistic note. On Wednesday, 9 June, I wrote an article quoting extensively survivors' accounts of the loss of the *Sir Galahad*, which made it clear that the ship was given inadequate protection and that there was anger and bitterness over the incident. I handed it to the MoD Press Officer Martin Helm, but when I saw him again five days later, after that week's edition of the paper had been published, he told me that it hadn't been sent. . . . The suppression of the piece was a simple act of censorship because it was felt the article might lower morale. In the event, there was little in the conduct of the war for the British forces to regret or feel ashamed of, but if there had been, it seems highly likely that nothing would have been allowed to be published about it while hostilities were in progress.

Occasionally, changes were made to reports somewhere along the line, without the reporters' knowledge, which deliberately altered the entire sense of the story. A line in a dispatch by John Shirley – 'Only the weather holds us back from Stanley' – somehow became 'Only the *politicians* hold us back'. John Witherow found that a description he'd written of the 'failure' of the Vulcan bombing raids on Stanley was changed to read how 'successful' they were. One of the MoD minders claims that 'a certain lieutenant-colonel on the

Falklands used to rewrite whole paragraphs relating to the Scots Guards which he didn't like.' The minder would wait until he'd gone and then change them back again.

Many of these problems arose because the journalists were wholly dependent upon the military for their communications. They were rarely around to see their copy transmitted – they were tens of miles away, dug in on a hillside or marching with their units. The reporters had to rely on the honesty of the authorities. The number of stories which went missing or were altered suggests that the military and the MoD were always ready to 'improve the image' of the war wherever possible. When Robert Fox reported on the disaster at Bluff Cove in which *Sir Galahad* and *Sir Tristram* were attacked, with heavy loss of life, he was

> enjoined by the MoD PRO in charge, Martin Helm, 'to print only the good news', i.e. that eleven Mirages had been shot down, allegedly, that day. Eventually even he realized the impossibility of such a policy and that every and any report emanating from the Force would have to lead on the Bluff Cove bombings.

The reporter who was most successful in his coverage of the war was the journalist most willing to report only the 'good news'. When Max Hastings of the London *Standard* was asked after the war whether he thought his positive approach had helped him, he replied: 'It may have done. It'd be foolish to deny it. Obviously the task force is more likely to give help to those whom they think are writing helpful things than those who are not.'

Almost all the journalists came to identify to a greater or lesser extent with the forces around them. 'The world of the Falklands campaign was so enclosed,' wrote Robert Fox, 'that it was hard not to identify with the troops on the ground; in the heavier engagements it was the only means of psychological survival.' Hastings subscribed to this view to a much greater degree. 'I've always had an enormous affection for the British Army and for the British forces,' he told *Panorama* after the war. 'I felt my function was simply to identify totally with the interests and feelings of that force.' He was asked whether, if morale were low, he would censor himself. 'Absolutely, absolutely. . . . When one was writing one's copy one thought: beyond telling everybody what the men around me are doing, what can one say that is likely to be most helpful to winning this war?' So great was Hastings's commitment to the cause that on 1 June he was allowed to use SAS satellite communications to dictate a report about them direct to their headquarters at Hereford: an unprecedented gesture from such an elite and secretive regiment.

Hastings, a lanky, bespectacled figure in his mid-thirties, is a military historian (author of the much-acclaimed *Bomber Command*) as well as a reporter used to covering the world's conflicts. 'Anybody with experience of war corresponding knows one has to be obsessed with communications,' he explained later. 'You need to treat problems of communication as if they were matters of life and death.' While most of the other reporters were content to stay with the units to which they had been assigned at the time of the landings, Hastings broke the rules, striking out and spending a few days with different units all over the island. He said later:

> We were all urged by the Ministry of Defence people that what we must do was stay with our units from beginning to end of the war . . . and some journalists very honourably did precisely that. I never felt – and again I said on *Canberra* – there was going to be an Eagle Scout badge at the end of the campaign for who suffered most. What is going to count is who got the most out, so one simply had to move from unit to unit according to who was doing something. When 42 Commando were

going up Mount Kent I went with them, and again up Mount Harriet. I went on one of the frigates, and then in the build-up I was allowed to write about one of the helicopter squadrons, so that one simply had to move around units where something was going on. But I think it was true that those who actually obeyed instructions felt afterwards most betrayed. For instance, at one point 45 Commando were about to carry out an attack on Mount Kent, and we were told that the only way, if we wanted to join the attack (that is, myself and Robert Fox of the BBC), was to go yomping with them and we joined them. They had been already yomping for three days with their dispatch correspondents and they were already very tired. We yomped with them for another two days up Mount Kent, then when we got up Mount Kent, the first person I saw was Brigadier Thompson. I said, 'Looking forward to the attack tomorrow night?' and he looked astonished and said, 'Not tomorrow night, there'll not be an attack. We'll be lucky if we get one in a week.' So I simply shrugged my shoulders, hitched a ride back in a helicopter, and said to the others, 'I don't see any point in sitting on Mount Kent for a week. One can't file useful dispatches just sitting up here.'

Wherever Hastings went, he wrote. 'Every time I passed him,' says Kim Sabido, 'he was sitting in a greenhouse, surrounded by tomatoes, a little cigar in his mouth, hammering away at a portable typewriter balanced on his knee.' Hastings produced a stream of articles, concentrating not so much on being first with the news – which was where many of his Fleet Street colleagues made their mistake – but on writing 'colour' pieces about everything around him.

I felt the most important thing was to start writing stories about every aspect of the task force, whether it was frigates, the air war, helicopter pilots or whatever. I just started moving around on my own doing these things and actually I was ticked off several times by MoD press officers for doing so much moving around, but I thought that they by then had proved themselves quite incapable and unsuited to organize any facilities for the journalists, and therefore it was entirely up to us to organize any facilities for ourselves. When it came to filing copy, whenever it was humanly possible I went physically to a ship in order to punch the tape myself. On the odd occasions when I did not do so, when like many others I handed helicopter pilots my copy, it was never seen again, and I do not blame the helicopter pilots for that.

Hastings loathed the MoD minders more than any other reporter: they impeded him in his headlong flight for copy. Virtually all the correspondents disliked the public relations men. They 'were held,' claimed Patrick Bishop, 'in equal contempt by journalists and taskforce members alike.' But it was Hastings who decided to make his anger known publicly, in an article written at the beginning of the second week in June. Tailored specifically for the *Standard*'s Londoner's Diary, the piece claimed that 'among the correspondents animosity towards the Argentines is nothing like as bitter as towards the Ministry of Defence public relations department.'

The most pitiful figures in all this are the Ministry public relations men on the spot, the minders as they are known without affection among the reporters. Not an impressive group from the first, since the task force entered the war zone these unhappy bureaucrats have become mere flotsam drifting meaninglessly from ship to ship, occasionally enforcing the latest restrictions from London, earning equal contempt from both reporter and military.

The final straw for the exhausted hack coming back to the ship from the mountains is to discover the minders, who pass their days reading newspapers in the wardroom, comfortably ensconced in their bunks, while the hacks doss down in sleeping bags on the floor. Retribution is promised when hostilities are over.

At the foot of this fulmination, Hastings added a note to the Diary's staff: 'I am most anxious that this is used in the hope of punitive action later.'

Before transmitting the article back to the UK, two of the minders attached their own comments to it, addressed to the Ministry of Defence. Senior press officer Martin Helm referred to 'Hastings's latest epic . . . an inaccurate distortion written in a fit of pique at being denied access to the phone'. Alan George, an MoD PR with whom Hastings had just had an argument about communications, added his own terse postscript for Neville Taylor: 'Grateful you contact my solicitor, Mr R. Wilson of Chethams, 19 Buckingham Street, London, to consider whether Hastings's piece is actionable, and please advise us all accordingly.' When the various messages reached London, the Ministry of Defence – inexplicably, and to the anger of Helm and George – released the entire text of all three for publication. The war between press and press officers, hitherto private, was now out in the open.

The minders are still seething about the Hastings incident, in particular the imputation that they were little short of cowards, sheltering in comfort well out of danger. 'Alan George sat through every air attack in San Carlos Water,' says one, 'the only person – minder or journalist – to do so. So when Hastings wrote what he did, Alan was a bit miffed, to put it mildly. He'd hardly had any sleep – he'd been bombed for eight days.'

It wasn't only the minders who were irritated. Hastings – grabbing 'all sorts of means of transport – small boats, moving constantly' – also became increasingly unpopular with a large section of the press contingent on the Falklands.

It gradually dawned upon some of the harder-bitten journalists that the Old Carthusian, Oxford-educated Hastings, so much more like one of the officers than a reporter, was beating them out of sight. Under a pooling arrangement, the press in London drew freely on the reports of one another's journalists, and Hastings's by-line dominated the newspapers: sometimes his stories even pushed out the dispatch from the paper's own correspondent. There were murmurings in the Falklands about 'favouritism', while in London the newspapers of the Express group, for whom Hastings worked, were jubilant about the success of their man. 'Only two names have dominated the Falklands war,' boasted the *Sunday Express*, 'Galtieri and Max Hastings.' That, commented Robert Fox, 'seems to cover a rather narrow political spectrum'.

Hastings's popularity among his colleagues reached its nadir in the final hours of the war, when he achieved his greatest coup: he became the first journalist to enter Port Stanley. The whole sequence of accidents, confusion and over-zealous military security which made up the last day of the land campaign proved a fitting climax to the whole war.

At midday on 14 June, with the British forces on the outskirts of Port Stanley, word spread that there were white flags flying over the capital. Max Hastings, naturally, was with the unit farthest forward, 2 Para, and the road into Stanley beckoned ahead. 'It was simply too good a chance to miss,' he wrote.

> Pulling off my web equipment and camouflaged jacket, I handed them to Roger Field in his Scimitar, now parked in the middle of the road and adorned with a large Union Jack. Then with a civilian anorak and a walking stick that I had been clutching since we landed at San Carlos Bay, I set off towards the town. . . .

Forty minutes later, having pretended to be from *The Times* and having talked to an Argentinian colonel, Hastings walked back into the British lines 'with the sort of exhilaration that most reporters are lucky enough to enjoy a few times in a lifetime.' His main priority now was to get back to *Fearless* and persuade the MoD minders to transmit the story immediately. 'When I came out of Stanley, Brigadier Thompson, extremely kind, realizing one had a marvellous scoop, arranged a helicopter for me to get back to the fleet to file my copy.' After 'a frenzied half-hour wait', during which Hastings tried to get on board three successive helicopters, the transport ordered by the brigadier arrived. Other reporters were milling around the British line, and Robert McGowan, Alastair McQueen, Derek Hudson, Ian Bruce and Leslie Dowd gave Hastings a 'pooled' dispatch they had written on the surrender for him to give to the MoD minders on *Fearless*; David Norris handed him a separate dispatch.

Hastings arrived at *Fearless* a few minutes before 4 p.m. local time 'to collect one of the Ministry of Defence public relations men'.

> I ran headlong into their cabin to seize one bodily and take him with me to a ship with transmission facilities. But I blurted out the essentials of my story to a disinterested audience. 'I am afraid that there is a complete news blackout,' declared the most senior of their number, a Mr Martin Helm. 'You cannot communicate at all until further notice.' Could he, I asked after an initial seizure, contact the Ministry to demand the lifting of the ban? No, such a call was covered by the ban itself.

What had happened was that John Nott had given instructions that no press were to be allowed to file copy. 'There was,' said Neville Taylor, 'an understandable and natural desire in London that that sort of announcement should be made first in London, preferably in Parliament.' There was an additional fear that a 'premature' disclosure from the Falklands might 'prejudice' the formal surrender negotiations which had not yet begun. Helm received a signal from Sir John Fieldhouse in which he was 'categorically told nothing could go back'.

> A bitter argument followed [wrote Hastings], in which it was put to him that Argentinian radio was already announcing a ceasefire, and that it was quite impossible to conceive what injury to British security might be done by a dispatch reporting my visit to Port Stanley. Mr Helm and his colleagues were unmoved. I went miserably to bed, to lie sleepless with rage towards the system which had so effortlessly thwarted me.

Brian Hanrahan, Michael Nicholson and their television crew were on Two Sisters Mountain when news of the white flags flying over Stanley came through. Hanrahan described what happened next:

> We went back to the brigade headquarters and saw the helicopter tasker there and tried to arrange the helicopters to split, so that Bernard Hesketh could go up into Stanley in order to film what was the end of the hostilities and I could head back to *Fearless* in order to send out reports and catch up with Bernard the next morning. At that moment, an officer came along and said that the order from Commander Land Forces Falkland Islands was that no journalist was to be allowed into Stanley and neither was a journalist to be helped – I think that was his word – to get back to *Fearless*. We had a disagreement about what the word 'helped' meant. His interpretation was that we were not to go back to *Fearless*: mine was that they should not divert helicopters to take me to *Fearless*.

Faced with this total refusal to 'help', there was nothing for the television men to do but to set off down the side of the mountain on foot. Every time a helicopter went by, they waved at it frantically, until eventually one stopped.

> It was a small Scout helicopter [recalled Nicholson], which should only take two passengers, but the sergeant pilot got five in the back, including our camera, all our burdens, our haversacks, and the crewman stood outside on the skids, and we got over to Fitzroy that way at 10 mph.

Like Hastings, Nicholson could scarcely believe it when Helm told him about the news blackout.

> I was on *Fearless* at ten to ten. With *News at Ten* I had ten minutes to go with this incredible story of the end of the war. ... Most of it was merely descriptive passages of how Stanley was taken and the war looked as if it was over and tonight the General was in Stanley negotiating a ceasefire. We could not see how that could in any way jeopardize the ceasefire negotiations. ...

While Nicholson and Hastings argued with Helm, Mrs Thatcher was announcing the news in the House of Commons: 'They are reported to be flying white flags over Port Stanley.' Once again, the war correspondents suffered the frustration of hearing the news announced over the World Service, without being able to do anything but hope to follow up with their own eyewitness accounts much later.

A little over two hours later, at 8.30 p.m. Falklands time (12.30 a.m. in London), General Moore arrived by helicopter at Government House in Port Stanley to conduct the surrender negotiations with the Argentine commander, General Menendez. It was a moment of triumph, mingled with great anxiety in case anything should go wrong. Moore had already forbidden any reporters to set foot in Stanley and was horrified to learn of Max Hastings's escapade earlier that afternoon.

Outside Government House the ubiquitous Martin Helm was on hand with two official photographers, and he asked Moore if he was willing to have the surrender filmed. 'I said "No",' recalled Moore.

> My reasoning was, and remains, that I was concerned with only one thing, and that was obtaining a surrender. I felt if there was half of a tenth of a 1 per cent chance that having the thing filmed might put Menendez off surrendering, and I did not know him, it would be a risk it could not be proper for me to take, and on those grounds I said 'No'.

It was a tense meeting. 'We were in a very poor way by 14 June,' stated Admiral Woodward. 'He was down to six rounds per gun that night; I had three frigates badly situated in terms of capability; we were running out of speed.' Sir Terence Lewin was listening to a running commentary on the negotiations on an open line to the Ministry of Defence, routed through SAS communications via Hereford.

Outside the negotiating room, Helm was waiting with his two official photographers – one from HMS *Fearless*, the other a Royal Marine commander – in the hope of getting a picture of the surrender being signed. But before Helm had a chance to get a picture of any sort, General Menendez agreed to capitulate and left, unescorted, with his officers. 'It was so quick,' explained Helm, 'we did not realize they were leaving.' Helm went in to see Moore and asked if it might be possible to get Menendez back in for a quick photography session: 'He said that unfortunately it was too late. They had already left.' For the first time in a modern conflict Britain had failed to get a single picture of her moment of triumph. Nor was a film cameraman or any journalist allowed to witness the evening of victory in Port Stanley. 'Posterity did not feature too much,' summed up David Nicholas.

Back on *Fearless*, Max Hastings was roused from his bed at

3 a.m. London time to be told that the news blackout, which had lasted for ten hours, had now been lifted. Refusing to trust the MoD minders to do anything, he made his way to the communications room and personally telexed to London the story of his triumphant march into Stanley.

What of the other copy, entrusted to him that afternoon by his fellow journalists? Hastings swears he gave it to one of the minders immediately he had punched out his own story. 'Fortunately, I took the precaution of doing so in the presence of a witness.' Although David Norris's piece eventually made it to London, the 'pooled' report by Robert McGowan and his colleagues disappeared: what happened to it remains a mystery to this day.

The absence of other stories enhanced the impact of Hastings's dispatch. It was the biggest scoop of the war, so complete that to its author it very nearly proved fatal. The other reporters were furious when they heard what had happened. At the Upland Goose, Port Stanley's hotel, Max Hastings was confronted by an angry Ian Bruce. According to one eyewitness:

> Max was sitting by the piano, when Bruce started yelling at him in a loud Glaswegian accent, which translated into something like, 'Hastings, you have lost my story and now I am going to kill you,' and then he pulled out an Argentinian bayonet. Patrick Bishop's face was one of studied amusement as to where Bruce would plunge the dagger. Then Derek Hudson piped up and said, 'This is neither the time nor the place to murder Max Hastings,' and Bruce was dragged off him. Poor Max went very white.

After a few days the owner of the Upland Goose actually refused to take journalists as guests. He told Alan Percival he was going to complain to the Press Council. The correspondents, he said, were 'worse than the Argies'.

*   *   *

In the last week of the war, Kim Sabido, the young reporter for Independent Radio News, filed a story that was bitterly critical of the media's behaviour on the Falklands. 'We have all been acting to a smaller or larger degree like overblown egos auditioning for parts in some awful B war movie,' Sabido told his listeners, and described how one minder had told him, 'If I had a pound for every time I've read "I dived for cover" or "The bomb burst just a few feet away", I'd be rich.' Sabido accused some reporters of outright lying – 'perpetrated, I believe, in a blind desire to be first with the news instead of just trying to be truthful' – and alleged two particular instances of reporters fabricating stories: 'those journalists who claimed to have read through binoculars street names in Stanley when still 10 miles behind the front line and within sight of nothing more than an Arctic ration pack', and the broadcaster who 'described in graphic detail how planes cartwheeled across the sky in the first dogfight of the war when he was, according to colleagues, locked below decks some 80 miles from the action'.

There were other examples of bogus stories which Sabido didn't quote. One 'eyewitness account' of the rescue of survivors from Bluff Cove was, swear the minders, broadcast by a journalist who was further up the coast with a large hill between himself and Bluff Cove at the time. Another reporter filed a false story about motorcycles being fitted with rocket launchers. Some journalists listened to broadcasts on the World Service, rewrote them and sent them back to their newspapers as if they were first-hand accounts. Five reporters arrived to cover the attack on Mount Kent with their reports on the action already written, based upon an inaccurate briefing: they had described the assault as having been preceded by a 'heavy bombardment', when in fact the plan was to mount a silent attack. The journalists held a hurried meeting. Two of the reporters were unhappy, but the consensus was to let the inaccurate stories – by now on their way to *Fearless* for clearance – be transmitted unchanged.

'When the final roll of honour comes to be drawn up for both British and Argentines alike,' said Sabido, 'I would humbly suggest that with some very noble exceptions . . . we the reporters will not be on that list.' Sir Frank Cooper gave vent to some justified exasperation to the Commons Defence Committee:

> I have not seen or heard a single admission, if I may say so – and I am not being beastly to the media – that any of them got anything wrong or that every single correspondent was not a knight in shining armour riding a white horse in search of the absolute truth.

After the war, Surgeon-Commander Morgan O'Connell, a psychiatrist sailing with the task force, described in the *Guardian* the symptoms of battle stress that he noticed in the men under his care: 'emotional tension, hypersensitivity to noise, explosive rage, a feeling of helplessness, amnesia and regression to childish behaviour'. Of all the groups during the war he found that the journalists fared the worst: 'They had no group cohesiveness. They were in competition with each other all the time, so they couldn't draw the same security from their group.'

Out of the twenty-eight correspondents who started with the task force, three dropped out, suffering from varying degrees of strain. Few of those left in Port Stanley at the end of the war had any desire to remain on the islands for a day longer than necessary. John Witherow and Patrick Bishop have described some of the ploys considered by the journalists in order to get off the Falklands quickly:

> chartering a seaplane from Chile, taking a hospital ship with the casualties to Montevideo and, most far-fetched of all,

trying to leave via Argentina with the prisoners on *Canberra*. Others boarded RFA *Resource* with the assurance she would reach Ascension within a week. The captain explained that his none-too-swift ammunition ship would have to do 35 knots to arrive in that time. Nevertheless, a number embarked and once at sea were told there had been a change of plan and they were bound for South Georgia. They managed to get a helicopter back to Stanley.

A straw poll was held to allocate seats on the first Hercules flight back to the UK; when it was completed, the list of successful journalists was stolen and hidden behind the bar. Offers of hundreds of pounds were made for a seat; none was accepted.

Most reporters were glad to have covered the war, but few wished to repeat the experience. Brian Hanrahan said he would 'probably be quite pleased' to be asked, 'but I am not sure I would be altogether pleased to go through it all again'. Hastings, characteristically, was more positive.

> One felt an enormous sense of privilege to have the opportunity to be there. After so many years in which one has been reporting on one aspect or another of national failure, it was enormously moving to see and to record a national success. Whether the war should have been fought at all, whether it was necessary, whether it was a good thing – one is almost dismayed to have to think about those things because you lose that magical sense one had in Stanley when the war ended. You thought, Gosh, one's actually taken part in a great British success. And it is saddening to come back to the real world.

Robert Fox echoed the same sentiments:

> One feels mildly affronted for it to be suggested that such an extraordinary experience, which so nearly cost me my life, was worthless. The days in that wild landscape, the companionship

of many of the men in the field were enjoyable more often than not; fear and danger were exhilarating too. . . . *For me it was an existential dream.* [Author's emphasis.]

Around 1,000 British servicemen were killed or wounded during the Falklands campaign; Argentina suffered over 1,800 casualties. Yet the final dominant impression of the media's coverage of the war is its unreality.

In part this was a reflection of the nature of the conflict itself. The *Observer*'s Neal Ascherson described an editorial conference in London as divided between 'those who thought something real was taking place and those who assumed they were having a gaudy dream'.

As the Falklands war ended, the Israelis attacked Lebanon. Night after night, British television carried pictures of suffering and destruction. Yet images of death and injury hardly featured at all in the media's coverage of the fighting in the South Atlantic.

To take one example: on 27–8 May, 250 Argentine soldiers were killed in a *single* attack, yet, as Peter Preston, editor of the *Guardian*, pointed out, 'We had pictures of Argentinian helmets on bayonets after Goose Green but not a body in sight throughout.' The first television film of British casualties following Goose Green was not transmitted for over two weeks: ironically, it was shown on 14 June, the night Mrs Thatcher announced the cease-fire, and followed pictures of her appearance in Downing Street listening to patriotic crowds singing 'Rule Britannia'.

The media also played their part in converting the war into what Bishop and Witherow described as a 'national drama' with 'all the cathartic effect of a Shakespearean tragedy'. Lieutenant David Tinker, a 25-year-old officer on HMS *Glamorgan*, described one encounter with the media at the time of the Pebble Island raid on 14 May:

The BBC were on board and grandiosed everything out of all proportion (Antarctic wind, Force 9 gales, terrific disruption done, disruption of entire Argentinian war effort, etc.). Mostly, they sat drinking the wardroom beer and were sick in the Heads: the weather was in fact quite good.

More than 1,000 men lost their lives in the struggle for the Falklands. Tinker was one of them – killed along with twelve other members of *Glamorgan*'s crew when she was hit by an Exocet missile on 12 June.

The newspapers just see it as a real-life 'War Mag' [he wrote on 28 May] and even have drawings of battles, and made-up descriptions, entirely from their own imagination! If some of the horrible ways that people died occurred in *their* offices, maybe they would change their tone. Let us hope it ends quickly.

CONCLUSION

Closing the Emergency Press Centre on 18 June, Ian McDonald told reporters that he had found the past ten weeks 'totally engrossing and tremendously exciting' and ended by quoting Prospero's final speech in *The Tempest*:

> Now my charms are all o'erthrown,
> And what strength I have's mine own,
> Which is most faint. . . .

That afternoon Ian McDonald left public relations for good. Three weeks later he took up a new post as head of the Adjutant General's secretariat.

Michael Nicholson celebrated his return home by buying a new house in a tiny village in Sussex. It became commonplace, as the weeks went by after the end of the war, to say that the media and the Navy must put the bitterness of the campaign behind them and learn to live together. The phrase took on a new shade of meaning for Nicholson, who has discovered that his neighbour in that enclosed community is the captain of *Hermes* – Lyn Middleton.

Six of the reporters who sailed with the task force either wrote or collaborated on books about the Falklands. Patrick Bishop and John Witheroe wrote *The Winter War*; John Shirley contributed to the Insight book *The Falklands War*; Max Hastings joined Simon Jenkins to write *Battle for the Falklands*; Robert Fox wrote *Eyewitness Falklands*, and he and Brian Hanrahan had their dispatches from the South Atlantic published as a book by the BBC. 'Never in the field of human conflict', commented one reviewer, 'has so much been written by so many so quickly.'

Seventeen task-force correspondents gave oral or written evidence to the House of Commons committee investigating the MoD's handling of the media. Over a period of five months, under the benign gaze of the committee's chairman, Sir Timothy Kitson, the protagonists of the information war paraded in front of MPs.

A few scenes linger in the memory. Dr John Gilbert, a junior Defence Minister in the last Labour Government, cross-examining Sir Frank Cooper and accusing him of *'suppressio veri suggestio falsi* – suppression of the truth and the suggestion of what is false, in the course of which you do not tell a single lie', with Cooper bristling at what he called an 'obnoxious suggestion'. Max Hastings, beaming with pleasure at the recollection of his triumphs while at the same time trying to look modestly at the floor. Brian Hanrahan's quiet accusations of news management: 'I am sure there were times when information was messed about for reasons which had nothing to do with military information.' Admiral Woodward's opinion of the minder on *Hermes* – 'I am a great believer in setting a thief to catch a thief. I am not sure whether Mr Hammond was a thief in press affairs', a comment which revealed as much about the Navy's attitude to the media as a volume of evidence. Finally there was the undisguised irritability of Sir Terence Lewin at having to give an account of himself to the committee: 'We won, which I assume was what the Government and the public and the media all wanted us to do. . . . I am somewhat surprised that there is a need now to have this great post mortem into the media aspects of the campaign in the South Atlantic.' 'I do not think,' replied Kitson, 'we should get into a discussion this afternoon as to whether it is right to hold an inquiry.'

The wounds caused by the Falklands war did not heal

quickly – least of all those inflicted within the Ministry of Defence. In October an internal MoD document was leaked to the Commons committee revealing that guidelines *had* been drawn up as early as 1977 to deal with the media in 'situations of crisis and increased tension . . . outside a NATO context'. The paper, entitled 'Public Relations Planning in Emergency Operations', laid down details of 'responsibilities for co-ordination' within the MoD PR department, and its recommendations had a specific relevance to the Falklands crisis:

> For planning purposes it is anticipated that twelve places would be available to the media, divided equally between ITN, BBC and the press. . . . The press should be asked to give an undertaking that copy and photographs will be pooled. Within the overall seat allocation and bids from the media every effort should be made to include a radio reporter in the party.

As the Ministry had been insisting that – in Cooper's words – 'there was no pre-planning' for coping with the media in a Falklands-style operation, the revelation of this five-year-old contingency plan caused considerable embarrassment. Ian McDonald was forced to confess that he had never even heard of it. It had been leaked by the Army deliberately to give the despised 'administration' within the MoD a rough time. 'It was done by the Green Jackets,' claims one furious official, 'the biggest shits in Britain.'

The Defence Committee was also encountering divisions within the media. The MPs discovered that Cooper's non-attributable briefings were all recorded by the MoD and asked for the tapes to be released. Neville Taylor, 'mending fences' and 'trying to establish better relations and a better understanding' with the media, consulted the defence correspondents concerned, and *they* voted by nine to seven not to give the committee access to the tapes. Taylor explained that they had 'expressed the view that the principle was important'. Timothy Kitson was angry and exasperated: 'Here we are inquiring into the problems, trying to be helpful to the media, doing all we possibly can to be reasonable about this inquiry, and then we find they are consulted about some tapes which, in fact, we are entitled to see and should see. . . .' The committee had run up against the symbiotic relationship, fostered by the lobby system, which had allowed misinformation to be so easily planted in the first place.

The Falklands conflict may well prove the last war in which the armed forces are completely able to control the movements and communications of the journalists covering it. Technology has already overtaken the traditional concepts of war reporting. The combination of lightweight video cameras and commercial satellites may mean that commanders will hear news of fighting as quickly through watching television as through normal military sources. 'You will never have it easier than the Falklands,' Sir Frank Cooper told the Commons Defence Committee:

> If any of us sit down and think for a moment that if there was a Soviet incursion into some part of Europe, what would actually happen in terms of war, diplomacy and the media, I think we would all find very great difficulty in answering all those questions to anybody's satisfaction at the moment. Obviously, we shall need to look at the whole question of whether there should be some form of censorship. Is any form of censorship practical in the modern world? It is highly unlikely we would get anything as simple as that again in a real shooting-type war.

'In a few years' time,' said John Nott, 'I think the task of censorship, with satellites, will become an impossible one.'

The British Government might be able to impose censorship on British satellite stations. It cannot expect to control foreign or international ones. If Britain were to be involved in joint military action with the Americans, would one population be given more information than the other? How could any censorship authority keep track of the sheer volume of material transmitted from the battlefield and from capitals around the world?

> I think the only conclusion I can safely reach [said Cooper] is that nobody has thought about this in anything like the depth that needs to be done to try and find out answers to difficult questions. Indeed, there are no simple or short answers to any of these issues. These are major and fundamental questions which will have a bigger impact on any kind of warfare than we have ever supposed to be the case.

The Ministry of Defence is setting up a committee to investigate the subject, under the chairmanship of 'a distinguished retired general'. Its terms of reference are 'To consider – not least in the light of the Falklands operation – whether any new measures, including the introduction of a system of censorship, are necessary to protect military operations. . . .' The MoD has also decided to sponsor a two- or three-year research project that will study the relationship between the armed forces and the media in time of war.

But this concentration on the long-term implications of censorship should not divert attention from the central lesson of the 'information war'. The episodes which caused the most disquiet, and which have been described in this book, were not necessarily unique to the Falklands crisis. The instinctive secrecy of the military and the Civil Service; the prostitution and hysteria of sections of the press; the lies, the misinformation, the manipulation of public opinion by the authorities; the political intimidation of the broadcasters; the ready connivance of the media at their own distortion ... all these occur as much in normal peace time in Britain as in war.

The Falklands crisis had one unique and beneficial side-effect. Its limited time-scale and crowded succession of incidents made it an experience of great intensity. It briefly illuminated aspects of British society usually hidden from view. It *exposed* habitual abuses by the armed forces, Government, Whitehall and the media; it did not *create* them. And although the war itself is over, the fighting here goes on: its first casualty – as always – truth.

SELLING HITLER

The Story of the Hitler Diaries

CONTENTS

ACKNOWLEDGEMENTS

This account is based upon interviews with the main participants in the Hitler diaries affair; upon the many hundreds of
pages of prosecution evidence generated by the subsequent
trial; and upon the so-called *Stern Report* – the findings of the
internal commission set up by *Stern* to examine how the fiasco
occurred. Almost all of this information came to me on the
understanding that its various sources would not be identified
publicly. It would be invidious to try to single out the few who
did speak freely; I hope I shall be forgiven if I thank them here
collectively rather than individually.

My editor at the BBC, David Dickinson, was once again
extremely understanding. My colleague Jane Ellison collaborated on the research, from the first interview to the last
document: without her help, this book could not have been
written.

R.H.
September 1985

Note
Most of the financial transactions concerning the Hitler
diaries were conducted in Deutschmarks. In April 1983, when
the diaries were published, the rates of exchange were:

£1 = 3.76 marks
$1 = 2.44 marks

DRAMATIS PERSONAE

WILHELM ARNDT: Adolf Hitler's personal servant, entrusted with escorting the Führer's 'testament to posterity' out of Berlin in April 1945

THE MARQUESS OF BATH: Owner of the world's largest collection of Hitler's paintings

HANS BAUR: Hitler's personal pilot

RANDOLPH BRAUMANN: 'Congo Randy', a close friend of Gerd Heidemann

WILLIAM BROYLES: Editor-in-chief of *Newsweek*

GERDA CHRISTIAN: One of Hitler's secretaries

BARBARA DICKMANN: Television journalist hired by *Stern* to help launch the Hitler diaries

CHARLES DOUGLAS-HOME: Editor of *The Times*

MANFRED FISHER: Managing director of Gruner and Jahr, owners of *Stern*

DR MAX FREI-SULZER: Swiss 'handwriting expert'

FRANÇOIS GENOUD: Swiss lawyer representing the families of Hitler, Goebbels and Bormann

FRANK GILES: Editor of the *Sunday Times*

ROLF GILLHAUSEN: *Stern* editor

OTTO GUENSCHE: SS adjutant who burned Hitler's body

MAJOR FRIEDRICH GUNDLFINGER: Luftwaffe pilot who flew Wilhelm Arndt out of Berlin in April 1945

GERD HEIDEMANN: *Stern* journalist responsible for obtaining the Hitler diaries

GINA HEIDEMANN: Wife of Gerd Heidemann

DR JOSEF HENKE: Senior official of the West German Federal Archives

DR JAN HENSMANN: Deputy managing director of Gruner and Jahr

PETER HESS: Publishing director of Gruner and Jahr

WOLF HESS: Son of Rudolph Hess

ORDWAY HILTON: American 'handwriting expert'

DAVID IRVING: British historian

EBERHARD JAECKEL: Professor of History, University of Stuttgart

MEDARD KLAPPER: Arms dealer and confidence trickster who alleged he was in touch with Martin Bormann

PETER KOCH: *Stern* editor

PETER KUEHSEL: Financial director of Gruner and Jahr

KONRAD KUJAU: Forger of the Hitler diaries

EDITH LIEBLANG: Konrad Kujau's common law wife

HEINZ LINGE: Hitler's valet

BRIAN MACARTHUR: Deputy editor, the *Sunday Times*

WERNER MASER: West German historian

ROCHUS MISCH: Führerbunker switchboard operator

MARIA MODRITSCH: Konrad Kujau's girlfriend

REINHARD MOHN: Chief executive, Bertelsmann AG

SS GENERAL WILHELM MOHNKE: Commander of the Führer-bunker

RUPERT MURDOCH: Chairman, News International; owner, *The Times*, *Sunday Times* and *New York Post*

HENRI NANNEN: Founder and publisher of *Stern*

LYNN NESBIT: Senior Vice-President, International Creative Management

JAMES O'DONNELL: Author, *The Berlin Bunker*

DR KLAUS OLDENHAGE: Official of the West German Federal Archives

MAYNARD PARKER: Editor of *Newsweek*

LEO PESCH: Journalist employed in *Stern*'s history department

BILLY F. PRICE: Collector of Hitler paintings from Houston, Texas; author, *Adolf Hitler: The Unknown Artist*

AUGUST PRIESACK: Self-styled 'professor' and expert on Hitler's art, consulted by Fritz Stiefel and Billy Price

KENNETH RENDELL: American 'handwriting expert'

ARNOLD RENTZ: West German forensic chemist

FELIX SCHMIDT: *Stern* editor

CHRISTA SCHROEDER: One of Hitler's secretaries

GERD SCHULTE-HILLEN: Manfred Fischer's successor as managing director of Gruner and Jahr

RICHARD SCHULZE-KOSSENS: One of Hitler's SS adjutants

WILFRIED SORGE: Member of the management of Gruner and Jahr, responsible for selling the Hitler diaries to foreign news organizations

FRANZ SPOEGLER: Former SS officer who offered Heidemann forged correspondence between Churchill and Mussolini

FRITZ STIEFEL: Stuttgart businessman, collector of Nazi memorabilia

JAKOB TIEFENTHAELER: Collector of Nazi memorabilia who acted as agent for Gerd Heidemann when he tried to sell Goering's yacht

HUGH TREVOR-ROPER (Lord Dacre of Glanton): Master of Peterhouse, Cambridge; Independent National Director, Times Newspaper

THOMAS WALDE: Head of *Stern*'s history department

GERHARD WEINBERG: Professor of Modern History, University of North Carolina

PETER WICKMAN: *Stern* correspondent based in London

LOUIS WOLFE: President, Bantam Books

SS GENERAL KARL WOLFF: Heinrich Himmler's Chief of Staff; Military Governor of northern Italy, 1943–45

PROLOGUE

On April Fool's Day 1983 the distinguished British historian Hugh Redwald Trevor-Roper, first Baron Dacre of Glanton, was telephoned at his country home in Scotland by the Assistant Editor of *The Times*, Mr Colin Webb.

Among his many honours, Trevor-Roper had, in 1974, accepted an invitation to become an Independent National Director of Times Newspapers. For nine years his telephone had rung periodically with news of strikes, sackings and closures. But this call had nothing to do with routine *Times* business. It concerned a discovery of great historical significance. It was strictly confidential. The German magazine *Stern*, said Mr Webb, had discovered the private diaries of Adolf Hitler.

Trevor-Roper, a former Regius Professor of History at Oxford, was startled and immediately sceptical. 'I said to myself, there are so many forgeries circulating in the "grey market": forged documents about Bormann, forged diaries of Eva Braun, falsified accounts of interviews with Hitler. . . .' Besides, it was well known that Hitler disliked putting pen to paper and had virtually given up writing in his own hand altogether after 1933. As far as he was aware there was no evidence, either in the German archives or in the recollections of Hitler's subordinates, to suggest that the German dictator had kept a diary. If he had, and if it had now been discovered, it would certainly rank as one of the greatest historical finds of modern times: Hitler, as Trevor-Roper himself had written, was the twentieth century's Genghis Khan, the 'political genius' whose murderous influence upon mankind was still being felt four decades after his death. If this diabolical figure, contrary to all accepted beliefs, turned out to have kept a *diary*, it would provoke a sensation.

Webb explained that *Stern* was offering to sell the foreign serial rights in the diaries. Rupert Murdoch, the owner of Times Newspapers, was considering bidding not merely for the British and Commonwealth, but possibly for the American rights as well. The syndication negotiations were about to begin. In the meantime the diaries themselves were being kept in a bank vault in Switzerland. Webb said that Murdoch wanted an expert's opinion before making an offer for the diaries. Would Trevor-Roper, as an authority on the period and a director of the company, be willing to act as an adviser? Would he fly out to Zurich and examine the material?

Trevor-Roper said he would.

In that case, said Webb, *Stern* would expect him in Switzerland at the end of the following week.

By the time Adolf Hitler had passed his fifty-second birthday, there was no longer a human being left in history who could provide a precedent for his impact on the earth. In January 1942, whilst he picked at his customary vegetarian supper at his headquarters in East Prussia, his soldiers were guarding U-boat pens on the Atlantic coast, shivering in dugouts on the approach roads to Moscow, sweating in tanks in the Libyan desert. In less than twenty years, he had passed from brawling provincial politician to imperial conqueror. He was remaking the world. 'Mark my words, Bormann,' he announced one evening over dinner, 'I'm going to become very religious.'

'You've always been very religious,' replied Bormann.

But Hitler was not thinking of himself as a mere participant in some future act of worship: he was to be the object of it.

'I'm going to become a religious figure,' he insisted. 'Soon

I'll be the great chief of the tartars. Already Arabs and Moroccans are mingling my name with their prayers. Amongst the tartars I shall become Khan. . . .'

When the warm weather returned he would finish off the Red Army. Then he would 'put things in order for a thousand years'. Giant roads would be built into Russia and the first of twenty million Germans, 'soldier-peasants', would start making their homes in a colony whose frontier would extend 250 miles east of the Urals. The Russians, denied churches and schools, educated only to a point at which they could read road signs, would be confined to vast, disease-ridden cities, patrolled from the air by the Luftwaffe. The Crimea would be exclusively German. Moscow would be razed to the ground and turned into an artificial lake. The Channel Islands would be handed over to the Strength Through Joy organization 'for, with their wonderful climate, they constitute a marvellous health resort'. Every nation would have its part to play in Hitler's New Order. The Norwegians would supply Europe's electricity. The Swiss would be hotel keepers. 'I haven't studied the problem as regards Sweden,' joked Hitler. 'In Finland, unfortunately, there is nothing to be done.' Opponents would be confined behind barbed wire in the lengthening chain of concentration camps now opening up in the Eastern territories. At the first sign of trouble, all inmates would be 'liquidated'. As for the Jews, they would simply be 'got rid of'. The future was a vista of endless conflict. A man's first encounter with war, stated Hitler, was like a woman's first experience with a man: 'For the good of the German people, we must wish for a war every fifteen or twenty years.' And in Berlin, renamed Germania, at the centre of this ceaselessly warring empire, would sit the Führer himself, in a granite Chancellery of such proportions that 'one should have the feeling that one is visiting the master of the world'. The Berghof, his private home on the Obersalzberg, would, in due course, become a museum. here, propped up in bed, while the rest of the household slept, Hitler had found the inspiration for his dreams, gazing out 'for hours' at 'the mountains lit up by the moon'. When his dreams were reality, it would become a place of pilgrimage for a grateful race. 'I can already see the guide from Berchtesgaden showing visitors over the rooms of my house: "This is where he had breakfast. . . ." I can also imagine a Saxon giving his avaricious instructions: "Don't touch the articles, don't wear out the parquet, stay between the ropes. . . ." '

Almost half a century has now passed since Adolf Hitler and his vision were buried in the rubble of Berlin. All that remains today of the Berghof are a few piles of stone, overgrown with moss and trees. But the repercussions of his career persist. '*Si monumentum requiris, circumspice,*' concludes Alan Bullock's study of Hitler: 'If you seek his monument, look around.' The division of Germany, the exhaustion of British power, the entrenchment and paranoia of Soviet Russia, the denials of freedom in the Eastern half of Europe, the entanglement of America in the Western half, the creation of the State of Israel and the consequent instability of the Middle East – all, in a sense, have been bequeathed to us by Adolf Hitler. His name has become a synonym for evil. Even the physical act of uttering the word 'Hitler' necessitates a grimace. In 1979, the British historian J. H. Plumb described him as a 'curse', the 'black blight' that overshadowed his youth:

> The trauma of Hitler stretched over fifteen years for my genera-
> tion, breaking lives, destroying those one loved, wrecking my
> country. So it has been difficult, well-nigh impossible, to think
> calmly of that white, moustachioed face, eyes ablaze like a
> Charlie Chaplin turned into a nightmare. Even now when I recall
> that face and hear that terrifying, hysterical, screeching voice,
> they create a sense of approaching doom, disaster and death.
>
> Yet hard though it may be, Hitler has to be understood. . . .

In an attempt to come to terms with this phenomenon there were, by 1980, according to one estimate, over seventy biographies of Adolf Hitler in existence. There are twice as many biographies of Hitler as there are of Winston Churchill; three times as many as there are of Roosevelt and Stalin. Only Jesus Christ has had more words devoted to him than Hitler. The public appetite for these books is enormous. In 1974, Joachim Fest's biography sold over 250,000 hardback copies in Germany alone. Two years later, John Toland's *Adolf Hitler* sold 75,000 copies in the United States (at $15 each) and went into four printings within weeks of its publication. When David Irving began on *his* study he wrote that 'it was possible to speculate that "books on Hitler" outnumbered page for page the total original documentation available. This proved a sad underestimate.' By 1979 the British Library and the Library of Congress listed over 55,000 items relating solely to Hitler and the Second World War. There are specialist books about Hitler's childhood, his years in Vienna and his service in the army; at least half a dozen works are devoted specifically to his last days and death. There have been investigations into his mind, his body, his personal security, his art. We have first-hand accounts from his valet, his secretary, his pilot, his photographer, his interpreter, his chauffeur and a host of adjutants, ministers and generals. From one doctor (Morell) we know all we ever want to know – and considerably more – about the movement of Hitler's bowels; from another (Giesing), the appearance of the Führer's genitalia. We know that he liked cream cakes, dumb blondes, fast cars, mountain scenery; that he disliked lipstick, modern art, opinionated women and the screech of an owl.

The detail is immense and yet, somehow, the portrait it adds up to remains oddly unconvincing. Despite the millions of words which have been poured into explaining the gulf between Hitler, the private individual, and Hitler, the political prodigy, the two remain unreconciled. 'We seem to be left with a phantom,' wrote J. P. Stern, 'a centre of Nothing.' This inner emptiness helped enable Hitler to use himself like a tool, changing his personality with shocking abruptness to suit the task in hand. The charm of an Austrian gentleman, the brutality of a gangster, the ranting of a demagogue, the assurance of a diplomat succeeded one another in a kaleidoscope of performances which left his innermost thoughts a mystery. In the 1930s, an astonished official watched him carefully work himself into an artificial rage for the sole purpose of frightening an English diplomat; the performance over, he returned to his advisers chuckling, 'Gentlemen, I need tea. He thinks I'm *furious*.' Hitler remained an enigma, even to his most intimate advisers. 'I got to know Adolf Hitler more closely in 1933,' wrote Joachim von Ribbentrop at the end of the war.

> But if I am asked today whether I knew him well – how he thought as a politician and statesman, what kind of man he was – then I'm bound to confess that I know only very little about him; in fact nothing at all. The fact is that although I went through so much together with him, in all the years of working with him I never came closer to him than on the first day we met, either personally or otherwise.

'When a decision has to be taken,' Hermann Goering told one diplomat before the war, 'none of us count more than the stones on which we are standing. It is the Führer alone who decides.' And General Jodl, at Hitler's side throughout six years of war, was equally baffled. 'To this very day,' he wrote in 1946, 'I do not know what he thought or knew or really wanted.' He was utterly self-contained, mysterious, unpredictable, secretive, awesome. He was, as Hugh Trevor-Roper put it, 'the Rousseau, the Mirabeau, the Robespierre and the Napoleon of his revolution; he was its Marx, its Lenin, its Trotsky and its Stalin.' What a sensation it would cause if it were now discovered that such a man had left behind a *diary*. . . .

On Friday, 8 April 1983, exactly one week after his initial conversation with *The Times*, Hugh Trevor-Roper presented himself at terminal 2 of London's Heathrow Airport. There he was met by *Stern*'s London representative, Peter Wickman, and at 11.15 a.m. they took off for Zurich.

Wickman, plump and garrulous, proved an amiable companion and the sixty-nine-year-old historian was soon launched into one of his favourite topics of conversation: the inordinate superiority of Oxford over Cambridge. (He once said that leaving an Oxford professorship for a Cambridge mastership was rather like becoming a colonial governor.) It was not until the stewardess had served lunch that the two men settled down to business.

Wickman gave Trevor-Roper a twenty-page, typewritten document, bound in a clear plastic cover and entitled *Plan 3*. Based on the so-called diaries, it told the story of how Hitler's deputy, Rudolf Hess, had undertaken his abortive peace mission to Britain in May 1941. The accepted view among historians was that he had made his dramatic flight on his own initiative. But according to the diary entries quoted in *Plan 3*, Hitler knew of Hess's intention in advance.

On 25 June 1939, Hitler was alleged to have written in his diary:

> Hess sends me a personal note about the England problem. Would not have thought that this Hess is so sharp-witted. This note is very, very interesting.

Other entries followed:

> *28 June*: Read the Hess note again. Simply fantastic and yet so simple.

6 July: Hess should work over his thoughts which he has informed me about in his note and I anticipate seeing him for a one-to-one meeting.

13 July: Have also talked to Hess again. As soon as he has thought everything over properly, he will call me back. I would not have thought Hess capable of this. Not Hess.

22 July: Have Goering with me once more. I carefully inquire what range our best planes have. Hess said that one would have to build a special plane and that he was already working on the plans. What a man. He does not want any more said to Goering about his plan.

Finally, Hitler was supposed to have outlined three contingency plans:

1 Should the mission go well and Hess be successful, he acted in agreement with me.
2 If Hess is arrested in England as a spy, then he informed me some time ago of his plan, but I rejected it.
3 Should his mission fail completely, I declare Hess acted in a fit of delusion.

When it became clear that Hess's mission *had* failed, 'Plan 3' had duly been adopted. This, according to *Stern*, was the solution to one of the great mysteries of the Second World War, proof that six weeks before the invasion of Russia, Hitler had made a genuine attempt to negotiate peace with Britain.

Even as he took detailed notes from the document, suspicions began to accumulate in Trevor-Roper's mind. *Stern*'s version of the Hess story was in conflict with all the available evidence. Albert Speer, for example, had been outside Hitler's study door at the precise moment that the Führer had learned of Hess's flight to Britain. 'I suddenly heard', Speer recalled, 'an inarticulate, almost animal outcry.' Trevor-Roper had been told the story by Speer in person. He had subsequently described in his own book, *The Last Days of Hitler*, how the Nazi leadership had been hastily summoned to the Berghof to discuss the damage Hess had done: hardly the behaviour one would have expected if Hitler had known of Hess's intention in advance. He told Wickman immediately that he thought the *Stern* story was rubbish and Wickman, who had long nursed his own private doubts, agreed.

By the time the plane landed in Zurich, Trevor-Roper was finding it difficult to keep an open mind about the diaries. He was almost certain it was a wasted journey, but having come so far he thought he might as well at least see them. The two men took a taxi into town, dropped off their luggage at the Hotel Bauer au Lac, and while Trevor-Roper waited, Wickman telephoned ahead to the bank where the diaries were being kept. The *Stern* people were already waiting. Wickman told them that he and the historian were on their way over.

Shortly after 3 p.m., Trevor-Roper was ushered into a ground floor room of Zurich's Handelsbank. At the end of a long table, three men rose to meet him. One was Wilfried Sorge, the salesman who had flown round the world alerting newspapers in America, Japan, Italy, Spain and Britain to the existence of the diaries. Another was Dr Jan Hensmann, the financial director of *Stern*'s parent company, Gruner and Jahr. The third German was *Stern*'s bullet-headed editor-in-chief, Peter Koch.

When the introductions had been completed, Koch gestured towards a side table. On it were fifty-eight volumes of diaries, carefully piled up in a stack more than two feet high. Another set of documents was in a metal safety deposit box. There was a bound volume of original drawings and paintings. There was even a First World War helmet, allegedly Hitler's. This was no mere handful of notes. It was, as Trevor-Roper later described it, 'a whole coherent archive covering 35 years'. He was staggered by its scale.

He picked up a couple of the books. They were A4-sized, with stiff black covers. Some bore red wax seals in the form of a German eagle. Others were decorated with initials in gothic script. Most carried typewritten labels declaring them to be the property of the Führer and signed by Martin Bormann. The pages inside were lined, some densely filled with old Germanic script, some bearing only a couple of sentences, some completely blank. At the foot of each page was Hitler's signature – a jagged oscillation in black ink, like a seismographic record of some distant earthquake.

The *Stern* men met Trevor-Roper's queries point by point. They produced three separate reports from handwriting experts authenticating the documents. They described how the diaries had come into their hands. They confirmed that the magazine knew the identity of the supplier. It was enough.

> When I entered the back room in the Swiss bank [wrote Trevor-Roper in *The Times*], and turned the pages of those volumes, my doubts gradually dissolved. I am now satisfied that the documents are authentic; that the history of their wanderings since 1945 is true; and that the standard accounts of Hitler's writing habits, of his personality, and even, perhaps, some public events may, in consequence, have to be revised.

Twenty-four hours later Rupert Murdoch was sitting in the same bank vault leafing through the diaries with the former head of Reuters at his side translating their contents. By mid-afternoon on 9 April he had offered the delighted Germans $3 million for the world rights.

What happened next is described in detail later in this book: how Murdoch and the *Newsweek* company fell into an ill-tempered auction which at one stage pushed the price of the diaries up to $3.75 million, until *Stern*'s greed and *Newsweek*'s alleged unscrupulousness punctured the whole deal; how *Stern* nevertheless managed to sell subsidiary rights in the diaries to newspapers and magazines in America, Britain, Austria, France, Italy, Spain, Norway, Holland and Belgium – a contract carefully calculated to squeeze the last marketable drop out of Adolf Hitler, dividing the diaries into twenty-eight separate extracts whose publication would have spanned more than eighteen months; how news of the diaries' discovery was rushed into print despite growing evidence that some of the material was of post-war origin; and finally how this elaborate but increasingly shaky pyramid of subsidiary deals and serial rights was sent crashing two weeks later by a short laboratory report from the Federal police.

The diaries, announced the West German state archives on 6 May, were not merely fakes: they were '*eine plumpe Fälschung*', a crude forgery, the grotesquely superficial ('*grotesk oberflächlich*') concoction of a copyist endowed with a 'limited intellectual capacity'. The paper, the binding, the glue, the thread were all found to be of post-war manufacture. By the time this was disclosed, the management of *Stern*, in the course of more than two years, had handed over twenty-seven suitcases full of money to enable their star reporter, Gerd Heidemann, to obtain the diaries. $4 million had disappeared, making the Hitler diaries the most expensive and far-reaching fraud in publishing history, easily dwarfing the $650,000 handed over by McGraw-Hill for the faked autobiography of Howard Hughes. Scores of reputations apart from Trevor-Roper's were damaged by the diaries fiasco. At least four editors in three different countries lost their jobs as a result.

The affair was a reminder of Adolf Hitler's continuing hold on the world's imagination. News of the discovery of the diaries made headlines in every nation; it ran on the front page of the *New York Times* for five consecutive days. Shrewd businessmen showed themselves willing to pay enormous sums for material of which they had read only a fraction. It did not matter that the diaries' content was perfunctory and tedious: it was sufficient that it had been written by *him*. The diaries briefly put Hitler back in the arena of international diplomacy, a weapon in the Cold War which his career had done so much to create. Radio Moscow alleged that 'the affair of the Hitler diaries clearly reveals the CIA style'. America's Ambassador to the United Nations, Jeane Kirkpatrick, suspected the communists of producing the diaries 'to sow distrust between the United States and its German friends'. In the middle of the furore, the East German leader, Erich Hoenecker, cancelled his planned trip to Bonn complaining of a hostile Western press campaign: repeated allegations that the diaries originated in an East German 'forgery factory' were bitterly resented in Berlin. When the real forger, Konrad Kujau, confessed to the police on 26 May, it was difficult to believe that so much international confusion could have resulted from the work of this jaunty and farcical figure.

How did it happen? How did a hard-headed German publishing company come to spend so much money on such palpable fakes, and persuade almost a dozen foreign partners to invest in the project? To answer that question, we have to go back more than forty years: back through the expanding market in Hitler memorabilia, back through the activities of the surviving members of the Führer's inner circle, right back to the figure of Hitler himself, malevolent to the last, but no longer confident of his destiny, preparing for death in his bunker in the spring of 1945.

PART ONE

*'For mythopoeia is a far more common
characteristic of the human race (and perhaps
especially of the German race) than veracity. . . .'*

HUGH TREVOR-ROPER,
THE LAST DAYS OF HITLER

ONE

On 20 April 1945, Adolf Hitler celebrated his fifty-sixth and final birthday. Russian artillery shells were falling on the centre of Berlin and 6000 Soviet tanks were moving into the outskirts of the capital. Bremen and Hamburg in the north were about to fall to the British; Stuttgart, in the south, to the French. The Americans had captured Nuremberg and the Stars and Stripes was being unfurled over the podium from which Hitler had once addressed the annual Nazi Party rally. To escape the constant Allied air attacks, the Führer and his staff were now forced to live cooped-up in a bunker fifty-five feet beneath the Reich Chancellery. 'It was not', observed Martin Bormann in his diary, 'exactly a birthday situation.'

At 2 p.m. Hitler shuffled out of his bedroom exhausted from lack of sleep. His doctors gave him three injections, including one of glucose. His valet administered eyedrops. He wrapped himself in a heavy grey overcoat, turned up the collar, and slowly climbed the spiral staircase out of the bunker and into the Chancellery garden to inspect a waiting contingent of Hitler Youth. Their leader, Arthur Axmann, was shocked by his appearance: 'He walked with a stoop. His hands trembled.' He passed along the short line of boys and patted a couple of them on the cheek. He uttered a few hoarse and scarcely audible words about his faith in an ultimate victory, turned, and retreated back underground to preside over the day's main war conference.

That same afternoon, while Hitler and his general were surveying what remained of the German armed forces,

Sergeant Rochus Misch, the bunker's switchboard operator, took the opportunity to slip upstairs into the fresh air for a cigarette. He was standing smoking amid the rubble of the Ehrenhof, the Chancellery's Court of Honour, when two men appeared. One was Sergeant Wilhelm Arndt, a wounded veteran of twenty, who acted as one of Hitler's personal servants. The other was a young soldier-valet named Fehrs. Between them they were dragging a large metal trunk. Misch offered to help.

There were approximately ten trunks which had to be loaded on to the back of an antiquated, three-wheeled delivery truck parked in the courtyard. It was heavy work. Misch reckoned that each of the metal containers weighed over one hundred pounds. To heave one on to the back of the truck took two men. Misch did not ask what was in them and Arndt did not tell him. 'It was only', he recalled, 'when Arndt, now in full field uniform and armed with a machine pistol, clambered on top of the chests, that I realized it must be a mission with a one-man escort.' The truck drove out of the courtyard. Misch watched it disappear. 'Poor Arndt,' he reflected years afterwards. 'At the time we all thought he was the lucky one, escaping embattled Berlin and heading for the mountains.'

Arndt was taking part in a mission known as Operation Seraglio: the evacuation from the Berlin bunker of about eighty members of Hitler's entourage, together with a mass of official government papers, personal property and valuables. Their destination was the so-called 'Alpine Redoubt' in the south of Germany, near Berchtesgaden, where the Nazis had a half-formulated plan to establish a new centre of command in the event of the capture of Berlin. The evacuation was being conducted by air. General Hans Baur, Hitler's personal pilot, who was responsible for the provision of aircraft, had managed to muster ten planes for the operation, dispersed between four different Berlin airstrips. The lorry carrying Arndt and the metal trunks was directed towards a grass runway at Schoenwalde, about ten miles north of the city. Two planes were waiting there. One was to be piloted by a Luftwaffe flying officer named Schultze; the other by a veteran of the Russian front, Major Friedrich Gundlfinger.

Allied aircraft had been celebrating Adolf Hitler's birthday all day with an almost continuous stream of air raids on Berlin. At 10 p.m. they struck again. Arndt and the other passengers heading in convoy for Schoenwalde were obliged to stop and seek shelter. The raid lasted four hours. At the airfield, Schultze and Gundlfinger were growing increasingly anxious. Time was running short. They had to take off under cover of darkness to avoid the Allied fighters which now had command of Germany's skies during the day. The two pilots discussed tactics. Schultze favoured flying high to make use of every available scrap of cloud cover. Gundlfinger preferred hedge-hopping at low altitude.

The passengers finally began struggling on to the airfield shortly before dawn. Arndt attended to the stowing of the trunks in Gundlfinger's plane, then clambered in after them. He was one sixteen passengers. Schultze took off first. Gundlfinger followed a few minutes later, at about 5 a.m. on the morning of 21 April. His destination lay 350 miles to the south: Ainring, near Salzburg, the airfield closest to Berchtesgaden.

In the event, Gundlfinger completed less than one-third of the journey. He had been in the air for little more than half an hour and had just passed what was left of the city of Dresden when something went wrong. Possibly the plane was shot up by a patrolling American fighter; possibly it was hit by fire from a German anti-aircraft battery which mistook it for an enemy plane. At any rate, it was next seen shortly before 6 a.m. skimming the treetops in flames before crashing into the

Heidenholz forest close to the Czech border. Villagers from the nearby hamlet of Boernersdorf ran to the scene. The plane – a large Junkers 352 transport aircraft – had ploughed nose-first into the ground and was burning fiercely. Trapped in the wreckage, a figure writhed and screamed at the onlookers for help. But the intense heat and the ricochets of exploding ammunition made rescue impossible. The aircraft had to be left to burn itself out.

Schultze, meanwhile, had also run into trouble. Shortly after taking off he had discovered that one of his fuel pipes was fractured. He was forced to divert to Prague, then still in German hands, to refuel. It was 8.30 a.m. when he finally landed at Salzburg, expecting to find Gundlfinger waiting for him. All the other eight planes were there. But of the major and his aircraft there was no sign. This information was relayed to General Baur in Berlin and he, in turn, broke the news to Hitler that one of the planes involved in Operation Seraglio was missing. Hitler, he recalled, 'became very pale' and asked which one. Baur said it was the one with Arndt on board, at which Hitler appeared 'very upset'. According to Baur, he then uttered the words which were to cause so much mischief almost forty years later. 'In that plane,' he exclaimed, 'were all my private archives, that I had intended as a testament to posterity. It is a catastrophe!'

'After I'd seen how much that affected the Führer,' said Bauer, 'I tried to calm him and explain that Gundlfinger was an old fox from the First World War, that the Americans wouldn't have got him that easily: probably he'd made an emergency landing somewhere. But we didn't know, and our investigations were without success.'

On 22 April, the day after Arndt's disappearance, with heavy fighting reported in the suburbs of Berlin and with no sign of the counter-attack he had ordered, Hitler at last admitted defeat. 'That's it,' he shouted, scattering a handful of coloured pencils across the map table. 'How am I supposed to direct the war in such circumstances? The war's lost.' He walked out of the military conference. At about 4 p.m. he summoned Julius Schaub, the crippled soldier who had been his secretary, bodyguard, companion, messenger boy and valet for more than twenty years. Together they opened the steel safe in Hitler's bedroom. Four feet high and three feet wide, it was brimming with his personal papers. The material was stuffed into suitcases, carried up into the Chancellery garden, tipped into a bomb crater and set on fire. Hitler stood for a while in the fading light, watching as this record of his private affairs went up in smoke. 'Richelieu once said, give me five lines one man has penned,' Hitler is reported to have lamented subsequently. 'What I have lost! My dearest memories! But what's the point – sooner or later you've got to get rid of that stuff.' To complete this task, he instructed Schaub to fly to Berchtesgaden and destroy all his remaining personal files.

Schaub is believed to have arrived at the Berghof on his errand of destruction on the night of 26 April. Berchtesgaden, which had been subjected to a 300-bomber raid the previous day, was in a chaotic state. The homes of Bormann and Goering had been badly damaged. One wing of the Berghof was wrecked. Schaub was in an equally dilapidated condition. Eva Braun's sister, Gretl, who met him in the Führer's apartments, was shocked to discover him drunk and on the arm of his mistress. He had flown down bearing Hitler's keys but whether he actually carried out his master's instruction and destroyed everything is unclear. According to a US intelligence report, Gretl confided to an American undercover agent a few months after the war that in her view 'Schaub probably selected the most interesting things with the help of his mistress and hid them away.' In the 1970s, the British historian David Irving, an indefatigable hunter of original documents, received information that Schaub had 'sold Hitler's papers to a former magistrate now living on Lake Starnberg in Bavaria'. The magistrate, however, 'proved unapproachable'.

Before lurching off into the Führer's private quarters with his girlfriend, Schaub handed Gretl a letter which had been entrusted to him in Berlin two days earlier by Eva Braun. 'My darling little sister,' it began.

> How it hurts to write such lines to you. But there is nothing else to do. Each day and each hour may be our last, and so I must use this last opportunity to tell you what must be done . . . . Please keep your head high and do not doubt. There is still hope. It goes without saying, however, that we will not let ourselves be captured alive.

In what was effectively her last will and testament, she provided a list of friends who were to receive her effects.

> In addition I must request the following. Destroy all of my private correspondence, especially the business papers. . . . Destroy also an envelope which is addressed to the Führer and is in the safe in the bunker. Please do not read it. The Führer's letters and my answering letters (blue leather book) I would like packed watertight and if possible buried. Please do not destroy them. . . .

In a reference to Gundlfinger's plane and its cargo of Hitler's property, Eva asked her sister if Arndt had arrived 'with the letter and suitcase? We heard here only that the plane had been attacked.' The letter ended 'with heartiest greetings and a kiss'. A few days later, Eva Braun achieved her life's ambition and married Adolf Hitler. On 30 April, the couple killed themselves and their bodies were set alight.

The following morning, at almost exactly the same moment as the charred corpses of the newly-weds were being interred in a shell hole in Berlin, their personal effects were being burned in Berchtesgaden. The rooms of the Berghof were systematically emptied of clothes, furniture, linen and crockery. The contents were taken outside and destroyed to prevent them falling into the hands of the approaching Americans. Hitler's library of 2,000 books, along with his collection of press cuttings, was hidden in a nearby salt mine. (These volumes, each with a garish swastika bookplate bearing the inscription '*Ex Libris Adolf Hitler*', were later found by American troops, transported to Washington, and in 1953 catalogued as a collection by the Library of Congress.)

On this same day, 1 May, Gretl decided the time had come to comply with her sister's last request. For assistance she turned to a young SS major named Johannes Goehler. According to a post-war investigation by US intelligence, 'Gretl said that she would like him to take charge of the safekeeping of a large chest of letters which had been entrusted to her. They were letters between her sister, Eva Braun, and Hitler. The chest, about the size of an officer's trunk, was in a cave near the Berghof.' Goehler promised to help. He rang one of his subordinates, SS Captain Erwin Haufler, and instructed him to send a truck to Berchtesgaden immediately. That night Eva Braun's chest, along with a clothes basket, was evacuated to the local SS headquarters in Fischhorn Castle in Austria.

For the next week they stood, objects of intense curiosity, in a corner of Haufler's office. The basket, which was open, was found to contain Eva Braun's photograph albums of life at the Berghof, 'a few small framed pictures' and some rolls of film. The trunk was locked. After several days of speculation, Haufler and his SS cronies eventually plucked up the courage to break it open. Inside was a treasure trove of Hitler memorabilia. There was an assortment of the Führer's architectural drawings: 'made in pencil,' Haufler told the Americans after the war, 'depicting floor plans and the like. I saw one sketch which seemed to represent a church.' There was a box of Hitler's stationery. There was a book belonging to Mussolini and another, in Eva Braun's handwriting, in which she had made notes of her letters to Hitler. There was an album entitled 'Enemy Propaganda in Stamps'. 'Then there was a pair of black trousers,' recalled Haufler, 'badly ripped, or rather slit, and also a coat, which was field grey,' bearing the insignia of the German eagle. This, the SS men correctly assumed, was the uniform Hitler had been wearing at the time of the attempt on his life in July 1944: in an emotional moment, the Führer had sent it to Eva to keep as a souvenir. But what most captured the soldiers' interest were the letters. The trunk was three-quarters full of them: 'at least 250,' estimated Haufler, with another thirty or forty postcards. These were Hitler's letters to Eva Braun, a lovingly preserved record of their ten-year relationship. Haufler picked up one. 'My dear Pascherl,' it began, 'I send you my heartiest greetings.' It was signed 'your Adolf Hitler'.

Precisely what happened next is unclear. According to Haufler, he handed the trunk over to his administrative officer, Franz Konrad, with instructions to burn it to prevent its contents falling into Allied hands. But Konrad, a notoriously corrupt SS captain, whose activities during the German occupation of Warsaw had earned him the title 'King of the Ghetto', disobeyed him. In the final hours of the war he sent a truck loaded with looted treasure to his brother's house in the nearby Austrian town of Schladming. Hidden among the canned food, the liquor and the radios were two suitcases and a metal trunk with Eva Braun's name tag attached to it. 'Make sure you get through,' the driver alleged Konrad told him. 'If you get stopped on the way, take the two bags and the chest and make off. If everything else should go wrong, you must save those three things.'

Acting on this information, on 24 August 1945, agents

from the US Counter-Intelligence Corps (CIC) raided the home of Konrad's brother and seized the Hitler uniform, Eva Braun's private photograph albums, her silverware, the notes she had made of her letters to Hitler, and the stamp collection. A second cache of material, which Konrad had given to his mother to hide, was recovered in October. This haul included twenty-eight reels of colour film – Eva Braun's home movies of her life with Hitler. All these objects were turned over to the American Army and shipped back to the United States. But of Hitler's letters, by far the most interesting items, there was no sign. Thirty years later, David Irving once more set out to track them down. His conclusion, after months of inquiry, was that they were discovered near Berchtesgaden by one of the CIC officers who promptly stole them for himself. They have now disappeared into the archives of a private collector in the USA.

In addition to the property of Eva Braun, Konrad also appears to have stolen the correspondence between Hitler and the leader of the SS, Heinrich Himmler. The files had been transferred for safekeeping from Himmler's headquarters to the library at Fischhorn Castle where they were kept in a steel cabinet, guarded by Himmler's orderlies. After Hitler's suicide, Konrad was assigned to help destroy them, but admitted to the Americans after the war that he put a set of the most interesting documents to one side. Shortly afterwards he turned up at the home of his secretary, Martha von Boskowitz, and gave her a package 'about 18 inches long, 6 inches thick and 4 inches wide'. He told her that the tightly wrapped parcel contained his 'personal letters' and asked her to hold on to them, 'in case anything should happen to me'. About six weeks later another SS man called and took the package away. It, too, has disappeared.

In the course of their investigations, the CIC also began picking up rumours of the existence of Hitler's 'diaries'.

According to Colonel Wilhelm Spacil of the Reich Main Security Office (RSHA) Franz Konrad boasted to him at the beginning of May 1945 that, in addition to all his other treasures, he was in possession of 'the diary of Hitler, written on very thin paper' which he had hidden in a specially made zinc box. The CIC asked Captain Haufler what he knew of such diaries. Haufler described how two weeks before the end of the war he had been at the Berghof when an air raid alarm sounded. He and Gretl Braun, along with the Berghof's housekeeper, Frau Mittelstrasser, took shelter in the underground bunker. The two women showed him around part of the labyrinth of tunnels which extended for nearly two miles beneath the mountain.

> I was only allowed to stand at the doorway to the Führer's room [recalled Haufler]. Frau Mittelstrasser pointed out several things in the room: for example, there were 5000 phonograph records stored there. Among other things, she pointed out the 'personal notes' of the Führer. These were contained in four or five large books which stood near the desk. Of course, everyone knew that Hitler kept a diary. The books were firmly bound, and not quite as big as a *Leitz-Ordner* [a loose-leaf file]. I can't tell you anything more about them, for I only saw them from a distance, and didn't even have them in my hand. I never saw these books again.

In the absence of any other hard information, the CIC investigation petered out. Gretl Braun dismissed Haufler's story. 'Hitler didn't keep any diaries,' she told a CIC agent. 'The books which were standing in the air raid shelter in the Berghof were not diaries, but rather minutes of the day's activities, which were kept by whoever was the Führer's adjutant at the time.' And Franz Konrad, despite prolonged interrogation, insisted that he knew nothing of such books, that Spacil was mistaken, that he must be muddling the 'diaries' with Eva Braun's notebooks which he confessed to having stolen. At the height of the debate over the Hitler diaries' authenticity in 1983, the *Sunday Times* clutched at the straw offered by the CIC files. Quoting only the testimony of Spacil and Haufler, the paper used the information to try to refute claims that there had never been any suggestion that Hitler kept a diary. But given the paucity of evidence, and even allowing for the unreliability of the witnesses, the likelihood is that the references to 'diaries' which creep into a couple of CIC reports are actually the result of a misunderstanding.

The Third Reich had dissolved into chaos. In Berlin, in Munich, in Berchtesgaden, Allied soldiers as well as German picked through the detritus of Hitler's Germany and carried off whatever seemed of value. A gang of Russian women soldiers ransacked Eva Braun's apartment in the Berlin bunker and emerged, according to one witness, 'whooping like Indian squaws', waving Frau Hitler's underclothes above their heads, carrying off lamps, vases, bottles, carpets, crystal glass, Hitler's monogrammed silver, an accordion, a tablecloth, 'even a table telephone'. At the Berghof, French and American troops wrenched off light-fittings and doorknobs and pulled out the springs from the Führer's bed. Eventually, every inch of plaster was stripped from the walls; stairs and handrails were torn up; the members of one enterprising unit even took a sledge-hammer to Hitler's marble fireplace and sold off the pieces as ashtrays. At the Führerbau, the monumental stone building on the Königsplatz in Munich where Hitler had met Chamberlain and Daladier, dozens of GIs plundered the storerooms, using a wooden crate as a stepping stone as they explored the waterlogged basement. When one anonymous soldier from the US 14th Division staved in the lid of the crate he found yet another hoard of

Hitler's private property: two gold-plated pistols, a swastika ring, a miniature portrait of the dictator's mother painted on ivory, a framed photograph of Hitler's favourite dog, Blondi, a gold watch bearing the initials 'A.H.' and valuable monogrammed crystal glasses, carefully wrapped in newspaper. 'The next thing I picked up was a diary,' recalled the soldier, many years later. 'It was a red diary with gold lettering and Hitler's insignia on it, his initials on it. But I flashed right through it and it was all in German. I just threw it right aside and it dropped into the water on the floor.' He returned to retrieve it some time later but the 'diary', or whatever it was, had gone. There are many such stories. As recently as 1984, a family in British Columbia found a crateful of personal papers belonging to Heinrich Hoffmann, Hitler's court photographer, lying discarded in their attic: it had been brought back by their father at the end of the war and forgotten. Years later it is impossible to guess how much of historical value may have been carted away from the wreckage of Nazi Germany and may still come to light.

Retrieving such documentary evidence as exists, it is conceivable that of five sets of Hitler documents supposedly destroyed in the spring of 1945, four of them – the private files held at the Berghof, the letters to Eva Braun, the correspondence with Himmler and even possibly part of the cargo entrusted to Arndt – may actually have survived. Only the contents of the safe in Berlin, whose incineration was personally supervised by the Führer, can definitely be regarded as lost.

This tantalizing state of affairs was to provide the perfect scenario for forgery.

TWO

Outside the entrance to the Führerbunker in Berlin, a shell crater was strewn with sheets of charred paper. Rummaging beneath the blackened litter, a Russian soldier discovered a pair of scorched and crumbling bones. He called his commanding officer over. 'Comrade Lieutenant Colonel!' he shouted, 'there are legs here!'

Thus, on 2 May 1945, if the Soviet writer Lev Bezymenski is to be believed, Private Ivan Churakov of the 1st Byelorussian Front stumbled on the most sought-after Hitler relic of them all. 'So!' exclaimed Stalin when he first heard of the Führer's death, 'that's the end of the bastard. Too bad that we did not manage to take him alive.'

Disinterred from the crater, the remains of Hitler and Eva Braun were placed in a pair of rough wooden boxes and taken to the Soviet Army headquarters in the northern Berlin suburb of Buch. Hitler's corpse had been so badly damaged by fire that parts of it disintegrated on the mortuary table. According to the official autopsy report, the left foot was missing; so was the skin: 'only remnants of charred muscles are preserved.' The mouldering cadaver was displayed in a clearing in a wood outside Berlin at the end of May to one of the Führer's bodyguards. By August it was in Moscow, where, quite probably, it remains to this day. ('Hitler's body', boasted one Russian official in 1949, 'is in better keeping with us than under the Brandenburg Gate in Berlin.') Hitler's teeth – a bridge of nine dentures in yellow metal and a singed lower jaw consisting of fifteen teeth – were handed over to the

Soviet counter-intelligence agency, SMERSH. These, together with the dictator's Iron Cross, his party insignia and the teeth of Eva Braun, were last seen in Berlin in May 1945 in a cigar box, being offered around by a SMERSH officer to fashionable German dentists for identification.

But, abetted by the Russians, even in this reduced form, Hitler was still capable of making mischief. The autopsy report and the various proofs of Hitler's death were suppressed by the Soviet Union for more than twenty years: officially, to have them 'in reserve' in case an imposter appeared claiming to be 'the Führer saved by a miracle'; in reality, to embarrass the British and Americans. At least twice in the Kremlin and once at the Potsdam Conference, Stalin lied to the Allies, telling them that Hitler had escaped and was in hiding. As part of his campaign against fascist Spain, he even suggested that Hitler was being sheltered by General Franco. Senior Soviet officers in Berlin, who had at first admitted to the discovery of the body, hastily changed their stories and followed Stalin's line. The Soviet newspaper *Izvestia* went so far as to allege that Hitler and Eva Braun were living in a moated castle in Westphalia in the British Occupation Zone of Germany.

The post-war appetite for stories about Hitler and the Nazis, which was to culminate in the diaries fiasco, found its first sustenance in this confusion. Throughout the summer of 1945, newspapers trampled over one another to bring their readers the 'true story' of the Führer's fate. First Hitler was said to be working as a croupier in a casino in the French resort of Evian. A few days later he resurfaced as a head waiter in Grenoble. Then, in bewildering succession, he was reliably reported to be a shepherd in the Swiss Alps, a monk in St Gallen, and an Italian hermit living in a cave beside Lake Garda. Some newspapers maintained that Hitler was posing as a fisherman in the Baltic, others that he was working on a boat off the west of Ireland. He had escaped by airplane. He had escaped by submarine. He was in Albania. He was in Spain. He was in Argentina.

Hitler's progress across the world's front pages was followed with increasing embarrassment in Whitehall. When the Russians hinted that the British might be shielding him in Westphalia, the Government decided to act. In September 1945, Brigadier Dick White, a senior official in the British security service, later to be chief of both MI5 and MI6, was asked to prepare a report on what had happened to Hitler. He was given six weeks to complete the task. White delegated this urgent mission, code-named Operation Nursery, to a particularly bright young intelligence officer named Hugh Trevor-Roper.

At the outbreak of war Trevor-Roper had been at Oxford completing a biography of Archbishop Laud. Recruited into British signals intelligence, the twenty-six-year-old research student was obliged to switch his mind from the study of seventeenth-century clerical politics to the analysis of intercepted German radio traffic. He became one of the foremost experts on the German intelligence service, the *Abwehr*. He had a penetrating intellect, a sharp tongue, and a natural combativeness which caused one of his superiors in the Secret Intelligence Service to threaten him with court martial.

He arrived in Germany in the middle of September. His method of solving the mystery of Hitler's fate owed something to the novels of Agatha Christie. He was the amateur detective; the Führerbunker the country house where the crime had been committed; its survivors the witnesses who could provide the vital clues. He quickly demolished the stories of some of the more obvious fantasists: the doctor who claimed to have treated Hitler for a lung wound sustained during fighting around the Berlin Zoo; the female Gestapo agent who swore she could take him to the Bavarian estate where Hitler was living in a secluded foursome with Eva, Gretl, and Gretl's husband, Hermann. To uncover the truth he compiled a list of everyone who had attended Hitler in his final days and travelled the country tracking them down. He interrogated Keitel, Jodl, Doenitz and Speer. In their prison camps he questioned the Führer's SS guards. At Berchtesgaden he caught up with two of Hitler's secretaries, Johanna Wolf and Christa Schroeder; he almost captured a third, Gerda Christian, when he turned up at the home of her mother-in-law – he missed her by only a couple of days. By the time he came to write his report he had found seven witnesses who were with Hitler in the final week of his life, including the chauffeur, Erich Kempka, who provided the gasoline with which his master's body was burned, and a guard, Hermann Karnau, who witnessed the funeral pyre.

On the night of 1 November 1945, Trevor-Roper presented a summary of his findings to an audience of sceptical journalists in the Hotel-am-Zoo in Berlin. One of them, the *Newsweek* correspondent, James P. O'Donnell, later recalled the confident impression he made: a 'dapper' figure in his wartime uniform, crisp and sarcastic, 'a master of tart understatement'.

That evening, Trevor-Roper told for the first time the story of Hitler's death which has since become familiar: the final appearance of the Führer, accompanied by Eva Braun, to say goodbye to his staff; their retirement to his sitting room; their deaths – his by a revolver bullet, hers by poison – and their subsequent cremation in the garden of the Chancellery. Trevor-Roper fixed the time of death as 'shortly after 2.30 p.m. on 30 April 1945' and he concluded with a magisterial rebuke to the press:

> There is no evidence whatever to support any of the theories
> that have been circulated and which presuppose that Hitler is

still alive. All such stories which have been reported have been investigated and have been found to be quite baseless; most of them have dissolved at the first touch of fact and some of them have been admitted by their authors to have been pure fabrication.

'As of that evening,' wrote O'Donnell, 'most of the international press stationed in Berlin was finally convinced that Hitler was indeed dead.' His handling of the case earned Trevor-Roper the title 'The Sleuth of Oxford'.

The inquiry was an unprecedented opportunity for an ambitious young historian. With the permission of British intelligence Trevor-Roper turned the information he had collected into a book. *The Last Days of Hitler* appeared in 1947. It was hailed in Britain as 'a masterpiece'. In the United States, Arthur Schlesinger Jr declared it 'a brilliant professional performance'. The book has since been reprinted thirteen times in Great Britain alone. By 1983 its world-wide sales amounted to almost half a million copies. Trevor-Roper bought a Bentley on the proceeds and for a while was said to hold the record for driving from Oxford to London in under an hour.

Behind the Iron Curtain, the book was banned. 'The Polish edition was stifled in the publisher's office,' wrote Trevor-Roper, 'the Bulgarian edition destroyed by the police on its appearance.' The Russian positon remained unchanged. 'It was never allowed that Hitler might be dead. It was assumed, and sometimes openly stated, that he was alive.' This doctrine officially remained in force until 1968 when the communist author Lev Bezymenski was allowed to publish the autopsy report in his book *The Death of Adolf Hitler*. Even then the truth had to be distorted for political effect. In his anxiety to avoid being captured alive, Hitler appears to have simultaneously pulled the trigger of a revolver held to his head and bitten on a glass ampoule of cyanide clenched between his teeth. But despite the unanimous evidence of the witnesses in the bunker that they heard a shot, despite the fact that the autopsy report itself stated that 'part of the cranium' was 'missing', Bezymenski insisted that Hitler had only taken poison and had thus died 'like a dog': it was apparently still important to the Soviet Union that Hitler should be depicted as too cowardly to take the soldier's way out. Twenty-three years after the concealment of its discovery, the corpse had not lost its propaganda value.

Rersearched at first hand in the interrogation cell and the secret service registry, *The Last Days of Hitler* was unique: the insight of an historian combined with the scholarship of an intelligence officer on active service. Trevor-Roper was given access to the diaries of Goering's chief of staff, General Koller, as well as those of Schwerin von Krosigk, the Minister of Finance. He was the first to make use of the diary kept by Hitler's valet, Heinz Linge, discovered by a British officer amid the ruins of the Chancellery in September 1945. In the middle of November, after the completion of his original report, he was summoned back to Germany from leave in Oxford to authenticate Hitler's last will and testament. Shortly afterwards, in pursuit of two missing copies of that document, he led a group of CIC officers in a midnight raid on a house near the Austrian border. After a long interrogation session he finally broke the resistance of a German major who admitted possessing a copy of Hitler's will. The major led him into the garden of his home and in the darkness broke open the frozen ground with an axe to retrieve a bottle: 'breaking the bottle with the axe, he drew out and handed to me the last missing document. . . .'

Such colourful adventures set Trevor-Roper apart from more conventional academic historians. His experience taught him that Nazi documents could surface unexpectedly in all manner of unlikely places. He also appreciated that it was sometimes necessary to deal with unorthodox and even unsavoury characters. One could not afford to be too squeamish. In 1952, he met François Genoud, a Swiss lawyer whom he described at the time in the *Sunday Express* as 'an unrepentant Nazi sympathizer'. Genoud, a former member of the SS, whose name was later to be linked with the Palestine Liberation Organization, had obtained over a thousand type-written pages known as the *Bormann-Vermerke*: the 'Bormann Notes'. They were meticulously kept in Martin Bormann's personal custody and he had written upon them, 'Notes of fundamental interest for the future. To be preserved with the greatest care.' They proved to be the transcripts of more than three hundred of Hitler's mealtime monologues: the interminable, rambling soliloquies which had passed for conversation at the Führer's dinner table and which had been recorded on Bormann's orders as if they were Holy Writ. The material legally belonged to Genoud. After the war he had acquired the copyright in Hitler's literary estate from the dictator's sister, Paula. Similar contracts had been agreed with Bormann's widow and the heirs of Josef Goebbels ('these poor people,' Genoud later called them, 'whose rights and property have been plundered'). Trevor-Roper edited, introduced and helped arrange publication of Genoud's material, which appeared in 1953 as *Hitler's Table Talk*.

Fascinating, yet simultaneously tedious and repellent in its grinding prose and vertiginous imagery, the book captures the authentic voice of Hitler. Lunch might find him lecturing Dr Porsche on the superiority of the air-cooled engine; over dinner he would hold forth on the origins of the planet. He had an opinion about everything: the inability of the English to perform Shakespeare, the 'harmfulness of cooked foods', the legends of ancient Greece, the toad ('a degenerate frog'), Winston Churchill ('an utterly immoral, repulsive creature'), the 'negroid' appearance of Eleanor Roosevelt, prelunar civilization and the mental capacity of a dog. In his brilliant introductory essay, Trevor-Roper depicted Hitler's mind as 'a terrible phenomenon, imposing indeed in its granitic harshness and yet infinitely squalid in its miscellaneous cumber – like some huge barbarian monolith, the expression of giant strength and savage genius, surrounded by a festering heap of refuse – old tins and dead vermin, ashes and eggshells and ordure – the intellectual *detritus* of centuries'.

For Trevor-Roper, *Hilter's Table Talk* was the first of a series of such commissions. In 1954, he edited Martin Bormann's letters. In 1956 he wrote the introduction to the *Memoirs* of Dr Felix Kersten, the faith-healer and masseur who treated Himmler and other senior Nazis. When Genoud produced what purported to be the final entries of the *Bormann-Vermerke* in the late 1950s, covering the last few weeks of the war, Trevor-Roper provided the foreword. For more than thirty years, if a publisher had documents from the Third Reich whose presentation required the imprimatur of a well-known academic, he was the first person they turned to. In the 1970s, when the West German company of Hoffmann and Campe acquired, from mysterious sources behind the Iron Curtain, 16,000 pages of Josef Goebbels's diaries, Trevor-Roper was appointed to edit the section devoted to 1945. And all the time he continued to turn out articles and essays about the Nazis and their Führer, many of them written in a vituperative style typical of academic debate in general, and of Trevor-Roper's technique in particular. He denounced the so-called 'memoirs' of Hitler's sister-in-law Bridget as a fake. He ridiculed the inaccuracies of *A Man Called Intrepid*. He attacked A. J. P. Taylor's thesis about the origins of the Second World War as 'demonstrably false'. Errors were punished, positions defended.

'Trevor-Roper', complained Taylor in 1983, 'thought he had taken out a patent in Hitler.'

THREE

Hitler's bunker in Berlin was blown up by the Russians in 1947, his house at Berchtesgaden by the Americans in 1952. The motive in each case was to deny any renascent Nazi movement a shrine. But interest in Hitler could not be destroyed. It continued to grow, like weeds amidst the rubble.

Although *The Last Days of Hitler* put a stop to much of the outlandish speculation about the Nazi dictator's fate, it did not end it entirely. A close personal following of cranks, misfits, fantasists and criminals continued to attend Adolf Hitler in death as in life. In December 1947 a German pilot calling himself Baumgart swore in an affidavit that he had flown Hitler and Eva Braun to Denmark a few days before the end of the war. 'Baumgart afterwards retired to a lunatic asylum in Poland,' noted Trevor-Roper. Six months later a film actor from the South Tyrol named Luis Trenker produced what he claimed were Eva Braun's diaries. *Wochenend*, a romantic magazine for women, based in Munich, undertook to publish them. For a short time, *Wochenend*'s breathless readers were treated to Eva's intimate reminiscences: how Hitler forced her to wear leather underwear, how naked dances at the Berghof turned into midnight orgies, how Hitler feared water but loved having his feet bathed. It was exotic drivel of a high order, but unfortunately a few weeks later it was officially declared a forgery. In 1950 the proprietor of *Tempo Der Watt*, a pro-Nazi magazine, claimed to have heard from Martin Bormann that Hitler was living in a Tibetan monastery. 'We shall not give up the fight as long as we live,' Bormann was quoted as saying. A French magazine reported sightings of Hitler, minus his moustache, in Caracas, Buenos Aires and Tokyo. In 1956 *The Times* reported rumours that recordings of Hitler's voice, allegedly made in the previous twelve months, were being produced and sold in West Germany.

Another German periodical, *Herzdame*, adopted a fresh approach in the autumn of 1949. Hitler, it revealed, had fathered an illegitimate son in Munich some time before the First World War. The son, Wilhelm Baur, had committed suicide shortly after his father, in May 1945, but his children – the Führer's grandchildren – were still alive, 'somewhere in Germany'. This baseless story nevertheless engendered a spate of imitations until, by the mid-1970s, there were enough Hitler children clamouring for attention to fill a sizeable nursery. Most were straightforward confidence tricksters like Franz Weber-Richter who swindled 15 million pesos and 50,000 marks out of a group of ex-Nazis in Argentina: their suspicions apparently were not aroused even by his additional claim to have spent eighteen months on the planet Venus. In 1965 the daughter of Tilly Fleischer, a famous German sportswoman who had competed in the 1936 Berlin Olympics, was persuaded by her boyfriend to compile a book, *Adolf Hitler Was My Father*. Extracts appeared in a German picture magazine under the headline 'If Only Hitler Knew', before police put a stop to the hoax. Claimants were still coming forward twelve years later. In 1977 a Frenchman, Jean Lorret, told an international press conference in a fine display of filial loyalty that he had decided to reveal the secret of his parentage in order 'to let the world know that Hitler was not impotent'. The stories have varied over the years but two characteristics have remained constant: their inherent implausibility and the willingness of someone, usually a journalist, to believe them.

*   *   *

Mercifully, despite the fears of the Allies, the post-war interest in Hitler generally centred on the man rather than his ideology. To this day there has been no popular resurgence in support for Hitler's ideas. In 1983, the West German government estimated the numbers of active neo-Nazis at less than 2000, a feeble legacy for a movement which once dominated every level of German society and conquered much of continental Europe. One of the most singular features of the Nazi phenomenon was the extent to which National Socialism ultimately proved to be totally dependent upon its creator. Hitler occasionally used to picture himself as a spider at the centre of an enormous web. Without him, in the spring of 1945, this complex system of interlocking institutions, which had once appeared so powerful, simply melted away. It was not merely Hitler's state which died with him: the beliefs which had underpinned it died too. As Professor J. P. Stern put it, people who had once followed him had 'real difficulty in recalling the message now that the voice was gone'. Afterwards this served to focus yet more attention on Hitler. How did he do it? What was he like?

To begin with, in Germany at least, the enormity of Hitler's career made it difficult even to ask such questions. The period from 1933 to 1945 was largely ignored in school curricula. Anyone displaying Nazi mementoes or even publishing photographs of the period was liable to prosecution. Hitler was a subject of acute sensitivity. At late as 1962 the West German embassy in London felt compelled to make an official protest over a British television play, *Night Conspirators*, which imagined that after seventeen years of exile in Iceland, Hitler had returned to Germany. *Mein Kampf* was banned. When Hutchinson's, owners of the British copyright, decided to republish it, the Bavarian State authorities declared their 'strong opposition'. 'The German authorities regret our decision,' acknowledged the publishers in a note at the front of the book, 'thinking that it may prove damaging to new understandings and friendships.' In 1967, when a publisher in Spain also proposed a new edition, the Bonn government intervened and bought the Spanish rights itself to stop him.

But in the decade which followed, this reticence about the past was gradually transformed. The curiosity of a generation born after the collapse of the Third Reich coincided in 1973 with the fortieth anniversary of the Nazis' rise to power. That year saw an unprecedented surge of interest in Adolf Hitler, a tide of books, articles and films which the Germans dubbed the '*Hitler-Welle*': the Hitler Wave. Joachim C. Fest, a former editor-in-chief of NDR television, published his monumental biography, the first comprehensive account of Hitler's life in German to appear since 1945. Fest began his book with a question unthinkable a decade earlier: 'Ought we to call him "great"?' *Hitler* became a bestseller, serialized in *Stern* and described as 'the Book of the Year' at the Frankfurt Book Fair. The Führer's domination of the display stands at Frankfurt was such that the German satirical magazine *Pardon* hired an actor to impersonate him. Their 'Hitler' visited the Fair to demand a share of the royalties. He was arrested.

The effects of the Hitler Wave were felt across the world. In America more than twenty new books about Hitler were published. Two film producers, Sandy Lieberson and David Puttnam, released a documentary, *Swastika*, which included the Eva Braun home movies seized by the CIC in 1945: the cans were discovered by a researcher in the archives of the US Marine and Signal Corps. In February, Frank Finlay starred in *The Death of Adolf Hitler*. Three months later, Sir Alec Guinness appeared in *Hitler: The Last Ten Days*. The film was banned by the Jewish management of the ABC–EMI cinema chain. The Israelis denied it a licence. 'The figure of the assassin', complained the Israeli Censorship Board, 'is represented in a human light without giving expression to the terrible murders for which he is responsible.'

Guinness confessed that in playing the part he had found it 'difficult not to succumb to Hitler's charm. He had a sweet smile and a very sentimental Austrian charm.' The BBC, despite protests, showed Leni Riefenstahl's Nazi propaganda film, *Triumph of the Will*. To Hutchinson's commercial pleasure but editorial embarrassment, the reissued *Mein Kampf*, despite an artificially high price to discourage mass sales, had to be reprinted twice. A delegation from the British Board of Deputies tried to dissuade the company from bringing out a paperback edition. They failed, and Hutchinson's sold a further 10,000 copies. Foreign language editions appeared in Denmark, Sweden and Italy. The *Sunday Telegraph* wrote of 'the astonishing resurgence of the Hitler cult'. *Time* reported a 'worldwide revival' of interest in the Nazi leader: 'Adolf Hitler's presence never vanishes. His career is still the fundamental trauma of the century.'

The 1970s also witnessed a corresponding boom in sales of Hitler memorabilia. In the immediate aftermath of the war this activity, too, had been discouraged by the German authorities. In 1948 a ruling by a denazification court that 'Hitler was an active Nazi' enabled the State of Bavaria to seize his personal property – principally his private apartment in Munich, some money owed to him by a Nazi publishing company, and a few valuable paintings. (Eva Braun's home, bought for her by Hitler in 1935, was also confiscated and donated to a restitution fund for the victims of Nazism.) Three years later, the Bavarian government made use of its powers to prevent Hitler's former Munich housekeeper, Frau Anni Winter, from selling a trunkful of the Führer's private property. Under the terms of Hitler's will, she was entitled to 'personal mementoes' sufficient 'for the maintenance of a modest middle-class standard of living'. She inherited such relics as Hitler's gun licence, his Nazi Party membership card, some of his watercolours, a copy of *Mein Kampf* and the original letter from President Hindenburg inviting Hitler to become Chancellor in 1933. For these and other treasures, Frau Winter was offered $250,000 by an American collector. The authorities promptly intervened and impounded the bulk of the collection, leaving her, bitterly resentful, with what they imagined to be a handful of valueless scraps.

But following Frau Winter's death, in 1972, these supposedly worthless items were put on sale at an auction in Munich. Telephone bids were taken from all over the world for lots which included family photographs, an eleven-word note for a speech and a War Loans savings card. Prices were reported to have 'exceeded all expectations'. The average price simply for a signed Hitler photograph was £450.

In the succeeding years the Nazi memorabilia market took off spectacularly. Hitler's 1940 Mercedes touring car – five tons of armoured steel and glass, twenty feet long with a 230 horsepower engine and a 56-gallon fuel tank – was sold in Arizona in 1973 for $153,000. A rug from the Reich Chancellery fetched $100,000. A millionaire in Nevada paid $60,000 for the crateful of Hitler's personal property rescued from the basement of the Führerbau. The Marquess of Bath acquired Himmler's spectacles, removed from his body after his suicide. He also bought a tablecloth which had belonged to the Commandant of Belsen concentration camp. A military dealer in Maryland, Charles Snyder, sold locks of Eva Braun's hair for $3500, and – following a deal with the official American executioner – strands from the ropes which hanged the Nuremberg war criminals.

It was against this background, in 1973, with the Hitler Wave at its height, that Mr Billy F. Price of Houston, Texas heard of a new prize about to come on the market. Mr Price – owner of Hitler's napkins and cutlery and on his way to possessing one of the world's largest collections of Hitler paintings – discovered through contacts in Germany that Hermann Goering's old yacht was for sale. Price expressed an interest. But before he had time to put in a bid, the boat was sold. The purchaser, he learned later, was a figure hitherto unknown in the close-knit memorabilia market: a German journalist named Gerd Heidemann.

PART TWO

'For in his male he hadde a pilwe-beer,
Which that he seyde was Oure Lady veyl:
He seyde he hadde a gobet of the seyl
That Seint Peter hadde, whan that he wente
Upon the see, til Jhesu Crist hym hente.
He hadde a croys of latoun ful of stones,
And in a glas he hadde pigges bones.
But with thise relikes, whan that he fond
A povre person dwellynge upon lond,
Upon a day he gat hym moore moneye
Than that the person gat in monthes tweye;
And thus, with feyned flaterye and japes,
He made the person and the peple his apes.'

GEOFFREY CHAUCER: 'THE PARDONER',
General Prologue to *The Canterbury Tales*

FOUR

The boat was lying low against the harbour jetty when he first saw her, ageing and dilapidated, with the freezing waters of the River Rhine seeping into her hold. She had been built in 1937 and presented as a gift by the German motor industry to Hermann Goering, architect of Hitler's rearmament programme and commander-in-chief of the Luftwaffe. The sumptuously finished motor yacht took its place amongst the other trappings of the Reichsmarschall's grandiose lifestyle: his luxurious private train, his 100,000 acre hunting estate, his enormous hoard of looted art treasures. In honour of his first wife, who had died prematurely in 1931, Goering named her *Carin II*. The yacht survived the wartime air raids guarded by three soldiers in a private anchorage in Berlin. She also survived the death of her owner in Nuremberg in 1946. During the Allied occupation she was impounded by Field Marshal Montgomery and presented to the British Royal Family who rechristened her the *Royal Albert*. Following the birth of the Prince of Wales, she was renamed the *Prince Charles*. In 1960, after more than a decade in the service of the British Rhine Flotilla, the Queen returned the yacht to Goering's widow, his second wife, Emmy.

It was on a bleak day in January 1973, thirteen years later, that Gerd Heidemann found her moored on the waterfront in the West German capital, Bonn. She now belonged to the owner of a local printing works. More than eighty feet long, expensive to maintain, and in need of extensive repairs, the yacht had become a financial liability. The owner told Heidemann he wanted to sell her.

Heidemann subsequently maintained that at that time he had no particular interest in the Nazis. He was a photographer and reporter on *Stern* and had simply been commissioned to take pictures of the boat for a feature article. He was forty-one years old, his third marriage had recently collapsed, and he was looking for an opportunity to make some money. He concluded that the yacht, once renovated, could be sold for a large profit. A few weeks later, in March, he bought her for 160,000 marks. It was a huge sum of money for an ordinary journalist to find. He had to mortgage his house, a bungalow in the Hamburg suburb of Flottbeck, to raise it.

Heidemann knew little about sailing. For help he turned to an acquaintance, a twenty-five-year-old seaman named Axel Thomsen who was studying for his captain's qualifications at the naval school in Hamburg. 'I went down to Bonn and saw the ship,' recalled Thomsen. 'It was in a miserable condition. Of the three engines, only one diesel was working. She was also taking in water and had constantly to be emptied.' She was too badly damaged to withstand the open sea, and late that summer the two men sailed her back to Hamburg along the inland waterways of northern Germany. She had to be put in dry dock for a year to be made watertight.

Heidemann soon had cause to regret his impulsive investment. He had hopelessly underestimated the amount of work which *Carin II*'s restoration would involve. By 1974 he was in a financial trap: he could hope to sell the boat only if he completed the repairs; he could pay for the repairs only by selling the boat. Meanwhile, interest rates on the money he had already borrowed and the cost of keeping the yacht in dock bit deep into his salary. 'He permanently seemed short of money,' said Thomsen ten years later. 'He was always trying to pump loans out of other people. He was worried that things were going to be taken off him because he hadn't paid his debts.' In desperation, Heidemann even asked Thomsen to lend him 15,000 marks. Word went round the Hamburg shipyards that the naive and over-confident new owner of 'Fat Hermann's boat' was financially shaky. Neither for the first time in his life nor the last, Heidemann was in danger of making a fool of himself.

Gerd Heidemann was born on 4 December 1931 in the Altona district of Hamburg, the illegitimate son of Martha Eiternick. When his mother married a former sailor turned policeman called Rolf Heidemann, Gerd took his stepfather's surname. His parents were apolitical. Gerd, like most boys his age, was a member of the Hitler Youth. When, at the end of the war, the Allies produced evidence of the scale of the Nazis' atrocities, he went through the same sequence of emotions as millions of his fellow countrymen: disbelief, anger, guilt and a desire to reject the past.

A quiet and unassuming adolescent, Heidemann left school at the age of seventeen to become an apprentice electrician. The passion of his life was photography and eventually he found work as an assistant in a photographic laboratory. He went on to become a freelance photographer for the German news agency DPA, for Keystone and for various Hamburg newspapers. In 1951 he won his first commission from *Stern*. On 1 September 1955 he became a permanent member of the magazine's staff.

Twenty-eight years later, when his bewildered and humiliated employers were pressed into holding an internal inquiry into his activities at *Stern*, they found there was almost nothing to say about his early days on the magazine. 'His colleagues do not have any particular memories of him, except that he used to enjoy playing chess,' reported the inquiry. His shyness effaced him to the point of anonymity.

Stern had been founded in 1948 by a charismatic journal-ist and businessman named Henri Nannen. The magazine prospered on a diet of scandal, consumerism, crime and human interest, skilfully designed to appeal to a war-weary population. The picture stories Heidemann worked on give an idea of the quality of the magazine at that time. One was 'Germany's Starlets'; another, 'Hospitals of Germany'. He investigated organized crime in Sardinia and smuggling on the border between Holland and West Germany. On one occasion he was dispatched to Goettingen to locate the son whom Chou En Lai was rumoured to have fathered during the 1920s when he was studying in Germany. Heidemann found a woman who had once had an affair with a Chinese student called Chou; their son was killed in the war. Unfor-tunately, as Heidemann reported to Nannen, her lover turned out to be Chou Ling Gui – a different Chou entirely. Nannen's reply, according to Heidemann, was 'Chou is Chou' and the story appeared beneath the dramatic headline, 'Chou En Lai's Son Fell For Germany'. Looking back on his work during this period, Heidemann described it as 'mediocre'.

In the mid-1950s Nannen was astute enough to recognize that the shock and humiliation of the immediate post-war era was gradually being replaced by a growing public interest in the Nazis. Heidemann became involved in features about the Third Reich: Auschwitz, fugitive war criminals and the reminiscences of the widow of Reinhard Heydrich. 'Heidemann's routine activities were generally speaking out-side my daily concern,' Nannen told police in 1983. 'I had the impression that he was a competent researcher. I didn't know of any mistakes in his work.' There was something about this intensely serious young man, with his pale com-plexion and earnest expression, which reminded Nannen of a priest fresh from a seminary.

From 1961 Heidemann worked abroad as a war photo-grapher. He saw action in the Congo, in Biafra, Guinea Bissau, Mozambique, Iraq, Jordan, Israel, Uganda, Beirut and Oman. In 1965 he won an international press award at the Hague for the year's best photo-report: a feature about white mercenaries in the Congo. He frequently worked in a partnership with Randolph Braumann, a *Stern* reporter of the macho school, known to his colleagues in Hamburg as 'Congo Randy'. 'We both enjoyed war reporting and enjoying life and experiencing danger away from Europe,' recalled Braumann. In 1970 they covered the Black September civil war in Jordan and were almost killed trying to run from a Jordanian tank to a German embassy car Heidemann had parked nearby. Even Braumann was impressed by his photographer's exuberance under fire:

> We jumped out of the tank and were immediately shot at from a house a few hundred metres away. I threw myself to the ground but Heidemann marched up to the bullet-ridden car and shouted to me: 'Randy! Come on! It's just like *Kismet*!'

Braumann was awed by his composure. 'The man had absolutely no fear.'

Back in Hamburg, Heidemann attempted to recapture the excitement of his foreign adventures. According to Brau-mann:

> He used to collect war games and toy soldiers. In the cellar of his house was a great panoramic battlefield with enemy infantry and tanks, columns of pioneers, rocket silos, fighter aircraft – I really don't know where he got the time to build up such a huge installation. He used to buy the toys from all over the world. He had catalogues from New York, London, Paris and Hong Kong.

Visitors to the Heidemann household would be taken down to the cellar by their host to be shown the toy battlefield.

Later, upstairs, if they were particularly unlucky, Heidemann would bring out mementoes from his trips abroad.

> In the sixties [recalled Braumann] he'd collected everything he could about the Congo rebels. He had recordings, notebooks, photographs. As I knew quite a lot about them, I found it quite interesting when he played all his recordings for me. You could hear a lot of shooting on them. He called them 'Conversations Under Fire'. Other guests – among them his wife at the time, Barbara – found the whole thing idiotic. I was the only one amongst his friends who knew what it was like to drive round with these rebel convoys.
>
> Basically, we were both always longing to escape from Europe.

Heidemann's obsessional nature inevitably had its effect upon his personal relationships. He had first married in 1954, at the age of twenty-three, and had a son. A year later he and his wife were divorced. In 1960 they remarried and had a daughter. But in 1965 the marriage finally foundered. Divorced once more, in 1966 Heidemann married his second wife, Barbara. This relationship lasted for five years, until Barbara too tired of his collections, his stories and his frequent absences abroad. The couple separated in 1971.

As a journalist, Heidemann was a curious amalgam of strengths and weaknesses. In research he was indefatigable, hunting down documents and interviewees with a dogged persistence which earned him the title '*der Spürhund*' – the Bloodhound. His approach was uncritical and indirect. He flattered and insinuated and was often rewarded with the sort of confidences that a more aggressive approach would have failed to solicit. But this tendency to submerge himself in the opinions of others was Heidemann's principal failing. He was such a compulsive collector of information that he never knew when to stop, and although he strove to be more than a photographer and researcher, he failed to become one of *Stern*'s major writers. He lacked any sense of perspective. Invariably the editor would end up asking him to hand over his boxes of files and transcripts. Someone else would have to boil down the mountain of information into a story. According to *Stern*'s 1983 inquiry: 'He never actually wrote any of his reports himself.'

In 1967 Heidemann became involved in an exhaustive investigation to try to uncover the real identity of the German thriller writer, B. Traven. Long after the essentials of the story had been published in *Stern*, Heidemann continued his researches, to the exasperation of the magazine's editors who wanted him to work on other projects. He went to Chicago, San Francisco, Mexico and Norway. He toured German antique shops collecting Traven memorabilia. 'I acquired everything I could,' said Heidemann. Even the patience of Congo Randy became strained. 'Heidemann would talk about nothing else but Traven,' he later complained. In 1972, Heidemann asked Braumann to help him turn his information into a book.

> He showed me everything that he'd collected about Traven. There must have been at least twenty ring-folders full of material. I said: 'My friend, I'd have to read for half a year before I could even start.'

Undeterred, Heidemann spent almost a decade immersed in the Traven story. By the time he had finished he had seventy files of information. He became convinced that the writer was the illegitimate son of Kaiser Wilhelm II. As proof, he showed Braumann two photographs: one of a man he believed to be Traven, and another of the Kaiser's eldest son. 'Don't they look similar?' he asked. Braumann was not impressed. 'I thought the story was far too improbable. It was typical of Gerd Heidemann that he should believe in something so crazy and unlikely.'

Braumann thought it was equally 'crazy' that Heidemann, short of money and ignorant of ships, should have plunged himself into debt to buy Hermann Goering's yacht. But knowing this restless, diffident, obsessive man as well as he did he was not in the least surprised by what happened next. 'I knew that after the mercenary phase and the Traven phase there would be a new phase for Heidemann: the Nazi phase.'

By 1974, *Carin II* had at least been rendered watertight. She was taken out of dry dock and moored in a Hamburg marina. 'Only the most urgent repairs had been done,' recalled Axel Thomsen, 'because Herr Heidemann was deterred by the high cost involved. He said that further work was too expensive.'

With the yacht's renovation temporarily halted for lack of money, Heidemann set about researching her history. In Munich he made contact with Goering's daughter, Edda. She was in her mid-thirties, attractive, unmarried and devoted to the memory of her father. According to his colleagues, Heidemann had always been remarkably successful with women. Apparently Edda too saw something in this tall, slightly pudgy, quietly spoken journalist who listened so attentively to her stories of her father. Shortly after their first meeting, when Heidemann visited her to show her photographs of *Carin II*, the couple began having an affair.

Slowly, imperceptibly, through his ownership of the yacht and his relationship with Edda, Heidemann began to be drawn into a circle of former Nazis. A *Stern* reporter, Jochen von Lang, introduced him to former SS General Wilhelm Mohnke, the last commander of the German garrison defending the Reich Chancellery. The sixty-three-year-old General had lived quietly since his release from Soviet captivity in 1955. He even declined to attend the reunions of the SS *Leibstandarte Adolf Hitler*, the Führer's bodyguard, of which he was a founder member. One reason for Mohnke's low profile was that the British still had an outstanding war crimes charge against him, alleging he had been responsible for shooting prisoners at Dunkirk. Mohnke, silver-haired and craggy-featured, still lithe and powerful, looked as if he had stepped out of a Hollywood war film. 'Herr von Lang took me to the yacht,' stated Mohnke, 'where, among others, I met Edda Goering.' He and Heidemann established what he called 'a very friendly rapport' and were soon addressing each other with the familiar '*du*'.

Another SS general introduced by Jochen von Lang became friendly with Heidemann around this time: Karl Wolff, one of the most senior of the surviving Nazis. Wolff had been Himmler's liaison officer with Hitler. He was sufficiently close to the SS Reichsführer for Himmler to call him by a pet name, 'Wolffchen', an endearment which Heidemann later adopted. In Minsk in 1941, on the one occasion Himmler steeled himself to stand at the edge of a mass grave and watch his SS troops massacre a hundred naked men and women, it was Wolff who caught hold of him when he seemed to faint and forced him to carry on watching. Wolff was heavily implicated in the Final Solution. As the Nazis' military governor in Italy, he was alleged to have sent at least 300,000 Jews to the Treblinka death camp. He was also accused of arranging the liquidation of partisans and Jews in the Soviet Union. Wolff saved his neck by secretly negotiating with Allen Dulles the surrender of the German forces in Italy to the Americans. In 1946 he was sentenced to four years' hard labour but spent only a week in prison. In the 1950s Wolff became a successful advertising agent in Cologne. But in 1962 he was rearrested. Fresh evidence was produced, including a letter written in 1941 in which he professed to be 'particularly gratified with the news that each day for the last fortnight a trainload of 5000 members of the "Chosen People" has been sent to Treblinka'. He was found guilty of complicity in mass murder and sent to prison, but in 1971, in view of his 'otherwise blameless life', he was released. He was seventy-four when Heidemann met him: charming, energetic and unrepentant.

Heidemann began to hold regular Third Reich *soirées* on *Carin II*. About a dozen friends and former Nazis would be invited, with Wolff and Mohnke as the guests of honour. 'We started to have long drinking evenings on board,' recalled Heidemann, 'with different people of quite different opinions talking to each other. I had always been a passionate reader of thrillers. Suddenly I was living a thriller.' He started to devour books on the Third Reich. 'I wanted to be part of the conversation, not just to sit and drink whisky.'

Heidemann's only problem was the continuing cost of the yacht. Merely servicing the debts he had incurred in buying it was proving 'a bottomless pit'. In the hope of a solution, he decided, in 1976, to seek help from Henri Nannen.

The *Stern* of 1976 was very different from the *Stern* which Heidemann had joined in the 1950s. With the advent of the sexual revolution in the 1960s, it had begun sprinkling its pages with glossy pictures of nudes. Following the growth of protest politics, its editorial line had swung to the left, with strident articles on student unrest, the Vietnam war, and the perfidy of the NATO alliance. The magazine's financial strength was a reflection of the power of the West German economy. It sucked in enormous advertising revenue and regularly produced issues running to 300 pages. Always abreast of the latest fashion, with a circulation of over 1.5 million, it easily outsold its major competitors. Its publisher, Henri Nannen, shaped the magazine in his own image: prosperous, bulging, glossy and bumptious.

In 1976 this 'hybrid of money and journalism', as one of his left-wing writers called him, was sixty-three. He had never been a member of the Nazi Party, but he had a past which sat uneasily with his present position as purveyor of radical *chic*. He had appeared as a sports announcer in Leni Riefenstahl's film of the 1936 Berlin Olympics. He had written articles praising Hitler in *Kunst dem Volk* (*Art for the People*), a Nazi magazine. During the war he had worked for a military propaganda unit. *Stern*, under his guidance, gave extensive coverage to the Third Reich and there were some who detected an ambivalence in his fascination with the period. 'It was subconscious,' claimed Manfred Bissinger, Nannen's left-wing deputy at the time. 'For Nannen, the less bad the Nazi past turned out to have been, the less bad his role in it was.' He had a powerful personality and Heidemann revered him: according to Braumann, 'he obeyed his great master Nannen's every word'.

Heidemann had been pestering Nannen to visit *Carin II* for months. In the summer of 1976, Nannen finally agreed. He was, in his own words, 'surprised and fascinated' by what he saw. Heidemann had turned the yacht into a kind of shrine to its first owner. Goering's dinner service was on prominent display, as were Goering's tea cups and Goering's drinking goblets. On the table was Goering's ashtray, in the cupboard, his uniform. The cushion covers were made out of Goering's bathrobe. Working from old photographs, Heidemann had even tried to fill the bookshelves with the same books Goering had kept there. Most of these mementoes had been given to Heidemann by Edda Goering; the rest had been acquired from dealers in Nazi memorabilia. Heidemann showed Nannen an album filled with photographs and newspaper cuttings about the yacht which included a picture of Princess Margaret on a trip to Basle. 'Simply everything was there,' said Nannen later. 'The photographs didn't just come from one source. They couldn't have been forged. He'd actually collected the whole lot. I found it an incredible journalistic performance.'

Having put his employer in this receptive mood, Heidemann outlined his plan. Nannen recalled:

> Heidemann told me he needed a loan of 60,000 marks, otherwise he would be in difficulties. He was having to pay the interest on a loan of 300,000 marks he'd taken out to pay for the renovation of the Goering yacht. He needed money to put a new engine into his boat.

Heidemann proposed that he should write a book for *Stern* based upon the conversations he was holding with Mohnke, Wolff and other old Nazis. He told Nannen that he had already begun tape recording some of these reminiscences and had some interesting material on the Odessa network, the supposed Nazi escape route to South America. 'Because Heidemann had already reported on this subject for *Stern*,' said Nannen, 'I agreed.'

On 12 October 1976 Heidemann concluded an agreement with *Stern*'s parent company, the large Hamburg publishing house of Gruner and Jahr. He undertook to write a book provisionally entitled *Bord Gespräche* (*Deck Conversations*) with the subtitle 'Personalities from History Meet on Goering's Former Yacht *Carin II*'. The contract was unusually generous towards Heidemann. He was paid an immediate advance of 60,000 marks, but no date was stipulated for the delivery of the manuscript and he was not required to return the money should he fail to write the book. All he had to do was undertake to maintain *Carin II* in a satisfactory condition. The contract was signed, on behalf of Gruner and Jahr, by Henri Nannen and by the company's managing director, Manfred Fischer.

With the official blessing and financial support of his employers, Heidemann's descent into the world of the old Nazis now began in earnest.

FIVE

While Heidemann poured whisky and adjusted his tape recorder aboard *Carin II*, another journalist was also busy tracking down survivors of the Third Reich. One hundred and fifty miles south-east of Hamburg, in his office in West Berlin, James P. O'Donnell, bureau chief of *Newsweek* magazine, was compiling a card index of more than 250 people who had been with Hitler during his last days in the bunker. His researches were to have important consequences for Heidemann.

O'Donnell's first assignment in Berlin for *Newsweek*, in July 1945, had to been to visit the Führerbunker. The memory of those forty-five minutes beneath the ground – the stench of blocked latrines whose effluent flooded the narrow corridor, the blackened walls, the tiny rooms littered with broken glass and bloodied bandages – had stayed with O'Donnell ever since. 'Adolf Hitler', he wrote, 'exercises over my mind, and that of many others, I suspect, a curious kind of fascination.' He decided to write a book, an expanded version of *The Last Days of Hitler*, describing what had happened in the bunker. Between 1972 and 1976, operating out of Berlin, he visited scores of eyewitnesses, 'cruising Hitler's old autobahns, clocking more than 60,000 miles'.

Like Heidemann, he found himself increasingly fascinated by the network of characters he uncovered. Thirty years after the end of the war many of the people close to Hitler still kept in regular contact. Gossiping amongst themselves, divided into cliques, their relationships still traced ancient patterns of loyalty and animosity forged in the heyday of the Third Reich. Once, while he was interviewing Albert Speer at his home in Heidelberg, the postman arrived and handed Speer a package which turned out to contain an autographed copy of his book, *Inside the Third Reich*. Speer had sent it to Christa Schroeder, his favourite among Hitler's secretaries, whom he had not seen since his arrest and imprisonment in 1945. She had sent it back with a brief covering note saying that she was sorry, but she was returning the book because she had been 'ordered to do so'. 'Who has the power to issue such orders?' asked O'Donnell. 'The Keepers of the Flame,' replied Speer: the adjutants, orderlies, chauffeurs and secretaries who had formed Hitler's inner circle and who habitually referred to themselves as '*die von dem Berg*', 'the Mountain People', in memory of their pre-war days at Berchtesgaden. Speer, once Hitler's favourite, was generally detested for his 'betrayal' of the Führer at Nuremberg. For his part, Speer contemptuously dismissed them as the *Chauffeureska*.

It was this group that O'Donnell, and later Heidemann, succeeded in penetrating: the adjutants, Otto Guensche and Richard Schulze-Kossens; the pilot, Hans Baur; the valet, Heinz Linge; the chauffeur, Erich Kempka; and, above all, the secretaries, who maintained a fierce loyalty to their dead employer. To them he was still *der Chef*: the Boss. The oldest, Johanna Wolf, had been recruited to work for Hitler by Rudolf Hess in 1924 and had remained his principal private secretary for more than twenty years. *Stern* was reputed to have offered her $500,000 for her memoirs. She turned them down. 'I was taught long ago', she explained to O'Donnell, 'that the very first and last duty of a confidential secretary is to remain confidential.' None of Hitler's four main secretaries had married after the war; none had much money. When O'Donnell finally persuaded Gerda Christian to meet him at the home of an intermediary in 1975 she was working as a secretary in a bank in Dortmund. Of all the Keepers of the Flame, she was the most fanatical. 'Do nothing to let the Führer down,' was Frau Christian's repeated exhortation to her colleagues. She had divorced her husband, a Luftwaffe general, in 1946, and like the other secretaries, she chose to remain single. O'Donnell once asked her why. 'How could any of us have remarried,' she replied, 'after having known a man like Adolf Hitler?'

It was in the autumn of 1972 that O'Donnell first heard the story of Sergeant Arndt's ill-fated mission to fly the ten metal trunks out of Berlin. From Heinz Linge he had obtained the address of Rochus Misch, the bunker's switchboard operator. Misch, by then in his fifties, turned out to be the proprietor of a paint and varnish shop less than a mile from O'Donnell's Berlin office. Misch was happy to talk about his wartime experiences. The interview began in his shop and continued during a walk through the city. From a vantage point in Potsdamer Platz the two men stood for a while, looking out across the Eastern sector, to the grassy mound in the shadow of the Berlin Wall which is all that now remains of Hitler's bunker. It was not until the early evening, when they were sitting in O'Donnell's office, that Misch mentioned the loading of the chests on to the lorry and described Arndt's departure from Berlin.

> In my office [recalled O'Donnell] I had for years been using my own US Army officer's standard-issue footlocker to store back-copies of the overseas editions of *Time* and *Newsweek*. Misch spotted this, and in order to describe the German chests pointed to the footlocker: 'Something like that, only cheaper, and with wooden ribs.' To get the heft and thus a guess at the weight, Misch and I together were just able to lift it three feet into the air to simulate the 1945 loading operation.

Using this as a rough guide, O'Donnell estimated that Arndt had been escorting almost half a ton of documents. He decided to pursue the story further and a few months later drove down to the Bavarian village of Herrsching, on the shores of Lake Ammersee, to see Hans Baur.

Baur had tried to break out from the Führerbunker two days after Hitler's death but had been cut down by Russian machine-gun fire. He was hit in the leg and the wound had turned septic. 'There was no surgeon available,' Baur wrote later, 'so the German surgeon amputated with a pocket-knife.' O'Donnell found a tough and irascible old man of seventy-seven, who used his wooden leg as if it were an elaborate stage prop, noisily tapping it with his signet ring or occasionally hobbling round the room on it to enact some dramatic scene. In November 1945 he had been taken by cattle truck to Moscow's Lubianka prison where, night after night for weeks on end, he had been interrogated about Hitler's final hours. He was made to put his account down on paper, only to have the pages snatched off him and torn up before his eyes. Sometimes he was grilled on his own; sometimes the Russians dragged in other bunker survivors: the commander of Hitler's SS bodyguard, Hans Rattenhuber, his naval attaché, Admiral Voss, Otto Guensche and Heinz Linge. The questioning went on for three and a half years. In 1950 he was asked if he had ever flown Hitler to meet Mussolini. Baur answered that he had, four times. He was promptly accused of 'having taken part in war preparations, because during those discussions Hitler and Mussolini had hatched their criminal plot to attack the Soviet Union'. Despite Baur's horrified protests that he 'bore no more responsibility than a train driver', he was sentenced to twenty-five years in a labour camp. In the end, he spent ten years in Soviet captivity. He was released in 1955 and shortly afterwards he decided to write his memoirs. They were not designed to be a work of scholarship or history, but – as he told Trevor-Roper soon after his return to the West – a book to be read 'by the fire, in the evening, with pipe in mouth'. It was in this book, *Hitler's Pilot*, buried amid the anecdotes of his adventures with the Boss, that Baur had first described Hitler's reaction to the news that Arndt's plane was missing.

The original manuscript had contained ten pages on Operation Seraglio, but his publishers had cut them – as they cut more than two-thirds of his rambling reminiscences. Baur told O'Donnell that he had been anxious to set matters straight because of accusations from the relatives of some of those killed that the operation had been poorly planned. He had contacted the Luftwaffe's Graves Registration organization who told him – erroneously as it turned out – that the aircraft had crashed in a Bavarian forest (it had in fact crashed in what is now East Germany). That was all he knew. He had no idea what Hitler had meant by 'valuable documents' for 'posterity'.

O'Donnell considered what could possibly have been of such value to Hitler that its apparent loss could cause such distress.

From the autumn of 1942 onwards, a team of stenographers had taken down every word uttered during the military conferences at the Führer's headquarters. These verbatim transcipts were compiled at Hitler's insistence as a means of establishing his strategic genius and his generals' incompetence: 'I want to pin down responsibility for events once and for all,' he explained to one of the stenographers. If there was one set of records which Hitler intended as 'a testament to posterity' it was this. He stated at the time that his words were to be 'taken down for later historical research'.

One of Hitler's secretaries, Christa Schroeder, told O'Donnell that in her view it was these transcripts that were on board the crashed plane. Else Krueger, Martin Boorman's former secretary, agreed with her. She rejected O'Donnell's intial theory that the papers might have been the missing notes of Hitler's 'Table Talk' from 1943 to 1944: these were Bormann's responsibility and would have been among his files, not Hitler's.

At this point, in 1975, with the deadline for the completion of his book looming, O'Donnell decided he had taken the story as far as he could. He was content to have obtained a minor historical scoop: establishing for the first time a link between Baur's account of Hitler's reaction to the loss of Arndt's plane, and Misch's description of the evacuation of the ten heavy chests. To round off the story, and to cover all possible eventualities, he ended his account of the episode with what he hoped was an appropriately teasing last paragraph:

> As all police reporters know, documents have a way of surviving crashes in which humans are cremated. While even metal melts, a book or a notebook does not burn easily, above all when it is packed tightly into a container excluding oxygen. Paper in bulk tends, rather, to char at the edges. . . . One is left with the nagging thought that some Bavarian hayloft, chicken coop, or even pigsty may well have been waterproofed and insulated with millions of words of the Führer's unpublished, ineffable utterances, simply hauled away at dawn as loot from a burning German transport plane.

O'Donnell's book was published in Germany under the title *Die Katacombe* in 1976. Not long afterwards, General Mohnke, one of the book's main characters, presented a copy to Gerd Heidemann.

SIX

O'Donnell was aware of *Stern*'s increasing interest in the survivors of Hitler's court. 'During the years when I was on the road talking to the "Mountain People", and above all from 1975 on, *Stern* approached at least a dozen of the old Hitler retainers and encouraged them, in the words of Heinz Linge, "to get something, anything on paper".' Linge, who lived in Hamburg, recalled one occasion where he joined Wolff, Mohnke, Hanna Reitsch (the famous Nazi test pilot) and 'several others' aboard *Carin II* for a day trip to the North Sea island of Sylt. Linge described the yacht as 'a kind of sentimental bait for all of us old Hitler people'. In the course of the two-hundred-mile voyage, Heidemann 'between bouts of champagne and caviar' tried to entice his guests to dictate their memories into his tape recorder. The results were disappointing: hardly surprising, observed Linge, 'with so much champagne flowing'.

The Sylt excursion was, unfortunately for Heidemann, fairly typical. The rambling and tipsy old Nazis enjoyed his hospitality but produced little of practical value. By 1978 it was becoming apparent that Henri Nannen's 60,000 mark investment in Heidemann and his 'deck conversations' was not paying off. Around this time, Erich Kuby, an experienced *Stern* writer, joined forces with Heidemann to investigate the Nazis' relations with Mussolini. *Carin II* was supposed to be the key which would unlock the participants' memories. SS Major Eugen Dollmann, formerly a senior officer in the German security service in Rome, was among those lured aboard.

In the visitors' book aboard the yacht Kuby wrote that 'on this calm and quiet sea – if one can ever describe the Elbe as such – in the company of General Wolff, we allowed the Third Reich to come alive again'. But despite Kuby's melodramatic description, these sessions also proved to be largely worthless.

> Heideman's research practice [according to Kuby] consisted of switching on his tape recorder and letting it run as long as possible so that he didn't break into the flow of the other person's conversation with pointed questions. . . . During our work together, Heidemann delivered to me from time to time transcripts of all his tape recordings. I think that in total there were some 500 pages or so. But he wasn't filtering the information. He was simply writing it up word for word and a lot of it didn't even have any questions.

'Until this time,' said Kuby, 'I had no particular reason to think that Heidemann was pro-Nazi in any way. But as we worked on the project, my conviction about this began to waver.' His colleague, he realized, no longer had any 'critical perspective' in his dealings with the former Nazis: he was beginning to identify with them. Piecing together Heidemann's activities from now onwards is to witness a man slowly sinking into a mire of obsession and fantasy about the Third Reich.

Heidemann married his third wife at his fourth wedding ceremony in May 1979. His new bride was not Edda Goering, from whom he had parted a few years previously, but one of Edda's friends. Gina Heidemann had been introduced to her future husband in the early 1970s. She was a former *au pair* girl and airline stewardess, tall and elegant with long blonde hair. At the time her affair with Heidemann began she was still married to her first husband and had two children, daughters, aged nineteen and sixteen. She shared Heidemann's interest in the Nazis and had spent many happy hours on board *Carin II*. The two witnesses at the wedding were not Joseph and Heike Friedmann – Gina's closest friends and the couple who had first introduced her to Gerd – but SS Generals Wolff and Mohnke. 'We asked the Friedmanns whether they'd mind,' Gina explained to the *Sunday Times* in 1983. 'They are Jews you see. Joschi said that, no, he thought it would be interesting. And it was. They were all very interested in talking to each other.' Not all the Heidemanns' guests were as phlegmatic. 'My wife and I went to the wedding ceremony,' recalled Randolph Braumann, 'and I said to him, "Aren't you going a bit far? The SS as wedding witnesses?" "That's just a tactic," said Heidemann. "I need these people in order to get to the old Nazis in South America."'

Heidemann wasted no time in exploiting his contacts. On 24 June 1979, he and Gina set off on their honeymoon – accompanied by General Wolff. Their destination was South America, where the trio spent the next nine weeks looking for fugitives from the Third Reich. The lustre of Wolff's name ensured that the Heidemanns had access to some of the most notorious of the Nazi refugees. They visited Argentina, Chile, Paraguay, Bolivia and Brazil. They saw several high-ranking SS officers who had served in Italy. In Chile they met Walter Rauff, Wolff's former subordinate, who had been in charge of the mobile 'gassing vans', precursors of the gas chambers. He was wanted in West Germany for the murder of 97,000 Jews, mostly women and children. In La Paz in Bolivia, Wolff arranged a meeting with Klaus Barbie, the 'Butcher of Lyons', wanted by the French for torture, murder and complicity in the Final Solution. Barbie gave Heidemann a long interview, and the reporter afterwards referred to his 'friendship' with the war criminal.

'The point of the trip was to find Mengele and Bormann,'

Wolff told the police in 1983, 'or at least to find traces of them.' Josef Mengele, the notorious chief doctor at Auschwitz, had, it has since turned out, drowned in the sea at São Paulo only four months before Heidemann came looking for him: his trail, said Heidemann, was 'cold'. But the search for Martin Bormann was a different matter. From the summer of 1979 onwards, Heidemann was convinced that Bormann was alive.

Such a belief was not without precedent. By 1972, sixteen different 'Martin Bormanns' had been arrested in South America: there was Rohl Sonnenburg, for example, the forty-three-year-old priest picked up in 1966 by the Brazilian police in a monastery near Recife; there was Juan Falero, the itinerant Mexican carpenter who had never even heard of Bormann, who was arrested in Guatemala in 1967; five years later there was the case of the septuagenarian jute and banana planter Johann Hartmann, who was plucked from his shack in a remote Indian village in Colombia, photographed and fingerprinted, and reported all over the world as being Hitler's former secretary. All of the alleged Bormanns were later found to be innocent and released, but the speculation that Bormann had survived persisted. 'I believe that Martin Bormann is alive and well,' wrote Stewart Steven, Foreign Editor of the *Daily Express* in March 1972. 'His story would be certainly the most fascinating of all.' Eight months later, Steven collaborated with the American writer Ladislas Farago on a five-part 'World Exclusive' serialized in the *Daily News* in New York and the *Express* in London. According to the two newspapers Bormann was living as a prosperous businessman in Argentina. This 'great manhunt saga', as they called it, was accompanied by a 'snatched' photograph of an 'Argentine intelligence officer' face to face with his 'quarry' in the border town of Mendoza. Subsequent investigation established that the picture was actually taken outside a café in the heart of Buenos Aires and showed two friends talking. 'Bormann' proved to be a fifty-four-year-old Argentine high school teacher named Rudolfo Siri.

The journalist who did most to discredit the rumours that Bormann had survived was Jochen von Lang – the man who had first introduced Heidemann to Mohnke and Wolff. In 1965, von Lang had published an exhaustive investigation in *Stern* which concluded that Bormann had died during the break out from the Führerbunker on 2 May 1945. *Stern* was sufficiently confident of von Lang's conclusion to hire a bulldozer and a team of labourers to dig for his body in Berlin's Invalidenstrasse. They found nothing. But seven years later, on a snowy morning in December 1972, workmen excavating a site a few yards from the scene of the original *Stern* dig found two skeletons. Identified from dental records, one proved to be Hitler's last doctor, Ludwig Stumpfegger, and the other, Martin Bormann.

This evidence satisfied most people. The West German public prosecutors, who had been searching for Bormann since 1945, shut down their inquiry. Hugh Trevor-Roper, who had regarded the question of Bormann's survival as 'open' for twenty-five years, stated that it could now be 'closed'.

Ladislas Farago, naturally, disagreed. In 1974 he produced a book – *Aftermath* – supposedly containing new evidence that Bormann was still alive. The book's credibility was not enhanced by Farago's highly coloured prose style. ('Turning to Hugetti, he said, "I think this gentleman needs the picana." Dieter winced. He knew what the picana was – the dreaded torture instrument. . . .') The climax of Farago's imaginative tale was his personal confrontation with 'Bormann' in a convent hospital run by nuns of the Redemptorist Order 'somewhere in southern Bolivia':

I saw a little old man in a big bed between freshly laundered sheets, his head propped up by three big downy pillows, looking at me with vacant eyes, mumbling words to himself, raising his voice only once, and then only to order us out of the room rather rudely. 'Dammit,' he said, not only with some emphasis, but with a vigour that astounded me, 'don't you see I'm an old man? So why don't you let me die in peace?'

For this, Farago was reported to have been paid an advance by his American publishers, Simon and Schuster, of more than $100,000.

Heidemann, like Farago, believed Bormann had survived. He subsequently claimed to have been given information to this effect by Klaus Barbie. When he returned to Germany from his honeymoon on 30 August he told Braumann 'he was more convinced than ever that Bormann was alive: there was a whole series of indications'. He showed Erich Kuby a collection of twelve by ten inch photographs, which he had brought back from South America. 'They included a set of pictures supposedly of Bormann,' recalled Kuby. 'Heidemann said he had not taken them himself but had been given them.' As had been the case with the pictures of the Kaiser's son six years earlier, the photographs fascinated Heidemann. He spent hours poring over them, tracing the subject's profile and the shape of his ears. 'He was convinced,' said Kuby.

His employers on *Stern*, however, were less impressed. Before he left, Heidemann had persuaded them to help pay for the trip. His expenses – excluding air fares – amounted to 27,000 marks. But once again they found themselves with little to show for their money. 'After his return from South America,' noted the *Stern Report*,' although he had masses of tape recordings and transcripts, none of it produced very much which was usable for the magazine.' This failure, combined with the high cost of the South American expedition, put Heidemann's position on the magazine 'in jeopardy' for the first time in almost twenty-five years. Heidemann retaliated by spreading rumours that he was considering offers for his services from *Stern*'s rivals, *Bunte* and *Quick*.

The extent of Heidemann's gullibility, of his almost pathetic eagerness to believe what he was told, was clearly demonstrated in 1979. There was the affair of the 'Bormann' photograph; there was also the affair of the Churchill–Mussolini correspondence.

While working with Kuby, Heidemann had become involved with a former SS officer named Franz Spoegler. Spoegler, who had been one of Mussolini's German adjutants, claimed to have access to thousands of pages of transcripts of Mussolini's telephone conversations with his mistress, Clara Petacci. He also said he could produce some sensational correspondence between the Duce and Winston Churchill. Heidemann was enormously excited. 'Over a period of about eighteen months,' recalled Kuby, 'he was always chasing Spoegler to get hold of these documents.'

On 17 February 1979, Heidemann approached David Irving, who was in Hamburg to take part in a television programme. Irving had edited the diaries of Goering's deputy, Field Marshal Milch, and Heidemann – with his mania for collecting anything to do with *Carin II* – asked Irving for a copy of an entry referring to a conference aboard the yacht. Then he told Irving about the Churchill–Mussolini correspondence. 'He knew that I was writing a Churchill biography,' said Irving. 'He wanted to use me to get to English newspapers with these Mussolini letters.' That night, in his diary, Irving made a note of his conversation with Heidemann:

> He has at his private address a few letters from WSC to Mussolini, in English, dated up to 1941 (!) in which latter letter

for instance WSC complains about the pro-German attitude of the Pope. The purpose of the WSC letters (to which G. H. does not have Musso's replies) was to try to break Mussolini out of the Axis. The letters are both typescript originals and photocopies.

Irving was intrigued and immediately on his return to London he wrote Heidemann a letter 'in order to confirm in writing my interest in the Churchill letters to Mussolini which you mentioned'. Nine months later, at the end of November 1979, Heidemann rang the British historian and asked him to come to Hamburg as quickly as possible. On 2 December, Irving arrived at the Heidemanns' flat.

Heidemann [recalled Irving] took me into the office next to his living room. On the bookshelves were between 50 and 70 large loose-leaf folders. He opened two or three of them and showed me transcripts he had written up himself of conversations with Karl Wolff and other leading figures from the Third Reich. Some of the conversations had taken place in South America. ... He described Karl Wolff as someone who had opened doors. I think the name Mengele was mentioned.

From one of the folders, Heidemann produced photographs of correspondence between Mussolini and Churchill covering almost six years. The first letter, dated 20 May 1939, was from Churchill, urging Mussolini not to sign the co-called 'Pact of Steel' with Hitler. The last letter, from Mussolini, written in April 1945, was a cryptic appeal to the British Prime Minister to remember their 'earlier agreements'. In addition to the correspondence already in his hands, Heidemann, according to a memorandum Irving wrote shortly afterwards, had:

a two-page typed list from his source listing all the other correspondence on offer, giving dates and synopses of the letters concerned. They display a close knowledge of the politics of the era, for example in July 1940 (?) Churchill offering Mussolini a revision of the frontier between Uganda and Kenya to Italy's advantage if Italy would withdraw from the Axis; he also offers a separate peace to Italy, at France's expense. . . .

For a moment, Irving was electrified. Here was evidence of secret dealing between the leaders of two warring nations. If it were true, it would create a sensation.

Unfortunately for Heidemann, as Irving pointed out after a careful examination, the letters were obvious fakes. In what purported to be a handwritten Churchill letter to Mussolini dated 7 May 1940 there were four clues to suggest it was a forgery: the Chartwell letterhead was centrally placed rather than printed on the right; in the text, Churchill referred to his impending appointment as prime minister – something which did not occur for another three days and which at that stage he was unlikely to have anticipated; the letter contained a misspelling of 'wich' for 'which' – 'a common spelling error made by foreigners', commented Irving; and finally the handwriting itself, in his view, was 'slightly too ragged'.

This was a bitter disappointment to Heidemann. Spoegler, according to Kuby, had demanded 65,000 marks for the correspondence, and Heidemann told Irving he had 'mortgaged one-quarter of *Carin II*' to pay for it. Having spent more than a year pursuing the documents he now saw their authenticity virtually demolished in the space of an afternoon. When Irving returned to London, he sent a copy of the letter dated 7 May 1940 to Churchill's official biographer, Martin Gilbert, for his opinion. On 17 December, Irving wrote to Heidemann telling him that Martin Gilbert 'clearly dismisses the possibility of authenticity. . . . Under no circumstances should you part with more money unless you are absolutely convinced.' For Heidemann, the news that his investment had been wasted could not have come at a worse moment.

Despite the 60,000 marks he had been paid by Nannen in 1976, Heidemann's financial position had steadily worsened. To ease the problem temporarily, on 9 May 1977, under a scheme open to Gruner and Jahr employees, he had taken out a two-year company loan of 10,000 marks. Exactly a year later, on 9 May 1978, he had borrowed a further 30,000 marks. Adding together this new loan, the balance still outstanding on the old one, and the money he had been paid for *Bord Gespräche*, Heidemann at this point owed his employers 94,960 marks: considerably more than a year's salary.

In 1979, unable to extend his borrowing any further, Heidemann resorted to a new tactic to raise money. On 23 May, despite his failure to write the promised *Bord Gespräche*, he signed another agreement with Gruner and Jahr. In return for a further 30,000 marks he now undertook to deliver *three* books: a study of Mussolini, to be written in collaboration with Erich Kuby; a volume of autobiography, with the working title *Gerd Heidemann: My African Wars*; and a book about Nazi escape routes, *SS Export*.

The problem, as he confided to General Mohnke, was the cost of *Carin II*. He earned 9000 marks per month; the yacht alone took up 6000. In desperation, in June 1978, he finally decided he would have to sell her. He advertised her in the catalogue of the Munich auctioneers, Hermann, specialists in the sale of military memorabilia. His asking price was 1.1 million marks. The boat remained unsold. The consequences of this failure were to lead Heidemann directly to the Hitler diaries.

Mohnke suggested Heidemann try getting in touch with an acquaintance of his who might be able to help sell the yacht: a former junior member of the SS living in the town of Augsburg near Munich. His name was Jakob Tiefenthaeler.

Tiefenthaeler was fifty-three years old. He worked at the local US airbase where he was in charge of audio-visual instruction. He had an extensive network of old Nazi contacts, Mohnke, Wolff and Hans Baur among them. He was also deeply involved in the secretive world of Nazi memorabilia collectors, specializing himself in the acquisition of photographs from the Third Reich. At the beginning of 1979 Heidemann rang him. 'He said he'd got my name and telephone number from General Mohnke,' remembered Tiefenthaeler.

> I'd known Mohnke for a long time. Heidemann said in the telephone conversation that Mohnke had told him that I might be able to find buyers for his yacht. I asked Heidemann to send me technical details and pictures of the ship and I said that I'd try to find somebody.

Heidemann complained sorrowfully to Tiefenthaeler that he couldn't bear the thought of being parted from the yacht, that he'd turned it into a 'perfect museum' full of Goering treasures, but that the cost of berthing and insurance were such that he could no longer afford the luxury of keeping it.

Tiefenthaeler advertised the yacht in the United States for a price of 1.2 million marks. When this proved unsuccessful, he made contact with a millionaire Australian who ran a war museum in Sydney. Despite the fact that Heidemann twice dropped the price – first to 800,000 marks, then to 750,000 – the Australian pulled out. An Arab oil sheik from Abu Dhabi expressed an interest, but Heidemann was not keen: he told Tiefenthaeler he was worried that the yacht would be damaged in the hot sun. The Ugandan dictator Idi Amin sent a German mercenary, Rolf Steiner, to inspect the ship, but again the deal fell through. Amin would have loved to have cruised around Lake Victoria in Hermann Goering's yacht, but the problems of transporting it to that landlocked country were felt to be insuperable.

While Tiefenthaeler was busy pursuing these potential foreign purchasers, he gave Heidemann the name of a wealthy south German collector of Nazi memorabilia who might be interested in buying some of the smaller Goering pieces. Accordingly, some time in 1979 – it is difficult to be sure of the precise date – Heidemann turned up in Stuttgart. Seven miles east of the city, in the quiet suburb of Waiblingen, he found a small engineering factory belonging to Fritz Stiefel; immediately next door to it was Stiefel's house. He rang the bell and a thickset, taciturn man appeared.

According to Stiefel, Heidemann handed him a visiting card and introduced himself as a reporter from *Stern*. 'He said that the reason for his visit was that he wanted to ask me if I was interested in buying the table silver from his yacht, the *Carin II*.' Stiefel invited him in. Like some medieval pardoner peddling holy relics, Heidemann then laid out his wares. 'There was a small silver sugar bowl, a silver water goblet and a gold coloured match-holder,' recalled Stiefel. 'The Goering family crest was engraved on all the objects.' This trinketry appealed to Stiefel and he promptly bought it. 'I can't say exactly how much I paid for these objects,' he claimed subsequently, with an unconvincing show of vagueness. 'It was certainly over 1000 marks.' Heidemann tried to tempt his customer into buying a couple of larger items. Stiefel was interested in the reporter's expensive set of Goering table silver, but decided against taking it after consulting his wife. Nor did he want Goering's ceremonial uniform which Heidemann also produced for his inspection.

Returning to Hamburg, impressed by Stiefel's interest and by his obvious wealth, Heidemann telephoned Tiefenthaeler and suggested a new scheme: in return for an investment of 250,000 marks they should offer to make Stiefel a partner in the yacht. Tiefenthaeler promised to speak to Stiefel and shortly afterwards, towards the end of 1979, he rang Heidemann back. He was in a state of some excitement, having just been shown round Stiefel's collection of Nazi mementoes; among them, he told the reporter, was a Hitler diary.

SEVEN

On 6 January 1980, a few days after David Irving had passed on Martin Gilbert's judgement that the Churchill–Mussolini correspondence was faked, Heidemann returned to Waiblingen to see Fritz Stiefel.

Heidemann opened the conversation by outlining his proposal that Stiefel should become part-owner of *Carin II*. In his quiet, urgent voice he conjured up a glowing vision of the future: the yacht, fully restored to her former splendour, would be permanently moored off the coast of 'an island in the Atlantic' (Heidemann's suggestion was Jersey); it would be 'a floating museum' full of Nazi memorabilia, dedicated to the memory of Hermann Goering. Stiefel was unimpressed. 'I turned him down flat,' he said.

Disappointed in one fantasy, Heidemann grasped at another. Was there, he asked Stiefel, any truth in the rumour that he had a Hitler diary? The businessman, according to Heidemann, was 'startled' but after some hesitation agreed to show it to him.

Stiefel led Heidemann to an armoured steel door upon which was a large sign: 'BEWARE. HIGH VOLTAGE. DANGER TO LIFE.' Stiefel unlocked it, swung it open, and the two men stepped over the threshold.

Heidemann was later to tell colleagues of his astonishment at what he saw. The room was large and windowless. On display, in beautifully lit cabinets, was a staggering assortment of souvenirs from the Third Reich. There were swastika flags, Nazi uniforms, photographs, paintings, drawings, books. In one corner was an exhibition of porcelain made by concentration camp inmates; in another, a collection of military decorations, including a *Pour le Mérite*. It had to rank as one of the largest private collections of its kind in Germany.

Stiefel handed Heidemann a slim, A4-sized book, with hard black covers and gothic initials in the bottom right-hand corner which Heidemann took to be 'AH'. Stiefel allowed him to hold it briefly. He flicked through it. It covered the period from January to June 1935. There were a hundred or more lined pages; some were half full, some blank; some written in pencil, others in ink. Many of the pages bore Hitler's signature. The writing itself was virtually indecipherable. After a few moments, Stiefel took it back and locked it up.

Heidemann began asking questions. Where did the book come from? Stiefel said it was salvaged by local peasants from a plane crash at the end of the war. Who gave it to him? A man in Stuttgart, replied Stiefel, who had relatives in senior positions in East Germany – no, he wouldn't reveal his name. Were there more diaries? Stiefel said he understood there might be another twenty-six, each of them, like the one in his possession, covering a six-month period. That was all he could say.

Heidemann returned to Hamburg in a state of great excitement. In the *Stern* offices he described how he had actually *held in his hands* Hitler's secret diary. He had managed to memorize a few sentences about Eva Braun and her two pet dogs which he recited endlessly.

Any journalist claiming to have stumbled upon such a scoop would have expected to face a certain amount of scepticism. Heidemann was greeted by an almost universal incredulity, bordering on derision. This was, after all, the man who had had two SS generals officiating at his wedding, who had spent his honeymoon looking for war criminals, who had claimed to have a recent photograph of Martin Bormann and who had thought he could prove the existence of secret dealing between Churchill and Mussolini. When Heidemann broke the news of the Hitler diary to Henri Nannen in the *Stern* canteen, the response was frankly insulting. According to Nannen: 'My word-for-word answer was: "Spare me all that Nazi shit. I don't want to hear about it and I don't want to read about it."' Heidemann fared no better with Peter Koch, the magazine's aggressive deputy editor, who treated him as if he were mentally deranged. 'Keep away from me,' he shouted, 'with your damned Nazi tic.' He warned Heidemann to stay off subjects connected with the Third Reich and added, ominously, that 'he'd better produce something soon'. 'The trouble with *Stern*', complained Heidemann bitterly, 'is they don't want to hear about history any more.'

Only one man seemed to take Heidemann seriously. He was Thomas Walde, an earnest and sober character in his late thirties whose chief distinguishing feature was a large brown moustache. Walde had joined *Stern* in 1971 as an editorial assistant and had risen to become news editor. When, at the beginning of 1980, *Stern* had established a new department specifically to deal with historical stories, Walde had been put in charge of it. He had been in his office little more than a week when Heidemann turned up asking if he could come and work for him. Leo Pesch, Walde's young assistant, recalled how Heidemann told them 'he had seen a Hitler diary in the possession of a South German collector'. He would not stop talking about it. One evening in April, he threw a party for the history department on board *Carin II*. 'The idea,' said Walde, 'was to meet outside the context of the normal office routine. We wanted to get to know the boat. And we wanted to discuss future projects.' Among those 'future projects' was the Hitler diary.

Walde was interested in Heidemann's tale. The problem

was that almost nobody else was. 'Heidemann and Koch didn't get on,' he recalled, 'and Koch opposed Heidemann's request to research Nazi topics.' Walde therefore decided to embark on what was to prove a disastrous strategy. Without telling Koch and the other editors he went behind their backs and commissioned Heidemann to search for the Hitler diaries. 'I didn't believe in their existence,' he claimed later. 'I just hoped Heidemann would do enough research to kill the subject once and for all.'

The most obvious course was to try to discover the identity of the man who had supplied the diary to Stiefel; once he had his name, Heidemann reasoned, he could approach him directly. Stiefel, however, flatly refused to cooperate. Therefore, in the summer of 1980, Heidemann once again turned to the man from whom he had first learned of the diary's existence, Jakob Tiefenthaeler. Tiefenthaeler, who had by now given up his attempts to sell *Carin II*, told Heidemann that he understood the supplier was an antique dealer in Stuttgart named Fischer. Armed with this information, Heidemann and Walde waited one night until everyone had gone home and then began combing through every Fischer in the Stuttgart telephone directory: a task – given the commonness of the name Fischer in Germany – not unlike searching an English phone book for a particular Smith. When this yielded nothing, Walde asked *Stern*'s correspondent in Stuttgart to make discreet inquiries around the city about this mysterious dealer; again, there was no trace.

With this line of inquiry temporarily at an end, Heidemann adopted a fresh tactic. He knew from Stiefel that the diary supposedly came from a plane crash. From O'Donnell's book, *Die Katacombe*, and Baur's, *Hitler's Pilot*, he knew of the mysterious documents shipped out of the bunker whose loss had so distressed Hitler. He was convinced that this must be where Stiefel's diary originated. If he could substantiate the story of the plane crash by pinpointing its location it would be a strong argument in favour of the diary's authenticity. On Monday, 13 October 1980, he rang the Wehrmacht information bureau, the *Wehrmachtsauskunftstelle*, in Berlin to inquire if they had any information about the pilot of the missing plane, Major Friedrich Gundlfinger. He was not hopeful. Given the chaos in Germany in those closing days of the war it was asking a great deal to discover the fate of a single aircraft after an interval of thirty-five years. Heidemann was therefore surprised when, after a pause, a voice at the other end of the line replied that the bureau did indeed have records relating to Major Gundlfinger: he had died in a plane crash on 21 April, close to the little village of Boernersdorf near Dresden in East Germany on 21 April 1945; he was buried close to the crash site; his death certificate in the local register was 16/45.

From this moment, Heidemann and Walde were hooked and the tempo of their search quickened. Two days after Heidemann's discovery of the location of the crash site, on Wednesday 15 October, Walde travelled to East Berlin. Through a contact in the East German security service he arranged a visit to the Dresden area to be undertaken in one month's time. The cover story was that Heidemann was a relative of one of the victims of the plane crash. On Monday, 27 October, Heidemann went to see Hans Baur in Herrsching, who once again confirmed the details of Gundlfinger's last flight.

Heidemann's unexpected success left Thomas Walde with a problem and in the last week of October, while Heidemann was talking with Hans Baur, he took the opportunity of a vacation to think things over.

For the past three years he and a close friend, Wilfried Sorge, had left their wives and families and gone on an annual walking holiday together. The two men, almost the same age (Sorge was three years younger than Walde), had known one another for the best part of twenty years. They had both attended the same school in the small town of Uelzen, not far from Hamburg. Now they both worked for the same company: Walde as a *Stern* journalist, Sorge as a junior executive with *Stern*'s owners, Gruner and Jahr. They kept few secrets from one another.

Accordingly, when they were safely alone in the middle of a Bavarian forest, Walde told Sorge of his involvement with the Hitler diaries and of the difficulties he was now in. The trouble, said Walde, was that Peter Koch, who was likely to take over from Henri Nannen in the New Year as editor-in-chief, had expressly ordered Heidemann 'not to pursue any further researches into the Nazis'; Walde had disobeyed him. Meanwhile, Heidemann's tale about Hitler's diaries, far from being 'killed' by further investigation, was beginning to look as if it might be true. To compound his problems, Walde was about to undertake what he described as a 'risky journey' to East Germany, unable to tell his superiors about it because he had been deceiving them for the past six months. 'Herr Sorge advised me to take the chance,' recalled Walde.

Agreeing to keep the conversation confidential, they continued their walk.

But the sudden spectre of Hitler had clearly infected the holiday mood. Nursing their secret, the two men crossed over the border into Austria. They inspected Hitler's birthplace in Braunau, and the town of Leonding, near Linz, where the Führer had spent part of his youth, before returning to Hamburg on 31 October.

On 15 November 1980, Heidemann and Walde drove through one of the checkpoints from West to East Berlin, picked up Walde's contact who had arranged the trip, and travelled 120 miles south to Dresden. Another hour's drive brought them to a tiny cluster of farmhouses and barns, nestling amid hilly fields and woods three miles from the Czech border, in a region known as 'Saxon Switzerland'. With its tiny kindergarten and scattered population of 550, it was difficult to imagine a sleepier village than Boenersdorf.

The *Stern* men parked their car on the side of the main road outside Boernersdorf's small church. Behind it, in the cemetery overlooking the village, in the south-eastern corner, half hidden amongst the weeds and the long grass, they found eight weather-beaten wooden crosses. Attached to each one was a small white tile giving the name of the person buried there, the date of their birth and the day of their death: 21.4.45. They found Gundlfinger's grave and Wilhelm Arndt's; two graves were simply marked 'unknown man' and 'unknown woman'. This physical evidence of the plane crash thirty-five years earlier made a profound impression on the two men. 'The discovery of the graves', said Walde. 'was like another stone in the mosaic.'

Anxious to avoid drawing attention to themselves, Heidemann and Walde did not stay for long. They made notes of the names on the crosses and took some photographs. Half an hour later they returned to their car and drove back to Berlin.

Heidemann and Walde now sensed they were close to a breakthrough. On their return from East Germany, Walde informed Wilfried Sorge of the success of their visit.

The story as they had pieced it together seemed simple and credible. Papers of great value to Hitler undoubtedly had been loaded on to a plane in Berlin; that plane undoubtedly had crashed in East Germany; part of its cargo, a diary, had surfaced in the West. The remaining task was to find the link between the wrecked aircraft and Fritz Stiefel – and to find him before anyone else did.

A few days after their arrival back in Hamburg, Heidemann and Walde renewed their contact with Jakob Tiefenthaeler. They asked him to pass on to the mysterious 'antiques dealer' an offer generous enough to tempt him out of his seclusion. They were prepared, they told Tiefenthaeler, to guarantee a payment of 2 million marks in return for the complete set of Hitler's diaries; this sum could be paid, according to his preference, in either cash or gold. If necessary, they would be prepared to accept photocopies of the diaries rather than the originals. The whole matter would be dealt with in the strictest confidence: even if the West German government tried to force *Stern* to disclose the identity of the supplier, they would stand by the traditional prerogative of a newspaper to protect the anonymity of its informants. It was a remarkable offer, all the more so considering it was made without the knowledge of the magazine's editors. It showed the extent to which Heidemann and Walde had already convinced themselves that the diary held by Stiefel must be genuine.

While they waited for Tiefenthaeler to bring them the supplier's response, Heidemann, using the notes he had made from the graves in Boernersdorf, set about tracing the victims' relatives. On 1 December, in the Ruhr steel town of Sollingen, he found Frau Leni Fiebes, the widow of Max Fiebes, one of Hitler's bodyguards who had been among the passengers. She had been notified of her husband's death in 1948. She showed Heidemann the official report which had been forwarded to her, recording the discovery of:

> a male corpse with the remains of a grey-green uniform with two stars on the collar, a wallet containing a number of passport photographs, and the name Max Fiebes, Oberscharführer of the SS, born 27 March 1910 in Sollingen. No personal property could be found as it had been completely burnt.

This was of interest to Heidemann only in so far as it showed that oddments of paper could have survived the crash. But Frau Fiebes was at least able to give him the name of the plane's rear gunner, Franz Westermeier, and on 10 December, the indefatigable reporter tracked down his family in Haag in Upper Bavaria. Westermeier, he learned to his surprise, had actually survived the crash, thrown clear of the burning wreck on impact, together with an SS guard, Gerhard Becker. Becker had died of his injuries two days later, but Westermeier had lived on into old age, dying in April 1980 of a kidney tumour: Heidemann had arrived just eight months too late.

Another trail seemed to have gone cold, leaving them no further forward. All Heidemann and Walde could do now was hope that the offer being relayed by Tiefenthaeler would flush out their prey.

EIGHT

The New Year arrived, cold and bleak, with a symbolic reminder of Germany's Nazi past and the conflicting emotions it aroused.

On 6 January 1981, a crowd of about 5000 German naval veterans and right wingers gathered in the snow at Aumuehle near Hamburg for the funeral of Grand Admiral Karl Doenitz, Hitler's successor as leader of the Third Reich. Doenitz, who had died on Christmas Eve at the age of 89, had been a devoted Nazi and the West German government announced that it would be boycotting the ceremony. 'But in buses, cars and trains,' reported *The Times*, 'mourners came to his funeral, many of them old men with an upright military bearing, Iron Crosses glinting on their breasts and evident nostalgia for what Doenitz stood for.' Rudolf Hess sent a wreath from his cell in Spandau. Serving naval officers – some in uniform, despite an official ban – formed an honour guard around the grave. As the coffin, draped in the red, black and gold flag of the Federal Republic and bearing Doenitz's service dagger, was lowered into the frozen ground, the mourners broke into the militaristic first verse of '*Deutschland über Alles*'. At a rally afterwards, speakers from the extreme right were applauded as they denounced the craven behaviour of the republic's politicians. It was an ugly start to the year and the ensuing political row lasted several weeks.

SS General Wilhelm Mohnke, who lived close to Aumuehle, marked Doenitz's passing by arranging a small reception at his house on the day of the funeral. Otto

Guensche and Richard Schulze-Kossens, two of Hitler's SS adjutants, attended; so too did Gerd Heidemann. They all met at the graveside and then went back to Mohnke's for his little party. 'It was on this occasion,' remembered Mohnke, 'that Herr Heidemann told us for the first time that there were supposed to be Hitler diaries.' Heidemann described the story of the plane crash and revealed that he had discovered its location in Boernersdorf. When he insisted that a set of Hitler's diaries had survived, the three old SS men were sceptical. 'That was thought by the people there to be impossible,' declared Mohnke. Schulze-Kossens, who had helped found Hitler's SS honour bodyguard in 1938 and who had often been in the Führer's company, doubted if Hitler had had the time to write a diary. Heidemann was undeterred. Nothing could now shake his conviction that somewhere out there were Hitler's diaries.

Nine days later, his confidence appeared to be vindicated. On Thursday, 15 January, after an interval of more than seven weeks, Jakob Tiefenthaeler at last rang back. Herr Fischer, he reported, *was* interested in Heidemann and Walde's offer and had authorized him to pass on his telephone number. It was 07152 41981. The reporter noted it down. He could hardly contain his impatience. 'I remember that Herr Heidemann was in a real hurry to end the conversation,' recalled Tiefenthaeler. 'He thanked me and promised to keep in touch.'

Heidemann turned in triumph to Walde. 'I have the number.'

A man's voice, gruff and heavily accented, answered the number which Heidemann dialled. 'I have been trying to reach you for more than a year,' Heidemann told him. He talked about his ownership of *Carin II*, his friendship with the old Nazis and his collection of Third Reich memorabilia, before finally coming to the point. 'We are very interested in the diaries.'

Fischer said that he was a dealer in militaria. He was

originally from East Germany. His brother was still there – a general in the East German army. The general had been in touch with peasants in the area where Hitler's transport plane had crashed at the end of the war. In return for money and consumer goods he had acquired from them a hoard of material which had been salvaged from the burning aircraft and hidden locally for more than thirty years. It was not simply a matter of diaries, said Fischer. There were other Hitler writings involved, including a handwritten third volume of *Mein Kampf* and an opera.

An opera? Heidemann was taken aback.

Yes, said Fischer, an opera entitled *Wieland the Blacksmith* which Hitler had written in his youth in collaboration with his friend August Kubizek. There were also letters and papers belonging to Hitler and original Hitler paintings. Heidemann asked about the material's whereabouts. Some of it was in the West, said Fischer, but most of it was still in the East. He had already had offers for it from the United States.

Heidemann repeated the proposition he had made to Tiefenthaeler: 2 million marks for the diaries and a guarantee of absolute secrecy. Fischer sounded doubtful. His brother was prepared to deal only with discreet private collectors. He would never agree to the sale of the material to a publishing company: if this involvement ever became known, his career, possibly even his life, would be endangered. Again, Heidemann promised complete confidentiality. Fischer hesitated. He could, he supposed, keep *Stern*'s name out of it and pass Heidemann off to his brother as a wealthy Swiss collector. Certainly, he was adamant that if they were to do business, no one else could be brought into the arrangement. He would deal only with Heidemann. This suited the reporter perfectly and by the time the conversation ended, half an hour later, the foundations of a deal had been laid.

*   *   *

Heidemann and Walde now needed money and the following week was devoted to putting together a suitably tempting prospectus to obtain it. Heidemann assembled the information and photocopied the relevant extracts from *Die Katacombe* and *Hitler's Pilot* but as usual he passed his material on to someone else to write up – on this occasion, Walde. The two men gave the project the cover name 'The Green Vault', after '*Grünes Gewölbe*', the treasure chamber in Dresden Castle which housed a famous military museum. On Sunday, 24 January the document was completed. After outlining the story of the trunks full of documents, the plane crash and Hitler's reaction to it, the prospectus went on:

> Farmers found the crates containing the documents. One man from southern Germany, who was a visitor in East Germany, managed to rescue the treasure from the farmers and safeguard it. Many years later, it was smuggled into the West. Part of the archive is still in East Germany. For around 2 million marks I could obtain 27 handwritten volumes of Hitler's diaries, the original manuscript of *Mein Kampf* – so far unpublished – and an opera by the young Hitler and his friend August Kubizek, entitled *Wieland der Schmied*. There are also many other unpublished papers.
>
> The conditions are that the names of the people who brought the material out of East Germany should not be revealed and the money must be handed over to the supplier by me, personally, abroad. Part of the money has to be paid into East Germany.
>
> I have actually visited the place in question [Boernersdorf]. Dr Thomas Walde came with me. We were there last year. There can be no doubt about the authenticity of the material. I know personally almost all those who survived from Hitler's bunker and I have checked the story with them. If our company thinks that the risk is too great, I suggest that I should

seek out a publishing company in the United States which
could put up the money and ensure that we get the German
publication rights.

The document was signed by Gerd Heidemann. It was put
into a folder together with the extracts from the books of
O'Donnell and Baur, and the photographs which Heidemann
had taken in Boernersdorf.

Under normal circumstances, the next step would have
been for Walde and Heidemann to have taken their story to
Stern's editors. But the deception which the pair had been
practising for more than six months had boxed them in. Not
only would they have been accused of lying, they had no
guarantee that their story would have been accepted. Koch's
attitude towards Heidemann's Nazi fixation had not changed.
Only a few days earlier, according to the reporter, Koch had
called him in and instructed him to research a series about the
arms race. Heidemann had tried to avoid the assignment and
had broached the subject of the Hitler diaries but Koch had
brushed him aside angrily: 'You! Always with your SS
topics!' And Walde had another fear: *Stern* was short of
sensational stories at the moment. The magazine's aggrieved
editors, he claimed later, might have 'wasted the tale of the
diaries as a quick scoop'. It is also likely, although naturally
neither man has ever admitted it, that they realized the discovery of the diaries could make them a great deal of money.
Why should they simply give it away to their ungrateful
editors?

Walde had already initiated Wilfried Sorge into the secret.
At about noon on Tuesday, 27 January, the two journalists
visited him in his office to show him their 'Green Vault'
dossier. They told him that they needed 200,000 marks as a
deposit to secure the first volumes. Sorge promised to see
what he could do.

Four hours later Heidemann and Walde were summoned up to the offices of Gruner and Jahr on the ninth floor of the *Stern* building. Sorge had shown the folder to his immediate superior, Dr Jan Hensmann, the company's deputy managing director. Hensmann was enthusiastic and at once telephoned the firm's managing director, Manfred Fischer, to ask if he could spare a few minutes. 'Heidemann has found something,' said Hensmann. 'We need to talk about it.' Full of curiosity, Fischer made his way to Hensmann's office.

Five men took their places in the room for the first of what would eventually prove to be dozens of conferences on the diaries, extending over a period of more than two years. Heidemann and Walde were the journalists present; Hensmann was the financial expert; Sorge, the salesman; Manfred Fischer, the dynamic executive whose love of instant decision making was to start the whole calamity.

The dossier was handed to Fischer. He read it, fascinated, and began asking questions. 'Heidemann', he recalled, 'explained that many of the documents were in the hands of a highly placed officer in the East German army. The books had to be smuggled into the West by secret and illegal means. No names could be revealed in order not to jeopardize the informants.' Fischer asked what Henri Nannen thought of it all. Heidemann described Nannen's derogatory remarks in the *Stern* canteen; he talked of his 'difficulties' with Peter Koch; neither of them knew anything about it, nor should they be told. Walde pitched in to support Heidemann. Fischer was impressed by his manner of calm assurance; Walde, he said later, added a 'seal of authority' to the story.

Things might have gone very differently for *Stern* if at this point Fischer had insisted that the magazine's editors be let in on the secret. But Fischer was a supremely self-assured character. He had reason to be. At forty-seven he was the favourite protégé of the mighty Reinhard Mohn. Mohn controlled 88.9 per cent of Bertelsmann AG, the West German printing and publishing conglomerate with an annual turnover of almost $2 billion. Bertelsmann in its turn owned 74.9 per cent of Gruner and Jahr. Fischer was expected to take over the running of the entire Bertelsmann empire in the next few months. If Heidemann and Walde wanted to keep the discovery of the diaries secret from their editors for a while, he was not the kind of man to shirk responsibility for that decision. He was flattered that two such experienced journalists should turn to him. Personally, he did not blame them for being reluctant to trust Koch – Fischer did not like the *Stern* editor either: he was too abrasive and much too left wing for his liking. Fischer was excited at the prospect of obtaining Hitler's diaries. It would do him no harm to arrive at Bertelsmann with a reputation as the man who had engineered the biggest publishing coup of the decade. He postponed his next appointment and asked Walde and Heidemann how much they needed.

It was eventually agreed that Heidemann would offer, on Gruner and Jahr's behalf, 85,000 marks for each of the 27 volumes. The company would also be willing to pay up to 200,000 marks for the third volume of *Mein Kampf* and 500,000 marks for the remainder of the archive, including the pictures. Heidemann said that he needed 200,000 marks as a deposit. Ideally, he would like to fly down to Stuttgart that night. Fine, replied Fischer, he should have the money at once. He summoned the company's financial secretary, Peter Kuehsel.

Kuehsel, an accountant in his forties, had been with the firm for only three weeks. He wandered into the office and was suddenly ordered by Fischer to produce 200,000 marks in cash – immediately. It was after 6.30 p.m. and Kuehsel had been on the point of going home. He protested that all the banks were closed. 'Get the money,' said Fischer, and with a parting injunction to Heidemann to keep him fully informed, he departed for a reception being held by one of Gruner and Jahr's consumer magazines.

'I didn't know what the money was for,' Kuehsel said afterwards. 'It wasn't necessary for me to know. According to the company's internal rules, Dr Fischer could authorize payment.' The only bank he could think of which might still be open was the Deutsche Bank at Hamburg Airport; he rang and checked; they were. Heidemann, Sorge, Kuehsel and a representative of the company's legal department piled into a car and drove off into the night.

At the bank, a bemused cashier handed over 200,000 marks in 100-, 500- and 1000-mark notes. 'Herr Heidemann gave me a receipt,' said Kuehsel, 'and put the money into his briefcase.' Heidemann had booked himself on to the final flight out of Hamburg for Stuttgart. According to Kuehsel: 'We took Herr Heidemann to the departure hall. I told him he was carrying a lot of money and he had to be careful.' In addition to the cash, Heidemann had also taken the precaution of packing what he hoped would be his trump card in persuading Fischer to hand over the diaries – the pride of his collection, the full dress uniform of Hermann Goering.

Heidemann was now playing the part he relished most. Settled into his seat on flight LH949, a suitcase containing 200,000 marks at his side, he took off for Stuttgart on a secret mission to buy Adolf Hitler's diaries.

At Stuttgart airport, Heidemann hired a car and drove into the city to the International Hotel. He rang Gina to let her know he would not be coming home that evening and went to bed.

The following morning, using the address given to him by Tiefenthaeler, Heidemann drove to Fischer's shop at number 20 Aspergstrasse. The building was four storeys high, a solid, red brick affair, part of a terrace on a steep hill. Fischer's shop had a pair of windows at the front, heavily shuttered. Heidemann rang the bell. There was no reply; the place was deserted. He tried to peer through the windows at the back, but they too had heavy metal bars and lace curtains.

Heidemann waited in his car in the bitter January cold all morning with only the money and Goering's uniform for company. In the afternoon he decided to try to find Fischer's home. From the area code prefixing Fischer's telephone number, he worked out that his house must be in the Leonberg area, about ten miles west of the centre of Stuttgart. Heidemann drove through the darkening countryside, through neat fields and brightly lit villages, until, at about 7 p.m., he reached the tiny hamlet of Ditzingen. He drove past a row of small houses, parked by a phone box and rang Fischer's number. 'It's Heidemann,' he said, when Fischer answered, 'from *Stern*.' Fischer asked him what the weather was like in Hamburg. 'I'm not in Hamburg,' replied Heidemann. 'I'm five minutes away from your house.' Fischer gave him his address – it was literally only across the street – and moments later, Heidemann was ringing the doorbell of one of the small houses he had just passed.

The door opened to reveal a short, round-faced man with a bald head and drooping moustache.

NINE

In Konrad Paul Kujau, alias Konrad Fischer, alias Peter Fischer, alias Heinz Fischer, alias Doctor Fischer, alias Doctor Kujau, alias 'The Professor', alias 'The General', known to his many friends as Conny, Gerd Heidemann had at last met his match: someone whose talent for inventing stories was equal to his own capacity for believing them.

Konrad Kujau, who began by forging luncheon vouchers and who ended up responsible for the biggest fraud in publishing history, was born on 27 June 1938 in the Saxon town of Loebau in what is now East Germany. He had three sisters and a brother; of the five children, he was the third eldest. His father, Richard Kujau, was a shoemaker. Unlike Heidemann, whose background was relatively apolitical, Conny was reared in a typically working-class, pro-Nazi household. Richard Kujau was an active supporter of the Nazis from 1933 onwards and his beliefs rubbed off on his son: seven years after the end of the war, at the age of fourteen, Conny was to be found painting an enormous swastika on his grandmother's kitchen wall.

Kujau's childhood was overshadowed by the poverty which descended on his family after his father was killed in 1944. His mother was unable to support the family and they had to be sent away to various children's homes. Conny, the brightest in the family, did well at school but was too poor to stay on beyond his sixteenth birthday. In September 1954 he became an apprentice locksmith, a position he held for less than a year. Then came a succession of temporary jobs, none of them lasting for more than a few weeks, as a textile worker, a building-site labourer, a painter, and finally as a waiter in the Loebau Youth Club. In 1957 a warrant was issued for his arrest in connection with the disappearance of the Youth Club's microphone. Shortly before dawn on 7 June 1957, Kujau fled to the West.

He made his way first to the home of his uncle, Paul Bellmann, in West Berlin. But Bellmann had no room for his troublesome, nineteen-year-old nephew, and Kujau found himself in the first of a series of refugee camps. Rootless, alone, with no family to fall back on, the young Kujau was eventually resettled in Vaihingen, on the outskirts of Stuttgart. He lived in a succession of homes for single men and drifted into a world of casual labour and petty crime. His biography is written in his police record. In November 1959 he was arrested for stealing tobacco from a local cooperative and fined eighty marks. In 1960, together with an accomplice, he broke into a storeroom and stole four cases of cognac. He made so much noise he woke up two nightwatchmen who pursued and caught him. The police found he was carrying an air pistol, a small revolver and a knuckleduster. A court in Stuttgart found him guilty of serious theft and he went to prison for nine months. In August 1961, he was in trouble again, this time for stealing four crates of pears and a crate of apples whilst employed as a labourer for a fruit merchant; again, he spent a short period in prison. Six months later, working as a cook in a Stuttgart bar, he was arrested after a fight with his employer.

It was at this time that Kujau met and fell in love with a waitress at the same establishment, a homely girl named Edith Lieblang. Edith, like Conny, was plump, in her twenties, and a refugee from East Germany: she had worked as a salesgirl and was training to be a nurse when she decided to cross into the West in April 1961, a few months before the erection of the Berlin Wall. She came to seek her fortune and found Conny Kujau, upon whom, for a time, she seems to have been a steadying influence. In the summer of 1962 he rented premises in Plochingen, fifteen miles outside Stuttgart, and opened the Pelican Dance Bar. 'For the first time,' he claimed later, 'I began to make money.' He also began to rewrite his personal history.

To call Kujau a compulsive liar would be to underrate him. It would not do justice to the sheer exuberant scale of his deceptions. In 1962 he told people his surname was 'Fischer' and asked them to call him 'Peter'. He made himself two years older, by changing his date of birth to March 1936. He altered his place of birth from Loebau to Goerlitz. He painted a touching but sadly fictitious picture of his childhood: separated from his parents during the bombing of Dresden, he had, he said, been brought up in an orphanage until his mother found him with the help of the Red Cross in 1951. He had not been a waiter in the Loebau Youth Club but an 'organization manager'. He had attended the Dresden Academy of Art. He had been persecuted by the communists because his family was not working class. He had fled to the West to avoid conscription into the East German army. He had worked as a commercial artist in an advertising agency. There was no particular reason for most of these lies: Kujau simply liked telling stories.

By 1963 Kujau was once again in financial trouble. He gave up his dance bar and returned to Stuttgart to work as a waiter in a beer cellar. He soon resumed his old ways and for the first time his police record shows a conviction for forgery. He counterfeited twenty-seven marks' work of luncheon vouchers and was sentenced to five days in prison. According to the court records, Kujau – who was tried under the name Fischer – had added some new stories to his repertoire: he now claimed to have been born in June 1935, so adding yet another year to his age; he also pretended he was married.

In the year that saw his first conviction for forgery, Kujau persuaded the long-suffering Edith Lieblang to put up the money for his latest money-making scheme: window cleaning. He now had the distinction of having two criminal records, one under the name of Fischer, the other as Kujau. As Kujau he was actually supposed to be in jail, serving time under an old suspended sentence. The company therefore had to be registered in Edith's name as the Lieblang Cleaning Company, with the slogan, 'Guaranteed Clean as a Housewife'. Although the firm eventually picked up contracts from a large Stuttgart department store, a chain of fast-food restaurants and South German Television, Kujau and Lieblang initially did not make much money from the business. For seven years they could not afford to buy a flat together and continued to live apart, Edith working part time as a textile worker and as a waitress in a coffee shop.

In March 1968 the police carried out a routine check at the Pension Eisele, Kujau's lodgings in Alfdorferstrasse. Kujau was registered as a cook and waiter named Peter Fischer from Guerlitz. He told the police that he was a resident of Berlin and gave them his uncle's address. Unfortunately he was carrying papers which gave a different name (Konrad Fischer), a different address (Stuttgart) and a different date of birth. He was arrested. At the police station he gave a third version of events. His name, he said, was Peter Konrad Fischer, of no fixed address. He had given a false name because he was in fact a deserter from the East German army: he had escaped to the West in 1963 after training as a lieutenant in chemical welfare at the Rosa Luxemburg officer academy. A few hours later, he changed his story again: now he had come to West Germany immediately after leaving school in order to evade military service. He confused his interrogators in Stuttgart as he was subsequently to confuse journalists and the

Hamburg police in 1983, by appearing to give precise details which only hours of investigation would later establish to be false – in this case that he had entered West Germany using a friend's passport made out in the name of Harald Fuchs. Finally, his fingerprints proved that he was none of the people he said he was: he was the same old Konrad Kujau, conman and petty thief, who was wanted for evading a suspended jail sentence. Still protesting his innocence, he was taken away to Stuttgart's Stanheim Prison.

In the late 1960s, following Kujau's release from Stanheim Prison, the Lieblang Cleaning Company began to flourish. By 1971 it had half a dozen employees and was making an annual profit of 124,000 marks. Kujau and Edith bought a flat together in Schmieden, near Stuttgart, and Edith became Conny's common law wife. In 1970, the couple returned to East Germany for a visit to Loebau. Kujau now had a new idea for making money, one which was far more in tune with his private interests than cleaning people's windows. Since childhood he had been obsessed with militaria – guns, medals, uniforms – especially from the Nazi era. There was a flourishing demand for such objects in the West, and in the East, in the attics and junk shops of communist Germany, there was a ready supply. They were also cheap: on the black market, the western deutschmark was worth five of its eastern counterpart. Through his relatives in Loebau, Kujau let it be known that he was interested in buying military memorabilia for hard cash. Carefully worded advertisements were placed by his family on his behalf in East German newspapers: 'Wanted, for purposes of research – old toys, helmets, jugs, pipes, dolls, etc.' Kujau claimed to have been 'swamped' with relics as a result. It was an illegal trade. The East German government had introduced legislation to protect the state's 'cultural heritage', forbidding the unlicensed export of objects made before

1945. Kujau and Lieblang had to smuggle their merchandise over the frontier. Normally, the border guards did not bother to search them. It was not until 1979 that Kujau was stopped trying to carry out a sabre; Lieblang was also caught on one run and had her consignment confiscated.

Kujau at this time cut a curious figure, simultaneously comic and sinister. He was only in his thirties but his thinning hair, bulging waistline and old-fashioned clothes made him look much older. He loved weapons of all kinds. Guns and swords brought back from East Germany decorated the walls of his house. According to his employers, he frequently wore a pistol which, after an evening's consumption of his favourite drink of vodka and orange, he would fire into the air at random. Mostly he would shoot off a few rounds in a field by the Schmieden railway station, but he had been known to take potshots at bottles in his favourite bar. On 13 February 1973 he lay in wait outside the Balzac night club in Stuttgart for a man who had allegedly been slashing the tyres of vans belonging to the cleaning company. At 4 a.m., roaring drunk, he leapt out brandishing a loaded machine-gun. The man ran off. In the darkness and confusion, Kujau blundered into a doorway where he came face to face with a prostitute. The woman screamed. The owner of the night club and a waiter heard the commotion, overpowered Kujau and summoned the police. He told them his name was Lieblang. When the police raided his flat they found a machine-gun, a double-barrelled shotgun, three air pistols, three rifles and two revolvers. He confessed to having given a false name, apologized for being drunk and was let off with a fine.

By 1974, Kujau's militaria was taking up most of the couple's home and Edith's attitude became threatening. According to Kujau she told him: 'Either that goes out of the window or we separate.' Kujau then began renting the shop in Aspergstrasse, filling its fifty square metres of floor space with his collection. It became the venue for long drinking sessions at which Kujau would entertain some of his friends: collectors with strong heads and simple minds like the local policeman, Ulli Blaschke, who is occasionally supposed to have acted as Kujau's bodyguard; the post office official, Siegmund Schaich, a collector of military drinking jugs; and Alfons Drittenthaler, a blacksmith from the nearby town of Burlafingen. 'The President of Police came several times,' boasted Kujau. 'Sometimes a prostitute would sit next to the State Prosecutor. It would go on until late at night.' Another regular visitor was Wolfgang Schulze, a resident of Miami, who was Kujau's agent in the United States, dealing on his behalf with the extensive network of American collectors.

Business was conducted both by barter and by cash. Drittenthaler, for example, gave Kujau a nineteenth-century grenadier's helmet in exchange for 3000 marks and a reservist's beer mug; on another occasion, in a straight swap, he obtained a set of mugs from Kujau in return for three uniforms. Drittenthaler described Kujau's collection as 'very large and valuable'. It included an almost complete set of Third Reich decorations, 150 helmets, 50 uniforms, 30 flags and, according to Kujau, the largest collection of military jugs in West Germany. 'He told me that the majority of his things came from East Germany,' said Drittenthaler. 'He said that he had a brother there who was a general.' Using this flourishing business as a cover, Kujau was now able to exploit to the full what he had discovered to be his greatest and must lucrative skill: forgery.

By his own account, Kujau first discovered his latent artistic talent at the age of five when his next door neighbour in Loebau, a 'Professor Linder', taught him how to draw. From childhood, painting was his main hobby. In Stuttgart, in the early 1960s, he began to sell a few canvases. He discovered that there was an especially large market for pictures depicting battle scenes; he claims to have painted his first in 1962: 'They were simply torn out of my hands.' He developed a technique of putting his customers into the centre of famous scenes – one client was painted sitting in a staff car next to Field Marshal Rommel – and these paintings, according to him, could fetch as much as 2000 marks, 'a lot of money in those days'. It was in 1963 that Kujau applied his talent to copying out luncheon vouchers, his first known act of forgery. How he graduated from this to larger frauds is unclear. At his trial in 1984 he told a typically colourful story of how his talent was first spotted by the legendary Nazi intelligence officer and head of the West German secret service, Reinhard Gehlen. Kujau claimed that Gehlen gave him forty pages of handwriting and signatures to copy out in 1970 and thereafter hired him to do a number of freelance jobs. Gehlen is dead and the story impossible to check – which no doubt explains why Kujau told it.

What *is* clear is that in the 1970s Kujau began introducing forgeries into the genuine material he was smuggling out of East Germany. The Hamburg police later filled two rooms at their headquarters with examples of his handiwork. To an authentic First World War helmet he attached a faked note, supposedly signed by Rudolf Hess, stating that it had been worn by Hitler in 1917. To an ancient jacket, waistcoat and top hat he added an 'authentication' stating that it was the dress suit Hitler wore to the opening of the Reichstag in 1933. 'When I had completed a piece,' bragged Kujau after his arrest in 1983, 'I framed it and hung it on the wall. People went crazy about them.' He passed off a Knight's Cross, one of Nazi Germany's highest decorations, as having once belonged to Field Marshal Keitel. He could execute a passable imitation of the handwriting of Bormann, Hess, Alfred Rosenberg, Keitel, Goering, Goebbels and Himmler. The forgeries themselves were invariably crude. Kujau used modern paper. He created headed stationery simply by using Letraset. He aged documents by pouring tea over them. But he guessed, rightly, that his customers would never take them to experts to check. Public display of Nazi memorabilia was illegal and collections were generally kept, a guilty secret, behind locked doors.

At some stage, Kujau even executed an outstandingly clumsy forgery of the agreement signed by Hitler and Chamberlain at Munich. Spelling and grammar were not Kujau's strong suits, even in German; when, as in this case, he tried to forge something in English, the results were farcical:

> We regard the areement signet last night and the Anglo-German Naval Agreement as symbolic of the desire of our two peoples never to go to war with one another againe.
>
> We are resolved that method of consultation shall be the method adopted to deal with any other questions that may concern our two countries, and we are determined to continue our efforts to remove possible sources of difference and thus to contribute to assure the peace of Europe.

When it came to Hitler, Kujau had even more opportunities for forgery: not only could he copy Hitler's handwriting, he could also forge his paintings.

In 1960, the Marquess of Bath had paid £600 for two Hitler watercolours auctioned at Sotheby's: *The Parliament and Ringstrasse, Vienna* and *A View of the Karlskirche, Vienna*. It was the first step on the way to accumulating what eventually would be the world's largest private collection of Hitler's art. By 1971 he had forty-eight paintings in his 'Hitler Room' at Longleat; by 1983 he had sixty. Lord Bath acquired the pictures for posterity and confessed to a certain 'admiration' for the Nazi leader: 'Hitler did a hell of a lot for his country,' he explained. Other collectors followed Bath's example. Billy F. Price, owner of Price Compressors of Houston, Texas, built up a private exhibition of twenty-four paintings, housed behind bullet-proof glass in his company's boardroom. The cost of the paintings escalated as the demand grew. By the mid-1970s they were fetching over £5000 (15,000 marks) apiece.

The paintings' sole attraction was that they were by Hitler; their intrinsic merit was negligible. Hitler took a layman's view of modern art: Impressionists, Expressionists, Cubists and Dadaists were 'scribblers, canvas scrawlers, mental defectives or cultural Neanderthals'; once in power, he banned their work. (When someone demonstrated to him that one of the outlawed painters, Franz Marc, was capable of producing 'traditional' pictures, Hitler was genuinely puzzled. 'He could even draw properly,' he commented, 'so why didn't he do it?') Hitler himself was a painter of such meagre talent that he rarely attempted to depict human beings; he confined himself to stilted pictures of buildings and landscapes. Even to Kujau, a painter of limited ability, their technical poverty made them easy to copy. The other advantage, for a potential forger, was the scale of the Führer's output. Whatever Hitler lacked in artistic merit he made up for in industry. He is estimated to have produced between 2000 and 3000 drawings, sketches, watercolours and oils.

Kujau was not far behind, turning out fakes literally by the hundred. He added to their plausibility using his favourite trick of attaching a forged letter or certificate confirming their authenticity. On the back of a large painting of German infantrymen in Flanders in 1918 Kujau wrote, in Hitler's handwriting: 'I painted this picture in memory of the comrades who fell in the field.' Next to this he pasted a note supposedly signed by a Nazi official: 'This work was created by the Führer and Reichschancellor Adolf Hitler in the year 1934.' Close inspection of the painting reveals Lance-Corporal Adolf Hitler standing in the midst of the battle clutching a hand grenade. Another of Kujau's efforts, *Nude on Green Background*, was passed off as a painting by Hitler of his niece, Geli Raubel. 'Picture remains in flat. Adolf Hitler,' reads a scrawled note. 'Geli sat as a model for this for over twenty days.' Kujau earned tens of thousands of marks for such forgeries. He did not even have to go looking for customers: furtive, wealthy, and eager to believe, they came looking for him.

TEN

Fritz Stiefel, forty-seven years old, owner of a flourishing engineering works, first noticed Kujau's shop in Aspergstrasse in 1975 as he was driving past it. The windows were full of military memorabilia. Stiefel was a collector himself. He pulled up outside and rang the bell. The shop was deserted. He came twice more but on each occasion there was nobody there. Then one day he happened to be passing when a small, fat man appeared outside cleaning the windows. 'I spoke to him,' recalled Stiefel. 'He introduced himself to me as Fischer.' He was taken inside and shown around the Aspergstrasse collection. He bought a Nazi decoration for 650 marks. Before long, seduced by Kujau's patter, he had become the shop's best customer.

Stiefel collected militaria of all types, but his specialist interest was in documents and autographed photographs. He was amazed by Herr Fischer's ability to produce these. 'I assumed that he must have really good connections. He certainly gave me that impression. He told me often of his journeys to East Germany. He said he had relatives there.' Stiefel's gullibility was matched only by his willingness to spend money. Kujau could scarcely believe his luck. 'He always got excited when he saw something new,' he said later. 'If I'd told him I'd got Hitler's underpants he'd have got equally worked up.' In six years, according to the Hamburg state prosecutor, Stiefel spent approximately 250,000 marks in Kujau's shop. He bought 160 drawings, oil paintings and watercolours supposedly by Hitler, along with eighty handwritten poems, speech notes, letters and manuscripts. Stiefel's obsession led him into fraud. He transferred 180,000 marks from his company's accounts to the Lieblang Cleaning Company, allegedly to meet 'cleaning costs' but actually to pay for Hitler memorabilia. As a result, he was eventually forced to repay over 120,000 marks to the German tax authorities.

In return for this outlay, Stiefel acquired one of the largest collections of fakes in West Germany. His 'Hitler' pictures ranged from a design for Hitler's parents' tomb, dated 1907, to a portrait of Eva Braun at the age of twenty-four. Some of the paintings were drawn from Kujau's fervid imagination (for example, a series of cartoons purportedly drawn by Hitler for his regimental newspaper in 1916); others were copies of existing works. One female nude executed in chalk signed 'Adolf Hitler' and dated 1933 was a copy of a drawing by Erhard Amadeus Dier. Another, entitled *Female Nude, Chubby, Fraulein E. Braun* was a poor imitation of Julius Engelhard's *Bathing in the Bergsee*: when Kujau persuaded Stiefel to buy it, he actually showed him a copy of the Engelhard painting and, with characteristic cheek, accused *Hitler* of plagiarism. Kujau also sold Stiefel a leather box, lined with silk, which he had bought at Stuttgart railway station, containing 233 handwritten pages of the 'original manuscript' of *Mein Kampf*. Kujau had simply copied it, verbatim, from the published book. On the title page he wrote, also in Hitler's hand: '*The Struggle of the Times*, or *The Struggle* or *My Struggle*. Which title impresses more? Adolf Hitler.'

Kujau subsequently claimed that he copied out the *Mein Kampf* manuscript as a means of practising Hitler's handwriting and there can be no question but that he became extraordinarily proficient at it. He slipped in and out of other people's handwriting as he did his various pseudonyms and biographies, with complete ease. It is difficult to say with precision when he first hit on the idea of writing a Hitler diary. Kujau's American agent, Wolfgang Schulze, told Gitta Sereny of the *Sunday Times* that he handled 'unbound' sheets of Hitler writing supplied by his client as early as 1976. According to Kujau it was in 1978 that he sat down and began typing out a chronology of Hitler's daily life, using an official Nazi Party yearbook for 1935. Having done that he decided to see how it would look in Hitler's handwriting.

In the cellar of his and Edith's new home in Ditzingen were some school notebooks, bought for a few marks in a shop in East Berlin. Kujau had originally intended using them to keep a catalogue of his collection. Now he took one out, dipped his pen in a pot of black ink, and started to write. When the ink ran out, he switched to a pencil. 'It was easy,' he said later. As a finishing touch, he stuck some imitation metal initials in gothic script on the cover. The initials were bought by Kujau in a department store, were made of plastic in Hong Kong, and were in fact 'FH', not 'AH' as Kujau had thought. It was, like all his forgeries, slipshod and homemade. It would not have withstood an hour's expert examination.

Two weeks later, during one of Fritz Stiefel's regular visits to Aspergstrasse, Kujau brought out the book and laid it on the table in front of him. '*That*,' he told him, 'is a Hitler diary.'

Stiefel examined it carefully. 'He was not so much fascinated by the contents,' said Kujau, 'as by the initials I'd stuck on the front of it.' He asked if he could borrow it and Kujau agreed. 'I took it home with me and read through it,' recalled Stiefel. He then locked the book away in his safe with the rest of his faked Hitler manuscripts.

At around the same time that he received the diary from Kujau, Stiefel decided that the time had come when he should seek an expert's opinion on his remarkable Hitler archive. He asked Kleenau, a firm of Munich auctioneers who handled important manuscripts, if they could recommend an authority on Hitler's art and writing. Kleenau gave him the name of August Priesack.

'Professor' Priesack, as he styled himself, had been employed by the Nazi Party between 1935 and 1939 to track down Hitler's paintings. His task was to buy up as many as possible and sort out the genuine Hitlers from the fakes which, even then, were polluting the market. For Priesack, as for so many of the 'Keepers of the Flame', those years in the sun before the war, when he was young and enjoying the patronage of the Führer, represented the best time of his life. He had piles of yellowing press cuttings and photographs from the Third Reich, his private archive, stored in his cluttered Munich apartment. He was seventy-six years old, a former secondary school teacher, listed in the Munich police records as a well-known sympathizer with the ideals of the Hitler era. He was working on a book of previously unpublished pictures of the Nazi Party rallies. He had also been hired by the American millionaire Billy Price who was compiling a complete catalogue of Hitler's art. Stiefel invited Priesack to visit him in Stuttgart and evaluate his own collection.

For Kujau, this was a decisive moment. Hitherto he had had to fool only amateur enthusiasts. Now his work was to be judged by a supposed expert. In May 1978 he had signed an agreement with Stiefel guaranteeing that everything he had sold him to date and might sell him in the future was 'original' and 'contemporary'. Under the terms of the contract, if anything turned out to be fake, Kujau had to give Stiefel a complete refund. A great deal therefore depended upon Priesack's verdict. He need not have worried. The old man took one look at Stiefel's collection and declared it to be of 'great historical significance'. He pointed to a watercolour. 'I last held that in my hands in 1936,' he told Stiefel and Kujau. 'It was then,' said Kujau later, 'that I knew what kind of an expert *he* was. I had only finished that painting ten days before.'

Priesack was sufficiently impressed to contact one of Germany's leading authorities on Hitler: Eberhard Jaeckel, Professor of Modern History at the University of Stuttgart. Jaeckel, the author of *Hitler's Weltanschauung, A Blueprint for Power*, had been engaged for some years in the compilation of a complete collection of Hitler's writings from 1905 to 1924. Priesack had passed on to him some material from his own archive in 1974 (subsequently dismissed by Jaeckel as 'a few pieces of paper, copies, without any value'). Now he urged the historian to meet with Stiefel and his astonishingly well-connected supplier, Herr Fischer. Jaeckel, aware that important Hitler documents were in the hands of a number of private collectors, agreed. An appointment was arranged for Friday, 21 September 1979.

Priesack arrived at Stiefel's house before Kujau and Jaeckel. For the first time the industrialist opened his safe and showed him the Hitler diary. Priesack spent an hour reading through it. He was hugely impressed by the existence of such a book, although he had to confess to a certain disappointment in its contents. (Kujau had filled it almost entirely with lists of appointments and proclamations lifted out of the Nazi yearbook.) He made a few notes. 'I can only remember one page which I copied,' recalled Priesack. 'The others were really for the most part just headlines from the *Völkischer Beobachter* [the Nazi Party newspaper].' The fullest entry, the one written down by Priesack, was for 30 June 1935:

> The explosion catastrophe in Reinsdorf is all I needed. One ray of hope today was the dedication ceremony of the House of German Art in Munich.

But at any rate I can relax a bit with the architects. E. [Eva Braun] now has two little puppies so time does not lie too heavily on her hands.

Must have a word with E. about Goering, too. His attitude towards her just isn't correct.

All quiet on the health front.

Despite the triviality of the content, Priesack had no doubts that the book was genuine. When Kujau arrived he paid him an emotional tribute. 'You are our salvation,' he told the former waiter and window cleaner. 'You must find more documents. History will thank you.'

Jaeckel was also impressed by Stiefel's collection as the industrialist laid it out before him. 'There were drawings, paintings and documents signed by Hitler,' he remembered. He was handed the diary and 'leafed through it quickly'.

I remember a place where Eva Braun and a dog were mentioned. As far as I recall, only the right-hand pages were written in ink and signed by Hitler. . . . I was told it came from East Germany and had been kept there since 1945. The question of how it was brought to the West was not answered – I was told it could be dangerous to the people who'd brought it out. It was also suggested to me that there was a senior official involved in East Germany called Fischer.

Kujau watched Jaeckel going through the book. There was a discussion about how many more diaries there might be. Kujau said that he understood from his sources in East Germany that the diaries spanned thirteen years, from 1932 to 1945. Priesack cut in: assuming that each of the missing books also covered six months, there would be twenty-seven books in total. Jaeckel urged Stiefel to try to obtain them. Kujau claimed later to have sat and listened to all this 'in amazement'.

Jaeckel's particular interest was in material up to the year 1924. Stiefel had plenty to show him, including some previously undiscovered poems by Hitler written during the First World War. These included 'It was in a thicket of the Artois Forest', an illustrated ballad, and 'An Idyll in the War', a work in four verses in which 'Hitler' described how a German soldier delivered a Frenchwoman's baby:

As the medical orderly Gottlieb Krause heard as he came through
    Arras,
The sudden dull cry of a woman from the closest house:
I must help! was his thought, even a German in the field remains
    helpful,
And a newborn baby Frenchman arrived in the world with Gottlieb
    Krause's help.

And with his typical great care he looked after the child,
Washed it, cared for it, to show we're not barbarians
And held the babe with pleasure in front of his comrades;
This little worm knows nothing of Iswolski and Delcassé's intrigues!

Milk was rare and needed in a hurry; in the meadow grazed a cow,
And two soldiers from the next troop commandeered her at once,
And milked her! It ran in spurts and in rich amounts,
Shrapnel fell close by but didn't stop the work.

Right afterwards, he gave the bottle to the child he had delivered,
And pulled two zwieback out of his pocket for the mother
An idyll proving once again the German's noble creed,
If the Limeys haven't destroyed it, the house is still there.

Each verse had an accompanying illustration: the soldier tending the mother and her baby; the soldier showing the baby to a comrade; the soldier milking a cow; the soldier saying goodbye to the Frenchwoman with the child in her arms. Jaeckel saw no reason to believe it was not genuine. Attached to it and to most of the other pieces in Stiefel's collection was an 'authentication' on official Nazi Party stationery. The following year, Jaeckel reprinted 'An Idyll in the War' in his book of Hitler's early writings, along with *seventy-five* other forgeries produced by Kujau.

At the end of this productive meeting, Jaeckel gave Kujau a lift back into Stuttgart. The 'antiques dealer' had scarcely opened his mouth all afternoon. He struck the historian as 'reserved' and 'uneducated'. Jaeckel told him that if he could discover any more volumes of Hitler's diaries, he would very much like to edit them.

Kujau was by now leading a life of bewildering complexity. He was running the shop in Aspergstrasse. He was organizing the illegal export of memorabilia from East Germany. He was forging documents and paintings. He was still nominally in charge of the Lieblang Cleaning Company. He was answering to at least two different names. And as if this was not enough, he had now begun deceiving Edith by taking a full-time mistress.

Kujau's corpulent figure had long been familiar to the working girls of Stuttgart's red-light district where he was universally known as 'The General'. His favourite haunts were the Pigalle night club and the Sissy Bar. Using the money he was making from Nazi memorabilia, he entertained lavishly. The girl he was with was always well paid; the others were regularly bought bottles of champagne. In March 1975 he met Maria Modritsch, a twenty-five-year-old Austrian girl who was serving drinks in the Sissy Bar. She had left school at fifteen to work in a factory, come looking for work in West Germany and ended up as a bar girl. She was thin, quiet and of homely appearance. Kujau took a liking to her and they began what Maria primly called an 'intimate relationship'. She gave up work in the Sissy Bar and in May 1978, he set her up in an apartment in Rotenbergstrasse where she lived alone with her pet rabbit, Caesar. Kujau had a key, kept some clothes in the flat, and provided Maria with a monthly allowance of between 1000 and 2000 marks. 'Conny gave me a loan for the furniture,' said Maria. 'He had more money than I did and he spoiled me. He visited me almost every day. We would go out together. Then he would go back to his own flat. From time to time he'd stay overnight. As far as I'm aware, Edith didn't know about my existence.' Kujau told Maria he was married to Edith. 'It was not until later,' said Maria, 'that I learned he only lived with her.' She helped out in the shop occasionally and was under the impression that her lover was some sort of painter.

Three weeks after the meeting with Jaeckel and Priesack, on 15 October, Kujau and Maria went out for a drink. After some schnapps in the Korne Inn they moved on to the Melodie Bar. Shortly before midnight, a group of immigrant workers, Yugoslavs, burst into the bar brandishing guns. While most of the clientele threw themselves to the floor, Kujau, in a fit of drunken bravado, leapt to his feet and attacked them. In the ensuing struggle he was struck on the head and had to be taken to hospital with blood streaming from a three-inch gash in his forehead. He was interviewed by the police and once again could not resist spinning them a story. He was 'Dr Heinz Fischer', Maria was his secretary, he worked for the Baden-Wuerttemberg authorities. When this was checked and found to be false, he lied again. He was 'Dr Konrad Kujau', until last year a colonel in the West German army, and soon to become a professor. The police searched a briefcase he had with him and found artists' materials, an air pistol and a photograph of himself posing in the full dress uniform of a general. Kujau said that he had bought the pistol at an auction. He confided to the policeman interviewing him that it had once belonged to Field Marshal Rommel. The policeman told his colleagues that Kujau was either mentally unstable or a military fanatic.

This curious episode was not over yet. Less than a week later, Kujau was invited to return to the police station to explain why he was going around falsely claiming to have a doctorate. Charges were laid against him for misrepresentation. Even the most blatant confidence trickster would by now have given up, but Kujau swore that he was the author of eleven books on Nazi Germany, including *Adolf Hitler the Painter*, *Adolf Hitler the Frontline Soldier*, *Adolf Hitler the Officer*, and a five-volume study, *Adolf Hitler the Politician* – all published by the Ullstein company in Munich. He declared that as a result of his work he had been invited all over the world to lecture on the Nazis; he possessed not merely one but three doctorates, awarded to him by the universities of Tokyo, Pretoria and Miami. The incredulous police asked him for proof of these honours.

> The documents [stated Kujau] are at home, but my office is currently being renovated and everything is packed in cartons. These documents are also in the cartons and therefore I cannot show them to you at the moment. I shall have them photo-copied and sent to you as soon as the renovation work is finished. I should mention that although I received my award from the University of Tokyo in 1977, the date on the document is 1952. This is because in Tokyo the year 1952 corresponds to our 1977.

The police waited but the documents never materialized. The following July, Kujau was fined 800 marks for the misuse of titles. He described his occupation in court for the first time as 'painter'.

On 20 October 1979, five days after the fight in the Melodie Bar, ignorant of his supplier's difficulties with the police, Fritz

Stiefel invited Kujau and Edith to his house for a party. The celebration was supposed to be in honour of the birthday of Frau Senta Baur, wife of Hans Baur, but at the last moment Frau Baur was unable to attend. As a result there were only six guests: the Stiefels, Kujau and Edith, and the former SS man Jakob Tiefenthaeler and his wife.

It was a convivial evening. Stiefel had known Tiefenthaeler as a fellow collector for several years; Kujau had been introduced to Tiefenthaeler as 'Herr Fischer' by Stiefel over dinner the previous March, although on that occasion, said Tiefenthaeler, Kujau 'had kept very much in the background'. This evening was different: the drink flowed, and as the number of empty bottles steadily mounted, so did Kujau's loquacity. 'He said that he was a businessman,' recalled Tiefenthaeler.

> Then later he explained that he had an antiques shop in Stuttgart. He told me that he didn't have any employees there, that he was often away travelling, that for much of the time the place was shut. He also boasted that evening of his good contacts in East Germany. In this connection he told us that his brother was a general in the East German border service: he had a great deal of authority but that wouldn't exempt him from punishment if he was found to be involved in something illegal.

After a few more glasses, Kujau began talking about the Hitler diaries. According to Tiefenthaeler he boasted that 'he could bring to the West diaries which had been on board one of the Führer's planes' which had crashed in East Germany at the end of the war.

> These diaries had been hidden in a safe place by local peasants. He said there were 27 volumes, but he could only bring them out to the West one at a time. They had to come out at invervals of between one and two months: more journeys than that would be suspicious.

Tiefenthaeler, whose own Third Reich collection was largely built around autographs and pictures, was fascinated.

This is the first occasion on which Kujau is reported to have used the plane crash to explain the provenance of the diaries. When he had given the first diary to Stiefel sixteen months earlier he had merely said that he had 'got it from East Germany' along with his other militaria. At the meeting with Jaeckel only four weeks earlier he had been equally vague. This suggests that at some point in the period 21 September to 20 October, Kujau discovered the story of the crash.

According to Stiefel, he and Kujau had visited Hans Baur at his home in Herrsching some time around September 1979. Priesack had also been there. 'It was in the evening,' said Baur, 'and my wife and I went with them to have dinner in a neighbouring village.' Baur subsequently claimed to have no recollection of discussing the loss of Gundlfinger's plane, but the coincidence of this meeting with Kujau's adoption of the story suggests otherwise. Stiefel admitted to the police that he had certainly heard an account of the crash from Baur himself. Kujau, on the other hand, alleged he had first learned of it from August Priesack, and Priesack, who knew of the crash from Baur's book, afterwards admitted that he could have been the one who first put the idea in Kujau's mind. Whichever version is the truth – and it should be remembered that in Baur's book the whole episode had been available in outline to anyone who was interested since 1955 – this was the decisive moment in the evolution of the fraud. Suddenly to produce a Hitler diary and claim it had been smuggled out of East Germany might be enough to satisfy collectors as gullible as Stiefel. To produce that diary and also to be able to point to Hitler's distress at the loss of valuable documents in a mysterious air crash – that suddenly made the story seem much more plausible.

At the end of the evening's festivities, Stiefel put his guests up for the night. The following day was a Sunday. After breakfast the industrialist unlocked the metal door to his collection and showed Tiefenthaeler the diary. A few weeks later, Tiefenthaeler told Gerd Heidemann what he had seen and at the beginning of 1980, Heidemann himself visited Stiefel, saw the diary and heard the story of the crashed Junkers 352.

What gives Kujau's fraud from this point onwards a touch of real genius is that having made the connection between the wrecked transport plane and the diaries, he left it to others to research the background. Never did the victim of a hoax work more assiduously towards his own entrapment than Gerd Heidemann. While Kujau shuttled between his two mistresses and tended his shop in Stuttgart, it was the reporter in Hamburg who worked long hours and even risked dismissal to make the story of the diaries credible. For Heidemann, each step in his attempts to prove that the diary he had seen at Stiefel's could be genuine represented an additional investment of time and effort. It is not surprising that by the end he *wanted* to believe in the existence of the diaries so desperately: by then he had put more work into them than Kujau. It took him a year, but gradually, in 1980, the two men's paths began to converge.

Stiefel still kept the 1935 diary in his safe, but his importance in the affair now lessened. He disapproved of *Stern*'s left-wing reputation and refused to help Heidemann by revealing the identity of the diary's supplier. Tiefenthaeler, who had already acted as Heidemann's agent in his attempts to sell *Carin II*, now supplanted him. His motive was almost certainly financial. He admitted that Heidemann told him it would 'not do him any harm' to help *Stern* find the diaries; in 1983 Kujau referred to him, with a laugh, as 'Mr Ten Percent'. It was in the summer of 1980 that Tiefenthaeler told

Heidemann that the diary had been brought into the West by a Herr Fischer of Stuttgart. Heidemann and Walde had then spent hours trawling through the local telephone book. (The reason they never found him was that the Kujaus' home in Ditzingen was listed in the directory under Edith's surname, Lieblang.) A few months later, after their return from Boernersdorf in November, the *Stern* men had renewed their contact with Tiefenthaeler and asked him to transmit an offer to 'Herr Fischer' on their behalf. Tiefenthaeler did so in a letter to Kujau dated 29 November 1980:

Dear Conny,

I've got something to tell you which I don't think we should discuss on the telephone because you never know if the line is bugged or not. I assume that you'll be absolutely quiet about this matter and that you won't talk to anyone about it.

A large Hamburg publishing company has come to me with a request that I should establish contact between you and them. It's about the diaries of A.H. which you have or could obtain. I was quoted an offer of 2 million marks which would be paid [for the diaries]. In addition, these gentlemen were not so much interested in possessing the diaries as in taking photocopies. The diaries could stay, as before, in your possession. Should you indicate that you are interested in making contact, this would be done as quickly as possible. The whole thing would, of course, be handled in strict confidence and silence on both sides is a precondition. Should you prefer gold to currency, there would be an unlimited amount.

I would be very grateful if you could let me know as soon as possible what you decide – but please, not on the telephone.

Perhaps I should also mention that the wealthy company would take any risk entailed in publication as well as any legal consequences which publication might entail. The source of these volumes would never be named – in the case of a legal battle (the Federal Government versus the publishing company) the company would plead press confidentiality.

I have been officially assured of all these things and they are ready to conclude a contract with you in which all parties would be legally secure. Perhaps you would also allow me to point out, my dear Conny, that none of these gentlemen has been given your name by me. They know that a Herr Fischer is the key to these volumes, but they know neither your first name nor your address and they will not discover them from me, lest you take a negative view of this project. . . .

Please don't even mention this to Fritz [Stiefel].

Kujau was already wealthier than he had ever been, thanks to his activities as a forger. But considering that two million marks represented almost *ten times* the amount he was to make from his best customer, Fritz Stiefel, it is scarcely surprising that he succumbed to this offer. Even if this 'wealthy company' discovered that he was passing on fakes, he stood an excellent chance of getting away with something. His anonymity was guaranteed. If anything went wrong he could always fall back on the excuse that he was merely handling material which originated behind the Iron Curtain. Thus it was that at the beginning of 1981 he gave Tiefenthaeler permission to divulge his telephone number and his address in Aspergstrasse.

On 15 January a man calling himself Gerd Heidemann telephoned him in Ditzingen. They discussed the diaries. Kujau repeatedly stressed that he had to have a guarantee of absolute secrecy and that he would deal only with Heidemann personally. True to his past form he also embroidered the story, promising the reporter not simply diaries but a genuine Hitler opera and a third volume of *Mein Kampf*. Kujau knew that the more improbable his inventions sounded, the more likely people were to believe that he could not possibly be lying. He knew what he was doing. He knew Heidemann's type. He recognized beneath the affected calm the note of longing that signified the suspension of disbelief. It was all too easy.

Sure enough, on Wednesday 28 January, at about 7.15 in the evening, the telephone rang again. Kujau had a brief conversation, then turned to Edith. 'That was Heidemann,' he told her. 'He's on his way over.' Within five minutes he was opening the door to his latest, eager, moon-faced victim, who clutched in his hand a suitcase full of money.

PART THREE

'Swastikas sell – and they sell better and better.'
SIDNEY MAYER, publisher

ELEVEN

This first encounter between Kujau and Heidemann lasted for more than seven hours. To begin with, Heidemann later testified, Kujau appeared reluctant to agree to a deal. He told the reporter that he had already had an offer of $2 million for the diaries from America and that the Hearst newspaper group was considering serializing them. According to Edith Lieblang, Heidemann then opened up the suitcase and displayed 'a huge amount of money'. He offered it to Kujau as a down payment for the diaries. He repeated that his company was willing to pay 2 million marks for all the volumes. As an added inducement, Heidemann also produced the Goering uniform, which appears to have excited Kujau even more than the money. 'I had to have it,' he said later. 'I had all the other uniforms – Hitler's, Himmler's, Rommel's. My one thought was: "How do I get this uniform off this man?"' Kujau, according to Lieblang, promised the reporter 'that he could provide the diaries'.

After that, the atmosphere relaxed somewhat. Heidemann, whisky in hand, boasted of his contacts with famous Nazis like Karl Wolff and Klaus Barbie. He described how he had tracked down the crash site in Boernersdorf. He then started recounting his experiences as a war correspondent. By about midnight Edith was beginning to fall asleep. She went off to bed. But Heidemann and Kujau stayed up talking until almost 3 a.m., when the reporter at last left to drive back to his hotel in Stuttgart.

After snatching a few hours' sleep, at 10 a.m. he was back with Kujau again, this time in the Aspergstrasse shop. His main concern was the diary held by Fritz Stiefel. He was worried that word of its existence would leak out to a rival newspaper. According to Edith, he was 'insistent' that they should go and retrieve it. Kujau, who was worried about souring his relations with Stiefel, managed to put him off by telling him that the industrialist was on holiday in Italy. Heidemann was anxious to conclude at least some sort of legal agreement with Kujau before he left. He suggested that he should make contact with Kujau's lawyer and arrange for him to come to Hamburg to sign an agreement with the Gruner and Jahr legal department – an offer which Kujau hastily declined. Instead, the two men parted with a tentative verbal understanding. Kujau would deliver the books, Heidemann the money. He would call the reporter when he heard from his brother in the East. As a gesture of good faith, they swapped gifts. Heidemann left his genuine Goering uniform behind and returned to Hamburg bearing a faked Hitler oil painting. The relationship had started on an appropriate note.

At 11.30 the following morning, in *Stern*'s elegant riverfront headquarters – known, irreverently, around Hamburg as 'the monkey cliff' – Heidemann went in to see Wilfried Sorge to report on the outcome of his trip to Stuttgart. The supplier of the diaries, he told Sorge, was a 'wealthy collector' of Nazi memorabilia whose brother was a general in East Germany. Some of Hitler's diaries were already in the West. Initially they had come over the border in ordinary travel luggage. Now they were being smuggled across hidden inside pianos (pianos being one of East Germany's main exports to the West). The general would at once cease supplying the diaries if he thought they were for publication in *Stern*. Heidemann was therefore posing as a Swiss collector. He repeated: it was imperative that the company maintain absolute secrecy.

*   *   *

In Stuttgart, meanwhile, Konrad Kujau was having to do some explaining to Fritz Stiefel, not about the Hitler diaries, but about the other pieces of so-called Hitler writing he had sold to the collector.

Eberhard Jaeckel and his co-editor, Axel Kuhn, had gone ahead and reprinted material from Stiefel's collection in their book of Hitler's writings from 1905 to 1924. The book had been published the previous autumn. To their embarrassment, Anton Hoch of the Institute of Contemporary History in Munich had pointed out that some of Hitler's 'poetry' was obviously fake. In particular, 'Der Kamerad', a poem supposedly written by Hitler in 1916, was actually lifted straight out of a book of verse entitled *Poems of the Old Comrades* by Herybert Menzel, published in 1936. It might have been possible to argue that Hitler himself had merely copied the poem from some earlier edition of Menzel's work. But unfortunately, as Hoch pointed out, Menzel was only ten years old in 1916. Jaeckel contacted Stiefel to demand an explanation. The outraged Stiefel contacted Kujau.

On 5 February, exactly a week after concluding his agreement with Heidemann, Kujau joined Stiefel and Jaeckel for an emergency meeting in the professor's office in Stuttgart University. What most perturbed him, said Jaeckel, was the fact that 'Der Kamerad' had been accompanied by a letter on official Nazi stationery, signed by a party official, stating that the poem was unquestionably genuine. The fact that 'Der Kamerad' was such an obvious forgery meant that the letter was also probably faked. And similar letters had been attached to dozens of pieces of Hitler writing belonging to Stiefel which Jaeckel had printed in his book. It had to be assumed that they were all forged.

This was a nasty moment for Kujau. According to Jaeckel he 'seemed very unsettled by my doubts'. But he handled the situation adroitly. In view of the aspersions which had been cast, he said, he was prepared to be more specific about the source of the material. He then proceeded, with considerable cheek, to recount to the two men the story of the crashed Hitler plane exactly as it had been described to him for the first time by Heidemann the previous week. Kujau, recalled Jaeckel,

> told me in detail what had only been suggested in general before: that the pieces came from a plane that had crashed near Boernersdorf in 1945 on its way from Berlin to Salzburg. ... To strengthen his case he said that the journalist Gerd Heidemann had seen the graves of the plane's crew in Boernersdorf.

Having used the evidence of one victim in an attempt to soothe the anxieties of another, Kujau then retreated to his customary last line of defence. According to Jaeckel 'he said he couldn't add very much more because he was only the middleman. He didn't really know much about the documents or their historical context.'

There was little more that could be done. Jaeckel had no alternative but to begin preparing an announcement to place in an academic journal admitting that he had been duped. He advised Stiefel in the meantime to submit his material for forensic examination. As for Kujau, he went home to Ditzingen to begin forging the first volume of Hitler diaries for Gerd Heidemann.

To sustain him through his labours over the next two years, Kujau, like any conscientious professional writer, established a regular routine. He would get up at 6 a.m. followed, half an hour later, by Edith Lieblang. The couple would have coffee together and then she would drive off to Stuttgart to her job in the Café Hochland. Kujau would cook himself a heavy breakfast of fried potatoes and two fried eggs and, thus fortified, retire to his studio where he would work right through the day, without even stopping for lunch. When the police raided his premises in 1983 they carried out ten cartons full of books and articles accumulated by Kujau to help him establish Hitler's daily activities. There were 515 books and newspapers in his workroom, 106 additional periodicals in his cellar. Stuffed into them were thousands of bookmarks – playing cards, blotting paper, old bills and tickets, visitors' cards and toilet paper – marking passages required for the concoction of the diaries. Kujau would write out a rough draft in pencil and then transfer it in ink into one of the school notebooks kept in his cellar. His work became more sophisticated with time. To start with, he confined himself to writing about Hitler's early years in power – years full of laws and decrees with which he could fill the Führer's empty days and which did not require much research into complex political issues. In the evening, when Edith returned from work, she would cook them both a meal. 'Conny would lie stretched out on the sofa,' recalled Edith. 'We'd watch television and often he'd fall asleep. I had no idea what he did during the day. We gave one another a lot of space.' This sedentary regime was to last until the spring of 1983.

According to Kujau, he finished the first three volumes about ten days after the meeting with Stiefel and Jaeckel. To dress them up, he stuck a red wax seal in the shape of a German eagle on the covers, together with a label, signed by Rudolf Hess, declaring them to be Hitler's property. He bashed them about for a while to age them, and sprinkled some tea over the pages. He then rang Heidemann to tell him he had the books. Walde said later that these early diaries were not supposed to have come from East Germany 'but from the United States, where "Fischer" had offered them through a lawyer to an interested party'. Kujau flew up from Stuttgart with the diaries to be entertained by Heidemann on board *Carin II*. To celebrate the arrival of the first books, the enthusiastic reporter opened a bottle of sparkling white wine.

Only five men at Gruner and Jahr knew the secret of the diaries' existence. For them, Wednesday 18 February was a memorable day. Shortly before 10 a.m., four of the initiated – Gerd Heidemann, Thomas Walde, Jan Hensmann and Wilfred Sorge – trooped into the office of the fifth, Manfred Fischer. The doors were closed, Fischer instructed his secretary to make sure they were not disturbed, and Heidemann laid the diaries before them.

It appears to have been a moment of almost religious solemnity. Hensmann picked up one of the diaries. It was 'bound in black', he recalled, '1.5 centimetres thick'. Like most of the others, he could not read the old Germanic script in which it was written, but it undoubtedly felt genuine. 'I held it with great care in my hands,' he said later. Manfred Fischer was also impressed by the slightly battered appearance of the books. 'They were a little bit damaged,' he remembered. 'The tops of the pages were bent.' For Fischer, the arrival of these first Hitler diaries was 'a great moment' in his life: 'It was a very special experience to hold such a thing in your hand. The certainty that this diary was written by *him* – and now I have it in my grasp. . . .'

The diaries cast a spell over the room. The intense secrecy of the meeting; the thrill of handling contraband, smuggled at great cost and danger from the site of a wartime aircrash; above all, the presence of Adolf Hitler as contained in this unknown record of his intimate thoughts – all these elements combined to produce a highly charged atmosphere, a mood which in its turn created what Fischer subsequently called 'a sort of group psychosis'. The prospect of possessing something once owned by the Führer affected these cool, modern-minded North German businessmen just as it did the obsessive, ex-Nazi collectors in the South. 'We wanted to have them,' said Fischer of the diaries. 'Even if we'd only believed that there was a 10 per cent chance that they were genuine, we'd still have said, "Get them here."' Of all the figures in history, perhaps only Adolf Hitler could have exercised such an hypnotic fascination.

In this atmosphere, the five men now took a series of decisions which were to have profound consequences. Both Heidemann and Walde urged on the group the importance of maintaining absolute secrecy. If the slightest hint of the existence of the diaries leaked out, they told the three businessmen, the East German general would cease shipping the material. Heidemann, according to Hensmann, went further: 'He didn't merely warn of the need to protect his sources, but of the danger that human life itself might be threatened.' For this reason the two journalists argued strongly against bringing in any experts from outside to examine the diaries until the full set was in the company's possession. 'These reservations', stated Sorge, 'were accepted. They led to the decision to obtain further volumes before authentication tests were carried out.' Not even Henri Nannen and the three editors-in-chief of *Stern* would be told what was going on until all the transactions had been completed; that would probably, said Heidemann, be in mid-May.

All these proposals were accepted. 'It was unanimously agreed,' stated Hensmann, 'that we should continue with the project.'

The five men were now effectively bound together in a conspiracy against *Stern*. Without consulting a handwriting expert, a forensic scientist or an historian, Fischer that day committed the company to the purchase of 27 volumes of Hitler's diaries at a price of 85,000 marks each; plus a sum of 200,000 marks to be paid for the third volume of *Mein Kampf*. The total cost of the project would be 2.5 million marks. As the company's managing director, he signed a document authorizing the immediate transfer of 1 million marks from the company's main account for the obtaining of the diaries.

'We all had a kind of blackout,' he commented afterwards.

For all this talk of mental aberration, the businessmen's behaviour was not totally irrational. As publishers they knew the size of the potential market for any venture connected with the Third Reich. In Britain one publisher, Bison Books, had been built entirely on the strength of the public's fascination with the Nazis. *Hitler's Wartime Picture Magazine* was simply extracts from the Nazi propaganda magazine *Signal* stitched together in a single volume: it sold over a quarter of a million copies in Britain and the United States; between 1976 and 1978 it was reprinted eight times. Another picture book from the same publisher, *Der Führer*, edited by a former SS officer, Herbert Walther, was bought by more than 50,000 people. Bison's flamboyant founder, Sidney Mayer, was quite open about the reason for his success:

> I don't want to end up as Hitler's publisher. I would have thought the public was as sick of it as I am. But they are not. The booksellers always want more. Hitler sells. Nazis sell. Swastikas sell – and they sell better and better. It's the swastika on the cover that gets them. Nobody can out-swastika us. I've even thought of putting one on our vegetable cook book because Hitler was a vegetarian.

On the wall of his office, Mayer hung a large picture of himself with a small Hitler moustache and the caption 'Springtime For Mayer'.

If this was the market for what were basically retreads of material already seen, the marketing possibilities of Adolf Hitler's secret diaries were clearly stupendous. Gruner and

Jahr was well placed to exploit it. The company owned a string of successful West German magazines, including *Stern* and *Geo*. It had outlets in Spain, France and the United States (where it owned *Parents* and *Young Miss*). Gruner and Jahr had a turnover of almost half a billion dollars and controlled a total of twenty periodicals across the world.

Since 1972, three-quarters of the company's shares had been held by the West German multinational, Bertelsmann AG, the country's largest publishing group. Founded in 1835 to produce religious tracts, by 1981 the company had one hundred and eighty subsidiaries operating in twenty-five countries. In America it owned such well-known organizations as Bantam Books and Arista Records. Once this formidable publishing and marketing machine was thrown behind the Hitler diaries, profits could be expected which would easily recoup Fischer's initial investment of 2.5 million marks.

Hitler was going to make everybody rich, no one more so than Gerd Heidemann. Fischer accepted that the reporter had a special claim to the diaries project. He had pursued it in the face of outright opposition from the *Stern* editors. He was the only person with whom the supplier of the diaries would deal. Heidemann had already talked vaguely of taking over the project for himself. He could go into partnership with an American publisher. He could sell everything and try to finance the project himself. He could take up those job offers he claimed to have received from *Bunte* and *Quick*. He had even mentioned a Dutch oil millionaire named Heeremann, a former member of the SS, who was prepared to put up 1 million marks towards the purchase of the diaries, providing they proved that Hitler knew nothing of the extermination of the Jews. Fischer was understandably anxious to conclude an agreement with Heidemann. Immediately after the receipt of the first diaries negotiations began, and five days later, on 23 February, the two men signed a contract. Such was the secrecy of the project, the company's legal department was not told what was happening. Wilfried Sorge personally drafted the agreement in accordance with suggestions from Heidemann.

The first part of the contract set out the reporter's obligations:

> The author [Heidemann] will obtain for the publishing company from East Germany the original manuscripts of the diaries of Adolf Hitler from the years 1933 to 1945 as well as the handwritten manuscript of the third volume of *Mein Kampf*. The publishing company will place at the author's disposal for the obtaining of these manuscripts the sum of 85,000 marks per volume and 200,000 marks for *Mein Kampf*.

> The author will be of assistance to the publishing company in reaching a settlement with the heirs of Adolf Hitler. He will attempt to obtain the ownership of the rights and transfer them to the company. The company will compensate the heirs through the author.

> Together with Dr Thomas Walde, the author will work on the manuscript for a *Stern* series and for one, or perhaps several, *Stern* books. . . . Other collaborators (for example, historians) will be engaged only with the agreement of the authors.

> The authors give the company exclusive and unlimited publishing rights to this material in all its forms. They give over all their copyright and further rights to the publishing company. The publishing company will be able to decide to whom it will syndicate the material. The company will only transfer the rights to a third party for a fee, and any alterations to the material which make it substantially different to the original will require the approval of the authors.

> The authors will not be given any special fees for the production of the *Stern* series. *Stern* will receive rights to the series for

nothing. In return, it will release the authors for two years from their usual editorial work. Those two years will commence when all the original volumes have been obtained.

Next came details of his reward:

For the *Stern* books, the author will receive a royalty of 6 per cent of the cover price of every volume sold up to 10,000 copies. For sales in excess of 10,000 copies, up to a total of 50,000, the royalty will rise to 7.2 per cent. For sales above 50,000 copies, the royalty increases to 9 per cent.

As a share of the syndication sales made by the company, Heidemann will receive 36 cent; Walde, 24 per cent.

Ten years after the start of publication, the company will return the original manuscripts to the author. When he dies, the author will bequeath them to the Federal Government. Before the expiry of the ten year deadline, the author will be allowed to use the material for his own researches. . . .

As an advance against royalties, when eight volumes of the Hitler diaries have been delivered, the author will receive 300,000 marks. . . .

If neither the publication of the books nor the syndication of the material covers the advance, nor the sale of the original material, the author will repay the difference within a year from the time when the last payment was made.

If for any reason the publishing company is prevented from publishing the work, it will be entitled to withdraw from this contract. In that case, all the payments due to the author will fall through, and if the author publishes the work with another company, he will be obliged to pay the money back.

Despite the caveat continued in the final two clauses, this contract represented a substantial victory for Heidemann. It was inconceivable that if the diaries were genuine they would fail to cover the cost of his advance. Even if *Stern* never published the material, Heidemann could keep the money, unless he took the diaries elsewhere: in other words, even if they were forged, Heidemann would not be obliged to pay back the advance. That fact alone gives some indication of the management's complete faith that the diaries were genuine. Assuming publication went ahead, the potential profit to Heidemann was enormous. Worldwide sales of Hitler's diaries would exceed 50,000 copies by a factor of ten, perhaps a hundred; the royalties that would yield, coupled with a third of world syndication rights, would make Heidemann financially secure for the rest of his life. To have such a golden vision of the future shimmering on the horizon would tend to make the most sceptical journalist incline to a belief in the diaries' authenticity. Heidemann was not one of the profession's natural sceptics. He had already shown himself capable of believing any amount of rubbish about the Third Reich. It is scarcely surprising that his attitude to the diaries from now on was one of blind faith. Gruner and Jahr had given the one man they had to trust an overwhelming financial incentive to deceive himself – and them.

TWELVE

Heidemann's advance of 300,000 marks was not due to be paid to him until he had delivered another five diaries. But Manfred Fischer knew of Heidemann's chronic financial difficulties (the reporter had taken out yet another company loan two months previously for 28,500 marks) and as a gesture of good faith he arranged to have the money paid into Heidemann's account the day after the conclusion of their agreement, Tuesday 24 February.

The following day, Heidemann rang Sorge to tell him that a new shipment of the diaries had arrived. He needed 480,000 marks. Sorge walked along the corridor to the office of Peter Kuehsel, the finance director, and asked for authorization to withdraw the money.

Kuehsel, a new arrival at Gruner and Jahr, must have wondered what sort of company he had joined. A month ago he had been ordered to find 200,000 marks in cash after the banks had shut; he had driven to the airport, stashed the money in a suitcase like a cashier for a Mafia family; then he had watched as Heidemann headed off into the night with it. Now he was supposed to hand over another 480,000 in cash with no explanation as to what it was for. He was an accountant. It offended his sense of business propriety. He sought out Manfred Fischer. 'I asked Dr Fischer what the money was for and why payments of this size had to be made in cash,' he recalled. 'I asked in order that I could make a proper entry in the company's accounts.' Fischer realized that the circle of the initiated would have to be widened from five to six. 'He swore

me to secrecy,' said Kuehsel, 'and told me that Herr
Heidemann was on the trail of the Hitler diaries.' Fischer
warned Kuehsel that in all he would probably be called upon
to hand over about 3 million marks. Kuehsel stared at his
managing director in astonishment. 'I said it was a lot of
money.' Fischer then asked him for some technical advice
and the two men 'discussed how it could be dealt with from
the point of view of tax'.

When Sorge had received the authorization, he drove to
the main Deutsche Bank in (appropriately) Adolphsplatz.
The money, in 500- and 1000-mark notes was packed into a
suitcase and given to Heidemann.

This established a routine which was to last for more than
two years. Heidemann would hear from Kujau that a new
consignment of books was ready for collection. He would
then inform Sorge who would in turn approach Kuehsel.
According to the accountant:

> Herr Sorge would tell me two days beforehand when money
> was to be handed out to Heidemann and how much was
> needed. I then made contact with the main branch of the
> Deutsche Bank in Adolphsplatz and asked them that same
> day to make arrangements to provide the money. Sometimes
> Sorge or sometimes Heidemann would decide the denomi-
> nations of the notes. As far as I remember, it was mainly
> 500-mark notes; sometimes 1000-mark

When Heidemann returned from Stuttgart with the new
diaries he would make two photocopies on a machine
installed in his private apartment, one for himself and one
for the *Stern* history department. Crucial to the development
of the whole affair was the fact that Heidemann was one of
the few people at *Stern* who could decipher the handwriting
and make sense of the obsolescent script in which they were
written – a type of Gothic composition no longer taught in

German schools. For most of those in the diaries' circle, Heidemann effectively became the Custodian of the Writ, the medium through whom the oracle of the diaries spoke. Once he had made the photocopies, he would take the originals to Sorge or Hensmann on the ninth floor of the *Stern* building. If those gentlemen had time they would listen while he read out passages to them. After this ritual, the diaries were put into brown envelopes, sealed, and placed in the management safe. The secrecy which surrounded this procedure was very tight. The *Stern Report* subsequently described how

> The circle of those who knew about the diaries was carefully restricted. Written notes were avoided. If internal notes were required, they were supposed to be destroyed immediately. Those who knew about the project began to behave like a secret organization working underground.

Walde did not even tell his wife what he was working on.

This mania for secrecy makes it difficult to reconstruct some parts of the story. The only record of deliveries was kept by Sorge. It was handwritten and intelligible only to himself. On the left-hand side of a piece of paper he wrote the date and the amount of money paid to Heidemann. On the right he entered the number of volumes delivered. But, as the *Stern Report* noted, there was no record of 'the time lapses between the deliveries, nor the order in which they came: to this day nobody knows at what point a particular book arrived at *Stern*'. Heidemann was not expected to account for the money he received. 'It was quite clear to us', explained Sorge, 'that in this sort of business, Heidemann wouldn't be bringing back receipts, nor would there be any indication of who the money was being paid to.' Having already given the reporter a personal payment of 300,000 marks, and promised him hundreds of thousands more when the diaries were published, the management reckoned they could count on Heidemann's integrity.

Whenever Kujau had finished forging a new batch of diaries he would telephone Heidemann at his home in Hamburg and tell him that a lorryload of pianos containing a fresh consignment of the books had arrived from East Germany. These telephone calls, according to the reporter, would generally come at about 8 a.m., when he was lying in his morning bath. Heidemann would then hasten down to the Aspergstrasse shop. Kujau would give him an A4-sized package, three or four inches thick, containing the latest instalments. Heidemann would give him a sealed envelope full of money to be passed on to 'General Fischer'. Sometimes Heidemann would open the package of diaries in Stuttgart and Kujau, pretending not to understand the old Germanic script, would ask him to read aloud from them. Heidemann would do so, a performance frequently interrupted by 'ahs' and 'oohs' from Kujau, as the forger feigned amazement at such an extraordinary historical document. After Heidemann had gone happily back to Hamburg, Kujau, equally happy, would open the packet of money, which – though he was not aware of it – held considerably less than it had when Heidemann took it from the safe in Hamburg.

Of the 680,000 marks which by the end of February had been paid to him for the acquisition of the diaries, the likelihood is that Heidemann stole almost half of it. It is impossible to be certain about this: it is Kujau's word against Heidemann's, the word of a compulsive liar against that of an an inveterate fantast. Nevertheless, the balance of probability, for once, is on Kujau's side. According to both him and Edith Lieblang, the suitcase Heidemann opened up in their house on the night of 28 January contained 150,000 marks – not the 200,000 it had held when Heidemann had left Hamburg twenty-four hours earlier. In 1983, in a raid on Heidemann's

home, the police found a note confirming the reporter's agreement with Kujau, but at a much lower cost than Manfred
Fischer was aware of:

Private collection, Militaria, Stuttgart FA, E. Lieblang, 7000
Stuttgart 1, Aspergstrasse 20.

Documents and pictures	500,000 marks
27 diaries at 50,000 marks	1,350,000 marks
Mein Kampf	150,000 marks
Total	2,000,000 marks

Of the 85,000 marks being given to him for each volume in
Hamburg, Heidemann was passing on at most 50,000 and
keeping 35,000 for himself. In this way he pocketed 280,000
marks by the end of February alone.

The Hitler diaries project was less than one month old but
already it had at least three layers of mendacity. Kujau was
deceiving Heidemann; Heidemann was deceiving Kujau and
the management of Gruner and Jahr; and the management of
Gruner and Jahr was deceiving the editors of *Stern*.

On Monday, 9 March, Manfred Fischer travelled to Guetersloh, one hundred and fifty miles from Hamburg, for a meeting
of the senior management of the Bertelsmann group. In his
suitcase he had three of the Hitler diaries which he had
removed from the ninth-floor safe the previous evening.

A full board meeting of the company on 11 February had
confirmed Fischer as the next managing director of
Bertelsmann. He was to take up his new job at the beginning
of July, easing the workload presently being carried by Reinhard Mohn, head of the family which owned almost nine-
tenths of the company. Mohn would shortly be reaching the
firm's retirement age of sixty. Daily operating control of
Bertelsmann would be relinquished to Fischer. Mohn would

concentrate on broader policy issues as chairman of the company's board.

It would not be easy for Fischer to establish his authority, stepping straight into the place of such a powerful figure, especially as Mohn would also continue to oversee his work. The Hitler diaries were a means of establishing that he had vision, imagination, a capacity for taking decisive action – proof, in the words of the *Stern Report*, of 'his wide-ranging approach to the publishing business'.

At the Guetersloh headquarters, Fischer asked Mohn for a private meeting. The two men retreated to Mohn's inner office, his secretary was instructed not to let anyone pass, and Fischer brought out Heidemann's dossier. He handed it to Mohn and drew his attention to Baur's description of Hitler's distress at the loss of his valuable papers. 'We have now found them,' he said. With considerable pride he laid the diaries before Mohn. 'These are Hitler's diaries.'

Mohn leafed through them. His reaction was all that Fischer had hoped it would be. 'He was just as fascinated as we were,' he recalled. 'He thought it was just great.'

'Manfred,' said Mohn, 'this is the most important manuscript ever to have passed across my desk.'

His initiation brought the number within Bertelsmann who knew the secret of the Hitler diaries to seven.

Three days later, on 12 March, Fischer signed a contract with Thomas Walde similar to the one agreed with Gerd Heidemann. Walde's share of the profits would be a royalty of 4 per cent of book sales up to 10,000 copies, 4.8 per cent up to 50,000, and 6 per cent thereafter; from the sale of syndication rights he would receive 24 per cent of the gross revenue. His advance was 10,000 marks. Like Heidemann, he retained the right to veto the involvement of other historians on the project.

*   *   *

On 2 April, a small drinks party was held on board *Carin II* to celebrate the way things were going. Manfred Fischer and Jan Hensmann arrived at about 6 p.m. to find Heidemann, Walde and Sorge already waiting for them. For Fischer and Hensmann, this was their first visit to the yacht. Heidemann showed them around, pointing out his various treasures. 'He showed me Goering's shoehorn,' remembered Fischer, 'and the big loo, installed because Goering had such a big backside.' To Hensmann, the yacht 'gave the impression of being clean and cared for'. After the tour, the men sat around drinking whisky and soda for two hours discussing their triumph. Heidemann was particularly excited. His discovery, he said, would 'make the world hold its breath'.

But already the first doubts about the diaries were beginning to be expressed. Contrary to the agreed policy of strict secrecy, despite his repeated and melodramatic warnings that disclosure would jeopardize human life, Heidemann could not resist showing off his great scoop. Reading through one of the first volumes Kujau delivered, covering the first six months of 1933, he came across references to the Führer's élite troops, the SS *Leibstandarte Adolf Hitler*. Bursting with excitement he decided to contact a founder member of the *Leibstandarte* – his old friend Wilhelm Mohnke. In the spring of 1981 Heidemann rang the former SS general to tell him he had the first three diaries. 'I'll show you them,' he said to Mohnke. 'There are things about you in them.' Mohnke, who three months earlier, on the day of Doenitz's funeral, had disparaged the whole notion of 'Hitler diaries', hurried round to Heidemann's flat on the Elbchaussee where he was shown a 'black book'. He was unable to decipher the writing so Heidemann read out the relevant entries:

15 *March* 1933: Visit of the specially chosen men, and the

plans for the new *Standarte* [unit] of the SS in Lichterfelde. These SS *Standarte* must carry my name.

17 March 1933: The Christian Unions are training themselves to be apolitical. From today an SS *Standarte* is in place in Lichterfelde. As from now all the relevant security measures will be taken by these people. These people are particularly good National Socialists. The *Standarte* are now carrying my name and are sworn in to me.

18 March 1933: Visit to these *Leibstandarte*. They are very fine men. Stayed up talking to members of the Cabinet until very late at night.

Heidemann recited these banalities – typical of the diaries as a whole – and asked Mohnke for his opinion. Mohnke was not impressed.

I said to Herr Heidemann that several things in these diaries were simply not true. First, the SS *Standarte* never had their barracks in Lichterfelde. I belonged to that troop and in March and April 1933 we were in the Friesenstrasse, in the police barracks. Secondly, at that time this troop of men did not have the name *Leibstandarte*. Thirdly, the entry for 18 March 1933 was false: Adolf Hitler never visited this troop in the Friesenstrasse.

Heidemann listened to this apparently devastating judgement with equanimity. He had long ceased operating on a rational wavelength: doubts about the diaries' authenticity were something he was not programmed to receive. 'Perhaps,' he suggested to Mohnke, 'Adolf Hitler *planned* all that and was putting his thoughts down on paper.'

He was equally unperturbed when, in the spring of 1981, Eberhard Jaeckel published his apology in Germany's leading historical journal, admitting that documents in his collected edition of Hitler's early writings were forged. Jaeckel kept his word and did not name Stiefel personally – he described the documents as having 'been in the hands of a private collector, totally unknown to the public' – but he conceded that the doubts which had been expressed about their authenticity were 'justified'. This was not only embarrassing to Jaeckel. It was also embarrassing to *Stern*. When Jaeckel's book had first appeared, the magazine had paid him 3000 marks to reprint the Hitler poems under the title *Rhymes from 'H'*: Kujau's handiwork had thus been published in the magazine for the first time two and a half years before the launch of the diaries. Was it possible, wondered Walde, that the diaries came from the same source as the poems? Heidemann was dispatched to the Institute of Contemporary History in Munich to copy the forged documents and check if they too had originated from the Boernersdorf crash. Heidemann did not bother to contact Jaeckel. Instead he sent the documents directly to Kujau for him to inspect, then rang him a few weeks later to ask if he had ever seen them before. Kujau, not surprisingly, said he hadn't and Heidemann reported back to Walde that there was no need for them to worry.

The publication of Jaeckel's apology stirred Kujau to another act of forgery. All the doubts about the authenticity of the poems stemmed from the fact that '*Der Kamerad*' was not the work of Hitler and could not have been copied by him, because it was not written until 1936. Kujau attempted to calm the fears of Fritz Stiefel on this point by forging a letter, dated 18 May 1981, purportedly sent by a librarian at the East German 'State Archive for Literature' to his brother, 'General Fischer':

Comrade Fischer,

I inform you that the text of the document '*Der Kamerad*' was originally written, in a slightly different form, by Xaver Kern in the year 1871. This verse was published repeatedly under different titles until 1942, always with slight textual variations. It was also published in 1956 in *Volk und Wissen* (East Germany, volume nine). I will send you a photocopy of the original in the next couple of days.

(Signed) Schenk.

If Heidemann had bothered to check with Jaeckel, or if Jaeckel had troubled himself to speak to *Stern* about the forged poems, Kujau's activities would almost certainly have been exposed. As it was, his victims once again played into his hands and Kujau was allowed to carry on his lucrative business for another two years.

THIRTEEN

On 13 May 1981, Pope John Paul II was shot and wounded in an assassination attempt in St Peter's Square in Rome. When the news came through in the *Stern* building in Hamburg, there was an immediate editorial conference. This dramatic story had all the ingredients the magazine specialized in: violence, personal tragedy, conspiracy, espionage, international crisis, vivid pictures – *Stern* threw all its resources into reporting the event. Someone with experience of foreign investigations should go to Turkey, home of the would-be assassin. The ideal choice was Heidemann. Had anyone seen him? Where *was* Heidemann these days?

Henri Nannen had stepped down from the day-to-day editing of *Stern* at the beginning of the year to become the magazine's publisher. A triumvirate of editors-in-chief had replaced him: Peter Koch, responsible for politics, economics and foreign affairs; Felix Schmidt, in charge of the arts, entertainment and leisure sections; and a design expert, Rolf Gillhausen. Koch had already spent several fruitless sessions with Heidemann trying to force him to do some normal journalism for a change. Now, Schmidt undertook to track him down. He rang Thomas Walde, Heidemann's departmental head. Walde said the reporter was not available. 'I don't care where he is,' shouted Schmidt. 'Get him into my office.' In exasperation, he went to consult Nannen. 'Who is Heidemann working for?' he demanded. 'The editors or the publishing company?' Nannen said that obviously he worked for the editors and advised Schmidt and Koch to complain to the management.

Meanwhile, three floors above them, uncertain as to what he should do, Walde was speaking to Wilfried Sorge. Because Manfred Fischer was away the two men approached his deputy, Jan Hensmann, and explained the problem. Hensmann's objective was a quiet life. His advice was that Heidemann should feign illness; Walde could then lie to the editors and tell them that Heidemann was on sick leave. Neither of the journalists was enthusiastic about this idea. With great reluctance, Hensmann finally accepted that the time had come to inform the lucky editors of the scoop the management was acquiring for them. The diaries were fetched from the safe and arranged in a pile on a small table in the corner of his office. Hensmann then rang Koch, the most senior of the editors, and asked him to come upstairs.

Koch's first reaction on being shown the diaries was one of anger at having been deceived by the management. He rang down to Schmidt and Gillhausen in the *Stern* offices below and told them to come up and join him. Schmidt arrived a few minutes later to find his colleague 'bent over a pile of A4-sized books. Koch said to me that they were the diaries of Adolf Hitler and that Heidemann had got them.' Like almost everyone else in the company, they were unable to read the antiquated script. They could only concentrate on the diaries' external features. Gillhausen noted that most of the books had a 'black cover', 'a red cord and a red seal', and a note pasted on the front 'on which either Hess or Bormann had written that these books were the property of the Führer'. Hensmann said that Heidemann was not available for normal journalistic work because he was acquiring the books on the management's behalf. Large sums of money had been paid. Absolute secrecy was necessary.

The editors retreated to Koch's office to digest this

information. Their reactions were mixed. There was unanimous resentment at the way they had been treated: five months into their new jobs it did not augur well for the future. On the other hand, the editors did not have the slightest doubt that the books were genuine. They had to be. Over half a million marks had already been spent. It was impossible to conceive of the shrewd, conservative, financially cautious managers of Gruner and Jahr investing in anything unless they were absolutely certain of its value. The three had to accept that if they rejected the diaries, they risked going down in history as the editors who threw away one of the biggest scoops since the war.

That point was made with brutal frankness a couple of days later, when Manfred Fischer returned and chaired a joint meeting of journalists and businessmen to review the whole project. Koch, Schmidt and Gillhausen faced Heidemann, Walde, Sorge and Hensmann. Fischer was not in the least apologetic for having circumvented the editors. As far as he was concerned their inept handling of Heidemann had almost lost the company this tremendous coup. He had no doubts about the authenticity of the diaries. 'Do you think,' he inquired, 'that I would have committed so much money if I were not convinced?' If *Stern* did not want the diaries, they could be marketed elsewhere: Bertelsmann could exploit the world rights; Bantam Books could handle the American publication. Heidemann scarcely opened his mouth. It was Fischer who explained the story of the East German general and his brother in the West whose identity could not be revealed. The three editors listened without enthusiasm. Humiliated and offended by the management's behaviour, their attitude to Heidemann's great scoop was, and would remain for many months, one of sullen acquiescence.

On 27 May, Heidemann crossed the border into East Germany and returned to Boernersdorf. This time he was on his own. He wanted to discover more about the crashed transport plane. He found some eyewitnesses to the disaster. Helda Fries, wife of a local hotel owner, described how the plane fell out of the sky, clipping the tops of the trees in the nearby Heidenholz forest. One of its three engines was wrenched off before it hit the ground. Richard Elbe, a local farmer who had been in the fields in charge of some Russian and French slave labourers, was the first to reach the burning wreck. Bullets were exploding, people trapped inside were screaming and hammering to get out. In front of them, one survivor, Franz Westermeier, crawled out of the chaos. 'Come here you cowardly dogs,' Elbe recalled him shouting. 'Come here. You are just too scared.' But the heat was too intense for the rescuers to get close. A farmworker, said Elbe, called Eduard Grimme later pulled the corpses from the wreckage. 'They didn't look like people any more. The arms were gone and the legs and everything else was charred.' The remains were examined in the local morgue by a German medical officer. On one body was a cigarette case embossed with the symbol of Lufthansa and the words: 'In memory of 500,000 kilometres flying.' It had belonged to Gundlfinger. The remains of the plane were cordoned off by German police and SS men. But according to Erwin Goebel, son of the mayor at that time, 'many people managed to salvage parts from the aircraft and got richer for it, soldiers included.' Debris and pieces of luggage were scattered all over the forest. Richard Elbe had carried off two cockpit windows and used them to build part of a shed.

It was all very insubstantial – fragments of gossip, hazily recalled thirty-six years after the event. Nevertheless, it was something for Heidemann to grasp at. He bought the two old windows off Elbe and carted them back with him to Hamburg where he showed them off as further proof of the story.

On 1 June he received a further 225,000 marks. Shortly

afterwards he returned from Stuttgart with more books. There were now twelve Hitler diaries in the management safe.

In May, Manfred Fischer had let another member of the publishing company's management into the secret of the diaries' existence. He was Dr Andreas Ruppert, Gruner and Jahr's legal adviser. Fischer wanted his opinion of the legality of the whole project. Would *Stern* be able to publish the diaries? Who owned the copyright?

Ruppert reported back that determining ownership of Hitler's estate was complex, indeed almost impossible. Hitler's property, together with 5 million marks owed to him by the publishers of *Mein Kampf*, was confiscated, after a court case, by the State of Bavaria in 1948. Hitler's will was declared invalid and in 1951, the Bavarian authorities seized personal objects bequeathed by Hitler to his housekeeper to prevent her selling them. But the following year they had been unable to prevent the appearance of *Hitler's Table Talk*: the state apparently owned rights in Hitler's literary estate only as far as published material was concerned; previously unpublished material fell outside their control. It was impossible to predict how the Bavarians or the Federal Government would react to news of the diaries' existence. The situation was further complicated by the fact that various private deals had been arranged with Hitler's descendants. François Genoud, the Swiss lawyer and ex-Nazi, had signed an agreement with Paula, Hitler's sister, shortly after after the war. But Paula was long since dead. Meanwhile, the West German historian, Werner Maser, had a separate contract to act as a trustee for the Hitler family. It was decided, as a first step towards securing ownership of the diaries, to make a deal with Maser.

Maser was a controversial figure. Ten years previously he had written a bestselling biography of Hitler, translated into twenty languages, which was regarded as having dwelt, at suspicious length, on the positive aspects of Hitler's character and achievements. In 1977 he had written a book attacking the Allied handling of the Nuremberg Trials, stating that, in many instances, the hanged war criminals were victims of a miscarriage of justice. His relations with the left-wing *Stern* were strained. The magazine therefore approached him through his former assistant, Michael Hepp. According to Maser:

> [Hepp] rang me in the summer of 1981 and asked me if I was interested in talking to a journalist from *Stern*. I told him of my basic objection to newspapers like *Stern*. ... Herr Hepp said that this journalist was a very sensible man who also had a large collection of Hitler memorabilia. We agreed a date and shortly afterwards Hepp and Heidemann came to see me.

Heidemann arrived at Maser's home in Speyer, near Heidelberg, on 11 June. Without mentioning the diaries, he asked the historian to sell him the rights to any original Hitler material which he had already discovered or might discover in the future. After a week's haggling over terms, a handwritten contract was drawn up and signed on 18 June:

> Professor Dr Werner Maser received, as the administrator of Hitler's will on behalf of Hitler's descendants, a fee of 20,000 marks, paid in cash. For this sum he allows Gerd Heidemann the rights to all the discovered or purchased documents or notes in the hand of Adolf Hitler, including transcribed telephone conversations and other conversations which have so far not been published and which could be used for publication. Professor Dr Werner Maser gives to Gerd Heidemann all the rights necessary for this, including personal rights and copyrights. Dr Maser affirms he is empowered to do this on behalf of the family. This document is completed in the legal department in Hamburg and is valid in German law.

Heidemann then opened a suitcase and pulled out a bundle of money. He counted out twenty-two 1000-mark notes and handed them to Maser.

After delivering the twelfth diary, Heidemann suddenly announced a price increase. Instead of costing 85,000 marks each, the books would now cost 100,000 marks. The East German general, he told the *Stern* management, was insisting on more money: to continue supplying the books, he was having to bribe an increasing number of corrupt communist officials. This news was a disappointment to the company. They had originally expected to have all the books in Hamburg by mid-May; instead, by mid-June, they had less than half. But they certainly did not want to jeopardize the project at such a late stage. They had no alternative but to agree to pay. Not once did they suspect where the additional cash was really going.

After years of living in debt, Heidemann was now awash with money. Over the following months he and Gina went on a spending spree impressive even by Hamburg's wealthy standards. In one of the city's department stores he bought 37,000 marks' worth of furnishings to renovate their flat; he produced the money from his jacket pocket with the bank's seal still on the bundles. At the Luehrs travel agency he put down 27,000 marks in cash on the counter and booked first-class cabins for himself and his family on the maiden voyage of the luxury liner *Astor*. The staff had no difficulty in describing the event to the police in 1983 – years later they could still remember the difficulty they had trying to stuff all Heidemann's money into the till. Gina got two cars – a convertible BMW318 for 32,000 marks and a Porsche 911 for 26,000. The Heidemanns eventually moved into larger accommodation on the Elbchaussee, Hamburg's most exclusive street: not content with one, they rented two apartments. A fortune went on jewellery and carpets.

Inflated by *Stern*'s money, Heidemann's compulsion to collect Nazi memorabilia ballooned out of control. Some of it was presumably genuine, like Karl Wolff's SS honour dagger, for which Heidemann paid the old general 30,000 marks. Most of it, however, came from Konrad Kujau. It included a swastika banner which Kujau passed off as the 'Blood Flag', the famous symbol of Hitler's abortive beer hall *putsch* of 1923, preserved on Hitler's orders like a holy relic in honour of the sixteen Nazi 'martyrs' killed that day. In reality, Heidemann's 'Blood Flag' was simply an ordinary banner – of which there are thousands in existence – to which Kujau had added his usual forged authentication. The swastika was in an old glass case upon which was glued a note: 'As the condition of the flag has suffered greatly in the years of confiscation it is shown in the flag hall of the Brownhouse behind glass. According to the wishes of the Führer.'

Heidemann also received from Kujau three hundred oil paintings, sketches and watercolours supposedly by Hitler; Nazi Party uniforms, flags and postcards; and 120 so-called Hitler documents. In addition, he acquired what he believed to be the actual revolver which Hitler had used to shoot himself. Attached to it was a label in Martin Bormann's handwriting stating that 'with this pistol, the Führer took his own life'. Heidemann proudly showed it to Wilhelm Mohnke and Otto Guensche. The gun was one of the most palpable fakes in his collection: it was a Belgian FN, whereas Hitler was known to have used a much heavier weapon, a 7.65 millimetre Walther. Both men said as much to Heidemann. Guensche, in particular, was in a position to know. He had helped carry the bodies of Hitler and Eva Braun out of the bunker. Indeed he had actually picked up the suicide weapon from the bunker floor where it had slipped from Hitler's fingers. But as with the diaries, Heidemann could not be swayed from his belief in its authenticity. He seemed to read great significance into the fact that only one of the revolver's bullets had been fired.

Heidemann felt that such treasures should be exhibited in a setting worthy of their value. During his meetings with Werner Maser in June he raised the possibility of buying Hitler's childhood home in Leonding. Maser, who knew the area well from his earlier researches, offered to help. On 1 July, the historian and his wife, together with Heidemann and Gina, drove into Austria where Maser had arranged a meeting with the *Bürgermeister* and town council of Leonding. According to Maser:

> Heidemann offered to buy Hitler's parental home. A large sum was mentioned as the purchase price – I think it was 270,000 marks, I'm not sure exactly. Heidemann said that money was no problem and patted his wallet. It seemed to the gentlemen of the town council of Leonding rather dubious that a journalist from Germany should be travelling around with so much of his own money in his pocket. ... I asked Herr Heidemann on this occasion where he got the money from. He insisted it wasn't money from *Stern* but from his wife who had sold two hotels for about 9 million marks.
>
> From Leonding we drove on together to Braunau. Heidemann wanted to look at Hitler's birthplace and possibly even to buy that. For my part, I declined to put Heidemann in touch with the town authorities there. I had slight doubts about Heidemann. For a start, I was worried by the fact that he was wandering around with so much money and saying that the price was no object. The other thing was that the behaviour of Herr and Frau Heidemann rather repelled me when they talked about Hitler.

As part of their tour that summer, the Heidemanns and the

Masers also visited Berchtesgaden where they spent a while poking around in the rubble.

The idea of buying the house in Leonding was not a mere whim. Heidemann was serious. After his return to Hamburg, on 13 July, he wrote to the town council to repeat his proposal 'once again in writing'. Hitler's childhood home, said Heidemann, 'always meant more to him than his birthplace in Braunau':

> Adolf Hitler had a decisive influence on the history of our century. The world and the events of today are a consequence of his politics and his war. A complete knowledge of all the threads in his life and the politics of this man is the basic precondition for the understanding of history. In my opinion, the house of Hitler's parents is an ideal site for an historical museum, to be supervised by a trustee from your own town to ensure that the presentation is strictly factual.
>
> If the town authorities agree, I will purchase from the town, for an agreed sum, the relevant house and land. I accept the conditions this would entail – for example, not altering the use to which the property is put without the express approval of the town authorities.
>
> Should there be any complications in selling this piece of land to me as a citizen of West Germany, an Austrian historical institute could be found who would become the legal owner of the land and museum.
>
> I ask you to consider this offer in a positive way. I await your answer and remain yours, etc, etc.

The town council met to discuss Heidemann's offer three days later. Despite his assurances that his Hitler museum would be 'strictly factual' there was something about the reporter and his proposal which the burghers of Leonding found faintly sinister. Heidemann's scheme was rejected.

Thwarted in his plan to install his collection in Leonding,

Heidemann had a new idea. He decided to investigate the possibility of moving his Hitler memorabilia to South America and in the summer of 1981, he sought the advice of Klaus Barbie.

Heidemann had met Barbie in Bolivia two years previously, during his honeymoon tour with Gina and General Wolff. The two men had enjoyed a friendly relationship. Unfortunately, from Heidemann's point of view, a year after his return, in October 1980, *Stern* had decided to salvage at least something from the trip which they had financed. There had been a military coup in Bolivia in which Barbie, correctly, was suspected of having played a part. Despite strong opposition from Heidemann, the transcript of his interview with 'the Butcher of Lyons' had been used by another reporter as the basis for an article entitled 'New Power of Old Nazis'. The piece depicted Barbie as a brutal SS torturer. Barbie had not been pleased.

Hoping for a reconciliation, Heidemann wrote to him on 22 August 1981. He sent his condolences on the recent death of Barbie's son. 'I am very sorry', he added, 'that I have also caused you some sorrow.' He then explained how the transcript of their interview had been taken off him by *Stern*'s editors and given 'a completely different slant':

> Of course I tried with all the means at my disposal to prevent publication – sadly, in vain. For me, the matter has been a continuing source of embarrassment and my wife reproached me for it for months. If she could not understand my dilemma, I can, of course, expect even less understanding from you and your wife. I can only ask for forgiveness. I regret very much the loss of your friendship as a result of this stupid affair.
>
> Nevertheless I would like to entrust you with an important matter, and seek your advice on it.
>
> I have succeeded in securing a large part of Hitler's property

— extremely interesting notes, watercolours and oil paintings executed in his own hand; the pistol with which the Führer killed himself in the bunker (a handwritten letter from Bormann guarantees it); crates with documents from the Reich Chancellery; and, above all, the Blood Flag, still in its original case with the memorial plaque to the fallen of 1923. In my view, these relics of the National Socialist movement should, at the very least, be kept in a safe place by reliable men. You will understand that I do not want to store the flag for too long in Germany: here, the relevant laws and statutes are always getting tighter and tighter and there are frequent house searches for Nazi relics. Perhaps you can advise me where I could place these relics for safety?

In the hope that you will still be prepared to have anything to do with me, I await your answer and will then give you more details about my finds. With best wishes to your wife from my wife and myself,

Yours,

Gerd Heidemann.

There is no record of Barbie's reply.

FOURTEEN

On 1 July Manfred Fischer left Hamburg to take up his new appointment in Guetersloh as managing director of Bertelsmann. He was now in the first rank of European executives, controlling a company with an annual turnover of more than $2 billion. Bertelsmann had expanded so rapidly during the 1970s, growing by as much as 15 per cent a year, that its capital base had become thin; a period of retrenchment was required. Mohn had decided that Fischer was the best man to oversee this new policy: he did so on the basis of Fischer's reputation as a cost cutter. Similarly, to replace Fischer at Gruner and Jahr, Mohn chose another businessman supposedly with an ability to enforce stringent economy.

Gerd Schulte-Hillen was only forty years old. After leaving school he had spent a year in the Bundeswehr, then qualified as an engineer, joining Bertelsmann in 1969. He was promoted rapidly, from assistant manager in Germany, to technical manager of printing plants in Spain and Portugal. He was put in charge of printing for the whole of Gruner and Jahr and built a huge new factory for the group in the United States. Schulte-Hillen's appointment as managing director came as something of a surprise. He was a highly respected technician, but he had little experience of handling journalists, of whom he was felt to be slightly in awe. He was quickly initiated into Gruner and Jahr's great secret. 'I think it was in June 1981,' he recalled, 'that Dr Manfred Fischer swore me to secrecy and then told me that the Hitler diaries were being bought by the company.'

He was soon deeply involved in the operation. On 29 July, Heidemann received 345,000 marks for the next batch of diaries. A week later, on 5 August, he picked up another 220,000 marks. This meant that since January he had removed a total of six suitcases full of cash from the Deutsche Bank, containing 1.81 million marks. There were now eighteen diaries in the management safe.

The next day, Hensmann and Sorge went to see the new managing director in his office. Before any further payments could be made, they explained, Schulte-Hillen had to sign a fresh authorization for the transfer of the company's funds. Without hesitation, he signed a document endorsing Sorge to use another 1 million marks of the company's money. According to Schulte-Hillen:

> Somehow I thought – oh, you don't have to worry too much about that. I was still feeling my way into the job. I said to myself – well, two million has already been spent, it must be OK. Fischer himself did it, and now he's on the overall board of the company and is my boss. Who was I to question it? That was a mistake. The next time I was asked to give my approval for the payment of another million, the room for manoeuvre was even smaller.

Manfred Fischer, the man who had initiated the operation, was 150 miles away, grappling with the day to day running of a multinational company. Schulte-Hillen, a relatively inexperienced businessman in a new job with little experience of journalism, was merely carrying on what Fischer had started. Hensmann was a weak man. The finance director, Kuehsel, did what he was told. Sorge's objectivity was compromised by his friendship with Thomas Walde. Walde and Heidemann, both expecting to make a fortune when the books were published, were the last men to call a halt to the delivery of the diaries. The editors were sulkily refusing to show much interest in the management's scoop.

The whole project was out of control.

The only person who seemed to be showing any financial sense was Edith Lieblang in Stuttgart. She took charge of the envelopes full of cash which Heidemann was delivering and invested them in bricks and mortar. When it came to money, she said firmly, 'We didn't have "mine" and "yours".' In May the couple bought a new apartment in Wolfschlugen for 235,000 marks, together with a garage for 18,000 marks. In July she paid 230,000 marks for a flat in Schreiberstrasse. This was on the ground floor of a substantial, heavy masonried, four-storey block, tucked away at the end of a quiet street near the centre of Stuttgart. Schreiberstrasse became Kujau's new shop. He bought a large building at the back for 120,000 marks, installed heavy steel shutters and a security camera to scan the courtyard, and transferred to it his entire collection from Aspergstrasse. He hired a local taxi company to do the removals.

Kujau continued to work on the diaries during the day at home. Edith knew he was supplying Hitler diaries to *Stern* but claimed, somewhat implausibly, that she thought they were genuine: she did not know, she said, what Kujau was up to during the day when she was out working at the Café Hochland. 'I don't know what he did in my absence. I rarely went into his workroom. He used to clean it himself.'

Once he had done the research, it took Kujau, on average, only four and a half hours to forge a complete diary. His favourite source was a weighty, two-volume edition of *Hitler's Speeches and Proclamations 1932–45*, a daily chronology of the Führer's activities, compiled in 1962 by the German historian Max Domarus. Working against the clock to satisfy Heidemann's demand for diaries, Kujau resorted to wholesale plagiarism, copying out page after page from

Domarus. The Hitler Diaries – the object of one of the most extravagant 'hypes' in the history of journalism – were for the most part nothing more interesting than a tedious recital of official engagements and Nazi party announcements. Nine-tenths of the material being so carefully hoarded in the Gruner and Jahr safe was unpublishable. These, for example, are the entries for the first seven days of September 1938 – a typically uninspired week in the life of the Führer, as recorded by Konrad Kujau:

1) The Reich Air Defence Federation received its own insignia and flag. The founding of the 'Federation for the unity of Germany and Poland' was today announced by the Polish Prime Minister.

2) Opening of the exhibition 'Great Germany' in Japan (telegram). A youth delegation from Japan is received in Munich by Schirach (telegram).
Reception at the Berghof for Henlein. Conference.

4) Admiral Horthy has kept his word. As from today there is compulsory military service in Hungary.

5) Opening of the Party Rally 'Great Germany'.
Reception in the Nuremberg town hall.

6) Opening of the Party Congress. Proclamation.
Handing over of Reich insignia to the mayor of the town of Nuremberg. A cultural meeting.

7) Call to the Reichs Labour Service. Diplomatic reception in the Hotel Deutscher Hof.

The bulk of the diaries, especially the early ones, consisted of padding of this sort – a technique which reached a pinnacle of improbability in the entry for 19 July 1940, when Hitler was supposed to have devoted five pages to copying out the entire list of senior promotions in the German armed forces following the fall of France.

At the end of each month's entries, Kujau had 'Hitler' write a set of more general notes headed 'Personal'. It was in these sections of the diary, unfettered by chronology and so less vulnerable to checks for accuracy, that Kujau allowed the Führer to think aloud about the state of his affairs. There were occasional revelations: that the burning of the books in May 1933 'was not a good idea of Goebbels''; that some of 'the measures against the Jews were too strong for me'. But overall, the tone remained relentlessly trivial. Health was one recurrent theme: 'My health is poorly – the result of too little sleep' (April 1933); 'I suffer much from sleeplessness and stomach pains' (June 1934); 'My stomach makes it difficult to sleep, my left leg is often numb' (July 1934). Eva Braun was another regular source of concern: 'Although I have become Reichs Chancellor, I have not forgotten E's birthday' (January 1933); 'She is the sporty type – it has helped her very much to be in the fresh air' (October 1934). Occasionally, as in June 1941, these twin preoccupations met: 'On Eva's wishes, I am thoroughly examined by my doctors. Because of the new pills, I have violent flatulence, and – says Eva – bad breath.' It was for material of this sort that *Stern* was to end up paying roughly £50 per word.

Kujau turned out the diaries so quickly that he had soon exhausted the stock of school notebooks in his cellar. In the summer of 1981 he flew to West Berlin, crossed into the East, and in a taxi travelled from shop to shop, buying up the old-fashioned, black-bound volumes. He returned home the same day bearing twenty-two of them. The whole lot cost him 77 marks.

Shortly afterwards Kujau passed on to Heidemann some wonderful news from his brother in East Germany. Contrary to their initial estimate, it now appeared that there were more than twenty-seven diaries. The haul of Hitler writings salvaged from the Boernersdorf crash was much larger than had been thought.

Heidemann returned to Hamburg to tell Gruner and Jahr of this latest development.

On 23 August, less than two and a half weeks after he had been asked to authorize payment of 1 million marks, Schulte-Hillen had to sanction a second transfer of money, this time of 600,000 marks. Heidemann reported that the price of the diaries had shot up to 200,000 marks each. The East German general, he said, was now having to pay money to members of the Communist government as well as to other corrupt officials. The company once again felt that it had no option but to pay up. Indeed, perversely, the price rise increased the company's confidence that the diaries were genuine. 'We weren't surprised,' said one of the managers later. 'In fact, we expected it. Once you've bought part of a collection, you naturally want the rest. It's worth that much more to you. The seller knows that and takes advantage of it. It's normal commercial practice.'

Schulte-Hillen was hopelessly out of his depth. Every so often, Heidemann would come into his office, escorted by Sorge, and read extracts from the latest diaries out loud to him. The banality of the content meant nothing to the technically minded managing director. 'I didn't concern myself with the question of whether they were sensational or not. That wasn't my affair.' For Schulte-Hillen, struggling to read himself into his new job, the diaries were an exotic project bequeathed to him by his predecessor. 'I didn't really worry about the details,' he confessed. 'Sorge and Walde were Heidemann's principal points of reference.'

Heidemann now began fantasizing about his role as middleman between *Stern* and the diaries' supplier. Simply flying down to Stuttgart, handing over the money and picking up the diaries did not accord with his vision of himself as a sleuth reporter. He decided to glamorize the story. 'I remember a very hot day in the summer,' said Walde later. 'Gerd Heidemann arrived in the office in a blue suit looking unusually worked-up.' According to Heidemann, the lorry driver who used to bring the diaries out of East Germany had been replaced. Heidemann said he was now having to drive into the East himself and smuggle the documents illegally over the border. 'The whole thing seemed very dangerous to him,' said Walde. 'He didn't know what to do when he got to the frontier. He just put the envelope containing the diary under the car's mat.'

For the benefit of Schulte-Hillen, Heidemann further elaborated on the story. He told the managing director that he would drive down the autobahn to Berlin. At an agreed point on the journey, another car would draw alongside him with its passenger window open. With both cars travelling at the same speed, Heidemann would toss the packet of money through the open window. The vehicles would then exchange positions and the driver of the other car would throw him the diaries. The managing director had never heard anything like it. He told Heidemann he was 'crazy': 'I said he shouldn't do it, especially in view of his family responsibilities.' 'Don't worry,' Schulte-Hillen remembers Heidemann telling him, 'I'll do it.'

Despite his misgivings for Heidemann's safety, Schulte-Hillen was impressed, and now treated the reporter with even greater respect. He would not hear a word said against him. He would rebuke anyone who expressed doubts about Heidemann's heroism: 'When a colleague puts himself in personal danger in order to obtain things,' he used to say, 'he should be entitled to the trust of others.' When Heidemann complained to Sorge that his own car was too dilapidated for this kind of work and that he was having to use Gina's, Schulte-Hillen arranged for him to be given a brand new company Mercedes.

In fact, Gruner and Jahr had a strong motive for believing Heidemann's story. If they could swear on oath that the money for the diaries had been paid outside West Germany, they would enjoy substantial tax concessions. In November, there was a month-long series of negotiations to provide Heidemann with a special life insurance policy at Gruner and Jahr's expense. Heidemann insisted on a clause providing for the payment of ransom money in case they should have to buy him out of an East German jail. In the event of his death, his share in the profits from Hitler's diaries was to be given to his heirs. Heidemann joked that this generous policy might induce his wife to 'separation, Italian style'. This farce carried on until the first week of December, when Heidemann announced that the piano shipments had resumed.

Around this time Heidemann also complained to Schulte-Hillen that he had not received a salary increase for several years. He hinted that he might be forced to leave the company unless something was done. The managing director immediately called in Peter Koch, Felix Schmidt and Rolf Gillhausen and instructed them, in Koch's words, 'to take better care of Heidemann, to motivate him more'. The editors had not recommended Heidemann for a rise because they had not thought his work merited one. Now, under pressure, they once again started paying him regular annual increments. Schmidt was also told by Schulte-Hillen to give Heidemann a special bonus payment of 20,000 marks. 'The man needs recognition,' Schulte-Hillen told him, 'and he needs to be treated with special care.' Schmidt gritted his teeth and arranged this reward for the reporter who had spent a whole year deceiving his editors. '*Recognition . . . special care. . . .*' 'These words of the management', said Schmidt two years later, 'still ring in my ears.'

*　　　*　　　*

Heidemann's fiftieth birthday coincided with a call from Kujau to tell him that more diaries were ready for collection. Heidemann decided to take Gina down to Stuttgart with him and the couple spent the evening of 3 December having a celebration dinner with Kujau and Edith in the local Holiday Inn, close to the Munich motorway exit. It was the first time all four of them had been together. They got on well; Gina particularly liked Edith – 'a very nice lady,' she called her, 'very bourgeois'. There was champagne, and at midnight the gregarious 'Dr Fischer' led them in the singing of 'Happy Birthday'. Amid warm embraces, Gina presented her husband with a solid gold Rolex watch.

It had been a good year for the couple. Heidemann had at last found the recognition he craved so desperately. Soon he would be able to present the world with his magnificent story and he and Gina would be wealthy for life. The Heidemanns beamed at Kujau, the source of their good fortune. 'We owe you so much,' said Gina. Kujau grinned.

FIFTEEN

The New Year of 1982 witnessed further large withdrawals of cash from the Adolphsplatz bank by Gerd Heidemann: 400,000 marks on 14 January; 200,000 on 27 January; 200,000 on 17 February. On 1 March, after picking up another 400,000 marks, he and Walde were taken out to dine at Hamburg's Coelln Oyster Restaurant by Gerd Schulte-Hillen.

According to Walde, the purpose of the meal was for Schulte-Hillen 'to show some recognition to Heidemann and to get to know me better'. Between mouthfuls of oysters, the three men discussed the Hitler diaries. There were already more than two dozen volumes in the management safe. There seemed no sign of an end to the stream of books emanating from behind the Iron Curtain. Even so, the time was approaching when decisions would have to be taken about the form of publication. Obviously there would be those who would seek to denigrate *Stern*'s scoop. Some form of independent authentication would have to be obtained – not because there were any doubts about the material in the management's mind, merely to ensure there was a weapon available with which critics could be silenced.

Walde had already made contact with West Germany's two main police organizations, the *Bundeskriminalamt* (BKA) and the *Zollkriminalinstitut*. Without mentioning the Hitler diaries specifically, he asked them in general terms what sort of tests had to be done to determine the age of documents and the authenticity of handwriting; who could do such tests; how much they might cost; what materials the experts would require for testing. 'Because neither of these two authorities does work for private individuals, I tried to arrange for people who work there to do tests for us in a private capacity.' He had then rung the Institute for Contemporary History in Munich and the Federal Archives – the Bundesarchiv – in Koblenz, to make arrangements to collect copies of Hitler's handwriting; this could then be sent to the experts for comparison with *Stern*'s material. It should be possible to organize such tests within the next few weeks.

Assuming, as they all did, that the Hitler diaries would quickly pass through the formality of authentication, Walde, Heidemann and Schulte-Hillen discussed how the books might be marketed. Their discovery was a scoop, but their content, it had to be admitted, was meagre. Each diary contained an average of only 1000 words. Added together, Gruner and Jahr's two dozen volumes scarcely added up to a couple of chapters, never mind a book. The three men agreed that the material could not be printed as it stood. It would have to be 'journalistically worked on', setting quotations from the diary in their historical context. This would have to be done whilst the diaries were still arriving, in complete secrecy and without outside help – an enormous undertaking, especially since neither Heidemann nor Walde was a qualified historian.

Two days after the meeting with Schulte-Hillen, on Wednesday 3 March, Walde and Wilfried Sorge were invited round for the evening to Heidemann's flat. The reporter wanted them to meet an important contact of his who could provide *Stern* with important Nazi documents. According to Sorge Heidemann said 'he needed our presence if he was to appear to be negotiating seriously on *Stern*'s behalf'. That night in the elegant Elbchaussee apartment they were confronted by a seedy and furtive character in his mid-fifties, whom Heidemann introduced as Medard Klapper.

Medardus Leopold Karl Klapper exerted a hold over Heidemann similar to that exercised by Konrad Kujau. He spun large and elaborate fantasies about the Third Reich in which Heidemann believed and in which he invested large sums of *Stern*'s money. Klapper claimed to have joined the SS in 1944 at the age of seventeen and to have been one of Hitler's bodyguards in the final days of the war. He was now an arms dealer in Karlsruhe in southern Germany. Apart from the Nazis, Klapper's other obsession was with cowboys and Indians: his shop in Karlsruhe, called The General Gun Store, was designed to look as if it belonged in the American wild west. Heidemann had made his acquaintance in 1971 when he was working on crime stories for *Stern*. Klapper was a police informer. Like Kujau, Klapper dealt in Nazi memorabilia and occasionally ran a stall selling militaria in the Flea Market in Konstanz. When Heidemann was short of money in the late 1970s Klapper had sold a few Goering mementoes on his behalf: a French collector bought a silver cigarette case and some silver picture frames for 20,000 francs.

Klapper's speciality was buried Nazi treasure. He promised Heidemann he could lead him to a hoard of enormous value. It would not only provide the reporter with a great story for *Stern*, it would also make him rich. On 19 August 1981 – shortly after the collapse of his attempts to buy Hitler's childhood home – Heidemann opened up his suitcase to Klapper, paying him 25,000 marks in cash. 'He said he now had money "like it was growing on trees",' recalled Klapper. 'He showed me his pocket which was stuffed with 1,000-mark notes.' In return for the money, Klapper provided Heidemann with a photocopy of a map, purporting to show the whereabouts of 450 kilos of gold and platinum, dumped by the Nazis at the end of the war in the Stolpsee, a lake in East Germany. A few weeks later, Heidemann signed an agreement with some East German representatives. He put up an undisclosed amount of money in return for which the East Germans promised to provide the manpower to search the Stolpsee; the proceeds would be split fifty-fifty. Eventually forty engineers from the East German army equipped with tons of dredging machinery were involved in searching the lake; all they sucked out of the water, Heidemann later complained to Klapper, was 350 cubic metres of mud.

Undeterred, Heidemann continued to believe the arms dealer's stories. Confiscated receipts suggest that over the next eighteen months he paid him almost 450,000 marks. In particular, he believed the gun salesman's claim that Martin Bormann was still alive: this story, after all, accorded with his own, earlier obsession of 1979. Klapper played on Heidemann's gullibility, assuring him that eventually he would take him to 'Martin'. According to him, Bormann led a nomadic existence, shuttling between hideouts in Argentina, Paraguay, Spain, Egypt and Zurich (where he was being watched by the Israeli secret service). Klapper told Heidemann that if he was willing to undergo a secret ceremony called a '*Sippung*', he would be admitted to Martin's inner circle. As far as Heidemann was concerned, Klapper was clearly a very important individual indeed, which was why he wanted to introduce him to Herr Walde and Herr Sorge, his colleagues from *Stern*.

Klapper was more restrained in his storytelling when there were others present than he was when he had Heidemann on his own. He told Sorge and Walde that Bormann had set up a secret Nazi archive in Madrid, administered by a Spanish lawyer named Dr Iquisabel. Among other things, these documents allegedly proved that the Germans had built three atomic bombs by the end of the war. These documents could be made available to *Stern*, free of charge, providing the magazine agreed to deal with the material 'objectively'. Walde and Heidemann signed a contract promising to abide by this undertaking and in return Klapper pledged to deliver the documents from 'Dr Iquisabel' by the end of the month.

Needless to say, nothing came of this agreement. But Klapper maintained contact with Heidemann and the reporter continued to believe his stories: for example, that he had met Bormann and Josef Mengele at Madrid Airport and that Bormann lived in a big house with a garden and a car park in Zurich. Heidemann gradually became certain that through Klapper he was talking to Bormann, and that 'Martin' had chosen him to be his intermediary with the outside world. This fantasy became inextricably linked in Heidemann's mind with the discovery of the Hitler diaries until, by April 1983, when *Stern* eventually launched its scoop, Heidemann confidently believed that Bormann himself would appear at the magazine's press conference to authenticate them.

While Heidemann pursued these shadows from the Third Reich, Thomas Walde organized the submission of the diaries for expert analysis.

This should have been the moment at which Kujau's fraud was exposed. The forger, after all, had failed to take even the most rudimentary precautions. The diaries were written in ordinary school notebooks stained with tea. The initials on the front of at least one volume were made of plastic. The labels, signed by Bormann and Hess, stating that the books were 'the property of the Führer' were supposed to span thirteen years but were all typed on the same machine. The diaries' pages were made of paper manufactured after 1945. The binding, glue and thread which held them together all contained chemicals which proved them to be postwar. The entries themselves, dashed off by a man with no academic training, were pitted with inaccuracies. The ink in which they were written was bought from an ordinary artists' shop. Logically, the Hitler diaries hoax should have collapsed in the spring of 1982, the moment the experts started work. Instead, Kujau was once again saved from exposure by the behaviour of his victims.

Inside *Stern*, the idea that the diaries might be forgeries was unthinkable. The project had been allowed to reach a stage where cancellation would ruin careers and cost millions of marks; successful completion, on the other hand, would bring the participants enormous financial and professional rewards. From the start the *Stern* men had been prepared to suspend disbelief, to have faith that the books were genuine. Now, subconsciously, their minds had become closed to any other possibility. All of them, from Manfred Fischer and Gerd Schulte-Hillen downwards, had a vested interest in the diaries passing the experts' scrutiny as great as Konrad Kujau's: the trickster and his dupes were on the same side.

If *Stern* had been properly sceptical, the magazine would have commissioned a thorough forensic examination of a complete diary volume. Instead, they concentrated on securing the bare minimum of authentication felt necessary to satisfy the rest of the world. The process, consequently, was flawed from the start.

'The security precautions surrounding the authentication had to be very tight,' recalled Walde. 'We had to prevent word leaking out and jeopardizing the life of "Fischer's" brother in East Germany.' It was considered too risky to part with an entire book. A single page was cut out of the special volume devoted to the flight of Rudolf Hess which had been delivered to *Stern* the previous November. The page consisted of a draft, supposedly in Hitler's hand, of the Nazi Party's official announcement of Hess's flight to Scotland. This tiny sample was considered sufficient to determine the authenticity of the entire hoard of diaries. The text of the Hess statement was selected for analysis because it was already well known; the diary page on which it was copied out was to be passed off simply as a hitherto undiscovered Hitler document, part of a larger find which the magazine wanted checked. None of the experts was told that what they were actually authenticating were Hitler's diaries. This duplicity on *Stern*'s part, the product of its anxiety to safeguard its scoop, was to lead it to disaster.

On Monday, 5 April, Heidemann and Walde visited the Bundesarchiv in Koblenz to meet two of the archive's senior officials, Dr Josef Henke and Dr Klaus Oldenhage. They gave them what purported to be a handwritten draft by Hitler of a New Year greetings telegram, dated 1 January 1940, addressed to General Franco: this was one of the documents Kujau had supplied to Heidemann along with the diaries. The two journalists told the archivists that it was one of a set of documents which *Stern* believed it could obtain from sources outside the Federal Republic. In return for an assurance that after *Stern* had finished with it the material would eventually be donated to the Bundesarchiv, Dr Henke agreed to submit the telegram to the West German police for an official handwriting and forensic analysis. The following day, Walde sent the archivists two further original documents: a speech draft dated 29 December 1934 and a letter to Hermann Goering dated 17 October 1940. These too were drawn from the archive accompanying the diaries. In a covering note, Walde stressed the need for secrecy:

> Once again we ask you to treat the enclosed documents with absolute discretion and not to reveal the source. Your report should be completed as soon as possible in order to enable us to secure the other material should it prove genuine. Otherwise, we must assume that the documents which are still abroad will be sold to collectors in the United States.

Only on 7 April, in a postscript to his letter, did Walde announce that 'Herr Heidemann and I have decided to give you a copy of a further document'. *This* was the Hess statement, slipped in casually among the other papers, with no suggestion that it had been cut out of a diary. Two weeks later, on 21 April, the Bundesarchiv sent all the *Stern* documents (three originals and one photocopy) to the regional police headquarters in Rhineland-Pfalz for a handwriting analysis. For comparison purposes, they enclosed five authentic examples of Hitler writing from their own archives. They would have to wait a month for the results.

Walde, meanwhile, had embarked on a 7000-mile round trip to commission additional experts to give their opinions. On Tuesday 13 April, accompanied by Wilfried Sorge, he flew to Switzerland to see Dr Max Frei-Sulzer, former head of the forensic department of the Zurich police. Frei-Sulzer was living in retirement in the small lakeside town of Thalwil, but was always willing to undertake freelance work. According to Walde, he advised them not to bother with a paper test: 'With today's technology it is possible to make paper look any age you choose.' He agreed to conduct a handwriting analysis. Walde, swearing him to secrecy, provided him with two photocopies of documents from the *Stern* hoard: the Hess statement and a draft telegram to the Hungarian ruler, Admiral Horthy. As comparison material, Frei-Sulzer was supplied with the same copies of authentic Hitler writing that the Bundesarchiv had given to the Rhineland-Pfalz police. A third set of documents for comparison was provided by Gerd Heidemann from his private collection: a paper from 1943 recording the promotion of General Ewald von Kleist to the rank of Field Marshal, along with three signed Hitler photographs. Unfortunately for Frei-Sulzer, these supposedly genuine examples of the Führer's writings were also the work of Konrad Kujau, a confusion which meant that the scientist in some instances would be comparing Kujau's hand with Kujau's, rather than with Hitler's.

The following day, leaving Frei-Sulzer to begin his examination, Walde and Sorge flew from Switzerland to the United States to see a second freelance expert. They spent the night of 15 April in the Hyatt Hotel in Greenville, South Carolina, and early the following morning headed off to their final destination: the town of Landrum, an hour's drive to the north.

Ordway Hilton, like Max Frei-Sulzer, was an elderly man, living in retirement, happy to undertake freelance work. He had been employed by the New York Police Department for almost thirty years and was a distinguished member of his own particular fraternity – a contributor to the proceedings of the American Board of Forensic Document Examiners, the American Academy of Forensic Science and the American Society of Questioned Document Examiners. Hilton now operated from his house in Landrum to which, at 10 a.m. on Friday 16 April, he welcomed his two visitors from Germany.

The American was handed the originals of the two documents copied for Frei-Sulzer: the page from the Hess volume and the telegram for Horthy, together with an accompanying folder of 'authentic' Hitler writing for comparison, part of which was genuine and part from Heidemann's collection of forgeries. 'Some bore signatures that were his or that they told me were his,' he later recalled. 'Some were photocopies they said came from their archives.' Hilton promised to keep their visit secret and to deliver his verdict as quickly as possible.

Walde and Sorge began the long journey back to Hamburg unaware that the only result of their four-day mission was to botch one of *Stern*'s last chances of avoiding catastrophe. If only they had taken the Hess page to a practising forensic expert – for example, Dr Julius Grant, a freelance consultant based in London – they would have discovered within five hours that it contained chemicals of postwar origin and therefore had to be forged. But in their ignorance they chose to depend on the much less reliable and slower process of handwriting analysis. They compounded this error by selecting as experts two men unsuited to the task. True, Frei-Sulzer and Hilton both had international reputations – they were chosen because it was felt their approval would be an advantage in syndication negotiations in Europe and America. But Frei-Sulzer's speciality was investigating biological microtraces, not handwriting; and Ordway Hilton was handicapped by the fact that he could not even understand the language in which the diaries were written. Neither man was a specialist in Nazi documents. In 1983, an expert who was – Charles Hamilton, a New York autograph dealer – estimated that on the American market only Abraham Lincoln's signature commands a greater price than Hitler's. A page of the Führer's writing might fetch $15,000 and no man's autograph is more commonly forged: Hamilton reckoned to see a dozen forgeries a year. If Hilton and Frei-Sulzer had been aware of the extent of the market in Hitler fakes they might have been more suspicious of the gentlemen from Hamburg. And as if all this were not enough, Walde and Sorge had crowned the confusion by unwittingly introducing forgeries from Heidemann's collection into the process of authentication.

Little suspecting the potential for chaos they had left behind them, the two Germans returned to Hamburg. They remained supremely confident that within a month they would have proof that the diaries were genuine. Once that was in their hands, plans could at last be drawn up for publication.

SIXTEEN

At the same time as Walde and Sorge were landing in Hamburg, August Priesack and Billy F. Price arrived in London. They made an odd couple: the impoverished, white-haired Nazi 'professor', and the rich, barrel-chested, aggressive Texan, drawn together by a shared obsession for the paintings of Adolf Hitler.

When Price was not in Europe, searching salerooms and private collections for Hitler's art, he could generally be found in his native city of Houston, pounding round the artificial-grass running track in the grounds of the Houstonian Country Club, or driving across his farm taking pot shots at squirrels with a Magnum from his convertible Cadillac El Dorado, 'custom built for Mr Billy F. Price'. ('Did you give them your design?' 'Hell no, boy, I gave them my cheque.')

At first sight, Price seems a bizarre figure, but he is not unique. It has been estimated that there are 50,000 collectors of Nazi memorabilia throughout the world, of whom most are American, involved in a business which is said to have an annual turnover of $50 million. In the United States a monthly newsletter, *Der Gauleiter*, published from Mount Ida in Arkansas, keeps 5000 serious connoisseurs and dealers informed of the latest trade shows and auctions. Prices increase by 20 per cent a year. 'In the States,' according to Charles Hamilton, 'the collectors of Hitler memorabilia are 40 per cent Jewish, 50 per cent old soldiers like me and 10 per cent of them are young, fascinated by people like Rudel.' In Los Angeles, a collector enjoys himself in private by donning

Ribbentrop's overcoat. In Kansas City, a local government official serves drinks from Hitler's punch bowl. In Chicago, a family doctor has installed a reinforced concrete vault beneath his house where he keeps a collection of Nazi weapons, including Hermann Goering's ceremonial, jewel-encrusted hunting dagger. In Arizona, a used-car salesman drives his family around in the 1938 Mercedes which Hitler presented to Eva Braun; it cost him $150,000 to buy and he expects to sell it for $350,000.

In 1982 Billy Price was fifty-two and a multi-millionaire. ('Hell, if you can't become a millionaire in Houston, you're an asshole, boy.') His money was derived from his ownership of the Price Compressor Company Incorporated, manufacturers of nine-tenths of all compressors used in undersea oil exploration. Like Fritz Stiefel – whom he had met in Stuttgart – Price was a wealthy engineer, no scholar, whose success had given him the means to indulge his interest in Adolf Hitler. He had first become fascinated by the Nazis in the 1950s during his service with the US Army in Germany. While he was stationed in Europe he sought out former Nazis and witnesses from the Third Reich, including Rommel's widow. In the early 1970s, having made his fortune, he returned to begin buying memorabilia, particularly Hitler paintings, paying between $2000 and $12,000 for each one.

Hitler seems to hold a special interest for businessmen, particularly when – as in the case of Billy Price and Fritz Stiefel – they are self-made men. Hitler's career represented the most extreme, as well as the most monstrous, example of what an individual can do if he dedicates himself to the exertion of his will. 'People say Hitler couldn't have kept diaries,' said Price after the forgery had been exposed. 'They say he couldn't have done this, he couldn't have done that – shit, Hitler could paint paintings, he could write operas. Hell, he controlled more real estate than the Roman Empire within three years. There's nothing Hitler couldn't have done if he set his mind to it.' The years of Hitler's 'Triumph of the Will' coincided with the years when the philosophy of self-help was at its height – the Depression was an era of personal improvement courses and guides to success which culminated in 1938 with the appearance of Dale Carnegie's *How to Win Friends and Influence People*. Everything was possible, given the drive to achieve it. 'A man is not what he thinks he is,' wrote the American clergyman Norman Vincent Peale, 'but what he *thinks* he is.' 'My whole life', said Hitler in 1942, 'can be summed up as this ceaseless effort of mine to persuade other people.' With his studied mannerisms, his cultivated habit of staring into people's eyes, his hunger to read manuals and absorb technical data, Hitler was self-help run riot. 'I look at that picture,' said Price, staring at one of his Hitler paintings, of flowers in a vase, 'and I just can't imagine *what was going through the man's mind when he did it*.'

The gates to Price's farm are thirty feet high and topped by stone eagles – scale replicas of a set of gates designed for Hitler by Albert Speer. Beyond them, on the lawn outside his house, stand a tank and a piece of field artillery. The bulk of his collection is housed in his company's headquarters close to Houston's Hobby Airport. On one wall is a portrait of Rudolf Hess in Nazi uniform. In the lavatory is a painting of Hitler. In glass frames are a few small souvenirs – the bill of sale for the first automobile Hitler bought for the Nazi party; a laundry note in Hitler's handwriting; a letter, on prison stationery, from Goering to his wife at the time of the Nuremberg trial; and a letter from Goering to Field Marshal Milch. On a side table stands a large picture of Goering in a swastika-decorated silver frame. Next to it is a heavy, vulgar birthday card sent by Hitler to SS General Sepp Dietrich. There are busts of Hitler. There are two of Hitler's wartime photograph albums – silver-bound with SS flashes and swastikas in the corners and a large eagle on the cover; as one opens a book-plate flutters to the floor: '*Ex Libris Adolf Hitler*'. An ornate cabinet houses Hitler's cutlery and napkins. Price likes showing off his souvenirs but is anxious not to offend visitors. 'I do a lot of business with Jews,' he says. 'When Jews come I put it all away.'

The pride of Price's collection, the fruit of a decade's labour, takes up an entire wall at the end of his conference room: thirty-three Hitler paintings, insured for more than $4 million, arranged in an illuminated display behind armour-plated glass, protected by a sophisticated array of burglar alarms. The pictures are lifeless and uninspired: clumsy land-scapes, fussy reproductions of Viennese buildings, a couple of paintings of flowers, two crude architectural sketches, scraw-led in pencil, bought by Price from Albert Speer. The Texan's favourite is a watercolour of the Vienna City Hall, completed in 1911. 'Most knowledgeable people say he was not the best artist in the world, but I think he was certainly a good artist considering the amount of training he had.' Price claims to have bought the paintings 'in the interests of history': one day, he thinks, given current advances in technology, 'it might be possible to feed them into a computer to get a read-out on Hitler's brain'.

Price's dream, for the sake of which he had gone into partnership with August Priesack, was to track down every extant Hitler painting and drawing in order to catalogue them in a book which he would publish himself. Price had no personal liking for his companion: it was a relationship founded on necessity. 'Sure, I know Priesack's a Nazi. But if you want to know about Hitler, you have to hire Nazis. Hell, if I was going to investigate cancer, you wouldn't start saying to me, "Why are you hanging around all those cancer vic-tims?" would you?' Together the two men had done the rounds of the private collectors in America and Germany. It was this mission which in the spring of 1982 brought them to Britain.

In the final week of April they drove down to the West Country, to Longleat, one of the finest stately homes in England, ancestral seat of Sir Henry Frederick Thynne, sixth Marquess of Bath. Lord Bath, seventy-seven years old and deaf in one ear, but otherwise remarkably sprightly, took them up in his ancient lift to the third floor, a part of the house closed to the public. He unlocked a door next to the library and led Price and Priesack into a long, narrow room, cluttered with Nazi memorabilia. Dominating the scene at the far end was a life-size wax model of Hitler wearing a black leather overcoat and a swastika armband. But neither this, nor Himmler's spectacles, nor the Commandant of Belsen's tablecloth interested Price. What he had come to see was Lord Bath's private exhibition of Hitler paintings. It ran all along one wall, the finest collection in the world: sixty paintings – worth, in Price's opinion, $10 million.

A few days later, back in London, on the afternoon of Thursday, 22 April, August Priesack telephoned David Irving in his flat in Duke Street, Mayfair. Priesack explained why he and Price were in Britain and asked him if he would like to come round to their hotel for dinner that night. Irving agreed.

Priesack had been looking forward to meeting the British historian for a long time. Of all Hitler's biographers, Irving was the most controversial. In *Hitler's War*, published in 1977, he had quoted one of the Führer's doctors, who described how Hitler had expressed his admiration for an 'objective' biography of the Kaiser written by an Englishman. According to the doctor:

> Hitler then said that for some time now he had gone over to having all important discussions and military conferences

recorded for posterity by shorthand writers. And perhaps one day after he is dead and buried an objective Englishman will come and give him the same kind of treatment. The present generation neither can nor will.

Irving was in no doubt that he was the man the Führer had in mind. *Hitler's War*, ten years in the making, had been based on a wealth of previously unpublished documents, letters and diaries. Irving's aim was to rewrite the history of the war 'as far as possible through Hitler's eyes, from behind his desk'. This made for a gripping book, but one which was, by its nature, unbalanced. However 'objectively' he might piece together the unpublished recollections of Hitler's subordinates, they were still the words of men and women who admired their ruler. And confined to Hitler's daily routine, the biography had a curiously unreal quality: the death camps, the atrocities, the sufferings of millions of people which were the result of Hitler's war were not to be found in *Hitler's War* as it was reconstructed by David Irving.

Irving's stated purpose was to portray Hitler as an ordinary human being rather than as a diabolical figure of monstrous evil. It was an aim which was bound to arouse offence: 'If you think of him as a man,' says one of the Jewish characters in George Steiner's *The Portage to San Cristobal of A. H.*, 'you will grow uncertain. You will think him a man and no longer believe what he did.' Irving pilloried earlier biographers who had depicted Hitler as a demon: 'Confronted by the phenomenon of Hitler himself, they cannot grasp that he was an ordinary, walking, talking human weighing some 155 pounds, with greying hair, largely false teeth, and chronic digestive ailments. He is to them the Devil incarnate.' Central to Irving's thesis 'that Hitler was a less than omnipotent Führer' was his argument that Hitler did not order, indeed did not even know of, the Holocaust. It was an assertion which provoked uproar. In Germany, after a dispute with his publishers, the book was withdrawn from sale. In Britain, he became involved in a furious row with a panel of academics during a live edition of David Frost's television chat show. In America, the book was savaged by Walter Laqueur in the *New York Review of Books* and boycotted by the major US paperback publishers. Irving revelled in the publicity, aggressively offering to pay $1000 to anyone who could produce a document proving that Hitler was aware of what was happening in the extermination camps. He claimed that the book upset Jews only 'because I have detracted from the romance of the notion of the Holocaust – that six million people were killed by one man'.

Irving admitted that in writing *Hitler's War* he had 'identified' with the Führer. Looking down upon him as he worked, from the wall above his desk, was a self-portrait of Hitler, presented to him by Christa Schroeder. He did not smoke or touch alcohol. ('I don't drink,' he would say. 'Adolf didn't drink you know.') He shared Hitler's view of women, believing that they were put on the earth in order to procreate and provide men with something to look at: 'They haven't got the physical capacity for producing something creative.' He had married and had four daughters, but wished he had remained single: his marriage had been 'my one cardinal mistake . . . an unnecessary deviation'. In 1981, at the age of forty-three, he had founded his own right-wing political group, built around his own belief in his 'destiny' as a future British leader. With his black hair slanting across his forehead, and a dark cleft, shadowed like a moustache between the bottom of his nose and the top of his upper lip, there were times, in the right light, when Irving looked alarmingly like the subject of his notorious biography.

When Priesack rang he was hard at work on his latest project: a vastly detailed account of Churchill's war years, designed to prove his contention that Britain's decision to go to war with Nazi Germany had been a disastrous mistake. But by 1982, though Irving still had his smart home and his Rolls-Royce he was going through a hard time. He was in the middle of a rancorous and expensive divorce. He was short of money, and smarting from the reception given to his last two books – one of which, *Uprising*, had been dismissed by a reviewer in the *Observer* as 'a bucketful of slime'.

Irving arrived for dinner at the Royal Lancaster Hotel, overlooking Hyde Park, at 9.45 p.m. Billy Price and his wife were unable to join them, so he and Priesack dined alone. Priesack told Irving that he was in difficulties and needed his help. In October of the previous year he had at last brought out his book of unpublished pictures of the Nuremberg rallies. But on 27 November, the Bavarian authorities had decreed that the book contravened anti-Nazi legislation. They ordered that every one of the 5000 copies printed should be confiscated. 'The printers and every bookshop in Germany were raided in a dawn swoop,' noted Irving in his diary. 'On 31 December the order was revoked and the books were returned. On 11 January this year the wholly silly confiscation procedure was repeated.' Priesack asked Irving if he would be willing to appear as a character witness at his forthcoming trial. Irving agreed. 'It is difficult', he wrote, 'to distinguish between these practices and the book burnings of the thirties.'

But sympathetic as he was to Priesack's problems, it was another of the 'professor's' stories which most interested Irving that night:

He is in touch [he wrote in his diary] with a mystery man in Stuttgart whose brother is a major general in the East German People's Army and about to retire to take over a military museum in Germany.

They have a nice racket going: Stuttgart man has acquired

from his East German sources loads of Hitler memorabilia, for cash. These include the Führer's *Ahnenpass* [proof of ancestry], bound in green leather, and revealing that his paternal great-grandfather was identical with his maternal grandfather, 27 half-annual volumes of Hitler's diary, tooled in silver, including a reference to the 1934 Night of the Long Knives ('I have dealt with the traitorous swine'), oil and watercolour paintings by Hitler, medals, photographs, letters, etc. In return for this, 'hard' West German currency, Saxon and Thuringian medals have been bought for the military collection in East Germany.

Problem is that the Bavarian state might try to seize this hoard if they knew where in the Federal Republic it is now located, as they have laid claim to all Hitler's properties by means of a spurious postwar ruling setting aside the personal testament signed and witnessed in the Berlin bunker. Therefore nobody on our side is saying where this Stuttgart man is, or who.

Irving was always interested in documents. Documents were the lifeblood of his career. Probably no other historian in the world had spent as long as he had trawling through the wartime archives in Europe and America. He had tried to track down Eva Braun's diary in New Mexico. He had spent weeks fruitlessly searching an East German forest with a protonmagnetometer, trying to find the glass jar containing the final entries in Goebbel's diaries. Over the past twenty years, like the Zero Mostel character in *The Producers* with his constant trips into 'little old lady land', Irving had visited countless lonely old widows in small German towns, perched on countless sofas drinking cups of tea, made hours of polite conversation, waiting for the moment when they would invite him to look at 'a few pieces of paper my husband left behind'. In this way he obtained a mass of new material, including the diaries of Walther Hewel, Ribbentrop's liaison officer on Hitler's staff, and the unpublished memoirs of Field Marshal Richthofen. Priesack's story of the 'mystery man in Stuttgart' naturally intrigued him, and when he returned home to Duke Street that night he made a careful note of the conversation. He decided that when he was next in Germany he would make a few inquiries about these 'Hitler diaries'.

SEVENTEEN

Spread before him in his office in South Carolina, Ordway Hilton had nine samples of writing for analysis. His task was to determine whether two of them – the Hess document and the Horthy telegram – were genuine. The other seven pieces of material were supposedly authentic 'standards' which he understood had been 'identified as being in the handwriting of Adolf Hitler'. There were three photocopies from the Bundesarchiv: a short postscript signed 'Adolf H' at the end of a typewritten letter dated 1933; a handwritten letter to a party official dated 1936; and copies of eleven Hitler signatures, also from 1936. The other four samples were originals from Heidemann's collection: a handwritten note recording the promotion of General von Kleist dated February 1943 ('In the name of the German people as Reichs Chancellor and Supreme Commander, I award Colonel-General Ewald von Kleist the rank, dignity and protection of a Field Marshal of the German Reich. . . .'); and three signed photographs showing, respectively, Hitler with Goering, Schaub and Bormann, Hitler with Konstantin Hierl, leader of the Reich Labour Service, in May 1940, and Hitler standing with a group in front of the Eiffel Tower in Paris after the fall of France.

Hilton quickly noticed a puzzling discrepancy in this comparison material. Using a binocular microscope he could see that in the photocopies, Hitler signed the 'A' in Adolf with a cross-stroke 'slanting downward'. In the originals, this stroke was horizontal. Unfortunately for him and for *Stern*, he did not pay much attention to this seemingly trivial detail: signatures, after all, often vary over the years and the original documents were all dated at least four years after the photocopies.

Three and a half weeks after Walde's and Sorge's visit, on Tuesday, 11 May, Hilton completed what he described as 'an extensive examination' of the documents he had been given. His findings were exactly what *Stern* had hoped and expected. The Hess document, he wrote in his report, 'reveals a free, natural form of writing':

> Letters which should have looped enclosures below the line are more commonly a simple long curving stroke. The legibility and details of the single space letters are poor due to the compression of their vertical height. Variable forms are present such as the 't' with a separate cross stroke and with the closing made by a triangular movement at the letter base to connect the cross stroke to the body of the letter.
>
> These same habits are found in the known Hitler writing. . . . The lack of lower loop, the flattened single space letters, the variable use of letter forms, and the interruptions in the words especially at points when the letter forms are connected in other instances are all common to both the known and this page of writing under investigation. The combination of all these factors establishes in my opinion adequate proof that this document was written by the same person who prepared all of the known writings. Further there is no evidence within this writing which suggests in any way that this page was prepared by another person in imitation of the writing of Adolf Hitler, and consequently I must conclude that he prepared the document.

After studying the Horthy telegram he reached a similar conclusion. He was particularly impressed by the signature. 'The name Adolf has been condensed to a capital "A" followed by a straight crossed downstroke'; whilst in the signature of the surname:

> The H-form is rotated to the right so that it lies almost horizontal, and the balance of the signature projects downward at a steep angle. This form is typical of the 1940 signatures as can be seen on the photographs and on the von Kleist appointment. Thus all the elements of the signature to the Horthy telegram are consistent with Adolf Hitler's signature and must have been signed by him.

Hilton's report, couched in five pages of professional gobbledegook, was conclusive. But, based as it was on the assumption that all the documents he had been given for comparison were authentic, it was also completely wrong. It was scarcely surprising that the signatures in the Kleist document, the Horthy telegram and the photographs proved 'consistent'; they were all forged by Kujau.

At first sight, this mingling of genuine and false material would seem to suggest that Hilton was deliberately misled by the *Stern* men. In fact, neither the police nor *Stern*'s own subsequent internal inquiry found this to be the case. According to the *Stern Report*: 'Heidemann cannot be accused of imposing material on [the experts]. Walde and Sorge asked him for it.' Walde confirmed this. 'Heidemann', he told the police, 'left the organization of the authentication tests completely to me and Sorge. I have no reason to believe that he wanted to obstruct or twist the authentication of the documents.' The bungling of the tests was the result of straightforward incompetence, typical of the negligence with which the whole diaries affair was handled. Walde and Sorge, in commissioning Hilton, failed to differentiate between documents from the Bundesarchiv and material from Heidemann's collection. And Hilton, working in isolation 3000 miles away, unfamiliar with the script in which the documents were written, did not bother to check.

The American could at least plead in mitigation that his mistake was based on an initial error by *Stern*. The police department of Rhineland-Pfalz had no such excuse.

The police were busy. A routine request from the Bundesarchiv was low on their list of priorities. It was a month before one of their handwriting experts, Herr Huebner, was able to look at the material they had been sent. Huebner had four samples to check: a photocopy of the Hess announcement and originals of a message to General Franco, some speech notes and a letter to Goering. His comparison material, five original Hitler documents from the Bundesarchiv, was unpolluted by Heidemann's fakes. Nevertheless, in a brief report submitted on 25 May, Huebner declared 'with a probability bordering on certainty', that three of the *Stern* documents were genuine. He could not be quite so positive about the Hess communiqué because he had not seen the original, but in his opinion it was 'highly probable' that it was in Hitler's hand.

When this news was relayed to the *Stern* offices in Hamburg, champagne was opened in the history department. The fact that an official government agency had certified that the papers were genuine was an occasion which called for a celebration. There could be no doubt now. The world would have to accept that the magazine had obtained one of the greatest scoops in history. Only Heidemann seemed unaffected by the general jubilation. 'Aren't you pleased?' asked Walde. Heidemann replied that he saw no reason to celebrate: he had known all along that the diaries were genuine.

On 2 June, Walde wrote to Dr Henke at the Bundesarchiv to thank him for sending them the police report. 'Its result greatly pleased us. With the certainty that it has given us, we are going to intensify our efforts to obtain further original material.' Walde added that 'to thank you, and as a gesture to the Bundesarchiv' Gerd Heidemann would like to make them a gift of the originals of Hitler's speech notes and of the Franco telegram.

Nine days later came the third and final handwriting report. The meticulous Max Frei-Sulzer had been determined not to rush to a premature conclusion. On 4 June, unwilling to make a judgement on the basis of photocopies, he travelled from Zurich to Koblenz where he was met by Dr Henke and shown original Hitler material from the vaults of the Bundesarchiv. After Hilton had finished his report, Frei-Sulzer was given the originals of the Hess statement and the Horthy telegram, along with the photographs and Kleist document from Heidemann's collection. He also received a dossier containing copies of Hitler's writing from 1906 to 1945, pieced together by Heidemann to show how the Führer's writing had changed over the years; and a guide to the old-fashioned script in which the documents were written. By the time he had finished assimilating all this, he had been working on the project for two months and his analysis ran to seventeen pages.

'The script of Adolf Hitler', wrote Frei-Sulzer, 'is highly individualistic and offers a good basis for the examination of questionable handwriting.' He singled out fourteen special characteristics, analysed the *i*s, the *h*s and the *t*s, the gaps between the letters and the pressure that had been applied to the pen. He made large photographic blow-ups of individual passages, and at the end of it all his conclusion on the Hess communiqué and the Horthy telegram was unequivocal: 'There can be no doubt that both these documents were written by Adolf Hitler.'

What had gone wrong? The police report certainly appears to have been rushed. The Bundesarchiv's request had been treated as relatively trivial in comparison with the police department's real task of dealing with criminals. Their analyst had been provided with only a relatively small sample of hand-writing to work on, and in the case of the longest document, the Hess statement, he had only had access to a photocopy. He had no idea that he was putting a seal of approval to what ultimately would be an archive of sixty volumes of Hitler diaries. How was Herr Huebner to know that so much rested on his findings?

Of the two private experts, one was unable to understand the language in which the documents were written; the other was operating outside his specialist field. Both were misled by the introduction of fakes into supposedly genuine Hitler writing.

But even after allowance has been made for all these factors, it has to be said that the success of Konrad Kujau's forgeries casts serious doubts on the 'science' of handwriting analysis – or 'holography' as its practitioners prefer to call it. Freelance analysts are always under pressure to reach a definite conclusion. Their clients want to hear 'yes' or 'no', not 'maybe'. Hilton and Frei-Sulzer were not the first experts to fall into the trap of committing themselves to rash over-statements on the basis of flimsy evidence. In 1971, when Clifford Irving faked his notorious 'autobiography' of Howard Hughes, one 'holographer' gave odds of a million to one against the possibility that it could be anything other than genuine. The reputable New York firm of Osborn, Osborn and Osborn, specialists in handwriting analysis since 1905, declared that it would have been 'beyond human ability' to have forged the entire autobiography.

The Hitler diaries fiasco has close parallels with the Hughes case. Like *Stern*, McGraw-Hill, publishers of the auto-biography, were obsessed with leaks and failed to commission a handwriting analysis until late in the project: when they finally did so, they allowed the experts to see only a fraction of the material. The tests were not ordered in a spirit of impartial inquiry: they were required as ammunition to fight off the attacks of sceptical outsiders. Kujau and Clifford Irving were both fluent forgers. They did not give themselves away by being over-cautious, copying out words in the slow and tedious manner which produces telltale tremors: Irving, like Kujau, could write in another person's hand at almost the same speed as he could write in his own. When the discovery of the Hitler diaries was announced in *Stern*, Irving recognized at once that they were probably the work of a forger like himself. 'Once you have the mood,' he commented, 'you can go on forever. I know that from personal experience. I could write sixty volumes of Howard Hughes autobiography and they would pass. Once you can do one page, you can do twenty. Once you can do twenty, you can do a book.' Handwriting experts were useless: 'Nine times out of ten they come out with judgements their clients expect. . . . They're hired by people who want an affirmative answer.'

Clifford Irving and Konrad Kujau succeeded in the same way that most confidence tricksters succeed: by playing on two of the most ancient of human weaknesses – vanity and greed. There came a point during the duping of McGraw-Hill when one of Irving's confederates found it impossible to accept that a powerful company led by intelligent men could be stupid enough to accept their often ludicrous forgery. 'It's got to occur to them,' he said. 'How can they be so naïve?' In his account of the hoax, Irving recalled his answer:

> Because they *believe*. First they wanted to believe and now they have to believe. They want to believe because it's such a coup for them. . . . Can't you see what an ego trip it is? The secrecy part – the thing that protects you and me – is what they love the most. That takes them out of the humdrum into another world, the word we all dream of living in, only we really don't want to because we know it's mad. And the

greatest thing for them is that this way they can live in it part time. They're participating but they're protected by an intermediary. I'm their buffer between reality and fantasy. It's a fairy tale, a dream. And the beauty part for them is that they'll make money out of it, too. Corporate profit justifies any form of lunacy. There's been no other hoax like it in modern times. . . .

Twelve years later, the analysis fitted *Stern*'s behaviour to perfection.

EIGHTEEN

With the diaries' handwriting now apparently authenticated as Adolf Hitler's, work on the project within *Stern* intensified. Five people were now engaged virtually full time on the operation: Thomas Walde; Walde's thirty-five-year-old assistant, Leo Pesch; two secretaries; and Gerd Heidemann. To safeguard the secret of the diaries' existence, the group moved out of the main *Stern* building to new offices a few minutes' walk away. The diaries were also moved. Every few weeks, Manfred Fischer would empty the management safe of the latest volumes and take them back with him to his own office at Bertelsmann's headquarters in Guetersloh. Eventually, fearful of a robbery, Fischer and Schulte-Hillen decided to transfer them out of the country altogether, to a bank vault in Switzerland. Not for the first time, the saga of the diaries assumed the trappings of a cheap thriller. Safe deposit box number 390 was rented from the Handelsbank in Talstrasse, Zurich. Periodically Fischer himself would board Bertelsmann's private jet carrying a suitcase containing the diaries and fly to Switzerland. Herr Bluhm, director of the Handelsbank, would meet him and the two men would descend into the vaults. Bluhm would unlock two steel mesh doors, retrieve the large metal box, and discreetly turn his back while Fischer filled it with the latest diaries. One key to the box stayed with the bank. The other was taken back to Germany by Fischer and locked in the safe in Hamburg.

Gradually, a publication strategy for the diaries began to evolve. On Tuesday, 25 May – the day on which the

Rhineland-Pfalz police expert concluded that the writing he had been given was Hitler's – a conference was called to discuss the marketing of the material. Present were Wilfried Sorge, Thomas Walde, Peter Koch, Felix Schmidt, Leo Pesch, Henri Nannen and Gerd Heidemann; Schulte-Hillen presided. Neither of the two editors said very much. Their status within the company had recently been eroded still further, when *Stern*, humiliatingly, was scooped by its rival, *Der Spiegel*, over a trade union scandal. Peter Koch, who had originally turned down the story, had offered to resign. He had been allowed to stay on, but in the aftermath of the affair, neither he nor Schmidt was in a position to argue with the management. The fact that their mishandling of Heidemann had almost cost the company the diaries scoop as well hung, unspoken, over the entire proceedings.

Thomas Walde put forward the plan which he had discussed with Pesch and Heidemann. One of the most interesting documents so far delivered to Hamburg was the special diary volume Hitler had devoted to the Hess affair. This had been with the history department since November. Entitled 'The Hess Case', it consisted of a few pages of notes scrawled in the early summer of 1941, proving that the Führer had known all along of his deputy's flight to Britain. 'From November 1940,' Hitler had supposedly written, 'Hess was whispering in my ear that he thought as I did that England and Germany could live together in peace, that the sufferings of our two peoples could bring satisfaction to one person, namely the old fox in Moscow, Stalin.' The content was sketchy – little more than 1000 words – describing how Hess had evolved his plan, how Hitler had been 'kept informed about the preparations' and how he had been forced to deny all knowledge of the mission when the British had imprisoned Hess.

Now [concluded 'Hitler'] the last attempt to reach an understanding with England has failed.

The English people perhaps understand what the flight of Hess signified, but the ossified old men in London don't. If Providence does not help our two peoples, the fight will go on until one people is totally destroyed, the English people.

After the victory, the German people will also be ready to understand the flight of Party Comrade Hess and this will be appreciated for its worth.

16 May 1941
Adolf Hitler

Walde's proposal was that this material should be used as the basis for a sensational story to be published in January, the fiftieth anniversary of Hitler's accession to power. The Hess volume stood on its own. There was no need to refer to the actual diaries, whose existence could be kept secret for a few more months. The advantage of Walde's idea was that it would give the magazine a good cover story whilst also enabling it to test the water prior to the launch of the main diary hoard. The plan was accepted by the conference. The only mildly dissenting voice was Henri Nannen's. Would it not, he suggested, be a good idea to bring in Sebastian Haffner or Joachim Fest, recognized authorities on the Third Reich, to work on the material? The idea was angrily slapped down. This was *Stern*'s story, and *Stern*'s men should take all the credit. Neither Nannen nor the editors were aware that Heidemann and Walde had contracts with the management which enabled them to veto the involvement of outside historians.

Ten days later, on Friday, 4 June, Manfred Fischer, Gerd Schulte-Hillen and Jan Hensmann flew down to Munich to meet Olaf Paeschke, the head of Bertelsmann's international publishing division. It was agreed, without reference to the *Stern* editors, that Walde and Pesch would first turn the Hess material into a book, provisionally entitled *Plan 3*. This would then be serialized in the magazine. The idea of marketing the Hess scoop through the book publishing industry was attractive to the businessmen. It would enable Bertelsmann to bring its foreign companies into the action and take control of the syndication negotiations. Shortly afterwards, Paeschke briefed Louis Wolfe, President of Bantam Books in New York, on the contents of the forthcoming manuscript. Wolfe was a lucky man, said Paeschke. *Plan 3* would be 'the publishing event of the century'.

On 5 July, Leo Pesch went down to Koblenz to hand the Bundesarchiv the original of the Hess announcement and the Horthy telegram which had now been returned to *Stern* by Frei-Sulzer. These, together with the original documents already in the archive's possession, were then forwarded to the West German Federal Police for a final forensic examination to confirm the age of the paper and the ink. *Stern* had hoped for a quick result. But the police laboratories were involved in anti-terrorist investigations and were swamped with work. Weeks passed and despite occasional reminders from Walde, nothing was done. There was no particular sense of urgency in Hamburg. The documents had, after all, been authenticated by three different handwriting experts: the forensic tests were only a safety check.

Meanwhile, Heidemann carried on draining the company's special diaries account – 200,000 marks was withdrawn on 29 March, 600,000 marks on 21 May, 400,000 marks on 2 June, 200,000 marks on 10 June – and the Heidemann family spending spree continued. Precise details of what was bought and when will probably never be known. More than 80,000 marks was spent in auction houses, mainly to buy Third Reich memorabilia. Ninety thousand marks went on jewellery and carpets; 37,000 on furniture. A futile attempt to recover Mussolini's treasure, supposedly dumped in Lake Como at the end of the war, swallowed 185,000 marks. At least a quarter of a million marks was paid into one or another of Heidemann's six known bank accounts. To house his Nazi relics, the reporter rented a gallery in Milchstrasse, in the heart of one of Hamburg's most expensive shopping areas. In the middle of April, Gina visited an estate agent. 'She said she was interested in buying a large house with a view over the Elbe,' recalled the agent, Peter Moller. 'The price was no object.' Over the next year they maintained contact and he sent her details of property costing in the region of 1–2 million marks.

On 14 July, after Heidemann received the largest single payment for the diaries to date – 900,000 marks – contracts were signed to start the long-awaited renovation of *Carin II*'s hull. The yacht alone cost Heidemann a fortune. Experts were flown in from England. New engines were installed. The boat was rewired. The interior was refurbished. The total cost exceeded 500,000 marks. To restore the woodwork, Gunther Lutje, a Hungarian boatyard owner who had known Heidemann and *Carin II* for almost a decade, was paid 300,000 marks.

In his prosperity, Heidemann did not forget those who had helped him in the past. In June, Axel Thomsen, the young seaman who had sailed *Carin II* from Bonn to Hamburg, rang Heidemann to ask for a loan. He had heard that the reporter now had plenty of money. 'He said immediately that he was perfectly willing to lend me 6000 marks,' recalled Thomsen. 'Two or three days later he came to my house and gave me the money, in 500-mark notes. It was lying around in his briefcase.' Encouraged by Heidemann's readiness to help,

Thomsen rang him again two months later to ask for a further 13,000 marks. 'From his reaction, I could see that he was slightly hesitant, but he said he was willing to lend me the money. He said he felt duty bound to assist me. He said I could have it and that I should go round to his flat in the Elbchaussee to collect it.' When Thomsen appeared, Heidemann handed him an envelope containing 13,000 marks in cash. Thomsen put the money in his pocket. Heidemann asked him to make sure that Gina did not get to hear about it. Heidemann also remembered Hannelore Schustermann, the secretary from whom, in his hard-pressed days, he had been forced to scrounge money to go to the canteen. She was let into the secret of the Hitler diaries and went to work for Heidemann in his special suite of offices. The diaries, he confided to her, were going to make him a millionaire.

On 29 July, Heidemann flew to Spain and arranged to buy two holiday villas in the Mediterranean town of Denia, midway between the resorts of Valencia and Alicante. The two houses, which stood next to one another, cost him 390,000 marks in cash. In August, he suggested to Kujau that he should buy one of them. The two villas, he said, both had spacious cellars which could be knocked together to make a large underground vault. Heidemann proposed that they should each move their Nazi collections there. Together they would create the biggest museum of Third Reich memorabilia in the world. The plan came to nothing the moment Edith Lieblang got to hear of it. She told Kujau, in forceful tones, that she was 'absolutely against' it. 'It seemed to me completely worthless,' she recalled, 'owning it and only spending a couple of weeks a year in it. For 200,000 marks, I could go on holiday around the world until the end of my life.' Edith's word was final and Heidemann's dream of erecting a monument to the Führer amid the haciendas and cicadas of the Costa Blanca evaporated.

*   *   *

Not all the money Heidemann spent at this time belonged to *Stern*; at least some of it was his own. He was now drawing a salary of over 100,000 marks a year. He had received a bonus of 20,000 marks. He had already been given an advance of 300,000 marks by Manfred Fischer and his position as the sole contact between Gruner and Jahr and the 'antiques dealer' in Stuttgart meant that he found no difficulty in extracting more. His moodiness and periodic threats to take his great scoop elsewhere were guaranteed to throw the *Stern* management into a panic. Without him, the flow of diaries from East Germany would dry up. Like wealthy drug addicts, they were prepared to pamper their supplier: to ensure he continued to deal with them, they were willing to give him whatever he asked.

In June 1982 Heidemann told the company that in order to keep up the pretence of being a Swiss collector, he was having to buy additional material from the communist general: Nazi documents and paintings and drawings by Adolf Hitler. Although as a collector he was naturally interested in obtaining such items, he did not see why he should have to go on paying for them out of his own pocket. Gerd Schulte-Hillen accepted Heidemann's argument and on 11 June concluded a new contract with him, by which the reporter was to be paid a 'loan' of 25,000 marks for each volume of diaries he delivered. To date, there were thirty-five books in the company's possession. Heidemann was therefore entitled to receive 875,000 marks, minus the 300,000 marks advance paid to him in February 1981, and the 80,000 marks still outstanding for his unwritten books – *Bord Gespräche* and *My African Wars*. The money was described, for tax purposes, as an 'interest-free loan' to be recovered through 'profit-sharing and royalty fees' following 'the commercial exploitation of the diaries'.

But Heidemann wanted more than mere money. Incapable

of writing up the stories he researched, he had, throughout his career, suffered from an inferiority complex. Now, as he watched Walde and Pesch start putting together a book based on the material he had gathered, his resentment welled up in a demand for praise for his achievement. He craved respect and recognition. It was like dealing with a child. Gerd Schulte-Hillen had already had to cope with one of these bouts. On that occasion, at the end of 1981, he had forced the editors to give Heidemann a salary increase. In the summer of 1982, Wilfried Sorge warned him once again that the company's ageing prima donna was proving difficult. 'He was portrayed to me,' remembered the managing director, 'as being rather like a circus horse: because he'd made this find, you had to say "hello" to him and pat him on the head from time to time.'

Acting on Sorge's advice, on Monday, 28 June, Schulte-Hillen took Heidemann out 'for a meal on expenses'. They met in the Ovelgonne, a restaurant in a picturesque street overlooking the Elbe. For three courses, Schulte-Hillen listened patiently to Heidemann's stories. He heard of the reporter's adventures in Africa and the Middle East, of his experiences with the white mercenaries in the Congo, of his long search for Traven. Finally, over dessert, Heidemann invited him back to his home in the Elbchaussee to see part of his collection. 'He showed me drawings by Hitler,' said Schulte-Hillen, 'and the pistol with which Hitler was supposed to have shot himself.' The businessman inspected Heidemann's archive: the shelves full of history books and folders crammed with documents, all neatly arranged and catalogued. He congratulated Heidemann on his professionalism and, after a couple of hours, the two men parted on excellent terms.

Heidemann was given another opportunity to show off a few weeks later, when Henri Nannen also decided to visit him at home. Nannen had retired from daily involvement in *Stern* to devote himself to the erection of his own memorial: an art gallery in his home town of Emden, to house his collection of German Expressionist paintings. But to Heidemann – as to most West German journalists – Nannen, despite his retirement, *was Stern*, and he was determined to impress his old employer. Nannen parked his car beside the Elbe and got out to see Heidemann on his balcony, waving at him with one hand, and raising a glass of iced champagne to him with the other. Climbing the stairs, he suddenly realized that Heidemann not only had the top floor apartment, but the one underneath as well. Inside, the impression of luxury continued. 'The place was decorated in the very best taste,' recalled Nannen. 'There were some superb pieces of furniture – Queen Anne, I think – and on the walls were drawings. The first thing that hit me was the original manuscript of '*Deutschland über Alles*' by Hoffman. He also had the autographs of Bismark and Moltke, along with other historical documents under glass and in frames. I was astonished. Where has he got all this from? I thought.' Heidemann told him he had been forced to buy it from the supplier of the Hitler diaries in order to disguise the fact that he was interested only in the diaries themselves. 'He gave me some convoluted story and showed me thirty or forty Hitler drawings,' said Nannen. 'I'm something of an art historian. They seemed to me to be perfectly genuine.'

After seeing Hitler's suicide weapon, and a pair of busts supposedly sculptured by the Führer, Nannen inquired about the diaries.

Heidemann crossed the room, pulled a cord, and a pair of black curtains slid back to reveal a bookcase full of files. These were Heidemann's private photocopies of the diaries, each sheet protected by a transparent plastic cover.

'What do you want to see?' asked Heidemann.

'The Roehm *putsch*,' replied Nannen.

He was handed the relevant volumes and read a few pages. He found them 'unbelievingly boring' – a fact which further convinced him that they must be genuine: 'I couldn't believe that anyone would have gone to the trouble of forging something so banal.'

But although Nannen had no doubts that the diaries were authentic, his visit convinced him that Heidemann was a crook. Unlike Schulte-Hillen – who had known Heidemann for only a year – Nannen had been his employer since the 1950s. The change in the man's fortunes was startling. It was inconceivable that he could have moved from near bankruptcy to such affluence without robbing the company. Nannen left the Elbchaussee and immediately drove to the *Stern* building. Within ninety minutes he was in Schulte-Hillen's office. 'I've just come from Heidemann's,' he told him, 'and he's shitting on us – from a great height.' Schulte-Hillen asked if he meant that the diaries were forgeries. 'No,' said Nannen, 'but he's clearly pocketing our money.' Privately, *Stern*'s editors thought the same: Peter Koch had been in no doubt ever since he learned of the expensive renovation work being carried out on *Carin II*. But they could have warned Nannen that to raise such suspicions with Schulte-Hillen was useless. The managing director regarded himself as a good judge of character; he was convinced of the reporter's integrity; and having made up his mind, he was unshakeable. He reacted, in Koch's words, 'like a man with an allergy' whenever Heidemann's honesty was questioned. That afternoon, when Nannen told him of his fears, Schulte-Hillen stared at him with contempt. Heidemann, he said, was being well rewarded for his work: the only sort of person who would think that he was robbing the company was someone who was capable of committing such a crime himself.

Meanwhile, as the summer wore on, Thomas Walde and Leo Pesch worked hard on the manuscript of *Plan 3*. Heidemann appeared in the offices occasionally and continued to deliver new volumes of diaries, but they had no time to look at them. To help them with the background for the Hess book, the two would-be historians hired a team of freelance researchers. 'We employed them without telling them the context in which they were working,' said Walde. 'We simply asked them to do some research in certain areas.' At the beginning of September, after three months' intensive work, more than half the book was completed. On Monday, 6 September, chapters 2–7 were submitted to the editors of *Stern*. Walde explained in a memorandum to Felix Schmidt how the book would be structured. The first chapter would be an account of Hess's life in Spandau and of his relations with his family. 'We have already won over Hess's son,' confided Walde, 'but not yet Frau Ilse Hess.' Not until chapter 8 – which had still to be written – did the authors intend to introduce quotations from the Hitler notebook on the Hess affair. Then would come an account of Hess's experiences in Britain, the Nuremberg trial, and his sentencing to life imprisonment. There was to be no mention of the existence of the diaries.

Schmidt later described himself as 'amazed' at Walde's proposed treatment. He was a journalist. It was ridiculous, in his opinion, to start publication of the documents with a history lesson on Rudolf Hess. *Stern* should launch its scoop with an account of the discovery of Hitler's diaries. Once again the editors realized that decisions had been taken behind their backs. *Plan 3* was the child of the Bertelsmann marketing division, not the company's journalists, part of a long-term commercial scheme to exploit the diaries.

The sales strategy was based on two premises. First, to enable the company to recoup its investment, publication would have to be spread over as long a period as possible – somewhere between eighteen months and two years. Secondly, the company would have to find reliable foreign partners to syndicate the material. *Plan 3* would enable Bertelsmann to begin earning money, whilst leaving the bulk of the diaries untouched. The manuscript would be sold to news organizations all over the world. Only if they paid promptly, adhered to *Stern*'s publishing timetable, and generally behaved 'correctly', would they be told of the existence of the real prize – Hitler's diaries – and be offered a share in its exploitation.

The moment Walde and Pesch had finished the first part of the manuscript, Wilfried Sorge and Olaf Paeschke flew to New York to hold discussions with the management of Bantam Books. The talks took place on Friday, 10 September. They did not go well. The Germans wanted to draw on Bantam's experience of the American and British markets. They wanted to know which would be the best magazines and newspapers to approach. As far as Bantam was concerned, their interest was in a book, not a newspaper serial – especially as the two Germans were insistent that they should retain the syndication rights. As paranoid as ever, Sorge and Paeschke refused to reveal the secret of the diaries, leaving the American publishers with a feeling that they were being used. The talks ended, according to one of the participants, with a 'bitter feeling' on both sides.

Sorge flew back to Hamburg over the weekend. On Monday he went in to see Schulte-Hillen to brief him on his trip. The managing director wanted to know how much the diaries were likely to fetch on the world market. This was a difficult question to answer. Sorge had no idea of the total sales potential. The project was unprecedented. After the discussions in New York, it was clear that the author who might remotely be compared to Adolf Hitler was Henry Kissinger. His memoirs had been syndicated across the globe in 1979 in an intricate network of deals, simultaneous release dates and subsidiary rights, which was a wonder to behold. Hitler was probably bigger than Kissinger – 'hotter', as the Americans put it. Certainly, the company was looking at an income of upwards of $2 million.

Sorge's report did not please Schulte-Hillen. The company had already paid out 7 million marks – roughly $2 million – to obtain the diaries. Under the terms of the contracts agreed with Heidemann and Walde in 1981, Gruner and Jahr was entitled to only 40 per cent of the revenue from syndication sales. That figure made sense when there were only twenty-seven diaries; but now there were more than forty, the tally was still rising and the costs were going to be more than four times the amount originally predicted. Unless something was done, the company was going to end up making a loss. During a business trip to Majorca, Schulte-Hillen took the opportunity to tell Manfred Fischer that he had decided to renegotiate the original contracts. On 14 October, he summoned Heidemann and Walde to a meeting in a Cologne hotel and explained the problem.

Legally, both men would have been entitled to reject Schulte-Hillen's proposal. Nevertheless, they were forced to accept the logic of what he said. A new, handwritten contract was drawn up, under which both men would be entitled to the same percentage of the syndication revenue – but only after Gruner and Jahr had cleared its costs. Walde signed, reluctantly. Heidemann, characteristically, demanded something in return. He pointed out that he was giving up a probable income of 2.3 million marks. Schulte-Hillen had no alternative but to agree to pay him yet more 'compensation'. Under the terms of the contracts of February 1981 and June 1982, he had already received 1.1 million marks in advances and 'loans'. Schulte-Hillen arranged for that sum to be converted into a once-and-for-all 'fee' of 1.5 million marks.

Heidemann also extracted another concession. From now on, it was written into his contract that he was 'not obliged to reveal in fine detail the method by which the diaries were acquired, nor the names of his sources'. Schulte-Hillen took this as further evidence of Heidemann's integrity – of his determination to protect the lives of his suppliers. In reality, Heidemann's manoeuvre was almost certainly designed to cover up his own fraudulent activities: if he could prevent the company checking with Kujau, no one would ever know precisely how much he had paid for the diaries. Schulte-Hillen's concession, seemingly trivial at the time, was to have important consequences.

The day after the meeting in Cologne, Heidemann withdrew another 450,000 marks from the bank in Adolphsplatz.

NINETEEN

On Saturday, 20 November, the German People's Union (DVU), a right-wing political group, organized a meeting in the Westphalian village of Hoffnungsthal. The speaker – a regular favourite among DVU audiences, with his stirring denunciations of communists and socialists – was David Irving.

Irving arrived at the hall to be met by the unmistakable figure of Otto Guensche. The devoted SS major, whose claim to fame was that he had burned Hitler's body, was a local DVU supporter. 'He talks to nobody,' noted Irving in his diary, 'but has been an informant of mine for twelve years or more.' After a few pleasantries, Guensche abruptly asked the historian: 'What's your view of the Rudolf Hess affair?' According to Irving:

> I did not know what he was getting at. He continued, 'Do you think the Chief knew about it in advance or not?' I said I thought there were signs that Hitler approved of the idea in the autumn of 1940, but unless it was discussed by Hitler with Hess when they met briefly after the Reichstag session of 4 May 1941, Hitler was probably taken by surprise. Guensche said: 'He knew about it. I know.' I asked how. Guensche: 'I've seen the proof.'

Suddenly, Irving remembered his dinner with Priesack in London back in April.

> Acting on a hunch I said, 'You've seen the Stuttgart diaries

too?' He said he had, that they were beyond doubt authentic, and that in this particular case they reveal Hitler as deliberating different courses of action: what to do if Hess's mission succeeded, what if it failed, etc. The diaries also contain Hitler's character assessments of his contemporaries, showing him a better judge than has hitherto been supposed, etc. Guensche implied that he has seen the originals.

The conversation ended when Irving had to go up on to the platform to deliver his speech. Afterwards, hoping to pick up more information, he went back to Guensche's house for tea. But Guensche had not withstood ten years of interrogation in the Soviet Union in order to be tricked into disclosure in his own home. He refused to say any more about the diaries and Irving left frustrated.

Despite his elaborate show of concern for secrecy, Heidemann had always been remarkably indiscreet about the diaries. He had shown original volumes to former Nazis like Guensche, Mohnke and Wolff and to such shady contacts as Medard Klapper. On several occasions, Walde and Pesch had been forced to restrain him from boasting openly about his discovery to colleagues in the corridor at *Stern*. In 1981, he had sat his old friend Randolph Braumann down on the sofa in his apartment. According to Braumann: 'He said: "Are you sitting comfortably?" and then from under the sofa he pulled out a plastic bag stuffed with bundles of money. He said it was for the diaries and asked me not to tell anybody.' The following year, meeting Braumann in the *Stern* canteen, Heidemann had taken him outside to his car 'and produced a packet containing seven or eight books. He seemed very proud, positively euphoric.' Now *Stern* was to pay the price for Heidemann's showing off.

Returning to London twelve days later, Irving telephoned Phillip Knightley, the senior reporter on the *Sunday Times*, and told him of the existence of the Hitler diaries. 'He is interested,' wrote Irving in his diary. 'I said I'd let him have a note about it at his private address.' That same afternoon, Irving wrote to him, enclosing an account of his conversations with Priesack and Guensche, and stressing the usefulness of his reputation as a right-winger: 'I would be prepared to set up or conduct such negotiations with traditionally awkward German personalities as might prove necessary in an attempt to secure this material.' In return, he made it clear that he expected a 'finder's fee' of 10 per cent of the cost of the diaries. Knightley – who was about to return to his native Australia for four months – passed Irving's offer on to Magnus Linklater, the features editor of the *Sunday Times*. On Wednesday 8 December, Linklater telephoned Irving to confirm that the paper was interested. At 9.15 that night, Irving rang August Priesack in Munich to try to extract more information from him. The first part of the conversation concerned itself with the old man's forthcoming trial for 'propagating the swastika' in his book about the Nazi Party rallies.

'*You* promised to provide a reference for me,' said Priesack, reproachfully.

'Yes,' lied Irving, 'that's why I'm calling.' (He had found the old man, frankly, to be rather a bore and had never had any intention of allowing his name to be associated with such an obvious crank.) He then had to endure five minutes of Priesack alternately moaning about his persecution and bragging about the book on Hitler's art he was working on with Billy Price. ('The book is written by *me* in every way. But it can't be put out like that because the American has paid 400,000 marks for it – so he has to appear as the author.') At last, after a number of false starts, Irving managed to turn the conversation to the diaries. According to Priesack 'six or seven' were already in America, where they were to be published. 'That's interesting,' said Irving.

PRIESACK: They're just headlines from the *Völkischer Beobachter*.

IRVING: The whole twenty-seven volumes?

PRIESACK: Yes. He wrote them as something to jog his memory. . . . I've only seen a half-yearly volume from 1935, and there were in total only six interesting pages. You can read them in Hitler's handwriting here [i.e. in Priesack's apartment].

IRVING: Good. When I'm there, I'll—

PRIESACK: But I've also got *Mein Kampf*. The third volume.

IRVING: [*emits stifled cry*]

PRIESACK: Haven't you heard about that?

IRVING: When did he write *that*?

PRIESACK: He started that on the day after the seizure of power. *Mein Kampf Three*. I've got a few pages. They've not been sold. They'll probably end up in America because America pays better.

IRVING: Do you know where all this is? Can you find that out?

PRIESACK: Up to a point, yes.

IRVING: You are a real gold mine.

PRIESACK: [*laughs*]

After promising to send Priesack a character reference (describing him as 'a well-known scientist'), and suggesting he might come and see him in Munich in a few days' time, Irving hung up and switched off his tape recorder.

The following day in Hamburg, the Hitler diaries team received an unpleasant surprise. In the belief that it might shake loose some information from someone, somewhere in Germany, Irving had written letters to dozens of West German newspapers to alert their readers to the existence of the diaries. On Thursday, 9 December, these seeds of mischief began sprouting in news columns and letters pages across the country:

> I am of the opinion that German historians are guilty of failing to explain to the German public the facts behind the Nazi crimes against the Jews. We know that Adolf Hitler's own diaries – 27 half-yearly volumes, including the first six months of 1945 – have entered the Federal Republic as a result of horse-trading with a major-general in the East German Army. They are however in private hands in Baden Wuerttemberg [the area of Germany which includes Stuttgart] and German historians are taking no notice of them. The Hitler diaries would surely clear up any doubts about whether he knew or did not know of Auschwitz, Treblinka and Majdanek.

Among the thirteen West German newspapers which eventually carried Irving's letter was Kujau's and Stiefel's daily paper, the *Stuttgart Zeitung*.

The effect of this burst of publicity on the furtive circle of south German collectors was dramatic. Like insects whose stone has been kicked away, they scurried for cover. Kujau rang Heidemann to warn him that Irving was on their trail. The reporter told him to put as much pressure as he could on Stiefel to ensure he kept quiet: above all, Irving must not get to see the 1935 diary which Stiefel still had in his safe. Kujau contacted the industrialist and warned him that he had heard from his brother that sixty-four East German generals had been summoned to Berlin in an effort to flush out whoever was supplying the diaries. Stiefel panicked. Convinced that he would be raided by the police at any moment, he packed his entire collection – his medals, papers, paintings and concentration camp china – and shipped it out of the country to his holiday home in Italy. He also wrote to Priesack. 'I must ask you,' he told him, 'under the terms of our agreement, to return to me all the copies and photographs which are in your possession and which come from us.'

At four o'clock in the afternoon, Heidemann spoke to Irving on the telephone. He pleaded with him to keep quiet about the diaries. Not all the material, he said, was in the West: he was having to make repeated trips into East Germany and his life would be in danger if there were any more publicity. Irving replied that Priesack had told him that most of the material had already been smuggled out. 'What has Priesack got?' asked Heidemann. For a moment, Irving – who had not yet seen any of the material – was stumped for an answer. Recalling his conversation with Guensche he replied that Priesack had a letter from Hess to Hitler dated May 1941. As the conversation went on, Heidemann began to realize that Irving was bluffing. He did not know the scale of the archive in *Stern*'s possession. He thought that some of the books were still in America. He did not know about Hitler's special volume on Hess. Almost all his information was either two years old or based on nothing more than regurgitated gossip. 'Priesack', he warned Irving, 'is talking about things of which he knows nothing.'

At the end of the conversation, Heidemann reassured his colleagues in the history department that the leak was not as serious as it appeared. He played them a tape recording of his telephone call from Kujau during which 'Conny' told him not to worry about Irving. According to Leo Pesch, Heidemann told them that ' "Conny" was putting so much pressure on Stiefel, there was no way he would hand over his diary volume to Irving.'

That same day, Heidemann collected another 450,000 marks from Sorge.

In London, Irving began transcribing the tape of his telephone call to Priesack. It was a laborious task and took him until after midnight to complete. At 2 a.m. he drove round to the offices of the *Sunday Times* in Grays Inn Road and left a copy of the transcript in reception addressed to Magnus Linklater. He fell into bed, exhausted, half an hour later.

Linklater found Irving's envelope when he came into the office the next day. He was in a dilemma. Obviously he wanted to pursue the story. On the other hand, it was not wise, in his opinion, for the *Sunday Times* to become involved with a man of Irving's reputation. Irving's suggestion – that he should fly out to Hamburg and Munich at the paper's expense in order 'to identify and talk with the Stuttgart source' – filled him with unease. Instead, he decided to do some checking of his own. He rang the German historian Hermann Weiss at the Institute for Contemporary History in Munich and explained what Irving had told him. Weiss's reaction was that the story was rubbish: it was inconceivable that there were any such 'Hitler diaries'. The *Sunday Times* also contacted Gerd Heidemann, whose name had been given to them by Irving. Heidemann, according to Linklater, confirmed he was involved in trying to obtain Hitler material, but said that as a result of recent publicity much of it had 'gone back' over the border to East Germany.

Early in the morning on Wednesday, 15 December, five days after receiving Irving's transcript of his conversation with Priesack, Linklater rang Irving at home. He told him that the *Sunday Times* could not afford to fly him to Germany: 'We don't have the large sums of money to throw around that we used to have.' They would much prefer to send Hermann Weiss or one of their own reporters down to see Priesack. The paper wanted to involve someone who was 'neutral'. Apologetic for the obvious inference in this remark, Linklater offered to pay Irving £250 for having given them the information in the first place. 'We don't want you to think we are trying to go behind your back,' he said. He offered to give him time to think it over. Irving thanked him for his honesty and said he felt inclined to accept his offer.

As soon as Linklater had hung up, Irving telephoned a contact at the German publishing company Langen Mueller. He told them that if they wanted to secure Hitler's diaries they should move fast because the *Sunday Times* was on to them. By mid-afternoon, the publishers had called him back and offered to pay his air fare if he would inspect the material on their behalf. Irving immediately booked seats on a flight to Munich. He had no intention of being double-crossed by the *Sunday Times*.

At the same time in Hamburg, Heidemann and Walde were being presented with a formal copy of the agreement sketched out in Cologne in October with Gerd Schulte-Hillen. Once the company had recovered its costs, the revenue generated by the diaries would be divided up between the journalists and Gruner and Jahr – and for the first time, in recognition of his work on the Hess manuscript, Leo Pesch was to be given a slice of the cake. Heidemann would receive 36 per cent of the money; Walde, 16 per cent; Pesch, 8 per cent; the company would take the remaining 40 per cent. These percentages would apply both to the sale of the syndication rights and to the sale of the actual diaries themselves.

An appendix to the contract set out in detail exactly how the agreement might work in practice. Supposing syndication sales brought in 10 million marks: the company would immediately claim 9 million to defray its own costs; of the remainder, Heidemann would receive 360,000 marks, Walde 160,000 and Pesch 80,000 – Grunder and Jahr's 40 per cent share would yield it 400,000 marks. If the books were sold – say, to an archive or a collector – for an additional 5 million marks, the company would immediately take half to cover its initial outlay. Of the remaining 2.5 million marks, Heidemann would then take 900,000, Walde 400,000 and Pesch 200,000; again, the company's share would be 40 per cent – 1 million marks. In other words, despite the readjustment insisted upon by Schulte-Hillen, the journalists still stood to become rich men as a result of the diaries' publication.

Although individual volumes, mainly from the war years, were continuing to come in, the Hess manuscript was now finished. The most difficult task had been securing the cooperation of Frau Hess, from whom Walde and Pesch had wanted information about her visits to see her husband in Spandau. The Hess family had called in a lawyer who had insisted on payment of a fee of 5000 marks as well as a guarantee that the family's 'political standpoint' would be represented when the story appeared in *Stern*. It had finally been agreed that this would be done in the form of an interview.

A copy of the manuscript of *Plan 3* was sent to Henri Nannen for his approval while Felix Schmidt briefed the head of *Stern*'s serialization department, Horst Treuke. Schmidt told Treuke to begin planning on the assumption that they would be running the Hess story in the summer of 1983. He also let him into the secret of the existence of the diaries. Treuke, startled by the news, asked if they were sure they were genuine. Schmidt reassured him. Did he seriously think that Schulte-Hillen would have paid out nine million marks to buy a set of forgeries?

David Irving arrived at August Priesack's apartment at 8.30 a.m. on Sunday morning. The much-vaunted 'archive' was spread out on the floor. 'It consisted', recalled Irving, 'of some twenty folders, A3-sized, with photographs stuck on the front and photocopies of documents of the entire Hitler period, from his birth to the end of his life. A special folder covered the years from 1939 to 1945.' When Stiefel had called Priesack in to look at his collection in 1979, he had rashly provided the 'professor' with photocopies of much of his Hitler material, including half a dozen sheets covering the most interesting entries from the 1935 diary. Several times, while Irving was skimming through the material, the telephone rang with urgent messages. The caller was Fritz Stiefel, but despite pressure from Irving, Priesack refused to identify him. He referred to him either as 'Fritz' or 'the client'. He said that he was in trouble for having said as much as he had, that according to 'Fritz' the entire higher command of the East German Army had been summoned to Berlin for an inquiry into the rumours that one general was smuggling Hitler's diaries to the West.

If he was ever to get to the diaries, Irving knew that he needed to speak to this mysterious 'client'. He decided to trick his doddering old host. 'I persuaded Priesack – who would not give me Fritz's other name however hard I tried – to telephone him reassuringly from the neighbouring room.' Irving crept across to the door and counted the clicks as Priesack dialled the number. In this way he managed to make out the prefix code. ('It's easy. You know the first number is "o" and you can work out the rest from that.')

Making an excuse that he had to go out for a while, Irving left Priesack's apartment and found a neighbouring telephone office. 'I checked all the phone books and found that the area code was for Waiblingen, and the number was for one Fritz Stiefel, whose address I thus obtained.'

The search took Irving several hours. By the time he returned at 5.30 p.m., Priesack had already finished entertaining another visitor. Wolf Rudiger Hess, son of Rudolf Hess, had called to inspect the letter supposedly sent by his father to Hitler in May 1941. 'He had roundly denounced the handwriting as a forgery,' noted Irving. 'If that is faked, what else might not be too?'

Promising to try to arrange a publisher for him, Irving managed to persuade Priesack to part with his precious folders.

Next morning, Irving left Munich for Stuttgart. He caught a train to Waiblingen and marched, unannounced, up to Fritz Stiefel's front door. 'Reluctantly, he appeared,' recalled Irving, 'and reluctantly invited me in.' The historian explained that he had not telephoned because 'one never knew who was listening in'. Stiefel said that if he had phoned him, he would have told him there was no point in coming. 'He approved my method of gaining entry this way and congratulated me.' To thaw the atmosphere further, Irving produced from his inside pocket one of his most valuable possessions: one of Adolf Hitler's monogrammed teaspoons from the Berghof. Whenever Irving was researching in Germany, he carried it with him, a talisman to charm reluctant old Nazis into helping him. 'That spoon', says Irving, 'has opened a lot of doors.' Stiefel examined it and then went and fetched one of his own to show Irving.

Having compared cutlery the two men settled to business. Irving asked about the Hitler diaries and Stiefel – as Heidemann had predicted – proceeded to lie. A local dealer, he said, had been to see him a few years earlier and shown him a diary. He had kept it for one or two weeks and then given it back. Irving asked if there was any way of finding out where the other volumes were. Stiefel 'answered that he'd heard they'd all been sold to an American'. The industrialist would not reveal the American's name, nor would he identify the diaries' supplier.

All Irving's hard work and cunning appeared to have been in vain. His only consolation was that he had managed to get hold of Priesack's photocopies.

On Tuesday, 21 December he flew back to London. He rang Alan Samson, his publisher at Macmillan, and told him about the diaries. Samson was interested and they arranged an appointment for the following day.

Irving did not begin a detailed examination of the Priesack material until 8.30 the next morning. He sat in his first-floor study, pulled out his own folder of authenticated Hitler writing and then began indexing Priesack's papers 'to try to get an impression of their value'.

Whatever allegations may be levelled at Irving as an historian – and there have been many – there is no doubting his ability to sniff out original documents. Over the past twenty years he had become only too familiar with the scale of the trade in forgeries. He had himself almost been fooled by a faked 'diary' of the German intelligence chief, Wilhelm Canaris. He therefore approached Priesack's papers critically – and almost at once he began finding discrepancies. The writing of words like 'Deutsch', 'Nation' and 'NSDAP' which recurred regularly varied in style from document to document. The most damning piece of evidence as far as he was concerned was a letter purporting to have been written by Goering in 1944. The word 'Reichsmarschall' in the printed letterheading was misspelt '*Reichsmarsall*'. 'By lunchtime,' he wrote in his diary, 'I was unfortunately satisfied that the Priesack collection is stuffed with fake documents.' He cancelled his appointment with Macmillan and rang Priesack. 'There are such huge variances,' he told him, 'that the documents cannot be genuine.' Priesack, according to Irving, 'gasped'. If Stiefel's documents were fakes, how reliable was the rest of the businessman's memorabilia? At that moment, one of the largest printing companies in Italy was busy producing several thousand copies of Billy Price's book, *Adolf Hitler as Painter and Draughtsman*, which was full of pictures from Stiefel's collection.

'Does this mean', asked Priesack, 'that the watercolours are also forged? They come from the same source.'

Irving replied that he was no art expert. He could not answer that question. He did however say that in his opinion 'the entire story about East German involvement' was 'part of an elaborate *Schwindel* to prevent the purchasers from showing their acquisitions around. . . . I urged him to advise Fritz Stiefel to buy nothing more from this source.'

According to Irving's diary, Priesack was fawning in his gratitude. There were those, he said, who believed that Irving should be given the title 'doctor'. He disagreed: in Germany, the name 'David Irving' was honour enough. To which Irving, angry at having wasted his time, and weary of this tiresome old man, added in his diary the single word: *Schmarn*.

But if Irving's visit to Germany had done little to restore his own fortunes, it did at least bring profit to August Priesack.

So far, using Kujau to pressure Fritz Stiefel into keeping quiet, Heidemann had been able to contain the damage done by Priesack's disclosure. Now, the reporter acted to seal the leak altogether. Hard on the heels of David Irving, Heidemann travelled down to Munich to see Priesack. He offered him 30,000 marks in cash for his archive – a sum which Priesack, scraping a living on a school teacher's pension, was happy to accept. 'This is worth a lot to me,' Heidemann told him. 'Now I will own everything Stiefel has.' He did not mention *Stern*'s diaries. Priesack assumed that he and Stiefel were simply rival collectors. Anyway, the reason for the offer was of less interest to him at that moment than the 500- and 1000-mark notes his visitor now pulled out of his briefcase. If Heidemann wanted to throw his money about buying up photocopies, who was he to complain?

TWENTY

Nineteen eighty-three was going to be a big year for Gerd Heidemann and he and Gina were determined to greet it in style. At a cost of more than 5000 marks, the couple flew to New York to attend the annual New Year's Eve Ball at the Waldorf Astoria.

As 1982 came to an end, Gerd Heidemann's behaviour was – if anything – even odder than usual. Two-and-a-half years after his honeymoon visit to South America, he was once more obsessed by Martin Bormann, gripped as if by a bout of some recurrent tropical fever. He was utterly convinced by Medard Klapper's stories that Bormann was still alive, presiding over a circle of old Nazis, shuttling between various countries in Europe and the Middle East. Klapper gave Heidemann Bormann's telephone number in Spain and Bormann's Spanish cover name, 'Martin di Calde Villa'. He showed him a house in Zurich where the 'Bormann Group' had its headquarters and allowed Heidemann to photograph the building. He was always on the point of taking the reporter to meet Bormann – only to have to tell him, regretfully, a few days later, that 'Martin' couldn't make the appointment. Heidemann commissioned one of his oldest colleagues, a photographer named Helmut Jabusch to fly to Zurich to take pictures of 'one of the most prominent Nazis': he even booked airline tickets, but once again, the assignment fell through.

On November 1982, Klapper gave Heidemann six Polaroid photographs of an old man whom he claimed was Bormann. The reporter paid him 25,000 marks for the pictures which he then began showing to colleagues. He pointed out to Felix Schmidt that the man in the photograph – who wore, as Schmidt recalled, 'a Basque cap' – had a birth mark on the left side of his forehead, exactly as Bormann had. According to Schmidt: 'Heidemann explained that it was possible to make contact with Bormann. Everything had to go through a middleman but he was sure he would meet Bormann shortly, either in Zurich or in Cairo. The Nazis who surrounded Bormann were going to allow him to meet him. Heidemann always spoke of Bormann as "Martin".' Schmidt was incredulous: not least, because it was *Stern* that had actually proved that Bormann was dead. He began to have doubts about Heidemann's mental health and confided his worries to Peter Koch. Koch shook his head. 'With Heidemann,' he said, 'anything's possible.' Heidemann sent one of the photographs to Max Frei-Sulzer, who was commissioned to investigate it for fingerprints. The versatile Frei-Sulzer reported back on 21 November that he could not reach a positive conclusion: 'Unfortunately, at the critical place there are several prints on top of one another which cannot be separated. The others are so fragmented, there is no question of being able to evaluate them.' There was only one clear print, said Frei-Sulzer: its owner was unknown.

His colleagues at *Stern* treated Heidemann's behaviour at this time as if it were no more than a minor eccentricity. It does not seem to have occurred to any of them that a man capable of obvious self-delusion over Martin Bormann might be equally unreliable on other matters. Leo Pesch recalled that Heidemann now seldom came into the office. When he did so, it was to show them the photograph and to 'talk very intently about Bormann'. Pesch and Walde regarded it as a 'half-crazy story' and used to have 'teasing conversations' with him about it. It was another example of Heidemann showing off, trying to convince people of his importance. 'My impression

SELLING HITLER

was that Heidemann had lost more and more contact with reality through his success,' Pesch said afterwards. 'In my view, Heidemann had a great deal of vanity. Again and again, quite unprompted, he would tell colleagues stories about the diaries and about Martin Bormann.' The general view was that funny old Heidemann was up to his usual tricks; as long as it didn't interfere with his real work, the best thing was to humour him. 'Our main concern', admitted Walde, 'was that Heidemann might be diverted by this myth about Bormann from the task of obtaining the diaries.'

Was there a connection between the two stories? Heidemann certainly acted as though there were. Whenever he came across a flattering reference to Bormann in the diaries, he photocopied it and gave it to Klapper to pass on to Bormann. Klapper reported back that 'Martin' was so pleased, he had hung an enlargement of one extract on his study wall in Madrid. Heidemann also talked about Bormann to Kujau. During one of these conversations, the forger told Heidemann that his East German brother could obtain Hitler's gold party insignia, allegedly given to Bormann at the end of the war. Heidemann reported this to Klapper who subsequently passed on 'Martin's' confirmation that the story was indeed correct. Heidemann told Kujau and shortly afterwards, a reference to the decoration appeared in the final volume of the diaries.

Further evidence of possible collusion between Kujau and Klapper surfaced at the beginning of December 1982. Every reference in the Hess special volume was being checked methodically against published sources to make certain it contained no errors. The name of one SS captain, supposedly appointed by Hitler to watch over Hess, proved to be almost indecipherable. Even Wilfried Sorge was called in to give an opinion. Lautman? Lausserman? Eventually, the consensus was that the name was Laackman. Because Walde and Pesch could find no mention of the name in any of their reference books, they asked Josef Henke of the Bundesarchiv to undertake a search on their behalf in the closed records of the Berlin Document Centre. Three weeks later, Henke sent them thirty photocopied pages of SS Captain Anton Laackman's military record. Heidemann also asked Klapper to check with Bormann. In January, Klapper returned with three *original* pages from Laackman's personal file which he told Heidemann he had removed from Bormann's office in Spain. There was no question but that the documents were authentic. Once again, the Bormann story and the Hitler diaries appeared to be substantiating one another.

Naturally, the Laackman papers did *not* come from Bormann. They were stolen, at Klapper's request, along with other Nazi documents, by a corrupt employee of the West German state archives, named Rainer Hess. But Heidemann was not aware of that. For him, the production of the papers was the clinching proof that Bormann was still alive.

Months later, after the diaries were exposed as forgeries, the *Sunday Times* used this episode as the basis for its assertion that 'Klapper played a pivotal role – perhaps the central role – in the diary fraud.'

The kindest thing that can be said about the *Sunday Times* investigation is that it overstated its case. If Laackman's name had not appeared in any book, and Kujau could have forged the diary entry only on the basis of documents supplied by Klapper, the evidence that the two men were working together to trick Heidemann would be conclusive. But Laackman's name *does* appear in a book. It occurs – as the *Sunday Times* was forced to admit – on page 221 of the Nazi Party's Yearbook for 1941: police discovered it, carefully marked by Kujau, when they raided his home in 1983. Moreover, the Hess volume was forged by Kujau in 1981. If the planting of Laackman's name was part of a carefully laid plot, it is hard to see how he could have known fourteen months in advance that *Stern* would fail to spot the reference in the 1941 Year-book and ask Klapper to obtain the documents.

It is possible there was a link between Kujau and Klapper. The fact that both men, proven liars, deny knowing one another, is no proof to the contrary. But if they were work-ing together, they have covered their tracks with great care. The only place in which the Bormann story, the hunt for secret Nazi treasure and the discovery of Hitler's diaries all came together with any certainty was in the overwrought imagination of Gerd Heidemann.

Now that *Plan 3* had been completed, sale of the syndication rights could begin in earnest. On Wednesday 5 January, Manfred Fischer turned over control of the safe-deposit box in Zurich to Dr Jan Hensmann, deputy managing director of Gruner and Jahr. The following day, Hensmann, Wilfried Sorge and Gerd Schulte-Hillen, accompanied by Olaf Paeschke representing Bertelsmann, flew back to New York for a second round of negotiations with Bantam Books.

Knowing the extent of the market for books on the Second World War, Bantam was enthusiastic about the project. *Plan 3*, based on new writings by Hitler, with its revelation that the Führer authorized Hess's peace mission, would make headlines all over the the world. If the hardback edition appeared that autumn, the paperback could tie in with Hess's ninetieth birthday in April 1984. But once again, the discussions foundered. Bantam's President, Louis Wolfe, wanted to involve expert historians in the project. He also demanded extensive guarantees of compensation should the book's authenticity be called into question – an open-ended commitment which the Germans were reluctant to make. A more serious problem concerned newspaper rights. Bantam was prepared to offer $50,000, but their visitors were insistent on retaining syndication rights for themselves. Wolfe 'found it difficult to grasp what Shulte-Hillen and Hensmann actually wanted'. He was not aware that *Plan 3* was regarded in Hamburg merely as a trial balloon for a much bigger scoop. Wolfe could not understand it. He thought that 'the whole thing was being handled in an amateurish way'.

While the businessmen were arguing in the United States, David Irving was preparing to speak to a packed meeting in West Germany. At noon on 9 January, 2000 supporters of the DVU jammed into one of Munich's enormous beer cellars to listen to Irving speak at the memorial meeting for Hans-Ulrich Rudel, the highly decorated fighter pilot who had lived in exile in Brazil and Paraguay, an unrepentant admirer of Adolf Hitler until the end of his life. 'I spoke first,' noted Irving, 'and was interrupted by a huge roar of applause as I called the Bonn politicians *Charakterschweine* for not allowing military representation at the Rudel funeral.'

At the end of the meeting, Irving drove across town to see August Priesack to return his Hitler documents. The material was so riddled with fakes, he told him, he was not going to waste any more time trying to sort it out. He showed Priesack the misspelt Goering notepaper. 'He indicated by his manner that he had already noticed that, but did not consider it important. At this I mildly exploded: "If even the printed letter head of the second most important man in Germany contains a printing error, how can the document be anything other than a fake?" He implied that in 1944 even Goering would be happy to have headed notepaper, printing error or not. I did not even bother to discuss that remark.' Priesack said that he thought he should contact Gerd Heidemann. 'Why contact him?' asked Irving. 'It is quite obvious from these documents that they are fakes.' He told Priesack that he suspected Fritz Stiefel had a hand in the forgeries. Priesack flushed and insisted that was not the case. 'Throughout the half hour conversation he kept putting his hand on my shoulder,' noted Irving, who was as fastidious as the Führer about physical contact. 'At one stage he even held my hand, which was not pleasant.'

Priesack accompanied Irving out to his car. 'I don't suppose I shall be seeing you again?' he said. 'He seemed sad about that,' recalled Irving in his diary, 'though not at all about the prospect of the money he had lost.' (Irving did not know that Priesack's apparent stoicism was that of a man who had sold his collection – fakes and all – to Heidemann for 30,000 marks). The historian drove off in a bad mood. *He*, at any rate, had lost money. Even allowing for the expenses paid to him by Langen Mueller, he reckoned he had spent 2000 marks he could ill afford. 'But', he wrote that evening, 'I do not regret that as it would have been much worse if I had proceeded any further before realizing that his files of documents were largely forgeries.'

'I suspect', he added, 'that Heidemann has also been tricked.'

The following day in New York the negotiations between Gruner and Jahr and Bantam Books finally broke down. In their hotel suite that evening, the Germans discussed what they should do next. The English language market was largely a mystery to them. Clearly, if they were to exploit their property to the full, they would need some professional advice. Sticking to their original model of the Kissinger memoirs, they decided to enlist the help of Kissinger's agent, Marvin Josephson. Josephson was the head of International Creative Management (ICM), the largest artistic agency in the world. Josephson did not handle their business personally. Instead, the *Stern* men were referred to Lynn Nesbit, Senior

Vice President of ICM, whom they were told was the company's expert on magazine rights.

According to Ms Nesbit, at a meeting with Sorge, she undertook to handle 'the North American serial rights to a document called *Plan 3*', based on original, unpublished notes written by Adolf Hitler. She did not bother to check its authenticity herself. Sorge told her that *Stern* had a series of expert reports which proved that the Hitler material was genuine. The magazine would be willing to show these reports to potential purchasers. 'The word "diary" was never mentioned to me,' she recalled. If she had known she was actually representing sixty volumes of Hitler's diaries, she would have been 'much more sceptical':

> It seemed totally plausible that a 4000-word [*sic*] document could have been hidden all these years. *Stern* has a reputation for reliability and they were putting their own reputation on the boards with this. If it had been just a person with no journalistic credibility and nothing at stake, I would have been much more suspicious.

Sorge was insistent that the material should be offered only to 'reputable' organizations. *Time*, *Newsweek* and the *New York Times* were the obvious candidates. Ms Nesbit promised to arrange a series of meetings at which Sorge could meet potential clients. Her tentative estimate of the market value of *Plan 3* in the United States was $250,000.

The next week in Hamburg was a busy one for Gerd Heidemann. On Tuesday, 18 January he finally signed the revised contract, drafted in October, finalized in December, guaranteeing him 36 per cent of the syndication revenue once the company had cleared its costs. This immediately entitled him to claim 300,000 marks – the balance owing on his 'compensation' settlement of 1.5 million. On Wednesday, he withdrew 150,000 marks in cash from the Adolphsplatz bank, telling Sorge he needed it for the next batch of diaries. On Saturday he was in Munich with Gina, at the invitation of August Priesack, for the launching party of Billy F. Price's book, *Adolf Hitler as Painter and Draughtsman*.

For Mr Price, millionaire compressor manufacturer and connoisseur of the Führer's art, Saturday, 22 January was a great day. He had already spent at least $100,000 on producing his book and to celebrate its publication he spared no expense. A room was booked at the Four Seasons, one of the most expensive hotels in Munich. There was plenty of fine wine and food. The guest list read like a Berghof reception.

There was Frau Henriette Hoffmann von Schirach – daughter of Hitler's photographer, Heinrich Hoffmann and widow of Baldur von Schirach, leader of the Hitler Youth and Gauleiter of Vienna. When she was a young girl, Hitler had taught Henriette to play the piano; when she was a bride, he had been best man at her wedding. She was suing the United States Government for the return of two Hitler paintings, allegedly stolen from her house at the end of the war and now hanging in the National Army museum in Washington. Price was paying her legal fees.

There was Frau Gerda Christian, most dedicated of Hitler's secretaries. Next to her was her old colleague, Christa Schroeder, 75 years old and ill with a kidney complaint. She had helped Price with his book and sold him some pictures from her own collection. In return, Price was paying her medical bills.

There was Frau Schmidt-Ehmen, wife of one of Hitler's favourite sculptors, and Eva Wagner, descendant of his favourite composer. There was Peter Jahn, the Viennese 'art expert', who had worked with Priesack cataloguing Hitler's paintings in the 1930s and who had helped the Marquess of

Bath acquire much of his collection. There was one of Hitler's doctors. There was Bormann's adjutant. . . .

Price moved among them, proud and prosperous, in a dark three-piece suit, signing copies of his book. He realized, he said later, that the only reason most of his guests wanted to know him was that he was rich – 'but what the hell?' He felt he was performing a service to history by gathering together Hitler's art. What he did not know was that of the 725 pictures in his book, at least 170 were the work of Konrad Kujau. At one point, Fritz Stiefel – who had supplied the pictures to Price – approached the Texan and asked him actually to autograph a copy of the book for his 'good friend Conny Fischer'. But for some reason, Price never signed the book. 'God', he declared afterwards with revivalist fervour. 'stayed mah hand.'

For Gerd and Gina Heidemann, the reception was filled with familiar faces and when the time came to leave, a tipsy Frau Heidemann thanked their host for 'a wonderful party'. Gerd Heidemann invited Price to come to Hamburg to see his own collection of Hitler's art. He confided to his fellow devotee that he had 'something big' himself coming out in a few months' time. 'He couldn't tell me what it was,' recalled Price, 'and I didn't question him too much about it.'

A few days after the party, Price took up Heidemann's offer and visited him at his home in the Elbchaussee. The Texan had met plenty of Hitler obsessives, but seldom anyone as far gone as Heidemann: 'Priesack's in love with Hitler. But Heidemann's more in love with Hitler than anyone I've ever met in my life.' He was impressed by much of the reporter's collection but even he – who had been taken in by Stiefel's pictures – found some of it 'ridiculously fake'. Heidemann showed him one painting (admittedly, one of Kujau's more exuberant efforts) which almost made him burst out laughing: a portrait, supposedly by Hitler, of King Farouk of Egypt.

Price was still shaking his head about the episode a year later. 'Hell, man. *King Farouk*. No *way* would I accept that.'

Another foreign visitor entertained by Heidemann in the two Elbchaussee apartments at this time was Gitta Sereny of the *Sunday Times*.

According to David Irving, he had warned the *Sunday Times* in a telephone call on 30 December that the material he had seen was 'dangerously polluted with fakes'. But the newspaper was not inclined to take his word for anything, let alone the authenticity of Adolf Hitler's diaries. They decided to send a reporter of their own to make contact with Heidemann, and Gitta Sereny was the obvious choice. Brought up in Austria before the war, she was trilingual in English, French and German, and a regular contributor on Nazi subjects. In 1974 she had written *Into that Darkness*, an examination of Franz Stangl, Commandant of the Treblinka extermination camp. She was also, as it happened, a personal enemy of Irving's, having published a damning attack on *Hitler's War* in the *Sunday Times* when it first appeared in 1977.

Over the course of two days, Heidemann and Sereny spoke for about eight hours. He took her on a tour of his archive. She found his collection 'breathtaking'. Filed away, protected by clear plastic covers, was a series of what appeared to be 'extraordinary' documents, including the original of Hitler's order to liquidate the Soviet commissars. He showed her a letter from Karl Wolff in which the general appointed him his literary heir and executor. He showed her his library of negatives from the Hoffmann photographic archive. The walls of the Heidemanns' two flats were crammed with Hitler paintings. 'I was stunned,' she recalled, 'absolutely stunned.'

I had seen examples of Hitler's painting before at Albert Speer's. These things looked exactly the same. There were about three dozen hanging round the Heidemanns' bed. I said: 'Jesus Christ, doesn't this stuff give you nightmares?' Gina said: 'Oh no, we couldn't possibly sleep without them.'

Heidemann told Sereny that he was making regular, clandestine trips to East Germany. He assured her that the Hitler diaries existed. He was not, however, prepared to say whether they were in his possession. Although Heidemann struck her as a man obsessed by the Nazis, characterized by 'an extraordinary political and intellectual naïvety', she believed he was telling the truth. If anyone could obtain the diaries, he could.

Inadvertently, despite his concern not to give anything away, Heidemann also provided her with a clue to the origin of the diaries' trail. He mentioned Professor Eberhard Jaeckel as an historian who knew something about the East German material. From her hotel in Hamburg, Sereny telephoned Jaeckel who confirmed that some years previously he *had* seen something: not a diary exactly, but a 'yearbook'. Sereny asked him if he thought it was authentic. He said it was 'interesting'. He would not go any further on the telephone. 'Come down to Stuttgart,' he said. Sereny asked if he could introduce her to the person who obtained the diary. Jaeckel replied that if she came down, it might be possible for them to go and see some people. Sereny telephoned Magnus Linklater in the *Sunday Times* office with this exciting news. But to her amazement, he refused to authorize a trip to south Germany. The paper's new owner, Rupert Murdoch, had demanded that the editorial department reduce its costs: the *Sunday Times* was gripped by what Sereny later called 'a rabid economy drive'. Even in sending her to Hamburg for two nights, Linklater had risked incurring the wrath of the editor, Frank Giles. She had to return to London at once.

If the *Sunday Times* had not decided on this false economy, the events of the next three months would probably have developed very differently. Sereny would have met Jaeckel and learned of the forgeries printed in his book of Hitler's writings. She would probably have met Stiefel. She might even have met 'Herr Fischer'. 'I could have stopped the whole goddam thing right there,' she complained later. As it was, the *Sunday Times* passed up one of the few remaining chances of uncovering the hoax. The impending fiasco, swollen by the profligacy of West Germany's journalism, was abetted by the parsimony of Great Britain's.

TWENTY-ONE

On Wednesday, 16 February, Wilfried Sorge arrived in the international departure lounge of Hamburg airport to catch a flight to Denmark. It was almost two and a half years since that stroll in the Black Forest when Walde had first told him of the hunt for Hitler's diaries. Now, with a copy of *Plan 3* in his luggage, he was about to depart on the first stage of a three-week odyssey to sell the story to the world. In terms of his career, Sorge – like Walde and Heidemann – had a great deal staked on the Hitler diaries. To have been entrusted with such an important mission, six weeks short of his fortieth birthday, was a clear sign of the young executive's growing stature within the company. Gruner and Jahr were counting upon him. Schulte-Hillen personally was watching the way he handled things.

Sorge was well equipped for his mission. Immaculately tailored, endlessly charming, permanently tanned, he was the epitome of expense-account smoothness. The strategy which he was about to put into action had been agreed in Hamburg after consultations with Bertelsmann and ICM. A list of foreign companies had been compiled to whom the Hess story would be offered. In some countries – the United States and Spain for example – several news organizations would be approached at the same time, in order to encourage competition and push up the price. In others, such as France and Italy, Sorge would deal with one company exclusively.

Sorge flew first to Copenhagen for discussions with Bertelsmann's agent in Scandinavia. From there he caught a transatlantic flight to New York. Lynn Nesbit had arranged three interviews for him. At the offices of *Newsweek* he met the magazine's editor-in-chief, William Broyles, and its managing editor, Maynard Parker. Peter Koch had mentioned the project to Parker during a visit to America shortly before Christmas. At the time he had been rebuked for his indiscretion, but Sorge found that the notion of publishing original Hitler material had taken hold at *Newsweek*. Broyles and Parker told him they were very interested and would probably be submitting an offer. At *Time*, the response of William Mador, former Bonn correspondent, also sounded promising. The only person who did not seem enthusiastic was the woman who represented the *New York Times*. After a few days in the United States, Sorge flew back to Europe – to Amsterdam, where he discussed the prospects for Holland and Belgium with the Bertelsmann people. Then it was on to France, to make a sales pitch to *Paris Match*. From there, Sorge flew south to Madrid to see representatives from the magazine *Cambio 16* and the newspaper *El Pais*. Leaving Spain, he headed east: first to Milan for a meeting with the publishing group Mondadori, then on again for the longest leg of the journey so far – to Tokyo, and the ancient mysteries of the Far Eastern market. . . .

It was during one lunchtime the following week, while Sorge was midway through his sales trip, that Heidemann met Henri Nannen and Peter Koch in the street near the *Stern* building. They passed on some devastating news. It had been decided to abandon the current publishing plan in favour of launching the scoop with the story of the diaries' discovery. Heidemann hurried back to the special office to tell Leo Pesch and Thomas Walde. In the afternoon, Heidemann and Walde went over to see Koch to find out what was going on.

Neither Koch nor Schmidt had ever been happy with the

idea of starting with the serialization of the Hess scoop. It might make sense commercially, but from a journalistic point of view it was ridiculous. The sensation was in the fact of the diaries' existence, not in the single revelation of Hitler's knowledge of Hess's flight, buried in the biographical detail of *Plan 3*. Alone, Koch and Schmidt had been unable to convince Schulte-Hillen and the *Stern* management. But now they had a powerful ally. Henri Nannen had taken the manuscript of *Plan 3* home to read over Christmas. 'I was amazed to find that it was simply the Hess story with Hitler quotations in it,' he recalled. He gave the book to a girlfriend for her opinion. She was forty-two. What did she think her generation would make of it? 'She found the story interesting, but she didn't appreciate its historical importance, and she didn't grasp at all that she was looking at part of a sensational find of Hitler's diaries.' When Nannen returned from his holiday in January he told Schulte-Hillen that he was in danger of squandering his investment by being overcautious: 'If one had Hitler diaries, one should start the story with this announcement, and with the story of the find.' Henri Nannen was one of the most successful journalists in West Germany. Schulte-Hillen listened to him with respect. He endorsed Nannen's decision.

The meeting in Koch's office that afternoon was noisy. Heidemann was horrified by the new idea. He returned to his old argument that premature publication would endanger lives and jeopardize the supply of the remaining diaries. Koch was sarcastic: the reporter had already spent more than two years bringing in the books; how many more were there? Schmidt and Gillhausen also arrived to add their support to Koch. Schmidt was worried that if they delayed much longer, David Irving or some rival organization would obtain photo-copies of the diaries. Gillhausen – the most junior of the editors, but nevertheless respected as a man with a 'nose' for a good story – added his opinion. 'His feeling', recalled Walde, 'was that the newsworthy part came in three little paragraphs before the end. The whole story should be published the other way round, starting with the story of the find.'

Walde shared Heidemann's fears. He also had two additional concerns: he did not want to see his book swamped by the controversy which would be aroused by the announcement of the diaries' discovery; and secondly, he wanted to write the story of the find himself – something which would be impossible if he had to prepare extracts from the diaries as well. Suddenly, he saw his dreams of becoming an authority on Hitler disappearing into the maw of *Stern*'s accelerating timetable. But Koch had been pushed around by his own staff for long enough. According to Walde he 'threatened' him. He said that 'he would take the work on the diaries out of my hands if I persisted in obstructing publication by my "inflexible" behaviour'.

'Despite my huge reservations about whether publication was possible in the time allowed,' said Walde, 'I gave in. That was my big mistake.'

Walde had one particularly good reason for being alarmed by the decision to speed up publication. Although the company had obtained three reports authenticating the handwriting of its Hitler archive, no part of it had yet been subjected to forensic tests. If he had contacted a freelance chemical analyst, these could have been performed in a matter of days. Walde's mistake had been to rely upon the West German Federal Police, the *Bundeskriminalamt* (BKA). On 5 July 1982, under the auspices of the Bundesarchiv, the BKA had been sent the originals of the material studied by the handwriting experts – the Hess statement and the Horthy telegram – with a request that they conduct tests to determine the age of the paper. Later, they had also been sent the various signed Hitler photographs and the Kleist document. Nothing

happened. Despite occasional reminders from Walde, the
BKA forensic experts continued to concentrate on their official police work. In December, *Stern* had asked for their
request to be given 'the highest priority'. Still nothing had
been done. Now the unpleasant meeting with Koch gal-
vanized the history department into making a new approach,
this time enlisting the help of the Bundesarchiv. On Tuesday 1
March, Leo Pesch telexed Dr Oldenhage, pleading with him
to contact *Stern* as quickly as possible: 'We have some urgent
deadline problems regarding the expert reports.'

On Friday, 4 March, Wilfried Sorge, jet-lagged in his bedroom
in a hotel in Tokyo, was telephoned by Peter Hess, Gruner
and Jahr's publishing director, and summoned back to Hamburg. 'What's happened?' he asked. 'The whole publishing
concept has been changed,' he was told: he must return
immediately 'in order to pitch the sales strategy in line with
the new plan'. Sorge was bitter at this news. In the space of a
single telephone call, thousands of miles of air travel and days
of meetings and planning had been ruined. He had no choice
but to book himself on the first available flight back to
Germany.

In New York, Lynn Nesbit's contract to sell *Plan 3* was
terminated. She received a fee of $10,000 for her efforts.
Newsweek, which had already submitted a tentative offer of
$150,000 for the serial rights to the Hess book, was told that
Stern had changed its mind. From Hamburg, telexes were
dispatched to all Sorge's potential customers informing them
that they 'could no longer be offered the material'.

The following Tuesday, Gerd Schulte-Hillen convened a
meeting in a conference room on the ninth floor of the *Stern*
building. It was attended by all those involved in the diaries

project: Nannen, Gillhausen, Koch, Schmidt, Walde, Heidemann, Pesch, Sorge, Hess and Hensmann. The history department's flickering hope that the new publication plan might be abandoned was crushed by Schulte-Hillen's opening words. 'Gentlemen,' announced the managing director, 'the time has come. We intend to publish.' Nevertheless, Walde, Pesch and Heidemann were determined to make one last stand. The source of the diaries, they warned, would be threatened, and important volumes had yet to be delivered. Walde reported that they had no books from the year 1944: 'If we did not get hold of those volumes ... we would be unable to settle some very important questions about the Third Reich.' Imagine what Hitler might have written about the German response to D-Day or the July bomb plot. Sorge supported his old schoolfriend. Speaking as a salesman, he would find it much easier to offer the diary archive in its entirety, rather than having to tell customers that part of it had not yet arrived.

Schulte-Hillen was not convinced. He accepted the argument of Nannen and the editors: to start with the Hess story and not to mention the diaries was the wrong way of doing things. If they delayed any longer there was a danger of leaks. They should go ahead and begin printing the story in May.

That settled, the conference went on to take a series of decisions on the timetable for publication. The existence of the diaries would be revealed in eight weeks' time, in *Stern*'s issue of 5 May. To wring the last ounce of sensation and profitability out of the diaries, serialization would be divided into three separate periods, spaced out over a period of eighteen months. In May and June, the magazine would run eight weekly instalments, covering the story of the diaries' discovery, the Hess flight and the Nazis' rise to power. There would then be a break over the summer. In the autumn they would relaunch the scoop with a ten-part series based on the pre-war diaries. This would be followed by a second and much longer interruption while the final extracts were prepared. Finally, in the autumn of 1984, *Stern* would publish another ten extracts based on the diaries from the war years. Heidemann was instructed to deliver the missing volumes by 31 March. Another *Stern* reporter, Wolf Thieme, was given the task of putting together the story of how the diaries were found – once again, Heidemann was expected to turn over all his information for someone else to write up.

The magazine, concluded Schulte-Hillen, had less than a month to product the first eight-part series: it would need to be shown to potential foreign customers during syndication negotiations at the beginning of April.

Early the next morning, the peripatetic Sorge was back at Hamburg airport to catch the first flight to London. He had already scheduled meetings with potential British customers before *Stern* changed its publication strategy. In view of the importance of the British market, it was decided to go ahead with the London sales trip as planned. At Heathrow, Sorge was met by *Stern*'s bureau chief in London, Peter Wickman, and the two men drove to their first appointment: with Sir David English of Lord Rothermere's Associated Newspaper group.

English, editor-in-chief of the *Daily Mail* and the *Mail on Sunday*, listened to Sorge's presentation of the Hess story. His immediate worry was the possibility that the Hitler document might be a fake. He had been caught himself, when editor of the *Daily Mail*, by forged correspondence supposedly originating from Lord Ryder. Another worry was the reputation of the *Mail on Sunday*, to whom the Hess scoop would be given as ammunition in its circulation battle with the *Sunday Express*. The *Mail on Sunday*'s editor, Stewart Steven, was the man who had helped Ladislas Farago track down Martin

Bormann for the *Daily Express* in 1972 only to discover, too late, that 'Bormann' was actually an innocent Argentine high school teacher. English told Sorge he was interested in *Stern*'s story, but he would require absolute guarantees of authenticity before going any further.

In the afternoon, Sorge and Wickman went to see their other possible client, Times Newspapers. Colin Webb and Charles Wilson attended the meeting on behalf of *The Times*, Brian MacArthur for the *Sunday Times*. Before revealing what he had to offer, Sorge made the three men sign a pledge of secrecy. They were more interested in the story than David English, but before they could make any commitment, they would have to consult the editors of the two papers and their proprietor, Rupert Murdoch. The secrecy pledge was amended to allow these three gentlemen to be informed of *Stern*'s scoop.

Sorge spent the night in the Savoy Hotel and the following morning returned to Hamburg.

Heidemann dreaded the impending launch of the diaries. His comfortable existence of the last two years – the suitcases full of money, the flattery of his superiors – was bound to come to an end. He would cease to have a hold over the company. He would suffer the humiliation of watching while the diaries were passed to other writers for exploitation. Already, he had been forced to entertain Wolf Thieme in his gallery in Milchstrasse and tell him the story of the diaries' discovery. This meeting had posed another problem for Heidemann. It was safe for him to talk about the evacuation of documents from Berlin and the loss of the plane. He could describe how he had located the crash site using Gundlfinger's name. He could talk of the local peasants who had salvaged material from the wrecked aircraft. But then, of necessity, there was a gap of more than thirty years, until the books started accumulating in the management's safe in Hamburg. Heidemann explained to Thieme that he could not say any more without jeopardizing the lives of his informants. Naturally, he did not tell Thieme the other reason for his reticence: that if Kujau's identity were ever disclosed, and if the garrulous relics dealer ever spoke to anyone else from *Stern*, it would only be a matter of time before the company discovered he had been defrauding them for the past two years.

To try to ward off publication, with all its attendant hazards, Heidemann used every argument, cajolement and threat at his disposal in a desperate attempt to make the company change its mind. On Thursday, 17 March he went to see Schulte-Hillen and handed him a closely typed two-page memorandum 'for his eyes only'. The managing director, said Heidemann, must destroy it as soon as he had read it. 'Dear Herr Schulte-Hillen,' it began,

> Before you reach any irrevocable decisions, I would like once again to put my reservations on paper. I cannot guarantee that the missing diaries will be in Hamburg by the beginning of May 1983. There is no way that they will be with us by the beginning of April. How are the sales negotiations to proceed if we cannot offer those who are interested a complete set of diaries? Are we to answer questions by admitting that we have not had the nerve to wait as long as it takes to have the last diary in our hands? Are we to say to those interested that we are worried there might be photocopies of the diaries on the market? What do we do when the main protagonists [in the negotiations – i.e. Sorge] are insisting that the diaries can only be sold as a complete package and we should wait until the autumn? Of course I am of the opinion that we should have the complete story of the find and several issues prepared and ready to go in order to be able to begin publishing immediately should any photocopies

surface. But this danger is very slight: my business partner in East Germany is counting on the fact that the 'Swiss collector' will eventually buy other things from him. . . .

Heidemann went on to list fourteen separate sets of Hitler documents which his 'business partner' had told him were on offer:

1. Six diary-like volumes which Hitler wrote alongside the diaries which are known to us.
2. Adolf Hitler's handwritten memoirs, *My Life and Struggle for Germany*, written in the years 1942–44.
3. Hitler's book about women, in which there are said to be descriptions of his experiences with women.
4. Hitler's plan for the solution of the Jewish question, written after the Wannsee Conference on 28 January 1942, in which he gives Himmler precise orders as to what is to happen to the Jews (eighteen handwritten pages).
5. Hitler's handwritten *Documents about Himmler, Ley and Others*, including notes about the Jewish origins of those concerned.
6. Hitler's notes from 18 April until his death on 30 April 1945.
7. Goebbels's notes following Hitler's suicide.
8. Hitler's handwritten testament and marriage documents (twenty-one pages).
9. Hitler's documents about his supposed son in France.
10. Hitler's documents about his origins and relatives.
11. *Secret Thoughts about Different Military and Political Problems*.
12. Hitler's book about Frederick the Great.
13. Hitler's book about King Ludwig II of Bavaria.
14. Hitler's opera, *Wieland the Blacksmith*.

Heidemann added that there were 'three hundred other

drawings and watercolours by Hitler' also available in East Germany.

Heidemann was not necessarily lying when he outlined this fantastic catalogue to Schulte-Hillen. He appears to have genuinely believed what Kujau told him: that these documents could be rescued from behind the Iron Curtain and that premature disclosure might lose *Stern* the chance of obtaining them. Not all the items were new to *Stern*. For example, Kujau had first offered to sell *Wieland the Blacksmith* to Heidemann at the beginning of 1981. The forger had hit on the idea after reading the memoirs of August Kubizek. In *The Young Hitler I Knew*, published in 1955, Kubizek described how Hitler set about writing an opera, a sub-Wagnerian epic of rape and murder, set in the rugged wastes of Iceland, complete with flaming volcanoes, icy glaciers and winged Valkyries in shining helmets rising from the waters of 'Wolf Lake'. In the end, *Wieland the Blacksmith* was too much even for Hitler, and he abandoned it, after a few weeks' work, in 1907. The incident provided Kujau with a perfect cover story for another fake, and for more than two years he kept promising to supply the opera to Heidemann. The imagination recoils at the thought of what Bertelsmann's marketing department might have done with a Hitler opera – especially as one of the company's American subsidiaries was Arista Records. Mercifully, *Wieland the Blacksmith* was one piece of Hitleriana that Kujau never got round to forging. (He would have done it, he said later, but for the fact that he did not read music.)

Another of the new documents – the biography of King Ludwig II of Bavaria – was also familiar to Heidemann. One of the first diaries the reporter delivered to Hamburg contained a description of a visit supposedly made by Hitler to the town of Hohenschwangau. 'During my address,' noted 'Hitler' on 12 August 1933, 'I mention that in earlier years I once wrote a small book about Ludwig II. This must be in Munich.' Thus

Kujau, with characteristic cheek, used one forgery to prepare the way for another.

In his memorandum, Heidemann warned Schulte-Hillen that it would be impossible to obtain all these treasures by 31 March – the managing director's 'target date' for the completion of *Stern*'s archive. Therefore, said Heidemann, he proposed to deliver the material to 'other interested parties', and asked to be released from his contract with Gruner and Jahr.

Schulte-Hillen was not impressed by Heidemann's bluster. The reporter had threatened to resign so often over the past few years, the bluff no longer carried any conviction. It was not that Schulte-Hillen saw anything inherently implausible in such documents as Hitler's 'book about women', it was simply that the time had passed when he was prepared to tolerate this sort of procrastination. Besides, the company already had enough Hitler material to fill *Stern* for the next eighteen months. He was a stubborn man, and he had made up his mind. They would begin publishing the diaries in May.

Schulte-Hillen also ignored Heidemann's request that he should burn the memo. When he had finished reading it, he locked it away in the same file as Heidemann's various contracts. Afterwards he mentioned the episode during a conversation with Henri Nannen. To Nannen, Heidemann's determination to try to postpone publication was further evidence of fraud. 'Heidemann', he thought, 'was only really interested in providing further material in order to obtain further payments.' But recalling Schulte-Hillen's reaction the last time he had aired his suspicions, he said nothing.

Three days later, Sorge announced to his clients that in addition to the Hess story, *Stern* was now offering to sell syndication rights in Adolf Hitler's diaries. Interested organizations were invited to send representatives to inspect the material in Zurich at the end of the first week of April.

TWENTY-TWO

The first intimation that there might be something seriously wrong with *Stern*'s great scoop came a week and a half later. Walde had at last succeeded in persuading the West German Federal Police to carry out the long-awaited forensic tests. On Tuesday, 22 March he telexed Dr Henke and Dr Oldenhage at the Bundesarchiv to tell him he had fixed an appointment to hear the results the following Monday morning. He hoped they could both make it: 'Colleague Heidemann will attend for us.'

At 10 a.m. on 28 March, Heidemann, Henke and Oldenhage duly assembled at the police headquarters at Wiesbaden. It was assumed that the meeting would be a formality. The material had, after all, been authenticated by three different handwriting analysts. The police expert, Dr Louis Werner, appeared. He had been given nine samples to examine: the Hess statement, the Horthy telegram, the Kleist document, the draft telegram to Franco, some speech notes, a letter to Goering and the three signed Hitler photographs. His conclusion : of the nine documents, he thought at least six were forgeries.

To begin with, Heidemann could not believe what he was hearing. He asked Dr Werner to elaborate. Werner explained that under ultraviolet light, six of the samples, including all the signed photographs and the Horthy telegram, appeared to contain a substance called 'blankophor', a paper-whitening agent which as far as he was aware had not come into use until after the Second World War. In his opinion, it was therefore impossible that they could have been written at the time their dates indicated. He proposed to consult an expert from the Bayer chemical company for confirmation. In addition, the Kleist document contained glue of recent manufacture, and one of the letters had been typed on a machine built after 1956.

Heidemann asked about the other three samples, which included the Hess statement, the only page to come from the actual diaries. They, at least, were definitely genuine? Not necessarily, replied Werner. He could not be sure until he had carried out further tests.

How long would that take?

A week.

Heidemann asked if he could borrow the telephone. Werner told him to go ahead. In the scientist's presence, he rang Walde and repeated what he had just heard. He handed the received to Werner.

Walde asked the expert if he could absolutely guarantee that the Hess document was a fake. Werner said he couldn't: he would have to carry out further tests. These would necessitate damaging the page by cutting away part of it which could then be broken down into its separate components.

Greatly relieved, Walde thanked him and asked him to put Heidemann back on the line. Walde told Heidemann to retrieve the material and return with it to Hamburg immediately.

The two men discussed this unexpected setback the next day. There was no question in their minds that the material was genuine. They had three handwriting reports to prove it. Clearly, there had been a misunderstanding somewhere. Perhaps the documents had become contaminated with whitener in the course of their travels around Europe and North America during the previous year. Perhaps Werner had made a mistake. Or perhaps somehow a few dubious papers *had* been mixed up with the genuine material.

Heidemann rang Kujau and explained what had happened. 'Oh, don't worry about the BKA,' Kujau assured him. 'They're all mad there.' He told Heidemann that he had encountered this problem before. According to a police official *he* knew, paper whitener had been in use since 1915. Werner was talking nonsense.

Heidemann relayed this conversation to Walde. They agreed, as a safety check, to arrange further forensic tests, this time specifically concentrating on material from the diaries. They did not bother to tell *Stern*'s editors or management of Werner's preliminary assessment.

To launch Hitler's diaries, *Stern* was planning the biggest publicity campaign in its history. There would be a press conference in Hamburg. There would be advertisements in all West Germany's leading newspapers. There would also be a special television documentary, packaged and ready to sell to networks throughout the world.

On Thursday, 31 March, Wilfried Sorge called in the head of *Stern*'s TV subsidiary, Herr Zeisberg, and briefed him on the story of the diaries' discovery. Could he have a forty-minute film ready by 3 May, to coincide with the launch? Zeisberg said it was possible. They discussed who they might commission to make it. The obvious choice as producer was Klaus Harpprecht: he had made programmes on historical subjects, he had an excellent reputation, and he had worked extensively in America – an important qualification, as Sorge wanted to include an American element to help US sales. As presenter, they picked Barbara Dickmann, an experienced journalist, occasionally tipped as a potential German equivalent of ABC's Barbara Walters.

Peter Koch approved their choices. He called Dickmann at

her office in Bonn that afternoon. Would she come to a confidential meeting at his home in Hamburg next Monday? She asked him what it was about. Her refused to tell her over the telephone. Intrigued by Koch's secretive manner, she agreed.

In American, Maynard Parker of *Newsweek* telephoned Gordon Craig, Professor of History at Stanford University. Swearing him to secrecy, Parker told him about the Hitler diaries and asked if he would be willing to advise *Newsweek* on their authenticity. Craig, author of *The Germans*, was not an expert on Hitler: his speciality was the eighteenth and nineteenth centuries. He advised Parker to ask someone else. Parker asked him if he could recommend anyone. Craig suggested Gerhard Weinberg of the University of North Carolina. Parker said he would try him.

Craig promptly rang his old friend Weinberg. He could not go into details, he said, but 'off the record' *Newsweek* would be getting in touch with him very shortly. Weinberg, fifty-five years old, quiet and punctilious, had managed to pursue his profession in peace for more than three decades and had only limited experience of journalists. 'I don't think that's very likely, Gordon,' he said.

'You'll see,' insisted Craig. 'They'll be in touch.'

In London, Peter Wickman spoke with Sir Edward Pickering, executive vice chairman of Times Newspapers. Pickering said the company wanted to send a historian out to Zurich to give them an opinion on the diaries: 'We thought we'd ask Trevor-Roper.' He was not only considered an authority on Hitler, he was also one of the company's five Independent National Directors. Wickman said that *Stern* did not mind who Times Newspapers nominated as long as it was someone discreet. The next day – Friday, 1 April – Colin Webb, assistant editor

443

of *The Times*, tried to contact Trevor-Roper.

For the 'Sleuth of Oxford', the years since the publication of *The Last Days of Hitler* had been filled with honours and success. In 1957, his friendship with one Conservative prime minister, Harold Macmillan, had helped bring him the post of Regius Professor of Modern History at Oxford University; and in 1979 Margaret Thatcher granted him a peerage. He was an honorary fellow of two Oxford colleges, a member of three London clubs, and a Chevalier of the Legion of Honour. In 1954 he had married Lady Alexandra Howard-Johnston, elder daughter of Field Marshal Earl Haig, and the couple had become renowned for grand dinner parties at which Trevor-Roper would occasionally appear in velvet smoking jacket and embroidered slippers. His friend, the philosopher A. J. Ayer, 'admired his intellectual elegance' and 'appreciated his malice'.

Intellectually, even in private, Trevor-Roper could be faintly menacing; in print, he was devastating. An attack on one historian's work (on the Elizabethan aristocracy) was described as 'a magnificent if terrifying work of destruction' and brought him a rebuke from the venerable R. H. Tawney: 'An erring colleague is not an Amalekite, to be smitten hip and thigh.' In the course of one intellectual dogfight with Evelyn Waugh on the subject of the Catholic church, Waugh advised him to 'change his name and seek a livelihood at Cambridge'. Trevor-Roper did so in 1980, taking the title Lord Dacre of Glanton and becoming Master of Peterhouse, the oldest and most conservative college in Cambridge. Since then, anecdotes of the running battle between the college's High Church fellows and their anti-clerical Master had reached mythical proportions within the university. At his first dinner on High Table, Trevor-Roper was said to have objected to the consistency of the soup. '*Gentlemen*,' he announced, 'only have *clear* soup at dinner.' The following evening's menu began with *Potage de Gentilhomme*, a soup thick enough for the Master to stand his spoon in.

Trevor-Roper was not at home in Peterhouse when Webb tried to reach him on the telephone. It was Good Friday, and he and Lady Alexandra had retired for Easter to Chiefswood, their country house in Scotland, once the property of the novelist, Sir Walter Scott. Here, Trevor-Roper was able to escape the in-fighting of Oxbridge and affect the habits and costume of a laird of the Scottish borders; and it was here, on 1 April, that Webb tracked him down, told him of Hitler's diaries, and asked him to fly to Zurich the following week.

On Easter Sunday, Peter Koch made several trips to Heidemann's home on the Elbchaussee to pick up drawings and paintings from the reporter's collection. The idea was to take them to Zurich and exhibit them alongside the diaries to create the right atmosphere for the negotiations. It was the first time Koch had seen Heidemann's lifestyle at first hand, and he was shocked by its luxuriousness. As he was led from room to room he tried to reckon up in his mind how much this would cost in rent. Ten thousand marks a month at least, he thought. Heidemann said he found it rather cramped. 'He told me he was thinking of buying a *house* on the Elbchaussee,' recalled Koch. 'It was a place with a view of the Elbe.' A house like that would cost over a million marks.

Heidemann pointed out some of his treasures. 'There was a whole pile of antiques,' said Koch. 'There were some old walking sticks, drawings by Rembrandt and Dürer, a memento of Napoleon. . . . He also told me he had about three hundred paintings by Hitler.' Heidemann produced Hitler's suicide weapon, with Bormann's note attached to it. 'There was also a ladies' pistol, which was supposed to have been Eva Braun's.' Heidemann told him it had all come from the Boernersdorf crash. Koch asked him how he had paid for it.

The reporter told him the company had compensated him for buying it with a payment of 1.5 million marks.

Heidemann mentioned this quite casually, apparently assuming that Koch already knew of it. It was the first Koch had heard of any special payment and he confronted Schulte-Hillen with the story at one of the company's routine financial meetings the following week. 'He behaved as if he didn't know anything,' Koch remembered. 'Then he asked his deputy, Hensmann, if he knew anything. They both looked very embarrassed, running their hands through their hair and behaving as if they had great difficulty in remembering. They hesitated and then they said they had made a special payment of 1.5 million marks to Heidemann.'

Koch told Felix Schmidt what the management had done. They were both angry. Money had been paid out to a member of their staff behind their backs, and they had learned of it only by accident. But they were not surprised. The longer the affair went on, the more private deals they seemed to discover. What might they stumble on next?

For all those involved in the Hitler diaries project, the pace of events now began to accelerate.

On Monday, 4 April, Klaus Harpprecht and Barbara Dickmann, together with executives from *Stern*'s television company, arrived at Peter Koch's apartment to meet Sorge, Walde, Pesch and Heidemann. The two television journalists were informed of the existence of the Hitler diaries. Koch said that *Stern* wanted a film ready to launch the scoop. It would almost certainly be bought by one of the West German networks, and probably by foreign stations as well. It would have a budget of 160,000 marks. Harpprecht and Dickmann were worried about their reputations as impartial reporters. To avoid being seen to be making a publicity puff for *Stern*, they asked for editorial freedom to make the film as they wished. Sorge and Koch readily agreed to their demands: all the information contained in the film would have to come from *Stern*, and most of the potential interviewees – old Nazis like Karl Wolff and Hans Baur – were acquaintances of Heidemann's; in the time available, there was no chance of the television team carrying out independent investigations of their own.

On Tuesday, Heidemann withdrew another 300,000 marks from the diaries account.

On Wednesday, Walde telexed Dr Werner at the police headquarters in Wiesbaden: 'I cannot yet give you our company's decision regarding the material for authentication. We will ring you or your colleague on Monday 11 April to inform you what material can be given to you, and when.'

On Thursday, Dr Klaus Oldenhage of the Bundesarchiv drove up from Koblenz to the Gruner and Jahr offices for a meeting with the company's lawyers.

In March, Gerd Schulte-Hillen had suddenly learned some shocking news. After more than two years of paying out money for the diaries, he was informed by the Gruner and Jahr legal department that the company did not actually own the diaries. The lawyers had revised their earlier opinion; the agreement with Werner Maser, they warned him, was probably worthless. It was impossible to say with certainty who held the copyright on the diaries: it could be the Federal Government; it could be the State of Bavaria; it might even be some distant relative of Hitler's of whose existence no one was aware; at any rate, it was not Gruner and Jahr. Schulte-Hillen found himself preparing to hold syndication negotiations which technically involved the handling of stolen property. There was only one hope: an agreement with the Bundesarchiv.

The Federal Archives had known of the existence of *Stern*'s hoard of Hitler's writing for more than a year, ever since

Walde had sent them samples for handwriting analysis. Legally, they were aware that ownership of the material might well be theirs anyway, as the archive's lawyers thought that the copyright was vested in the West German Government. On the other hand, it was undeniable that without *Stern*'s expertise and money, the documents would never have come to light. At his meeting with the lawyers in Hamburg on Thursday, Oldenhage therefore announced that the Bundesarchiv was prepared to do a deal with the magazine, allowing them exclusive rights to the material for a limited period – on condition that eventually the originals would all be deposited in the Bundesarchiv. A contract was drawn up. To avoid accusations that the authorities were giving special treatment to *Stern*, the agreement was in Heidemann's name.

'Herr Gerd Heidemann', stated the contract, 'has access to unpublished written and typed documents belonging to Adolf Hitler.' The material came from 'outside the Federal Republic of Germany' and was 'of political and historical significance'. (Oldenhage still had no idea that the documents in question were Hitler's diaries.) The Bundesarchiv agreed to give Heidemann 'unlimited newspaper, book, film, TV and audio-visual rights in the material for him to dispose of as he thinks fit'. The rights would remain his for 'as long as the material has a marketable value', a period which was not to exceed ten years. At that point, the documents would revert to the Bundesarchiv 'in order to preserve them and allow them to be used in a proper historical context'.

For *Stern*'s lawyers, the agreement was a triumph. It was, of course, still possible that when the diaries were launched, some unknown descendant of Adolf Hitler would step out of the shadows to claim his inheritance. But now the magazine would have the West German authorities on its side. The contract also gave the company's salesmen a legal document to wave at potential purchasers in the syndication talks.

Gruner and Jahr had secured ownership in its scoop a bare twenty-four hours before the sales negotiations began.

That night, the principal figures in the first stage of those negotiations began moving into position. Sorge, Heidemann and Koch flew from Hamburg to Zurich, while Hugh Trevor-Roper travelled south from Scotland to London to be ready to catch a flight to Switzerland the next morning.

Trevor-Roper had finished breakfast and was preparing to leave for Heathrow on Friday when the telephone rang. It was Charles Douglas-Home, the editor of *The Times*.

The grandson of an earl, the nephew of a prime minister, educated at Eton, commissioned in the Royal Scots Greys, a dedicated hunter of the English fox – Douglas-Home's qualifications to edit *The Times* were perfect to the point of caricature. Trevor-Roper knew him well, and liked him: as one of the five independent directors of the paper he had supported his candidature for the editorship on the grounds that he was 'more academic' than his rival, Harold Evans. Nevertheless, he was not pleased at being bothered by Douglas-Home that morning.

In the course of the previous week, Trevor-Roper had had several conversations with *The Times*. He had told them that it would be impossible for him to reach an instant decision about the diaries' authenticity. He had been assured that he would not be required to do so. He should get a feel of the diaries in Zurich, and on his return to London he would be given a typed transcript of the material up to 1941. Only after he had studied that would he be required to deliver a verdict. The purpose of Douglas-Home's call ran contrary to that understanding. The editor of *The Times* told Trevor-Roper that Rupert Murdoch was taking a personal interest in the project, that he was determined to secure serial rights in the diaries, that there were rival news organizations equally determined, and that Murdoch wanted to be in a position to make his bid quickly. He could not afford to sit around while transcripts were studied; if he did, he would lose the deal. Douglas-Home therefore asked Trevor-Roper if he would ring London from Zurich *that same afternoon* with a preliminary assessment of the diaries' authenticity.

Trevor-Roper was 'very irritated' and 'surprised' by the request. It was ridiculous to expect him to reach a conclusion so quickly. But, 'under the pressure of events' and with assurances from Douglas-Home that this would only be an interim opinion, he agreed.

The next four hours were a blur of taxis and airports. Shortly after 9.30 a.m. he was picked up by car and driven to Heathrow. At 10.30 a.m. he met Peter Wickman. At 11.15 a.m. he took off on a Swissair flight to Zurich. He read the outline of *Plan 3* on the aircraft and thought it so phoney that his entire journey was wasted. At 1.50 p.m., Swiss time, he landed in Zurich. Wickman hurried him through immigration and customs. At 2.30 p.m. they dropped their luggage off at their hotel. At 3 p.m. he was led into the entrance hall of the Handelsbank, taken through a door immediately to his left, and found himself staring – 'astonished' – at fifty-eight volumes of Hitler's diaries.

This was the first occasion on which a trained historian had seen their treasure and the *Stern* men had prepared for it thoroughly. The diaries had been brought up from the vault and arranged in a neat pile on a table at the end of the room, embellished by other Hitler documents, paintings, drawings and memorabilia, including a First World War helmet, supposedly authenticated as Hitler's by a note from Rudolf Hess. Seen in its entirety, the archive looked stunning in its scope and variety. As Trevor-Roper bent over the stack of books, Sorge, Koch and Hensmann swiftly surrounded the elderly gentleman.

Trevor-Roper's specialist field – *The Last Days of Hitler* notwithstanding – was the sixteenth and seventeenth centuries. He was not a German scholar. He was not fluent in the language and had admitted as much in a review of *Mein Kampf* published a decade earlier: 'I do not read German', he confessed, 'with great ease or pleasure.' Written in an archaic script, impenetrable even to most Germans, the diaries might as well have been composed of Egyptian hieroglyphics for all the sense Trevor-Roper could make of them. He had to rely on the *Stern* men for translation. The conversation was entirely in English.

Sorge, who had spent three months perfecting his sales patter, did most of the talking. He showed Trevor-Roper Heidemann's dossier of how Hitler's handwriting had changed over the years. He showed him the extract in Baur's book in which the pilot referred to the Führer's anguish at the loss of Gundlfinger's plane. He showed him photographs of the graves in Boernersdorf. He talked of their 'star reporter', Heidemann. He gave him the reports of three independent handwriting experts who all confirmed that the writing they had seen was Hitler's. He pointed out that the diaries were not the only cargo salvaged from the plane. He handed him a box full of drawings and paintings. As Trevor-Roper leafed through the books, listening to Sorge, his doubts 'gradually dissolved'.

Recollections of the meeting vary between the participants, but on at least two points it would seem that Trevor-Roper was deliberately misled. He was told that the age of the paper had been chemically tested and found to come from the right period. This was not true. He was also told by Peter Koch that *Stern* knew the identity of the 'Wehrmacht officer' who had originally kept the material in East Germany, and that this same individual was the supplier of the diaries. This, too, was false. Heidemann was the only man who had dealt with Kujau and knew the route by which the diaries had supposedly reached the West.

Trevor-Roper has never been renowned as a trusting and simple soul. Nevertheless, it does not seem to have occurred to him that his hosts might lie to him. *Stern* stood to gain a fortune if the syndication negotiations proved successful: for that reason alone, their statements should have been treated with scepticism. But Trevor-Roper trusted them. He could see no reason why *Stern* should choose to sell forgeries. They might not be a particularly reputable organization, but he believed them to have high professional standards. As he put it afterwards in characteristic terms: 'I took the *bona fides* of the editor as a *datum*.'

'I was also impressed', he said, 'by the sheer bulk of the diaries. Who, I asked myself, would forge sixty volumes when six would have served his purpose?'

He was struck by *Stern*'s 'almost neurotic fear of leakage'. At one point, Koch produced a sheet of paper and wrote out in longhand a pledge of secrecy which he asked Trevor-Roper to sign. He was not to discuss what he had seen with anyone except those authorized to discuss the project on *The Times*. Trevor-Roper asked why he had to give such an undertaking. 'In case *The Times* doesn't buy the diaries,' replied Koch. 'It seemed a reasonable request,' recalled Trevor-Roper, 'so without thinking any more about it, I signed.'

By the time Trevor-Roper left the bank, he was convinced that the diaries were genuine. He did not like the fact that *Stern* had refused to tell him the name of its supplier, but then, in his experience, an insistence on anonymity was not unusual: 'Both the papers of Bormann and the diaries of Goebbels have come to publication through persons who have never been identified; and no one doubts that they are genuine.' He went straight back to his hotel, the Baur au Lac, and from his bedroom telephoned Charles Douglas-Home. 'I think they're genuine,' he told him. Douglas-Home, excited, thanked him for calling and said he would ring him back in an hour.

Believing that he would have an opportunity to study a transcript of the diaries on his return to Britain, Trevor-Roper had done no preparation for his visit to Zurich. He had not brought out a sample of Hitler's writing or any kind of chronology of the dictator's life with which to carry out a random check of the diaries' contents. The only thing he had brought, jotted on a scrap of paper, was the telephone number of a German historian he knew and respected — someone with whom he had planned to discuss the diaries. The historian whose name he had written down was Eberhard Jaeckel.

'If I had rung him,' lamented Trevor-Roper afterwards, 'he would have told me of his experience. He would have warned me.'

But it was not until Trevor-Roper was back in his hotel that he remembered the pledge of secrecy he had signed at the bank. He did not dare break it. He decided not to call Jaeckel.

The telephone rang. Trevor-Roper answered it, and a voice announced: 'Rupert Murdoch's office. I have Mr Douglas-Home on the line for you.' Trevor-Roper realized at once that the editor of *The Times* must have gone straight from speaking to him to see the proprietor.

'I've spoken to Rupert,' said Douglas-Home. 'We're both coming out to Zurich tomorrow.'

Trevor-Roper said that he was in a hurry to get back to Britain. He wanted to resume his holiday in Scotland. What flight were they coming on?

Douglas-Home told him not to worry. They were coming in a private plane.

Months later, the historian looked back and saw this as the decisive moment in the developing disaster:

What I should have done was insist on waiting for a transcript before giving my verdict. I should have said that in my view the diaries were *superficially* genuine. I should not have been so enthusiastic on the telephone.

If I'd refused to commit myself and reserved my position, then I'm quite sure Murdoch would have insisted on an answer. But I would have stood my ground. As it was, I lost the initiative. And I never regained it.

There was no liking between Murdoch and Trevor-Roper. The Australian tycoon regarded the Master of Peterhouse as a typical English establishment waxwork of the type he had been forced to acknowledge in order to purchase *The Times*. He was also 'too clever by half': Harold Evans described the historian at board meetings of Times Newspapers, sitting with 'eyes screwed up behind pebble glasses ... permanently sniffing the air for *non sequiturs*'. For his part, Trevor-Roper thought Murdoch 'an awful cad'.

When the millionaire bought *The Times* and *Sunday Times* in 1981, he had been obliged to sign an agreement designed to safeguard the integrity of the papers. The undertakings subsequently proved a feeble restraint, but at the time they had seemed to promise a curb on Murdoch's legendary ruthlessness. According to Evans, Trevor-Roper had boasted that 'we have Leviathan by the nose'. He was about to discover, as scores of others had done before him, that Leviathan was not so easily restrained.

TWENTY-THREE

On Friday night, the *Stern* team took Trevor-Roper out for a meal in one of Zurich's most expensive restaurants. The following morning, he flew back to Britain.

As Trevor-Roper left Switzerland, Murdoch arrived. With him on board his private jet he brought his tough Australian lawyer and business adviser, Richard Searby, along with Sir Edward Pickering and Charles Douglas-Home. Gerald Long, the former chief executive of Reuters and deputy chairman of News International, flew in to join them on a separate flight from Paris. Peter Wickman met them in the lobby of the Baur au Lac and took them through to a private dining room for lunch.

Around the table, there was an unmistakable feeling of anticipation. Murdoch sat next to the senior *Stern* negotiator, Jan Hensmann. Wickman sat beside Douglas-Home. Koch talked with Maynard Parker and William Broyles who had flown in from New York to make an offer on behalf of *Newsweek*.

Murdoch seemed particularly excited. In the spring of 1983, his corporation News International controlled more than thirty newspapers and magazines, four book publishers, three television companies and a variety of firms specializing in transport, energy and leisure. He ruled his empire in a manner not dissimilar to that which Hitler employed to run the Third Reich. His theory of management was Darwinian. His subordinates were left alone to run their various outposts of the company. Ruthlessness and drive were encouraged, slackness and inefficiency punished. Occasionally, Murdoch would swoop in to tackle a problem or exploit an opportunity; then he would disappear. He was, depending on your standing at any given moment, inspiring, friendly, disinterested or terrifying. He never tired of expansion, of pushing out the frontiers of his operation. 'Fundamentally,' Richard Searby, his closest adviser, was fond of remarking, 'Rupert's a fidget.'

The sudden decision to buy the Hitler diaries was a perfect example of Murdoch in action. He loved the concept of The Deal – spotting the opening, plotting the strategy, securing the prize. Already, in Zurich, he had his eyes on more than simply the British rights, which were all that *Stern* had originally offered him. Sure, the diaries could run in *The Times* or the *Sunday Times* (he would work out which later). But they could also run in the *New York Post* and the *Boston Herald* and *The Australian* and in one of the outlets of New Zealand's Independent Newspapers group (of which he owned 22 per cent). He had also recently acquired a 42 per cent stake in the Collins publishing company: he was aiming to buy the book rights to the Hitler diaries as well. It was this ability to spread the cost of his purchases throughout his many holdings which made Murdoch such a formidable force in international publishing. The Hitler diaries deal was exactly what he was looking for: he would publish the book, serialize it in three continents, and – given that he had recently joined forces with Robert Stigwood to produce Associated R & R Films – he might even make a movie which he could eventually show on Channel Ten, his television station in Sydney. The Hitler diaries potentially were a model for the internationally integrated media package.

After lunch, the *Stern* men took Murdoch and his entourage over to the bank. Seated around the table in the ground floor conference room, Sorge read out extracts from a typed transcript, Gerald Long provided a simultaneous translation, while Murdoch skimmed through a handful of diaries, nodding intently. He had no doubts that Hitler would help sell his papers. The diaries were sensational. At one point, he asked the Germans if they were sure their security was good enough: in his view it was possible that the Israeli secret service might try to seize the material.

A couple of hours later, back in *Stern*'s suite at the Baur au Lac, Murdoch made Hensmann an offer. He told him he wanted to bid for syndication and book rights. Hensmann said he could not discuss a book deal – Bertelsmann was insisting that Bantam retained the first option. Disappointed, Murdoch submitted an opening bid for American, British and Commonwealth serial rights. Hensmann considered it too low. Murdoch and his team retired to confer and to make some telephone calls. Shortly afterwards, they returned. News International, announced Murdoch, was willing to offer $2.5 million for the American rights, plus an additional $750,000 for serialization in Britain and the Commonwealth.

Three and a quarter of a million dollars. It was a good offer. It would clear Gruner and Jahr's costs and still leave them European and Asian serial rights and a percentage of the booksales. Hensmann, provisionally, agreed. He said he would give Murdoch a final answer at 5 p.m. on Monday. The two men shook hands and the News International team returned to London.

Meanwhile, Broyles and Parker were inspecting the books for *Newsweek*. They too considered the diaries a wonderful story. Serialization would attract tens of thousands of readers and give them a coveted boost in their ceaseless circulation battle with *Time*: whereas *Newsweek* sold roughly 3.5 million copies around the world each week, its rival had sales of almost 6 million.

The Hitler diaries appealed to Broyles in particular. A

Texan, a former marine, only thirty-eight years old, he had been appointed editor the previous September. It had been as surprising choice. Broyles's background had been in glossy magazines – *Texas Monthly* and *California*. He had no background in immediate news coverage. Announcing his arrival, *Newsweek*'s owner, Katherine Graham, had declared: 'He will add a whole new dimension.' He had, and *Newsweek*'s staff did not like it. He appeared to be more interested in features than news. Fashion, show business and social trends seemed to be his priorities. When *Time* led on the massacre of hundreds of Palestinians in the Lebanon, *Newsweek*'s cover story was the death of Princess Grace of Monaco. Broyles's editorial standards were attacked, but he tried to keep above the intrigue. He saw it as his task to provide long-range direction; he did not bother with the day-to-day running of the magazine. Just as the Hitler diaries suited Murdoch's style of running his company, so they fitted Broyles's approach to editing *Newsweek*.

Returning from the bank at about 8 p.m., the Americans offered Hensmann $500,000 for serialization rights in the diaries. Hensmann, sitting on Murdoch's offer of $3.25 million, found this 'totally unacceptable'. *Newsweek* doubled its offer to $1 million. Hensmann told them he wanted $3 million for the American rights. He would not take less. Broyles and Parker said they would have to return to New York. They would telephone him on Monday with an answer.

Back at the bank, Wilfried Sorge supervised as a guard carried the diaries down from the negotiating room to the vault. He watched to make sure the volumes were safely stowed, locked the deposit box, and took a taxi to the airport. He managed to catch the last flight home. It was his fortieth birthday party in Hamburg that night and he had no intention of missing it.

* * *

At his house in Chapel Hill, North Carolina, Gerhard Weinberg was telephoned by Maynard Parker.

Weinberg was fifty-five, a neat and bespectacled man, fastidious in his personal and professional habits. His origins were German Jewish. His family had fled the Third Reich when he was twelve and he now spoke in a broad New York accent which gave no hint of his German background. His name was not generally well known like Trevor-Roper's, but among professional historians he was respected as a careful scholar. In 1952 he had helped compile the US armed forces' *Guide to Captured German Documents*. He was the author of a two-volume study of Hitler's pre-war foreign policy that had taken him more than a decade to complete. He did not like to be hurried and he did not care for journalists – their sloppiness, their deadlines, their assumption that one was willing to drop everything 'to jump to their tune'.

Weinberg's first reaction to the alleged discovery of Hitler's diaries was the same as Trevor-Roper's: he thought it was improbable but was reluctant to dismiss it out of hand. It was true that there were no references to diaries in any of the reminiscences of Hitler's subordinates. It was also well known that Hitler had a strong personal aversion to writing in his own hand. (Weinberg knew this well, having enjoyed a minor historical scoop himself in the 1950s when he discovered the Führer's private testament of 1938 – the longest passage of Hitler's handwriting in existence; after drafting the will, Hitler had told his associates that the task had demanded 'a quite special effort on my part, since for years I've had the habit of writing directly on the machine or dictating what I have to say'.) However, Weinberg – professionally cautious – considered that 'too many things turn up which are not supposed to exist'; if the entries were short enough, the discovery of a diary might not be too far fetched.

The fact that Murdoch had already had *his* expert over to

Zurich put added pressure on *Newsweek*. Parker said he wanted Weinberg to fly to Switzerland to look at the diaries. How soon could he go? Weinberg replied that he was going to work as a visiting professor at Bonn University for three months over the summer. He was flying out to Germany on 22 April – what if he was to go early and inspect the diaries then? No use, said Parker: he wanted Weinberg in Zurich next week. The historian protested that he had classes in North Carolina on Monday, Wednesday and Friday. Cancel them, said Parker. Weinberg refused. He consulted his diary. 'I could go after my last class on Monday,' he said, 'as long as you can guarantee to get me back in time for my next one on Wednesday. Talk to your travel people.'

The morning of Monday, 11 April found Sorge back in Zurich, exhausted after having snatched only four hours' sleep in the past two days. At the bank he met the television presenter Barbara Dickmann, Heidemann and the *Stern* film crew who had arrived to shoot the opening sequence of the documentary; Sorge's attendance was required because he was the only person with keys to the safety deposit box.

The lights were set up outside the vault, the camera began turning, and Heidemann self-consciously walked into shot. He plodded woodenly over to the deposit box, opened it, pulled out one of the diaries and began reading.

By mid-afternoon, the filming was finished, and for the second or third time that day Heidemann took the opportunity to slip out to attend to some mysterious 'business' in Zurich. Barbara Dickmann asked him what he was doing. Heidemann replied that he was trying to make arrangements to drop in and see Martin Bormann who lived nearby.

Meanwhile, in Hamburg, London and New York, the negotiations to buy the diaries continued.

For *Newsweek* it was clear that to stay in the game they would have to match the News International offer. On Monday, back in the Gruner and Jahr headquarters, Hensmann received a telephone call from the United States informing him that the magazine was now prepared to offer $3 million for the American serialization rights. The deal was conditional on their being satisfied that the diaries were genuine. Broyles and Parker wanted to return to Zurich the following day and show the books to their nominated expert, Gerhard Weinberg. Hensmann agreed. This opened up the enticing prospect for Gruner and Jahr of pushing up the price by playing off *Newsweek* and News International against one another.

In London, Rupert Murdoch had already become suspicious that something was going on behind his back. Throughout the day, he made a number of attempts to ring Hensmann, without success. Each time he was told that Hensmann could not be reached. Finally, towards the end of the afternoon, the German rang him.

The deal was off, said Hensmann. *Newsweek* had made him a very attractive offer for the American rights. Murdoch could still have serial rights in the diaries in Britain and the Commonwealth for $750,000, but if he wanted the complete package, including United States rights, he would have to pay $3.75 million – $500,000 more than Murdoch had originally offered in Zurich.

Murdoch was furious. He understood that the handshake had clinched the deal. He unleashed a torrent of invective down the telephone which a shaken Hensmann was later to describe as 'bitter'.

Wilfried Sorge was at Zurich Airport to catch the evening flight to Hamburg when he was paged over the public address system. It was Hensmann. 'I don't want you to come back. I want you to stay there,' said the deputy managing director.

'*Newsweek* are coming to see the diaries tomorrow.'

Wearily, Sorge returned to the Baur au Lac.

Across the Atlantic, Gerhard Weinberg's last class at the University of North Carolina – a two-hour seminar on Nazi Germany – was coming to an end. At 4.15 p.m. Weinberg dismissed his students, drove twenty miles to the local airport, Raleigh-Durham, and caught a flight to New York. There was a limousine waiting at La Guardia Airport to rush him through the heavy evening traffic to the inter-continental terminal at JFK. Maynard Parker and William Broyles were already there waiting for him. Half an hour later, the three men boarded the overnight Swissair flight to Zurich.

Settled into their seats in the first-class section, the *Newsweek* men handed Weinberg the reports of the three handwriting experts. He read them carefully. 'It looks good,' he said when he had finished. 'If these people say the hand-writing is correct, that's fine by me.' Only one thing puzzled him: nowhere in the report was there any mention of diaries. He told Broyles and Parker that before they bought the books, they ought to have a specific volume checked. He also raised the question of copyright.

'We'll buy that off *Stern*,' replied Parker.

Weinberg shook his head. 'Mr Parker, it's not as easy as that.'

In the course of his work with original documents, Weinberg had acquired some understanding of the complexities of West German copyright law. As he understood it, literary rights in *unpublished* papers could not be confiscated. Although the State of Bavaria claimed ownership of *Mein Kampf*, it had no jurisdiction over Hitler's private diaries.

'I tell you what will happen,' warned Weinberg. 'Hitler's heirs will wait until you've printed millions of copies – and then they'll sue you.'

*   *   *

Weinberg, Broyles and Parker landed in Zurich shortly after 9 a.m. on Tuesday morning and went directly to the Handelsbank. They had no time to waste: the professor's irritating insistence on being back in North Carolina in time to take his next class had forced *Newsweek* to book him on a 3 p.m. flight to New York out of Amsterdam. At the bank they were met by Sorge and also by Heidemann, who had stayed overnight in Zurich after the previous days's filming. The introductions were friendly. Heidemann especially struck Weinberg as charming and anxious to help.

The session began with Heidemann reading aloud extracts from the diaries for 1940 and 1945. Sorge then invited the Americans to help themselves to whatever volumes they wanted from the stack in front of them.

Weinberg had brought with him a copy of the diary of Hitler's valet, Heinz Linge, covering the second part of 1943. Linge's daily notes of Hitler's activities were available for inspection in the National Archives in Washington but had never been published: if the *Stern* diaries were poor quality fakes, discrepancies with the Linge record would swiftly expose them. Unfortunately, the entries in the *Stern* diary covering the last three months of 1943 were so sketchy, Weinberg was unable to make an adequate comparison. He then asked to see the volumes covering the battle of Stalingrad. These were no use either. There was no typed transcript available and the handwriting was so bad that Weinberg was unable to decipher it. He pulled out a few other volumes at random. Nothing in them struck him as false. He noted that there was a page missing from the volume devoted to the Hess affair, and a statement witnessed by a notary indicating that it had been sent away for analysis. He looked up the entry for the Munich conference in 1938 and found a startling tribute from Hitler to the British prime minister, Neville Chamberlain:

He almost outwitted me. This smoothie Englishman.... I
would have imposed quite different conditions on Mussolini
and Daladier [the French prime minister], but I couldn't do so
with this cunning fox, Chamberlain.

The entry impressed Weinberg, who nodded sagely as he read
it. 'This accords with my own theories,' he announced.

Half-way through the examination, a third *Newsweek*
journalist arrived. He was Milan Kubik, the magazine's
bureau chief in Jerusalem, flown in by the Americans to
inspect the Jewish angle. Broyles and Parker introduced him
and explained his presence on the grounds that the magazine
expected there to be 'enormous interest' in the Hitler diaries
in Israel. Throughout the meeting, the *Newsweek* editors kept
probing the material for information which would appeal to
their American readership. At one stage, Parker asked to see
the volume covering the Battle of the Bulge in the winter of
1944, but Heidemann told him it was one of the four books
which had yet to be delivered from East Germany.

Two things, meanwhile, had struck Weinberg, who was
carefully reading through the diaries. One was the fact that
almost every page carried Hitler's signature. No one in his
right mind, he thought, would have risked forging hundreds
of signatures; it seemed a strong argument in favour of authenticity.

He also pointed out to Broyles and Parker that most of the
diaries began with a handwritten note stating that if anything
happened to him, Hitler wanted the books to be given to his
sister Paula. This could pose further copyright problems, said
Weinberg, strengthening the case of any heirs of Hitler who
cared to argue that the diaries were actually their property.
Sorge and Heidemann, already aware of the problems over
copyright, looked at one another in embarrassment: that had
not occurred to them, they said.

Weinberg also wanted to know why no German scholar had been showed any of this material. Sorge replied that they were worried about leaks. He asked who Weinberg would recommend. Weinberg said he was thinking of a very reliable historian – Eberhard Jaeckel of Stuttgart. Had they heard of him? The *Stern* men replied that they had. 'It was clear to me', recalled Weinberg, 'that they didn't want to involve Jaeckel.'

At 2 p.m., Weinberg's self-imposed deadline expired and the *Newsweek* party had to leave. In order to obtain Weinberg's assessment, Broyles, Parker and Kubik had to fly with him to Amsterdam. The historian admitted he was 'astonished' by what he had seen. He had not been able to find fault with the diaries. On balance, he inclined to the view that they were authentic.

This was what *Newsweek* wanted to hear. At Amsterdam airport, Weinberg caught his flight to New York. The three *Newsweek* journalists boarded a flight to Hamburg to clinch the deal.

Stern's London office was based in Peter Wickman's house in Barnet, miles out of town in the northernmost fringe of the capital. On Tuesday morning, as the *Newsweek* contingent sifted through the diaries in Zurich, Wickman's telex machine suddenly clattered into life with an urgent message from the Gruner and Jahr headquarters. It was a contract requiring Rupert Murdoch's agreement, offering him the British and Commonwealth rights in the Hitler diaries for $750,000. It included a 25 per cent penalty clause should News International default on the deal.

Following Hensmann's instructions, Wickman delivered the contract to Murdoch personally in his office in *The Times* building in Gray's Inn Road. Murdoch scarcely glanced at it before handing Wickman his own version – roughly twenty pages long, drawn up by his lawyers, reiterating the terms he understood had been agreed in Switzerland on Saturday.

Wickman made his way back up to High Barnet and began feeding the pages into a telecopier, transmitting Murdoch's counter offer back to Hamburg.

The next day, Wednesday, 13 April, Heidemann and Barbara Dickmann continued their work on the *Stern* television film, driving to Herrsching, near Munich, to interview Hans Baur.

The Baur family detested the media, even when it came in the friendly and uncritical form of Gerd Heidemann. The eighty-five-year-old ex-Nazi hobbled over to them on his wooden leg and stared at the camera with undisguised hostility. Then a former Munich policeman arrived, 'in a state of extreme agitation', according to Dickmann, claiming he had been summoned by Baur to protect the family. On his advice, Frau Baur went round the house taking down photographs of her husband with Hitler and packing away various Nazi mementoes. Heidemann, the Baurs and the ex-policeman then disappeared into another room while Dickmann and the crew waited to hear whether they would be allowed to film.

After twenty minutes, the group reappeared. According to Baur, Heidemann had shown him one of the diaries: 'a black book with red cord and a red seal . . . I was of the opinion that it was Hitler's writing.' The camera was set up and Baur described the plane crash and Hitler's distress.

When the interview was over, the atmosphere relaxed. The retired policeman, who came from Luxembourg, turned out to be a collector of Nazi relics. He told Heidemann, in Dickmann's presence, that 'his circle of friends was almost exclusively composed of prominent ex-Nazis'. He suggested that they should 'set up an agency for Hitler relics in Munich'. Heidemann told him about the Blood Flag and offered to sell it to him. When the time came to leave, the two men made an appointment to have dinner together.

Listening to this conversation merely served to confirm

Barbara Dickmann's feelings about Heidemann. The man was 'unable to distance himself professionally from the events of the Nazi era'. Although she had known him for little more than a week, she had already spent many hours with him, driving between locations. Being trapped in a car with Heidemann had not proved a pleasant experience. 'I couldn't avoid having to listen to his stories,' she recalled.

> He talked to me constantly about his friend 'Martin'. He told me incredible stories about 'Martin's' life after the collapse of the Third Reich. He said that 'Martin' was in Switzerland, that he was being watched over by the Israeli secret service.
>
> Heidemann also indicated that he had original material belonging to Hitler supposedly containing the 'ten theses' of Hitler's Final Solution.

He had told her during filming in Zurich on Monday that he was trying to arrange a meeting with Bormann. Later, he showed her his set of Polaroid pictures and confided to her that he was going to meet him on 20 April, Hitler's birthday, when he would be given important documents. (Martin subsequently cancelled the meeting.) He showed her his collection of relics: 'several glass cases in which he had helmets, uniforms, a brown shirt, a pair of trousers, a damaged watch, weapons, drawings allegedly by Hitler, a swastika flag, a Party book of Hitler's, his passport and all sorts of other things'.

Dickmann was shocked by Heidemann's behaviour. He seemed 'euphoric' about his access to senior Nazis, gripped by 'sick fantasies'. Their relationship became 'increasingly cool'. When the television team returned to Hamburg, she was worried enough to seek out Peter Koch and tell him what his reporter was up to. Koch reassured her: Heidemann always immersed himself in whatever he was researching – it was part of his technique for gaining access to circles which were normally impossible to penetrate. She could rely, said Koch, on the fact that Heidemann 'was not a Nazi and that once he'd finished his researches he'd be normal again'.

Meanwhile, as Heidemann and Dickmann were leaving Hans Baur in Herrsching, Rupert Murdoch's draft contract was arriving on Jan Hensmann's desk in Hamburg. *Stern*'s chief negotiator regarded it as 'completely unacceptable'. News International had refused to improve its offer in the face of *Newsweek*'s bid. Hensmann decided to sign a deal with the Americans.

Broyles, Parker and Kubik, who had arrived in Hamburg the previous night, were informed that their offer of $3 million for the American serial rights had been accepted. The *Newsweek* representatives were taken to the special suite of offices occupied by the diaries team. As a gesture of good faith, Peter Koch was authorized to give them the story of the find as it had been written by Wolf Thieme, together with the rough text for the first four instalments of the *Stern* serialization.

It was at this point that word came from the nearby Four Seasons Hotel that two emissaries from Rupert Murdoch – Richard Searby and Gerald Long – had arrived to discuss the News International offer. They wanted to come over to the *Stern* building straight away.

Confronted by this embarrassing situation, Hensmann dispatched Wilfried Sorge to the Four Seasons. He was to tell them to go home – the deal with Murdoch was off.

Sorge relayed the message.

He had often seen negotiators lose their tempers, but he had never before witnessed anything to compare with the reaction of the two Murdoch men. Searby was normally smooth and urbane; Long, beetle-browed and pugnacious, looked, even in his lighter moments, as if he would enjoy nothing more than a good Victorian eviction, preferably involving widows, orphans and a tied cottage. When Sorge told them that the diaries had been sold to *Newsweek*, both men blew up in anger. 'They were beside themselves with rage,' he recalled: as close as men could come to physical violence without actually resorting to it. But despite the threats and accusations of bad faith, Sorge refused to yield.

Later that night, after he had calmed down, Searby rang Sorge at home to ask him what the hell was going on. Privately, Sorge was beginning to have doubts himself about the way Hensmann was handling the negotiations, but in his conversation with Searby he remained loyal to his superior.

'Murdoch's people,' he recalled, 'went away with nothing.'

In London, Peter Wickman received another urgent communication from Hamburg. *Stern* wanted to use three quotations from Trevor-Roper to launch the diaries. The quotes they had in mind were, first, that the discovery of the diaries 'was the most important historical event of the last ten years'; secondly, that 'it was a scoop to equal Watergate'; and thirdly, that it would 'make it necessary, at least in part, to rewrite the history of the Third Reich'. All three lines were actually the work of Peter Koch, but he instructed Wickman to ask Trevor-Roper if he would allow them to be attributed to him.

For Wickman, this was the latest in a series of bizarre requests from Hamburg. *Stern*'s mania for secrecy was such that he now had to make any telephone calls connected with the diaries from a public call box in case MI6 had bugged his phone. He was also sick of having to shuttle back and forth between Hensmann and Murdoch. It was with some embarrassment that he rang Trevor-Roper and relayed Koch's request.

Trevor-Roper was not enthusiastic. 'I didn't like any of the quotes,' he recalled, 'and said so to Wickman.' Nevertheless, reluctantly, he agreed to put his name to the statements that the diaries represented the most important historical discovery of the decade and a scoop of Watergate proportions. He rejected the third one about the rewriting of history – he had yet to see the promised transcript of the diaries.

Wickman telexed Trevor-Roper's reply to Germany.

On the morning of Thursday, 14 April, Gerd Schulte-Hillen arrived back in Hamburg from his trip to the United States. He had barely walked through the front door of his house when the telephone rang.

It was Rupert Murdoch.

It is a measure of Murdoch's tenacity as a businessman, and also of his determination to secure the Hitler diaries, that even after Long and Searby had been sent back empty-handed, he still believed he could salvage his deal with Gruner and Jahr. He subjected Schulte-Hillen to an harangue about the behaviour of Jan Hensmann. He complained that he had been double-crossed, his associates insulted. What was going to be done about it?

Schulte-Hillen apologized. He said he had only just returned from abroad.

Murdoch wanted to know whether the negotiations could be reopened. He was now willing, he said, to pay $3.75 million for the English language world rights, matching *Newsweek*'s latest offer.

Schulte-Hillen now made the first of what was to prove a succession of extremely costly mistakes. He noted Murdoch's offer and promptly invited him to attend a new round of negotiations in Hamburg the following day. He then drove over to the Gruner and Jahr office and, overruling Hensmann's objections, instructed him to issue a similar invitation to *Newsweek*.

Broyles and Parker had made two round trips to Europe in six days. They had assumed that an agreement had been reached. Hensmann's call to New York to tell them that the deal was off and that they had to come back a third time produced an outraged response. 'They were not pleased,' said Sorge. But if *Newsweek* wanted the diaries they had no alternative. They agreed to come.

A few hundred yards away, in the headquarters of the diaries team, Thomas Walde was at last getting round to sending a fresh sample of the diaries for forensic analysis. Under the supervision of a Hamburg notary, blank pages had been cut out of two of the books – one was removed from the Hess volume, one from a volume covering 1933. The two sheets of paper, marked 'Hess' and 'August 1933', together with another of the Hitler documents accompanying the diaries – a draft telegram to Mussolini – were parcelled up and given to Walde's secretary, Hannelore Schustermann, to take down to the Bundesarchiv in Koblenz. 'It is urgent,' wrote Walde in a covering letter to Dr Henke, 'and a particular priority should be given to the two blank sheets. A thousand thanks and best wishes.'

Henke, still ignorant of the diaries' existence, forwarded the material to a forensic chemist named Arnold Rentz who lived a few miles outside Koblenz. Rentz undertook to deliver his verdict within the next week.

Shortly before noon on Friday, 15 April, representatives of *Newsweek* and News International arrived at the Gruner and Jahr headquarters. There was an immediate shock for the Germans. The two organizations – which Schulte-Hillen had eagerly expected to come ready to bid against one another, pushing the price still higher – arrived *together*. Rupert Murdoch headed the News International delegation; Mark

Edmiston, President of *Newsweek* Inc., led the Americans. Tired of *Stern*'s sloppy and amateur tactics, the two men had decided to join forces. They would share the costs and split the diaries between them. The details had yet to be worked out, but considering there were supposed to be twenty-eight separate instalments, there was plenty of Hitler material to go around. Extracts of particular interest to the Americans could run in *Newsweek*, those relevant to Britain could go to Murdoch. The rest could be carved up between them at a later date. For now, the first priority was to end the uncertainty and reach a final agreement. Watching the supposed rivals conferring together, Sorge was deeply disappointed. They would be able to set their own price. There was no chance now that *Stern* would get the $3.75 million which up until yesterday had been on offer.

The negotiations took place around the large conference table in the managing director's office, with its imposing view out over the Elbe. Schulte-Hillen, Murdoch and Edmiston did most of the talking, turning occasionally to their advisers for clarification on particular points. The number of men present at any one time varied between ten and twenty – lawyers, journalists, accountants and executives, neatly dressed in two and three-piece suits, briefcases full of circulation figures, memoranda, balance sheets and legal opinions. For the next eleven hours they haggled over simultaneous release dates and standard extracts as if *Stern* was offering nothing more unusual than franchises in a new kind of fast food.

The two biggest sources of contention were the order in which the diaries were to be serialized and the time scale over which they would be published. Edmiston maintained that the American public didn't give a damn about Rudolf Hess and his peace mission to Britain. They wanted to know about the murder of the Jews. The whole series, as far as *Newsweek* was concerned, should begin with the Holocaust. Schulte-Hillen rejected that. Many of the diaries had not yet been tran-scribed. The only section which had been properly checked was that relating to Hess. With publication less than a month away, it was too late to change. To maximize revenue, *Stern* wanted to tease out the diaries for as long as possible: the only way to do that was to publish the books in chronological order. Again, Edmiston objected. As one of the Americans put it afterwards: 'We were especially bothered by the idea that *Stern* was trying to drag this out for almost thirty instalments. If it were 500,000 words, that's one thing, but it's only 50,000 words. We thought they were trying to slice the salami very thin.'

Eventually, after some hours of discussion, the meeting began to grope towards a compromise. Perhaps the diaries could be published grouped under themes: 'Hitler and the Jews', 'Hitler and his Women', 'Stalingrad' and so on.

After dinner, the conference moved on to copyright. This was the most worrying area for *Stern* and the company fielded three lawyers to try to handle it. Schulte-Hillen and his col-leagues were acutely aware of the fact that if anyone pirated the diaries, it might well prove impossible to stop them. Indeed, if a rival organization could somehow get hold of a descendant of Hitler, they might be able to sue Gruner and Jahr for the return of the diaries. Thankfully, *Stern* could at least fall back on the agreement between Heidemann and the Bundesarchiv – this, they claimed, would be enough to pre-vent any breaches of copyright.

Edmiston and Murdoch agreed to have their lawyers check over that aspect of the contract the following morning.

At 10.30 p.m. the main outstanding issue was the money. Schulte-Hillen suggested they should reconvene the following day. The News International and *Newsweek* people shook their heads. It was essential that this was finally straightened out tonight. Schulte-Hillen again suggested a postponement.

Edmiston was sarcastic. Was Schulte-Hillen, he asked, planning to fix the price on his own?

There was an uneasy shifting around the table.

Very well, said Schulte-Hillen. How much would they offer?

Surprisingly, Murdoch and Edmiston had not planned to take advantage of their alliance to reduce the price. They were confident that the diaries would easily generate enough extra revenue to recoup the cost.

The original offer stayed on the table, announced Edmiston. 'We'll stick to $3.75 million.'

To Sorge, who had been expecting the worst, this was an enormous relief. He was therefore startled to hear Schulte-Hillen's reply:

'We no longer think that is enough. We want $4.25 million.'

There was a moment's pause, and then an explosion of exasperation. Both Edmiston and Murdoch said that they had never encountered such bad faith in the course of negotiations. They stood up, and like courtiers to a pair of princes, all the lawyers, journalists, accountants and executives immediately followed suit. Jackets were taken off the back of chairs, cigarettes were stubbed out, papers were shovelled into briefcases, and in a dramatic display of contempt, the Americans, British and Australians filed out of the room without another word.

The *Stern* team was left alone.

Hensmann had slipped out earlier in the evening. Only Schulte-Hillen, Sorge and the three lawyers were left. Beneath them, the eight floors of offices and corridors were dark and deserted. Schulte-Hillen began shuffling the documents in front of him. He suggested they prepare for the following day's talks. The other four looked at him incredulously. It was obvious to all of them there were not going to *be* any more talks. After a week of intensive negotiations, 'the deal', as the *Stern Report* later put it, 'which had once seemed so certain for $3.75 million, had burst like a bubble'.

TWENTY-FOUR

Early the next morning, Schulte-Hillen and Sorge tried ringing
Murdoch and Edmiston in their hotel suites. It was, as Sorge
had feared, hopeless. Edmiston said that he had no further
interest in the diaries: Gruner and Jahr should pretend that he
was no longer in Hamburg. Murdoch refused even to come to
the telephone. A few hours later, the *Newsweek* and News
International teams flew home.

It was a decisive turning point in the development of the
diaries affair. The initiative had passed out of *Stern*'s hands.
From self-confident salesmen they had, overnight, been
reduced to anxious supplicants. There were no other potential
clients to turn to who were in the same league as Murdoch
and *Newsweek*. *Time*'s interest had always been lukewarm.
The *New York Times* had turned down the Hess story within
six hours of being told about it. Associated Newspapers had
only offered £50,000 for *Plan 3*, and had made that condi-
tional on the most stringent guarantees of authenticity. Even
more worrying for the *Stern* men was the realization that
Newsweek and Times Newspapers between them now knew
an enormous amount about the diaries. Each organization
had been allowed to send in an expert to read through the
material; journalists from both groups had had extracts read
out to them; and *Newsweek* had actually been handed the
complete story of the find and the first four instalments of the
Stern series.

It was the thought of what *Newsweek* might do, with its
worldwide sales of more than three million copies, which

most terrified the Germans. There was nothing to stop Broyles and Parker breaking the news of the diaries' existence and running pirated extracts. They could have their story on the news stands by Tuesday, 26 April – in less than ten days' time.

Over the weekend, an emergency meeting of *Stern*'s editors and management reviewed the situation and concluded that they had only one option. Their next issue was due out on Thursday, 21 April – there was no way they would be ready to run the diaries by then. The following week, 28 April, would be too late to beat *Newsweek*. Accordingly, they would have to change their publication date. Monday, 25 April would give them the maximum amount of time, while still allowing them to head off the Americans. In the meantime, it was decided that Schulte-Hillen and Peter Koch should fly to New York to try to salvage some sort of agreement.

On Sunday, 17 April, Hugh Trevor-Roper came south from Scotland to Cambridge, ready for the start of the University's summer term. On Monday he was telephoned at the Peterhouse Master's Lodge by Colin Webb of *The Times*, who told him of the collapse of the negotiations.

The news came as a surprise to Trevor-Roper. The *Stern* television people had asked him to give them an interview for their documentary. He had agreed. They had offered to come to Cambridge, but he had insisted on flying to Hamburg: he wanted to meet this 'star reporter' Heidemann and see what else he had in his collection. He was supposed to be going the next day. What should he do now?

Webb said that *The Times* would still like him to go. Murdoch, now in New York, was confident he would soon be in a position to buy the diaries – on his terms; the Germans had nowhere else to go.

*   *   *

477

Schulte-Hillen and Koch arrived in New York on Monday evening. They began telephoning around town, trying to speak to *Newsweek* and Murdoch. No one would return their calls.

In Zurich, the diaries were removed from the Handelsbank and locked in a safe in the Schweizer Bankgesellschaft, where security was much tighter. After Murdoch's warning about the Israeli secret service, the Germans were determined not to take any chances.

On Tuesday, a conference of *Stern*'s senior editors and heads of department met to discuss their special Hitler edition. It would be the biggest in the magazine's history: 356 pages thick, with a 48-page supplement devoted to the diaries – half in colour, half in black and white. The print run would be increased to 2.3 million copies. The expected boost in sales would cover the additonal production costs, estimated at 720,000 marks. The meeting was secret. Only those staff who needed to know were to be told that *Stern* was about to publish Hitler's diaries.

Trevor-Roper came through customs at Hamburg Airport on Tuesday and was met by a fat, pale man in glasses. There was a brief period of pantomime thanks to Trevor-Roper's assumption that he was merely the chauffeur sent by *Stern* to collect him. Eventually, Heidemann made himself understood: *he* was the Bloodhound, the German equivalent of Woodward and Bernstein, the man responsible, in Trevor-Roper's reluctant words, for 'the greatest scoop since Watergate'. The historian apologized and said he was very pleased to meet him.

It took fifteen minutes for Heidemann to drive Trevor-Roper from the airport to his archive in Milchstrasse. Before

478

the television interview he wanted to show off his collection to the famous historian – it satisfied the same craving for recognition which Nannen and Schulte-Hillen had found it politic to feed. Trevor-Roper found himself conducted down a quaint, narrow street of small boutiques and art galleries, into a curiously arranged apartment. It consisted, he recalled, of four corridors laid out in the shape of a 'hollow square'. There were no sleeping or washing facilities. Heidemann explained that he used it solely as a museum.

Trevor-Roper found the contents 'staggering'. There were hundreds of folders full of documents and photographs from the Third Reich. Some had been sold to Heidemann by Karl Wolff and Heinrich Hoffmann and were unquestionably authentic. There was, for example, an SS file on an expedition to Tibet organized by Himmler, part of the Reichsführer's crackpot research into 'Aryan bloodlines'. The file contained carbon copies of the outgoing correspondence and originals of the incoming. Trevor-Roper was in no doubt that it was genuine.

At least two of the corridors were crammed with Nazi memorabilia. Then, turning the corner, came a section devoted to Mussolini. Finally, Heidemann conducted Trevor-Roper into an area with a few mementoes of Idi Amin. 'Those', he said, pointing to a pair of voluminous white cotton drawers, 'are Idi Amin's underpants.'

For the first time, the former Regius Professor of Modern History began to eye his host uneasily. Until now, he had assumed that Heidemann was simply a thorough journalist. Suddenly it occurred to him that the reporter was slightly odd. He seemed to have an obsession with dictators. Trevor-Roper started to dislike him. The more he talked, the more phoney he seemed. Like Koch and Nannen before him, Trevor-Roper found himself wondering how Heidemann could afford such an obviously expensive collection.

After this guided tour, Heidemann took his guest over to the Atlantic – one of the most imposing and luxurious hotels in Hamburg, looking out across the Alster to the *Stern* building. *Stern* had reserved Trevor-Roper a room for the night. In another part of the hotel, the film crew was waiting. Trevor-Roper took his place in front of the camera and recorded a brief interview. Despite his personal misgivings about Heidemann, he was still convinced that the diaries were genuine and he said so. Heidemann was delighted.

Trevor-Roper had been looking forward to a quiet meal alone with a book followed by an early night before his flight back to London. But Heidemann insisted that they dined together. He led the protesting historian into the bar.

Heidemann ordered meals for them both and began drinking heavily. He became loquacious. Trevor-Roper experienced the sequence of emotions familiar to those who had had the misfortune to be trapped in a conversation with Heidemann: bewilderment, disbelief, distaste and an overwhelming sense of claustrophobia.

He told Trevor-Roper that he had access to an important archive of Nazi documents which Martin Bormann had deposited in Madrid in 1938.

Trevor-Roper pointed out that such an action by Bormann was rather unlikely – Madrid was in Republican hands in 1938.

Perhaps it was somewhere outside Madrid, said Heidemann. Or perhaps it was 1939. Anyway, it was certainly true; he had been told the story personally – by Martin Bormann.

Trevor-Roper smiled, assuming that Heidemann was making a joke. But the reporter was serious. He pulled out his wallet and produced a photograph. 'This is a picture of Martin, taken recently.'

The historian studied the photograph. It showed a man in

his mid-sixties – an obvious impostor, considering that Bormann would by then have been eighty-three.

Heidemann would not be dissuaded. Martin, he insisted, was alive and living in Switzerland. . . .

The evening crept by with more stories of Heidemann's Nazi contacts, until Trevor-Roper at last felt able to make a polite excuse and escape to his bedroom.

In retrospect it is difficult to understand why Trevor-Roper's uneasiness and scepticism about Heidemann did not begin now to extend to the diaries he had seen in the Swiss bank. In fact, his reaction was almost exactly the opposite. He reasoned that if he, after half a day's acquaintance, found Heidemann unreliable, *Stern*, after employing him for thirty years, must surely have known what he was like and been all the more careful about checking his stories. He was under the impression that this had been done. As far as he was concerned, the diaries had been authenticated by three handwriting experts and by forensic analysis; their provenance in the Boernersdorf air crash was entirely credible; their contents had been thoroughly investigated by *Stern* over a period of several years; and the magazine's editor had assured him that the supplier of the diaries was known to them and had also been checked.

Heidemann reminded Trevor-Roper of the late Ladislas Farago, the American writer who claimed he had seen a decrepit Bormann propped up in a large bed in 1973 surrounded by Bolivian nuns. Farago had visited Trevor-Roper in Oxford and had exhibited a similar naïvety and readiness to believe whatever he was told, combined with a genuine talent for unearthing documents and information.

With these complacent thoughts, the historian retired to his bed, his belief in the Hitler diaries unshaken.

Murdoch's handling of the negotiations had been masterful.

By Tuesday, isolated in New York, Koch and Schulte-Hillen found themselves effectively reduced to begging the Australian to buy the syndication rights. When he finally consented to resume negotiations, he was able to dictate his own price. His original offer for the British and Commonwealth rights had been $750,000. Now, he picked them up for little more than half that sum – $400,000. The money was to be paid over the next two years. The first instalment of $200,000 was handed over on signature of the contract. (Shortly afterwards, Murdoch also acquired the American rights for a bargain price of $800,000.)

The continuing silence from *Newsweek* convinced the Germans that the magazine was indeed going to steal their story. Further negotiations were useless. The pair had the feeling that they were being deliberately kept waiting around in a New York hotel in order to hold up publication in Hamburg.

On Wednesday, Schulte-Hillen telephoned Reinhard Mohn and confessed to the Bertelsmann owner that he had made a mess of the negotiations – in his words, he had 'over-pokered' his hand. He also rang Hensmann and issued orders confirming that *Stern* would publish its scoop the following Monday. The discovery of the diaries would be announced in a statement on Friday.

Koch and Schulte-Hillen caught the next plane back to Germany.

In the offices of *The Times* and *Sunday Times* that Wednesday, very few people knew of the impending acquisition of the Hitler diaries. Those who did were mostly confused or apprehensive.

Phillip Knightley had arrived back at the *Sunday Times* on Tuesday after four months in Australia. That night he had gone out for a drink with Eric Jacobs, the editor responsible for commissioning the long articles on the front of the paper's

Review section. He wouldn't be requiring anything for a while, he told Knightley. He understood he was going to be running the Hitler diaries in that space.

The next day, Knightley went in to see Magnus Linklater, the Features Editor. 'These Hitler diaries,' he asked, 'they're not the ones that David Irving put us on to in December, are they?' Linklater said they weren't – they'd been offered to the paper by *Stern*. A few minutes later, Knightley bumped into the *Sunday Times* editor, Frank Giles, in the lavatory. He told him he was worried about the rumours he was picking up regarding the diaries. It all sounded very suspicious.

'You're right to be cautious,' replied Giles. 'But don't worry. It doesn't concern us. Murdoch's going to run them in *The Times*.'

Knightley was still anxious. He asked if he could submit a memorandum setting out his reservations.

By all means, said Giles, but keep it to one page. Murdoch's attention span was notoriously short; there was no point in giving him anything longer than a few hundred words to read.

What was nagging away at the back of Knightley's mind was the memory of another set of wartime documents which had been bought for the *Sunday Times* fifteen years earlier – the diaries of Benito Mussolini. These had been offered to the Thomson Organization, at that time the owners of the *Sunday Times*, for £250,000. A series of expert examinations had failed to find anything wrong with them, and £100,000 had been handed over as a down payment to a Polish-born arms dealer who was acting as middleman. Further large sums had been paid out in expenses – for example, Vittorio Mussolini, the dictator's son, had been given £3500 in cash in a brown paper bag in order to buy himself a sports car in return for agreeing to renounce his claim on the diaries. In the end, the books had turned out to be the work of an Italian woman called Amalia Panvini and her eighty-four-year-old mother,

Rosa. The affair had cost Thomsons a fortune and made the *Sunday Times* a temporary laughing-stock in Fleet Street. Knightley – one of the few reporters left on the paper who remembered the affair – had been cautious of so-called 'finds' of wartime papers ever since.

It took him the rest of Wednesday to write his memorandum. Point by point, he drew attention to the similarities between the forgery of 1968 and the 'scoop' of 1983. The Mussolini fiasco should have taught the *Sunday Times* some lessons:

1 You cannot rely on expert authentication. Thomson engaged five experts, including the author of the standard work on Mussolini, the world's greatest authority on paper, a famous handwriting expert, an internationally known palaeographer and an academic who authenticated the Casement Diaries. *Not one expert said that they were fake*.

2 You cannot rely on people close to the subject. Vittorio Mussolini, Mussolini's son, said that the diaries were definitely his father's.

3 You cannot rely on legal protection. Slaughter and May [a firm of solicitors] did the negotiations for Thomson. They did not succeed in recovering a single penny when the diaries turned out to be fakes.

4 Beware of secrecy and being pressed to make a quick decision. The Mussolini con men were able to bring off their sting by pressing Thomson to make a quick deal. Absolute secrecy was essential, they said, to prevent the Italian government from stepping in. Both manoeuvres prevented proper examination of the background of the salesmen and the provenance of the diaries.

Questions to consider:
1 What German academic experts have seen all the diaries?

Has, for instance, the Institute of Contemporary History seen them?

2 What non-academic British experts have seen all the diaries? Has David Irving seen them?

3 How thoroughly has the vendor explained where the diaries have been all these years and why they have surfaced *now*: the fiftieth anniversary of Hitler's accession to power.

The crux of the matter is that secrecy and speed work for the con man. To mount a proper check would protect us but would not be acceptable to the vendor. *We should insist on doing our own checks* and not accept the checks of any other publishing organization.

Knightley's intuition was subsequently proved correct in almost every detail: the authentication had been inadequate; the supposed involvement of East German officials and the fear that the copyright might not be secure had fostered a climate of secrecy, bordering on paranoia; no German historians had been allowed to see the diaries; no explanation had been given as to where the diaries had been kept for more than thirty years; and Times Newspapers had not carried out its own checks, apart from sending Trevor-Roper on his brief expedition into the Swiss bank.

Knightley sent his memorandum to Frank Giles to be forwarded to Murdoch. He never heard another word about it. It was too late. Murdoch had bought the diaries and now his priority, like *Stern*'s, was to beat *Newsweek* into print.

Trevor-Roper arrived home in Cambridge late on Wednesday night. He was talking to his wife in her sitting-room at about midnight when he received a transatlantic telephone call from Murdoch and Charles Douglas-Home in New York. Murdoch told him that *Stern* was bringing forward its publication date to Monday. News International had acquired syndication rights in the diaries. 'I think we'll put them in the *Sunday Times*,' he said. The announcement of the discovery would be made on Friday morning, in less than thirty-six hours' time. Douglas-Home cut in. 'We want a piece from you for Saturday's *Times*. Can you do it?' Trevor-Roper said he thought he could, if he wrote 'flat out'. It was agreed that the article would be picked up from Peterhouse by dispatch-rider on Friday morning.

In Hamburg on Thursday, Sorge and Hensmann tied up the loose ends with *Stern*'s smaller, European syndication partners. *Paris Match* bought the diaries for $400,000. The Spanish company Grupo Zeta paid $150,000. Geillustreerde Pers of the Netherlands handed over $125,000 for serial rights in Belgium and Holland. Norshe Presse of Norway bought the diaries for $50,000. The Italian rights went to Mondadori, publishers of the magazine *Panorama*, although as a precaution they decided at this stage to buy only the first four instalments for $50,000. Added together with the $1.2 million paid by News International for the English language serialization, this meant that the Hitler diaries had so far realized $1.975 million – less than *Stern* had originally hoped for, but still one of the largest syndication deals in history. And, of course, there were still the world book rights to come.

The Peterhouse Master's Lodge is a large and stately Queen Anne house on the eastern side of Trumpington Street, opposite the college. This spacious and well-proportioned home was regarded by Trevor-Roper as one of the more attractive aspects of being Master of Peterhouse. ('The only drawback', he remarked, 'is that the college comes with it.')

Throughout Thursday, 21 April, Trevor-Roper sat in his first-floor study, trying to write his article for *The Times*. Although justifiably renowned for his literary style (A. J. P.

Taylor called him 'an incomparable essayist'), he had always found writing 'terribly painful'. Deadlines especially were a torture to him. He never used a typewriter, always a fountain pen, and liked to 'write, sleep on it, and then rewrite'. Today he had no time for such luxuries. At length, having sorted through his notes and cleared his mind, he set to work.

'A new document' – he began – 'or rather, a whole new archive of documents – has recently come to light in Germany. It is an archive of great historical significance. When it is available to historians, it will occupy them for some time. It may also disconcert them. It is Hitler's private diary, kept by him, in his own hand, throughout almost the whole of his reign. . . .

On Thursday night in his laboratory in the small town of Bad Ems outside Koblenz, Dr Arnold Rentz completed his analysis of the three sheets of paper *Stern* had sent to the Bundesarchiv the previous week.

When he had commissioned him, Dr Josef Henke had told Rentz that the tests were a matter of the utmost urgency. The chemist therefore worked late in order to be able to give Henke the results the following day. He had some good news, and some bad.

PART FOUR

'After all, we are in the entertainment business.'
RUPERT MURDOCH ON THE HITLER DIARIES

TWENTY-FIVE

Friday, 22 April.

At 9 a.m. a motorcycle dispatch-rider from *The Times* arrived at the Peterhouse Master's Lodge.

Trevor-Roper was entitled to feel a certain professional pride as he handed over his article. It was long – over 3000 words – and had been difficult to write, but he had finished it in a day and submitted it on time. It was an impressive piece of journalism, if not of scholarship.

His career had always been marked by a curious dichotomy. There was Hugh Trevor-Roper, patient historian, author of learned works on such *esoterica* as the sixteenth-century European witch craze, the ancient Scottish constitution and the life of the fraudulent Sinologist, Edmund Backhouse, 'the Hermit of Peking'. And then there was Lord Dacre, man of public affairs, newspaper director, pundit, MI5 officer and Hitler expert. His article for *The Times* represented the triumph of the intelligence officer over the scholar. His authentication of the Hitler diaries was not based on a careful analysis of their content – it could not be, he had scarcely bothered to read a single entry. It was based almost entirely on circumstantial evidence.

He confessed that to start with he had been sceptical ('the very idea of Hitler as a methodical diarist is new'). But then he had 'entered the back room in the Swiss bank, and turned the pages of those volumes, and learned the extraordinary story of their discovery' and his doubts had 'gradually dissolved'. What most impressed him, he wrote, were the other parts of the Hitler archive shown to him by *Stern* in Zurich and by Heidemann in Hamburg:

> ... it is these other documents – letters, notes, notices of meetings, mementoes, and, above all, signed paintings and drawings by Hitler, all covering several decades – which convinced me of the authenticity of the diaries. For all belong to the same archive, and whereas signatures, single documents, or even groups of documents can be skilfully forged, a whole coherent archive covering 35 years is far less easily manufactured.
>
> Such a disproportionate and indeed extravagant effort offers too large and vulnerable a flank to the critics who will undoubtedly assail it. ... The archive, in fact, is not only a collection of documents which can be individually tested: it coheres as a whole and the diaries are an integral part of it.
>
> That is the internal evidence of authenticity. ...

Trevor-Roper's entire misjudgement was founded upon the *non sequitur* contained in that last, fatally confident sentence. The fact that the archive spanned thirty-five years and included paintings and other documents did not, except in the most superficial sense, provide 'internal evidence of authenticity'. If such internal evidence existed, it was to be found in the detailed content of the diaries themselves. But no German scholar had even been allowed to see them, let alone check every entry; at least twenty volumes had not yet been transcribed into typescript; and Walde and Pesch, the only journalists apart from Heidemann who had access to the diaries, had thoroughly examined only one volume: that devoted to the flight of Rudolf Hess. (Ironically, the authenticity of the Hess book was the one feature of the diaries which still worried Trevor-Roper. 'We must not jump to premature conclusions,' he wrote. 'There are many mysteries in the case of Hess.')

The 'external fact' which impressed Trevor-Roper was the plane crash and Hitler's reaction to it: 'a clue which connects him, by a thin but direct line, with this archive'. The outburst in the bunker, together with the extent of the material accompanying the diaries, 'seems to me to constitute clear proof of their authenticity'.

The world, he concluded, would have to revise its opinion of Hitler to take account of the fact that he was 'a compulsive diarist'.

> In fact, we must envisage him, every night, after he had apparently gone to bed ... sitting down to write his daily record: and perhaps more too, for the archive contains not only the diaries but whole books by Hitler – books on Jesus Christ, on Frederick the Great, on himself (the three subjects which seem equally to fascinate megalomaniac Germans) – and a third volume of *Mein Kampf*. If Hitler (as he said in 1942) had long ago found writing by hand a great effort, that may be not so much because he was out of practice as because he already suffered from writer's cramp.

As this hasty compilation of donnish jokes and misunderstanding sped down the M11 to London, Felix Schmidt opened the regular *Stern* editorial conference in Hamburg. It was 11 a.m., German time.

He had a brief announcement to make, he said. His statement was simple and to the point. Over the past few days, colleagues had probably heard rumours of an impending scoop of great importance. He was now pleased to be able to let them in on a secret which had been kept by the magazine for the past two years. *Stern* had acquired the diaries of Adolf Hitler and would begin publishing them on Monday.

The news was met with gasps and whistles of astonishment.

Simultaneously, the magazine was issuing a public statement announcing its discovery to the world. 'Following evaluation of the diaries,' it claimed, 'the biography of the dictator, and with it the history of the Nazi state, will have to be written in large part anew.'

At 11.15 a.m., *Stern*'s news department began sending out the telexed message – to the German press agency, DPA, to Association Press, to Reuters, to United Press International, to West German radio and television. . . .

It was at this point, with the juggernaut already beginning to roll, that Thomas Walde received a telephone call from Dr Josef Henke at the Bundesarchiv. Henke had received the results of Rentz's forensic analysis. The two blank pages which had been cut from the diaries did not contain paper whitener and therefore could have been manufactured either before or during the Second World War. The Mussolini telegram, however, *did* contain whitener and Rentz was convinced the paper was made after 1945. Rentz's findings supported those of the West German police in March: while the diaries might be genuine, much of the accompanying archive (whose existence had done so much to convince Trevor-Roper) was faked.

Walde thanked Henke for his help and asked him to rush Rentz's written report to Hamburg as quickly as possible.

At first sight, this news was not too disturbing for *Stern*: the diaries, after all, were what mattered, and Heidemann had already told Walde that, according to 'Fischer', the other material did not necessarily come from the Boernersdorf crash. But considered more carefully, the implications of the Rentz report were frightening. Three handwriting experts had concluded that the draft telegrams to Admiral Horthy and General Franco (similar to, and from the same source as, the Mussolini telegram) were written by the same person as the author of the page from the Hess special volume. If they were fakes, how much reliance could be placed on the handwriting authentication? And Rentz had been able to establish, by the apparent absence of whitener, only that the two diary pages *might* be from the right period: they could still be made of paper manufactured after 1945 by an old-fashioned process (as indeed eventually proved to be the case). Thus, at the very moment that news of *Stern*'s scoop was being flashed around the world, the magazine received indications about its authenticity which were, at best, ambiguous.

As soon as Walde had finished speaking to Henke, he went off to find Peter Koch to tell him the news. Koch, newly returned from America, was understandably alarmed. Walde tried to reassure him: according to Heidemann, he said, whitener was in use before the war; and even if the Mussolini telegram was a fake, it did not originate from the same source as the diaries.

Koch was still not happy. He told Walde that they must inform the management at once. They collected Felix Schmidt on the way, briefed him on what had happened, and together all three went up to the ninth floor to see Schulte-Hillen.

Koch explained the situation and made a short speech. At any moment, he declared, a wave of scepticism was going to descend upon them. They were going to be attacked by academics and newspapers all over the world. They had to be absolutely confident that the story was watertight. There was only one way they could be sure. Heidemann must be made to divulge the name of his source. Koch was worried. 'I told Schulte-Hillen,' he recalled, ' "Heidemann has greater trust in you than in me. Please ask him to write down the exact course of events. You can then read the piece of paper and lock it away in a safe. You don't even need to give it to me to read. Just tell me that the source is OK." '

Schulte-Hillen agreed. He asked his secretary to get Gerd Heidemann on the telephone.

The reporter was not in Hamburg. He was eventually

traced to the Bayerischer Hof, an expensive hotel in the centre of Munich.

Schulte-Hillen explained the problem and asked him to write down, in confidence, the complete story of how he had obtained the diaries. Heidemann refused. 'I asked him again,' recalled Schulte-Hillen, 'emphatically.' It was no use. According to the managing director:

> He told me that as an experienced journalist he knew that anything that was written down could also be copied and anything that was said could be passed on to other people. He was not so unscrupulous that he would endanger the life of his informant. He could not live with his conscience if he put someone else's life in danger.
>
> When I tried to pressurize him further, he became quite irritated and said: 'What is it that you want of me? I won't tell you. I swear to you on the lives of my children that everything is in order. It has all been properly researched. The books are genuine. What more can you ask of me?'

Schulte-Hillen was once more struck by what seemed to him Heidemann's obvious sincerity. 'I too have children,' he said afterwards. 'Heidemann's oath impressed me.' He let the matter drop. In any case, under the terms of his contract, Heidemann had the right to keep the identity of his supplier secret. The managing director told the editors that there was nothing he could do. They would all have to trust Heidemann.

In London, Frank Giles, editor of the *Sunday Times*, summoned two of his senior colleagues, Hugo Young and Magnus Linklater, to his office. He was, recalled Linklater, 'obviously very flustered'.

Giles was not a member of Murdoch's inner circle. He had been only on the fringes of the group which negotiated to buy the diaries – vaguely aware of what was going on, unenthusiastic, yet comforted by his belief that they would be running in *The Times*. His *sang froid* had been shattered the previous day by a brisk, transatlantic announcement from Murdoch that the Hitler diaries were going to be serialized in the *Sunday Times* after all: now that *Stern* would be appearing on Monday, Sunday had become the perfect day to print the extracts. It would enable the paper to avoid the risk of rivals getting hold of advance copies of the German magazine and printing pirated extracts from the diaries twenty-four hours ahead of them.

Murdoch was not a proprietor who encouraged dissent. Even strong editors found it hard to stand up to him. Giles was not a strong editor. He was sixty-four years old, sleek and aristocratic, a lover of Glyndebourne, fine French wines and classical music which he listened to on his Sony Walkman. His relationship with Murdoch was akin to that between a rabbit and a stoat. The proprietor made no secret of his habit of ripping into Giles's editorial decisions. He once announced jauntily to Harold Evans that he was 'just going over to terrorize Frank'. Murdoch's office on the sixth floor of *The Times* building looked directly across into Giles's at the *Sunday Times*. Evans recalled how the Australian tycoon 'would stand up with a big grin and with his fingers pointed like a pistol fire bang! bang!' at Giles working with his back to the window. The subject of this imaginary target practice was in no position to stop Murdoch from doing what he wanted with his newspaper.

Giles told Young and Linklater that the *Sunday Times* would be serializing the Hitler diaries. They would prepare the ground on Sunday with extensive coverage of their discovery. The two men were 'aghast'. How could Giles countenance something as irresponsible as running the diaries without allowing the paper's own journalists to make independent checks? Had he not seen Knightley's memorandum? Had he forgotten the Mussolini diaries?

Giles, according to Linklater, raised his hands to his ears.

'I know, I know,' he said. 'But I don't want to hear about all that. The deal's been signed and we're going to have to do it.'

Minutes later, Arthur Brittenden, Times Newspapers' Director of Corporate Relations (their press officer), announced that the Hitler diaries would be running in the *Sunday Times*. 'It's not been decided how many Sundays,' he told the *New York Times*, 'because the complete translation is not yet finished. But I think we'll run it for two or three weeks, then there will be a gap and we'll pick it up again.'

By coincidence, many of the leading characters in the British subplot of the affair came together for lunch on Friday at the Dorchester Hotel. The Dorchester was hosting the UK Press Awards, an annual ceremony at which Britain's journalists present prizes to one another in recognition of their professional skill. Charles Douglas-Home was holding forth to a woman sitting next to him. 'It's just been announced,' he told her. 'It's the greatest historical find of the century.'

Sitting at the table, Gitta Sereny of the *Sunday Times* asked what he was talking about.

'The Hitler diaries,' said Douglas-Home.

'Are you running them?' she asked.

'No. You are.'

Sereny relayed the gist of this conversation to Phillip Knightley, sitting a few yards away. Knightley hurried back to the office and sought out Magnus Linklater. Linklater gloomily confirmed that the news was true. '*The Times* is running an article by Trevor-Roper tomorrow saying they're genuine. Why don't you talk to him?'

It was 3 p.m. In the Master's Lodge, Trevor-Roper was preparing for a visit to the opera when Knightley called him.

The historian's tone was confident and reassuring.

'The one thing that impressed me most', he told Knightley, 'was the volume of the material. I asked myself whether it all could have been constructed out of the imagination and incidental sources. I decided that it could not.'

Knightley reminded him that there had been thirty volumes of the purported Mussolini diaries. Trevor-Roper was unperturbed: 'I *know* Hitler's handwriting. I *know* his signature. I *know* the changes in it between 1908 and his death. It seemed to me that an operation of forgery on that scale was heroic and unnecessary.' He pointed out that they were not dealing with some shady characters operating on the fringes of the law, but with one of the wealthiest and most widely read magazines in Europe: 'The directors of *Stern*, one must assume, do not engage in forgery.'

By the time he hung up, Knightley – who recorded the call – felt much happier. Trevor-Roper's reputation was impeccable. It was inconceivable that he could be so emphatic about the diaries' authenticity without good cause. 'I must say,' Knightley recalled, 'he went a long way to convincing me.'

Trevor-Roper and his wife left the Master's Lodge shortly after 3.30 p.m. to join a party of Cambridge dons and their families on an excursion to the Royal Opera House at Covent Garden. The historian still felt fairly confident about his judgement of the diaries. But the conversation with Knightley had been vaguely disconcerting and as he settled down in his seat on the party's private coach, somewhere in the recesses of his mind, something began to stir.

Three thousand miles away, America was waking up to the news of the diaries' discovery. All the major US wire services were running the *Stern* announcement, and across New York, in the offices of publishers, agents and newspapers, telephones were ringing with demands for information.

At Bantam Books, Louis Wolfe confirmed to the *New York Times* that he had heard of the Hitler diaries. 'An offer was made,' he admitted, 'but we were never sure exactly what was being offered, so it seemed much simpler to have our parent company handle it out of its group office in Munich. To the best of my knowledge no one in the United States has signed a contract to publish a book based on Hitler's diaries.' Wolfe's Vice-President, Stuart Applebaum, was also fielding calls. 'We have a great interest in the possibility of doing a book someday related to the diaries,' he told the *Washington Post*, 'but at this time we have no plans to publish one. Nor do we have any deal to do one.'

At ICM, Lynn Nesbit struggled to answer a deluge of questions. Yes, she had been hired to represent *Stern*. No, she was no longer their agent. Yes, she was paid a commission. No, she wouldn't disclose the amount. . . .

Almost every big American magazine found itself pressed to issue a statement. *Time*'s was terse ('We have had an interest'); *Life*'s was baffled ('We haven't been involved at all; we just heard about it today'); the *National Enquirer* tried to pretend it was on the point of clinching a deal ('right now we are involved in negotiations with *Stern*'). The longest came from *Newsweek*, read out by the magazine's publicity director, Gary Gerard: '*Newsweek* does not have an agreement with *Stern* for publishing rights to the Adolf Hitler diaries. We are covering the story as news.'

Newsweek's behaviour went much further than merely 'covering the story as news'. At a morning editorial conference it was decided to ransack the material handed over in Hamburg. Hitler would go on the cover. Inside the magazine, thirteen pages would be devoted to the diaries (as opposed to four for the week's main story, the bombing of the US embassy in Beirut which left forty-seven dead). The advertising department was instructed to prepare an extensive publicity campaign. Full-page advertisements were taken out in six major US newspapers, including the *New York Times* and the *Washington Post*; these were to be backed up by thirty-second television commercials in twelve American cities.

As it happened, this was the day on which *Newsweek*'s nominated expert, Gerhard Weinberg, was due to fly to Germany to take up a temporary teaching post in Bonn. Maynard Parker was nevertheless determined to extract an article from him. Weinberg dismissed his last class on the campus at Chapel Hill at 11 a.m. He and his wife caught a flight to New York and at 3 p.m. were met at La Guardia airport by two *Newsweek* reporters and a photographer. The journalists steered the professor into a corner of the arrivals lounge and thrust a copy of Trevor-Roper's *Times* article into his hands – the text had just been wired over from London. Weinberg skimmed through it: '*doubts dissolved . . . satisfied documents authentic . . . standard accounts Hitler's personality have to be revised . . . astonishing archive. . . .*' Weinberg, who had always respected Trevor-Roper's scholarship, was startled by the lack of equivocation. Such a ringing endorsement seemed to him 'in itself to be a strong argument in favour of the diaries' authenticity'. Trevor-Roper, he reasoned, must know something he didn't'. He told the *Newsweek* reporters that in view of the article, the diaries, in his opinion, were now more likely to be genuine than not.

The *Newsweek* men still needed more information to complete their coverage. Weinberg was equally determined to catch his flight to Germany. The only solution was for one of the journalists, Steven Strasser, to fly out with him, interview him on the plane, and file a piece by telephone from Germany. The photographer stood Professor Weinberg against a wall and took a few hasty pictures. Then Weinberg, his wife, and Mr Strasser left to catch the afternoon flight to Frankfurt.

*　　*　　*

Peter Koch's prediction of the hostility the diaries would arouse was already coming true.

In Stuttgart, Eberhard Jaeckel – although, like Weinberg, 'shaken by Trevor-Roper's position' – declared himself 'extremely sceptical'. He had seen a so-called 'Hitler diary' some years before, he said, and decided it was forged.

'I have not seen their evidence, but everything speaks against it,' Werner Maser told Reuters. 'It smacks of pure sensationalism.'

'I am extraordinarily sceptical,' announced Karl-Dietrich Bracher of Bonn University. 'It would be a total surprise and I consider it highly unlikely.'

A spokesman for the Federal Archives in Koblenz confirmed that they had arranged for the examination of 'about ten pages' of Hitler's handwriting for *Stern*, but denied having authenticated any diaries.

The loudest condemnations of all were emanating from London.

David Irving reckoned he was due for some luck. For two years, everything had gone wrong for him. His marriage had ended in an acrimonious divorce. He was being pursued by the Inland Revenue. His political activities had collapsed due to lack of funds. He was on the point of being evicted from his flat. Most of the furniture had been taken by his wife and entire rooms were left stripped and abandoned while he was reduced to squatting in one corner. By the spring of 1983, he was in desperate need of money and a boost for his flagging career. And now, as if in answer to a prayer, Adolf Hitler came to his rescue.

Ever since 10 a.m., when a reporter from *Der Spiegel* had called to tell him of *Stern*'s impending announcement, he had been inundated with inquiries from around the world – Reuters, *Newsweek*, the *New York Times*, the *Observer*, the *Sunday Mirror*, *Bild Zeitung*, Independent Radio News, the

BBC ... 'As soon as I rang off, the phone rang again,' he noted in his diary. 'Quite extraordinary.' His answer to all of them was the same: the Hitler diaries were fakes, and he had the evidence to prove it.

He was 'shocked' by *Stern*'s decision to publish. He was certain that the forgeries he had received from Priesack in December originated from the same source as Heidemann's diaries. Thankfully, he still had photocopies of the material – letters, drawings, a few pages from the original volume for 1935 (the one Kujau had forged in 1978 and given to Fritz Stiefel). With the Hitler diaries fast becoming the hottest news story in the world, these worthless scraps had suddenly become a potential gold mine. Irving's priority now was to make money as quickly as possible.

In between constant interruptions from the telephone, he wrote to the *Sunday Times* drawing their attention to the fact that he had given them an 'exclusive lead to these documents' before Christmas and demanding as commission a percentage of the price paid for the diaries. He then set about marketing his information. *Der Spiegel* offered to pay him for his photocopies. *Bild Zeitung*, a mass-circulation West German paper, promised to meet his expenses and provide a fee if he would fly out to Hamburg to confront *Stern* at its press conference on Monday. One of the *Sunday Times*'s main rivals, the *Observer*, paid him £1000 for his help in compiling an article which derided the diaries' authenticity; another, the *Mail on Sunday*, gave him £5000 for his documents and a statement that the diaries were forged.

This was only the beginning of an extraordinary resurgence in Irving's fortunes. No one now cared about his reputation as a right-wing maverick. Seeing their circulations threatened by the Hitler scoop, newspapers and magazines which would have treated him as a pariah twenty-four hours earlier queued up for quotes. By the end of the afternoon Irving had emerged as *Stern*'s most vociferous and dangerous assailant.

At 9.30 p.m., a BBC taxi picked him up and took him to Television Centre where he appeared in a live studio confrontation with Charles Douglas-Home. Irving waved his fakes at the camera. Douglas-Home was unperturbed. 'I have smelt them,' he said of the diaries. 'I'm a minor historian and we know about the smell of old documents. They certainly smelt.'

At that moment, sitting in the audience at the Royal Opera House, Covent Garden, Times Newspapers' star witness was beginning to have second thoughts. Borne along by the momentum of deadlines, midnight phone calls and departure times, infected by the pervading atmosphere of excitement and secrecy, he had scarcely had time for an hour's calm reflection all week. Now, as the other academics and their wives concentrated on the music of Verdi's *Don Carlos*, Trevor-Roper's thoughts were elsewhere, ranging back over his experiences in Hamburg and Zurich, with one incident in particular gnawing at his mind.

On Tuesday, Heidemann had shown him a letter, supposedly by Hitler. It was dated 1908 and addressed to a girl with whom Hitler was supposed to have been infatuated during his days in Vienna. The incident had been described by August Kubizek in *The Young Hitler I Knew*. In retrospect, this letter 'disquieted' Trevor-Roper. It fitted in 'just a little too neatly' with the known historical record. 'Could this letter have been forged for this purpose?' he wondered. And why was it with Hitler's papers? Why wasn't it with the girl's? Until this moment he had taken the existence of such supplementary material, which helped to make up the sheer bulk of the archive, as an almost unanswerable argument in favour of the diaries' authenticity. Suddenly he saw the flaw in this logic. For the first time since leaving the Swiss bank, he allowed his mind to approach the *Stern* find from a different angle.

> I began to consider the whole archive with the mind of a forger. How would a forger of Hitler's diaries proceed? I decided that he would concentrate on a period when Hitler's movements were well documented, and, outside that period, select only detached episodes for which public evidence was accessible. He would also, since his main material would be derivative or trivial, vary it where he safely could with interesting deviations. The diaries, I noted, had a discomforting correspondence with this model. They were continuous from 1932; before that there were isolated episodes; and an interesting variation was suggested in the affair of Rudolf Hess.

Trevor-Roper had always had doubts about the Hess book: 'That Hitler, with his political brain, should have sanctioned such a mission – it was insane.' Now, these doubts and his reservations about the 1908 letter began to set off a fearful chain reaction in his mind. Why hadn't any German experts seen the material? And Heidemann – the memory of that awful evening at the Atlantic swam back into his memory – Heidemann could so easily have been deceived; 'he was not a critical spirit'. Trevor-Roper's confidence in his judgement began rapidly unravelling.

'If at that moment,' he said later, 'I could have stopped the course of events, I would have done so.'

He briefly considered groping his way out of the dimly lit auditorium to find a telephone. He rejected the idea. He knew the workings of a modern newspaper sufficiently well to appreciate that there was no chance of stopping his article now. At that moment, less than a mile away, in the print-room of Times Newspapers, twelve hours after it had been picked up from his home, 400,000 copies of it were coming off the presses.

TWENTY-SIX

Hugh Trevor-Roper arrived home in Cambridge in the early hours of Saturday morning. He went to bed but was soon up again. Shortly after 7 a.m. he went down to collect the morning's edition of *The Times*. The story dominated the front page:

38 years after Bunker suicide

Hitler's secret diaries to be published

- Hitler approved the 'peace' flight to Scotland in 1941 by his deputy, Rudolf Hess, but then declared him insane.
- He ordered his troops not to destroy the British Expeditionary Force trapped at Dunkirk in 1940 in the hope that he could conclude a negotiated peace.
- He thought Neville Chamberlain, whom history has judged harshly, was a skilled negotiator and admired his toughness.

Trevor-Roper opened the paper. His own article was spread across an entire page:

> 'When I had entered the back room in the Swiss bank, and turned the pages of those volumes, my doubts gradually dissolved. I am now satisfied they are authentic.'

Secrets that survived the Bunker

BY HUGH TREVOR-ROPER

Reading the article spurred Trevor-Roper into action. At 8 a.m. he began making a series of telephone calls.

506

He rang Charles Douglas-Home and told him he now had 'some doubts' about the authenticity of the diaries. 'They were not doubts such that I could say I disbelieved in the diaries,' he recalled – but they were serious reservations. Douglas-Home took the news with remarkable calmness. He told the historian that there had been a good deal of publicity on television the previous evening, with David Irving emerging as 'prosecuting counsel'. He said that he, too, personally regretted the deal with *Stern* – the Germans were unpleasant to deal with, arrogant and paranoid. They still hadn't supplied a complete transcript of the material. The conditions they had imposed were 'insulting'. They would have to see what developed over the next few days.

Trevor-Roper also spoke of his doubts to Colin Webb. Next, he rang Peter Wickman. *Stern* wanted him to attend the press conference to launch the diaries on Monday. Trevor-Roper told Wickman he would take part only if he were given an opportunity to put some questions to Gerd Heidemann beforehand. In addition, he wanted to see a typed transcript of the Hess volume. Wickman promised to see what he could do.

One good reason for Douglas-Home's stoicism in the face of Trevor-Roper's sudden nervousness was the fact that he was no longer responsible for the diaries. That burden had passed on Thursday to Frank Giles at the *Sunday Times*. A fatal breakdown in communication now occurred. Douglas-Home believed that Trevor-Roper's doubts were relatively minor; if they were serious, he assumed the historian would pass them on to the *Sunday Times*. But Trevor-Roper was relying on Douglas-Home to spread the word of his unease around Gray's Inn Road. He did not think of calling them direct. 'I had had no dealings with the *Sunday Times* myself,' he explained. 'I had been employed solely by *The Times*.' He sat at home in Cambridge and waited for Knightley or Giles to ring him. He was 'surprised that they didn't call; it would seem the thing to do'.

Meanwhile, happily ignorant of Trevor-Roper's change of heart, the staff of the *Sunday Times* were racing against the paper's deadline to do justice to a story endorsed by the historian as the greatest scoop since Watergate. Professional instincts were now overriding natural scepticism. Magnus Linklater (co-author of *Hoax*, the story of the faked Howard Hughes autobiography) and Paul Eddy, the head of the paper's Insight team, were responsible for putting together the coverage. *Stern* would not allow them to talk to Heidemann directly. Quotations from the diaries were having to be extracted from the Germans by Anthony Terry, the *Sunday Times* representative in Hamburg, who translated them and telexed them to London. Even as they worked, Linklater and Eddy were conscious of how phoney they sounded. According to the telexes, Hitler had written some peculiar entries.

[*On Goebbels's affair with a Czech actress*]
The little Dr Goebbels is up to his old tricks again with women.

[*On Himmler*]
I shall show this deceitful small animal breeder with his lust for power; this unfathomable little penny-pincher will find out what I am about.

[*On the July 1944 bomb plot*]
Ha, ha, isn't it laughable? This scum, these loafers and good-for-nothings. These people were bunglers.

The two journalists discussed what they should do. 'We agreed,' said Linklater afterwards, 'that the honourable course would have been to have refused to touch it. But as Paul said, if we did that we would have to resign. We both laughed about that, so we carried on – like a couple of hacks.'

Phillip Knightley was also searching his conscience. His task was to write an article setting out the reasons for the diaries' authenticity and their importance as an historical source. 'I agreed to do it on the understanding that my name wasn't to be attached to it. Then someone pointed out that it would look odd if the article appeared anonymously and I was asked to reconsider.' Knightley went off to consult John Whale, the *Sunday Times*'s religious correspondent, 'a great moral force on the paper'. Knightley showed him what he had written and asked him what he should do. Whale advised him to agree to the request – he had been sufficiently detached in the piece to cover himself against the possibility that the material was fraudulent. (Only one sentence – the first – later returned to haunt Knightley: 'Hitler's diaries', he wrote, 'have been submitted to the most rigorous tests to establish their authenticity.')

The edition of the paper which emerged after all this agonizing was extraordinary: a testament to the skill of the journalists and the old rule that anything about the Nazis, once embellished with swastikas and pictures of Hitler, has a quality of compulsion. 'We did a hell of a good job on it,' said Linklater. 'It was gripping stuff. Professionally, we were all very pleased with it.'

Dominating the front page, spread over eight columns, headed 'WORLD EXCLUSIVE', was an article promising the reader 'The secrets of Hitler's War'. There was a super-imposed picture of Gerd Heidemann holding the diaries; behind him, looking out over his shoulder, staring hypnotically at the potential purchaser, was an enormous close-up of Hitler's face. The story spilled over on to page two and was backed up by articles on pages sixteen, seventeen and eighteen. The centre spread announced 'HITLER'S SECRET DIARIES' in letters almost two inches high. There were photographs of Hitler and Eva Braun, of extracts from the diaries, of Goebbels, Himmler and Bormann, of the graves in Boernersdorf and of Heidemann solemnly holding up the salvaged window from the crashed plane. 'Look at that,' said Brian MacArthur, the deputy editor, when the first proofs arrived in the newsroom. 'You will never see another front page like that as long as you live. It is sensational.'

It is a tradition on the *Sunday Times* that, as the presses begin to turn, the senior members of the staff gather in the editor's office for a drink. Shortly after 7 p.m., Linklater, Eddy, MacArthur, Knightley and their colleagues trooped in to see Giles. There was a mood of self-congratulation. The paper looked so good, it almost convinced the people who had written it. Over a glass of wine, the conversation turned to the following week's paper: who would attend the *Stern* press conference, who would handle the serialization. . . . Giles suggested they should invite Trevor-Roper to write an article demolishing 'all these carping criticisms' about the diaries' authenticity. This was considered a good idea. Giles picked up the telephone. What followed has entered the mythology of Fleet Street, a scene etched in the memory of the witnesses, 'told and retold over the milk-bars of Fleet Street', as Evelyn Waugh once wrote of a similar moment in *Scoop*, 'perennially fresh in the jaded memories of a hundred editors. . . .'

'Hugh? . . . Frank Giles. . . . Very well, thank you. . . .'

There had been a murmur of conversation in the room, but this gradually died away as more of the *Sunday Times* men began listening to one side of the telephone conversation.

'. . . I think we'd like just a quiet, scholarly, detailed piece, rebutting. . . .'

There was a pause. 'Frank didn't go white exactly,' recalled Knightley, 'but his tone suddenly changed.'

'Well, naturally, Hugh, one has doubts. There are no certainties in this life. But these doubts aren't strong enough to make you do a complete 180-degree turn on that? . . . Oh. I see. You *are* doing a 180-degree turn. . . .'

The editorial conference froze into a tableau of despair: MacArthur, who had slumped against the wall, now slid gently to the floor; Linklater sat with his head between his knees; Knightley silently pounded the table; nobody spoke.

After Giles had hung up there was, according to one partici-pant, 'a tense fifteen-minute conversation'. Should the presses be stopped? That would require Murdoch's agreement. He was in New York. Someone went off to try to reach him. It was decided that Giles should ring Trevor-Roper back and insist that if he had doubts, he should not air them in public at *Stern*'s press conference but should reveal them exclusively in the following week's *Sunday Times*. Everyone left to enable the editor to make the call in peace; as they did so, his ebullient wife, Lady Katherine Giles, burst through the door carrying her husband's supper in a hamper. She stayed with him while he made the call and emerged a few minutes later to reassure everyone: 'Frank was *marvellous*.' Meanwhile, Brian Mac-Arthur was speaking to Rupert Murdoch who had been tracked down in the United States. MacArthur outlined the problem caused by Lord Dacre's change of heart. Should they stop the print run and remake the paper?

'Fuck Dacre,' replied Murdoch. 'Publish.'

Sunday, 24 April.

As 1.4 million copies of the *Sunday Times* were distributed across Great Britain, the assault on the diaries' authenticity intensified. Lord Bullock, author of *Hitler: A Study in Tyr-anny*, made the same point as a number of critics of the scoop: how could Hitler have written about the attempt on his life in July 1944, when his right arm was known to have been damaged in the blast? Bullock called for an international commission of French, British, American and Jewish historians to be appointed to examine the diaries. The *Sunday Times*'s rivals, using the information bought from Irving, were having a field day. 'Serious doubts cast on Hitler's "secret diaries",' claimed the *Observer*. 'THE DAMNING FLAWS IN THE HITLER DIARY,' alleged the *Mail on Sunday*. 'All too splendid, too neat, too pat to be anything but a gigantic hoax.' In Germany, a succession of Hitler's former aides, few of them under seventy, was wheeled out for comment. 'We often used to eat at about three or four o'clock in the morning,' said Nicolaus von Below, the Führer's air force adjutant, 'and only after that did Hitler go to bed. He had no time to write anything. It's all a complete lie.' Richard Schulz-Kossens echoed von Below: Hitler 'never had time' to keep a diary. 'The Führer never made notes by hand,' insisted Christa Schroeder.

At 8.30 a.m., David Irving was picked up by a *Mail on Sunday* car and driven to the airport to catch the 10.35 a.m. flight to Hamburg. He was met at the other end by Jochen Kummer, a senior reporter on the mass-circulation *Bild Zeitung*. Irving was to be their 'torpedo' at the *Stern* press conference the following day. 'We agreed a fee of £1000 plus expenses,' noted Irving in his diary.

A couple of hours later, Trevor-Roper also arrived at Heathrow, accompanied by two minders from the *Sunday Times*, Paul Eddy and Brian MacArthur. At the airport he found himself 'pursued by massed cameras'. 'The whole story had been blown up into a sensation,' recalled Trevor-Roper. Microphones were thrust at his face. 'I do believe the diaries are genuine,' he said, 'but there are complications. I will not put a percentage figure on my belief. I admit there are problems. . . .'

In Hamburg the three men met Anthony Terry, and Trevor-Roper once again checked into the Atlantic Hotel to await the arrival of Gerd Heidemann.

It was late afternoon by the time Heidemann arrived. He apologized for having kept Trevor-Roper waiting. He had just flown in from Munich, he said, where he had been talking to Frau Ilse Hess. Trevor-Roper told him there were certain points he wanted clarified before he was prepared to endorse the diaries at the press conference. Would Heidemann tell him, once again, how the diaries came into *Stern*'s possession?

This posed a problem for Heidemann. Since he had last spoken with Trevor-Roper, *Stern* had received the results of the Rentz forensic investigation. Heidemann was now aware that although the diaries might still be genuine, the accompanying archive was probably forged. Kujau had assured him that the two sets of material came from different sources. But how could Heidemann square that with his original assertion that there was one plane crash, one salvaged cargo, and one supplier? His solution was to add a new twist to his story. Heidemann now told Trevor-Roper that the diaries had been brought out of the East by a former Wehrmacht officer currently living in West Germany. The reporter said he had collected the first diaries from Switzerland. *Other material had been delivered to him in Hamburg by the Boernersdorf peasants.*

Trevor-Roper was immediately suspicious. This was the third version of the story he had heard, he said. Originally, in Zurich, he had been told by Peter Koch that the diaries' supplier lived in East Germany: that was why his name could not be disclosed. Then, in Hamburg last week, Heidemann had told him that the so-called 'Wehrmacht officer' lived in Switzerland and could not be identified for tax reasons. Now he was supposed to live in West Germany and only to have supplied the diaries, not the additional material. Which version was correct?

Heidemann blustered. He was not responsible for anything Koch said. Koch knew nothing. Koch knew only as much as he, Heidemann, chose to tell him.

The historian was insistent. He would not authenticate the diaries unless Heidemann gave him the full story of their discovery. They should start again from the beginning. How had the diaries come into *Stern*'s possession?

'In interrogation,' Trevor-Roper once observed, 'pressure must be uninterrupted.' That afternoon in the Atlantic Hotel he drew on the skills he had learned in the prisoner of war cages of Germany in the autumn of 1945. Remorselessly, he battered away at Heidemann's story in a way that no one had done since the diaries had first begun to emerge in Hamburg. Heidemann pulled out document after document from his briefcase. 'I'll produce anything if you just won't put me through the mincing machine.'

Trevor-Roper read through the Hess special volume. It was ludicrously superficial. He had no doubts now. It was a forgery.

'Can you give me', he demanded, 'any reason why I should believe in this Wehrmacht officer?'

'No,' said Heidemann. 'Why should I?'

'Well, then, why should I believe?' retorted Trevor-Roper.

There was real anger in the exchanges; old resentments flared. 'You are behaving exactly like an officer of the British secret service,' shouted Heidemann. 'We are no longer in 1945.' After putting up a stubborn resistance for more than an hour, the reporter declared that he had had enough and stalked out of the room, refusing to attend a dinner that *Stern* was supposed to be giving in Trevor-Roper's honour that evening.

Trevor-Roper, too, considered boycotting the meal. In the end he agreed to attend only in the hope of extracting the name of the diaries' supplier from Peter Koch. But to the historian's astonishment, Koch, when confronted with his earlier assertion that *Stern* knew the identity of the 'Wehrmacht officer', calmly denied ever having made such a claim. Trevor-Roper threatened to stay away from the following morning's press conference. The *Stern* men were unmoved. The dinner ended, according to the subsequent *Stern Report*, with 'an icy atmosphere around the table'.

After the meal, Trevor-Roper discussed his dilemma with Paul Eddy, Brian MacArthur and Anthony Terry. They urged him not to recant in public at the press conference. He should at least wait until he had returned to Britain. The three *Sunday Times* men were persuasive, and by the time they left him at midnight, the historian was half convinced. He was crossing the lobby of the hotel on his way up to bed when he unexpectedly ran into an old friend – Sir Nicholas Henderson, Britain's former ambassador in Washington and Bonn. The two men retreated to the bar and drank beer until 2 a.m. Henderson's advice was unequivocal. Trevor-Roper should state his reservations as quickly and publicly as possible. He would not have a better opportunity than the *Stern* press conference in a few hours' time. Trevor-Roper decided 'to sleep on the matter'.

Monday, 25 April.
'The big day,' wrote Irving in his diary.

The special issue of *Stern* was already piled up on the news-stands to greet the early morning commuters. More than two and a quarter million copies had been printed over the weekend. 'Hitler's Diary Discovered,' proclaimed the cover, displaying a stack of black-bound volumes, topped by one bearing the Gothic initials 'FH' (the 'F' still assumed by *Stern* to be an 'A'). Coverage of the diaries sprawled across more than forty pages, with extracts blown up to three or four times their original size. There was Hitler on Ernst Roehm:

> I gave him the chance to draw the consequences, but he was too cowardly to do so. On my orders he was later shot.

Hitler on the *Kristallnacht*, the 'Night of Broken Glass' in 1938, when Jewish shops and synagogues were smashed and thousands of Jews sent to concentration camps:

> Report brought to me of some ugly attacks by people in uniform in various places, also of Jews beaten to death and Jewish suicides. What will they say abroad? The necessary orders will be given immediately.

Hitler on the Russian attack on Berlin in April 1945:

> The long-awaited offensive has begun. May the Lord God stand by us.

There were pictures of Hitler in the Reichschancellery in 1945, Hitler with Mussolini, Hitler writing at his desk, Hitler holding a bunch of flowers, Hitler with Hess; the only other person shown as often was Gerd Heidemann: Heidemann on *Carin II*, Heidemann with the diaries, Heidemann in Boernersdorf, Heidemann with Wolff, Heidemann with Guensche and Mohnke – the entire issue was a monument to one man's obsession, a tasteless and hysterical trampling over thirty-eight years of post-war German sensitivity about the Nazis. *Stern* was already under attack for its handling of the diaries; this tactless treatment was to earn the magazine the odium of almost the entire West German press.

In the Four Seasons Hotel, Irving was up early. He prepared for the morning's combat with a haircut in the hotel barber's followed by a heavy German breakfast. The restaurant, he found, was 'packed with journalists and television teams, poring over this morning's *Stern*'.

Trevor-Roper woke at 8 a.m. to a telephone call from Charles Douglas-Home. How was he feeling? Trevor-Roper said that he had talked to Heidemann, that his doubts had not been assuaged, that they had, in fact, increased. Douglas-Home urged him not to 'burn his boats' at the press conference.

By 10.30 a.m., the *Stern* canteen was packed with journalists. More than two hundred had converged on Hamburg from all over the world. There were twenty-seven television crews. All the seats were taken and reporters and photographers squeezed into every corner, squatting, and in some cases lying full-length, beneath the platform at the far end of the room. Incongruous yet unnoticed, in the centre of it all, sat General Wilhelm Mohnke, attending by special invitation of Gerd Heidemann. Each of the journalists was issued with a press kit: twenty pages of information about the diaries and a set of seven photographs. Also included were copies of the Rentz forensic reports on the two diary pages; the Rentz finding on the Mussolini telegram was omitted, giving the impression that his tests had been a hundred per cent in favour of the authenticity of the *Stern* material.

At 11 a.m., the stars of the conference filed in to a battery of flashes from the photographers: Peter Koch, Felix Schmidt, Thomas Walde, Gerd Heidemann and Hugh Trevor-Roper. The professor was startled by the size of the audience, the hot and noisy atmosphere, the brilliance of the television lights. It looked, wrote one journalist afterwards, like 'a Sadler's Wells set for hell'.

Peter Koch's introduction was aggressive. He denounced the attacks on the diaries' authenticity. Eberhard Jaeckel was making assertions about material he had not even seen. 'If we as journalists behaved in such a manner,' said Koch, 'we would be accused of superficiality.' David Irving – sitting half-way down the room – he dismissed as an historian 'with no reputation to lose'. 'I am a hundred per cent convinced that Hitler wrote every single word in those books,' insisted Koch. 'We paid a lot of money for the diaries, but when it comes to informing the reader, nothing is too expensive.'

The press was then shown the *Stern* documentary film, *The Find*. Trevor-Roper watched his own endorsement of the diaries, recorded the previous week, with his head in his hand. When the programme finished, a young woman pushed her way through the cameras to the tables at the end of the canteen and tipped out the contents of two parcels: a dozen volumes of the Hitler diaries. It was a *coup de théâtre* – 'as if,' said Brian James of the *Daily Mail*, 'Hitler had suddenly thrust an arm out of the grave'. The photographers scrambled for close-ups. The *Stern* men tried to shield the contents to prevent any premature disclosure. Koch thrust a handful of diaries at Gerd Heidemann, who was persuaded to stand up, with great reluctance, and pose with them for the cameras. Koch invited questions. Almost all of them were directed at Trevor-Roper.

In his own mind, the historian had already concluded that the diaries could well be false. 'Having once admitted it to myself,' he said later, 'I felt I must attend the press conference and admit it to others.' With head tilted back, eyes focused on some indeterminate point in the middle distance, he began to recant. 'The question of the authenticity of the diaries is inseparable from the history of the diaries. The question is: are these documents linked necessarily to that aeroplane? When I saw the documents in Zurich, I understood – or, er, mis-understood – that the link was absolutely established. . . .' The diaries 'might' be genuine, he said, but 'the thing looks more shaky' – there was, after all, 'such a thing as a perfect forgery'. He ended with a swipe at *Stern* and Times Newspapers:

> As a historian, I regret that the, er, normal method of historical verification, er, has, perhaps necessarily, been to some extent sacrificed to the requirements of a journalistic scoop.

One of Trevor-Roper's Oxford pupils, Timothy Garton Ash, covering the press conference for the *New Republic*, described the performance as 'rather like watching a Victorian gentleman trying to backpedal on a penny farthing'.

Someone asked the historian about the damage the affair

had done to his reputation. Trevor-Roper took a meditative sip from a glass of water. 'I suppose my personal reputation is linked to anything I say. I am prepared to express my opinion, and if I am wrong I am wrong, and if I am right I am right. I don't worry about these things.'

Until Trevor-Roper's contribution, the press conference had been going well for the *Stern* men. Now they sat, stony-faced, with arms folded, as the proceedings began to disintegrate around them. David Irving leapt to the microphone in the centre of the hall, incensed at Koch's description of him as a man without any reputation. 'I decided to play hardball,' he wrote in his diary afterwards. 'I am the British historian David Irving,' he declared. 'I may not have a doctorate, or a professorship, or even the title "Lord", but I believe I have a reputation in Germany nevertheless.' He demanded to know how Hitler could have written of the July bomb plot in his diary, when *Stern*'s own film had just shown the dictator meeting Mussolini a few hours after the explosion, and having to shake hands with him with his left hand. He brandished his photocopies. 'I know the collection from which these diaries come. It is an old collection, full of forgeries. I have some here.' The television cameras swung away from the *Stern* dignatories and on to the gesticulating figure in the middle of the room. 'Reporters stormed towards me,' recalled Irving, 'lights blazing, and microphones were thrust at me.' A Japanese film crew was trampled in the rush and a fist fight broke out. Chairs and lights were scattered as chaos rippled across the crowded floor. From the platform, Koch shouted that Irving should ask questions, not make speeches. Irving's microphone was switched off. But it was too late. Irving challenged *Stern* to say whether the diaries' ink had been tested for its age. There was no answer. 'Ink! ink!' shouted some of the reporters. 'Torpedo running,' whispered Irving to one of the journalists sitting next to him as he sat down. The local NBC correspondent approached and asked if he would leave immediately to take part in a live link-up with the *Today* show, now on the air in America. Irving agreed. 'All most exhilarating,' he noted, 'and I left a trail of chaos behind me.'

As Irving was going out of the *Stern* building, Gerhard Weinberg was coming in. The American academic had been unpacking in Bonn on Saturday, finishing off his interview with Steven Strasser of *Newsweek*, when Peter Koch telephoned him. Koch had pleaded with him to attend the press conference. Weinberg had told him that it was impossible – he had his first class in Bonn at 10 a.m. on Monday; he wouldn't cancel it. ('It took him some time to realize I wasn't being difficult,' said Weinberg. 'I was just being me.') But Koch was persistent: he would fix the travel arrangements to ensure that the professor did not miss his class. Accordingly, the instant his lecture finished, at 11 a.m. on Monday, a *Stern* driver rushed Weinberg from the university campus to the airport. From Bonn he was flown in the company's private plane to Hamburg, then driven straight to the *Stern* office. At 12.30 p.m. he took his place on the platform.

Weinberg repaid *Stern* for its trouble and expense by raising fresh doubts about its scoop. 'All the handwriting authentication I have seen', he told the world's press, 'pertains to documents other than the diaries, except one page said to have been cut out of one diary. In other words, the memorandums from the American handwriting expert and the German police handwriting expert refer to Hitler's handwriting, but not to Hitler's handwriting in the diaries. In fact, they probably didn't know the diaries existed when shown this evidence.' It was 'inappropriate' to cite the analysis of one set of documents and apply it to another.

Koch stared at Weinberg in horror, but the professor had not finished yet. In his careful, pedantic manner, he continued: 'One question has troubled me from the outset – that no knowledgeable expert on the Third Reich has been allowed to study the whole text to see if there are any textual absurdities. I mean, we're not living on a South Sea island here, they wouldn't have had to have gone outside the Hamburg city limits to find experts who would know. It is vital now that a group of experts from all over the world should be given the chance to test these manuscripts.' Koch cut in to say that, of course, experts would be given the opportunity to study the diaries. There were shouts of 'When?' and 'Set a date.' 'When the journalistic evaluation has been completed,' replied Koch.

The news conference, which had begun so well for *Stern*, broke up after more than two hours in complete disarray. It was not merely a public relations disaster; the failure to produce convincing evidence for the diaries' authenticity also had legal implications. One of *Stern*'s lawyers, Herr Hagen, had warned Schulte-Hillen on Friday in a confidential memorandum that the magazine's coverage was such that the company risked prosecution for disseminating Nazi propaganda. *Stern*'s defence, obviously, would be that it was furthering historical research. But that argument could collapse if historians regarded the diaries as being of dubious value. The State of Bavaria could use the uncertainty as a pretext to withdraw the publishing rights it had conceded through the agreement with the Bundesarchiv. Watching as the press conference disintegrated, Hagen decided that 'only a quick and definitive judgement on the diaries' authenticity could save the situation'. With the consent of the *Stern* management, he arranged for three of the diaries – the Hess special volume and books from 1934 and 1943 – to be handed over immediately to Dr Henke of the Bundesarchiv, who had attended the conference. Henke promised to deliver a judgement to Hagen swiftly and privately. The lawyer was relieved. The prospect of a court battle to try to establish that *Stern* was not sympathetic to the

Nazis, with Gerd Heidemann possibly called as a witness, did not bear contemplating.

Trevor-Roper felt a sense of relief as he left the *Stern* building. His action might have come as 'a painful surprise' to his hosts, but he had done as his conscience dictated. After a light lunch with the three *Sunday Times* journalists, he caught an after-noon flight back to London.

Trevor-Roper hoped he might now begin putting the whole affair behind him. He was over-optimistic. One of the first things he saw on his arrival at Heathrow was a placard advertising the London *Standard*. Its front-page banner head-line was 'Hitler Diaries: Dacre Doubts'. 'My heart sank,' he recalled.

At home in Cambridge the telephone had scarcely stopped ringing since his departure for Germany on Sunday. He found his wife deeply upset. Reporters were camped on his doorstep. His first act was to instruct the Porter's Lodge not to put through any more calls. It was impossible to stroll across the road to Peterhouse without running the gauntlet of journalists in the street outside. Instead, he had to leave through his garden, shin a back wall, cut through a car park and sneak into the college a few yards further up the street. He had to keep up this performance for the rest of the week.

Pictures of the *Stern* press conference were carried on all the evening news bulletins and dominated the following morning's papers. The stories all focused on Trevor-Roper: 'I'm Not Sure Now Confesses Hitler Diary Professor', 'Hitler: The Great Retreat', 'Boffins' Battle on Nazi "Diaries"', 'Fists Fly in Hitler Uproar', 'I'm Not Quite so Sure, Says Dacre'. The *Guardian* wanted to know why he had decided to 'risk his reputation by pronouncing the diaries genuine after only the most cursory examination?' His former colleague at Oxford, A. L. Rowse, wrote an article headed 'The trial of Lord Dacre' describing him, at the age of nearly seventy, as 'a young man in a hurry'. 'I have always had reservations about him,' said Rowse, 'since he started writing at Oxford as my protégé.' A limerick did the rounds of Cambridge senior common rooms:

> There once was a fellow named Dacre,
> Who was God in his own little acre,
> But in the matter of diaries,
> he was quite *ultra vires*,
> And unable to spot an old faker.

The final insult came in a solicitor's letter sent on behalf of Rachel, Lady Dacre. She was a distant cousin who had arranged for the ancient Barony of Dacre to be called out of abeyance in her favour in 1970; she had strongly objected to Trevor-Roper's decision to use the same name when he was awarded a life peerage in 1979. Now she had her lawyers warn him always to use his full title – Lord Dacre of Glanton – so as not to embarrass her side of the family in the light of his action over the Hitler diaries.

'Life', said Trevor-Roper, subsequently reflecting on the period, 'was torture.'

TWENTY-SEVEN

But what was torture to one historian was food and drink to another. After his triumph at the press conference, David Irving spent the rest of Monday writing articles and giving interviews. 'Adolf Hitler is still big box office, from Hamburg to Harlem,' he wrote in the *Daily Mail*. He described Heidemann as 'a typical nice guy. He does not believe that villains exist in this world; he is the kind of man who believes the claims of tyre advertisements.' For the readers of *Bild Zeitung* he outlined seven reasons why the diaries had to be forgeries. He was inexhaustible. At 3.30 a.m. on Tuesday morning, he was roused in his hotel room in Hamburg and rushed to a local television studio for a live link-up with the ABC programme *Nightline*. 'Twenty million viewers again,' recorded Irving gleefully in his diary. 'Paid 700 marks in cash as requested.' From the studio he was taken back to his hotel. He grabbed another two hours' sleep and after breakfast heard from *Der Spiegel* that they were willing to pay him 20,000 marks for his photocopies and his story. '*Very* satisfactory,' he noted. 'That brings the total up to about £15,000 in three days.' In the afternoon, he flew to Frankfurt to take part in a West German television debate on the diaries' authenticity.

Meanwhile, in the United States, the full extent of *Newsweek*'s alleged perfidy was at last apparent. Monday had seen the airing of the magazine's television commercials, none of which made any mention of doubts about whether the diaries might be genuine. Casual readers of the accompanying newspaper advertisements would also have had the impression that *Newsweek* had bought the diaries and that there was no question surrounding their authenticity:

> These controversial papers could rewrite the history of the Third Reich from Hitler's rise to power to his suicide in the ruins of Berlin.
>
> They shed new light on his character, his plans for war, Munich, the miracle of Dunkirk, the flight of Rudolf Hess, his military campaigns, his relations to his lover, Eva Braun.

The patient reader had to wade through to the fifth paragraph before coming to the throwaway question 'Are they real?' Maynard Parker, responsible for putting together the *Newsweek* treatment, was subsequently unrepentant about this aggressive salesmanship: 'The advertising department had earlier deadlines than ours, but I do not feel that the ads misrepresent what is in the magazine.'

This was true. Although *Newsweek* gave some space to the views of the sceptics, the overwhelming impression left by its extensive coverage was that the diaries were genuine. The magazine actually ran more extracts than *Stern* – seventeen individual quotations, culled during the course of the syndication negotiations. Here was an 'awestruck' Hitler on Josef Stalin ('How on earth does Stalin manage it?'); Hitler on Mussolini ('He does not have the courtesy to face me'); on the Wehrmacht High Command ('These old officers let themselves be hung with titles, decorations and property, but they don't obey my orders'); and a 'tender and sentimental' Hitler on Eva Braun ('Eva had to endure much suffering'). The Germans were predictably outraged. 'That was a nice dirty trick,' Peter Koch complained in an interview with *Time*. 'We would like to sue. We were cheated and I guarantee *Newsweek* will regret what they did.' There was a separate article on the forensic and handwriting examinations commissioned by *Stern*, there was 'A Scholar's Appraisal' by Gerhard Weinberg and a piece on 'Hitler and the Holocaust'. The magazine concluded with a prediction that the discovery of the diaries would force the world 'to deal, once again, with the fact of Hitler himself'.

> Germans will have to wonder anew about their collective, inherited guilt. Jews will have to face their fears again. All of us will have to ask once more whether Hitler's evil was unique, or whether it lurks somewhere in everyone. Those speculations have been trivialized for years in gaudy paperback thrillers and made-for-television movies. Now the appearance of Hitler's diaries – genuine or not, it almost doesn't matter in the end – reminds us of the horrible reality on which our doubts about ourselves, and each other, are based.

Newsweek's behaviour over the Hitler diaries was widely criticized in the United States. An editorial in the *New York Times* entitled 'Heil History' poured particular scorn on the magazine's assertion that the question of whether or not the diaries were genuine 'almost doesn't matter':

> Almost doesn't matter? Almost doesn't matter what really drove the century's most diabolic tyranny? Almost doesn't matter whether Hitler is reincarnated, perhaps redefined, by fact or forgery?
>
> Journalism should take no solace from the customary excuse that it must deal with history in a hurry. And scholars in such a hurry, their second thoughts notwithstanding, can hardly be called historians.

Newsweek gave enormous play to the diaries, but the magazine was not alone in seeing it as the most important story of the moment: the *New York Times* itself ran it on its front page on Saturday, Sunday, Monday and Tuesday; the mass-circulation tabloids gave it even greater space. By the fifth day the Hitler diaries affair had turned into a kind of giant soap opera – an international entertainment playing on almost every radio and television network and newspaper front page in the world. And what a story it was – Hitler's bunker, old Nazis, a wartime plane crash, a trail across the Iron Curtain, millions of dollars, Swiss bank vaults, secret documents, a punch-up in front of the cameras, dramatic changes of heart, the Rewriting of History, Lord Dacre, David Irving, Rupert Murdoch, Gerd Heidemann. . . .

It seemed that every academic who had ever written about Hitler was at some stage called upon to comment. Professor Donald Watt, the editor of the most recent English language edition of *Mein Kampf*, thought the diaries 'odd'. John Kenneth Galbraith called them 'impossible'. William L. Shirer said they were 'outlandish . . . a hoax'. I don't think serious historians will touch these things for a long time,' said J. P. Stern, the author of *The Führer and the People*. Professor Gordon A. Craig called it 'one of the most sensational finds of the century'. 'The question is of little importance,' was A. J. P. Taylor's characteristic comment. 'Who cares about Hitler nowadays?'

There was a section of opinion which held that the material, even if genuine, should not be published. What had caught the popular imagination was the fact that these were Hitler's *diaries*. A diary was something intimate and human. How could a figure who had caused so much suffering be allowed to speak in ordinary language, to justify what he did? It directly touched the point George Steiner had made: 'You will think him a man and no longer believe what he did.' The Chief Rabbi of Great Britain, Immanuel Jakobovits, put this argument in a letter to *The Times* which was extensively quoted around the world, especially in West Germany:

As a human being – victim and survivor of history's most monstrous tyranny – I protest vehemently against the publication of the so-called Hitler diaries. Whether they are authentic or not is quite immaterial to the outrage of resurrecting the incarnation of evil and his propaganda, rehabilitating him for a generation which knew not this master gangster.... Hailing this find as 'the biggest literary discovery since the Dead Sea Scrolls' is a sacrilege which only compounds the insult to the millions who perished and suffered under this tyranny.

Nineteen eighty-three marked the fiftieth anniversary of the Nazis' rise to power. But although more than a generation had passed since the end of the war, the reaction aroused by the diaries showed how potent a symbol Hitler remained. It was not simply fresh proof of the accuracy of the old cliché about the fascination of evil; the comments also revealed how little attitudes towards Hitler had changed. In the communist world, the Hitler portrayed in the diaries was denounced as an agent of capitalism. Similarly, some conservatives in the West, in their comments on *Stern*'s Hitler, were blinded to any other consideration by their overwhelming mistrust of the Soviet Union. Both responses were a curious echo of those of the 1930s.

On the day of the *Stern* press conference, Professor Karl-Dietrich Bracher of Bonn University dismissed the diaries as forgeries and speculated as to who might be responsible. He noted that this was a Hitler who was supposed to have expressed admiration for the shrewdness of the arch-appeaser, Neville Chamberlain; who had allowed the British Army to escape at Dunkirk; who had sanctioned Hess's peace mission in 1941. Perversely, it was Hitler's enemies in the West, Churchill and Roosevelt, who were portrayed as the warmongers. Bracher suggested that the diaries were 'an

attempt to manipulate German history at a politically sensitive moment'. Perhaps the diaries were the work of a foreign
power? The 1980s, after all, were 'a time of intense debate
about the deployment of new NATO missiles in West Germany' – at such a moment 'there was a growing audience for
history unfavourable to the United States and Britain'. Werner Maser alleged the diaries were the work of an official
'forgery factory' in Potsdam in East Germany 'where Hitler
letters and Hitler notes are produced to earn hard currency
for the East Germans'. This theme was developed in Britain in
a radio interview by George Young, a former deputy director
of MI6 and a noted cold warrior. Without any evidence –
without even having seen the diaries – he alleged the affair
might be part of 'an East German official disinformation
effort':

> The east German security and intelligence service has a
> document-faking or disinformation section. No doubt they
> would be capable of doing this. . . . It would suit the Russians'
> book to sow mistrust in any shape or form, particularly among
> the West Germans. NATO croaks and groans quite a bit these
> days and anything that sows doubts about the past may create
> mistrust about the present.

At a press luncheon in New York on Tuesday, the American
Ambassador to the United Nations, Mrs Jeane Kirkpatrick,
also detected in the diaries the hand of an Eastern intelligence
agency. 'I have no doubt', she claimed, 'that there are those in
central Europe today who would, and indeed do, attempt to
sow distrust between the United States and its German
friends.'

The communists nurtured suspicions of their own. The
Soviet Union lost 20 million dead in Hitler's war; the memory
was still a decisive influence on Russia's foreign policy.
Moscow had not officially confirmed Hitler's death until

1968 and remained acutely sensitive to what it saw as any attempt to rehabilitate the Nazis. On Monday, Professor Sergei Tikhvinski, a leading Russian historian and a member of the Soviet Academy of Science, denounced the Hitler diaries as 'a most obvious act of political sabotage'. At 6.30 on Wednesday evening, Soviet television described the diaries' publication as 'an attempt to whitewash the chief fascist criminal'. Ninety minutes later, Radio Moscow International broadcast a similar opinion to its listeners in France, where *Paris Match* had just begun its serialization:

> The phantom of the human Führer ... is an attempt to make allowances in advance in the eyes of public opinion for those in the USA and in NATO headquarters who are working out new versions of limited warfare, or other wars for Europe, using the pretext of the old myth of the threat from the East – the one that allowed Hitler to unleash the Second World War.

'These "diaries"', claimed the official news agency Tass, 'are intended to propagandize Nazism among the young generation, to distract them from the fight for peace and put them on the path of right-wing nationalist forces in the Federal Republic.'

In Berlin, the East German Foreign Ministry issued an official statement: 'The German Democratic Republic regards the publication of the Hitler diaries in *Stern* as a belated attempt to rehabilitate Hitler.' Western journalists who applied for permission to visit the site of the crashed plane in Boernersdorf found that visas were granted with unusual speed. The East Germans were eager to allow foreigners to speak to the local farmers who, virtually without exception, derided the idea that documents could have been salvaged from the burning wreck. Suddenly, after centuries of calm, the peaceful village was invaded by the western media. Ignorant of the furore about the diaries, a rumour went round

Boernersdorf that the reason for the influx of cameramen and reporters was that two of the graves in the churchyard, marked 'Unknown man' and 'Unknown woman', contained the remains of Hitler and Eva Braun.

On the night of Tuesday, 26 April the leading western protagonists in the controversy were brought together on West German television. ZDF, one of the country's two national networks, cleared its evening schedules to mount a debate on the diaries' authenticity. Peter Koch and Gerd Heidemann flew down from Hamburg to the television studios in Wiesbaden. At Frankfurt Airport they ran into another participant on his way to ZDF, David Irving. The three men shook hands – 'Koch unwillingly,' wrote Irving in his diary.

The programme began with the screening of *The Find*, which ZDF had bought off *Stern* for 175,000 marks. The film was followed by an interminable and crowded discussion of the sort beloved by West German television. Four historians – Walther Hofer, Andreas Hillgruber, Eberhard Jaeckel and David Irving – faced Peter Koch in Wiesbaden. Gerhard Weinberg took part down the line from Bonn. Trevor-Roper was persuaded to sit in a studio in London – an isolated figure who spoke throughout in English (evidence of his unease with the German language which did not go unnoticed in the West German newspapers the following day). Gerd Heidemann was prevented from taking part by Peter Koch: his belief that the diaries had been authenticated by Martin Bormann would not have enhanced *Stern*'s credibility.

Trevor-Roper went further than he had done at the press conference. The burden of proof once again rested with *Stern*, he said. 'I also believe that some of the other documents which I have seen in Mr Heidemann's house and which come from the same source are forgeries.'

Koch, undeterred, put up a spirited defence of the diaries.

There was no question but that they were genuine, he insisted. They had been tested by handwriting and forensic experts and most of *Stern*'s critics were motivated by commercial jealousy. Even Irving, a master at hijacking the medium for his own purposes, was impressed by his 'manful' performance. 'At the end he put his Hitler diary on the table and challenged me: "Now, Herr Irving, put your 'diary page' next to it and let's see which is genuine." Fortunately, the cameras were off or it would have been difficult: the pages were clearly different. . . .'

The debate was a victory for *Stern*. Afterwards, at about midnight, as Koch and Heidemann were driving back to the airport, they passed Irving and Jaeckel walking down the hill from the studio to their hotel. They pulled alongside and asked the two historians if they wanted a drink. Irving and Jaeckel agreed.

In this private conversation Koch gave vent to his bitterness about *Newsweek*. It was only because of the Americans, he complained, that *Stern* had been forced to rush into print so precipitately. But for *Newsweek*, they would have had more time to check the documents and could have prevented the damaging publicity which now surrounded the diaries. Irving said *Stern* had been foolish to trust *The Times* and *Newsweek* while refusing to take a West German historian into its confidence. 'I suggested he should show [the diaries] to a *sceptical* historian like Jaeckel. Jaeckel nodded, puffed his pipe sagely, and was staggered when Koch then turned to him and asked if he would, in principle, agree to assess all sixty diaries, after signing an undertaking incorporating a savage financial penalty if he revealed the contents.' The idea was discussed for a while, but by the time the drinking session broke up at 2 a.m., it was obvious there was no room for agreement: Jaeckel was 'too fixed in his hostility' to the diaries.

*　　　*　　　*

When Peter Koch walked into the *Stern* editorial meeting in Hamburg a few hours later, he was greeted by a round of applause from his colleagues for his 'valiant defence' of the diaries on television the previous night. Emboldened by this success, *Stern* now planned a counter-attack on its critics. They would take the fight into the heart of the enemy camp with a lightning campaign on American television. Koch would fly over to New York the next day with one of the diaries and offer himself for interview on every available US television and radio network.

That same afternoon, *Stern* recruited a valuable new ally to its cause. Wolf Hess emerged from a two-hour meeting with Koch and the other editors to announce to reporters that he had no doubts that the magazine's scoop was genuine. 'I will ask the Allied authorities to allow my father to comment on the diaries.'

Rudolf Hess had celebrated his eighty-ninth birthday in Spandau prison on Tuesday. The family had been trying to secure his release for years. The appearance of the diaries now offered them a fresh chance to focus attention on his plight. Wolf Hess agreed to accompany Koch, at *Stern*'s expense, on his American tour. He also sent a telegram to the American, British, French and Soviet Ambassadors appealing to them to let his father examine and authenticate the diaries 'as the sole living and direct eyewitness'.

David Irving arrived back in London on Wednesday afternoon and rushed straight round to see his bank manager, arriving late and perspiring for his appointment. To his surprise, he found him 'very friendly': he had followed his client's progress over the past few days with great interest. That did not, however, lessen his distress at the fact that Irving's overdraft stood at £26,700, unchanged since January; it must come down. Irving, as he noted in his diary, was at last able to give him some good news. 'I said I have earned about £15,000 since Friday in various ways (TV, newspaper articles and contracts, etc.) and this money is due *now*; I guarantee to let him have £6000 in two weeks. He is very happy. God knows what I would have had to offer at the interview without the happy events since Friday.'

Despite the scepticism being heaped upon the diaries by experts from West Germany and abroad, Gerd Heidemann betrayed no trace of anxiety. He was undoubtedly aware by now that there were some problems with his material: both the police and Arnold Rentz had found that part of the archive he had obtained from Kujau was false; he also knew that the faked diary pages which Irving was hawking around Europe came from the original Fritz Stiefel diary, a volume which had finally come into his possession at the end of March. But self-deception was one of the strongest traits of Heidemann's character. He had no difficulty in accepting Kujau's excuses – that the dubious telegrams came from a different source, that paper whitener was in existence before the Nazis came to power, that the Stiefel diary was a 'party yearbook' and not part of the main diary archive. Nor was his delusion that the diaries were genuine entirely without foundation. He could point to the three handwriting analyses which had found that the page cut from the Hess special volume was in Hitler's hand. He could also call in support the two forensic tests, neither of which had established that the diary's paper was of the wrong date. He exuded confidence. When the Austrian magazine *Profil* asked him whether he was alarmed by David Irving's claim that he had a sample of the diaries, Heidemann's answer was that Irving was bluffing – he 'has no original and has never seen an original'. Was he, at least, concerned by Trevor-Roper's change of heart? 'Of course not,' he replied. 'I know where the diaries come from. . . . My informant is neither an old Nazi nor a wanted war criminal, but he won't go public because he doesn't want huge press attention and I won't name him because I promised not to.'

Heidemann's unshakeable conviction that the diaries were authentic soothed the worries of his colleagues. Throughout the week which followed the press conference, *Stern* presented a united front to the world. Brian MacArthur, the head of the *Sunday Times* team staying at the Four Seasons Hotel, shared the doubts of his British colleagues. 'But when you see their absolute confidence,' he said to Gitta Sereny after one meeting with the *Stern* men, 'their total calm in the face of this almost universal disbelief, then all one can think is that they know something they are not telling; that they have something up their sleeves, some sort of absolutely reliable confirmation of authenticity.'

On Thursday, 28 April Heidemann announced that the missing diaries had at last arrived in a consignment of pianos delivered to Saarbruecken. He visited Peter Kuehsel in his office and arranged to pick up the final instalment of 300,000 marks at 9.30 a.m. the next morning.

On Friday, he met Konrad Kujau in Hamburg and took delivery of the last four volumes.

Kujau had been watching events unfold from Stuttgart with some interest. On Friday, when the evening news had announced the diaries' discovery, he had telephoned Maria Modritsch and told her to switch on her television. He had viewed the coverage of Monday's press conference and found it 'unbelievable'. Could he get away with it? He was confident enough to believe that he could: he had, after all, been forging Nazi documents for the best part of a decade and had so far managed to avoid detection. Surely *Stern* would not be publishing the material unless it had already succeeded in fooling enough experts to put him in the clear? When Ulli Blaschke, his friend in the police force, saw him in the Beer Bar in Stuttgart at the height of the controversy, he brought up the subject of the diaries and asked Conny whether he thought they were genuine. Kujau solemnly assured him that in his opinion they were.

The forger has provided a colourful account of his final transaction with Heidemann that Friday. According to him, they met in the archive in Milchstrasse. Outside, the public debate about the diaries was still raging; inside, the telephone scarcely stopped ringing. Heidemann received the diaries and handed him in return 12,000 marks and an IOU for a further 100,000. He then told Kujau that he had a plan showing the location of a hoard of Nazi treasure in East Berlin, buried 'two spades deep'. Heidemann suggested that Conny and Edith should go over together and dig it up. He would pay them 20,000 marks as a reward. 'Oh yes?' replied Kujau. 'You'll be coming to hold the lamp, will you?' The reporter said he couldn't: it was impossible for him to cross the border at the moment. Kujau immediately suspected that Heidemann planned to tip off the East German police and arrange for him to disappear into a communist jail. He declined the offer and returned to Stuttgart.

A few hours after saying goodbye to Kujau, Heidemann rang David Irving in London.

Since his return to Duke Street, Irving had been pondering the events of the past few days. He was forced to admit that as far as attacking the authenticity of *Stern*'s diaries went, he had 'squeezed the lemon dry'. He asked himself what he could do to recapture the initiative, and he came up with one answer: he could announce that he had changed his mind and declare the diaries genuine.

There were a number of factors which made this an attractive idea, apart from the obvious injection of fresh publicity it would provide. One was temperamental. Irving had always relished his role as an *enfant terrible*. He liked being outrageous, making liberal flesh creep. Now, for the first time in his career, his stand on the diaries had put him on the side of conventional opinion. It was not his style and he found it disconcerting.

He had also begun to have genuine doubts about the wisdom of the uncompromising line he had adopted. He had been shaken by the sheer quantity of *Stern*'s archive when he had seen it in the ZDF studio on Tuesday night. Perhaps there *was* a genuine set of Hitler diaries somewhere, which had served as a model for the forgery in his possession? One of his objections to the *Stern* material had been that Hitler had suffered from Parkinson's disease in the final weeks of his life. Now he had to admit, having seen them, that the final entries did slant sharply to the right, as if oblivious to the lines on the page – a classic symptom of Parkinsonism. And finally, there was the fact that the diaries did not contain any evidence to suggest that Hitler was aware of the Holocaust – *Stern* might help substantiate the thesis of *Hitler's War*.

Irving told Heidemann that he was on the point of changing his mind. He had given an interview to the BBC that morning announcing his reservations. Heidemann asked him when it would be broadcast. Next Wednesday, replied Irving. 'Heidemann', he wrote in his diary, 'urged me to say it *now* as Peter Koch is going on television in New York on *Monday* with his counter-attack.' Irving promised to think it over.

Meanwhile, that afternoon, Radio Moscow had resumed its attack on the diaries with a heavy-handed 'satirical broadcast' to West Germany. Its target was a new one: not *Stern*, but the rest of the republic's press, at that moment filling its pages with reports of the affair. The broadcast took the form of a story set in the office of the editor of *Die Welt*. The editor wants to know what he should put in the paper over the next few weeks. The home editor suggests unemployment, which is about to reach three million. The foreign editor suggests the deployment of American missiles. The editor-in-chief 'explodes':

> 'You are quitters. The hit of the coming months is the diaries of our Führer. Granted, the copyright is in the hands of our business rivals. To hell with them. Nobody can stop us discussing the authenticity of the diaries. We shall quote from the diaries in every edition and in every column. You [he says to one reporter] will have to take care of statements by historians from abroad. You [to another] provide interviews on the subject with comrades-in-arms of the Führer. What is important is to make the Führer appear as respectable as possible. And you, well you go to Berchtesgaden, to the former residence of the Führer. He says in his diary that his favourite alsatian, Blondi, always stopped at the gate during walks. You take samples of the soil there and give them to the laboratory. If these soil tests are compatible, then . . .?'
>
> 'The diaries are authentic,' the reporter bursts out.
>
> 'That's right,' the boss says, grinning. 'Let's get to work now. And don't say a word about missiles or unemployment.'

For once, Hugh Trevor-Roper had other things on his mind apart from the Hitler diaries. Friday, 29 April was an important occasion in the life of Peterhouse – the day of the annual college Feast, an ancient ritual of good food and fine wine. The guest of honour was the Lord Chancellor, Lord Hailsham, who arrived in mid-afternoon to take tea with Trevor-Roper and his wife in the Master's Lodge.

It was now four days since the historian had given orders to have all telephone calls to the Lodge stopped at the porter's switchboard. It was inconvenient, particularly with a member of the Cabinet in the house. In some trepidation, Trevor-Roper decided to rescind the instruction. The telephone rang almost immediately. 'I'll answer it,' said Hailsham.

It was the *Observer*.

'I'm afraid Lord Dacre is not at home at present,' said the seventy-five-year-old Lord Chancellor. 'May I take a message? I'm his butler.'

It was an amusing end to what was otherwise one of the more unpleasant weeks of Trevor-Roper's career.

TWENTY-EIGHT

As the crisis over the Hitler diaries worsened, Rupert Murdoch flew back from New York to London. The *Sunday Times*'s reputation was clearly in jeopardy, but Magnus Linklater was struck by Murdoch's apparent lack of concern. He seemed almost bored by the diaries: they were yesterday's deal; his restless mind had already moved on to other matters. In commercial terms, the question of whether or not the diaries were genuine was of only minor importance. In the past week, sales of the *Sunday Times* had increased by 60,000 copies. As long as the controversy continued, circulation was likely to remain buoyant. Besides, under the terms of News International's agreement with Gruner and Jahr, his money would be refunded if the diaries proved to be fakes. Whatever the final verdict on authenticity, Murdoch would not suffer. At a meeting with the journalists involved in the project he readily agreed that if the situation worsened, he would suspend publication. They wanted to know how much worse things had to get. Murdoch said he would pull out of the deal only if there was a 55 per cent chance that the diaries were forged – in other words, the onus was on the sceptics to substantiate their doubts, not on *Stern* to justify its faith. This irresponsible formula was, none the less, regarded at the time as a major concession on Murdoch's part.

The psychology which was leading *Stern* to disaster now began to operate on the *Sunday Times*. The reporters involved on the story had no desire to see their paper humiliated; they *wanted* to believe that the diaries were genuine and set out to find evidence to keep their hopes alive. Brian Moynahan was dispatched to Boernersdorf where he managed to find a fifty-one-year-old quarryman named Helmut Schmidt who had been thirteen when the Junkers 352 had crashed. Schmidt told Moynahan that he had seen one of the survivors sitting dazed on the ground clutching a wooden case more than two feet long and eighteen inches wide. 'He hung on to it like this,' he claimed, at which point, according to Moynahan, 'Schmidt, working on his allotment, gripped his hoe until his veins rose.'

While Moynahan tramped round Boernersdorf, in London Elaine Potter ploughed through some of the US Counter-Intelligence Corps files. She extracted the story of how the CIC picked up rumours of a 'Hitler diary' during its investigations in the Berchtesgaden area in 1945.

In Hamburg, Gitta Sereny interviewed Heidemann. The reporter gave her the variation on his original story which he had given to Trevor-Roper on Sunday: the diaries had stayed in the hayloft in Boernersdorf for only a few days; they had been brought to the West by an officer in 1945; this officer was now over seventy and had given Heidemann the documents on condition his name should never be divulged; Heidemann claimed to have talked to him only 'two days ago'. 'Here,' wrote Sereny, 'is one of the indispensable links demanded by critics who have questioned the authenticity of the diaries.'

Frank Giles presided over this rearguard action with his customary diffidence. When the *Sunday Times* journalists in London expressed their concern about the affair and asked him to address a union meeting, he turned them down. He told them he was going away on holiday to Corfu. 'Even if I were here,' he added, 'I must tell you that I do not think that this matter is appropriate for the chapel.' Publication of the diaries would go ahead in his absence, he informed the editorial conference, and would stop only if the diaries were conclusively proved to be forgeries.

On Sunday, the paper appeared with a somewhat more muted front page than it had presented the previous week:

> Hitler's Diaries – the trail from the hayloft
> *Stern* challenges David Irving
> 'No shred of doubt,' says Heidemann

The editor of the *Sunday Times* then left the country.

David Irving spent the day sending out invoices to newspapers and magazines, billing them for his work attacking the diaries' authenticity. Shortly before noon, a reporter from the *Daily Express* rang to ask if it was true that he was suing the *Sunday Times* for failing to pay him his commission for putting them on to the Hitler diaries. 'Not suing,' replied Irving, 'just asking.' He then told him to 'hold on to his hat' and gave him what he modestly described as 'the story of the day': that he now believed the diaries were genuine.

The *Express* ran the story in its early editions, and at 11 p.m. a sub-editor from *The Times* rang to ask if the report in the *Express* was correct. Irving said it was.

The Times immediately put it on its front page.

The following morning, as *The Times* in Britain announced Irving's belief that the diaries were genuine, *Der Spiegel* appeared in Germany carrying his assertion that they were fakes. 'Hitler's Diary: Find or Forgery?' was the title on the magazine's cover; the contents left little doubt of *Der Spiegel*'s opinion as to the correct answer. It was a devastating assault, attacking the *Stern* scoop for 'bad German, bad punctuation and banality'. *Der Spiegel*'s reporters had tracked down the SS man who discovered the Boernersdorf crash and using his testimony they picked Heidemann's research apart. The Junkers' fuselage had been made of metal, not canvas, as *Stern* had claimed; the plane had ploughed straight into the ground, not ended up on its roof; gold bars, pistols and ammunition had been salvaged, but no papers. In contrast to the carefully cultivated image of 'the Bloodhound' which *Stern*'s public relations department had built up of Heidemann, the reporter was depicted as an obsessive friend of old Nazis, whose discovery had been inadequately checked and blown up into an international sensation. 'If it all goes wrong,' Peter Koch was quoted as saying, 'the editors will charter Heidemann's boat, sail it to Heligoland and pull out the plugs.' Much of the information had been provided by Irving and the centrepiece of the attack was a reproduction of a page from his fake diary.

Der Spiegel's attack was bad enough news for one day, but worse was to come when the company's lawyer, Dr Hagen, arrived at the Bundesarchiv.

Josef Henke had handed the three diary volumes given to him after the *Stern* press conference to the Federal Institute for Forensic Investigation in Berlin. On Monday, he was able to give Hagen the scientists' preliminary findings. All three volumes contained traces of polyamid 6, a synthetic textile invented in 1938 but not manufactured in bulk until 1943. The binding of the Hess special volume – supposedly written in 1941 – included polyester which had not been made until 1953. Ultraviolet light had also shown up fluorescent material in the paper. These results had yet to be confirmed in writing, said Henke, but *Stern*'s scoop was beginning to look extremely dubious. In addition, although the archive's researchers had had time for only a brief check of the diaries' written content, they had already found a couple of textual errors: two laws relating to agriculture and student organizations were not passed on the dates given in the diaries.

Hagen hurried back to Hamburg to pass on this information.

At about 6 p.m. Schulte-Hillen convened a crisis meeting in

his office on the ninth floor of the *Stern* building. Wilfried Sorge did not attend (he was on holiday in Italy), nor did Koch, who was in the United States preparing his media campaign, but all the other leading figures in the affair were present: Jan Hensmann, Felix Schmidt, Rolf Gillhausen, Henri Nannen, Gerd Heidemann and Thomas Walde.

As Hagen reported the Bundesarchiv's findings an atmosphere of barely suppressed panic spread through the room. Only Heidemann seemed unmoved, sitting wrapped in his own private world as the others began shouting at him. Felix Schmidt was enraged by his calmness. How could he sit there, he demanded, and act as if none of this concerned him? It was imperative that he reveal the name of his source; otherwise, publication of the diaries should be stopped. Heidemann remained silent. 'You either belong in a madhouse or a prison,' Nannen told him. He added that in his opinion, the magazine's editors could not be allowed 'to dangle like this any longer'.

Schulte-Hillen now spoke up, and for the first time he addressed Heidemann sharply: he wanted to speak to the reporter alone – immediately. The two men left the room.

Before the emergency meeting began, the managing director had been approached in private by Felix Schmidt, who had suggested that Heidemann might be keeping the identity of his supplier secret because he had stolen some of the money. As far as Schmidt was concerned, that no longer mattered: the important thing was to find out whether the diaries were genuine. He had pleaded with Schulte-Hillen to try once more to persuade Heidemann to tell him the whole story, if necessary by promising him 'that if he has pocketed some of the money, it will not be held against him'.

In another office, away from the others, Schulte-Hillen confronted Heidemann. 'I asked him to tell me the whole story,' he recalled, 'leaving nothing out.' Heidemann, reluctantly, agreed. According to Schulte-Hillen:

Heidemann told me that the south German collector was called Fischer. This was the first time I had heard the name. Herr Fischer was supposed to have a sister in East Germany who was married to a museum director called Krebs. For a long time, Frau Krebs had been putting advertisements in East German newspapers asking for militaria. One day, an old man from the Boernersdorf area had contacted Frau Krebs and asked if she was interested in handwritten documents belonging to Adolf Hitler. Frau Krebs had been so taken aback by this offer that she had told her brother, an army general. . . .

At last, Heidemann was telling Schulte-Hillen the truth – or, at least, the truth as he had been given it by Kujau. 'General Fischer' had been to see the old man and obtained the names of peasants in the Boernersdorf area who had hidden material salvaged from the plane crash. The documents turned out to be the Hitler diaries. The general had kept them hidden for some years, before offering them for sale through his brother in south Germany. Heidemann said that at least three other communist generals were involved in smuggling them out of the East, including one from the Ministry of State Security; he added that he knew their names. 'I asked him to tell me them,' recalled Schulte-Hillen. 'He said he would have to check in his archive, then he could show me them in writing.'

Heidemann disappeared for two hours and returned at about 11 p.m. His 'evidence' turned out to be two letters addressed to an East German general, whose name had been blacked out. Schulte-Hillen was disappointed. 'What am I supposed to make of this?' he asked. The letters proved nothing. Heidemann said he was sorry, but 'the originals were in a safe place to which he had no access'.

Schulte-Hillen reported back to the group assembled in his

office. The story of the diaries' discovery, as Heidemann had explained it, seemed plausible to him. But he still did not have a full account, and given Heidemann's insistence that it was a matter of life and death for people in East Germany, he did not feel able to put any more pressure on the reporter.

What has frequently – and accurately – been described as a 'bunker mentality' now descended on the headquarters of *Stern*. Surrounded by enemies, cut off from reality, the leaders of the magazine began deploying phantom divisions in a frantic attempt to stave off the impending disaster.

Surely they could somehow prove that paper whitener had been in use before the war? Henri Nannen spent the night reading through chemistry books. In an old dictionary he came across a pre-war entry for a substance called 'blankit'. Wolf Thieme spoke to a contact of his in the Bayer chemical company who told him that the paper whitener 'blankophor' might have been used on an experimental basis in the 1930s. Early on Tuesday morning, Hans Shuh, the head of *Stern*'s business section, was summoned to Nannen's office and instructed to write a detailed article on the history of the paper industry. Meanwhile, a statement, resonant with hollow bravado, was issued to the news agencies, signed jointly by Nannen, Schmidt and Schulte-Hillen:

> For a week *Stern* has been accused, with ever-increasing shrillness, of publishing forged Hitler diaries. Professor Werner Maser spoke in detail of an East German forgery factory near Potsdam. In spite of repeated demands, Maser could not provide any proof of this.
>
> Professor Broszat, the director of the Institute of Contemporary History in Munich, demanded that all the diaries be laid before an international historical commission. *Stern* immediately turned down this demand. Historians, like doctors, diverge in their diagnoses. One day the English historian

Trevor-Roper confirms the authenticity of the diary and the next day doubts it. The writer David Irving behaves in an opposite manner.

But at least doctors are bound by an oath of confidentiality. Historians, it is now clear, are under no such obligation. Laying all the documents before an historical commission would, as Henri Nannen, *Stern*'s publisher, has pointed out, compromise the exclusivity of the material.

Even the handwriting and forensic tests, commissioned by *Stern* before publication from well-known experts, have been misinterpreted by the press, television and radio, and partly pronounced false. Certain newspapers have not hesitated even to raise political suspicions about *Stern*'s editors.

But this discussion concerns material from recent history of extreme delicacy. *Stern* has therefore, despite its opinion, taken into account Professor Broszat's demand, and will allow an immediate inspection of the material by experts from West Germany, Switzerland and the United States.

Until these tests, carried out on the broadest basis by highly responsible bodies, have been completed and yielded a clear result, the chief editors, publisher and printer of *Stern* believe that any further discussion will serve no purpose.

Heidemann and Schmidt promptly withdrew from a discussion programme on Austrian television which they were scheduled to take part in that night.

As a first step in this new process of verification, the Bundesarchiv was informed that more diaries would be made available for a full textual and chemical analysis. Only one condition was attached: if the diaries proved to be forgeries, *Stern* was to be informed well in advance of any public announcement – at least the magazine would be able to run the story of its own folly as an exclusive.

On Wednesday, 4 May accompanied by a company

manager and a lawyer, Leo Pesch arrived in Zurich and removed fifteen volumes of the Hitler diaries from the bank vault. The group split up. The manager went direct to Koblenz to hand over four books to the Bundesarchiv for a check on the contents. Pesch and the lawyer drove to the Swiss forensic laboratories in St Gallen and gave the scientists eleven diaries for microscopic examination.

On the same day, from Hamburg, Gerd Heidemann set off on a two-day trip to Bavaria. He planned to visit a former employee of the Berghof now living in an old people's home near Berchtesgaden – she would swear, he was sure, to having seen Hitler write a diary. He told Walde that he would also stop off at an old printing works in Miesbach, south of Munich. The factory had at one time been run by the SS and he was certain he could obtain enough samples of pre-war paper to prove that whitener had been in use in the 1930s. And then there was Hitler's chauffeur's girlfriend – she would swear that Erich Kempka had told her before he died that Hitler used to write notes in the back of his Mercedes.

They must all trust him, said Heidemann. Everything would be fine.

In America, Peter Koch, supported by Wolf Hess, had embarked on what *Newsweek* described as a 'media blitz', with invitations to appear on *Good Morning America*, *The CBS Morning News*, *The Today Show* and *Nightline*. He gave a long interview to the *Washington Post* whose reporters were impressed by the confidence of this 'balding, trim man, sunburned from an outing at Jones beach over the weekend'. He was in combative mood. 'I expected the uproar,' he told another group of journalists, 'and expected that many incompetent people would denounce the diaries as fakes. This is because every other publishing house will envy our story and every historian will envy us.'

One man following Koch's publicity tour with interest was Kenneth Rendell, a forty-year-old handwriting expert based in Boston. Rendell had been retained by *Newsweek* when the magazine was bidding for the diaries at the beginning of April. 'Anticipating my imminent departure for Zurich,' Rendell recalled, 'I organized about a hundred samples of authentic Hitler writing, researched scientific tests that might date the material and prepared myself for a sizeable challenge.' Then, to his disappointment, the deal with *Newsweek* had fallen through, and he had been forced to watch the affair unfold from America. Koch's visit, bearing diaries from 1932 and 1945, gave him an opportunity to have a look at the material at first hand.

Rendell caught up with Koch at the Manhattan studio of CBS at breakfast time on Wednesday, as Koch was preparing for his appearance on the *Morning News*. Koch knew of Rendell's reputation and had no objections to letting him look at the diaries. Repeatedly interrupted by technicians, Rendell began his examination on the studio floor. 'Even at first glance,' he wrote later, 'everything looked wrong.' The paper was of poor quality, the ink looked modern, none of the writing was blotted ('a sloppiness I didn't expect from Hitler'), and the signatures seemed to him to be 'terrible renditions'. His immediate reaction was that both diaries were forged – the 1945 volume especially was a 'fiasco'.

At the end of the broadcast, Koch invited the American expert to continue his analysis in *Stern*'s New York office that afternoon. Rendell arrived with an assistant, an 80-power microscope and a dossier of genuine Hitler writing. The microscope showed 'no examples of tracing or other glaring technical errors', so Rendell tried a different technique. At his request, the *Stern* staff photocopied the twenty-two pages of the 1932 diary. 'We began,' he recalled, 'the tedious process of snipping out all of the capital letters and pasting them on sheets of paper. In all we assembled separate collections of twenty-one letters, and an additional assortment of numbers. We compared the diary characters with authentic characters we had pasted up earlier. . . .'

At 9 p.m., Rendell broke off his examination for the night. 'It doesn't look good,' he warned Koch.

Across the Atlantic, in Koblenz, the President of the Bundesarchiv, Hans Booms, had been given four of the diaries by the *Stern* lawyer. He took them home with him to read. He was shocked by the content, but not in the way he had expected: it was indescribably *dull*. At midnight he turned to his wife. 'I don't care whether they are real or forged,' he told her. 'They are so boring, so totally meaningless, it hardly makes any difference.'

TWENTY-NINE

The next morning, 5 May, *Stern* appeared carrying the second instalment of its serialization of the diaries. The magazine, which had reverted to its normal habit of publishing on Thursday, devoted its cover and thirty-four inside pages to the story of Rudolf Hess's flight to Scotland. Hitler was quoted as describing the Duke of Windsor in an entry for 1937 as 'a glowing National Socialist'; Winston Churchill was dismissed in 1939 as 'the greatest poisoner in London'. The issue was also notable for a ranting editorial by Peter Koch, written before he left for America, entitled 'the Falsifiers', smearing *Stern*'s critics as part of an international conspiracy founded upon envy. Irving and Maser were historians without reputations to lose; so too, now, was Eberhard Jaeckel for daring to criticize the magazine's scoop. As for Trevor-Roper, Koch hinted that he had changed his mind partly because of his wartime connection with British intelligence. They were all contemptible. *Stern* welcomed the abuse of such people. 'More enemies,' wrote Koch, 'more honour.'

It was a masterpiece of mistiming, for at that moment, disaster was racing towards *Stern* from at least five different directions: from Koblenz, where Booms had handed over the diaries to a team of scholars to check for errors; from the forensic laboratories in Berlin which had taken samples of material from three of the diaries; from the police laboratories in Wiesbaden, whose scientists had now been handed those three volumes and were running their own tests; from the forensic institute in St Gallen; and from New York, where, at

10 a.m., Kenneth Rendell had resumed his handwriting investigation.

Within three hours, Rendell was in a position to prove what he had suspected the moment he saw the diaries. The capital letters E, H and K in the 1932 volume had striking dissimilarities to the same letters in authentic examples of Hitler's writing. 'Koch was stunned when he saw my evidence laid out on a conference table,' recalled Rendell. 'This type of systematic analysis was unimpeachable.' He wanted to know how the American could have concluded they were fakes so quickly, when three other handwriting experts had been convinced the diaries were genuine. 'He had the impression', said Rendell, 'that all of the comparison documents provided by his magazine had come from the German Federal Archives. But I showed him that a careful reading of the authentication reports indicated that most examples were from the dossier of *Stern* and its reporter Gerd Heidemann.'

Rendell – who was reportedly paid a retainer of $8000 by *Newsweek* – wanted to tell Maynard Parker of his findings at once. Koch pleaded with him to keep quiet for the time being; *Stern* would fly him to Europe and give him the opportunity to study the entire archive if he would deal with them exclusively. Rendell agreed.

At 1.30 p.m. New York time (7.30 p.m. in Hamburg), Koch telephoned Schulte-Hillen.

The managing director of Gruner and Jahr had taken to his bed with a fever. 'Rendell thinks the diaries are forged,' said Koch when he eventually tracked him down. Groggily, Schulte-Hillen agreed with his suggestion that they should invite Rendell to Hamburg to inspect the diaries. But he refused to panic: he would wait, he told Hoch, for the Bundesarchiv's verdict which *Stern* had been told would be given to them the next day. Besides, Rendell had spent only a few hours with the material; Frei-Sulzer, Hilton and Huebner had been allowed weeks and they had all been certain it was genuine.

Schulte-Hillen was still feeling confident when Manfred Fischer paid him a visit at home later that evening. Fischer had left Bertelsmann the previous November: despite Reinhard Mohn's excitement at the purchase of the Hitler diaries, the relationship between the two men had not worked smoothly. Nevertheless, Fischer had continued to maintain an interest in the project he had started in 1981. But over the past week, his pride had turned to dismay. The Hitler diaries could turn out to be the 'biggest deception of the century', he warned his successor. 'I fear we have allowed ourselves to be led by the nose.'

Schulte-Hillen shook his head. He was sure Fischer was being pessimistic. Anyway, they would both know for certain tomorrow.

The events which would eventually turn Friday, 6 May 1983 into 'Black Friday' as far as the participants in the diaries affair were concerned began at 11 a.m. when the two *Stern* lawyers, Ruppert and Hagen, turned up at the Bundesarchiv to see Hans Booms.

Booms now had full reports from the scientists at Wiesbaden and Berlin. Reduced to its basic components, *Stern*'s great scoop had proved to be a shoddy forgery. The paper was a poor quality mixture of coniferous wood, grass and foliage, laced with a chemical paper whitener which had not existed before 1955. The binding of the books also contained whitener. The red threads to the seals on the covers contained viscose and polyester. The labels stuck on the front and supposedly signed by Bormann and Hess had all been typed on the same machine. The typewriter came from the correct period – it was an Adler Klein II, manufactured between 1925

and 1934 – but although an interval of seven years supposedly separated the labels attached to the 1934 diary and
the Hess special volume of 1941, there was no evidence of
wear in the typeface: the labels had been written in quick
succession. The four different varieties of ink used in the
books were of a type commonly found in West German
artists' shops; they did not match any of the ink known to
have been widely used during the war. And by measuring the
evaporation of chloride from the ink, the scientists established
that the Hess volume had been written within the last two
years, whilst the writing in the 1943 diary was less than
twelve months old.

Booms told all this to Hagen and Ruppert. They were, he
recalled, 'deeply shocked' and 'shattered': 'I can still hear
their arguments: "Heidemann is certain. He absolutely swears
on it. As far as he's concerned, it's quite impossible that we
could be dealing with a forgery...."'

But there could be no doubt. In addition to the forensic
evidence, the Bundesarchiv had discovered a number of textual errors: for example, a law passed on 19 January 1933
was entered in the diary under 19 January 1934. It did not
take the archivists long to discover the forger's main source:
the two-volume edition of *Hitler's Speeches and Proclamations*, compiled by Max Domarus. 'It became apparent to us',
said Booms later, 'that if there was nothing in Domarus for a
particular day, then Hitler didn't write anything in his diary
that night either. When Domarus did include something, then
Hitler wrote it down. And when an occasional mistake crept
into Domarus, Hitler repeated the same error.' One such
mistake was an entry by 'Hitler' recording that he had
received a telegram from General Ritter von Epp con-
gratulating him on the fiftieth anniversary of his joining the
army; in reality, the telegram was *from* Hitler *to* von Epp.
Kujau had copied the error word-for-word into the diary.

Throughout the half-hour conversation, Booms was repeatedly interrupted by telephone calls from Berlin, Wiesbaden and Bonn. Suddenly, Hagen realized what was happening: the two forensic laboratories, both official organizations, were reporting direct to the Federal Government. Booms confirmed that this was the case. But what about the guarantee of confidentiality? That no longer applied, answered Booms. The affair was now 'a ministerial matter'. There would be a government news conference to announce that the diaries were fakes at noon.

The two *Stern* lawyers scrambled to a telephone to alert Hamburg to what was about to happen. They reached Jan Hensmann. Hardly anyone seemed to be around. Hensmann rang Schulte-Hillen who left his sick bed immediately to come in. Hensmann tried to find Nannen.

Nannen was at Hamburg airport, preparing to fly to Rome for a ceremony to open *Stern*'s new Italian office. A stewardess told him he was wanted urgently on the telephone.

'It's all a forgery,' wailed Hensmann.

Nannen asked how he could be certain. The Bundesarchiv, said Hensmann. They were going to announce it in less than thirty minutes.

The sixty-nine-year-old publisher dropped the telephone, sprinted through the terminal, abandoned his luggage and his car, and jumped into a taxi. At the office, he dictated a statement acknowledging the Bundesarchiv's findings and promising a full investigation. The message was rushed to a telex machine but it arrived just five minutes too late to beat the official announcement.

The news that the diaries were forgeries had been whispered to the West German Minister of the Interior, Friedrich Zimmermann, during a debate in the Federal parliament. Broad smiles appeared as the news spread along the Government bench.

Zimmermann told the Chancellor, Helmut Kohl. 'Now that is something,' laughed Kohl. *Stern* was an old enemy of the Christian Democrats: the discomfiture of Nannen and the rest of 'the Hamburg set', as Kohl dismissively called them, was a pleasant prospect to brighten the Government's day. Zimmermann hurried out of the Chamber to brief the press.

Zimmermann's determination to announce the news immediately was not motivated solely by party considerations. The legacy of Adolf Hitler was too important to be bandied about as *Stern* had done. Any West German government would have been sensitive about the diaries; the fact that the scandal had blown up on the fiftieth anniversary of Hitler's accession to power, at a time of intense interest in the Nazis, made the matter especially delicate. There was no question of the Interior Ministry permitting the Bundesarchiv to suppress the news that the diaries were forged while *Stern* tried to wriggle off the hook. The whole business was out of hand. It could no longer be left to a collection of scoop-happy journalists.

'On the basis of an analysis of the contents and after a forensic examination, the Federal Archive is convinced that the documents do not come from Hitler's hand but were produced after the war,' Zimmermann told reporters. 'I regret most deeply that this analysis was not undertaken by *Stern* before publication.' A press conference giving more details would be held shortly by the Bundesarchiv.

A few minutes later, the German Press Agency put out a rush statement: 'HITLER DIARIES ARE POST-WAR.' It was two weeks, literally to the hour, since the same agency had issued the announcement of *Stern*'s scoop.

In the *Sunday Times* offices in London there had been, according to the paper's own account, 'an air of considerable elation' all morning. *Stern* had finally agreed to lend the newspaper two volumes of the diaries to enable it to carry out its own forensic tests. A *Stern* courier had flown in from Hamburg and handed them personally to Rupert Murdoch. Someone suggested to Murdoch that they should have the books photocopied. Murdoch would not allow it. He had given his word, he said, that they would be used only for scientific evaluation.

The atmosphere of self-congratulation was punctured abruptly at noon. Peter Hess, the publishing director of Gruner and Jahr, rang through from Germany with the news that the diaries were forgeries. 'It's staggering, shattering,' he said, stammering out his apologies. 'We still just can't believe it.'

Murdoch told his journalists to photocopy the diaries.

Arthur Brittenden issued a statement to Associated Press: 'The *Sunday Times* accepts the report of the German archivists that the volumes they have examined contain materials that demonstrate the diaries are not authentic. In view of this, the *Sunday Times* will not go ahead with publication.' News International announced it would be seeking an immediate repayment of the $200,000 it had paid as a first instalment for the diaries.

In Hamburg a debate was underway as to what *Stern* should do next. Astonishingly, Henri Nannen thought the magazine should cut out all the references drawn from the Hitler diaries and continue with its series about Rudolf Hess: it was still an interesting piece of journalism in his opinion. The others were horrified. The magazine would be torn apart by its critics if it tried to carry on as if nothing had happened. Nannen was forced to back down.

At the Itzehoe printing works, thirty miles north-east of Hamburg, the third issue of *Stern* to be built around the Hitler diaries was already being printed. By the time the arguments on the editorial floor had ended and the order had been given to stop the presses, 160,000 copies of the inside pages and 260,000 covers had already been printed. An additional 70,000 magazines were actually finished and in lorries on their way to the distributors; they were recalled only after frantic telephone calls. Every trace of the issue was pulped, losing *Stern* a quarter of a million marks in the process. The cover picture of Rudolf Hess was replaced by a photograph of a new-born baby.

At 2.30 p.m. Felix Schmidt addressed a hastily convened editorial conference. Everyone had to set to work to remake the next issue, he told them. He refused to answer detailed questions. Confused and angry, the *Stern* department chiefs drifted away. At 5 p.m. the entire staff held a meeting and elected a committee to negotiate a new code of conduct with the management.

In Cambridge, Hugh Trevor-Roper's telephone was once again ringing incessantly. 'I just don't want to say anything about it,' he told one reporter. 'I think I should only comment to Times Newspapers.'

In America, Leslie Hinton, the associate editor of Rupert Murdoch's *Boston Globe*, confirmed that the paper had been on the point of running extracts from the Hitler diaries. 'We have suspended our plans to publish,' he said in a statement to UPI, 'in view of what the German archivists said today.'

David Irving was in Düsseldorf on another speaking tour for the DVU when he heard the news from his secretary in London. It was a disastrous turn of events. He hastily dictated a statement for the press accepting the Bundesarchiv's ruling but drawing attention to the fact that he was the first person to declare the diaries fakes. ('Yes,' said a reporter from *The*

Times when this was read out to him, 'and the last person to declare them authentic.') NBC sent a television crew to interview him after his speech to an audience of right-wing extremists in the nearby town of Neuss. 'They questioned whom I was speaking to,' Irving recorded in his diary, 'but I ducked the issue. As I was sitting down for the interview the whole audience streamed past behind the cameraman, several of the nuttier of them wearing the uniform and badges of the *Vikinger Jugend* [a fanatical sect of young neo-Nazis]. Fortunately NBC did not observe *them*.'

For Konrad Kujau, the newsflash announcing that the diaries were forgeries was the signal to pack up and leave Stuttgart as quickly as possible. Things had already started becoming uncomfortable for him. Stefan Aust, the editor of *Panorama*, West German television's leading current affairs programme, had managed to reconstruct the trail back from David Irving through August Priesack to Fritz Stiefel. Working from a clue dropped by Priesack that the supplier of the diaries was apparently a dealer in militaria named Fischer, Aust had begun trailing round every antiques shop in Stuttgart until someone remembered a Herr Fischer who had kept a shop in Aspergstrasse. Neighbours there told Aust that Fischer had moved to Schreiberstrasse. Aust had arrived on Thursday to find the shop deserted. He had driven straight round to see Fritz Stiefel to confront him with this information, and whilst there had actually spoken to Kujau on the telephone. 'Tell me where you are,' insisted Aust, 'and I'll come over.' Kujau had managed to stall him. But now that the diaries had been exposed, it was obviously going to be only a matter of time before a dozen other journalists followed Aust's path to Stuttgart.

According to Maria Modritsch, her lover turned up on her doorstep at 7 p.m. on Friday, accompanied by Edith Lieblang.

'There was a conversation between us,' recalled Maria. 'Conny told Edith that I was cleaning for him.' Kujau insisted that all three of them leave Stuttgart immediately. Both women knew too much for him to be able to leave them behind. 'Conny wanted to go to the Black Forest,' said Maria, 'but then he took up my suggestion that we go to Austria.'

Shortly afterwards, the forger, his common-law wife and his mistress all clambered into a car, and this bizarre *ménage à trois* headed off to the Austrian border.

Gerd Heidemann had been incommunicado all day, driving around the countryside between Berchtesgaden and Munich trying to find evidence to shore up his crumbling scoop. The *Stern* executives were itching to get their hands on him. So too was Gina, who was having to field telephone calls from their apartment in the Elbchaussee. She refused to believe what the Bundesarchiv was saying. 'I am not surprised,' she told Gitta Sereny. 'We expected something like this.' Was she saying the diaries were genuine? 'Yes.' Those who said the diaries were fakes, she insisted to a reporter from the *New York Times*, were trying to 'suppress the truth'. 'It's terrible, but no matter what happens, we will always believe in the diaries. . . . It would have been a joy to tell the world about the Führer. We have received letters and telegrams above all from young people who are overjoyed finally to learn the truth.' Between conversations with journalists, Gina managed to reach the couple's friend, Heinrich Hoffmann, the son of Hitler's photographer, who was also in Bavaria, undergoing treatment in a private clinic. Did he know where her husband was? Hoffmann said he did not. It was an emergency, said Gina, Gerd must ring her immediately. 'Shortly afterwards,' recalled Hoffmann, 'Heidemann rang.'

He told me he was in the neighbourhood, but had no time to drop by. He asked how I was. I told him that his wife had rung and that he was being looked for. He said: 'Yes, that's the reason I'm in a rush – to get the last plane from Munich to Hamburg. . . .' I then rang Frau Heidemann and said: 'You can relax. Gerd's all right and he's on his way back home.'

According to Heidemann's own account, he had heard the news of Zimmermann's announcement towards the end of the day on the car radio. He was 'completely shattered'. At 8 p.m. he rang the *Stern* office, and was briskly informed that they had been trying to find him all day and that a private plane was waiting on the tarmac at Munich to bring him straight to Hamburg.

The plane touched down shortly after 11 p.m. A *Stern* representative was waiting for Heidemann at the airport with a car to take him to the office. Gina was also there. At first she had been told by *Stern* to keep away, but she was determined to meet her husband. *Stern* had relented, but its official had instructions to make sure the couple did not try to rehearse a story together. 'All Gerd could say to me in the car', recalled Gina, 'was: "I know they are genuine. I know." He looked shaken to the core.'

Heidemann faced a grim reception committee in the managing director's office: Henri Nannen, Felix Schmidt, Rolf Gillhausen and Gerd Schulte-Hillen had been waiting for him all evening. 'We are going to uncover the full story of this forgery and lay it before our readers,' Nannen had promised in an interview on West German television that night. 'We have reason to be ashamed.' No one was in any mood to listen to excuses. 'What do you have to say?' demanded Schulte-Hillen.

Heidemann said he was sure that most of the diaries were genuine. He needed more time. He wanted to meet a contact in East Berlin.

Schmidt interrupted him. 'Stop playing around. I'm sick of this performance. Let's get down to the real issues.'

Very well, said Heidemann. He opened his briefcase and placed a cassette recorder on the table. He switched it on and played his interrogators a recording of a fifteen-minute telephone conversation he had had from Munich with Medard Klapper. Klapper promised the reporter that Martin Bormann was now willing to fly over from South America to authenticate the diaries – he was an old man, he no longer feared prosecution, he would come and help Heidemann out of his predicament. Heidemann switched off the tape. The four *Stern* officials looked at one another. After a while, Schulte-Hillen spoke. 'How is Bormann proposing to get here?' he inquired.

'In a Lear jet,' said Heidemann.

There were angry and frustrated shouts from around the table. Felix Schmidt pointed out that a Lear jet did not have the range to cross the Atlantic: it would fall into the sea in mid-flight.

The atmosphere became progressively more unpleasant as Heidemann still refused to name his source. 'Lives are in danger,' he insisted. 'Nonsense,' said Schmidt. '*We're* the ones in danger.' Heidemann replied that his supplier had returned to East Germany to try to obtain the original score of Wagner's *Die Meistersinger*, one of Adolf Hitler's most treasured possessions which had also been on the Boernersdorf plane.

It was after midnight. Schulte-Hillen was unwell and Henri Nannen was beginning to fall asleep. The four senior *Stern* men decided to get some rest and Heidemann was taken downstairs to Felix Schmidt's office to face a fresh set of examiners: Thomas Walde, Wolfe Thieme and another *Stern* journalist, Michael Seufert. This session lasted until dawn.

Meanwhile, in another office, Gina Heidemann was also being subjected to some detailed questioning. Heidemann had once described driving her car over to East Germany to carry out one of the dramatic exchanges of money for diaries on the Berlin autobahn; had she been with him? Gina said she had, an answer which did not help Heidemann's credibility as at that moment he was denying that his wife had ever accompanied him. At 2.45 a.m., Gina telephoned Gitta Sereny at the Four Seasons Hotel. Sereny had flown over to cover the story of the forgery for the *Sunday Times*. 'They've got Gerd upstairs,' whispered Gina. 'They are putting him through the mangle.' By the time she emerged from the *Stern* building shortly after 3 a.m. she was in a pitiful state. She went to Sereny's hotel. 'Her hair', wrote the reporter, 'usually neat and attractive, was tangled, and she looked as if she was in an advanced state of shock. She was trembling and crying.' Did she now believe the diaries were fakes? 'I don't know what to think,' she replied. 'Gerd always believed and swore they were genuine.' Who was the supplier? 'That's what they want to know. That's what they are asking him up there.'

As light began to break over Hamburg, Heidemann's defiance at last started to wilt. He was forced to accept that journalists from rival organizations would soon be swarming over Stuttgart. 'We simply cannot cling to the principle of protecting our informants any longer,' said Walde. At 5 a.m., Heidemann handed over 'Herr Fischer's' home telephone number. 'He used to live in Ditzingen,' said Heidemann, but he'd moved a year ago. 'I said to him: "Give me your new address", but he refused to give it to me so we always spoke on the telephone.' This was the break *Stern* needed. At 5 a.m., Seufert called the head of the magazine's Frankfurt office and told him to try to trace the owner of the number.

Was it possible, someone asked, that 'Herr Fischer' had forged everything?

'He can't have forged it,' replied Heidemann. 'He's far too primitive.'

THIRTY

Stern was given a predictable savaging in the West German press the following day. One paper denounced the magazine for its 'megalomania' in claiming it would rewrite the history of the Nazi era, 'as if this history had not already been written by the sixty million victims of the Second World War'. Another called the scoop 'a stinking bubble from the brown swamp'. An editorial in *Die Welt* summed up what seemed to be the mood of the entire country:

> Two days before the thirty-eighth anniversary of the Nazi defeat on 8 May 1945, one thing is certain: the history books on Hitler and the Third Reich will not be rewritten. Hitler's diaries, which *Stern* presented to the world at enormous cost in money and wordage, are a forgery. . . . Mr Zimmermann is to be thanked for the fact that this upsurge of sensationalism, involving a massive attempt to falsify history, has been stopped in its tracks. Fortunately, the matter has been clarified before irreparable damage was done to the consciousness of the German people and the world.

It was clear that some heads from within *Stern* would have to be offered up to appease public opinion; the only question was – whose heads should they be?

Early on Saturday morning, Schulter-Hillen telephoned Reinhard Mohn and submitted his resignation. Mohn refused it. 'You do not carry the main responsibility,' he told him. Throughout the morning, members of the boards of Gruner and Jahr and Bertelsmann telephoned Schulte-Hillen to pledge their support. By lunchtime there was a clear consensus that the editors rather than management should face the consequences of the disaster. Koch arrived back from New York to find Nannen, Schulte-Hillen, Gillhausen and Schmidt locked in conference in Nannen's office, passing the poisoned chalice from one to another. Schulte-Hillen had the backing of Mohn, therefore he was excused. Nannen was already in semi-retirement. Gillhausen was responsible only for the design of the magazine. . . . Koch quickly realized that it was he and Schmidt who were expected to drink. At 2 p.m., a lawyer was called in to represent them, as the meeting turned from a general discussion into a specific negotiation over severance pay.

It seems grossly unfair that Koch and Schmidt – who had never trusted Heidemann and who might, indeed, have dismissed him in 1981 – were made to carry the responsibility for the collapse of what had always been the management's scoop. Certainly, the two editors felt this to be the case, and their threats to take the issue to an industrial tribunal brought each of them enormous financial compensation: 3.5 million marks (more than $1 million) each, pre-tax, acording to the *Stern Report*, conditional on a pledge of secrecy that they would not reveal the story of how the diaries affair had been handled within the company.

In London, the two diary volumes handed over to the *Sunday Times* had quickly been confirmed as forgeries. Dr Julius Grant, the forensic scientist who had established that the Mussolini diaries were forgeries, took only five hours to locate traces of post-war whitener in the paper. Norman Stone, one of Hitler's most recent biographers and one of the few scholars in Britain who could read the outdated German script, rapidly concluded that the diaries were fakes. There were inconsistencies and misspellings; above all, the diaries were full of trivia and absurd repetitions. On 30 January 1933, the day upon which Hitler assumed power, the diarist had recorded:

> We must at once proceed to build up as fast as possible the power we have won. I must at once proceed to the dissolution of the Reichstag, and so I can build up my power. We will not give up our power, let there come what may.

'This reads almost like a "Charlie Chaplin" Hitler,' wrote Stone. The *Sunday Times* itself admitted that nothing 'had prepared us for such an anticlimax'.

In Frank Giles's absence, it fell to his deputy, Brian Mac-Arthur, somehow to frame an explanation for the behaviour of the newspaper, whose front page headlines had changed in two weeks from 'World Exclusive: The secrets of Hitler's war' to 'The Hitler Diaries: the hunt for the forger'. The statement which eventually appeared probably earned the paper more derision than anything else it had done in the past two weeks. 'Serious journalism', it began, 'is a high-risk enterprise.' It went on:

> By our own lights we did not act irresponsibly. When major but hazardous stories seem to be appearing, a newspaper can either dismiss them without inquiry or pursue investigations to see if they are true. No one would dispute that the emergence of authentic diaries written by Adolf Hitler would be an event of public interest and historic importance.
>
> Our mistake was to rely on other people's evidence. . . .

The statement ended:

> In a sense we are relieved that the matter has been so conclusively settled. A not-proven verdict would have raised difficult problems about publication.

This remarkable piece of self-justification masquerading as apology was subsequently attacked by a number of writers.

The Hitler diaries affair was not an example of 'serious journalism', but of cheque-book journalism, pure and simple. And, as has become clear since, a 'not-proven verdict' would probably have led the *Sunday Times* to continue serialization: Murdoch's 55–45 formula required the balance of probability to tilt decisively *against* authenticity. To add to the paper's embarrassment, its colour supplement had already been distributed containing a twelve-page pictorial guide to Hitler's career: it was too late to recall.

'What has happened to the *Sunday Times*?' asked an article in the *New York Times*, commenting on this front page statement. 'Rupert Murdoch has, for one thing, with his talent for turning what he touches into dross.' Murdoch himself has been quoted as making three comments on the affair:

> 'Nothing ventured, nothing gained.'
> 'After all, we are in the entertainment business.'
> 'Circulation went up and stayed up. We didn't lose money or anything like that.'

The last statement is certainly true. *Stern* returned to News International all the money it paid for the diaries, and the *Sunday Times* retained 20,000 of the 60,000 new readers it acquired when it began publishing the scoop.

When he had first heard that the diaries were forgeries, Gerd Heidemann had managed to cope with the news relatively calmly. The finality of the verdict had not sunk in. He still clung to the hope that the Bundesarchiv might be wrong. But by Sunday he was suffering from a bad case of delayed shock. His confidence had been shattered by his rough treatment overnight in the *Stern* building. And that, he realized, was only the beginning. Now that his three-year-old dream of bringing Hitler's testament to the world was in ruins, it would simply be a matter of time before questions began to be asked about what had happened to the money.

He later testified that his depression was such that he had considered shooting himself: he did, after all, have Hitler's so-called 'suicide weapon' and five bullets with which to do it. For part of the weekend he lay, in a state of collapse, in the lower of the family's two apartments, refusing to move. Barbara Dickmann telephoned from Rome to find out what was happening and was shocked by Heidemann's emotional state: 'He was crying, emphasizing again and again that it would become clear that most of the diaries were genuine, that I had to trust him, that he hadn't landed me in it.'

On Sunday morning, having not heard a word from Heidemann for more than twenty-four hours, Thomas Walde, Leo Pesch and Michael Seufert set out to try to find him. 'We were worried that he might be suicidal,' recalled Walde. They tried telephoning him, but there was no answer. They drove over to *Carin II*; the yacht was deserted. At about midday, they turned up outside the Heidemanns' Elbchaussee home. 'We rang the bell,' said Pesch later. 'His elder daughter appeared at the window. After much toing and froing, the door was finally opened and we were let into the flat by Frau Heidemann.' The three men told her they needed to speak to her husband. Gina said that he was staying with friends somewhere in Hamburg; she would fetch him. The *Stern* reporters were left alone while she went downstairs, apparently to try to persuade her husband to come out of his hiding place in the apartment below. Ten minutes later, the doorbell rang.

'I looked through the spyhole,' related Pesch, 'and I saw Heidemann, in his shirt sleeves, lying crumpled up on the floor by the steps. He was groaning, "Open up, open up." His wife was next to him and was trying to get him to his feet. I opened the door and Heidemann – who didn't seem able to stand – staggered to a chair and dropped into it. He was crying and choking. It was about ten minutes before he could speak.'

Heidemann presented a wretched spectacle, but his colleagues' visit was not principally motivated by concern for his health. *Stern* had been working flat out since dawn on Saturday to piece together the story of the hoax. Using information and the telephone number supplied by Heidemann, the magazine's reporters had located 'Fischer's' home and shop and found them shuttered and deserted; neighbours said that Conny and Edith had gone away. *Stern* had soon established that 'Fischer's' real name was Kujau and that his highly placed East German relatives – the museum keepers and the general – were, respectively, a municipal caretaker and a railway porter. Walde, Pesch and Seufert were under instructions to obtain more information and once Heidemann had regained his composure, they began asking him the same old questions all over again.

Seufert produced a photograph of Kujau which the magazine had already obtained from his family in East Germany. Was this 'Fischer'? Heidemann replied immediately that it was. Seufert told him that the man's real name was Kujau. According to Pesch: 'Heidemann assured us – and I believed him – that this was the first time he'd heard the name Kujau.' The questioning went on until seven o'clock in the evening and resumed again at midday on Monday.

In the interim, Heidemann received a telephone call from Kujau. The forger told him he was calling from a telephone box in Czechoslovakia where he was still trying to locate the score of *Die Meistersinger*. Heidemann taped the call. He was desperate. He told Kujau that the diaries were fakes. 'Who could have forged so much?' he demanded.

'Oh my God,' wailed Kujau, 'oh my God.'

Heidemann told him that they would both probably end up in prison.

'Shit,' exclaimed Kujau. 'You mean we've already been connected?'

'*Stern*'s going to file charges against me for sure,' said Heidemann. 'The papers are saying that I did it.'

'That's impossible.'

'Come on,' pleaded Heidemann. 'Where did you get the books from?'

'They're from East Germany, man.'

Heidemann confronted him with *Stern*'s revelation that he had lied about his relatives in East Germany.

Kujau admitted it, but said that it hadn't been his idea: 'they' had made him do it.

Heidemann later replayed this conversation with Kujau to Leo Pesch during the interrogation on Monday. 'It wasn't at all clear who "they" were supposed to be,' Pesch recalled, 'and Heidemann didn't press him. . . . During the telephone conversation, Heidemann kept referring to the Wagner opera score. He still seemed to believe that Kujau had delivered him some genuine material.'

Reporters and photographers had been lurking around the Heidemanns' home for several days. By Tuesday Heidemann had recovered sufficiently to invite them in for an impromptu press conference. Dozens of journalists jammed into his study, pinning Heidemann against a bookcase full of works on the Third Reich. Accompanied by his lawyer, he was described as looking 'drained' and 'subdued'. He was asked why he was still refusing publicly to identify the diaries' supplier. 'Because this man was probably also deceived,' replied Heidemann. 'He is trying on his own to clear up where they came from and if they are forgeries. While he is investigating the affair for me and while I still have some faith in him, I cannot betray his name to the public.' He would not comment on rumours that the man's name was Fischer.

The same day, *Stern* announced that Heidemann had been

'summarily fired' and Henri Nannen disclosed that the company would be pressing charges with the Hamburg State Prosecutor for fraud. Nannen said that, in his opinion, Heidemann had always believed in the diaries, but had been blinded by 'dollar signs in his eyes' and had stolen at least some of the magazine's money. 'Heidemann has not just been deceived,' he told reporters, 'he too is a deceiver.' Nannen also revealed that *Stern* had paid more than 9 million marks for the diaries.

A few hours later, the West German television programme *Panorama*, presented by Stefan Aust, scooped *Stern* by two days and named Heidemann's source as Konrad Fischer, alias Konrad Kujau.

Needless to say, Kujau had not been in Czechoslovakia hunting for the score of *Die Meistersinger* when he rang Heidemann on Monday. He was in the Austrian industrial town of Dornbirn, close to the Bavarian border, holed up in the home of Maria Modritsch's parents. Conditions were cramped and the atmosphere was understandably tense. 'Conny and Edith slept together,' said Maria, 'and I slept in the living room.'

Kujau's plan had been to stay away from Stuttgart until things cooled off. But it quickly became apparent that this was not going to happen – indeed, things were hotting up. Kujau was sitting watching the Modritschs' television when his picture was flashed on the screen as the man who had allegedly supplied Heidemann with the Hitler diaries. When it was also announced that *Stern* had paid out 9 million marks for the material, Kujau shot out of his chair. *Nine million marks*? He had received only a quarter of that sum. The deceiver had been deceived. The forger was full of moral outrage at Heidemann's dishonesty. 'He was bitterly upset,' recalled Edith. Kujau was certain that the reporter, believing him to be behind the Iron Curtain looking for the Wagner opera, had deliberately betrayed him: once his name was known, he would then never have been able to get back over the border; he would have conveniently disappeared into the clutches of the secret police, leaving Heidemann to enjoy the millions of marks which should rightfully have been Kujau's – such, at least, was the forger's conviction.

Kujau telephoned his lawyer in Stuttgart and learned that the Hamburg State Prosecutor was looking for him and proposed to raid his home and shop. It was clear that it was all over. On Friday 13 May Dietrich Klein of the Hamburg Prosecutor's office, accompanied by a group of police, broke into Kujau's premises and, watched by a crowd of reporters, began removing evidence: ten cartons and two plastic sacks full of books about Hitler, correspondence, newspaper cuttings, a signed copy of *Mein Kampf* and artist's materials. There were also Nazi uniforms, military decorations, swastikas and photographs. Screwed to the wall above the entrance to Kujau's collection was a coat of arms with the motto 'Fearless and True'.

Klein was in Kujau's house, sifting through his property, when the telephone rang. 'This is Klein speaking,' said the prosecutor. 'This is Kujau speaking,' came the reply. Kujau told the official that he understood he wanted to speak to him. He was willing to come forward voluntarily. He told Klein he would meet him at a border post on the Austrian frontier early the following morning.

At 8 a.m. on Saturday, Kujau said goodbye to Edith and Maria and made his way to the German border where Klein was waiting with a warrant for his arrest.

Kujau had agreed to give himself up. He had not agreed to tell the truth. During the long journey north to Hamburg he asked the prosecutor what would happen to him. According to Kujau, Klein told him that if he was not the man who wrote the diaries, he would be free in ten days; if he was: 'It could take a long time.'

'I decided', said Kujau afterwards, 'to tell him Grimms' fairy stories.'

Kujau's tale – which he stuck to throughout the next week – was that he was simply a middleman: the idea that he was the forger of the diaries he dismissed as 'absurd'. He claimed to have met a man known only as 'Mirdorf' in East Germany in 1978 who had offered to supply him with Hitler material. In this way, Kujau said he had obtained a diary and given it to Fritz Stiefel. Later, when Heidemann had heard about the story, he had pressured him to provide more diaries. Kujau told the prosecutor that as a result he had renewed his contract with Mirdorf, who had promised to obtain them. The books had then emerged from East Germany over the next two years through another man called Lauser. Above all, Kujau denied emphatically the allegation that he had been given 9 million marks for the books. He had passed on no more than 2.5 million, of which he had taken 300,000 in commission.

Kujau's story sounded wildly improbable, and Klein had no difficulty in demolishing large sections of it almost at once. For example, when Maria Modritsch was interrogated, two days after her lover's arrest, she identified the shadowy 'Mr Lauser' not as a Swiss businessman but as 'a man who used to come to the Sissy Bar to fix the juke box'. And if Kujau had not been aware that the diaries were forged, demanded Klein, why did he have in his house more than six hundred carefully marked books and newspaper articles detailing Adolf Hitler's daily movements? And why had the police also found several empty notebooks identical to the so-called diaries?

The questions were unanswerable. But what eventually proved most effective in breaking Kujau's resistance was the image the police could conjure up of Heidemann. Whilst he languished in prison, the reporter was still enjoying his free-dom in Hamburg, telling everyone he had handed over all the money to Kujau. The idea of it was intolerable. On Thursday, 26 May, his thirteenth day in custody, Kujau confessed in writing to having forged more than sixty volumes of Hitler's diaries. To prove his guilt, he wrote out part of his confession in the same gothic script he had used in the diaries. As a final, malicious embellishment, he added that Heidemann had known about the forgery all along.

It had been clear to Heidemann for some time that he had become the subject of a criminal investigation. Within hours of Kujau's arrest, on Saturday, 14 May the Hamburg police had raided the family's home on the Elbchausee along with his archive in Milchstrasse; *Carin II* had also been searched and impounded. Heidemann's collection of Nazi memorabilia and many of his private papers were seized. Four days later, the police carried out a second raid. It turned up 'nothing new' according to the prosecutor's office, but it made it obvious to Heidemann that his days of freedom were drawing to a close.

He read of Kujau's arrest in the newspapers and reacted to the growing rumours that 'Conny' was the forger with incre-dulity. 'I don't believe it at all,' he told Reuters: Kujau would have had to have been a 'wonder boy' to have forged so much. 'If these diaries are not genuine,' Heidemann confided to his friend Randolph Braumann, 'then there must – somewhere – be some genuine ones. Kujau cannot have made it all up alone – all those complicated historical situations. Maybe Kujau copied them up from genuine diaries which still exist somewhere.'

Heidemann told Braumann that he was feeling 'completely *kaputt*, flat out' and Gina warned him that her husband was 'terribly depressed'. The company Mercedes had been taken away; their credit cards had been cancelled; they were social lepers. Braumann felt very sorry for them. On Monday, 23 May he rang and invited the couple round for a drink that evening. Gina doubted whether Heidemann would leave the flat. 'He's depressed again,' she said.

The Heidemanns eventually turned up at 10.30 p.m., and stayed drinking with Braumann and his wife until three o'clock the next morning. Heidemann was listless and full of self-pity. The other three tried to make him pull himself together, but he simply sat slumped in his chair, shaking his head. 'Everything seems to have collapsed at the same time,' he complained. 'Everything has crumbled. If only a scientist would appear and prove that the diaries, or at least some of them, were genuine.'

Braumann said that what was so astonishing was that the diaries were such primitive forgeries. Heidemann said that it was easy to say that now: 'But I never doubted. It all seemed to fit together so well. One thing followed another: first the Hitler pictures, then the things that he'd painted in his youth, then the writing from his time in Vienna, then his application to the school of art and his rejection by the professors – everything genuine, everything proven; then the positive results on the diaries. No one ever dreamed it could all have been forged.'

Braumann asked about the two police raids.

'They've taken everything away,' said Heidemann. 'Documents, photographs, all the paperwork – everything, without a receipt.'

'He was really apathetic,' recalled Braumann, 'like a man who had seen all his hopes and dreams destroyed. He didn't drink very much. His thoughts seemed to be stuck in a groove, going round and round on the subject of where the diaries came from, whether they were genuine or whether they were false.'

'I don't want to be remembered,' said Heidemann, 'as the man responsible for the greatest flop in newspaper history.'

Braumann promised to do all he could to help Heidemann, but time had run out. Three days later, Kujau implicated him in the forgery and at 10 p.m. on the night of Thursday, 26 May the reporter was arrested at his home and taken into custody.

A variety of theories have been advanced to explain the origin of the Hitler diaries. Radio Moscow alleged that the whole affair was a CIA plot 'intended to exonerate and glorify the Third Reich'. The CIA, claimed the Russians, had provided the information contained in the diaries and trained the forger. Its aim was 'to divert the attention of the West German public from the vital problems of the country prior to the deployment of new US missiles' and to discredit the normally left-wing *Stern*. In this version of events, Kujau was an American stooge:

> Half a century ago the Nazis set fire to the Reichstag building and accused the insignificant provocateur Marinus van der Lubbe of arson. Van der Lubbe was supposed to provide proof against the communists, and he did. Now, another van der Lubbe has been found, a small-time dealer, possessed by the mad idea of going down in history, psychologically as unstable as van der Lubbe. Even now the West German bourgeois press predicts that this new van der Lubbe will testify against East Germany. This is not just the normal style of the CIA: one clearly also detects the hand of the [West German] intelligence service and the Munich provocateurs from the circle around Franz Josef Strauss.

(The fact that the writer Fritz Tobias had established more than twenty years previously that the Nazis did not set fire to the Reichstag, and that the blaze *was* the work of van der Lubbe, is apparently still not officially accepted by the Soviet

Union.) The Hitler diaries, wrote *Izvestia*, 'parted the curtains a little to reveal the morals of the Western "free press" and the political morality of bourgeois society'.

Henri Nannen, on the other hand, told the *New York Times* that in his view the affair could have resulted from 'an interest in East Germany to spread disinformation and destabilize the Federal Republic'. According to *Stern*'s rival, *Quick*, East German intelligence concocted the diaries and transported them to the West 'to provide a spur for neo-Nazis and to resurrect the Nazi past as a means of damaging the reputation of the Federal Republic'. The West German authorities took the allegations seriously enough to ask the central police forensic laboratory to examine the diaries to see if their paper and ink could have originated in the East. The anti-communist hysteria surrounding the fraud was sufficiently widespread to be cited as a reason by the East Germans for cancelling the planned visit to Bonn of their leader, Erich Hoenecker.

Another conspiracy theory was put forward by the *Sunday Times* in December 1983 after a lengthy investigation into the hoax. According to this account, the Hitler diaries were organized as a fund-raising operation by the SS 'mutual aid society', HIAG, which pays out funds to old SS men who lost their pensions at the end of the war. Despite the paucity of evidence put forward to support its thesis, the paper stated flatly that 'most or all of the money' paid out by *Stern* 'went to HIAG'. The idea was dismissed in West Germany and since appears to have been quietly dropped by the *Sunday Times* itself: not one word has appeared in the paper about the subject since 1983.

Most of these theories about the diaries reveal more about their authors than they do about the fraud. Because the figure of Adolf Hitler overshadows the forgery, people have tended to read into it whatever they want to see. To a communist the affair is a capitalist plot; to a capitalist, a communist conspiracy; to a writer on the Third Reich, fresh evidence of the continuing hold of the Nazis on West German society. This is not surprising. Hitler has always had the capacity to reflect whatever phobia afflicts the person who stares at him – as the columnist George F. Will wrote at the height of the diaries controversy, Hitler 'is a dark mirror held up to mankind'. Equally, it flattered the victims of the fraud to believe that they were not gulled by their own paranoia and greed for sensation, but were actually the targets of a massive 'disinformation' operation or giant criminal conspiracy, trapped by something too complex, powerful and cunning to resist. How else could a successful and worldly publication like *Stern* have fallen for such obvious fakes? How else could they have paid out so much money? How else could the story have been bought by someone as shrewd as Rupert Murdoch and launched, unchecked, in such a distinguished publication as the *Sunday Times*? Anyone who took the magnitude of the fiasco as their starting point was bound to look for an appropriately sophisticated plot as the only possible explanation. When Konrad Kujau crawled out from beneath the wreckage of *Stern*'s million-dollar syndication deals, people refused to believe that such an odd individual could be responsible.

There are many unanswered questions relating to Kujau, of which the most important are how and why did he learn to forge Nazi documents with such skill; his craftsmanship certainly suggests that at some stage he may have learned his trade by working for someone else. But, although it is possible that Kujau may have had an accomplice to help him write the diaries, it would appear, on present evidence, that there was no extensive conspiracy to rob *Stern*. The fraud swelled to the proportions it did only because of the incompetence displayed within Gruner and Jahr. How could anyone possibly have guessed in advance that the magazine would have behaved so foolishly? The editors, presented with a *fait accompli*, relied upon the management; the management relied upon Heidemann and Walde; Heidemann and Walde relied upon Kujau; and between them all, they managed to bungle the process of authentication. A competent forensic scientist would have established in less than a day that the diaries were forgeries: any conspirators would have been aware of that. Only the uncovenanted stupidity of *Stern*, along with a series of flukes, prevented the fraud from being exposed long before publication. The Hitler diaries affair is a monument to the cock-up theory of history. If HIAG or some similar group had really been so desperate for 9 million marks as to contemplate crime, they would have been far better served to have staged an old-fashioned bank raid.

But money need not have been the only motive behind the appearance of the diaries. It has also been suggested that they were concocted in an attempt to rehabilitate Hitler. Gitta Sereny, responsible for the *Sunday Times* investigation, has claimed that the diaries' content is 'totally beyond' Kujau's abilities, that a 'coherent psycho-political line' emerges, presenting Hitler as 'a reasonable and lonely man'. The suggestion is that Kujau was told what to write by someone else: the candidate put forward by the *Sunday Times* was Medard Klapper, 'the central organizer of the conspiracy'. Again, this now seems highly improbable. In the first place, it greatly exaggerates the sophistication of the diaries. They read like the handiwork of a fairly uneducated man, obsessively interested in Hitler, who has cobbled together whatever he can lay his hands on from the published sources – they read, in other words, like the handiwork of Konrad Kujau. Secondly, the idea that Medard Klapper of all people might be the political brain behind the whitewashing of Hitler seems somewhat unlikely. Is the man who promised to introduce Heidemann to Martin Bormann once he had undergone a

'*Sippung*' any more credible as an author of the diaries than Kujau? HIAG would have had to be desperate.

But above all, it is the crudity of the forgery which belies the idea that it might be the product of a Nazi conspiracy. If this was a serious attempt to present an untarnished Hitler, one would at least have expected the conspirators to have taken some elementary precautions. They would not have used paper containing chemical whitener; they would have avoided such Kujau touches as plastic initials and red cord made of polyester and viscose; they would not have relied so completely on the work of Max Domarus as to have copied out his errors.

What *is* sobering is to speculate on what might have happened if these precautions *had* been taken. After all, *Stern* and News International stopped publication only because of the conclusiveness of the forensic tests carried out in the first week of May. If those tests had found nothing substantially wrong, the diaries would have been printed and would now stand as an historical source. No doubt they would have been dismissed by most serious scholars, but nevertheless they would have been bought and read by millions. Thomas Walde and Leo Pesch would have produced their book on Rudolf Hess and become rich men; Gerd Heidemann would have retired with his Nazi memorabilia to southern Spain; and Konrad Kujau, ex-forger of luncheon vouchers, having thrown students of the Third Reich into turmoil, would no doubt have continued flooding the market with faked Hitler memorabilia.

Instead of which, on Tuesday, 21 August 1984, after more than a year in custody, Heidemann and Kujau were led out of their cells and into a courtroom incandescent with television lights and photographers' flash bulbs to stand trial for fraud. Heidemann was accused of having stolen at least 1.7 million of the 9.3 million marks handed over by *Stern* to pay for the diaries. Kujau was charged with having received at least 1.5 million marks. Edith Lieblang, although not being held in prison, was also required to attend court with her lawyer, accused of helping to spend Kujau's illegal earnings.

The two men had both been transformed by the events of the past sixteen months. Heidemann looked worn out and seedy. He had grown a beard in captivity which only gave further emphasis to the unhealthy prison pallor of his skin. His first act on arriving in the courtroom was to head for the corner. When anyone spoke to him, he would look away. It was common knowledge that he had suffered some kind of nervous collapse in jail.

Kujau, in contrast, had developed into something of a star. He had sold his life story to *Bild Zeitung* for 100,000 marks. He gave regular television interviews from his prison cell. He slapped backs, exchanged jokes with his warders, kissed female reporters, and happily signed autographs 'Adolf Hitler'. And he lied: expertly, exuberantly and constantly. Every reporter who interviewed him came away with a forged diary entry as a souvenir and a different version of his career. He drove Heidemann mad with frustration. While the reporter sat alone in his cell, poring over a meticulous card-index of the events of the past three years, trying to work out what had happened, he could hear Kujau regaling a reporter with some new account of his adventures; occasionally, like a tormented beast, Heidemann would let out a howl of rage. He would not speak to Kujau; he would not look at him. It was a far cry from the days when Gerd and Gina and Conny and Edith would meet and toast with champagne their good fortune at having met one another.

On its opening day, the Hitler diaries trial drew an audience of 100 reporters, 150 photographers and television crewmen and around sixty members of the public. It was front page news for the first couple of days; thereafter interest dwindled until eventually the audience numbered only a half dozen regular court reporters and a handful of curious day trippers. The proceedings became so monotonous that in the middle of September one of the magistrates had to be replaced because of a chronic inability to stay awake.

Heidemann denied stealing any of *Stern*'s money. However, from his private papers and known bank accounts, the prosecution had no difficulty in establishing that he had spent almost 2 million marks more than he had earned since 1981, even allowing for the 1.5 million marks paid to him as 'compensation' for obtaining the diaries. The prosecutor also told the court that, although he would only be attempting to prove the smaller figure, he believed Heidemann could have stolen as much as 4.6 million marks. Heidemann's defence was that the money had been paid to him by four anonymous investors as payment for a stake in one of the reporter's Nazi treasure hunts. As Heidemann refused to name these gentlemen, his story lacked credibility. His defence lawyers managed to persuade the court to accept as evidence a series of tape recordings made by Heidemann of his telephone conversations with Kujau. These had been edited together by the reporter and effectively proved his contention that he had not known the diaries were forged. Unfortunately, whenever the discussions turned to the matter of payments, the tapes abruptly ended, strengthening the prosecution's case that Heidemann had not handed over all of the money.

Kujau's defence was handled by a lawyer of feline skill and left-wing opinions named Kurt Groenewold. At first sight Groenewold was an unlikely choice to defend a Nazi-obsessed forger: he was one of West Germany's leading radical lawyers, a friend of the Baader-Meinhof group, a solicitor who numbered among his clients the CIA 'whistleblower' Philip Agee. But it turned out to be an inspired partnership.

Groenewold's defence of Kujau was based on the argument that he was a small-time con man who had been lured into forging the Hitler diaries only by the enormous sums offered by the capitalists from Bertelsmann. Whilst Groenewold dragged *Stern* into the centre of the proceedings, exposing the negligence which had allowed the fraud to reach the proportions it did, Kujau was able to play the role of a likeable rogue whose cheerfully amateurish work had been exploited by the salesmen from Hamburg.

On Monday, 8 July 1985 the media returned in force to Hamburg to record the verdict. After presiding over ninety-four sessions of testimony from thirty-seven different witnesses, the judge found all the defendants guilty. Heidemann was sentenced to four years and eight months in prison. Kujau received four years and six months. Edith Lieblang was given a suspended sentence of one year. The judge said he could detect no evidence of a wider conspiracy. *Stern*, he announced, had acted with such recklessness that it was virtually an accomplice in the hoax.

More than two years had passed since the diaries were declared forgeries. More than 5 million marks of *Stern*'s money remained – and, at the time of writing, remains – unaccounted for.

The Hitler diaries affair had a traumatic effect upon *Stern*. Its offices were occupied by journalists protesting at the management's appointment of two new conservative editors. There were hundreds of abusive letters and phone calls. The overwhelmingly left-wing staff found themselves being greeted on the telephone by shouts of 'Heil Hitler!' Politicians treated them as a laughing stock; prominent West Germans pulled out of interviews; young East German pacifists refused to cooperate with a planned *Stern* feature article on the ground that the magazine was 'a Hitler sheet'. Circulation slumped.

Before the scandal, the magazine reckoned to sell around 1.7 million copies. This figure climbed to a record 2.1 million in the week in which the diaries' discovery was announced. After the revelation that they were forgeries, circulation fell back to less than 1.5 million. Apart from the loss of advertising and sales revenue, the cost to the magazine was estimated by the *Stern Report* as 19 million marks: 9.34 million for the diaries; 1.5 million for Heidemann; 7 million (before tax) as compensation to the two sacked editors; and miscellaneous costs, including agents' fees, publicity and the expense of destroying thousands of copies containing the second instalment of the Hess serialization.

Gradually, most of the main participants in the story left the magazine. Dr Jan Hensmann departed at the end of 1983 to become a visiting professor at the University of Munster. Wilfried Sorge resigned in the spring of 1984 to run a small publishing company. Thomas Walde left Hamburg to work in another outpost of the Bertelsmann empire. Leo Pesch went to Munich to work for *Vogue*. Manfred Fischer, who initiated the purchase of the diaries, is currently the chief executive of the Dornier aircraft corporation. Felix Schmidt is now editing the main West German television guide. Peter Koch, at the time of writing, has not re-entered full-time employment. Gerd Schulte-Hillen, however, *is* still the managing director of Gruner and Jahr: he must be a very good manager indeed.

In Britain, Frank Giles returned from his holiday to find himself the target of a vicious whispering campaign. In June 1983, 'after discussions with Mr Rupert Murdoch', it was announced that he was to retire prematurely as editor and assume the honorific title of editor emeritus. According to a story which did the rounds at the time, Giles asked what the title meant. 'It's Latin, Frank,' Murdoch is said to have replied. 'The "e" means you're out, and the "meritus" means you deserve it.'

Newsweek, which ran the Hitler diaries on its front cover for three successive weeks, was widely criticized for its behaviour. 'The impression created with the aid of provocative newspaper and television advertising', said Robert J. McCloskey, the ombudsman of the *Washington Post*, 'was that the entire story was authentic.' The morality of selling Hitler 'bothered us', confessed Mrs Katherine Graham. William Broyles appeared to disagree: 'We feel very, very good about how we handled this,' he told the *New York Times*. Seven months later, he resigned as *Newsweek*'s editor. Maynard Parker who had been expected to succeed him, was passed over. Insiders blamed the Hitler diaries. 'That episode killed Parker,' said one. 'There were expressions of high-echelon support, but it was poor judgement and everyone knew it.'

In the aftermath of the Hitler diaries affair, David Irving's American publishers tripled the print run of his edition of the Führer's medical diaries. Excerpts were published in Murdoch's *New York Post* and in the *National Enquirer*. But all publicity is not necessarily good publicity: not long afterwards Irving was arrested by the Austrian police in Vienna on suspicion of neo-Nazi activity and deported from the country; he is still banned from entry.

In 1985, Hugh Trevor-Roper published a collection of his work entitled *Renaissance Essays*. It was hailed by most critics as 'brilliant'. The Hitler diaries, tactfully, were not mentioned.

Fritz Stiefel, Kujau's best customer until Heidemann appeared, announced that he would not be suing the forger for damages. 'I have one of the biggest collections of fakes in the world,' he said, 'and that, too, is worth something.'

Adolf Hitler as Painter and Draughtsman by Billy F. Price and August Priesack was banned in West Germany, but appeared in the United States at the end of 1984 as *Adolf*

Hitler: The Unknown Artist. A large section of it was the work of Konrad Kujau, but it would have cost a fortune to rip out the fakes and reprint the book. The Kujaus therefore were left sprinkled amongst the Hitlers, and nobody, apparently, cared: 'Even the suspect pictures', claimed a limp note of explanation in the book's introduction, 'generally reflect Hitler's known style.' The remark echoes that made by *Newsweek* about the Hitler diaries: 'Genuine or not, it almost doesn't matter in the end'.

Perhaps it doesn't. Certainly, the trade in Nazi relics has not been depressed by the revelations of wholesale forgery thrown up in the aftermath of the diaries affair. Shortly before Christmas 1983, Christies of New York auctioned seven pages of notes made by Hitler in 1930 for which the purchasers, Neville Rare Books, paid $22,000. In London, Phillips, Son & Neale, fine art auctioneers since 1796, held a sale entitled 'Third Reich Memorabilia' which netted over £100,000. Four small Hitler paintings, at least one of which had the look of a genuine Kujau about it, raised £11,500. Also up for sale were such curiosities as Reichsführer SS Heinrich Himmler's vanity case, removed from his body after his suicide and described in the catalogue as 'a small leather vanity wallet with fitted compartments containing comb, metal mirror, penknife by Chiral with gilt niello-work to sides, the wallet embossed in gold "RF-SS"'. Meanwhile, at the other end of the scale, operating from his garage in Maryland, Mr Charles Snyder continued to sell locks of Eva Braun's hair, allegedly scraped from her comb by an American officer who looted her apartment in Munich.

Here, rather than in any grand conspiracy, lies the origin of the Hitler diaries affair. Why would anyone pay $3500 for a few strands of human hair of dubious authenticity? Because, presumably, *he* might have touched them, as he might have touched the odd scrap of paper, or painting, or piece of uniform – talismans which have been handed down and sold and hoarded, to be brought out and touched occasionally, as if the essence of the man somehow lived on in them. The Hitler diaries, shabby forgeries, composed for the most part of worthless banalities, were no different. 'It was a very special thing to hold such a thing in your hand,' said Manfred Fischer, trying to explain the fascination which he and his colleagues felt when the first volume arrived. 'To think that this diary was written by *him* – and now I have it in my grasp. . . .' After millions of dollars, two years, and a great deal more stroking and sniffing in offices and bank vaults, the diaries appeared, and have now taken their place as one of the most extraordinary frauds in history – a phenomenon which Chaucer's Pardoner, six centuries ago, with his pillow cases and pig's bones, would have recognized at once.

GOOD AND FAITHFUL SERVANT

The unauthorized biography of
BERNARD INGHAM

For my mother and father

CONTENTS

PREFACE

'Albion'

'... what greatly concerns me and many other Socialists is that there are thousands of highly moral, upright and indeed religious people who are nevertheless Tory to the bone. They are quite frankly enigmas to simple souls like me.'

BERNARD INGHAM, 1965[1]

One day towards the end of February 1964 a small left-wing magazine in the north of England acquired the services of a new columnist. The *Leeds Weekly Citizen* was the journal of that city's Labour Party. The columnist was anonymous. He signed himself simply 'Albion'. As time passed, Albion's outspoken views became famous among local party members. He was at once a familiar and yet mysterious fixture on the Leeds socialist scene. His articles, 800 to 1,000 words long, ran almost every week for more than three years until suddenly, in April 1967, as abruptly as he had surfaced, Albion vanished.

This gentleman (for gentleman he clearly was) begged a number of questions, of which the most obvious was his choice of pseudonym. 'Albion' is the ancient and poetical name for Great Britain: the sort of alias one might expect to see adopted by some mystical, flag-draped, right-wing nationalist. But the Leeds Albion was not that sort of chap at all. In his first column he declared himself proudly to be 'a politically active trade unionist'.[2] In his second, he attacked Britain's possession of nuclear weapons, calling the Conservative Prime Minister, Sir Alec Douglas-Home, a 'political fossil ... dangerous ... bomb-happy'. By column number three, Home ('the incurable waffler') had been rechristened 'Sir Alec Strangelove'.

> He suffers, in particular, from the disability of arrogance, which is an hereditary, though not exclusive, disease of those reared in the main forelock-touching belts of Great Britain. (13 March 1964)

Home was not the only member of the 'terrible Tory tribe' to feel the thud of Albion's pen between his shoulder blades. When Home's successor as Conservative leader, Edward Heath, made a speech, he apparently 'revealed his party's stagnant mind in all its revolting crudity'. The Chancellor of the Exchequer, Reginald Maudling, was an 'arthritic slug' who 'should hang down his head and cry'. The Minister for Science and Technology, the once and future Lord Hailsham, was usually referred to simply as 'Mr Quintin "Bonkers" Hogg'. As for Enoch Powell, even before his notorious 'rivers of blood' speech, he was 'an anarchist without the sense he was born with ... a menace to civilized society'.[3] Albion, it soon became apparent, did not discriminate much between Tories. He loathed them all:

> As a party they do not give a tinker's cuss for the consequences of Capitalism – the crawling anthill of the South-East and the under-employed, under-privileged muckheap of the North – until they become electorally dangerous. (10 April 1964)

> In the Tory state of the future it is obviously intended that we should all be crawling madly over each other after tax concessions like ants in search of building materials. Our motivating

force is not to be anything more than hard cash; not a vision of a better future for society, brighter hope for a largely down-trodden world, a worthier, fuller corporate life. Not on your Nelly. Just a bit more filthy lucre for yourself if you're pre-pared to flog your guts out for it.

Well, I can tell you one who won't have any truck with this sort of apology for existence, not to mention life, if he can avoid it. And that's me. I don't mind flogging my guts out. I don't even mind a bit more filthy lucre for myself.

But Ted Heath and his bandits are not going to have the privilege of treating me like a gormless greyhound. For that is what I would be if I fell for their diabolical plan.

Under their scheme I – and millions like me – would be like the greyhound given the essentially hopeless task of running against the elite who are also given 10 yards start. (22 October 1965)

What it amounts to is this: we are to establish in Britain if, God forbid, the Tories ever get the chance, two classes of citizenship – those who help themselves and those, poor dears, who either don't or can't. If you can't make the first class compartment there will be a place for you in the cattle wagon, providing, of course, you're suitably docketed ... What do they think we are? Serfs? (11 February 1966)

So who was Albion? A regular reader of his column would soon have picked up enough clues to form a rough picture. He was a north countryman. He was irascible. He had been born into a fairly poor background, brought up, he said, in a 'two-up and one-down' terrace house, 'built into a damp hillside'. He had failed his eleven-plus, an exam which he denounced as 'stupidly cruel'. He was an ardent trade unionist ('all companies – public or private – should be made to hand over audited accounts to Trade Unions who are negotiating with them so that they can really have the facts and not some managing director's fiction'). He was passionate in his commitment to full employment, which he called 'the foundation of happiness in the home'.

Sometimes he sounded like a Marxist, talking about the 'economic and social purpose of Socialism'. 'Serf' was one of his favourite words. He began one column 'Dear Fellow Serfs'; three months later, he was addressing his 'fellow slaves'. At other times he sounded more like a lay preacher, his language hinting at a chapel upbringing: for thirteen years, he thundered in July 1964, 'this nation has bowed down before the Golden Calf'. Capitalists, he maintained, 'worship on a much higher altar than Britain, mankind or even God. They have no other gods before Mammon.'[4]

As for Albion's profession, the likeliest bet appeared to be journalism. For one thing, his work seemed to take him to Conservative as well as Labour party meetings; for another, he had a journalist's preoccupation with the media. He denounced 'the Tory Press' as 'part of the Tory election machine': if it 'can convince us that the Tories are going to win,' he wrote in August 1964, 'then it will have done its job'. To correct the imbalance, he urged the creation of a socialist press: 'members of the Labour Party and the Trade Unions had better get interested in the idea of owning their own newspapers pretty quickly'. And if they didn't, Albion had another and, as it turned out, prophetic suggestion: they should employ 'full-time officials who would at least be able to try to make the most of the hostile media'.[5]

Now it is an axiom of politics that as a person gets older, so they tend to move crab-wise across the political spectrum, from left to right. But few, at first glance, can have scuttled quite so far or quite so quickly as Albion of the *Leeds Weekly Citizen*. For in 1979, twelve years after his last appearance in print as a scourge of the capitalist classes, to the astonishment of his old friends, he moved into Downing Street as Chief

Press Secretary to Margaret Thatcher, Britain's most ardently pro-capitalist Prime Minister.

That Bernard Ingham and Albion are the same person is beyond doubt. Surprisingly, it has taken a quarter of a century to put the two together. It was in January 1990 that an old colleague of Ingham suggested I try to find back copies of the now defunct *Leeds Weekly Citizen*; another recalled the pseudonym under which his column appeared. One had only to read this to know its author. 'These are facts and interpretations which I defy anyone to dismiss as prejudiced bunkum,' concluded one column on 26 August 1966. 'I may be prejudiced but I try hard not to talk balderdash.' Anyone who has ever had dealings with Ingham knows that 'bunkum and balderdash' is his favourite phrase, regularly employed to knock down some errant reporter's speculative story.

Albion's voice is unmistakably Ingham's: gruff, no-nonsense, didactic, colloquial, colourful, aggressive, humorous, chippy, sometimes surprisingly querulous. I was soon able to match internal evidence from the column with the facts of Ingham's life: for example, that he had failed his eleven-plus. His choice of pseudonym was significant. Albion was the name of the street in which the *Yorkshire Post* and, at that time, the *Guardian* had their Leeds offices; Ingham worked there from 1959 to 1965. More importantly, the 'two-up and one-down' terrace house 'built into a damp hillside', in which the columnist had grown up, turned out to be part of a small row in the Yorkshire weaving town of Hebden Bridge. Ingham's childhood home was in Albion Terrace. So when he picked his alias, he was making a proud nod not to Britain's heritage, but to his own.

How could he do it? That was the question which I encountered again and again in the north of England from people who had known Bernard Ingham when he was, in the words of one, 'the kind of bloke who would stop on the way to his own wedding to argue with someone who was rude about the Labour Party'. How could he work for Margaret Thatcher? Not just work for her, but be part of her inner circle for more than eleven years – indeed, on a twice-daily basis, in meetings with the media, become her very voice? 'I believe what I write,' Albion had asserted in 1966.[6] How, then, did a believer in full employment come to defend policies which produced more than three million unemployed? How did a man who believed in extending trade union rights come to advocate their strict curtailment? And if Albion found Home, Heath, Maudling and Hailsham impossible to stomach, how on earth could he bring himself to make common cause with a Tory Prime Minister far to the right of any of them? One purpose of this book is to trace that ideological journey: a trail, it is worth remembering, followed by millions of working-class voters in the 1970s and 1980s, many of them former Labour supporters with an upbringing similar to Ingham's. In that sense, he is representative of a type.

As to the book's theme, that is summed up in the biblical quotation which provides its title:

> Well done thou good and faithful servant: thou hast been faithful over a few things, I will make thee a ruler over many things: enter thou into the joy of thy lord. (Matthew, xxv, xxi)

Ingham was not the 'rough-spoken Yorkshire Rasputin' to whom John Biffen once jokingly referred. He was not really a Machiavelli or a Svengali or an *éminence grise* or any of the other (as he might put it) bloody foreigners to whom he was regularly compared. His role was much more that of an ultra-loyal servant; a courtier; one might almost say, a willing tool. Like one of those legendary butlers who has been with the same family for years, he would render a service before his employer had even thought of asking for it. 'Bernard is not a Conservative,' claimed one intimate of the Prime Minister.

'He is a fully paid-up member of the Thatcher Party.' He was a True Believer. He was One of Us. 'These last six years,' he told the Media Society in 1985, 'I have been able to operate with the confidence of a Prime Minister constant of purpose and resolve.' Asked what it was about her he most admired, he always answered 'guts'.

Ingham was duly rewarded for his devotion. After his arrival in Downing Street, there were three different Chancellors of the Exchequer, four Home and five Foreign Secretaries. Elections passed. Cabinet and Private Secretaries came and went (or, in the case of Mr Charles Powell, came and stayed). A hundred ministers were bundled out of the back door of Number 10, occasionally speeded on their way by a non-attributable briefing from the Chief Press Secretary. But Ingham, like his mistress and the Mississippi, just kept rolling along. By 1990 four years had elapsed since she last rejected an offer from him to resign, two years since the Civil Service last dared try to remove him. Theirs was the longest partnership between an official and a Prime Minister in British political history.

This fact alone would render Ingham a figure of interest. But in 1989, Margaret Thatcher did indeed make him 'a ruler over many things'. She placed her Chief Press Secretary at the head of the entire Government Information Service (GIS), with responsibility for the careers of all 1,200 of its members. For forty years previously, fearful of charges of politicization, care had been taken to keep the two posts separate. Moreover, through his chairmanship of the weekly Meeting of Information Officers (MIO), he had oversight of the burgeoning Whitehall advertising budget, which by 1989 was running at £168 million per annum.

Even by the standards of British democracy, a bizarre situation had now been reached. Margaret Thatcher's longest-serving official adviser, a uniquely-placed confidant, who had already held his office almost twice as long as any of his predecessors, was effectively in sole charge of the Government's propaganda machine. Ingham was so devoted to her, and she so trusted him, that he was almost an extra lobe to her brain. Ministers regularly scanned the papers to find out what he was saying about them. Some were careful about what they said in front of their own information officers lest it got back to Ingham and, through him, the Prime Minister. Yet technically he was a neutral civil servant. He was not accountable to Parliament. If he did not wish to speak to MPs, as the Westland affair showed, he did not have to do so. He was not accountable to the electorate. In fact, he took care to shield himself from its gaze. His words could not be attributed to him. His media briefings were conducted off the record at meetings which could not be televised because officially they did not exist.

It was at this point that Mr Ingham – his personality, his career, his position and his methods – suggested themselves as a legitimate subject for study. This is the result: the first biography of a British civil servant to be written whilst he was still in office.

It is not an honour which Mr Ingham has taken kindly to having thrust upon him.

The reader has a right to know the relationship between a biographer and his subject. I first met the Prime Minister's Chief Press Secretary in 1982, during research for a book about the media and the Falklands war. In 1987, I became Lobby correspondent of the *Observer* and, for the next two years, attended his weekly Downing Street briefings for the Sunday press. To me, he was consistently courteous and helpful. To him, I suspect, I must have been a regular pain in the neck – and never more so than in November 1989, when I sent him a letter telling him I intended to write this book and asking for an interview. His reply was a single sentence, polite but succinct: 'I think I would prefer that those who write books about me do so without my assistance.'

I make no complaint. In his place, I might well have said the same. Besides, on a purely practical level, I soon discovered that Mr Ingham's fondness for giving lectures laced with autobiography had already placed a surprising amount of material on the record. In addition, more than eighty friends and colleagues, past and present, were willing to give me an interview. Most asked to remain anonymous; those who did not are named in the text where appropriate. I thank them all for their time and trouble.

I would like also to record my gratitude to the staffs of the Leeds University Library, the Hebden Bridge Library, the British Newspaper Library, the West Yorkshire Archive Service, the *Hebden Bridge Times*, and the libraries of the *Guardian* newspaper, both in London and Manchester.

For helping me with advice, or for lending me various books, documents and photographs, I would like to thank Diverse Productions, Barry Flynn, Andrew Grice, Joe Haines, Ian Hellowell, Lord Houghton of Sowerby, David Hughes, Nicholas Jones, Sir Dick Knowles, Mrs Alice Longstaff, Richard Norton-Taylor, Peter Preston, Laurence Rees, Sally Soames, Neville Taylor and Donald Trelford. Anna Ford kindly gave permission to use the cartoon of Mr Ingham by her husband, the late and much-missed Mark Boxer. Tony Benn generously agreed to let me quote from his diaries.

My editor, Susanne McDadd, had the original idea for a book about Mr Ingham, was unflaggingly enthusiastic, and was ably assisted at Faber and Faber by Julian Loose. My agent, Pat Kavanagh of Peters, Fraser and Dunlop, gave good advice, as always. And my wife, Gill Hornby, read the book chapter by chapter as it was written: her suggestions made it a much better – or at any rate, a less worse – book than it would otherwise have been.

Where, despite the best efforts of those mentioned above, errors have occurred, I am solely responsible.

ONE

Dear Bernard

'The thing about you and me, Bernard, is that neither of us are
smooth people.'

MARGARET THATCHER[1]

The lights came on in the bungalow in Purley just before
6.00 a.m. By 7.00, he was at the wheel of his car – a vehicle,
paid for out of his own pocket, invariably modest, deter-
minedly British (in 1990 it was a Ford Escort). As he drove to
work through the still-quiet streets south of the Thames, he
listened to the news on Radio Four and to tapes of Elgar. By
7.30, he was at his desk on the ground floor of Downing
Street, gutting the morning's newspapers, as he had done all
his life. He began with the tabloids: 'they get my blood going'.
By 9.00 he had finished, and a secretary was typing up his
1,200-word summary of their contents for his employer.

Bernard Ingham's daily précis of the press was a staccato
compilation of snappy quotations, facts and figures. He was
punctilious about including the bad news as well as the good:
it was 'not a sanitised version,' he once explained, 'you have
to reflect the media as it is'.[2]

'There was generally a line from the leaders,' according to
one of his former assistants: '"the *Sun* calls you the Iron

Lady, the *Guardian* calls you a silly old cow" – that sort of thing. The first part consisted of items just about her; then came a section on the Government; then general matters; then economics and industrial disputes.' The moment it had been copied, the press summary was run upstairs to the Private Office. By 9.30, it was on the Prime Minister's desk. And that – unless someone, later in the day, drew her attention specifically to an article or editorial – was as close as Margaret Thatcher came to reading the papers. (Weekends were slightly different: at Chequers over breakfast she was said to glance through the *Sunday Times* and read the opinion pages of the *Sunday Telegraph*.)

According to Michael Alison, her former Parliamentary Private Secretary, she set great store by Ingham's labour-saving digests: 'She's better informed after a ten- or twenty-minute perusal of Bernard's briefings than she would be if she sat down for two hours and read the papers herself.'[3] No other Prime Minister relied on an official to interpret the press for them in this way. It placed Ingham, from the start, in a uniquely influential position – a kind of gatekeeper of information, deciding which facts were worth ushering into the Presence and which should be turned away.

On Tuesdays and Thursdays, when Parliament was in session, the press summary was finished a little earlier and formed the agenda for a morning meeting to prepare for Prime Minister's Questions. At least five people met the Prime Minister in her study. In 1990 they included Sir Brian Griffiths, the head of the Number 10 Policy Unit; Peter Morrison, her current Parliamentary Private Secretary; either Charles Powell or Andrew Turnbull from the Prime Minister's Private Office; John Whittingdale, Mrs Thatcher's young Political Adviser; and Ingham, the only member of this kitchen cabinet whose memory of such meetings went back to 1979. John Wakeham, the minister responsible for co-ordinating Government presentation, would sometimes call to offer advice. By 10.00, the group would have compiled three lists: of subjects likely to be raised by the Opposition, of information required to make an effective counter-attack, and of helpful questions to be 'planted' in advance with the more malleable Tory back-benchers.

Back in his office, Ingham then chaired his own meeting. His bow-fronted room overlooking Downing Street was spacious. There were a couple of armchairs and a sofa upholstered in a rough, mustard-coloured fabric; a large safe for classified documents; a television and a video recorder; and a desk at which he sat with his back to the window. A single line from Hansard, greatly enlarged, hung framed on the wall:

> *The Prime Minister*: Mr Ingham acts in accordance with the duties of his office.

His staff – a deputy, three full-time press officers and a junior on a six-week attachment – were given their orders: Get me *this* from the Ministry of Defence . . . Find out *that* from those buggers at the Foreign Office . . . Environment is making its announcement at *what* time? . . . At 10.45 they trooped back in with the result of their researches. At 11.00, Ingham briefed the Lobby in his office. About twenty reporters turned up. He ran through the Prime Minister's engagements and answered questions about not only her work but that of the entire Government. What he said here helped shape the coverage of both the lunchtime news and the London *Evening Standard* – and they in turn helped determine the main themes of the day.

The briefing was followed by routine administrative work, correspondence, and possibly lunch with a journalist. At around 3.00, if it was a Tuesday or Thursday, he looked in at the Prime Minister's room in the House of Commons, then took his place in the Press Gallery at 3.15 for Questions. He had become a familiar part of the Westminster furniture over the past eleven years, sitting hunched over his notebook, scribbling his famously accurate shorthand, his bushy eyebrows – now leaping in exasperation, now knitted in a frown – dancing around like a pair of tiny ginger field mice in the mating season. 'He is large and craggy and rather loopy-looking,' wrote Craig Brown, when he was Parliamentary sketch writer for *The Times*, 'like one of the background soldiers who used to be employed on Dad's Army.' (Ingham retaliated in a speech two years later by describing Brown, not altogether inaccurately, as looking 'like Dylan Thomas pulled through a hedge backwards'.)[4]

After a swift cup of tea in the Press Gallery canteen, he climbed the spiral stone staircase to the Lobby room in the eaves of the Palace of Westminster for what is known as 'the four o'clock' – the second of the two daily Lobby briefings – this one attended by thirty or forty reporters. Then it was back to Downing Street and more work until 7.30 or 8.00 p.m. If he was eating in town rather than returning straight to Purley, he would often finish his meal and go back to the office to check all was well. In that case, it might be midnight before he got to bed. And so it went on for more than a decade: twelve hours a day, five days a week, forty-seven weeks a year, not counting the constant telephone calls at home during the night and at weekends, not including the endless foreign trips (two European summits a year, the annual Group of Seven summit, countless 'bilaterals' with foreign heads of government, and always at least two full-scale overseas tours).

Few colleagues, even those who had worked with him for twenty years, knew much about his private life. His wife Nancy, a former policewoman, was always an off-stage figure. 'I've met Nancy, but very rarely,' said Neville Taylor, who was Head of Information at the Department of Health and Social Security when Ingham arrived at Number 10. 'Like many husbands and wives, they're two totally, totally different characters. She's very quiet.' Nancy made the headlines only once, in April 1987, when the IRA sent a letter bomb to the Inghams' home address: it arrived at lunchtime, she took one look at its Ulster postmark and, with admirable coolness, placed it on the front step and dialled 999.

Their son John took a degree in history at Durham in 1980 and won a Fulbright Scholarship to George Washington University. On his return from the US, he decided to follow his father into journalism. 'Bernard asked his friends where might be the best place for him to start,' recalled Geoffrey Goodman, former industrial editor of the *Daily Mirror*. 'I said that in his job he could surely just pick up the phone and someone would help out. But he said no, he'd never do that.' And he never did. John Ingham had to work his own way up through trade magazines and regional newspaper offices before finally landing a job in London in 1990, as defence correspondent on the *Daily Express*.

Many accusations were flung at Ingham, but nobody, not even his bitterest critic, has ever suggested that he put on airs and graces or abused his position for personal gain. His house was as modest and unpretentious in 1990 as it was when he moved into it in the 1960s. You would not find the Inghams – unlike the Powells – at smart dinner parties or on the cocktail circuit. 'Bernard is a workaholic,' said Neville Taylor.

> I don't think there is any time in his life for anything other than work, and I don't think there ever has been ... There is this drive, this total and permanent drive, to do this job better than any other bugger's going to do it. He will go for weeks – and I mean, literally, weeks – before he gets round to reading something that somebody's sent him to read because

it was urgent six weeks ago. Bernard will quite honestly say: 'I
just haven't had time . . .'

Even when his wife was almost killed by a runaway lorry in
1982, and had to spend three months in hospital, Ingham
refused to take a day off.

Occasionally, the strain took its toll on his health. Ingham
still suffers from the asthma which afflicted him in childhood
and which prevented him – to his chagrin – from doing his
National Service. A visitor to Number 10 in 1984 noted that
Ingham had difficulty mounting the one flight of stairs to the
Prime Minister's study: a chest cold had activated his asthma
and he was panting heavily.[5] There was also a stage when he
suffered blackouts and was ordered by his doctor to stop
drinking and lose weight. But, for the most part, he thrived on a
diet of adrenalin and mugs of coffee. 'I am still a journalist at
heart,' he claimed. His life was one long, rolling deadline.

Only one other person shared such a gruelling workrate for
such a long period at the heart of the Government, and that was
Margaret Thatcher. A mutual capacity for early starts, long
hours and little sleep was one of the planks on which they built
their relationship. 'He fell under her spell very quickly,'
remembered Goodman. 'He spoke of her with great admiration, first and foremost because of her workrate. I'd say "What
does she do in her spare time?" and he'd say "She doesn't
watch television or read books because she just works".' Her
idea of an annual holiday was a week in Cornwall; his was a
fortnight mucking-out on his brother's farm. 'She is not a
relaxed person,' Ingham told one reporter. 'I'm not either. We
work hard.' To another he confided that he and Thatcher had
'an instinctive rapport . . . My parents regarded hard work as
the greatest virtue, and it was impressed on me from the earliest
age that education never did anyone any harm . . . She had a
fairly hard upbringing, too.'[6]

They treated these similar backgrounds in completely different ways. Ingham nurtured his roots, returning to them whenever possible. He hung watercolours of the Yorkshire countryside (by his friend Donald Crossley) on his walls at home and in Downing Street. He kept up old friendships, proudly inviting acquaintances from his school days and their children to look round Number 10. He made no attempt to disguise his accent; if anything, he hammed it up. To him, the north was a place to which he looked forward to retiring. Margaret Thatcher's approach was in sharp contrast. She loathed Grantham and bent all her immense will to fighting her way out of it. She has virtually no old friends. She married a millionaire from Kent and took elocution lessons to obliterate the last, embarrassing trace of Lincolnshire from her voice.

But all of us, as Ingham once observed, 'are mightily conditioned by our upbringing; few of us escape its consequences or can shake it off like dust from the feet'.[7] The weaver's son and the grocer's daughter, whatever the superficial differences, shared a common inheritance: both were reared in a culture suspicious of metropolitan sophistication, which emphasized the virtues not only of hard work, but of thrift and self-reliance, of discipline and respect for authority. They were practical people; they favoured plain speaking to oratory, facts to theory. Thatcher talked of her father as Ingham did of the people of Hebden Bridge, as a repository of sound, old-fashioned common sense. Here was the basis of what Ingham called the 'instinctive rapport' between them. 'Chemically, it worked right from day one,' claimed a civil servant who was employed in Downing Street in 1979. Donald Grant, Chief Information Officer at the Home Office, also described the 'chemistry' as 'quite amazing'.

It gave Ingham the confidence to be frank in his advice. 'He was not afraid to argue with her if he thought she was wrong,' insisted one insider. 'If he wanted to say something, he said it – you know, wham, bam, he argued back.' Every so often, in the privacy of her study, if one of his briefings had blown back in his face, she would rage against the Lobby system: 'Bernard, just don't do it any more. Just stop talking to them.' To which he always replied: 'You can't do that, Prime Minister. If you did, it would only start up again.' More than once, standing around in a television hospitality suite after an interview, as she reached for another glass of whisky, he was known to tap his watch and loudly tell her it was time to go home.

If his employer resented this occasional bluntness, she did not show it. She knew she was always the boss. Even after eleven years he invariably called her 'Prime Minister'. She referred to him, possessively, as 'my Bernard', or even 'dear Bernard'. 'He's a sort of rock of loyalty,' said her speechwriter, Sir Ronald Millar. 'I think his loyalty to her is something that she absolutely appreciated.' Mrs Thatcher's favourite poet is Kipling; her favourite poem, 'Norman and Saxon', in which an eleventh century Norman baron passes on this advice to his son:

The Saxon is not like us Normans. His manners are not so polite.
But he never means anything serious till he talks about justice and
    right.
When he stands like an ox in the furrow with his sullen set eyes on
    your own,
And grumbles, 'This isn't fair dealing,' my son, leave the Saxon
    alone.

She seemed to cast Ingham in the Saxon's role, as a man of old-fashioned, ox-like reliability. He responded in kind. 'The Prime Minister knows her own mind,' he once declared. 'She allows me to get on with my job. She has guts and she supports me.

'I like people with guts.'[8]

TWO

Hebden Bridge

*'I want a Government that redistributes wealth. I want a
Government that relieves the lowly paid of the magnified
miseries of poverty in an affluent society. And I want a
Government that produces a society which affords its children
an equal opportunity in life. And if the shortest route to
securing these, and many other desirable objectives, means
pursuing the idea of "consensus", then I'll pursue it.'*

BERNARD INGHAM, 1966[1]

Hebden Bridge, a place to which Bernard Ingham constantly
alludes and frequently returns, stands on the River Calder in
the West Riding of Yorkshire, on the road from Halifax to
Burnley. 'Lower the window, lad,' Ingham once commanded a
Guardian colleague as they passed through it on the train.
'Take a good sniff of that air, because you're nearer to Heaven
now than you ever will be on earth.'

They do things differently in Hebden Bridge. The local
delicacy is dock pudding, a dish made from the leaves of a
common weed, sweet dock (*polygonum bistorta*), chopped up
with nettles, boiled with oatmeal, then fried with bacon fat to
make a kind of slimy green patty, of which the Prime Minister's
Press Secretary is particularly fond. The Yorkshire dialect is

thick, studded with words the rest of the country has long forgotten: *carr* (to sit), *gang* (to go), *bahn* (going). There is even a local phrase book. '*Smarrerweeim*?' translates as 'What's the matter with him?' '*Astageniter*?' is 'Have you given it to her?' In a speech in 1990 to mark the fortieth anniversary of the local high school, Ingham spoke with warmth of the 'modesty and unpretentiousness' of his home town:

> This was perhaps most beautifully brought out when a *Financial Times* reporter, staying in Hebden Bridge for the General Election, was asked by the waitress if he wanted coffee.
>
> 'Yes,' he said. 'Cappuccino.'
>
> 'Nay lad,' she said, 'you'll have to go to Leeds for that.'

Hebden Bridge is the place he comes from, the place he talks of retiring to. The *Hebden Bridge Times* is still delivered each week to his home in London. One of the yardsticks by which he judges whether a problem is just a passing media squall or a serious storm is whether they are discussing it in the pubs of Hebden Bridge. So it is in Hebden Bridge that we should begin.

Ingham is a Yorkshire name. Members of his family have lived in the Hebden Bridge area for at least three generations. His father, Garnet Ingham, was born at the turn of the century in Charlestown, a small village a couple of miles to the west of the town. He was the eldest of seven children – after him came Maud, Florrie, Arthur, Harold, Clare and Annie – all of them the progeny of the redoubtable Harry Ingham, weaver, who lived to be ninety-four. Garnet was called up to fight in the First World War and joined the Royal Naval Air Service. But he never saw action. The Armistice was signed while he was still in southern England, training. He returned to Yorkshire where, in 1927, he married Alice, then twenty-four years old, the only daughter of the splendidly-named Greenwood Horsfall, of Queen's Terrace, Hebden Bridge.

'In her younger days,' according to her obituary in the *Hebden Bridge Times* in 1967, 'Mrs Ingham was well known in the district as an elocutionist.' She is still remembered by some of the older inhabitants as a 'right good singer' who used to play a leading part in the amateur productions of the Hebden Bridge Light Opera Society. But, like most of the town's 6,000 inhabitants, it was on the weaving sheds that her living depended. When her children were growing up, she worked part-time as an 'odd weaver': someone who was paid by full-time weavers to mind their looms for them while they were off sick or away for a few hours.

Garnet, apart from his brief spell in the armed forces and a period of war-work in a local engineering factory during the early 1940s, was a weaver all his working life. He was employed at the Windsor Shed, in the northern part of Hebden Bridge, owned by the Olympia Manufacturing Company, and also at a grim Victorian fortress in the centre of town called Nutclough Mill. Each weaver operated perhaps four looms. With 250 employees to each shed and up to 1,000 heavy metal looms running at full speed, opening the door to the factory was like walking into a wall of noise. In the words of David Fletcher, a historian who was raised in Hebden Bridge, 'it hit you like a solid substance; you could feel your whole body vibrating in time to the machinery'. Over the roar of the looms, the weavers communicated with one another like deaf-mutes. It is unwise in Hebden Bridge, even today, to make an unflattering remark about someone on the other side of the street. Plenty of sharp-eyed elderly residents remember how to lip-read.

Noise was not the only form of pollution produced by the mills. For the best part of a century, unchecked by law or public protest, they spewed their dirt into the air and their filth into the waters of the River Calder. The effects were worsened by Hebden Bridge's geography. Its mills and grey stone houses jammed the narrow valley floor and clung, sometimes at precarious angles, to the steep hillsides overlooking the river, forming a cauldron of smog. To quote David Fletcher again:

> Hebden Bridge was a very demoralizing place in which to grow up. The streets and houses were dingy, and the air was smokey, especially on still winter mornings. Sometimes you would go for days and the place would stay dark, with a roof of smoke trapped in the valley. You'd go to school on your bike with a handkerchief over your face, and by the time you arrived, the material would be filthy. If you went into the woods and ran your hands down the bark of the trees, they'd be smeared with soot. We didn't have silver birches; we had black birches. Depending on what dye they were using further up the valley, the streams would run blue, black or maroon.

The air which Ingham urged his *Guardian* colleague to sniff thirty years later was the product of the Clean Air Acts of the 1950s: a very different substance to that which he breathed as a child.

He was born, plain Bernard, in the Royal Infirmary, Halifax, on 21 June 1932. A brother, Derek, arrived two years later. As a child he suffered badly from asthma. So did his mother. She was to be a semi-invalid for the last few years of her life, before dying of pneumonia at the age of sixty-four. Derek also contracted pneumonia, in May 1937, when he was three. The Inghams could not afford an ambulance, and he had to be transported to and from hospital by the local greengrocer. The memory of this episode later stirred 'Albion' to a vigorous defence of the National Health Service:

It represents a tremendous advance on the inherently vicious private enterprise system of Dr Finlay's time, and the 1930s. That was when my parents, for example, ran up for them, the colossal bill of £120 when my brother contracted double pneumonia.[2]

Garnet and Alice had to borrow the money, and were still paying it back years later.

A few months after his brother's illness, Bernard began attending the Central Street School, a Victorian establishment bounded on three sides by mills and warehouses. His nickname was 'Bunny' Ingham. He was tall for his age, red-haired and raw-boned. As he grew up he became rather fat: years later, in his teens, he and some friends would have to abandon a cycling holiday in Devon after his weight had buckled the spokes of his back wheel. 'He tended to be "Big Daddy" in a group,' recalls one of his schoolmates, Peter Marsland. 'He wasn't brash, but in a quiet way you knew who the leader was.' Cricket and football were his main interests. But he was bright enough at his class work and certainly expected to pass the eleven-plus. Unexpectedly, through sheer panic as much as anything else, he flunked it. He later recalled the shame of how 'after consistently coming out top or second in the class virtually from entering primary school I failed miserably in the eleven-plus and had to go to bed for several days with asthma brought on by the nervous strain imposed by the examination'.[3]

It was a traumatic experience and, again, it was to help shape his political views. In the mid-1960s, when Harold Wilson denounced the 'educational apartheid' of the grammar school system, and his Labour government legislated to end it, he had few more enthusiastic supporters than Ingham. In the *Leeds Weekly Citizen* of 14 January 1966, he attacked 'the anxiety, pain and often downright cruelty' it inflicted.

> There are millions being made into second class citizens by an
> archaic education system, and we are not on this earth to
> perpetuate a second class system riddled with the strength-
> sapping pox of class tensions and injustices ... This also
> implies that I want an end to public schools as such and the
> fee-paying sector. I do. It is the only way that we shall get a
> real head of steam behind our educational system.

Fortunately for Ingham, there *was* a fee-paying scheme available in Hebden Bridge in 1943. Parents whose children had
failed the eleven-plus were allowed to buy them a place at the
local grammar school. Garnet and Alice, in their son's words,
'scraped enough money together' to pay the fees and Bernard
went after all. Had he not, he would have stayed another
three years at Central Street and then left at the age of
fourteen, probably to work in one of the local mills. As it was,
he recovered his academic confidence sufficiently to be placed
in the A-stream at Hebden Bridge Grammar School, consistently coming a creditable fifth or sixth in a class of about
twenty-five.

Outside work and school, the Ingham family's attention
was divided between two institutions. One was the Hope
Street Baptist Church. Bernard's parents, like most of the
town's citizens, were regular worshippers. His aunts helped
teach Sunday School and he and Derek were strictly brought
up in the Nonconformist tradition. They were expected to
devote a large part of their spare time to the church. In 1947,
for example, Hope Street's basement was flooded, destroying
the electrical system which powered the organ. For six
months, the Ingham boys were required to pump it manually.
'The hymns were fine,' recalled Derek, 'but then they decided
to do Handel's *Messiah* at Christmas. The Hallelujah Chorus
nearly killed us.'

The other institution was the Labour Party. Garnet was of

that generation for whom Baptism and socialism were two halves of the same faith. He was the auditor of his local union, the Todmorden Weavers' and Winders' Association; a director of the Hebden Bridge Co-operative Society; and a member of the Executive of the Sowerby Constituency Labour Party. Round-faced, bespectacled, with thick wavy hair and a ready smile, he became one of the town's best-known citizens. 'Garnet were a right good man', is the sort of comment still made about him. 'A right kindly man; had a good word for everybody.' Hilary Varley, whose family knew the Inghams through the church and the local Trades Club, retained a similar impression: 'Garnet was a lovely man. He ran the Labour Party. He *was* the Labour Party.' Bernard's mother, who also did her bit for the socialist cause as secretary of the town's Co-operative Women's Guild, is remembered as 'quiet' and 'supportive'.

His parents' opinions were readily absorbed by their eldest son. Bernard's headmaster, Herbert Howarth, once had to ask the tyro politician to remove a pile of Labour Party pamphlets from the school library. 'I am all in favour of politics,' Ingham recalled Howarth admonishing him, 'but I will not have party politics in this school.'[4] Nevertheless, during the 1945 general election, the voice of the thirteen-year-old Ingham could be heard piping 'Vote Labour' from a loudspeaker van parked outside the school. Perhaps these modest efforts swayed a few minds; at any rate, on 25 July the Labour candidate for Sowerby, John Belcher, defeated the sitting Conservative MP, Malcolm McCorquodale, by 7,000 votes.

From this point onwards, the Ingham household's preoccupation with politics intensified. In March 1946, Garnet became the first candidate to stand for the local council with the official backing of the Labour Party (hitherto, all councillors had stood as independents). He polled 790 votes, only narrowly missing election – 'a good figure for a first contest,' commented the local paper. The following year he tried again. On 29 March 1947, under a dull and rainy sky, the citizens of Hebden Bridge turned out to vote at the polling station in Central Street School. Counting began at 8.00 p.m. 'The space available for the public was packed,' recorded the *Hebden Bridge Times*, 'and a keen interest was taken in proceedings.' Two hours later, with the street lamps doused and in almost pitch darkness, the town clerk posted the results outside the *Times*' office in Market Street. With 906 votes, Garnet Ingham was elected – the first socialist councillor in the history of Hebden Bridge.

That same year, Bernard became a founder member, and subsequently Secretary, of the Hebden Bridge League of Labour Youth. In November 1947, he helped organize a meeting for John Belcher in the town's Little Theatre. The MP mounted an outspoken attack on the 'vicious' and 'unscrupulous' attempts of Mr Churchill to divide the nation, and concluded with a little homily on 'the importance of youth in the ranks of the Labour Movement'. According to the *Hebden Bridge Times*, 'a vote of thanks to Mr Belcher was moved by Bernard Ingham'.[5] At the age of fifteen, he had made his first speech – and his first appearance in print.

These were good years for the Inghams. Four decades later, it became fashionable to blame the Attlee Government – with its dreary insistence on 'planning' and 'welfare' – for precipitating Britain's economic decline. But in places like Hebden Bridge it was simply the best thing that had ever happened. 'The valley,' Ingham subsequently recalled, 'was humming. It was a good place to live. The future looked better than the past.'[6]

Garnet and his family were typical beneficiaries of the government they had helped elect. They left the cramped conditions of Albion Terrace and moved to a new housing estate in Mytholmroyd – the local pronunication is 'Mar-thamroyd' – a mile from Hebden Bridge. Number 1 Birchen-lee Close was a post-war prefab, boasting such undreamed-of luxuries as an indoor lavatory, a spacious kitchen and bath-room, and three bedrooms. Round the corner from the Inghams, in Aspinall Street, lived the future Poet Laureate, Ted Hughes. (Hughes was two years older than Bernard, and they did not meet until Ingham was working in Downing Street; since then, however, they have kept in touch.)

When it came to building the socialist New Jerusalem, Garnet was a Stakhanovite. Most of the other councillors were self-employed businessmen who could take time off whenever necessary. Mill workers, on the other hand, were employed in two shifts on a rota basis: 6.00 a.m. till 2.00 p.m., and 2.00 p.m. till 10.00 p.m. Undeterred, Garnet managed to strike a deal with a fellow weaver who preferred to spend his mornings in bed. For the next 13 years he worked the early shift only, leaving his evenings free for council and Labour Party business. This meant getting up at half past four every morning to catch a bus to work at 5.20 a.m. In the evening, after a hurried meal, he would return to Hebden Bridge, to the council's imposing Victorian offices in St George's Street, where he sat on half a dozen committees, including housing, health and highways. It might be nine or ten o'clock at night before he returned home. The council's records show him to have been one of the most assiduous attenders: in 1949, for example, out of eighty meetings held, he was present at seventy-two. Eventu-ally he gave up all outside interests, including his beloved membership of the Hebden Bridge Brass Band, to concen-trate on council work.

Garnet Ingham was never a militant, but he was passionate about the aims and achievements of the Labour Party. He regularly berated the council for its 'disgraceful' failure to invest its funds in the Co-operative Society Bank which, he said, offered a higher rate of interest than its competitors. He spoke proudly of the 'pioneers' of the Sowerby Labour Party who, in the early years of the century, 'practically gave their lives in the service of the movement' but who had had the courage to stick to their convictions.[7] He was no theorist: his brand of socialism was very much of the practical, municipal, gas-and-water kind. In 1951, when he stood for re-election, his address to the voters concentrated on health and hygiene: 'it is imperative that no attempt should be made to deter the onward march of the past few years'.[8] He lost on that occasion, swept away when the tide turned against the Labour Government nationally. But he was re-elected the following year and, on 20 May 1957, despite the fact that Labour had only two seats on the council compared with the Conservatives' eleven, was unanimously nominated as Leader. There were affectionate tributes to what one Tory councillor called 'a rabid old socialist'. Some of the phrases used to describe him – that when he had an idea 'he stuck to it with great stubborness' and that he 'had a reputation for calling a spade a spade' – would later be applied equally readily to his son. 'I am proud to be associated with the Labour movement,' responded Garnet, the Leader's chain of office glinting on his chest. 'This is not said in a belligerent attitude, but out of respect for the achievements of the Labour Party over the past fifty years.'[9]

'Garnet,' in the words of one elderly resident of Hebden Bridge, 'were red hot Labour.'

If Bernard Ingham had been born ten years later he would almost certainly have gone to university. But in the 1940s such a prospect was far beyond the horizons of the average son of a Yorkshire weaver. 'My parents' attitude,' recalled Derek, 'was that they made sure you got a good education at school. After that it was up to you to get the best job you could.' Ingham's original plan was to become a geography teacher. Then, in the autumn of 1948, the *Hebden Bridge Times* ran an advertisement for a trainee journalist. Ingham applied. According to him, they 'made me an offer I could not refuse: the post of junior reporter at thirty bob a week, with use of your own bike to cover Luddenden Valley on Mondays'. He started that October. He was sixteen.

Ingham often refers to these early days of his in journalism. His manner on such occasions is invariably that of a self-made Yorkshire businessman, wi' brass in t'bank, discoursing at a school prize-giving on the homespun virtues of his humble youth. Indeed, this is how Ingham actually expressed it at the local school in 1990:

> Working on the *Hebden Bridge Times*, cheek by jowl with your readers, was the finest preparation for the life I now lead. You either got it right or you got it in the neck, right there in Market Street, Bridge Gate or Hangingroyd Lane.

It was a favourite theme. Covering council meetings, he declared, was 'the finest background for any real life in politics, because you got to know how a country worked from the bottom up.' In 1986, he told an audience in the City of London:

> I share the view Lord Kemsley expressed in his *Manual of Journalism*, a copy of which I acquired when it was first published in 1950 ... Lord Kemsley wrote: 'There is no more important responsibility to the community than that of journalists.' Those words 'responsibility to the community' were the very bedrock of my training. Responsibility to inform. Responsibility to be accurate. Responsibility to be fair. In short, responsibility to the reader.[10]

Asked to lecture on the theme 'The Right to Know' in 1983,

he told his audience of newspaper editors that there was no such thing: 'And I am bound to tell you that my training as a journalist put far greater emphasis on responsibilities, duties and obligations than ever it did on rights.'[11]

The *Hebden Bridge Times*, this apparently inexhaustible fount of civic virtue and journalistic excellence, was then housed in a disused eighteenth-century church in the centre of town. It was an odd place to find a newspaper office. Visitors had first to make their way through a small graveyard, filled with sombre reminders of stories past:

> In Memory of
> Henry Riley; whose short existence was marked
> with continued Misfortune, and because he became
> poor, was cruelly murdered on the 2nd of Oct 1818
> in the 37th Year of his Age. He has left a Widow &
> eleven Children to lament his Loss.
> Nor Angel's Blessings, nor the Murder'rs Prayers
> Can wipe away a desolate Widow's Curse;
> And though he shed his Heart's Blood for Atonement,
> It will not weigh against an Orphan's tear.

Beyond the grave stones, fixed to the Ebenezer Chapel's smoke-blackened frontage, was a sundial with the dolorous inscription *Quod petis umbra est* ('What you seek is but a shadow'). If Ingham's first years as a reporter really were marked by such a heavy sense of seriousness and duty, one can begin to see why.

The gloomy atmosphere lingered inside. 'You'd go in,' remembered Derek Ingham, 'and the reporters were in a dark room on the left, sitting at a long table, with perhaps one telephone between the lot of them.' In 1948, the two senior journalists were veterans of the Hebden Bridge scene, Jack Holroyd and Walter Marsland. Running round the walls, at a height of four feet, was a tidemark, a relic of the same flood which had damaged the organ in Hope Street the previous year. The paper was set in type in a room upstairs. If the compositor had a query, he would fling open a trapdoor above the reporters' heads, swear, and toss down the offending piece of copy, screwed up in a ball. The reporter would flatten it out, make any necessary corrections, screw it up again and throw it back, accompanied by a few choice words of his own.

The *Hebden Bridge Times* then consisted of eight pages, published weekly. Once a month the front page was given over to the council's minutes, which were published almost verbatim. Another staple was the magistrates' court ('Butcher Burnt Cow's Hide/Slaughtered Animal Himself – Fined £50/ Horseflesh Dealer to Appeal Against Sentence'). There were the usual births, marriages and deaths. Nature Notes were provided by 'Tawny Owl' ('Don't forget that empty bird table; do it now!'). Advertisements were basic ('Do your false teeth ROCK, SLIDE or SLIP?'). The frequent announcements placed by the Ministry of Food reflected the austerities of post-war rationing. One, a list of recipes for various kinds of dumpling (fish, herb, cheese, curry, sweet and baked), concluded with the bathetic message: 'Good News! There's plenty of Ryvita in the shops now and it's down to only 2 points a packet!'

Bernard's special beat, for which his bicycle was essential, was village news: the whist drives in Luddenden Foot; the old-time dancing nights in Lumb or Heptonstall; bowling club socials ('the Embassy Band played for dancing') in Sowerby Bridge; the talks by the likes of Mr S. Weatherill of Todmorden 'on the signalling system of the railways' or by the Rev. H. Godfrey, who spoke to the Providence Methodist Church on 'Real Romance'. On one celebrated occasion, Ingham found himself interviewing a talking dog in the Spotted Cow at Drighlington. The prosperity of the *Hebden*

Bridge Times, like that of most successful local papers, was based on the sound commercial principle of printing as many readers' names as possible. Ingham's job was to lick the end of his pencil and make sure he spelled them correctly. To that end, the paper paid for him to learn shorthand one morning a week at the Todmorden Technical College, where he cut an incongruous figure, the only boy in a class of more than thirty girls.

As it happened, one of the biggest news stories in the history of Hebden Bridge occurred in the very month that Ingham joined the paper. On 7 October 1948, the government set up the Lynskey Tribunal to investigate allegations of corruption against the constituency's MP. John Belcher, for whose election Ingham had campaigned, was by now Parliamentary Secretary at the Board of Trade. He was accused of receiving various gifts in return for dropping an investigation into a firm of football pools promoters. The 'bribes', to a modern eye, seem almost pathetically tawdry: a week's holiday in Margate, a gold cigarette case, a suit. Nevertheless, in January 1949, Belcher was found guilty. In February, in 'the very depths of unhappiness and wretchedness', he was obliged to resign his seat.

The man chosen to replace him was Douglas Houghton, a well-known trade union leader and broadcaster. The executive of the Sowerby Labour Party, of which Garnet Ingham was a member, had no say in the matter: the leadership in London imposed the candidate they thought most likely to win a by-election. More than forty years later, aged ninety-two, Houghton could still recall Garnet: 'a staunch, middle-of-the-road chap; always eloquent on the side of reason; one of the sobersides in the constituency.' He could remember Bernard, too: 'a ginger-headed boy who worked in my campaign; on election day he ran messages between the headquarters and the polling booth'. Among those who came up to speak for Houghton was his former deputy at the Inland Revenue Staff Federation, the youthful MP for South Cardiff, James Callaghan. On 17 March, Houghton duly held the seat with a majority of 2,000. The *Hebden Bridge Times*, normally published on a Friday, kept the printers waiting and managed to get the news on to its front page.

In 1951, Ingham entered what he later called 'my most idyllic and productive years in journalism'. The paper's two senior reporters departed: Jack Holroyd to go to the *Burnley Express* and Walter Marsland to the *Halifax Courier*. That left young Bernard, effectively, to produce the paper on his own.

> I wrote at least fifteen columns a week – roughly 15,000 words; sub-edited the lot – that is, cut the stories to fit and wrote the headlines; wrote the editorial column, to my enormous pride and satisfaction; laid out the front page and the sports pages; and then on Thursday mornings put some of the pages to bed, even locking up the forms, the metal frames holding the type together. And the forms had to be locked up properly because they had to be carried down the stairs from the first floor of the old Ebenezer Baptist Chapel and out through the front door, through the graveyard to the waiting taxi in Market Street. The paper was printed in Todmorden ... One bit of bad workmanship and the *Hebden Bridge Times* would have been a page short that week – lying in tiny pieces on the pavement or on the floor of the taxi.[12]

In the interests of accuracy, it should be recorded that Ingham's frequently repeated claim – that 'I had the direct responsibility for producing and editing a local weekly thrust upon me at the age of nineteen'[13] – is contested by Kenneth Lord, son of the paper's owner at that time, who insists *he* was in charge. But if, over the years, Ingham has slightly exaggerated his role, it scarcely matters. Certainly, he had done well enough chronicling the comings and goings in Hebden Bridge to be offered, in 1952, a better job. The *Yorkshire Post*, based in Leeds, needed an extra pair of hands at its Halifax office to help cover news in the West Riding. Ingham applied for the post, and got it.

Superficially, not much changed in his life. Halifax is only seven miles from Hebden Bridge, and he continued to live at home with his parents for the next four years. But in fact this was a decisive moment, for his ambition was beginning to pull him beyond his home town. 'I used to say that Hebden Bridge was like Colditz,' his brother recalled. 'Everyone was planning their escape.' Unlike many of his contemporaries, whom he returns to visit trailing clouds of glory, Bernard made it.

He was ambitious. He was already famous for working extremely hard. He had absorbed, and would continue to revere, the values of a small town in the north of England. Yet he had taken the first opportunity to leave it behind. He had been brought up a Nonconformist. He had a respected father, a councillor, who had sacrificed much of his spare time to civic duties, and from whom he had inherited a passionate interest in politics. In all these respects the young Bernard Ingham already had a surprising amount in common with the woman who, nearly thirty years later, would become his boss.

THREE

Reporter

*'I feel for the reporter ... I have shared with him his perishing
funerals, his sodden agricultural shows, his grisly murders, his
eerie ghost hunts, his endless doorsteps, his high living at trade
union conferences ...'*

BERNARD INGHAM, LECTURE TO THE WORSHIPFUL
COMPANY OF STATIONERS AND NEWSPAPER MAKERS, 1986

At the age of twenty Bernard Ingham's life settled into a daily
routine which was to last for the next four years. He would
rise early and leave the house for Halifax. Mostly he went by
bus; occasionally, according to his colleagues, he even
walked: a two-hour trudge beside the River Calder. Halifax at
that time was like Hebden Bridge, only larger: a gritty, smoky
Victorian textile town of some 75,000 inhabitants, bounded
by steep hills. The local offices of the *Yorkshire Post* and
Yorkshire Evening Post were above a printer's shop in Hor-
ton Street, near the railway station. These Dickensian premises had battleship grey lino on the floor, on to which flowed
piles of yellowing cuttings and back-copies. Ingham's first
task each morning was to telephone the police and fire
stations and the local hospital and check if anything had
happened overnight. If it had, he would ring the story through
to the *Post*'s news desk in Leeds. Then he would don his

raincoat and cloth cap and walk down to the County Court building to check what cases were on that day. The police headquarters were conveniently arranged in the same building, and at 9.00 a.m. an inspector would brief reporters.

After that, breakfast was taken in the Star Café in Rawson Street, where a cup of tea and a cigarette could be had for sixpence. Here would gather the cream of the Halifax press corps: Stan Solomon, Alan Cooper and Max Jessup of the West Riding News Service; Jack Knott and David Illingworth of the Bradford *Telegraph and Argus*; Bryan Harwood of the Halifax *Courier*; and Bernard Ingham and his partner on the *Yorkshire Post*, an experienced journalist named Tom Dickinson. The gossip would go on until a few minutes before 10.30. Then they would grab their notebooks and set off at a brisk trot back to the court in time for the start of the first case.

The popular image of a journalist – a solitary creature, endlessly in pursuit of a scoop – is only partially true. Reporters are wolves rather than foxes. Most of the time they hunt in packs. This was especially so in a small town like Halifax in the 1950s where a limited supply of news – crime, sport, the council, the activities of the locally-based Halifax Building Society and British and Foreign Bible Society – had to satisfy the appetites of half a dozen papers. The journalists' main object was to make sure they missed nothing. Accordingly, they filled in for one another. Illingworth of the *Telegraph and Argus* might cover the morning's court case, while Ingham of the *Post* headed up to the Chamber of Commerce. Afterwards, they would exchange notes. Often they would even go on the same stories together. Illingworth had a motorbike and sidecar and he and Ingham would chug up and down the Calder Valley covering the parish councils.

The emphasis was on providing the reader with a good service of news; the reward was never to see your name in print. Everything Ingham and Dickinson wrote for the *York-shire Post* was attributed, if at all, to 'our Halifax staff'. Indeed, from the day he walked into the Ebenezer Chapel until the day he received his first by-line, Ingham had to wait more than twelve years. Three headlines from the beginning of 1953, credited to 'our Halifax staff', give the flavour of what would have been considered major stories:

Thieves took cup tie money from shop

Fire in theatre as 1,000 watch show
Audience left without panic

Mill worker dies from smallpox
Two suspect cases at Todmorden

Ingham was renowned among his colleagues for two qualities: dogged thoroughness and first-rate shorthand. The most famous story about him, endlessly retold by Yorkshire journalists, is that he once rang Halifax police station on Christmas Day and, on learning that a man had fallen off his bike and broken his arm, missed Christmas lunch to interview him. That tale, sadly, proves on investigation to be apocry-phal. But the fact that it is still so widely believed shows how well it captures his spirit. 'The man used to turn out twelve stories a day,' recalled Stan Solomon. 'It was phenomenal. He never bloody stopped.' Covering council meetings, where others might take four or five pages of shorthand notes, Ingham would take twenty or thirty. His colleagues would leave in the evenings for a drink and he would still be there, sorting through reams of paper or banging out a story with two fingers on an old Underwood typewriter.

This thoroughness and capacity for hard work shone through in other ways. In 1954 David Illingworth got married and moved to a new house. The 22-year-old Ingham could not afford to buy the couple a present, so he offered to dig their front garden instead. For weeks thereafter, whenever he had a day off, he would turn up, spade in hand. 'He didn't just dig it,' remembered Illingworth. 'He riddled the soil. He carted away bricks and boulders. He'd go on for hours. There were blisters on his hands. It got to the point where we just used to give him the key to the house so he could use the lavatory, and leave him to get on with it. To this day, the front lawn is a yard lower than anywhere else in the garden because of the amount of rubble he took out.'

By this time, Ingham had marriage plans of his own. Nancy Hoyle was a policewoman, Halifax born and bred, more than eight years his senior. She was often to be found behind the desk in the police station when the reporters went for their morning briefing – a pleasant, unpretentious woman, remembered for a capable manner and a quiet sense of humour. One day, Ingham took Bryan Harwood of the *Courier* to one side. 'He said to me: "I do like that police lady, Nancy Hoyle. I'd like to take her to the pictures. Will you introduce me?" So I did. He was quite chuffed.' (Such a liaison was not uncommon. 'Provincial journalists,' says one of Ingham's northern colleagues, 'tend to marry policewomen, nurses or barmaids: they're the only women they meet.')

Nancy came from an Irish family. Her father, Ernest Hoyle, a joiner by profession, was dead. She lived with her mother, Nora, in the terraced house where she had been born. The policewoman and the reporter carried on a discreet courtship for a couple of years – so discreet that when the workaholic Ingham announced he was getting married, some of the Star Café regulars were amazed. There was a slight complication in so far as Nancy was a practising Roman Catholic. Her Nonconformist fiancé was thus obliged to take instruction from a local priest, Father MacMahon, before a wedding could be countenanced. The ceremony eventually took place on 3 November 1956 at St Columcille's Church in Pellon,

Halifax. Ingham was twenty-four, his wife a month short of her thirty-third birthday. 'The bride wore a cocktail gown of gold brocade,' reported the *Hebden Bridge Times*, 'and was given away by her brother.' The best man was Derek Ingham. Following a reception in the town's Co-operative Café (a concession to Garnet Ingham, perhaps), 'the couple left for their honeymoon in Keswick'.[1]

They returned to a new home. Sixty-two Gleanings Avenue was a small, semi-detached house in Norton Tower, a windy hilltop on the outskirts of Halifax. Nancy gave up work, and a little over a year later she gave birth to the couple's first and only child. An announcement in the *Hebden Bridge Times* in February 1958 recorded the birth of 'a son, John Bernard. *Deo Gratias*.'[2]

Ingham served seven years in Halifax for the *Yorkshire Post*. At length, in 1959, this long apprenticeship was rewarded with a transfer to the paper's headquarters in Leeds. Eighteen months later he was given a further promotion. He was made the paper's northern industrial correspondent. From now on he had a by-line. At last he could take full credit for his prodigious output of news stories (when he had finished his day's work in Leeds, he became famous for asking the news editor if there was anything more he could do). Few editions passed without some contribution from him – on the coal or motor industries ('Six ton coal lump sent to Solid Fuels Exhibition at Grimethorpe', 'Skilled workers in short supply'); or on a takeover or a strike ('Merger of liquorice kings', 'Plan for peace in car works'). Only when it came to features was his touch less sure. This, for example, was his idea of a catchy opening to the 'Inside Industry' column on 24 April 1961:

Life, as the saying goes, is full of temptations as well as surprises. This is particularly true so far as top executives are concerned when they come to deal with the problem of management succession.

It was one of the points made most forcibly at the seminar held this week in Harrogate by Ashley Associates Ltd, the Manchester firm of executive selection consultants . . .

This leaden prose style, only a minor disadvantage in his early years as a journalist, was later to prove a decisive handicap.

That problem, however, lay in the future. In the early 1960s, the northern industrial scene suited him well. His upbringing in Hebden Bridge and his background in the Labour Party gave him a rapport with the local trade unionists, especially the Yorkshire miners. He relished their company. Years later he was still telling the story of a fellow industrial correspondent's attempt to interview a striking miner at Rossington Colliery, near Doncaster.

> The office car he was driving had seen better days – a relic of the '30s. It hissed, puffed, creaked and groaned its way down the pit lane and shuddered to a halt in the yard. As my colleague untied the string to let himself out he heard the crouching miner observe 'Hey up lads, here comes t'capitalist press'.[3]

Ingham got on well with his fellow reporters. Monty Meth, then freelancing for the *Daily Worker*, who became a friend, remembers a colleague who was 'objective and diligent in the extreme', who had brilliant shorthand and 'would do three or four stories where others would be content to do one'. Joe Haines, then with the *Scottish Daily Mail*, who was to become an adversary, remembers 'a very convivial evening' during a TUC conference when 'we were both stuck in a rather shabby hotel on the south side of Blackpool. He was Labour. We had a sympathy of political view.'

Through these contacts, towards the end of 1961, Ingham

learned that the *Guardian* was looking for a reporter to work in its Leeds office, a few doors down from the *Yorkshire Post* in Albion Street. There were disadvantages in such a move. He would lose his by-line. His work would appear under the tag 'by our own reporter'. He would be a smaller fish. But then he would be swimming in a much larger pond. He applied for the job.

Ingham was interviewed first by Mike Parkin, the *Guardian*'s Leeds correspondent. Parkin preferred writing about the lighter, more whimsical side of northern life. Ingham these days was concentrating on politics, industry and regional planning: the sort of worthy subjects which needed to be covered, but which few of the *Guardian*'s specialists, based in London, wanted to trail up and write about. Parkin thought him the ideal candidate. Harry Whewell, the paper's northern news editor, came across the Pennines to meet him. Finally, Ingham was dispatched to Manchester to see the *Guardian*'s editor, Alastair Hetherington. He was approved, hired, and started work at the beginning of 1962.

'Bernard looked like a grafter,' recalled Whewell. 'He *was* a grafter. He just laboured away.' Whewell would speak to him on the telephone from the Manchester news room every morning to assign him his day's work. By chance, several of the ledgers in which the news editor recorded who was doing what have survived. They bear out what every ex-colleague of Ingham remembers: that whereas most reporters undertook to do one or two pieces, he would often submit ideas for five or six. In 1963 alone, Whewell's ledger records 351 stories assigned to Ingham: 133 connected with trade union or industrial matters; 121 with politics and regional policy; the rest mainly devoted to agriculture, tourism or fishing (covering the latter, he fell victim to the *Guardian*'s legendary capacity for typographical errors, and was recorded as interviewing 'a machine biologist').

In the course of that year he attended the conferences of the TUC in Brighton and the Labour Party in Scarborough. He was with the National Union of Public Employees at Bridlington and with the Confederation of Shipbuilding and Engineering Unions at York and Margate. He followed Lord Hailsham across the north-east of England. With John Cole, the *Guardian*'s labour correspondent, he toured Scotland. He was hungry to get his copy into the paper and became a master of the 'Sunday-for-Monday' story: by coming in on his day off and filing an article when fewer journalists were competing for space, he stood more chance of seeing it printed.

Not all his work was quite so serious. In January 1963 he covered the world needle-threading contest. In the same month he reported on the case of a fox and a terrier trapped together in a snow-bound crevice at Hardcastle Crags (the fox escaped, Ingham was able to assure the *Guardian*'s readers, while the dog was rescued and 'went home to a liver and whisky dinner').[4] He described such marvels of science as the development of antibiotics for fish and the strengthening of eggshells. Best of all, in July 1963, was a piece about a peripatetic Yorkshire crab – the first Ingham story, as far as one can tell, ever to make it on to the *Guardian*'s front page:

175-MILE CRAWL BY CRAB?

By our own reporter

A Yorkshire crab now holds the record for the longest known journey by an East Coast crab.

One tagged off Whitby last year by the staff of the Fisheries Laboratory at Burnham-on-Crouch has turned up in a seine net in Aberdeen Bay, about 175 miles away as the crab crawls. Previously the longest known journey was by a Norfolk crab which covered 124 miles from Norfolk to Yorkshire in 21 months ... Mr E. Edwards, of the Fisheries Laboratory, who has just completed tagging another 1,000 crabs off the Yorkshire coast, says a pattern is already emerging. Apparently there is a tendency for the female to wander northwards and for the male to stay where he is.[5]

Parkin found his new colleague to be 'the very embodiment of the Protestant work ethic; a demon worker'. Ingham sat hunched over his desk in their dingy one-room office, smoking so heavily that by the end of the day the air would be thick with stale fumes and the floor littered with cigarette stubs. He smoked cheap Woodbines – not, in Parkin's view, 'because he couldn't afford better cigarettes, but because he thought it was a good working-class smoke: none of your nonsense'. He had turned into a young man of stern values, contemptuous of people he thought had had it soft. He was good-natured rather than witty; dogged, decent, serious. As a journalist he was renowned both for the quantity of facts he would stuff into a story and for their unerring accuracy. But if he was asked to speculate or embroider he was lost, and his sentences, notoriously, 'went on like a club bore's story':

> Yet at least one firm in Sunderland so far speaks only highly of the Board of Trade even if it owes its presence on the Pallion industrial estate there to a combination of circumstances stemming from the Board's policy of refusing industrial development certificates in London for new industrial buildings and extensions of more than 5,000 square feet.[6]

That particular specimen, from January 1964, lurches on bewilderingly through 58 words without the assistance of a single punctuation mark.

Ingham by now was notorious for the vehemence of his political views. In Halifax he had made no secret of his socialism. 'He was not just violently anti-Tory,' recalled Stan Solomon, 'he had a vitriolic hatred of them.' Bryan Harwood remembered him as 'steeped in politics; always on about wanting to get into politics'. Like his father, he was a strong union man. He had joined the National Union of Journalists aged sixteen. In Halifax, he had been chairman and treasurer of the local NUJ; in Leeds, vice-chairman. At the 1959 General Election he gathered together a group of Yorkshire journalists to help produce Labour's campaign material.

As the years passed, he became increasingly dogmatic. He could always be provoked into an argument. The man who rented the *Guardian* its office in Albion Street, Ken Ridge, would come in with a gleam in his eye and the sole intention of goading Ingham to fury. No matter how busy he was, his quarry would invariably break off from his work and rise to the bait. 'Gutlessness' was what he claimed to despise most. 'The Tories could kick you in the teeth,' he was fond of remarking, 'and all you would say is: "Sorry, did I hurt your boot?"' His style of debate was demotic, hectoring, often pedantic. 'I gave you an argument,' he would say, 'and all you've given me is an assertion.' One night he was laying down the law to Mike Parkin and Harry Whewell over dinner in Whitelocks, a Leeds hostelry famous for the sawdust on its floor. He became so agitated, his newly-fitted false teeth flew out and skittered across the dining room. Ingham paid no attention. He carried on talking. Eventually Whewell had to tell him to stop and put his dentures back in.

At the beginning of 1964, Ingham's involvement in the Labour Party suddenly intensified. For some reason, he must have let his subscription lapse – at any rate, in February 1964 he simultaneously joined the West Leeds constituency party, and arranged for the Fabian Society, of which he was a member, to nominate him for inclusion on Labour's list of candidates for the City Council. His nomination paper has been preserved. Under 'experience', he wrote of himself: 'Has had a great deal of experience in writing political articles. Has spoken at weekend schools and seminars on "The Press" and also on "Regional Development"'. Under 'adult education' he disclosed that he had taken classes in 'public speaking' at the National Council of Labour Colleges, an organization similar to the Workers' Educational Association, but with a decidedly more Marxist tinge. Clearly, and with typical thoroughness, Ingham had been schooling himself for a political career.

On the evening of 11 February 1964 he was summoned to the Leeds Trades Hall to be interviewed by the Executive Committee of the City Labour Party. According to notes of the meeting made by Dick Knowles, the party's full-time agent, when 'asked why he wanted to go on the Council, Ingham replied: "Planning, Housing, Transport"'. As a known party sympathiser, he must have passed muster, for Knowles noted laconically underneath: 'Moved. Agreed.'[7] Ingham was on the candidates' list – the first step on the road.

The following week, he struck a deal with Solly Pearce, a wealthy Jewish tailor who ran the party's newspaper, the *Leeds Weekly Citizen*. The *Citizen* was unique – professionally produced from a building in Queen Square, well regarded, half a century old, the only official Labour Party weekly of its type. Pearce was always keen to fill his pages. Ingham was always keen to express his views. A columnist was born.

Albion made his debut on 28 February 1964 with an attack on the Prime Minister, Sir Alec Douglas-Home: 'no greater harm could have befallen the country than to have had inflicted upon it by a manifestly undemocratic process, however normal, a Prime Minister who is irrelevant to the problems both at home and abroad.' This, as we have seen, was mild stuff, no more than a polite clearing of the throat, compared with what was to come. In the *Guardian* office, Mike Parkin would occasionally look up from his work to find that his colleague's face, ruddy at the best of times, was turning even redder than usual. That was the sign that Ingham was writing his column.

Five months earlier, Ingham had been with the *Guardian*'s team at Scarborough for the Labour Party conference. It was there that Harold Wilson had made his famous speech about a 'new' Britain being forged by the 'white heat' of technology. The excitement it generated was reflected in the *Guardian*'s own front page report, written by John Cole, which hailed Wilson's performance as 'superb . . . the best platform speech of his career', proof that the Labour leader's 'hard political shell covers a sincere and reforming spirit.'[8]

This enthusiasm for Wilson was all the rage in the period 1963–4 and Ingham, in the guise of Albion, was in the vanguard of the cheering crowd. 'Britain under Harold Wilson,' he asserted on 12 June, 'could be sure of thoughtful, professional leadership.' The Conservative Party was perceived, even by many of its supporters, as out of step with the times. Or, as Ingham put it characteristically on 3 July:

> The plain fact is that this raddled lot with their class approach to wages and salaries on the one hand and capital gains and dividends on the other are incapable of securing the co-operation that could produce the conditions necessary for 'controlled development' of the economy.

Or, even more characteristically, on 8 August:

> The trouble with Sir Alec and the whole terrible Tory tribe is that they are stuck with a feudal mentality in a potentially brave new world of social, scientific and technological revolution.

But there was more to Ingham's column than the mere following of intellectual fashion. It did not spring from some temporary infatuation with Harold Wilson and the wonderful world of science. It was founded on the bedrock of an absolute loathing of the Conservatives. 'From now on,' he wrote on 17 April, 'everything must be subordinated to the task of demolishing this battered remnant of an opponent still arrogant in its cowardice.' The Tory Party stood for everything he despised. The words seethed and foamed from his pen with a fluency he could never manage in his everyday journalism. Conservatives were public school southerners who had had it easy – snobs, 'fossils', 'goons', parasites living off unearned income, 'contemptuous of the common man's intelligence', 'diseased' and 'bonkers', forever looking down their long noses at the likes of him, expecting the workers to be grateful for their television sets and similar crumbs from the rich man's table:

> Everywhere the call – nay the demand – is for gratitude. But everywhere, fellow serfs, crude humanity refuses to be grateful for the fruits of this paternal feudalism ... As for my television set, I had that in 1959 when I was last told I'd never had it so good. But I still rebelled at the polling booth, because this is one serf who has not the slightest intention of being grateful for small mercies when others have huge mercies for, in my opinion, less effort, less ability, less application and less work.[9]

These, it is worth bearing in mind, were not the passing protests of some teenage militant. They were the settled opinions of a man of thirty-two. As the opinion polls continued to point to a Labour victory in the coming election, Ingham was jubilant. 'Night is upon the Tories,' he chortled in April 1964. 'And night must fall.' In August he was rubbing his hands in anticipation: 'All the rag bag lot of them are about to meet their Waterloo.'[10]

'Labour will win,' he predicted on the eve of polling. 'My estimate is by a margin of at least thirty-six seats. This would be enough to lift Britain out of the feudal strife into which the country could sink with Sir Alec.'[11] He was over-optimistic. On 16 October 1964, Harold Wilson scraped into Downing Street with a majority of four. It may not have been a victory on the scale he had hoped for, but few can have celebrated the end of the Conservatives' 13-year reign more joyfully than Bernard Ingham.

Privately, he nurtured hopes of becoming a Member of Parliament himself. To several friends he confided his ambition of seeking the nomination in his old home constituency of Sowerby. This was not an unrealistic ambition. Although Garnet Ingham had by now retired from the Hebden Bridge council to nurse his ailing wife, he would still have been a useful ally in any selection battle. Douglas Houghton, the sitting MP, was in his sixty-seventh year. Who better to succeed him than Ingham: a local boy, an ardent trade unionist, a founder member of the local League of Labour Youth, a reporter on a distinguished left-wing newspaper? His acceptance on to Labour's list of candidates was designed to plug the one hole in this promising curriculum vitae: the fact that he had never previously stood for public office.

At the beginning of 1965, he was selected to fight the Conservative seat of Moortown in the forthcoming local elections. It was a daunting prospect. Moortown was one of the Tories' safest wards: street after street of rock solid, respectable Yorkshire bourgeoisie. Nevertheless Ingham set about contesting it with his customary thoroughness. He wrote Labour's campaign pamphlet ('LEEDS/heart of a NEW region/ help LABOUR to make it really tick') which, in the opinion of Dick Knowles, was one of the best pieces of propaganda the city party ever produced. After three pages of facts and figures, headlines and pictures, came Ingham's own election address:

Dear Elector,

I have accepted an invitation to stand as Labour candidate for Moortown for three main reasons. I believe that:

1. As a journalist I have served an adequate apprenticeship for membership of a local authority;
2. I have something to offer Moortown, Leeds and Yorkshire through my broad understanding of their problems;
3. The Labour Party should be supported in its effort to bring about radical – and much-needed – changes in our society.

On May 13 YOU have an opportunity to lend your support by voting for ME. And if every Labour voter in Moortown takes the trouble to vote, Labour CAN take this so-called Tory citadel by storm.

Give me five minutes of your time on May 13 and I will give you many hours' service in return. My object is to serve you by securing imaginative, efficient and socially just local government.

Thank you.

Yours faithfully,

BERNARD INGHAM.

This appeal was rounded off with the slogan 'Let's get things done VOTE INGHAM' and was accompanied by a picture of the candidate, fat-cheeked and unsmiling.

He took time off from the *Guardian* to pound the streets, delivering his leaflet. He bussed in colleagues to help with the canvassing, among them Mike Parkin and two reporters from the Manchester office, Victor Keegan and R. W. Shakespeare. They even got up at dawn on polling day to deliver a last-minute appeal: 'if everyone who THINKS Labour VOTES Labour we can WIN'. By the end, Ingham had fallen prey to a syndrome common among first-time candidates in hopeless seats: he had convinced himself victory was within his grasp. It was pure self-delusion. In the local elections in May 1965

Labour performed badly everywhere. Moortown registered an 8.5 per cent swing to the Conservatives, and Ingham ran a very poor second:

Mrs L. E. Henson (Conservative)	5,532
Mr B. Ingham (Labour)	1,485
Mr K. R. Dunn (Liberal)	561
Mr P. Boyles (Communist)	190

For all his hard work, the result was exactly in line with others across the city.

In 1989, Ingham reminisced sweetly that he was 'comprehensively beaten by an extremely nice old lady.'[12] At the time, however, in the *Leeds Weekly Citizen*, his response to his defeat was less magnanimous. He ascribed Labour's poor showing in the local elections to

> stunning apathy on the part of Labour supporters and a relative eagerness on the part of reactionary minds to rush to the defence of their 'brass' ... The Socialistic notion had the same effect on Tory voters – most of whom have plenty to defend – as a bit of sun has on a chrysalis: it hatched them and sent them flitting about their business.[13]

In fact, although Albion's readers did not know it, by the time this article appeared its author had done a little flitting of his own. Defeated in Leeds on the Thursday night, on the following Monday morning he left Yorkshire to begin a new job – at the *Guardian*'s head office in London.

Ingham already had some limited experience of working in the capital. Occasionally in the previous year, if a member of the paper's labour staff had been off sick or on leave, he had been summoned down to spend a few days filling in. At that time the *Guardian*'s labour correspondent was Peter Jenkins. When, in the spring of 1965, Jenkins's deputy, Eric Jacobs, took a job as press adviser to the newly-created Prices and Incomes Board, the Yorkshireman was the obvious replacement.

At first, until he was able to move his family down, Ingham had to stay during the week at a grimy hotel behind the newspaper, only travelling home to Leeds at weekends. In the evenings, with nowhere else to go, he would hang around the Grays Inn Road offices long after his colleagues had gone home. Eventually he bought a bungalow in Purley, on the southern outskirts of London; Nancy and John joined him; they settled into a new life.

In leaving Leeds he had not abandoned his political ambitions. Far from it. He still talked hopefully about the Sowerby nomination. He maintained the Albion column, and thereby kept a toe in the water of Yorkshire politics. But the next couple of years were ones of gradual disillusionment as two of the institutions he respected most – the British trade union movement and the *Guardian* newspaper – badly let him down.

To begin with there were no apparent problems. The fearsome clique of labour correspondents was penetrated without too much difficulty. Monty Meth, his friend from the Leeds industrial scene, had also moved down south; he helped with introductions. The labour lobby tended to divide into two camps, one centred around Keith McDowall of the *Daily Mail*, and the other around John Grant of the *Daily Express*; Ingham gravitated towards the latter. With the Wilson government in office and with the trade unions approaching the peak of their power, these were the days when the labour correspondents were mighty barons in Fleet Street. The 'number ones' – men like Geoffrey Goodman of the *Daily Mirror* and Jenkins of the *Guardian* – supped, if not with princes, then at least with Cabinet ministers and general secretaries. Their deputies, the 'number twos' – men like

Ingham and the 26-year-old John Torode of the *Financial Times* – were expected to produce large amounts of copy. Both the *Guardian* and the *FT* prided themselves on a comprehensive service of labour news. Ingham and Torode formed an alliance. One might cover the transport workers while the other would ring round the executive of the seamen's union. They would then exchange information, much as Ingham had done with his colleagues in Halifax a decade earlier.

Yet again the same phrases about Ingham recur: 'brilliant shorthand', 'diligent in the extreme', 'a grindingly hard worker', 'accurate', 'absolutely straight', 'fair'. He was soon churning out news stories at a greater rate than ever. 'After 17 years of straining blood out of millstone grit,' he would later say, 'I found that government, considered in its widest sense, not merely served it up on a plate in London but often washed it down, too.'[14] What were all these pansy southerners complaining about?

Among the trade unions, he had particularly good contacts with the miners, especially those members of the NUM executive from the Yorkshire area. According to Harry Whewell: 'While all the other reporters tended to concentrate on the leaders, Bernard would be off in the pub with some ordinary delegate who was telling him things he wasn't supposed to.' Another valuable source was Vic Feather, then assistant general secretary of the TUC. Ingham and Feather found they had plenty in common: both were north countrymen, both down-to-earth no-nonsense types, both suspicious of Oxbridge intellectuals, yet both deputies to exactly such men – in Ingham's case, Peter Jenkins and in Feather's, George Woodcock.

Given a choice between the worker by hand and the worker by brain, Ingham favoured the former any day. His loyalty to the Labour Party was never in question ('we took it for granted,' said Geoffrey Goodman) but there was a type of socialism which he hated: the theoretical, the airy-fairy, the chic revolutionary, the 'look-at-me-how-radical-I am' tendency of the ultra-left. This was shown most strongly just before Christmas 1965 when Henry Solomons, the Labour MP for Hull North, suddenly died, cutting the government's majority to one and precipitating a by-election. Hull North was highly marginal. Labour's majority was less than 1,200. If ever there was a time for all good men to come to the aid of the party, this was it. Yet what happened? Richard Gott, a Labour Party member – a journalist on the *Guardian*, to boot – decided to stand as a candidate of the Radical Alliance. Gott was protesting at the Wilson government's support for America in the Vietnam War. Albion was outraged.

> He is prepared because of what I accept is a sincere abhorrence of the conflict in Vietnam personally to bring down the Labour Government. As an historian he will no doubt appreciate the niche in history that this would give him.
>
> As an individual he has a perfect right to seek this sort of glory, or infamy, depending on one's point of view. But as a member of the Labour Party he has no right at all. He surrendered his right to act in this way the minute he joined it . . . In this situation he classes himself – quite unjustifiably I'm sure – with the Trotskyists who use this party as a respectable cover for their disreputable activities . . . He is in these circumstances no better than the meanest Young Socialist who has been corrupted by that miserable bunch of intellectual bullies, whose main deficiency is intelligence, which inhabits the fringes of the Labour Movement.

Ingham's stance on the issue of Vietnam was equally robust:

> I take exception to those who clamour, often mechanically, for the immediate withdrawal of all foreign troops from Vietnam,

meaning, of course, American troops, and the holding of free elections which, in the circumstances of an immediate American withdrawal, would be just about as free as a Great Train Robber in Durham Gaol ... We shall not achieve a thing if the Americans pull out tomorrow. All that we shall do is sanction an even more horrible bloodbath ...

There has to be a negotiated settlement. And those who delay the return to the negotiating table are the people to whom Mr Gott and the Radical Alliance should direct their challenge. Not the Labour Government. Not Harold Wilson. Not Michael Stewart. This is the Government and they are the statesmen who want a negotiated settlement. And it is they who are trying to get it.[15]

(In the event, Gott's challenge fizzled out. In January 1966 Labour held Hull North with a majority of more than 5,000: a result hailed by Ingham as 'a magnificent Tory-shattering victory ... a real tonic.')[16]

For students of Bernard Ingham this article is something of a key text. There is, first, the overwhelming personal antipathy to the *Guardian* pointy-head, Gott, which no amount of weasel words ('what I accept is a sincere abhorrence ... quite unjustifiably I'm sure') can fully disguise. Secondly, with its thuggish denunciation of Trotskyists ('miserable bunch of intellectual bullies') and sympathy for the American presence in Vietnam (essential to prevent 'an even more horrible bloodbath'), it places him firmly on the Healeyite Right of the Labour Party. Thirdly, and most importantly, it shows what might be called Ingham's reverence for authority. It is genuinely incomprehensible to him that people should step out of line and question the wisdom of the 'statesmen' in charge of the nation's affairs: for 'this,' as he puts it in his most revealing phrase, 'is the *Government*'. Here, as early as 1965, inside the shell of a supposedly left-wing journalist, is the future Whitehall press officer struggling to get out.

For Ingham, Harold Wilson could do no wrong. He stood 'head and shoulders above all other political leaders'. He was 'the outstanding national leader in British politics today'. He had 'given the lie to that ridiculous myth about Labour's incapability of governing'. He was 'a Prime Minister with an obvious ability not merely to walk but to command the world's stage'. James Callaghan's Budget was a 'tour de force': 'a springboard from which to launch ourselves on what has already been called the Wilsonian Grand Design'.[17]

At the start of the General Election campaign in March 1966, Ingham proclaimed that 'Labour has exceeded the wildest dreams of those who hoped it would jerk this country out of the inertia into which it had fallen under Conservatism.' Even taking into account the audience at which it was aimed – the Labour faithful – this was laying it on a bit thick. He listed nine factors which made it essential for the Wilson Government to be re-elected, including its 'redistribution of wealth', its 'determination to intervene in industrial trouble spots', its 'substitution of the savage stop-go system with the controlled operation of a flat-out economy' (whatever that might be), and 'its drive for reform of the educational system on comprehensive lines'.[18]

Anyone who attacked the Labour Government was, in Ingham's eyes, an enemy. They were undermining the only party 'likely to act fairly and decently to all groups of people'. If the attackers came from within the Labour movement itself, they were even more reprehensible. They were traitors. When, two months after the election, the seamen went on strike, they received scant sympathy from Albion. Their claim – effectively, for a 17 per cent pay increase – threatened to sail a large hole through the Government's pay 'norm' of 3.5 per cent. The 'saddest part of this whole miserable affair,' wrote Ingham in the *Leeds Weekly Citizen*, 'is that brother has been set against brother.'

> The seamen who have gone on strike – and all the unions fighting the incomes policy – should realise once and for all what they are doing.
>
> If I need to spell it out, they are sabotaging the Government's chances of successfully applying the policies it was elected to carry out. They are conspiring to set back the progressive forces which were unleashed at the General Election.[19]

The strike dragged on for seven weeks and did indeed do immense damage to the Government, reducing exports by 20 per cent, draining £38 million from the gold and currency reserves, and contributing to a run on sterling which eventually turned into the 1966 July Crisis. Ingham spent much of his time covering the strike almost literally camped outside the headquarters of the National Union of Seamen (NUS) in Clapham. In the *Guardian* during the week he was a neutral, strictly factual Dr Jekyll; in the *Leeds Weekly Citizen* at the weekends he became an opinionated, foaming Mr Hyde. At the end of the second week he wrote an article entitled 'The Seamen's Strike: Why we should support the Government'. On 10 June he accused the unions not only of failing 'to show any gratitude towards the Labour Government' but also of lacking any 'intellectual appreciation of the situation'.

At least eight members of the NUS Executive had communist sympathies. They were famously denounced in the House of Commons on 20 June 1966 by Harold Wilson as a 'tightly-knit group of politically motivated men'. Three days before Wilson's attack, Ingham criticized:

> the bulk of moderate Labour MPs who have remained strangely silent about the strike, its consequences and implications.
>
> We were told that the 1964 and 1966 intakes into Parliament

were the brightest and best for many a long year. To me, the events of the last few weeks have proved neither their brilliance nor their worth; merely their dumbness ... A lot of things have needed saying over the past four weeks ... It grieves me that I have had to say them in the *Citizen*. I expect MPs to speak out against wrongs, including trade union wrongs ...

For Ingham, the seamen's strike was a kind of Damascene conversion in reverse: the point on the road at which he began to be blinded by doubts. Hitherto his vision of the world had been a simple one: the Tories represented a feudal, failed Britain; Labour stood for partnership and progress. Yet suddenly the unions – the institutions he and his family had set so much store by, which he had spent half his working life writing about – were ratting on their side of the bargain. They were behaving as selfishly as any capitalists. Worse, they were jeopardizing the very government they had helped elect. Meanwhile, the Parliamentary Labour Party was in the grip of a new intake of supine intellectuals, unwilling to confront a manifest wrong.

These feelings did not come hurtling out of an entirely clear sky in the summer of 1966. Six months earlier, Ingham had put his finger on what was to prove a central weakness of Labour governments for the best part of two decades:

Either we trade unionists believe what we say when we talk about the brotherhood of man and social justice or we don't. And if we are not prepared to practise what we preach – often, I suspect, so hypocritically from conference platforms – we should shut up.

We – and that goes for me as well as every other trade unionist – have to show that we have the humanity we so often deny to capitalists. If we don't we shall be branded by history as the biggest hypocrites since the Bible-toting Victorian (and

649

some Elizabethan) mill owners; the Sunday saints who literally overnight became or become Monday devils.[20]

But after the seamen's strike, these feelings coalesced to become almost an obsession. It was as if Ingham felt personally let down by the unions. From now on, week after week in the *Leeds Weekly Citizen*, he berated them with the indignation he had once reserved for the Tory Party. 'I might as well tell you before, instead of after, the event,' he wrote on 3 June, 'that if the busmen come out they will not have much sympathy from me.' In July, Frank Cousins, the left-wing former leader of the Transport and General Workers' Union, resigned from the Cabinet in protest at the Government's incomes policy. Ingham was derisive about this 'prima donna':

> Somehow I'm supposed to get worked up about the resignation of Frank Cousins ... And yet I can't. This is perhaps because I am one of those who can never make head or tail of what Frank Cousins says when he gets to a rostrum. And, believe you me, I try hard.[21]

He did not have much time for the leader of the white collar workers' union, either: 'I would never bank on Clive Jenkins supporting a Government which secured a drastic transformation of our society. The great strength of Clive's position is that he is insatiable.'[22]

Such blunt home truths did not, predictably, go down well with the more orthodox comrades who subscribed to the *Leeds Weekly Citizen*. The paper began to carry regular letters of complaint. One reader described Albion as the political equivalent of Ken Dodd. Ingham loved it. 'If all this does not provoke a fierce row in the correspondence columns of the *Citizen* then nothing will,' he wrote at the end of one anti-union diatribe. 'Blast away, please!' He delighted in taunting his readers: 'for too long I have felt able to get away with any outrage ... you are soul-destroying in your apathy.'[23]

The longer he wrote the column, the more self-revelational it became. By the end of 1966, the full Ingham persona, which twenty years later was to earn him from foreign journalists the nickname 'Bernie the Bear', was on vigorous display: earthy, irascible, rude, aggressive – often to the point of self-parody and, occasionally, beyond it. On 14 October he described how he had found himself the previous week with a 'group who were pleased to call themselves rising young executives'.

> And I happened to say some blunt things about our lily-livered national newspaper proprietors collapsing at the first whiff of grapeshot from the printing unions, breaching the [pay] freeze and then laying all the blame on to the Government for not doing its own dirty work.
>
> 'Good Lord,' one of them said, 'we've got a right communist here.'
>
> Had I anything more to do with this particular rising young executive he would neither rise nor continue to execute.

Ingham then described how one of these proto-yuppies, earning four times the national average wage, had denounced as greedy a man on £11 a week who had asked for more. 'I told him,' said Ingham (and it requires little effort of the imagination to hear him doing it), 'that if I were on £11 a week I would not merely want another £1 per week. I'd damn well get it.'

Ingham's column leapt out from the pages of the *Leeds Weekly Citizen* like a firework on a grey day. On 21 April 1967, Solly Pearce forgot to print Albion's by-line and the following week published a wry apology: 'We regret the absence of his "name" from the article, but discerning readers would have known from its individual style who was its writer.' They certainly would. Albion had now been making his inimitable contributions for more than three years. But henceforth the *Citizen*'s readers would have to manage without him. By coincidence, that very week, Ingham had filed his last dispatch from the political battlefield. He had ceased to be a columnist; indeed, he had ceased to be a journalist.

The exact sequence of steps which led to Ingham's resignation from the *Guardian* is difficult to retrace. Those who were involved, when questioned today, tend to be afflicted by flashes of amnesia. Who can blame them? Not many journalists would care to confess that they once helped deprive of a job the man who is now the most powerful press secretary in the country.

The basic cause was the nature of the *Guardian* itself. It was – and is – a progressive, liberal newspaper. But then there is no snob quite like a progressive, liberal snob. Whatever it is like today, a quarter of a century ago there was a definite division on the editorial floor between gentlemen and players. The gentlemen composed elegant leaders and leader-page articles, and provided the front-page stories. The players produced the other nine-tenths of the paper. 'People often spoke of the *Guardian* as a snobby paper,' remembered Harry Whewell. 'For instance, reporters would come into the Manchester office from some local paper to do shift work and no one would speak to them. Bernard, I think, was always a bit over-awed by the *Guardian*, and he felt it more when he got to London.'

The 'number one' labour correspondent was, by tradition, a gentleman; the 'number two' was a player. Peter Jenkins would cover the main story of the day and contribute to the discussions about the leader; Ingham did the rest. 'He found he was a bit of a dogsbody,' recalled one old *Guardian* reporter. 'He was the guy who stood shivering outside the Ministry of Labour waiting for the result of some arbitration.' Years later, in his regular homilies on media standards, there was always something heartfelt about the way Ingham spoke of the Poor Bloody Infantry of the newsroom: he once described ordinary reporters as 'an endangered species': 'One of my ambitions is to elevate the reporter in the hierarchy of newspapers. He is the prospector in the geology of news who digs and pans for the gold of which a service to the public is made.'[24]

'He was very nice to work with: extremely conscientious,' recalled Jenkins, who was two years younger than his deputy. 'He probably thought I was a bit flash and metropolitan.' Keith Harper, who currently has Jenkins's old job on the *Guardian* and who was then a young reporter, remembers Ingham as a red-faced figure, arms akimbo, always in the forefront of office politics, a human dynamo, 'the engine room of the labour coverage'.

> Peter would be turning out the airy features while Bernard hammered out four news stories a day. I remember him in shirt-sleeves in '67 coming in with bits of copy to the news desk complaining about Peter's absence but actually revelling in it because it gave him an opportunity to make a name for himself.

Matters were brought to a head early in 1967 when Harold Evans, editor of the *Sunday Times*, offered Jenkins the chance to write a column. Alastair Hetherington promptly offered him a similar role on the *Guardian*. Jenkins accepted. The post of labour correspondent now fell vacant.

Not surprisingly, Ingham believed the position should be his. He had been Jenkins's deputy for two years. He had worked hard. He had the contacts and the experience. But Jenkins was dubious: 'In those days, the labour correspondent's job was second only to the political correspondent's; it was a stepping stone to greater things.' Jenkins's immediate predecessor, John Cole, was now news editor; Cole's predecessor, John Anderson, was northern editor. Nobody could imagine Ingham in such a senior role on the *Guardian*. He was not, to be frank, regarded as officer material. He was not Oxbridge. He was not even redbrick. He lacked intellectual self-confidence and made up for it by what came across as a belligerent anti-intellectualism. His colleagues would have been amazed by the fluency of his Albion columns: under his own by-line his style was stilted, conventional, dull. In Jenkins's words: 'The view – and it was not just mine – was that Bernard's experience as an industrial reporter just down from the north was not up to being chief labour correspondent.'

Jenkins's refusal to recommend his deputy for promotion was the Black Spot for Ingham. Whatever chance he might have had vanished. There was a painful interview during which Ingham's alleged deficiencies were made brutally clear to him. The *Guardian*, he was told, had decided to bring in an outside candidate and, to Ingham, their final choice must have seemed a calculated slap in the face. John Torode, his colleague on the *Financial Times*, was only 27 years old – seven years his junior. He was also much less experienced. He had been a Fleet Street labour reporter for just eighteen months. What he did have was a university education. Oxford, Cornell and Harvard trumped Hebden Bridge, Halifax and Leeds.

Ingham took it very badly. 'It was pretty rough on him,' remembered Jenkins, 'because he'd moved his family down.' Keith Harper recalled him 'vociferously complaining about his lot . . . [He] felt very aggrieved.' Another *Guardian* reporter describes 'a terrible set-to in public' between Ingham and one of the paper's senior editors. Around the office there was considerable sympathy for him. For he had not been simply passed over; he had been humiliated. It had been made abundantly clear to him that, as things stood, his prospects of promotion were bleak. In his later years, Ingham was to reveal a profound contempt for his old profession and it may well be that it was formed, at least in part, by his experiences at the hands of the *Guardian* in the spring of 1967.

It was at this point, with his career precariously balanced, that a *deus ex machina* appeared. It assumed the form of Eric Jacobs, whose decision to leave the *Guardian* to work for the Prices and Incomes Board (PIB) had brought Ingham down to London in the first place. Jacobs, too, had now been offered a job by Harold Evans. Quite by chance, according to Jacobs, he rang his old friend Peter Jenkins to tell him he was going to the *Sunday Times*. Ingham, who shared an office with Jenkins, heard the news and spotted the opportunity in a flash. A few minutes later he rang Jacobs back. Would he be willing to recommend him, Ingham, as his successor as press adviser to the PIB? It was the perfect solution for all concerned. Jacobs, who was keen to leave as soon as a replacement could be found, was delighted to have a name – any name – to put forward. The PIB was anxious to fill the post at once. Ingham was keen to get out of the *Guardian*. The *Guardian* was happy to let him go. A couple of days later, he was offered a short-term contract to run from 1 May 1967.

If the Civil Service did not regard this as a permanent arrangement, neither did Ingham. He wanted a break from a newspaper where he felt badly done by. He also, with typically dogged determination, wanted to improve himself: to ensure he would not be treated in such a fashion again. 'I was told it would make me a better journalist,' he subsequently said of his move to the PIB. 'My intention at the end of it was to return to the practice of journalism all the better for the Whitehall experience.'[25] He thought he would be in and out in one year; two at the most. Nobody, least of all him, dreamed he would still be there nearly a quarter of a century later.

On 28 April, the *Leeds Weekly Citizen* published Albion's final column. '"No man is an island,"' he quoted. 'Yet if we rationalize Conservative philosophy, we soon discover that, in their view, man really is an island. And the bigger his island the better they think he is.' With that characteristic observation, he turned his back on the *Citizen*, resigned from the Labour Party (as he was obliged to do under Civil Service rules) – and disappeared into the anonymity of Whitehall.

FOUR

Press Officer

'Bernard Ingham came to see me. He's a very difficult man . . .'
TONY BENN, DIARY ENTRY, 30 OCTOBER 1975[1]

It is a prejudice widespread among journalists that all press officers, however grand their rank, are really just failed reporters. In the summer of 1967 this would have been a harsh but not wholly unfair assessment of Bernard Ingham. He was close to his thirty-fifth birthday and had been slogging away at his chosen profession for nearly nineteen years. True, he had risen from a local weekly to a Fleet Street daily. But by the mid-1960s there were ominous signs that he had gone as far as he was likely to get. Already, younger and less experienced men were streaking past him. He was not a fluent writer. He was not a scoop-monger. 'I never felt confident,' he once said of his work as a journalist, 'and never settled for not feeling confident.'[2] This was a revealing admission. The aggressive exterior and the phenomenal work-rate hid a more tentative spirit than might have been suspected.

Once, in a speech in 1986, he quoted Bismarck's maxim, that 'a journalist is a man who has missed his calling'. It was truer of Ingham than most. Having talked to his colleagues, ploughed through his journalism and read his Polonius-like

657

lectures on the profession – with their emphasis on duty, responsibility, service and respect for the integrity of government – it is hard to avoid the conclusion that he was not really cut out for what Francis Williams called the 'Dangerous Estate'. There are all sorts of journalists: the elegant and provocative essayists, the macho foreign correspondents, the show-offs who thrive on being first with the news, the hangers-on of the rich and famous, the gossips, the malcontents, the mischief-makers, the conspiracy theorists (it was a deputy editor of *The Times*, no less, who once advised any young journalist interviewing a politician to keep asking themself 'Why is this bastard lying to me?'). Ingham was none of these. He was a frustrated man of power. Instinctively, he respected rather than suspected authority. He should have been one of those curmudgeonly, northern, right-wing Labour MPs. And who knows? If Douglas Houghton had retired at the 1966 general election he might have become one. Instead, he happened upon the perfect substitute. He became a civil servant.

When Ingham walked into his new office in Kingsgate House, Victoria Street in May 1967, it was like coming home. 'I found, on the inside, how little I had known,' he said later, 'how much there was to learn, and how much enjoyment I could get out of trying to solve problems.'[3] The PIB, set up in 1965, had the power to poke its nose into every wage and price increase in the country. It had the statutory right to summon witnesses and collect information. Its rulings had the force of law. Ingham had long supported it: 'a bold and praiseworthy idea,' he called it.[4] Now his task was to boost its public image.

His predecessor, Eric Jacobs, had had a deputy and four or five clerks who would answer the telephones, write letters to members of the public, and snip out press clippings about the Board and its doings. Jacobs professed himself 'bored stiff'.

When the Treasury had suggested that he could manage with-out a deputy he had readily agreed. He finally left because it seemed to him there was 'nothing much to do'.

Ingham changed all that. A new deputy was hired. He took to coming in himself early in the morning to compile a detailed summary of the day's press. Like so many others, the Board's senior civil servant, Alex Jarratt, was immediately impressed by Ingham's 'immense capacity for work' and by the fact that 'he had strong views on most things'. According to Jarratt, Ingham and his predecessor 'could not have been more unalike. Eric was sophisticated and cultivated. Bernard was much more rugged and from a quite different back-ground. Eric was interested in concepts. Bernard was just very anxious to project the Board and its chairman, Aubrey Jones.'

In fact, rather like the blind man who didn't wish to cross the road, the reserved and donnish Jones didn't always want to be 'projected', Ingham-style. He acidly described his new press adviser as 'very zealous, to the point of excess.' Clive Jenkins recalled a meeting he had with Jones: Ingham attended and 'repeatedly interrupted to protect him.'[5] More than twenty years later, Jones could still recall a vigorous argument at Manchester Airport when he felt his press adviser was trying to browbeat him into doing something he had no wish to. Journalists also claimed to detect a different style at the PIB. Whereas the laid-back and gossipy Jacobs would happily leak stories over lunch, Ingham, in the words of one reporter, was 'a jailer of information'.

This combination of zeal and discretion may not have been to everybody's taste, but it certainly brought its practitioner a growing reputation in Whitehall. This was just as well, for eleven months after Ingham joined the civil service, Harold Wilson embarked on yet another administrative shake-up. In April 1968, the old Ministry of Labour was given cosmetic surgery, and rechristened the Department of Employment and

Productivity (DEP). The PIB was tossed in to add to the impression that this was some sort of dynamic new organization. On 5 April Barbara Castle was promoted from the Ministry of Transport to run the DEP as the new Secretary of State. She was now, albeit at several removes, Ingham's boss.

His fate was decided over Sunday afternoon tea two days later at Mrs Castle's country cottage. Denis Barnes, the Permanent Secretary, travelled down to see her to discuss personnel. The conversation turned to the question of who should be head of information at the new department. 'She wanted to import her man from Transport,' recalled Barnes. 'Well, the last thing I wanted to do was say "yes" to that. She already had a reputation for sacking people and bringing in her own team. I would immediately have been seen as being under her thumb.' Barnes's solution was to suggest she appoint the energetic new boy at the PIB, Bernard Ingham. There was one snag. The old Ministry of Labour already had a head of information: a former industrial correspondent in his fifties named Charles Birdsall.

There now occurs such a conflict of evidence and testimony regarding this crucial stage of Ingham's career that the only honest course is to offer both versions. According to Sir Denis Barnes: 'We had to pretend Birdsall was still chief information officer. He was very upset, but he wasn't so far off retirement. Bernard managed it very well and went out of his way to make sure his feelings weren't hurt.' Sir Alex Jarratt, who became Deputy Under Secretary at the new department, has a similar recollection: Birdsall, he has stated, was 'pushed to one side'. These memories are backed up by other sources. On 20 May 1968, the *Financial Times* reported Ingham's appointment as 'Director of Information' at the DEP. Ingham's own *Who's Who* entry reads simply: 'Chief Inf. Officer, DEP, 1968–73'. Barnes says that Ingham 'seemed to suit Barbara; he got on very well with her'. This impression was shared by other observers: 'He was very close to Barbara' (Geoffrey Goodman); 'He became very attached to Barbara' (Peter Jenkins); 'She had a high regard for him' (Alex Jarratt).

Barbara Castle's own version is, however, quite different. In her capacious diaries of the period, Ingham first appears on 18 May 1968, when our heroine is suffering from acute toothache and preparing for the Second Reading of the Prices and Incomes Bill:

> I tried to make progress with Bernard Ingham's rough redraft of my speech with very little success. Bernard has tried to liven up the ghastly officialese of the Department but I wouldn't say I have got myself a Kennedy-type speechwriter yet. However, he is still very new, poor man.

A footnote to this entry records flatly: 'When, to my great regret, Charles Birdsall retired, I brought Bernard Ingham over from the PIB where he was Press and Public Relations Adviser, to be my Chief Information Officer.' Yet Birdsall did not in fact retire until September 1969: Castle attended his farewell party and wrote in her diary that she would 'miss [him] terribly'.[6]

At first glance, there is an obvious explanation for this discrepancy: in order to save face, Birdsall was allowed to keep the title for eighteen months while Ingham actually had the power. But that is not Baroness Castle's recollection:

> Charles Birdsall was my main fellow . . . From the point of view of press contact and the general feel for how to handle the press, I thought Charles was a wonderful old boy . . . I didn't have that rapport with Bernard at all . . . I found him a bit dull, a bit stodgy . . . He didn't impinge on me at all . . . I can't say I was massively impressed by him.

Nor is it the picture drawn in her diaries. These show Birdsall ('a pocket dynamo of a man,' according to one former colleague, 'restless and unremittingly energetic')[7] to have been at her side throughout the first, turbulent eighteen months of her rule at the Department. On 24 April 1968, for example, 'poor devoted Charles' is still hanging around the office at 2.30 a.m.; on 18 October 'Charles was doing his usual magnificent stuff, seeing that the press got the picture right'; on 18 June 1969, after the collapse of *In Place of Strife* (see below), 'Charles could not have been more loyal and comforting'. Ingham, by contrast, merits half a dozen perfunctory entries, conspicuous for their lack of flattery. Therefore, unless memory and diary have both been severely edited, it would seem that Ingham was not nearly as important to Barbara Castle as his contemporaries suggest: not least because he can only have been her 'main fellow' from September 1969 (when Birdsall went) to June 1970 (when the Labour Government fell), a period of a mere nine months.

There is a slight but poignant element of unrequited love about all this, for if she scarcely noticed him, he obviously adored her. Jarratt detected in him an element of protectiveness, almost of chivalry. 'He was devoted to her,' recalled Geoffrey Goodman. 'He thought she was an outstanding person in every respect. I think it was partly the Yorkshire connection. One got the impression that here was red-haired Yorkshire Bernard devoted to red-haired Yorkshire Barbara.' A former *Guardian* colleague watched him in action with her during an official visit. 'She'd say: "Right, come along Bernard!" and you could see that he loved it. She was to him what a duchess was to Ramsay MacDonald.' He shared her accent, her background, her political beliefs. Above all, he admired her for trying to tackle the trade unions.

Castle's White Paper on the future of the unions, *In Place of Strife*, was published in January 1969. It contained three particularly controversial proposals: a twenty-eight day 'cooling-off' period for unofficial disputes, during which strikers would be obliged to return to work; compulsory pre-strike ballots in industries where the government believed a dispute would damage the economy; and the establishment of a Commission on Industrial Relations with the power to impose fines on trade unionists who breached its rulings. All this, of course, met with Ingham's warm approval. 'The Government,' he had written three years earlier, 'was not elected by trade unions to serve trade union ends. It was elected by the nation to serve the nation and – at least in the minds of many who voted for it – the wider cause of humanity.'[8]

He thus required no prodding from Barbara Castle to defend her policy: on this issue, both in 1969 and, ten years later, under Margaret Thatcher, he was more royalist than his Queen. 'When Bernard got on that side of the fence he became even more disillusioned with the unions,' remembered Peter Jenkins. 'People who wanted the Labour Government to succeed were increasingly frustrated with the bovine selfishness of the union bosses, and Bernard became very indignant.'

But from the start *In Place of Strife* was a doomed venture, an idea a decade ahead of its time. James Callaghan, then Home Secretary, opposed it. Labour's National Executive rejected it. A special conference of the TUC came out against it by a majority of 8 million votes. In desperation, the Government decided to produce a 'pop' version, written in the style of a tabloid newspaper, designed to appeal over the heads of the union leaders to the ordinary members. This was entrusted first to an official in Ingham's department, but Number 10 was unhappy with the result and passed it on to Joe Haines who had recently joined Harold Wilson's staff from the *Daily Mirror*. Haines rewrote it in a way which Ingham felt breached civil service rules on impartiality. 'I can remember,' Haines recalled, 'Ingham fuming at me: "The trouble with you is you're too political!" Which I think, given today's circumstances, is amusing.'

It hardly mattered. The pamphlet was never published. On 17 June ('the most traumatic day of my political life,' as Castle called it) the Cabinet rebelled and she and Wilson were obliged to capitulate to the TUC. 'You're soft, you're cowardly, you're lily-livered,' the Prime Minister railed at his colleagues, but he decided not to resign. This was one of the great turning points in British politics, clearing the way for the union militancy of the 1970s and the consequent rise of Margaret Thatcher. It was a turning point, too, in Ingham's life. According to Geoffrey Goodman: 'He was deeply disillusioned by the whole experience of *In Place of Strife*. It conditioned his attitude to the trade unions, without any question. The way the unions rounded on Barbara persuaded him that something had to be done to destroy their power and influence. That whole department, Bernard included, was in a state of shock.'

One year later, almost to the day, the Conservatives won the general election. The 'terrible Tory tribe,' as Ingham had once called it, was back – and this time he, as a civil servant, was obliged to work for it.

Ingham's political ambitions, at least in a party sense, had now been abandoned. He had resigned from the Labour Party on the day he entered Whitehall. Eighteen months later, at his request, his short-term contract had been converted into full, professional membership of the civil service. But he was obviously no ordinary mandarin. He had never tried to pretend that he was neutral. 'He made no secret of his political views,' recalled Neville Taylor, then a public relations adviser at the Ministry of Defence. 'There was a general awareness that this chap was different, because the rest of us didn't make a political comment, even among friends ... He was very open about his support for the Labour Government.'

The advent of a Conservative administration in June 1970

therefore left him in a peculiarly exposed position. Moreover, Edward Heath was pledged to introduce statutory controls on the unions. The Department of Employment was bound to be at the centre of a political storm and Ingham would have the crucial task of explaining its plans to the media. Could he do it? More importantly, would the new Secretary of State, Robert Carr, trust him to do it? According to Carr:

> Practically on my first day, Sir Denis Barnes came to see me and said Bernard Ingham wanted to have a word with me. What Bernard wanted to tell me was that he was still a committed supporter of the Labour Party and that he had stood as a local candidate. He said he wanted to tell me before anybody else did, especially as we were bound to be heading towards controversy over the Industrial Relations Bill. However he also said that, contrary to the views of most of the Labour Party, he was a passionate believer in creating a new framework of industrial law for the unions. He had been a very strong supporter of *In Place of Strife* – it wasn't just a matter of professional support. I made a few enquiries and everyone said he was very good: forceful, able, absolutely first class. So I kept him on.

Here was the clearest measure yet of how far Ingham had travelled politically, and how bitter was his disillusion with the unions. Five years earlier he had written in the *Leeds Weekly Citizen* that Tory plans to legislate on industrial disputes would be 'the kiss of death ... It is not in the Conservative nature, whatever they may say to the contrary, to wish to see a stronger and healthier trade union movement.'[9] In 1966, he had denounced the ideas which Heath now proposed to put into effect as 'dangerous drivel ... designed to appeal to the simple-minded':

> If you make procedures legally enforceable you have to have a means of enforcing them. This means fines and ultimately

imprisonment if you don't pay the penalty . . . But how do you enforce fines on, say 1000 miners? . . . If they refuse [to pay], do you send them to prison? And if you send them to prison, do you have enough cells to go round? Of course you don't. The whole miserable business would collapse the very day those 1000 miners marched to the doors of Armley Gaol and demanded instant incarceration.[10]

As it happened, this was one of Albion's more prescient pieces. By 1974, even the major employers' organization, the CBI, wanted the repeal of Heath's Industrial Relations Act, which they saw as inflammatory and unworkable. But at the time Ingham threw himself into the battle with a full heart, confident that Carr was only doing what Castle had tried and failed to do. He produced a series of five information films extolling the virtues of the Act ('for which, believe it or not,' he later claimed, 'there was a very brisk demand indeed').[11] He developed a considerable respect for his new boss, and the feeling was reciprocated. 'He knew his stuff,' said Carr.

Rather more unexpectedly, Ingham also got on well with Carr's successor, the charming, reformed alcoholic Etonian, Maurice Macmillan – a Treasury minister who was as startled as anyone else to find himself transferred to the Department of Employment. 'Bernard was frightfully good at covering for Maurice,' recalled Denis Barnes. Geoffrey Goodman also remembered Ingham saying how much he admired and respected Macmillan: 'What impressed Bernard was the way he handled the unions during this difficult period.' On one memorable occasion, in April 1972, Macmillan, Barnes and Ingham found themselves confronted outside the Department by a group of striking railwaymen, protesting at the Government's decision to order a ballot. Ingham was unimpressed. 'If you don't hold a ballot yourselves,' he growled at them, 'we'll hold the bloody ballot for you.'

Ingham's yeoman service during the industrial battles of the Heath years established his reputation in Whitehall. No longer was he seen as a creature of the Labour Party. Sir Donald Maitland, the former diplomat who had been brought back from the British embassy in Tripoli to serve as Heath's Press Secretary, was aware that Ingham supposedly had left-wing sympathies. 'But I would not have guessed that from his behaviour, from the way he carried out his job ... He was utterly reliable, a safe pair of hands, and gave me great support.' Maitland did not, at that time, rate him as the best information officer in the government, but certainly placed him 'in the top rank'.

These were the years of Edward Heath's grand, Gaullist press conferences in Lancaster House, as the Government struggled to put together a 'tripartite pact' with the CBI and the TUC to tackle the country's economic problems. Ingham was trusted enough to be part of a small, four-man team, chaired by Maitland, including Peter Middleton from the Treasury and Patrick Shovelton from the Department of Trade and Industry, which met weekly at Number 10 to co-ordinate press coverage. According to Maitland:

> Bernard's role was to mark the trade union side. He was not only on very good terms – terms of mutual respect – with the TUC, but also with the industrial correspondents. I had total confidence in his handling of that sector of these negotiations. His contributions at our own co-ordination debates were characteristic of Bernard: very much to the point, no mincing of words, short, concise ... He did have what people call 'northern directness'. He didn't go in for diplomatic niceties. He may have been a bit impatient: I wouldn't deny that. But I wasn't at the receiving end ...

For all the efforts of Ingham and his colleagues, the tripartite talks failed. Heath, like Wilson before him, had to impose a statutory prices and incomes policy. In November 1973, the miners began an overtime ban. A state of emergency was declared. With the country facing power cuts and on the brink of a three-day week, the Prime Minister played one of his few remaining cards. He brought back William Whitelaw from the Northern Ireland Office (where he had established a formidable reputation as a conciliator) and put him into the Department of Employment, replacing Macmillan. Whitelaw's brief, effectively, was to save the Government.

This, in turn, had alarming consequences for Ingham, for it quickly transpired that part of the price Whitelaw had demanded for his services was the right to bring across his own public relations officer from Belfast: Keith McDowall, former industrial editor of the *Daily Mail* and an old rival of Ingham from his labour corps days. Ingham fought desperately to retain a job he loved and at which he was held to be good. He enlisted the support of the Cabinet Office and of his superiors at the Department of Employment – to no avail. As Whitelaw subsequently explained: 'I was in a fairly powerful position because I didn't want to come back anyway . . . So they had to take it.'

At the beginning of December, Ingham had a series of painful interviews with Barnes and Whitelaw. 'I had to tell him that I was sorry,' said Whitelaw, 'that I had nothing against him personally, but that Keith McDowall had worked for me in Northern Ireland and I wished to bring him back. He obviously was disappointed because he enjoyed the job. He thought it was unreasonable.' At lunchtime on Wednesday 5 December, Barnes told him he would have to be sent home on what the Civil Service euphemistically called 'gardening leave' – suspended on full pay, whilst they tried to find him another job. It leaked to the press. It was deeply embarrassing. 'He was very upset,' according to Barnes. 'He took it badly.'

For a workaholic like Ingham, having to sit at home in
Purley as the country was gripped by the biggest industrial
crisis since 1926 must have been torture. Five weeks dragged
by. Eventually, in January 1974, he was given a new job. At
an annual salary of £8,000, Ingham was made Chief Information Officer at a new ministry: the Department of Energy.

The formation of the Energy Department, in the words of its
first Secretary of State, Lord Carrington, was an exercise in
'crisis management'. Electricity was being rationed, coal
stocks were dwindling, the price of oil had quadrupled. 'I was
plucked from the Ministry of Defence to go and head it,'
wrote Carrington. 'I went without enthusiasm ... For the
weeks that this lasted I retain no affection.'[12] Less than two
months later the Heath Government had fallen and Labour
was back in power.

Ingham might reasonably have hoped that with Whitelaw
gone, he could have returned to his old post at the Department of Employment. The new Labour Employment Secretary, Michael Foot, certainly toyed with the idea of reinstating
him. A few days after the formation of the government, he sat
near Peter Jenkins at a dinner party and asked his opinion of
Bernard Ingham. Jenkins gave a non-committal reply. The
idea was dropped.

Instead, Ingham passed the next fifteen months at Energy in
the congenial service of Eric Varley. Varley was exactly
Ingham's type of minister: a north countryman, a former
miner, moderate in his views, efficient in the dispatch of
business. His Chief Information Officer was soon making his
presence felt in the new department in his accustomed manner: part-gruff, part-cheerful; part-helpful, part-bully. Ronald
Custis, Varley's Private Secretary, had a 'friendly' but sometimes 'uneasy' relationship with him. They had a series of
running battles over access to classified information:

At the time [recalled Custis] there was a little bit of sensitivity about how much heads of information saw which wasn't relevant to their own departments. And I was applying the rules, saying 'No, you can't see this' or 'Yes, you may see that'. And he found this a bit upsetting and once or twice we had 'I'm-not-talking-to-you' sessions for a few days.

Another civil servant with whom Ingham had frequent rows was the deputy secretary responsible for energy conservation, Philip Jones. 'I often used to say to him,' Jones remembered, '"It's your job to present policy, not make it." He was always wanting to write great papers and there used to be stormy minutes flying between us as a result.' At heart, Ingham was what he always had been: a frustrated man of power. And although, in Jones's view, he 'ran the best public relations department in Whitehall', this propensity to argue and to involve himself in everyone else's business hampered his effectiveness:

If Bernard has a fault, it is that he gets over-assertive and over-aggressive and promotes policies more strongly even than their authors. The danger is that you get Bernard's policy rather than government policy.

Under an easy-going character like Eric Varley, this was less of a problem. But in June 1975, Ingham's world was turned upside down by the arrival of yet another Secretary of State. Tony Benn was a public school-educated, far-left intellectual, determined to go his own way, deeply suspicious of the entire civil service, at war with the media, semi-detached (to coin a phrase) from the Labour Government, the most controversial figure in British politics. He was, in short, Bernard Ingham's idea of a nightmare.

During his eight years as Prime Minister, Harold Wilson

appointed forty-two different Cabinet ministers. Of these forty-two, three published diaries. Of these three, Ingham worked for two: Barbara Castle and Tony Benn. This statistical freak may have been Ingham's misfortune; it is certainly of the greatest assistance to a biographer. 'I had a call from Bernard Ingham, my new press officer at the Department of Energy,' recorded Benn on 11 June 1975, the day of his appointment. For the next two and a half years, theirs was to be one of the most fascinating and well-documented relationships in Whitehall.

Benn had been demoted to Energy from the Department of Industry, and viewed his new job as the equivalent of a posting to run a Siberian power station: it was 'an absolutely major political reverse ... From the point of view of the party and the country, it was a position of disgrace, or intended to be.'[13] This attitude was not calculated to endear him to his new department. Nor was the reputation he brought with him. At Industry he had become famous for treating his civil servants, especially his Permanent Secretary, Sir Antony Part, as if they were Fifth Columnists. Part has left a telling description of what even their most routine tête-à-têtes about the ministry entailed:

> Usually for such informal talks the Secretary of State and his Permanent Secretary would sit in armchairs in a corner of the office. Mr Benn wished us to face each other across the long narrow conference table next to his desk. As he did at meetings with deputations, he put a block of paper in front of him and drew a line down the middle. As the conversation proceeded, he noted my remarks to the left of the line and any comment or counter-argument of his to the right of the line. This did not make for a relaxed atmosphere and occasionally it was as though he were pointing a pistol at my head. Metaphorically, I would watch his finger tightening on the trigger and when I

judged that he was about to fire I moved my head to one side. With any luck, I heard the bullet smack harmlessly into the woodwork behind me.[14]

As if to underline his contempt for the regular civil service, Benn trailed around with him two ideologically-sound 'special advisers': Frances Morrell and Francis Cripps. The trio was portrayed in the press as a nest of revolutionaries at the heart of the Government. Benn's house in Holland Park was routinely staked-out by the media. 'I'm sorry to see you lot going,' the Chief Information Officer at the Industry Department, Ray Tuite, told Frances Morrell as they packed their bags. 'There's been nothing like it since the Berlin airlift.' He had cause to be cheerful. Benn's relations with the press were now Ingham's responsibility.

For the first few weeks, all was quiet. 'Benn was sulking in his tent,' according to Ronald Custis, who had stayed on to serve as his Private Secretary. 'We saw very little of him. Then he appeared and the weight started flying around.'

What brought Benn dashing out of his tent was an economic crisis. On 30 June 1975, the pound lost more than five cents against the dollar. The next day the Cabinet went into emergency session. To strengthen sterling, the Treasury was demanding cuts in public expenditure and an incomes policy – both of them anathemas to the Labour left. Ingham saw Benn first thing in the morning on 2 July and asked him about his personal position. 'I told him I was strongly opposed to the proposed economic package,' recorded Benn, 'and that there were four options: to put up with it, to oppose it from the inside, to come out and oppose it constructively, or to come out and oppose it destructively. I thought opposing it from the inside was perhaps the best thing to do.'[15]

In theory, Benn's personal political position should have had nothing to do with Ingham: as a press officer, he was employed by the taxpayer solely to explain the policies of the Energy Department. In practice, of course, he was immediately sucked into the political controversy. Ingham suggested they brief his old friend, Ian Aitken, political correspondent of the *Guardian*, on Benn's thinking. Benn agreed. In the following morning's paper, Aitken reported that the Energy Secretary was 'known to have serious reservations' about the Government's direction.[16]

The real crunch came the following week, when the Cabinet had to vote on the Treasury's demands. On 10 July, minutes before he was due in Downing Street, Benn had a discussion about tactics with his media adviser. 'Bernard Ingham said the press would be interested today in whether or not I would resign,' wrote Benn. 'I told him I wasn't sure what to do but the movement wanted us to stay in. He thought I might have to explain to my constituents the agonizing choice I'd had to make.'[17] In the event, it was not Benn who explained his 'agonizing choice' to the country; it was Ingham, using the medium of an off-the-record briefing to John Bourne of the *Financial Times*.

Bourne's account ('"Grave doubts" by Left after marathon talks'), based in part on his conversation with Ingham, was the lead story in the following morning's *Financial Times*. It provided a good illustration of some of the baroque euphemisms of British political journalism, and of the grey area in which supposedly neutral civil servants operate. First came an account of the Cabinet's deliberations (a clear breach of the then Official Secrets Act, incidentally); then this explanation of Benn's position:

> Some left-wing ministers, led by Mr Anthony Wedgwood Benn, the Energy Secretary, expressed grave doubts about the policy. But Mr Wedgwood Benn has for the moment let it be known that he has no intention of resigning from the Government.

However, he is worried about the policies in the Government's White Paper, to be published at 11.30 today, because he believes they are bound to fail.

Some political friends of Mr Wedgwood Benn maintain that Mr Michael Foot, the Employment Secretary, would destroy himself by supporting the Chancellor's package. But they also claimed that Mr Wedgwood Benn's refusal to resign at the moment was because he regarded the economic situation as extremely serious and although very unhappy about today's measures, he thought he ought to do his best not to break Cabinet solidarity at this stage.

According to the same sources, Mr Wedgwood Benn believes that now for the first time a Labour Government is imposing pay cuts by law, that public expenditure reductions and higher unemployment are also in the wind – all points that ran counter to Labour's election manifesto . . .

'Mr Benn has let it be known . . . political friends of Mr Benn . . .' – it did not require Sherlock Holmes to detect Ingham's fingerprints all over this piece. It was too ham-fisted an operation even for Benn (whose more subtle ploy to distance himself from his Cabinet colleagues had been to walk into Number 10 with a copy of Labour's election manifesto tucked prominently beneath his arm). 'When I went into the office, Bernard Ingham told me he had been talking to John Bourne of the *FT* about how I thought the policy was bound to fail, and how I was anxious about wage cuts and public expenditure cuts and rising unemployment and so on. I was slightly nervous, as I think was Bernard, that they had printed it so fully.'[18]

Ingham was now experiencing at first hand the dilemma which had confronted Sir Antony Part. What was an official to do when his political boss, although opposed to Government policy, nevertheless refused to resign? In Part's words: 'To whom does his loyalty lie – his Secretary of State or the Prime Minister?' The dilemma was a particularly acute one for Ingham, who had built his career on his reputation for loyalty. Suddenly he was finding himself having to brief against the interests of the Government he served. More than that, he was briefing against his own deepest beliefs, for everything in his personal history suggests he would have been an instinctive supporter of the policy his minister opposed. The 'Social Contract' between Government and unions which Wilson, Foot, Denis Healey and Jack Jones were struggling to devise was exactly the sort of partnership for which Ingham had argued in the *Leeds Weekly Citizen* a decade earlier. Not surprisingly, his relationship with Benn began deteriorating fast.

The week after the Bourne briefing, Benn, accompanied by Ingham and Custis, travelled up to Aberdeen to inspect a North Sea oil rig. They spent the evening in Glasgow. 'We were due to come down on the night sleeper,' recalled Custis, 'and we found ourselves with a couple of hours and Benn said: "Let's go and see the chaps in the *Scottish Daily News*."' This was a pet project of Benn: a workers' co-operative, born three months earlier out of the ashes of the *Scottish Daily Express*, into which the sacked printers and journalists had been encouraged to invest their redundancy money in return for a Government loan of £1.2 million. According to Custis:

> We walked through this huge old printing shed, and there in one corner was a group of men working a machine and getting it ready to go to press and it was obviously doomed to failure. The whole atmosphere of the place was black. And here were all these chaps who had, in a sense, been duped into putting their redundancy money into this venture. They were obviously going to lose it all. But nevertheless in walked Benn

675

and there was a bit of hero worship going on . . . That was quite
a night.

Ingham knew enough about journalism to recognise a sinking
ship when he saw one (the paper closed in November) and the
whole incident left him, in Custis's view, not merely 'saddened
and depressed' but 'sickened'.

Benn's starry-eyed view of the working classes, his mugs of
tea, his regular quotations from the seventeenth-century
Diggers and Levellers, his well-aired obsession that the secret
service was out to get him – all these idiosyncrasies grated on
Ingham. 'At times one could find him very, very depressed,'
Custis remembered. 'He was glum and humourless. You could
sometimes go into his room late in the day and find him
slouched over his desk looking very fed up with things.' It was
around this time that Ingham swore one journalist to secrecy
and then confided his firm belief that his minister was 'stark
raving mad'. Word of his disenchantment filtered back to
Benn's ever-vigilant inner circle. 'I can't believe I'm doing this,'
one sympathetic left-wing journalist told Frances Morrell in
September 1975, 'but I heard the head of your PR department
vilifying Tony Benn so much I felt I had to come and tell you.'

Ingham, in turn, suspected Morrell of leaking confidential
information behind his back. 'PLAN TO MAKE BRITAIN
WORLD'S NUCLEAR DUSTBIN' was the *Daily Mirror*'s front-
page headline on 21 October. The *Mirror* reported that Britain
might soon be sent '4,000 tons of lethal waste' by Japan, in a
reprocessing deal worth up to £400 million. According to
'sources close to the secret talks . . . the contract could be signed
before Christmas'. The story spilled over on to page two.
'Would you fill your house with bottles of poison just because
someone paid you to do it?' demanded the paper's editorial.
'What a lethal legacy to leave to our children and our children's
children.'

The 'source' was undoubtedly inside the Energy Department. Ingham went immediately to see Benn and accused Morrell of being responsible for the story. Such was his agitation ('hot, flushed and angry,' according to one eye-witness) that Benn himself went off to find his special adviser. He was away for what seemed a suspiciously long time. When finally he returned with Morrell, she loudly denied any involvement. Ingham did not believe her, and the next day's *Mirror* seemed only to confirm his suspicion that Benn was now running his own private press operation within the department. Under the headline 'Well done the *Mirror* – Praise by Benn for Doomwatch Report' was a comment from the Energy Secretary actually praising the leak: 'The *Mirror* has performed a very valuable function and now there will be a lot of public pressure put on the Government and my department. This breakthrough by a big popular newspaper gives us the opportunity to discuss these problems.'

Ingham's reaction to this extraordinary statement, in which a damaging leak suddenly became a 'breakthrough', can be easily imagined. Certainly, he was not the sort to bottle his feelings and he appears to have confronted his Secretary of State. 'Bernard Ingham came to see me,' recorded Benn the following week. 'He's a very difficult man ... I think when Eric Varley was at Energy, he and Ronnie Custis did exactly what they liked. Eric is entirely guided by his civil servants. I think part of my problem has been trying to get control of those two.'[19] Benn suspected that Ingham would have taken over the running of the entire department if he had been given half a chance. Many years later, asked if he believed the rumours that Ingham was virtually Deputy Prime Minister under Margaret Thatcher, he replied: 'I wouldn't put it past him.'[20]

This battle of wills between Secretary of State and civil servant reached a farcical, indeed almost physical, climax a fortnight later, with the passing of the act which opened the North Sea oil pipeline. Benn wanted to make a ministerial broadcast to mark this historic step. Ingham advised against it 'on the grounds that it would not be interesting enough'.[21] Benn insisted and was eventually given permission by Number 10. But he was granted leave to give a radio talk only: the BBC had ruled that a television broadcast would be too party political and the Opposition would be entitled to a right of reply. Ingham and Custis duly accompanied Benn to Broadcasting House where he made his radio recording. 'Then,' recalled Custis, 'he said: "Well, let's go and do this television piece." We said: "No, you're not allowed to." And he went right to the door of the television studio and we were almost literally standing in his way and saying "No, you mustn't." He eventually said: "Well, have it your way. I'll get the Party on to this." We just came back and Bernard and I reported what had happened to Number 10.'

This seems to have been the final straw as far as Benn was concerned. He had already demanded the removal of Custis from his Private Office on the grounds that he was 'unsympathetic'. Now he set about securing the dismissal of Ingham. On his way out of Cabinet on 18 November he had a word about Ingham with Joe Haines, the Prime Minister's Press Secretary. According to Haines: 'He said he couldn't stand him and he wanted to know how he could get rid of him. He just thought that Ingham was obstructive to what he was trying to do.' Benn announced that he wanted to bring over his old press adviser from the Industry Department, Ray Tuite. Haines suggested they might arrange a straight swop, but he warned him (or so Benn noted in his diary) that 'Ingham was capable of creating trouble if I got rid of him.'[22]

Nevertheless, Benn was not prepared to let the matter drop. The next day he raised it with Jack Rampton, the department's Permanent Under Secretary.

I said, 'While we're on staff matters, I'm a bit worried about Bernard Ingham.' He told me Bernard had gone to see him, saying he feared he'd lost the confidence of Ministers. I said, 'I think that's true but it's a much deeper problem. He doesn't seem to take an interest and he's not very helpful.'

'He's an energetic chap,' Jack said. 'He has an idea of what a Minister should do and he bullies him until he does it.'

I said, 'On the principle that everybody does best what they most enjoy doing, wouldn't it be a good idea to give him a full-time job on energy conservation?'

'That might be one way of doing it or else I could have a word with Douglas Allen of the Civil Service Department and see what can be done.'[23]

In terms of personal relations between a minister and a press adviser, where trust is of the essence, this is about as bad as things could get. Each man was convinced the other was trying to undermine him. Yet ridding himself of Ingham was not as easy as Benn had hoped. Shunting him off to look after energy conservation was the best hope. But that could not be done immediately: no such division existed within the ministry, and it would take time to persuade the Treasury to put up the extra money. For a time, Geoffrey Goodman – an old friend of Ingham and one of the few journalists Benn respected – seemed to offer a solution. He had been seconded from the *Daily Mirror* to work for Harold Wilson at Number 10 as head of the Counter-Inflation Unit. When James Callaghan replaced Wilson in March 1976, Goodman decided to return to journalism. He nominated Ingham as his successor. 'Callaghan said to me: "Why him?" I said: "Because he's absolutely straight, he's worked for Labour and Conservative governments, and of all the Whitehall press people, he's the best."' Ingham was enthusiastic, but nothing came of it. Callaghan eventually appointed Hugh Cudlipp.

The weeks turned into months, and a curious thing happened. Ingham and Benn started to get on better. The air had been cleared. In addition, Ronald Custis had been replaced by Bryan Emmett, a civil servant more to Benn's taste, and who seems to have helped smooth relations. At the beginning of April, Ingham and Emmett took Benn out to lunch at a restaurant near the ministry. At the end of the month, they travelled back on the train with him from the NUM Conference. 'Every time I talk to them they tell me something interesting about the last Government,' recorded Benn. Among the matters discussed on this occasion was how the Energy Department's 'Switch Off Something' campaign during the three-day week had been 'purely political, designed to prolong the community's capacity to beat the miners; and how many Tories had thought the 1974 Election was a revolution.' Benn responded by describing the way he had been treated by Sir Antony Part at the Department of Industry. 'Gradually they are beginning to understand what it is all about,' Benn dictated into his diary that night. 'I like them both.'[24] On Ingham's side, too, a certain wary respect began to replace his earlier hostility. 'Stark raving mad' Benn might well appear on occasions; but on others he could be stimulating, inspiring and (a quality for which few were prepared) immensely charming.

In February 1977, Benn made a delightful speech at the Energy Department's annual party for journalists, during which he claimed that the ministry was run not by him but by the Press Office. As proof, he read out Ingham's characteristically thorough briefing paper on the evening's festivities: 'Tonight's party for the Press Office will give journalists the full opportunity to explore through casual conversations with Ministers and officials progress on two oil-related items ... Since all who will be representing the Department tonight will no doubt wish to maintain a consistent line if asked about these issues, it might be useful if I describe the line that the Press Office has been authorized to take.' The reporters laughed. Benn paused and looked up. 'I have to stop there because the last two paragraphs – which tell you the Press Office line – have been classified top secret by Sir Jack Rampton.'

'There was,' noted Benn, 'a lot of giggling and amusement.'[25]

In the meantime, after much clanking and groaning, the Whitehall machine was finally on the point of coughing up enough money to establish a proper Energy Conservation Division. Ingham's final months as Benn's Chief Information Officer were peripatetic – together they visited Brussels, Washington, Saudi Arabia, Norway and Luxembourg – until at length, on 12 December, Benn recorded their last press conference: 'he is leaving to take over as head of the Energy Conservation Department, something I suggested to Jack Rampton when I was getting on badly with Bernard, but I'm sorry to see him go now.'[26] Three months later, he was still grieving over the loss. One of the last entries under 'Ingham' in Benn's diary is for 22 March 1978. It reads simply: 'I miss Bernard.'[27]

The details of Ingham's twenty months in charge of energy conservation need not, mercifully, detain us long. Ingham himself subsequently referred to it as 'this rather agreeable life ... during which I rediscovered the luxury of reading books and listening to music uninterrupted by calls from newspapermen'.[28] He had reached the rank of Under Secretary. He was entitled to an entry in *Who's Who*, where he listed his recreations as walking, gardening and reading. He presided over a department of some thirty or forty. He helped launch the Government's 'Save It' campaign, an initiative which was later held to have had mixed results, concentrating as it did on domestic users rather than on the real profligates of power, industrial consumers. He launched a newspaper with the uninspiring title, *Energy Management*.

As an administrator he was a natural empire-builder, a tendency he had displayed ever since his days at the PIB. 'I felt he would be expanding his department at times more than it deserved,' recalled Philip Jones, one of his superiors. 'You would find, say, that if there was a need for regular discussions with the building societies, Bernard would create a building society section. Then he'd want more people and more space.' He was not a high-flier. He was an ordinary, competent, middle-aged civil servant. If he had stayed at the Department of Energy, according to Jones, he would, in due course, have been 'moved across to another Under Secretary's job. I doubt whether he had the ability to go up the policy-making ladder. He wasn't a deep enough thinker. I don't think he could have formulated, say, North Sea policy, or gas policy.'

By the summer of 1979 he was forty-seven years old and a pleasant, routine life beckoned: his son was away at Durham University; he and Nancy had time on their hands; he had a secure job and a pension; there would be weekends in Hebden Bridge, summers spent on his brother's farm on the dales overlooking Halifax; early retirement, perhaps, and a return to the north of England; whatever happened, the next fifteen years promised to be easier than the last fifteen . . . Then, quite without warning, these modest expectations were utterly transformed by a summons to see Sir Jack Rampton.

FIVE

Prime Minister's Press Secretary

'The Press Secretary is employed by the Prime Minister and for the Prime Minister, not by or for Fleet Street. He has no function in helping Fleet Street. Everything he says and everything he does is designed to help the Prime Minister first, and after that the Government as a whole. If, in the end, it means ditching another minister . . . then you ditch that minister.'

JOE HAINES, FORMER PRESS SECRETARY TO
HAROLD WILSON, 1989[1]

It was August 1979. The Labour Government had fallen three months earlier. Benn had gone from the Energy Department, taking his pint mugs of tea and his miners' lamps and his union banners with him. In his place was a Thatcherite Conservative, David Howell. The atmosphere in the complex of offices overlooking the Thames was noticeably less tense.

When Ingham arrived in the Permanent Under Secretary's office, Rampton took him by surprise. Was he, he inquired, happy in his work as an administrator? Were there any circumstances under which he would consider returning to the Government Information Service? Ingham replied that he preferred to stay where he was: 'Unless, I suppose, I am being asked to go to Number 10 as Chief Press Secretary. But that's not going to happen, so ...' Rampton said nothing. The conversation ended. But his smile, Ingham recalled, 'was more inscrutable than that of the Sphynx'.[2]

One of Margaret Thatcher's first actions on entering 10 Downing Street in May 1979 had been to appoint as her Press Secretary a man named Henry James. James was an experienced Whitehall hand who had started his career as a government press officer at the old Ministry of Pensions in 1951. Since then he had swung from branch to branch – from the Admiralty to Education to Downing Street to Housing back to Downing Street and on to Environment – before finishing at the top of his professional tree as Director-General of the Central Office of Information (COI) in 1974. He had since retired from the civil service and was working as public relations adviser to the main board of Vickers when Mrs Thatcher asked him to come back and work for her.

Why she did so is not entirely clear. True, James had done a couple of stints as a junior press officer at Downing Street; true, also, that the Parliamentary Lobby had let Mrs Thatcher know, whilst she was still Leader of the Opposition, that his would be a welcome appointment (she had sent her Parliamentary Private Secretary, Ian Gow, to make discreet enquiries). But he was nearing sixty and it quickly became apparent that he and the Prime Minister had no real rapport. He once sent her a memorandum about media arrangements for a forthcoming trip in which he claimed to have visited the location 'to case the joint'. Thatcher, a stickler for correctness, announced to one of her advisers that she had no idea what the man was talking about. In the words of one doyen of the Lobby: 'Our recommendation turned out to be a complete disaster. They just didn't hit it off. It became clear to us that he hadn't got her confidence and he had nothing to tell us. It was conveyed to her by the Lobby that this just couldn't go on.'

James had only been in place three months when Downing Street began putting out feelers for a replacement. The Head of the Home Civil Service, Sir Ian Bancroft, in strict confidence, asked for suggestions from the Permanent Secretaries. There were three potential candidates considered to have sufficient seniority: Donald Grant, Director of Information at the Home Office for the past five years; Keith McDowall, Ingham's old rival, who had just left the Department of Employment to become Managing Director of Public Affairs at British Ship-builders; and Bernard Ingham. What helped swing it Ingham's way was the enthusiastic lobbying of Jack Rampton, who insisted from the start that he had the ideal man.

There followed an intricate courtship, more like an oriental marriage negotiation than the appointment of a senior govern-ment official. After Rampton had established that Ingham, at least in principle, was interested in the match, he arranged for the bride and groom to be brought, discreetly, face to face. Mrs Thatcher was then engaged in her infamous tour of all the Whitehall ministries – a regal progress which, legend has it, had left several of her shattered hosts bobbing like driftwood in her wake. The Energy Department was next on her list. At the last minute, Ingham was invited 'to take tea and cucumber sandwiches with the Prime Minister' in the company of thirty-five colleagues. Rampton engineered a meeting. 'I talked to her,' said Ingham, 'for all of two minutes.'[3]

A few days later he was telephoned by Thatcher's new Principal Private Secretary, Clive Whitmore. Even at this late stage Whitmore was unwilling to come out openly and admit what was going on. He began by recalling that they had met on an open government seminar six months earlier. Then he asked if the Head of the Civil Service had been in touch with him. Ingham replied that he rarely spoke to Sir Ian, and 'had not recently had the pleasure.'

'Oh dear,' Whitmore groaned, 'not another cock-up.' He

asked Ingham if he had got the 'drift' of what was happening. Of course, Ingham had. He asked for time to think the matter over.

He sought the advice of his colleagues. Most urged him to go. 'It's the best place to give rein to your talents,' Philip Jones told him. Ingham was understandably excited by the prospect, but had two major reservations: he wondered whether he was up to it, and he doubted whether he could work with Margaret Thatcher. He was ambitious enough to take a gamble on the first; the second was more troubling. 'I'd put my bottom dollar,' one friend of his insisted, 'on Bernard having voted Labour in 1979.' Whatever else he was, he was not a Tory. But then – and this is what finally convinced him he should take the job – neither was she. Thatcher, like Ingham, had been born without privileges. She had never quite lost the aura of an outsider. She did not want to conserve Britain's institutions: she wanted to abolish a lot of them, or shake them up, or dismantle them. She was not a member of the Establishment. She was suspicious of it. She thought it had gone soft and let the country down. With all of this, and especially with her conviction that an economic recovery depended on a reduction in trade union power, Ingham was in full agreement. 'I think I'll do it,' he confided to one colleague. 'The thing is: we're both radicals.'

Alex Jarratt, his former boss at the PIB, had agreed to address a seminar on energy conservation Ingham was organizing in Birmingham. At the last minute, Ingham failed to appear. He had been summoned, Jarratt later discovered, to see Mrs Thatcher in her study at Number 10. Ingham thought this was his final interview. It was not. The decision had already been made. She merely outlined his duties and welcomed him aboard. He was in and out in twenty minutes.

So it was that on 9 September 1979 the Downing Street Press Office announced that its next head would be Bernard

Ingham. He was to begin work on 1 November at an annual salary of £16,714. In Fleet Street and Westminster and, indeed, in Conservative Central Office, the news was greeted with astonishment. In the words of Peter Jenkins: 'We all said: "She's appointed a Labour man!"'

It has been presented as if it were a baffling question: why did an ideologue like Thatcher choose a man like Ingham? In fact, there is a simple answer: she didn't. The civil service chose him. After her experience with Henry James she was happy to leave the appointment of her Press Secretary to her officials. This was not because she was in thrall to Whitehall – on the contrary, few Prime Ministers have more frequently spurned its advice – but because she gave the matter a generally low priority. 'Prime Ministers,' in William Whitelaw's words, 'have different approaches to the press. Some, like Wilson, never stopped reading the newspapers and were obsessed with what was written about them. Attlee never read any papers at all. Margaret Thatcher is much closer to Attlee than she is to Wilson.' That was why, where other leaders might have agonized over such a sensitive appointment, she was prepared to approve it on two minutes' acquaintance. She had been told, by people who were paid to know, that Ingham was the best. She accepted that judgement. Over the next decade, it was to be her relative indifference to what appeared in the press, as much as his ambition, which made Ingham so powerful.

Mrs Thatcher's surprise appointment moved Ingham from the periphery of the Government to its very heart. He was only the fifteenth man in history to serve as Press Secretary to the Prime Minister.

The post – or, at least, its forerunner – had been created exactly fifty years earlier, in 1929, by Ramsay MacDonald, Britain's first Labour Prime Minister. MacDonald wanted professional advice on how to handle what was then, as now, an overwhelmingly Conservative press. To provide it, he brought in an official from the Foreign Office News Department named George Steward.

No picture of Steward decorates any government office. Little is known of him. Yet, serving MacDonald, Stanley Baldwin and Neville Chamberlain in turn, he did as much as anyone to shape the way politics is reported in Britain. He took the Parliamentary Lobby system – which had been created in 1884 and which permitted certain journalists to wander the corridors and lobbies of the Palace of Westminster, talking freely to MPs and ministers, on condition they did not directly attribute what they were told – and imposed upon it a formal structure. Henceforth, he announced, he would brief the Lobby at daily meetings. Naturally, no journalist could afford to miss these events and they quickly assumed a pivotal importance. The system gradually became more rigid. In 1930, according to the Lobby's annual report for that year, 'definite times were arranged for conferences and rooms were provided at Number 10 for meetings'.[4] Three years later, Steward told the journalists that 'although he was formally appointed to act for the Prime Minister and the Treasury, he was also required to act for the Government as a whole in all matters of a general character' – a sweeping job description which, as the Lobby presciently recorded, carried 'certain dangers' as 'it may become too much a personal service of Prime Ministers'.[5]

It was indeed to prove a significant blow to the independence of the Cabinet, centralizing power in Downing Street by enabling Number 10 to impose its interpretation of events on the press. Chamberlain used Steward repeatedly to bypass the Cabinet and promote his policy of appeasing Hitler. In the autumn of 1937, for example, Lord Halifax, the Foreign Secretary, had received a private invitation to visit Germany.

The Foreign Office was anxious to play down the importance of the trip. Chamberlain's purpose was precisely the
opposite. Steward briefed the Lobby with the Number 10
version. The next day *The Times* and the *Daily Telegraph*
appeared with almost identical stories about the visit's vital
significance in the eyes of 'the Government' – an interpretation which horrified the anti-appeasers and caused delight in
Berlin. By exploiting his press secretary's contacts with the
Lobby in this way, Chamberlain was able to raise 'news
management,' in the words of the historian, Richard Cockett, 'almost to the level of an exact science.'[6]

Thereafter, every Prime Minister had a motive for keeping
a Press Office. When Labour returned to power in 1945,
Clement Attlee soon appointed Francis Williams, a former
editor of the pro-Labour paper, the *Daily Herald*, to be the
first official 'Adviser on Public Relations to the Prime Minister'. (Attlee had a famously other-worldly approach to the
press: when Williams arrived at Number 10 he found there
was not even so much as a news agency tape machine installed, and he only persuaded a suspicious Attlee to have one
put in on the grounds that it would enable the Prime Minister to keep up with the cricket scores; one afternoon, or so
the story goes, Attlee, ignorant of Williams's morning press
briefings, came rushing in demanding to know why his
'cricket machine' was carrying details of what had been discussed in Cabinet that morning.) In 1951, Winston
Churchill, who had an old-fashioned view of these matters,
did try to dispense with the Press Office. But he soon found
that its abolition was having such an adverse effect on the
Government's standing that he was forced to relent. In May
1952, Fife Clark, Press Officer at the Ministry of Health,
was appointed 'Adviser on Public Relations to the Prime
Minister and the Government'. As Churchill refused even to
have Clark under the roof of Number 10, he was obliged to

work out of an office in the old Treasury building next door.

Contacts between Government and the media now settled into a pattern which has persisted, virtually uninterrupted, until the present. Clark would see the Lobby twice daily, at 11 a.m. in his office and at 4 p.m. in the Commons. He was kept fully informed of Government policy through occasional monologues from Churchill and regular meetings with Rab Butler, the Chancellor of the Exchequer, and Viscount Swinton, the Commonwealth Secretary. Prime Ministerial press secretaries invariably rose and fell with their masters. In June 1955, after succeeding Churchill, Anthony Eden moved the Press Office back inside Number 10 and offered the job to William Clark, diplomatic correspondent of the *Observer*. This was hailed as an imaginative appointment – a phrase which generally preludes disaster, and so it proved. 'The PM is tired and fretful,' Clark noted in his diary at the end of his first six months.[7] When the Suez crisis erupted, there was a complete breakdown in confidence between the two men. Eden gave orders that his Press Secretary was to be kept away from all sensitive papers: 'you must stay down at your end of the building.'[8] Clark was driven to record in his diary what must be the most damning assessment any press officer has ever made of his Prime Minister.

> It seems to me that the PM is mad, literally mad ... My mood towards him is extraordinary. I never see him, worn, dignified and friendly, but a surge of deep and almost tearful compassion surges up in me: I leave him and my violent bitter contempt and hatred for a man who has destroyed my world and so much of my faith burns up again. Then I long to be free as a journalist to drive this government from power and keep the cowards and crooks out of power for all time. God, how power corrupts.[9]

Following this fiasco, Harold Macmillan, Eden's successor,

was understandably reluctant to bring in another outsider, and appointed Harold Evans, Head of Information at the Colonial Office. Evans, by common consent, was the most successful of Ingham's predecessors. He stayed for almost seven years – a record until Ingham overtook it in 1986. 'He understood better than most what power at the top is all about,' wrote James Margach, Lobby correspondent of the *Sunday Times*, 'he never attempted hard or soft sells and always avoided becoming involved even remotely with party politics.'[10] He had what has always proved the most essential prerequisite for the job: an easy relationship with the Prime Minister. Most mornings, he would climb the stairs to Macmillan's private flat for a 'gossip'. Macmillan would usually 'still be in bed, wearing a brown cardigan over his pyjamas and surrounded by dispatch boxes, having begun work on his official papers several hours earlier'.[11] Evans was allowed access to most papers in the Prime Minister's Private Office. There was also a standing instruction to the Private Secretaries to 'let Evans know' everything that was going on. Such was the effectiveness of Evans's emollient manner that, in his words, he had 'no serious disagreement' with the Lobby in the whole of his seven years, despite the fraught atmosphere of Macmillan's final months in office. When he left in 1963 they gave him a valedictory silver dish inscribed 'to Harold Evans, for seven years the flawless voice of 10 Downing Street'.

In 1964, Harold Wilson, like Eden, brought in a journalist. Once again, but for different reasons, it proved a less than satisfactory arrangement. Trevor Lloyd-Hughes had been the Lobby correspondent of Wilson's constituency paper, the *Liverpool Daily Post*, for the past thirteen years and the new Prime Minister thought that appointing an insider would smooth relations with the Parliamentary press corps. His plan backfired. Far from flattering the Lobby, this elevation of a provincial newspaperman offended the *amour-propre* of many in the national press. Suddenly they were obliged to go cap in hand for briefings to a man who only yesterday had been a junior member of the club. Aware of this, Lloyd-Hughes became anxious and uncommunicative. He took his new status as a civil servant so literally, according to Marcia Williams, Wilson's Political Secretary, that he shrank 'from any connection with any part of the work of the Government which could in any way be regarded as political'. He became 'more of a civil servant than the civil servants, and so impartial as to make his news statements sometimes sound devoid of content'.[12] Lloyd-Hughes, in his own words, resisted 'fiercely' any suggestion that he should play a political role: 'It is quite wrong for a civil servant . . . to peddle a party line.'[13]

Another reason for his relative ineffectiveness was that Wilson was obsessed by the press and wanted to deal with reporters personally. Against Lloyd-Hughes's advice, he instituted what became known as the 'White Commonwealth', regularly summoning selected political journalists to drinks in Downing Street. Editors and owners were invited down to Chequers for the night, often to hear their political correspondents trashed by the First Lord of the Treasury: David Wood of *The Times* should be given 'a golden handshake', Nora Beloff of the *Observer* was incapable of taking down 'a monumental scoop at dictation speed', and so on. Eventually, so preoccupied was Wilson, a second, 'political' press secretary was appointed, in the person of Gerald Kaufman. Finally, as if this were not enough, at the beginning of 1969, Wilson brought in yet another Lobby correspondent, Joe Haines, to serve first as Lloyd-Hughes's deputy and then, six months later, as his replacement when Lloyd-Hughes was made 'Chief Information Adviser to the Government' (a grand title which, according to Haines, 'didn't mean anything'). Haines never pretended to be neutral. He was always a Labour partisan.

Edward Heath had noted carefully how his predecessor had behaved and was determined not to do likewise. Having thought hard in Opposition, when he came to power in 1970, he appointed Donald Maitland, a career diplomat. 'You know what this job's about,' was Heath's only instruction. 'Get the facts out.'

Maitland was the first Number 10 Press Secretary since George Steward never to have had any journalistic experience. He had met and 'got on well' with Heath in the mid-1960s, when he was Head of the Foreign Office News Department. He was forty-seven: a short, tough-minded Scot, famous in Whitehall for having stood up to George Brown when he was Brown's Private Secretary ('You do not imagine, Foreign Secretary,' he is said to have remarked during one row, 'that a person of my stature has got where he is today by kow-towing to bullies?')[14] For him, the Downing Street Press Office was not the summit of his career; it was not an end in itself; it was just another job. 'I regarded this as a posting, like any other Foreign Office posting.' He thus looked on the Parliamentary press with a cooler and more impartial eye than most of his predecessors. There were by the 1970s, more than one hundred reporters in the Lobby and, to Maitland, 'the idea that this was a conversation which was not taking place seemed to me to have a slightly ludicrous character.'

Maitland soon became tired of seeing simple statements of fact refracted through the distorting lens of the Lobby. He would read (to quote his phraseology) that 'the Government were at pains to do so-and-so' or 'Government plans to do so-and-so suffered a setback,' when the reality was that they had taken no pains, suffered no setback. The reader was often unable to assess the relative weight of such judgements because the stories in which they appeared were seamless robes, with no indication as to where their material had been gathered. 'Everyone is entitled to comment and criticize,'

Maitland insisted. 'They should do so. But I don't think they should do so in presenting the actual statement of policy.'

Criticism of the Lobby system was familiar enough, even in the 1960s ('all this grey anonymity has really become a farcical charade,' wrote Anthony Howard, himself a former Lobby correspondent, in 1965).[15] But this was different. A Prime Minister's Press Secretary was in a position to do something about it. Accordingly, in 1972, Maitland suggested to the Lobby that 'as far as possible we should have briefings on the record but by mutual agreement we could go on to a non-attributable basis'. The journalists were at once suspicious, seeing in this a plot to make the Government's image more attractive: good news would be attributable; bad news would be off the record. They rejected Maitland's proposal. Maitland promptly came up with a new idea:

> Instead of coming to the Lobby with a piece of paper from which I read, and then have that 'processed' through the Lobby system, we would issue a press release. They would be given it on arrival so they could read it. Then they could ask me questions on that, on a Lobby basis.

This was tried a couple of times. It seemed to work. The sky did not fall in. As Maitland had shrewdly judged, once the news agencies and the broadcasters began carrying the Government's actual words, Fleet Street news editors wanted 'to have something which was in quotes' to put in their pages as well. This innovation was still being tried in April 1973, when Maitland's posting came to an end.

Joe Haines returned in March 1974 even more determined to forge the Downing Street Press Office into a political instrument. Out of the staff of eleven which he inherited, he promptly sacked five. 'For Joe,' wrote Marcia Williams, 'the building up of an efficient and loyal Press Office meant, quite rightly, having a staff who were loyal to him personally, and who thought and felt the way he did. In sum, he wanted a Labour-orientated organization.'[16]

Haines was one of the more colourful figures to occupy the Press Secretary's chair. A Labour councillor, born in Rotherhithe in 1928, brought up in what he called 'one of the worst slums in south-east London', he had the look of a Mafia hit-man and a wit to match. (Shown a film of the Ronan Point tower block disaster, his response was to murmer the slogan from President Nixon's 1968 campaign: 'The risks are too great for you to stay home.') He operated in Number 10 as if under siege – which, in a sense, he was. He surveyed the British press and concluded there were only two news organizations – the *Guardian* and the Mirror Group – which he could trust. 'I have long remembered,' he wrote a decade later, 'the occasion when three members of the Lobby, separately, went to the Conservative Chief Whip and told him what had been said at the four o'clock meeting.'[17]

After five bruising years as Wilson's press adviser, in power and out of it, Haines felt he owed the Lobby no favours and soon began tightening the screw. He stopped journalists travelling on the Prime Minister's plane during visits overseas. He abandoned the practice of answering questions across the whole range of Government activities, believing it was 'crazy' that he should have to speak for every Whitehall department. ('This greatly upset the Lobby,' he recalled. 'They were really put out that they actually had to make their own enquiries.') He adopted Donald Maitland's technique of issuing a regular press statement: it 'took up an enormous amount of bloody time [but] at least nobody could misreport it.' Finally, on 19 June 1975, he took the biggest step of all, writing to the chairman of the Lobby, John Egan, announcing his decision to end Downing Street's off-the-record briefings entirely:

From now on, it will be my general rule that if a statement needs to be made on behalf of the Prime Minister, that statement will be made on the record.

This will not lead to any loss of information to the general public. Indeed, they will then know its source. And it will eliminate the kind of extreme absurdity where, under the rules governing the present meetings, even the name of the annual Poppy Day seller who calls on the Prime Minister is given unattributably.

By the time Wilson's final premiership came to an end in March 1976, Haines had ceased to function as a Press Secretary in any traditional sense. He had stopped the Lobby briefings. He had palmed off the administrative work on to his deputy. He rarely talked to groups of journalists, except the Americans based in London ('they were a higher class of correspondent, frankly, and I could trust them and talk freely to them on political matters'). Instead, Haines became a sort of general Prime Ministerial factotum. He wrote almost all Wilson's speeches. He helped draw up the frequent (and extensive) Honours Lists. He acted as an informal adviser to the Number 10 Policy Unit. On one occasion, he even appointed a minister, suggesting her name to the Prime Minister and then interviewing her ('Harold didn't know who to give the job to, so he left it up to me').

Stormy though his relations with the Lobby were, Haines did not exceed his authority. He 'handled them in exactly the way Harold Wilson wanted,' wrote Bernard Donoughue, 'which was quite roughly at times'. Wilson's successor, James Callaghan, could be equally testy with the Fourth Estate but, perhaps wisely, chose as his Press Secretary a man quite different to Haines.

Tom McCaffrey, a professional civil servant, had been Callaghan's Chief Information Officer at the Home Office

from 1967 to 1970. He was known to be a Labour sympathizer but, like Maitland, he was nobody's poodle. A few weeks
after the new Home Secretary's arrival, McCaffrey had told
him bluntly that he was not living up to expectations. Callaghan rather admired him for his candour, or so he claimed.
At any rate, when Labour returned to power and he was made
Foreign Secretary he readily fell in with Haines's suggestion
that the 'politically sensitive' McCaffrey should join him at
the FO. Two years later nobody was surprised when Callaghan took McCaffrey with him to Number 10. On their first
night in the building, McCaffrey rang the secretary of the
Lobby and told him briefings would resume at 11.00 a.m. the
next day – a deliberately flamboyant demonstration that the
war was over; it was business as usual.

Callaghan trusted McCaffrey. 'It was thanks to him,' he
conceded, 'that I enjoyed a less barbed relationship with the
press than I might have done, for his patience and modesty
were greater than mine.'[18] McCaffrey, in turn, trusted the
Lobby system, of which he was a staunch defender. 'I believe
that as a result of Lobby meetings over the years the public
know more today than ever before of what the Government is
doing in their name,' he said in 1986.[19] Nevertheless, he soon
had direct and painful experience of what a combustible
device it had become.

In the spring of 1977, Callaghan was prevailed upon to
appoint his son-in-law, Peter Jay, as the British Ambassador
in Washington. On the morning of 12 May McCaffrey had
the delicate task of announcing this to the Lobby. Afterwards,
in the corridor, he fell into conversation with two old friends,
Robert Carvel of the London *Evening Standard* and John
Dickinson of the London *Evening News*. They asked him
what was wrong with the present incumbent, Sir Peter Ramsbotham. McCaffrey, caught off guard, replied to the effect
that he was stuffy and a bit of a snob. This accurately reflected

Callaghan's view, and that of the Foreign Secretary, David Owen, who had talked to McCaffrey about it a few weeks previously. A few hours later, the two London evening papers, the *News* and the *Standard* – one quoting 'the Callaghan camp', the other 'Government circles' – carried similar stories with an identical headline: 'SNOB ENVOY HAD TO GO'. Several Lobby correspondents on Conservative newspapers told Tory MPs that McCaffrey was the source.

The controversy which followed was immensely embarrassing, not only to McCaffrey (who offered to resign) but to the entire Lobby. There had, after all, been a time when such confidences were as sacred as secrets whispered in the confessional box. The swiftness with which McCaffrey's role was exposed was a warning that times were changing. The days of the old Lobby stalwart – of Jimmy Margach of the *Sunday Times*, who knew every Prime Minister from Ramsay MacDonald to James Callaghan; of Harry Boyne of the *Daily Telegraph*, who once appeared in the Commons in a morning coat; of Francis Boyd of the *Guardian*, who retired with a knighthood – the days when such men might spend thirty years with the same paper in the same place were passing, and with them went part of that deference to tradition, the shared assumptions, which had underpinned the Lobby system.

This, then, was the situation as Ingham inherited it at the end of 1979. As with so much else in Britain, the job he was about to undertake had never been properly defined. It had grown up, like the fabled unwritten constitution, according to custom and usage: mysterious, crenellated, sham-antique. By the late 1970s, most countries had a straightforward government spokesman – a political appointee who would brief the press, appear on radio and television, and promote the official line. But in Britain, the spokesman was not only anonymous: he acted in accordance with quasi-masonic rules drawn up in

Queen Victoria's time. A system which had been designed to preserve the quintessentially English atmosphere of a gentleman's club had been imported into the television age. Not surprisingly, it had begun to look rather shaky.

On the other hand, the very vagueness and secretiveness of the office – the fact that it had always meant different things to different administrations, that its anonymous holder spoke for both government and premier – rendered it a source of potentially enormous influence. The powers were there, waiting to be picked up. Given a sufficiently ruthless, determined Prime Minister and an appropriately ambitious, domineering Press Secretary, it was a superb instrument for imposing the views of Number 10 on the media, for preempting debate, and for undermining dissident ministers within the Government. Between them, Margaret Thatcher and Bernard Ingham were to use the Downing Street Press Office in a way which her predecessors – even men as astute and manipulative as Neville Chamberlain and Harold Wilson – would never have dared attempt.

SIX

The Yorkshire Rasputin

*'One would begin to imagine that we have in Mr Bernard
Ingham some sort of rough-spoken Yorkshire Rasputin who is
manipulating Government and corroding the standards of
public morality.'*

RT HON. JOHN BIFFEN MP, SPEECH IN THE HOUSE OF
COMMONS, FEBRUARY 1983[1]

For a man who relished being at the centre of events as much as
Ingham, entering the office of Chief Press Secretary at Number
10 Downing Street was like wandering into Aladdin's Cave. He
had only been in place three weeks when the Prime Minister
overruled the advice of the Cabinet Secretary, Sir Robert
Armstrong, and decided to make public the treachery of the
so-called 'fourth man', Sir Anthony Blunt. Her Chief Press
Secretary, naturally, was closely involved and he later described it as 'the best story I have ever worked on'.[2] On the day
Mrs Thatcher made her announcement, interest rates were
raised to 17 per cent, inevitably inviting charges of news
management. Ingham was alert to the danger. 'If only you
knew,' he recalled, 'how hard I worked to stop those two things
happening, because I thought it was Wilsonian to a fault . . .'[3]

Naming traitors, raising bank rates . . . This was high politics. There were no more minor officials fussing around,

stopping him from seeing Government documents. Now, Armstrong had instructions to send Ingham some Cabinet papers direct. If he wanted to read the others, he had merely to climb the stairs to the Prime Minister's Private Office and browse through them. After Cabinet meetings on Thursday mornings, either Armstrong or the Prime Minister herself would brief him on what had been said. The lad from the *Hebden Bridge Times* who had left school at sixteen – the man whom the *Guardian* had turned down because he wasn't clever enough – had finally made it. He could hardly believe his luck.

From his earliest years, Ingham had shown a capacity to identify completely with whatever task he was given. He was always ferociously loyal, whether it was to the Labour Party or to the *Guardian* or to Barbara Castle. Now he transferred his formidable powers of devotion to Margaret Thatcher. Partly this was due to sheer professionalism; partly to a streak of old-fashioned chivalry – a protectiveness towards a woman he saw as courageous and embattled. But mostly it was down to a passionate belief that what she was doing – knocking Establishment heads together, making the unions face up to the consequences of their actions, putting the emphasis back on traditional values – was long overdue. After twelve years in Whitehall during which, as a press officer, he had often been made to feel like a second-class citizen, he shared her instinctive hostility towards Oxbridge mandarins – he once spoke heatedly of 'the administrator's natural elitist arrogance and the intensely hierarchical and generally secretive nature of our Civil Service'.[4] When Mrs Thatcher made her famous remark, after a particularly rough press conference – that neither of them was a 'smooth' person – she was putting her finger on what made theirs such a strong working relationship. They were two of a kind.

The Lobby journalists soon picked up the Whitehall gossip

and concluded that Ingham, unlike his predecessor, was on the inside track. Indeed, the Prime Minister and her Press Secretary were held to be so close that he was credited with almost supernatural powers. What Bernard said today, ran the Lobby cliché, Thatcher would be thinking tomorrow. 'Ingham has learned to read her mind,' claimed Andrew Thomson, her former constituency agent. 'He does not need detailed briefings from her or other Downing Street officials. Hand him a pile of Government papers outlining the problem and setting down a series of choices of action and Ingham will know almost as quickly as the Prime Minister what decision to take.'[5]

When, soon after Ingham arrived, the Government began to run into severe political turbulence, he seemed almost to embody the Thatcherite spirit: embattled, aggressive, often brutally frank. The official guidelines for Government Information Officers, issued in 1980, state that an official 'should not get himself involved in the political battle by fierce advocacy of a controversial policy in his discussion with journalists.' But that was not Ingham's style. 'I got a bit worried at one stage that he seemed to have fallen out with virtually every political correspondent,' recalled one Whitehall Head of Information. 'The first twelve, eighteen months – the Lobby meetings were almost a shouting match.'

For a Government whose message was 'there is no alternative', there could have been no better-equipped delivery boy, either physically or temperamentally, than Ingham. At last he could give free rein to his natural obduracy and penchant for hectoring. 'I have been able to operate with a Prime Minister constant of purpose and resolve,' he subsequently boasted. 'That is why I spent the first two years playing spot the U-turn with the media – and why they never found one.'[6]

In this endeavour, Ingham's previous, well-known attachment to socialism and corporatism was not a handicap but an asset: he personally had travelled down that road in the 1960s, he frequently declared, and had found it led only to a dead end; it was time to try a different route. Like so many Thatcherites, he had the zeal of the recently-converted. To Jim Prior, the 'wet' Employment Secretary in the first Thatcher Cabinet, 'he was another of the left like Paul Johnson who, having decided to change sides, has moved right across the political spectrum,' the only difference being that Ingham 'did not qualify as an intellectual: he was more in the mould of a political bruiser.'[7] When, during an industrial dispute, one Lobby correspondent suggested Government mediation, Ingham was contemptuous: 'That's beer and sandwiches at Number 10. We tried that and look where it got us.' Another reporter with whom he had regular rows on industrial issues was John Cole – part of the *Guardian* team who had refused to promote him in 1967, and who had now resurfaced in his professional life as the BBC's political editor.

It was Ingham's passionate conviction that the trade unions had to be tamed and, like Thatcher, he chafed at Prior's cautious approach to union reform. During the steelworkers' strike of 1979–80, the Employment Secretary came under orchestrated attack from the Tory Right over the slow progress of his department's legislation. He resolved to defend himself and accepted an invitation from Radio Four's *The World at One*. 'Then my private office received a call from Number 10,' recalled Prior. 'Bernard Ingham was saying that I should not go on. That convinced me that I should appear.'[8]

The following year, in October 1981, Ingham briefed the Lobby on a threatened strike at British Leyland. 'It took the steelworkers thirteen weeks,' he said grimly, 'and the civil servants twenty-one weeks to realise that we meant business.'[9] Coming from a once-ardent trade unionist, industrial correspondent and Labour candidate, this tough-talking carried more conviction than it would had it come from some plummy ex-diplomat. In Peter Jenkins's words: 'He used to speak as if he was still of the Labour movement but could justify her policies.' In this sense, he represented a valuable propaganda weapon in his own right: that a man with his background could argue the Government's case so robustly was itself an indication that There Was No Alternative.

Indeed, there is an argument that the Thatcher persona of those crucial early years was, at least in part, an Ingham creation. Prior describes how important a part the right-wing press played in setting the tone of Cabinet debates. 'Battling Maggie Under Attack from Wets' would be the morning headline in the *Sun* or the *Daily Mail*. The issue would be thus reduced to a simple question: were you pro- or anti-Maggie? In October 1980, at the time when the Cabinet was agonising over cuts in public spending, the *Sun* proclaimed that 'Premier Margaret Thatcher routed the "wets" in her Cabinet yesterday in a major showdown over public spending. She waded into attack . . .' But, recalled Prior, 'this was not what had happened . . . When the *Sun* finally reported a month later that the Prime Minister and her Treasury team had not secured the cuts they sought, its headline typified the view that Margaret was somehow separate from her own Government: "Maggie at Bay: Tories baffled as the battle for £2 billion extra cuts is lost."'[10]

Ingham created a (literally) vicious circle: he would brief the Lobby emphasizing her toughness and determination; the following morning, he would relay the resulting headlines to the Prime Minister in his press summary; this would fire her up to be still more tough and determined, giving him yet more ammunition for his next Lobby briefing. This was certainly the opinion of Andrew Thomson, who observed her at first hand for six years:

In private she was at times cautious, hesitant and uncertain. So instead of waiting to see whether other ministers would be able to capitalize on her weaknesses, Ingham took the essence of Margaret Thatcher out to the media. He scoffed at the idea of U-turns. He disparaged fainthearts in the Cabinet. A crisis over proposals to cut planned rises in Government spending? Ministers would just have to find the cuts or she would sort them out. Listening to Ingham gave the media the certain impression that there was a ferocious tigress on the loose in Whitehall.[11]

'It was Bernard Ingham who made Margaret Thatcher what she is,' claimed one of Ingham's colleagues. 'He went out and sold the Prime Minister to the Lobby correspondents. But the Prime Minister he sold was not quite the woman she was, at least not at the time he was selling her.'[12]

One should be careful not to overstate the case. After all, Margaret Thatcher was not invented by her Press Secretary: there *was* a 'tigress on the loose in Whitehall', one which had prowled around for several months before he arrived in Downing Street. But it is equally true that Ingham – growling and red-faced, with his frequent snorts of 'Dammit!' and his eyeballs swivelling upwards in exasperation – took care to give no hint of the doubts which sometimes crowded in upon her in the precarious days of 1980–82. He was more furious, more impatient, more intolerant of the 'wets' even than she.

Lobby journalists are quick to spot such hints. Twenty years earlier, Harold Evans, Macmillan's Press Secretary, used to adopt for briefings what Macmillan called his 'Lobby face'. According to Evans: 'an outwardly relaxed and unhurried manner is a necessary part of the equipment of a spokesman, whose demeanour, no less than his words (sometimes more than his words) comes under close scrutiny. A poker face is part of the business...'[13] Evans's phlegmatic style helped reinforce Macmillan's reputation for unflappability. Ingham's approach was exactly the opposite. He did not merely speak for Thatcher, he out-Thatchered Thatcher – to an extent she may not fully have realized. On the rare occasions, usually before Prime Minister's Questions, when she studied the press at first hand, she often declared herself baffled at her own reflection. 'Why do they always make me out to be so angry?' she would inquire, with an air of apparently genuine innocence. In time, this, too, became part of Ingham's repertoire of complaints against the media. 'Mrs Thatcher it seems can never be happy, sad, sorry, ecstatic or bored,' he told the International Press Institute in 1985. 'The only emotion permitted is fury.' If that was the case, he was himself in large measure to blame.

Only very rarely, even in private, did he so much as hint at any doubts about Government policies. In 1980, unemployment rose by 830,000, the largest annual increase since 1930. Confronted by images of the Depression, with three million out of work, it would have been strange if Ingham had not felt his father's ghost at his back. 'I suppose you think I've sold out?' was his plaintive remark to one former *Guardian* colleague during this period. On another occasion, he and the Prime Minister went to lunch at the *Daily Mirror*. An argument broke out over unemployment. Ingham, uncharacteristically, sat silently, looking down at his plate. 'He never rebuked me for what I wrote,' recalled Geoffrey Goodman, who had remained a Labour supporter and who was present on that occasion. 'I would tease him about Government policy and he'd just shrug. It was a sign that it was the sort of thing he didn't want to get involved talking about.'

But such reticence, even despondency, was rare. 'The word that he most often uses,' according to his former colleague in the Government Information Service, Neville Taylor, 'is "screw": "Got to screw the Foreign Office" . . . "Can't understand the Lobby – just got to screw the buggers" . . .'

On 2 February 1982, when Margaret Thatcher's unpopularity was at its peak and the 'wets' were in open rebellion, Ingham screwed, stuffed and mounted his first Cabinet Minister.

What Ingham was to do to Francis Pym was not without precedent. On at least two occasions, Harold Wilson, like Margaret Thatcher, used the Downing Street Press Office to undermine ministerial colleagues. On 3 April 1969, he instructed Joe Haines to tell the Lobby that James Callaghan had been reprimanded at that morning's Cabinet for openly opposing *In Place of Strife*. In fact, as Barbara Castle noted in her diary, Wilson was 'unnerved' by Callaghan's coolness and, despite his tough promises, 'the thunderbolt never materialized'.[14] Nevertheless, the papers the next morning were full of Callaghan's supposed 'dressing down' at Wilson's hands. It was a fiction. Haines, taking individual correspondents to one side ('I wouldn't have dared do it to the Lobby generally') and whispering in their ears, had done his bit; but the Prime Minister had failed to do his. Six years later, in 1975, according to Haines:

> Harold told me that Hugh Jenkins [Minister for the Arts] was stupid and he was going to get rid of him. And as the *Evening Standard* had been running a big thing about the arts, he told me to have a word with Bob Carvel. So I went to Bob and told him that Hugh Jenkins was going to be sacked. I told him without equivocation because there was no equivocation. Except that after Harold saw the story and one or two people went to him and said 'You're not going to do this to old Hugh, are you?' he chickened out. And so Bob had a perfectly genuine splash and he kept coming to me and saying 'When's it going to come true?' And Harold kept saying 'Tell him to wait, tell him to wait.' And in the end it never happened.

Ingham had disapproved of Joe Haines precisely because of antics of this sort. Yet once he was in Haines's old job, he was soon up to similar tricks. On 6 January 1981, the Leader of the House of Commons, Norman St John Stevas, had the dubious distinction of becoming the first Cabinet Minister to be sacked by Mrs Thatcher. Naturally, Ingham was asked by the Lobby why the Prime Minister had dismissed him. He had gone chiefly because he was the most vulnerable of the 'wets', and sacking him would serve as a useful warning to the others.

But that was not what Ingham said. In the words of the *Daily Telegraph* the following day: 'sources close to her [a coded phrase for Ingham] were suggesting that he had borne the brunt of concern about open and at times inaccurate portrayals in the press of what had been going on in Government.' The *Daily Express* claimed Stevas had been sacked because he 'blabbed out of school'. A leader in *The Times* declared: 'One of the reasons for dismissing Mr St John Stevas was to provide a warning to other members of the Cabinet that leaks would not be tolerated.'

This 'guidance' from Ingham, coupled with remarks made by the Prime Minister in a television interview that afternoon ('Leaks there have been . . . I hope it will happen less and less') were too much for Stevas to bear. The next morning, having read the papers at breakfast, he was so upset he sat down at his typewriter in his home in Montpelier Square and tapped out a letter, full of errors and mis-spellings, saying he was 'greatly distressed and indeed angered' and demanding an apology. Mrs Thatcher had little option but to give him one, but it came dripping with disingenuousness: 'I believe it unreasonable that my remarks should have been interpreted in the way they apparently have been.'

The beauty of using the Lobby in this fashion was precisely this: that the stories which resulted were deniable; indeed, that they could be blamed on the 'unreasonable' behaviour of the reporters themselves.

The Stevas briefing, however, was only a curtain-raiser. He had, after all, been sacked: the briefing was merely salt in the wound. It was the treatment meted out the following year to Francis Pym which provided the first textbook example of the way Thatcher and Ingham were prepared to use the Lobby to undermine a senior colleague still in the Cabinet. Pym, formerly the Defence Secretary, who had replaced the hapless Stevas as Leader of the House, had always been a particular *bête noire* of the Prime Minister. She openly regarded him as a gloomy, disloyal, vacillating snob. On 1 February 1982, he made a speech to the Allied Brewery Trades Association which was unusual for its pessimism, even by his standards. 'This Government is completely committed to a long-term economic recovery,' he announced. 'But this cannot lead to an early return to full or nearly full employment, or an early improvement in living standards generally.' He spoke of a 'formidable challenge', of 'a very painful period of transition', of living standards which 'generally can only fall': 'We have to find ways of coping with higher levels of unemployment than we have been used to . . . Let nobody think it is going to be easy.'

Pym was saying nothing in public which the Treasury had not already warned ministers about in private. His words were literally correct. Newspapers as loyal to Mrs Thatcher as the *Daily Express* and the *Daily Telegraph* praised him for his courage and honesty. The Prime Minister, however, was incensed. Only four days previously, the Chancellor of the Exchequer had made a speech emphasizing the signs of recovery in the British economy. Now Pym had destroyed the Government's attempts to accentuate the positive, and done it, moreover, without even consulting Number 10. She could not disown him without sacking him, and he was too powerful for that. She therefore did the next best thing.

On the day following his speech, at 3.15 p.m., she rose in the Commons to take Prime Minister's Questions. The Opposition's blood was up and Michael Foot, the Labour leader, was quickly on his feet demanding to know whether she agreed with Pym. Thatcher's reply floored him: 'My Right Honourable Friend made an excellent speech last night, so good that I wish to quote from it.' This she proceeded to do, at length. In that case, inquired Foot, why had the *Daily Telegraph* given it such prominence (under the headline 'Bleak view of the economy by Pym')? 'Because,' said Thatcher, sweetly, 'it was a very good speech.'[15]

Down on the floor of the House, all might be smiles; but up in the Lobby room, the knife was flashing. Half an hour after the Prime Minister had sat down, Ingham was telling the journalists, non-attributably, a very different tale. According to the *Daily Telegraph* the following day:

> The Prime Minister was dismayed by some of Mr Pym's phraseology ... She was also angry that Conservative Central Office, which distributed the speech to correspondents early on Monday evening, did not give her office a copy at the same time ... Discount was being made for a general tendency towards pessimism by Mr Pym. There was an off-stage comparison of him with the wartime radio character whose lugubrious catch phrase was 'It's being so cheerful as keeps me going'.

The *Guardian* had almost exactly the same words:

> In spite of Mrs Thatcher's defence of Mr Pym, it was clear that the Leader of the House was by no means popular among his Treasury colleagues. He was compared to 'Mrs Mopp' whose wartime catch phrase on the *Itma* radio programme had been 'It's being so cheerful as keeps me going'.

(In fact, the phrase belonged to a character called Mona Lott; Mrs Mopp's slogan – which, under the circumstances, would have been rather an appropriate one for Ingham – was 'Shall I do you now, sir?')

The story was everywhere, and everywhere it took precedence over the Prime Minister's soft words. 'Maggie sends grim Pym to the doghouse,' chortled the *Sun*. 'If Mr Misery Pym does not believe the good news,' ran the paper's editorial, 'then he is not merely in the wrong job. He is in the wrong Government.' The *Daily Mirror* reported that 'the word being put around by Mrs Thatcher's friends yesterday was that Mr Pym was known to be a pessimist.' 'Maggie cross at Pym's gloomy view,' was the headline in the *Daily Express*. In the *Daily Mail*, which quoted 'senior Whitehall sources', it was 'Fury over Pym's bleak warning of gloom'. According to *The Times*: 'It was admitted openly in Government quarters that Mr Pym's speech on Monday night ... had upset Mrs Margaret Thatcher ... Mr Pym's main sin, in the eyes of Mrs Thatcher, was that he approved the release by Conservative Central Office of extracts of his speech which made little of the good news and much of the bad.'

The Lobby had witnessed some skulduggery over the years, but never anything quite like this. In 1969, Joe Haines had reported what he believed to be a fact – that Wilson had given Callaghan a dressing-down – and he had done it to correspondents individually. Similarly, in 1977, Tom McCaffrey had made his disparaging remarks about Sir Peter Ramsbotham off the cuff to two old friends. But never before had the Government's official spokesman, a civil servant, deliberately disparaged a minister for speaking what he saw as the truth – and done it, moreover, to the entire Lobby only moments after the Prime Minister had given an entirely different version of events. To Anthony Bevins, political correspondent of *The Times*, it was 'despicable for a servant of the

Crown to be backstabbing colleagues of the Prime Minister. He wasn't selling the policies of the Government. He was acting as her personal advocate. I had never seen that before.' John Nott, who had replaced Pym as Defence Secretary the previous year, later called Ingham's use of the Lobby 'sickening ... deplorable and malicious'.[16]

Was Ingham's action really any different to, or worse than, what had happened before – than, for example, Wilson's treatment of Hugh Jenkins in 1975? With hindsight, it is clear that it was significantly different and, in some respects, worse. Different because the disparaging of Pym was not some private tip-off, which would have been reprehensible, no doubt, but a recognized stroke in the dark art of politics; it was not inadvertent; it was a premeditated abuse of the main channel of communication between Government and media. And it was worse, because at least Haines had openly admitted that his role was a partisan one; Ingham had always insisted he was the neutral spokesman of the Government as a whole.

In the end, Ingham's style, like the style of his predecessors, was conditioned by the nature of his boss. What was also striking about this episode was that Pym never heard a word of complaint from the Prime Minister herself. He had to read it in the press. For a leader with a reputation for straight-speaking, it was an oddly devious means of issuing a reprimand. Donald Maitland was shocked by this sort of behaviour because, under Edward Heath, whatever that difficult and autocratic man's other faults, the situation 'could not have arisen':

> There was never any occasion when I commented on the performance of any member of the Cabinet, for the very good reason that the Prime Minister never discussed his Cabinet colleagues with me ... My relationship with Ted Heath was

obviously a very close one, but on no occasion did that arise in any conversation he had with me, and I didn't expect it to.

Margaret Thatcher, on the other hand, was notorious for keeping up a private running commentary on the failings of her ministers and their policies, as if the Government was in some way nothing to do with her. Stevas has described how she once stood on a chair during a party in Downing Street and announced herself to be 'the rebel head of an establishment government'.[17] Diatribes against her 'spineless' male colleagues occurred all the time when Ingham was with her: at the 9.30 a.m. meetings in her study, during her preparations for Prime Minister's Questions, on her long plane journeys abroad, in the evenings, after a reception, when she would kick off her shoes and hand round the whiskies to her Downing Street advisers. Knowing her as he did put Ingham in a quandary. When he was asked about her opinions at a Lobby meeting, how much should he disclose? A civil service smoothie would have answered 'Nothing'. But then, a civil service smoothie would not have been privy to such confidences in the first place, let alone have lasted eleven years as Margaret Thatcher's Chief Press Secretary.

Nevertheless, certain of her advisers were worried that, to adapt Attlee's phrase about Aneurin Bevan, where she needed a sedative she got an irritant. 'There's always a danger that Bernard exaggerates her reactions,' said one. 'She's going to react in the privacy of her own room with her close associates one way – like an actor in a hotel who's just read some bad reviews. But what can happen is that he sees her reaction in the morning, shares it, and then recycles it to the press. They wind one another up in private.'

How much of the 'fury', the intransigence, the distancing of the Prime Minister from colleagues, was Thatcher and how much Ingham? That was the question which increasingly preoccupied nervous ministers over the next decade. And, of course, there was never any way of telling. That was the point.

The invasion of the Falkland Islands, exactly three months after the Pym briefing, provided another graphic illustration of how much Ingham's views had changed. In his 'Albion' years, when he was opposed to nuclear weapons, he had been violently pacifist – an aggressive dove. Labour's failure to slash the defence budget in the mid-1960s he called 'an abject failure'. 'Whom are we defending ourselves against?' he asked in 1967. 'It hardly seems likely these days that Russia wants to chuck her weight about.' On this issue, he was an extremist, to the extent of advocating that half the defence budget – £1 billion – should be switched to 'agricultural, irrigational and medical development schemes which Mr Wilson, before he lost his idealism, so movingly pressed upon a receptive Labour Party Conference. Such a policy would soon sort out the men from the boys in the Labour Movement. We would soon discover then what socialism meant to many who now have the honour to call themselves socialists.'[18]

But on this, as on so much else, the wheel had turned. In the first week of the Falklands crisis, as the task force sailed, he gave a briefing to the Lobby correspondents of the Sunday papers, looking, in the words of one, 'like an old sea dog, with the salt spray lashing his face'. He was asked about reports that some Conservative MPs – most notably the Member for Clwyd, Sir Anthony Meyer – were opposed to the Prime Minister's stated willingness to use force. 'Is that what they're saying?' he demanded. He was assured that this was indeed the case. 'So it's true then,' he growled, glaring at the reporters, 'she is the only man among 'em!'

In the course of that extraordinary ten-week conflict, Ingham certainly did his share of hand-to-hand fighting: not in the South Atlantic, but rather in the treacherous terrain of Whitehall. His enemy – implacable, cunning and numerically superior – was located a few hundred yards east of Downing Street in the Ministry of Defence, commanded by the MoD's Permanent Under Secretary, Sir Frank Cooper.

Cooper, sixty years old and due to retire in a few months' time, had travelled with Thatcher to Bonn and Paris in 1979 and 1980, as well as to Washington on her first visits to see Presidents Carter and Reagan. He had observed her relationship with Ingham often enough and closely enough to have become distinctly wary. He had worked for Francis Pym for two years and had just seen what had happened to him at Ingham's hands. The Falklands operation was a purely military affair as far as Cooper was concerned. He wanted Number 10's influence kept to a minimum, and his first objective was to neutralize Ingham.

Ingham's primary aim was equally clear. In 1981, he had secured the appointment of a friend, Neville Taylor, the Chief Information Officer at the Department of Health and Social Security, to the equivalent position at the MoD. But Taylor had been ill. He was not due to take up his new duties for another two months. In the meantime, public relations at the MoD were being run by Ian McDonald, an assistant secretary previously responsible for pay and recruitment. Even in normal times it was a preoccupation of Ingham, amounting almost to an obsession, that all Whitehall heads of PR should be fully-trained information officers and not ordinary career civil servants. Now, with war imminent, he was especially keen to get one of his own kind in place at the MoD: first, because he thought they would do the job better; secondly because McDonald reported to Frank Cooper and was not under his direct control; thirdly because Margaret Thatcher's position as Prime Minister was in the balance and the presentation of news naturally had to take account of this political dimension. Thus, in the shadow of the greater conflict, were the battle-lines drawn for the lesser.

All Ingham's fears appeared to be borne out by the events of the first weekend. The Navy at first refused to allow any journalists to sail with the task force. Ian McDonald persuaded them to take ten: five places were to go to television, one to the Press Association (PA) and four to reporters from national newspapers; the winners were literally picked out of a hat. Naturally, this produced a howl of resentment from all those – the four other Fleet Street dailies and the eight Sunday papers, the regional press, Reuters, independent radio, the foreign correspondents based in London – who felt they had been unfairly excluded. The telephone began ringing in Purley on Friday night with calls from newspaper editors and executives, and it barely stopped all weekend. Ingham later recalled how, 'having spent the first four nights ... literally on the phone all the time, I said "This has got to stop".'[19] On Monday morning, using the authority of the Prime Minister's name but without actually consulting her, he instructed the MoD to increase the allocation of media berths on the task force. Eventually, some twenty-eight journalists sailed with the fleet: 'more people,' in Frank Cooper's view, 'than we could properly cope with'.[20]

More disturbing to Ingham even than the chaos surrounding press accreditation was McDonald's decision to end all off-the-record briefings. Defence correspondents, like most specialist journalists, operated their own mini Lobby system, as part of which they were given regular 'guidance' by Cooper. On the day of the Argentine invasion, McDonald severed these contacts on the grounds of security. Ingham was incredulous. 'I certainly took the view that when you are in a crisis of this kind, the last thing you do is withdraw the service to the media,' he said later. 'I think that is not the time to withdraw your service to your clientele.'[21]

Ingham acted quickly. He arranged with the DHSS for Neville Taylor to be relieved of his post and sent to the MoD nine weeks earlier than planned. Cooper made his counter-move equally smartly. When Taylor walked through the door on the morning of 13 April he was handed a letter welcoming him to the ministry and informing him that he was now in charge of all areas of public relations – except the Falklands. It was a bureaucratic master-stroke, justified by Cooper on the grounds that Taylor (who had not worked at the MoD for twelve years) needed time to reacquaint himself with military matters. The real reason, as Taylor swiftly discovered, was Cooper's deep-rooted suspicion of Ingham. 'I was known to have a rapport with Bernard,' recalled Taylor, 'which made Frank Cooper incredibly suspicious of me. He didn't trust me. This was a recurring theme throughout the Falklands – actual instructions from Cooper: "Don't tell that bugger anything about it."'

Ingham, who learned of Taylor's treatment with 'ill-concealed fury', now found himself in danger of becoming sidelined. On 8 April he had set up a 'co-ordinating commit-tee', with himself in the chair, which met at 10.00 a.m. each day in his office in Downing Street. The MoD, the COI, the Cabinet Office and the Foreign Office were all obliged to send representatives. The purpose, in Ingham's words, was 'to take stock of developments and their implications for the public; to bring the departments and offices up to date with events; to anticipate, in so far as this was possible, events over the next 24 hours; and to agree on or make recommendations about the action required.' Cooper saw through this ploy at once. Ingham was trying to run the entire information effort from Number 10. Once again, Cooper's response showed what a master he was at Whitehall in-fighting. He simply instructed McDonald not to attend. Instead, the MoD made it a point of principle to send the lowliest official in its news department.

As McDonald was the only information officer empowered to be present at the morning meeting of the Chiefs of Staff, Ingham's 'co-ordinating committee' was left with little to co-ordinate.

After a few days of this, Ingham complained to the Prime Minister. She was sympathetic and instructed Cecil Parkinson, Chairman of the Conservative Party and a member of the War Cabinet, to help him out. Parkinson summoned Cooper and the other Permanent Under Secretaries over for drinks on a couple of occasions in order (in his words) to let them know 'that they would have to explain to a member of the Cabinet why a junior representative had been sent to the key co-ordinating meetings'.[22] Cooper took the hint and McDonald duly started attending the Downing Street committee. Ingham also told Mrs Thatcher of his anger at the MoD's decision to abandon all off-the-record briefings; these were re-started in May. Both victories were a telling demonstration of Ingham's power. He might be outwitted sometimes by nimbler minds, but in any dispute he always had at his disposal the ultimate deterrent: the Prime Minister.

Cooper was not antagonistic towards Ingham because he regarded him as incompetent; on the contrary, he thought him a first-class political information officer. His concern was that Ingham would inevitably be tempted to let political imperatives override military ones. On 6 May, for example, two Harriers crashed in fog in the South Atlantic. As the task force had only twenty of these aircraft in the first place, and as no Argentine forces had been involved, the MoD wanted to delay the announcement of their loss. 'In no way do you tell the Argentines that you have lost 10 per cent of your capability,' argued Admiral Woodward, the task force commander. 'It's obvious.'[23] But 6 May was also the day of the local elections. In the House of Commons Press Gallery after Prime Minister's Questions, Ingham was asked if the official release of the bad news was being held up until the polls had closed. Such a cynical tactic would certainly have rebounded on the Government. As Ingham later explained: 'It is very often disadvantageous not to release information which is disadvantageous.'[24] He therefore urged an immediate announcement. The news was promptly released and the Navy, understandably, was dismayed.

As the fighting intensified, the tension in London between Downing Street and the MoD increased. It was soon an open secret among the journalists covering the war in Whitehall. 'We got the distinct impression,' said Bob Hutchinson, defence correspondent of the PA, 'that Number 10 was more than unhappy at the way the MoD were handling the war – *more* than unhappy – and there were times when Number 10 were briefing on subjects which the MoD refused to talk about.'[25]

It was obviously in the Government's interests to convey an impression of irresistible momentum. 'We're not going to fiddle around,' Ingham told the Lobby on 23 May, two days after the British forces landed on the Falklands. Later that week, on 27 May, Cooper was incensed to hear reports that Ingham had given a briefing hinting that Goose Green had already fallen. At that moment Cooper knew that the 2nd Parachute Regiment was only just beginning its assault. He telephoned Ingham and told him that if he ever did it again, he'd have his bloody head off. He hung up before Ingham could reply. He subsequently criticized the Downing Street Press Office in a radio interview:

> On one particular occasion they let out that something had happened that hadn't happened ... because, I think, they wanted to influence the political scene. Happily, it was captured quite soon afterwards. They may say that's a very fine distinction. I happen to think it's quite an important distinction in a wartime situation when lives are very much at risk.[26]

Eighteen paratroopers, including their commander, Colonel 'H' Jones, were killed in the assault on Goose Green, and there were bitter complaints from the survivors that the plan had been leaked behind their backs in London. Indeed, there were allegations from some military commanders that the entire operation was strategically unnecessary and had only been mounted due to political pressure at home. 'Goose Green,' said one anonymous 'very senior MoD civil servant' after the war, 'was a push from Number 10.'[27]

Two weeks later there was a further skirmish between Ingham and the MoD. On 8 June, Argentine aircraft attacked the landing ships *Sir Galahad* and *Sir Tristram*. Fifty men were killed. The MoD decided not to release the casualty figures. 'We knew from intelligence,' claimed the Chief of the Defence Staff, Sir Terence Lewin, 'that the Argentines thought they were very much higher.'[28] For the next three days, rumours were allowed, even encouraged, to swirl around Fleet Street and Whitehall that up to 800 men had been killed or wounded. Eventually, on 11 June, Ingham decided that the speculation had gone on long enough. It was proving politically damaging. He made it clear to the Lobby that fewer than seventy had died. The MoD was furious: the Downing Street briefing, said Neville Taylor, 'became the subject of pretty heated discussion between Bernard Ingham and myself.'[29]

Even after white flags had been hoisted over the Falklands and the war had been won, Ingham and Sir Frank Cooper continued to bicker about the part played in the conflict by the Number 10 Press Office. In July, Cooper told the House of Commons Defence Committee that Ingham had definitely not played a 'co-ordinating' role. Ingham read that, and in October sent the committee a paper claiming that his morning meetings had been throughout 'the main instrument of co-ordination' for media relations. The following month, he appeared before the MPs and blamed the discrepancy between their two versions on the fact that Cooper was not properly briefed. Finally, Cooper took his revenge at a major lecture, attacking Ingham's general role in Government in outspoken terms:

> the aim now is the management of the media with a very much higher degree of central control from Number 10 Downing Street and with the connivance of a part of the media. There is now public relations – which I would define as biased information. I suggest that the post of Chief Information Officer at Number 10 Downing Street is in fact a political job in a party sense and is not a job which it is proper for a civil servant to fill unless he or she resigns from the Civil Service on appointment.[30]

How much truth was there in Sir Frank's assertion? Undoubtedly, the Falklands War served further to cement the relationship between the Prime Minister and her Press Secretary. Ingham, although few in the media realized it at the time, had been operating under a considerable personal strain. On Tuesday 11 May – the day Margaret Thatcher attacked the BBC in the House of Commons for failing to support 'our boys' – Ingham was called away and told that his wife had been gravely injured in an accident. That lunchtime, Nancy Ingham had been shopping in the local market in Surrey Street when a runaway lorry had careered through the stalls and up on to the pavement, injuring nine pedestrians. She was trapped under the wreckage for several hours. Once in hospital she was found to have, among other injuries, a broken pelvis. The Prime Minister told Ingham to take leave. He refused.

This was devotion to duty of an order which surprised even those who knew him of old. Nancy, according to her brother-in-law, 'was on her back for three months'. She eventually had to leave hospital on crutches. 'Most of us,' in Neville Taylor's words, 'given the nature of our marriages and the nature of the injuries suffered by his wife, would have said: "Terribly sorry, even if there's a war on I've got to take half a day off". Bernard didn't. He snatched odd hours. He had a car, visited his wife, then came back again. It was hardly noticeable that there was anything else going on in his life.'

The Falklands War had transformed the Government's fortunes. From third place in the opinion polls it had moved to first. There was talk of a quick General Election to exploit the after-glow of victory. On 10 September, in the Cabinet Room, the Prime Minister convened the first meeting of the pre-election Liaison Committee, designed to co-ordinate the efforts of Tory Party and Government. Five ministers attended (Sir Keith Joseph, Norman Tebbit, John Biffen, Norman Fowler and John Wakeham), together with three senior party officials (the Chairman, Cecil Parkinson, the marketing director, Christopher Lawson, and the research director, Peter Cropper). Somewhat surprisingly, Bernard Ingham was also present.

The Liaison Committee's confidential minutes show how close Ingham now was to playing a party political role. The group, which met many times in the run-up to the election, was essentially concerned with propaganda. The gentlemen from Conservative Central Office undertook to revise a Government paper on the National Health Service and to publish a brochure to accompany it; to 'advise on a more appealing presentational approach of [sic] the Government's privatisation policies'; and to help combat the Campaign for Nuclear Disarmament. Ingham himself addressed the problem of deflecting the Labour Party's attacks on the high level of unemployment: 'the Government,' he said, 'must emphasize the importance of wealth creation'.[31] The Committee's work had nothing to do with the objective publication of facts and everything to do with securing an election victory for the Conservative Party.

Before any election could be contemplated it was necessary to deal with one last piece of unfinished business from the Falklands War. Early in the conflict the Government had been obliged to set up an inquiry under Lord Franks to investigate ministers' conduct prior to the invasion. The inquiry, which included two former Labour Cabinet Ministers, had been given access to all classified documents. There was a risk that its findings might puncture the post-Falklands euphoria, and with it the Government's new-found popularity. Publication was set for 18 January 1983.

Number 10's response was to mount two pre-emptive strikes. On 8 January, the week before the report appeared, the Prime Minister, accompanied by her Press Secretary, paid a dramatic secret visit to the Falklands. What could more graphically remind the nation, in the run-up not only to Franks but to polling, of the victory she had won? Ingham organised an RAF flight to ferry a couple of Lobby friends, Chris Moncrieff of the Press Association and John Warden of the *Daily Express*, down to the islands.

Words were easy to arrange; television pictures were more difficult. For reasons of security, the visit could not be announced in advance. Ingham did not even tell his wife where he was going. Despite strong hints dropped to ITN that it would be worth its while to send a team to the South Atlantic, they did nothing. When the Prime Minister landed, the BBC had the only crew on the Falklands. Ingham nonetheless was determined to have Mrs Thatcher's triumphal entry into Port Stanley shown on all news bulletins.

His first words to the BBC's reporter, Nick Witchell, waiting by the runway, were a demand that the material he and his crew were shooting should be given free of charge to ITN. Witchell replied that that was a matter for the BBC in London. Ingham responded in a menacing tone that he would have him thrown off the island unless he did as he was told. He then rang the BBC's Assistant Director General, Alan Protheroe, and ordered him to 'pool' the material with ITN. Protheroe, understandably, was reluctant. 'I really find it very difficult to accept that Number 10 can actually just declare a pool when necessary, Bernard.' Ingham began to splutter with indignation. A radio ham was recording the call, and the tape is a treasure. His Yorkshire vowels pierced the howl of interference across a distance of 8,000 miles like some latter-day Heathcliffe bellowing into a moorland storm.

> INGHAM: It is this childish behaviour that when indeed we have done you a signal service – a signal service – by keeping your people in the islands, as I say and to repeat, at considerable risks to ourselves – and I, I, I, I frankly don't believe that the British public, when it is explained to them, will understand this childishness. I do expect more actually from the BBC and I am deeply hurt.
>
> PROTHEROE: It would have been a lot easier if somebody in your office had asked us or told us twenty-four hours beforehand –
>
> INGHAM: I am sorry there is absolutely no question of us doing that, and you have got to get it into your mind, and the media has got to get it into its mind, that we don't operate for your convenience, we operate for the security of the Prime Minister! I'm fed up with this! I had it in Northern Ireland.

At considerable cost, the BBC had booked a satellite and flown engineers out to Ascension Island. The plan was for the film to be flown there from the Falklands on an RAF Hercules due to take off at 4.00 p.m. This provided Ingham with his trump card. 'No film is coming out tonight,' he threatened, 'unless I have your absolute assurance that it will be freely available to ITN and Independent Radio News.' He went on: 'I'm sure the Prime Minister, if I had to tell her what is going on, she would scarcely credit it.' Protheroe had no answer to that. He capitulated. 'When I get home,' shouted Ingham, 'we have got to have a meeting. We can't go on like this.' He hung up on the BBC and called Number 10 in triumph:

INGHAM: I've won!
DOWNING STREET: You've won?
INGHAM : Yep!
DOWNING STREET: What happened?
INGHAM: I rang Protheroe and I told him in no uncertain terms that he wouldn't get it back tonight unless it was freely available . . .

For the next five days, images of the Prime Minister – graciously accepting the cheers of the islanders, manfully firing an artillery piece, tearfully laying a wreath – dominated all networks. The visit was a great success, although Ingham privately confessed to finding the Falklands a gloomy and charmless place.

He had spent the first leg of the flight down, from RAF Brize Norton to Ascension, reading the Franks Report. ('In thirteen hours,' he said later, 'you can shift an enormous amount of work, even if you come up for air every five minutes.'[32]) Personally, he had never been in any doubt about where the blame lay for failing to anticipate the Argentine invasion. 'Typical bloody Foreign Office,' Neville Taylor recalled him grumbling. 'They didn't see this coming. Even when some of their own people were telling them something was going on they didn't take any bloody notice because they're all Arabists and Arabists don't know anything about the South Atlantic . . .'

However, the Franks Report did not bear out this trenchant analysis. It was an odd document. Its first 338 paragraphs gave a devastatingly detailed account of Government incompetence, from which the Foreign Office actually emerged better than either Number 10 or the MoD. Lord Carrington, the Foreign Secretary, was revealed to have sent three separate minutes to the Defence Secretary urging him not to withdraw HMS *Endurance* from the South Atlantic lest it send the wrong signal to Buenos Aires. Carrington, clearly, was alert to the danger. The Cabinet's Defence Committee, on the other hand, chaired by the Prime Minister, which had approved *Endurance*'s removal, did not even discuss the Falklands between January 1981 and 1 April 1982, the day before the Argentine attack.

But then came the final paragraph – 339 – at which point, in Lord Callaghan's memorable phrase, Franks 'got fed up with the canvas he was painting and he chucked a bucket of whitewash over it'. The Committee announced it did not feel 'justified in attaching any criticism or blame to the present Government' for the invasion of 2 April 1982.

For Ingham, with all the instruments of news management at his disposal, this was a gift: the opportunity for the second pre-emptive strike against Mrs Thatcher's opponents in as many weeks. The Franks Report was due to be presented to Parliament four days after her return from the Falklands. It was rumoured to be long (it actually ran to 109 pages) and the media, anxious to prepare comment and detailed analysis, were pleading for the chance to see embargoed copies a few hours prior to publication. This had been standard practice for years with Government White Papers. But in October, in retaliation for what he claimed was a 'disgraceful' breach of the embargo on the Falklands Honours List, Ingham had withdrawn this 'privilege', making good his threat to leave 'Lobby correspondents waiting outside Number 10 in the snow'[33] for official documents.

Now, confronted with requests for advance copies of the Franks Report, Ingham turned them down flat. He told the BBC that if they could cover Budget speeches without knowing their contents, they could do the same with Franks (another disingenuous reply, given that the report was seven times the length of the average Budget, took at least a day to read, and was much more detailed). Instead, the report was to be distributed at 3.30 p.m., at the moment the Prime Minister presented it to Parliament. Ingham planned to offer only one piece of assistance: he would meet the Lobby at 2.45 p.m., 'to point out the important paragraphs'.

This was too much, even for some Lobby journalists. Fourteen hours before the proposed briefing, in the early hours of 18 January, the Labour MP Tam Dalyell rose in an almost deserted House of Commons to reveal Ingham's plan. He had been forewarned of it by a Lobby correspondent: 'not a member of the left-wing press,' claimed Dalyell, but a reporter who was 'professionally and personally outraged' by Ingham's manipulative behaviour. To head off a Parliamentary row, the Prime Minister had to tell Ingham to postpone his briefing until after her statement. He was outraged by this fresh evidence of treachery in the Lobby. Never before had the mechanics of its operation been revealed in advance. He was still sore about it several days later when Roy Hattersley, author of a weekly column on press matters, asked him about the purpose of the reconvened briefing. Ingham snapped that he had merely been helping the Lobby 'find their way around Franks'. If people did not believe him, 'that is their problem'. According to an amused Mr Hattersley: 'He gave me that assurance in such bellicose language that failure to report his disclaimer would put my person at risk when next I meet the burly Mr Ingham.'[34]

Politically, despite the last-minute embarrassment, Ingham's handling of the Franks inquiry paid rich dividends. With only a couple of hours available to study the report, almost every paper and news bulletin portrayed it as a document essentially uncritical of the Government. It took some days for its implications to be properly digested. By the weekend, the coverage had become distinctly hostile ('Why the Falklands invasion could have been foreseen,' was the headline in the conservative *Sunday Telegraph*) but by then the Franks Report was the stuff of history. The Government had scored a short-term, knock-out victory – and, in politics, those are the only victories that count.

But in the longer term, and personally, Ingham had done himself considerable damage. A narrow line divides the anonymous civil servant from the official who is too powerful and controversial to ignore. Ingham crossed it in that third week of January 1983. On the Monday he was named on the floor of the House of Commons and accused of trying to manage the news. On the Tuesday, the allegation was reported in the press. On the Friday, the Channel Four programme, *The Friday Alternative*, broadcast the tape of his browbeating of Alan Protheroe. On the following Monday, the 24th, it was revealed that Ingham was considering taking legal action over the unauthorized transmission of a private conversation.

Then on Tuesday, the 25th, there was a fresh controversy. The *Daily Mirror* disclosed that 'a number of Irish journalists' had written to the Prime Minister complaining that Ingham had 'knocked microphones aside and made liberal use of his elbows, buttocks and shoulders' during her recent visit to Belfast: 'I admit I did bang into them with my backside,' the paper reported Ingham as saying, but he insisted that the reporters were 'behaving like sensitive plants and they should grow up'.

Harold Evans or Donald Maitland would never have spoken in such terms. Fife Clark would have shrivelled into a corner at the mere thought of being quoted by *name*. Even Joe Haines made it a rule that any member of the Downing Street Press Office who was identified in the media had to pay a forfeit of a bottle of wine. But it was not in Ingham's nature to let such slights pass. He fought back – in public. On 6 February, he took the unprecedented step of granting an on-the-record interview to the *Sunday Telegraph*. 'I do not bear grudges,' said the man who, for five months, had persistently refused to let the Lobby see Government papers in advance. 'I play no part in politics,' maintained the official who sat on a Liaison Committee with employees of Conservative Central Office. Most risibly of all, the Press Secretary who regularly turned Lobby briefings into what one colleague called 'shouting matches' was recorded as insisting: 'I keep my views to myself'.

Until this point, the discreet conventions of the Lobby had protected Ingham, more or less. When he had compared Francis Pym to Mona Lott, for example, not a single newspaper had named him as the source. But henceforth, such niceties would not be observed. Anonymity, like virginity, once lost, is gone for good: even prolonged periods of self-denial will not restore the *status quo ante*. In any case, Ingham was too colourful, too combative, too ready to give offence and too swift to take it, for him now to relapse back into the shadows as just another 'senior Government source'. From the episode of the Franks Report onwards, he no longer simply released the news; the manner in which he released it often *was* the news.

Proof of that came within twenty-four hours of the *Sunday Telegraph* interview, when Ingham became the first Prime Minister's Press Secretary to be the subject of a Parliamentary debate. True, the debate took place at breakfast time, lasted just fifty-six minutes and involved only two speakers. But such attention had never before been focused upon any civil servant, let alone one in Ingham's position. 'The Prime Minister's press relations,' stated Tam Dalyell, 'are being handled at senior level by someone whom I can only call a thug.' Protected by Parliamentary privilege, unfettered by the risk of a libel action, the MP let fly.

> Why do we have to tolerate a Lobby system in which able, gifted journalists are forced to become beholden to men in the position of Mr Ingham who threaten assistant directors-general of the BBC with 'incalculable consequences'? Why should men and women of calibre, chosen by editors to represent newspapers at Westminster, be put in the position of prostituting their profession by keeping in with truculent, arrogant bullies of the species that the Prime Minister's Press Secretary has clearly become?

The 'heady air of Downing Street has warped his judgement,' concluded Dalyell. He 'should be redeployed to other duties'.[35]

The minister required to respond to this diatribe was the new Leader of the House of Commons, John Biffen, who had patiently sat up all night awaiting the start of Dalyell's debate. He ridiculed the suggestion that Ingham was a sinister, all-powerful Machiavelli lurking at the heart of Number 10. 'One would begin to imagine,' he mocked, in a phrase which became justly famous, 'that we have in Mr Bernard Ingham some sort of rough-spoken Yorkshire Rasputin who is manipulating Government and corroding the standards of public morality.'

Biffen would not have been so sanguine had he known what lay in store for him at Ingham's hands.

SEVEN

Conducting the Orchestra

*'I have waxed eloquently indignant about the Tory plan for
bringing the Welfare State up to date. For "up to date" you
should read "to an end".'*

BERNARD INGHAM, ARTICLE IN THE
LEEDS WEEKLY CITIZEN, 25 MARCH 1966

*'. . . news stories about deaths due to the shortage of resources
for kidney dialysis machines and transplants would certainly
arise . . . the emotive nature of the subject created
presentational problems.'*

BERNARD INGHAM, QUOTED IN THE MINUTES OF THE
MEETING OF INFORMATION OFFICERS, OCTOBER 1983

On 1 May 1983, Ingham travelled to Cardiff to address a
conference of British newspaper editors. These large-scale
lectures were to become quite a hobby of his over the next few
years, and he devoted considerable care to their preparation.
After their delivery, he would have the text immaculately
reproduced, placed between printed covers, and circulated to
selected colleagues in Government and the Lobby. The contents invariably fell into three sections: first, a panegyric to
journalism as he practised it in his early years; second, a
contrasting of those high principles with the low standards

now prevalent in Fleet Street and broadcasting; third, a vigorous defence of the Government's integrity, with himself cast in the role of weary and misunderstood servant of the public good. The routine is so unchanging, the language so trenchant, it is difficult not to believe that he is – ever so slightly – sending himself up.

His speech in Cardiff on 'The Right to Know' set the pattern. He quoted approvingly the words of Sir Angus Maude, the minister responsible for co-ordinating Government presentation in the first Thatcher cabinet:

> When people talk about a right of access to information, I am not clear from what that right derives. The right is not written into the constitution. It does not arise from law ... I do not even accept that there is a moral right to know everything that goes on.

This was certainly, said Ingham, his own experience on the *Hebden Bridge Times*:

> I was taught that the newspaper I represented had no rights in the community beyond those of the ordinary citizen ... As for responsibilities, they were legion. But in essence the dominating obligation was to inform the reader accurately, objectively and comprehensively of matters affecting the public interest; to keep him abreast of developments; and responsibly to cultivate an informed public opinion. And don't miss anything, lad.
>
> I am not aware that this concentration on responsibilities to the virtual exclusion of rights was inimical to the public interest – or detrimental to our performance in the service of the community.

How different, how *very* different, from the media of the present day:

This is in part due, I suppose, to the changed attitude to authority. But it may also be that a second Watergate is pursued these days much as the Knights of the Round Table sought the Holy Grail. Too often these days the assumption seems to be that Government is either automatically wrong, naturally perverse, chronically up to no good, or just plain inept.

Nowadays, the stock in trade of most newspapers was speculation (as in 'The Government may be on the verge of . . .' or 'The Government could soon . . .') and breach of confidence (witness the widespread desire 'to lay hands on any document but preferably those marked secret'). Truth was defended by a thin blue line of '1,200 information officers engaged on a whole variety of communications tasks'. They were a much-maligned group. Ingham quoted Shylock: 'Sufferance is the badge of all our tribe.' The suggestion that they spent their time conspiring to 'manage' the news was nonsense.

> With respect, the Government does not manage the news. You do, you and the rest of the media are the real news managers. My colleagues and I present the news on behalf of the Government and offer an interpretation of its importance and significance. You either accept that interpretation or reject it . . .
>
> If by news management you mean I seek to present the case for the policies and measures of the Government I serve as effectively as possible, I plead guilty a thousand – nay 10,000 times . . . If by news management you mean I try to avoid the Government's coming out with five major announcements on the same day – or worse still on Budget Day, or even worse than that on Bank Holiday Monday, I again plead guilty . . .
>
> I only wish I was as sophisticated, as devilishly clever, as Machiavellian, as some make out. Not even a combination of Einstein backed up by the world's most advanced computer could achieve the presentational coups with which we – indeed I – have been credited.

This was to be the standard Ingham line for the next seven years, albeit with ever more lurid metaphors and increasingly apocalyptic diagnoses of the 'raddled, disease-wracked body' of the British media. None of the charges he levelled against the press – that it was over-mighty, irresponsible, speculative and unhelpful – was new; they are the traditional complaints of those in authority, as old as the press itself. ('The degree of information possessed by *The Times* with regard to the most secret affairs of State,' grumbled Lord John Russell to Queen Victoria 140 years ago, 'is mortifying, humiliating and incomprehensible.') But it was the first time he had made plain in public what many were aware of in private: that he had developed a deeply antagonistic view of his old profession.

Tony Benn had encountered this five years earlier, in 1978, when the science correspondent of the *Guardian*, Anthony Tucker, had complained to him that he was being victimized by Ingham. Tucker at that time supplemented his income by writing harmless articles for the Central Office of Information magazine, *Spectrum*, about astronomy and medicine. The magazine was distributed overseas to publicize Britain's scientific achievements. Tucker alleged that Ingham disliked him because of his outspoken anti-nuclear views and, in retaliation, had arranged for his COI work to be stopped. Benn investigated and found that this was indeed the case. Ingham had written a minute to the Director-General of the COI stating that Tucker was 'completely unreliable, that he had joined the anti-nuclear lobby and that his opinions "weren't worth paying for in washers"'. Benn tried to persuade Ingham to retract it, but found him 'rigid and dictatorial in his attitude'. He told Benn: 'I don't see why we should pay people to write articles for the Central Office of Information who are critical of the Government, who don't come for a departmental briefing and who are not balanced and objective.'[1] Tucker never worked for the COI again.

For Ingham, the media, essentially, were the enemy. He later likened Government press officers to 'riflemen on the Somme' shooting down an advancing army of hostile stories. Although he reserved the right to be sceptical about the information *he* was given to pass on ('I am never satisfied that anybody is ever telling me the whole truth and nothing but the truth, and I look them in the eye when I am in real difficulty and put them up against the wall and say, "Are you going to let me down?"'),[2] he appeared to regard similar suspiciousness on the part of reporters as a personal insult.

Yet they surely had good reason to be sceptical. Just as Margaret Thatcher had come to dominate the machinery of Government, so Ingham had established an unusual degree of personal control over its Information Service. He did this, like her, not by taking more powers, but by bending the existing structure to suit his ambitions, overcoming any opposition by sheer hard work and force of character.

Every Monday afternoon at five o'clock, in Conference Room 'D' of the Cabinet Office, Ingham would assemble some twenty-two heads of information from all over Whitehall. This weekly Meeting of Information Officers (MIO) had been established more than twenty years earlier to keep departments in touch with one another and was, by tradition, chaired by the Prime Minister's Press Secretary. In the past it was of limited importance. Indeed, several of Ingham's predecessors virtually ignored it. Donald Maitland, for one, never attended its meetings ('I didn't find that my presence was all that useful') nor did Joe Haines ('They were dreadfully boring ... I put all that kind of thing on to my deputy').

Ingham, by contrast, was soon treating it as a sort of below-stairs Cabinet, even to the extent of encouraging subcommittees on the economy and other policy areas, in imitation of the real thing. By all accounts, the MIO under Ingham resembled nothing so much as a butler's pantry during an Edwardian house party, where the butlers of the various guests would gather after hours and disport themselves according to the stations of their masters. Thus those information officers whose ministers were out of favour with Mrs Thatcher found themselves out of favour with Ingham. According to one participant: 'If someone said, "Look, is it a good idea to say this?" Bernard got very short: "You're the same as your bloody Secretary of State – always arguing!"'

> You didn't criticize Government policy because Bernard took that as a personal attack. People who tried got their fingers burnt, so they didn't do it the next week. I've heard colleagues say, 'Well, I've got to go to this bloody meeting but I'm not going to say anything.' It was similar to the Cabinet: there was no proper discussion, and if you criticized you had to be disloyal.

On one occasion, Ingham made an announcement and invited his colleagues to give their opinions. Nobody spoke. Whereupon, in the words of another member, 'Bernard got very red-faced and shouted, "Dammit, what point is there in having this meeting if nobody makes any comments?" So Janet Hewlett-Davies [Chief Information Officer at the DHSS] said, "The main reason, Bernard, is that if anyone seems to disagree they'll be regarded as hostile". Ingham grunted "Rubbish!" Everyone else was silent.'

For twenty years, ever since the days when his passion in argument had been sufficient to send his dentures flying, Ingham had loved to lay down the law. Even then, as a member of the Labour Party, he had been notably intolerant of dissenters. Now these twin characteristics of vehemence and authoritarianism were harnessed to the cause of Government presentation. His all-embracing approach was first adumbrated in 1980, a few months after his arrival at

Number 10, when he was asked to prepare a report on what the Government should do to encourage public support for the European Community. The point should be made, he wrote, in a phrase reminiscent of Albion, that a community of 250 million could achieve more than a 'debilitated nation of 55 million, however much the latter may trade on its past imperial glory'. Government publicity should stress this, 'with all the instruments of the orchestra, not only central Government, reading the same score, playing the same tune and coming in on cue'.[3] This potentially discordant ensemble was to be conducted by him through the MIO.

Departments were required to notify the Number 10 Press Office by close of business on Wednesday of all announcements and media engagements planned for the following week. This then became the central item on the agenda for the Monday afternoon meeting. The MIO's minutes are marked 'Restricted', the lowest of Whitehall's four security classifications: their release is defined officially as 'undesirable in the interests of the nation'. Nevertheless, in the autumn of 1983, three sets of minutes were leaked to Richard Norton-Taylor of the *Guardian*, revealing both the dominating role Ingham had assumed and the level of detail he insisted on discussing.

On 12 September, for example, he began by announcing that he had written to the Manpower Services Commission 'to express his concern' at its 'failure to observe its own embargo arrangements in the handling of its Annual Report'. He gave a '*tour d'horizon*' of current news issues following the summer break'. On the economy, he looked ahead 'to the New Year and beyond' and warned that 'Economic Departments should expect a rough ride'. He raised no objection to Cecil Parkinson, Secretary of State for Trade and Industry, appearing on *Panorama* to discuss the economy, but instructed the DTI Press Office to consult with the Treasury 'to ensure a comprehensive presentation of the economic policy and the state of the economy'. He circulated figures on the impact of break-fast television on early morning radio audiences.

Five weeks later, on 17 October, he was to be found bemoaning the circumstances of Parkinson's resignation over the Sara Keays affair ('the behaviour of the news media in creating news stories out of nothing caused great concern'). He thanked those present for their help in compiling a list of departmental achievements since the General Election: 'Ministers might find it a useful aid to presenting the Government's case'. He welcomed the visit of President Mitterrand of France as providing, in the week of a huge CND demonstra-tion, 'a useful opportunity' to stress the 'continued need for an independent nuclear deterrent' (no more talk now of Albion's 'bomb-happy' Tory Party). He warned of the 'presentational problems' caused by the shortage of kidney dialysis machines. He called for departments 'to make a prac-tice of preparing and circulating speaking notes for Ministers on topical issues': all such notes 'should be copied to the Prime Minister's Office'.

> At the instigation of the Chairman [Ingham], it was agreed that the Ministry of Defence should liaise with the Foreign and Commonwealth Office and the Home Office and Scottish Office to prepare a Ministerial speaking note on the Govern-ment's defence policies. It was further agreed that *Ministers should be encouraged* [author's emphasis] to use the platform provided by weekend newspapers to present these policies to the full. This would provide a 'trailer' to the NATO Nuclear Planning Group meeting which was to take place in Ottawa on 27–28 October.

At the MIO on 31 October, in the wake of the United States' invasion of Grenada, Ingham blamed the media's criticism of the Prime Minister on her 'failure to live up to their caricature of her, either as a Reagan "poodle" or as a warmonger'. At

the same meeting, he welcomed the decision of the Conservative Party Chairman, John Selwyn Gummer, to keep ministers
off the Radio Four *Any Questions* programme, leaving it
instead as 'the preserve of Government backbenchers'. On the
economic front, he regarded it as 'essential that the importance of continuing wage and cost restraint was put over in
Ministerial speeches' . . .

All this may seem at first glance the small change of
Ingham's work as Chief Press Secretary. But it is in its very
smallness that its fascination lies. For at the MIO, information officers were required not only to list every forthcoming
announcement – hospital closures, retail sales figures, crime
statistics and the rest – but to indicate whether these were
expected to be good or bad, and what dealings their departments were having with the media: would Minister A be on
Newsnight? should Minister B take part in a phone-in? In the
case of longer-term documentary programmes such as *Panorama* or *This Week*, the MIO might well go so far as to
discuss the names of individual reporters and producers: was
C to be trusted; did D not once give Minister E a rough ride?
In all these decisions, through the MIO, Ingham was consulted and became, effectively, the final arbiter. He made no
secret of this process. In October 1981, he spoke at a private
seminar organised by the Independent Broadcasting
Authority:

> Since ministers are not primarily in the entertainment business,
> they do not see why they should be the objective of blood
> sport, and we shall do our level best to deny you it. If you
> remain incorrigibly preoccupied with staining the sand with
> ministerial blood, please find a more sophisticated way of
> doing it than with the invited audience, replete with statutory
> Trot, bra-burner and barrack room brawler. Finally, do not
> expect me or my colleagues to move heaven and earth to help

you if you have a reputation for seldom, if ever, examining
anything constructively as distinct from destructively . . .

Television, he warned his audience darkly, was 'corrupting no
less of those who work for it than those who appear on it'.

Of course, Ingham was not in a position actually to forbid a
minister's appearance on a particular programme. But he
could make his feelings plain to that minister's Chief Information Officer (whose advice would usually be decisive) and he
could even lay down the 'line' Number 10 would like pushed.
Hence his directives, quoted above, that Government
speeches should stress 'the importance of continuing wage
and cost restraint' or that ministers should be 'encouraged' to
promote the deployment of Trident and Cruise missiles in the
Sunday papers.

As Ingham's reputation spread, the question which was
asked increasingly was whether this was not an abuse of the
system. In 1952, when Lord Swinton urged Winston
Churchill to re-establish a Number 10 Press Office, he conceded that 'a centralized information agency of this character
might, in the hands of an unscrupulous extremist Government, prove both a powerful and dangerous weapon of propaganda'.[4] Three decades later, there was a growing number
– including some Whitehall information officers – who
believed that Swinton's warning was fast coming true.

Ingham was seeking to do something which none of his
predecessors had attempted. He was trying to reconcile two
hitherto unreconcilable functions. He wanted to be both the
civil service spokesman for the Government as a whole, along
the objective lines of a Trevor Lloyd-Hughes, and to act as the
Prime Minister's ultra-loyal lieutenant, after the partisan style
of a Joe Haines. And in his urge to meddle in detail, to
centralize, to take personal control, to brook no opposition,
one is struck, once again, by the parallels between servant and

mistress. '*L'état, c'est moi*,' Louis XIV's famous motto, was often applied to Margaret Thatcher. What could be more natural than that her spokesman should seek, in his gruff tones, to embody the voice of the entire Government?

Behind his back there was considerable grumbling about Ingham's domineering manner, particularly his habit of answering for every department when he met the Lobby. 'I've never known anyone so keen to have all the minutiae and deliver it all himself,' claimed one independent-minded Chief Information Officer. 'I said to him: "What am I bloody well here for, if not to give out news?" He thought I was just trying to protect my territory. But if we'd got the news, why shouldn't we give it out?' These concerns erupted in public in the summer of 1983 when it became known that Ingham wanted to link all Whitehall information departments to Number 10 via a new computer system. He commissioned a plan, 'The Potential for Information Technology in the Information Service'. A mole in the MIO promptly leaked it to Fleet Street. 'Every morning,' complained an anonymous 'colleague' to *The Times*, 'departments would have to put up what was happening that day. If Number 10 did not approve of Minister X appearing on *News at Ten*, the appearance would be cancelled.'[5] It also emerged that Ingham was floating the idea of downgrading the post of Head of the COI and putting himself in charge of the Government Information Service.

Five days later, under the impassive gaze of the Director-General of the COI, Donald Grant, Ingham told the MIO that two quite separate ideas – the acquisition of information technology and changes in his own role and status – had been brought together to somehow suggest he aimed at becoming 'a so-called "Information Overlord"'. He dismissed the reports as 'inaccurate, ill-informed and possibly malicious'. But he did not, it was noted, deny that he had ambitions to aggrandize his role in some fashion. Ingham's denunciation of the leak was itself immediately leaked. That Thursday, the leader of the Social Democrats, David Owen, wrote to the Prime Minister asking her to explain what was happening and reminding her of the 'classical definition' of the role of the Government Information Service given by Lord Swinton in 1953: that it should

> give prompt and accurate information and give it objectively about Government action and Government policy. It is quite definitely not the job of the Government Information Service to try to boost the Government or try to persuade the press to.

It took Mrs Thatcher almost two weeks to reply, but when she did her answer was emphatic. Ingham, she said, was

> in an especially delicate and exposed position ... But it remains his duty to give prompt and accurate information objectively about Government action and policy. It is not his job to try to persuade the press to boost the Government ... I do not have and have never had any intention to centralize control of Government information in 10 Downing Street, and I have no plans to extend the responsibilities of my Chief Press Secretary.

Ingham got his computer system (after securing the support of the Cabinet Secretary, Sir Robert Armstrong), but his ambition to bring the Whitehall information machine under his personal control was balked – at any rate, for the time being.

Mrs Thatcher's declaration – that it was not Ingham's 'job to try to persuade the press to boost the Government' – seems at first sight to be so palpably false, it is a wonder it can have been made with a straight face. Only if one studies her reply more closely can one, perhaps, detect behind it the slippery hand of the civil service drafter. Technically, it was correct to state that persuading the press to boost the Government was not his *job*: in so saying she was not denying that that was what he *did*. On such subtle distinctions are Whitehall careers built.

Why was it necessary to go through these linguistic contortions? What was wrong with seeking to manipulate the press? Why not admit what everyone on the inside track knew for a fact: that Ingham devoted himself, body and soul, twelve hours a day to boosting the Government; that he used the MIO not as a channel for ensuring the smooth transition of facts from rulers to ruled, but as an instrument for even more high-octane Government-boosting?

The answer was simple. If it was once admitted that Ingham's job was to procure for the Government the most favourable coverage possible, and hence to increase its popularity, he could no longer be regarded as objective. If he was not objective, he was not acting in accordance with his duties as a professional civil servant. And if his behaviour was deemed improper, what of the MIO, whose members were instructed by Ingham to 'encourage' their ministers to do this, that or the other? Ingham's alleged neutrality, in other words, was the rock upon which the entire edifice rested. Remove it, and the theory of a Government Information Service whose sole function was to dispense objective facts would have come crashing down. Hence the necessity for the fiction that he did not 'persuade the press to boost the Government'.

It is hard to think of any other public official whose duties were so hedged around with half-truths and evasions. He was in a sense like the head of MI5 or MI6 – organizations whose existence for years was never officially admitted. He was there, but he was not there; he managed the news, but he did not manage the news; he was neutral, but he was not neutral: he ran the Government Information Service, but then again . . .

743

Another illustration of Ingham's actual, rather than his professed, role came just three months after Mrs Thatcher's assurances to Owen. At the Prime Minister's insistence, the 1983 Conservative election manifesto had promised the abolition of the Greater London Council (GLC). It had seemed a good idea at the time. Unexpectedly, however, in October, an *Evening Standard* poll had found 54 per cent of Londoners opposed to abolition. Tory GLC councillors were aghast at the plan, as were a substantial number of Conservative MPs and peers. To add to the Government's problems, the GLC was running a sophisticated advertising campaign.

On 30 December, Ingham addressed himself to the problem in a seven-page memorandum. He called for 'a plan of campaign ... comprehensive but flexible', which would 'treat, as a matter of urgency, dissident elements among the Government's own supporters to ensure they are neutralized if not positively harnessed to the Government's cause'. He also demanded 'remedial action with troublesome journals, whether national, provincial or specialist'; the placing of 'special articles' in sympathetic newspapers ('eg, *Sunday Express*, *News of the World*, regional press'); and ministerial appearances on 'phone-ins or discussion programmes, including the *JY Prog* [the *Jimmy Young Programme*]'. In addition, Ingham also proposed 'a comprehensive diary to which all Departments contribute relevant dates, events and Ministerial engagements which might be turned to good account'. It is difficult to square this memorandum, either with the Prime Minister's earlier assurances about her Press Secretary's role, or with Ingham's own statement to the newspaper editors in Cardiff in May that 'with respect, the Government does not manage the news'.

Ingham's 'plan of campaign' was soon in operation. In the first week of January 1984, the minister responsible for abolishing the GLC, Patrick Jenkin, began hawking round Fleet

Street an article explaining the Government's case. The *Sunday Times* turned it down. The *Sunday Express* published it on 15 January. On 18 January, Ingham's other measures were approved by a Cabinet sub-committee. On 20 January, details of his proposals leaked. 'As a Tory dissident I must confess I rolled about in my chair, laughing until the tears fell down my cheeks, at the news that Mr Bernard Ingham has drawn up a seven-page memorandum on how to "neutralize" us all,' wrote George Tremlett, a GLC councillor, in the *Guardian* three days later. 'Ye Gods and little fishes, has it really come to this? How long, I ask, will it be before the gentlemen in white coats come to take Mr Ingham away?'

These leaks were becoming a serious embarrassment to Ingham. He abhorred such breaches of trust, wherever they occurred. Fancy notions about civil servants having a 'higher duty' to Parliament or the nation passed him by. In September 1983, he told the MIO that the leak of a minute from Michael Heseltine about Cruise missile deployment was 'taken very seriously indeed'. When the culprit, a clerk in the Foreign Office named Sarah Tisdall, was discovered and jailed for six months, he applauded the sentence. He saw Clive Ponting, the MoD official who revealed details of the sinking of the *General Belgrano*, as a particularly odious viper. On 10 September 1984, on the eve of Ponting's trial at the Old Bailey, he told the MIO of his wish that the case be heard by a particularly severe judge: he only wished Judge Jeffreys of the 'Bloody Assizes' of 1685 was available. It was, presumably, a joke.

The best means of stopping leaks in the Government Information Service, in his view, was to make sure the right kind of person was appointed in the first place. Never had a Prime Minister's Press Secretary taken such a close interest in the careers of Whitehall's information officers. 'Bernard wanted the very best people to work in Number 10,' recalled one of his most senior colleagues, 'and he had no compunction in digging them out of other departments. And if people went to Number 10 and were no good he was quite ruthless about it.' One by one, the brightest entrants to the Information Service were given six-week attachments to the Number 10 Press Office. By the summer of 1984, Ingham had worked his way through more than thirty. Those he felt he could trust he backed for promotion.

But this alone was not enough. His associates speak of his strong desire, amounting almost to a sense of personal mission, to 'sort out' public relations in Whitehall. First, he wanted to end the practice whereby some departments – notably Trade and Industry, the Treasury and the Foreign Office – appointed ordinary civil servants to run their information offices. They were not 'professionals'. They had not worked for him at Number 10. They were in-house 'natives'. In the great symphony of Government presentation, as Ingham envisaged it, they were the ones who could be expected to hit the wrong notes.

Secondly, he wanted to improve press officers' pay and conditions of service. According to Neville Taylor: 'Bernard has had – and I have got to use the phrase – a great chip on his shoulder that until he got to Number 10 he never felt he'd been taken as seriously as an information officer as he would have been as an administrator . . . Throughout his career, he's had this feeling that it's unfair, that for the work we did we should have been at least one grade further up.'

And the third necessary reform, in his humble opinion, was that he should be placed formally in charge of the whole operation. Ever since its establishment in 1949, the Government Information Service had been technically subordinate to the Central Office of Information, a strictly non-political body, responsible for advertisements, exhibitions and public service films. Thus the Director-General of the COI (in 1984 it was Donald Grant, whom Ingham had defeated for the Press Secretaryship) was also Head of Profession for all full-time information officers. Theoretically, he was Ingham's superior. He was paid more. It was Grant who sat on the appointments boards and recommended the promotions. Although Ingham could – and frequently did – use his political muscle to defeat Grant on particular issues, he regarded the situation as ridiculous. What did the boss of the COI – stuck in a gloomy office block in Hercules Road in Lambeth – know about life at the sharp end, dealing with the media across the river in Whitehall day in, day out? He coveted the job. 'I believe it was the case,' recalled Neville Taylor, 'that he actually wanted to be Director-General of the COI and Press Secretary. I believe that to be true. I also believe it to be true that there was quite a debate within the Cabinet Office and Number 10 as to the way in which his power would be, could be, increased by combining elements of the two jobs.'

Ingham's tentative manoeuvring was brought temporarily to an end in the autumn of 1983, by the premature disclosure of his ambitions in the press. Asked on 31 October – by the indefatigable Tam Dalyell – about her intentions, the Prime Minister had been obliged to reply: 'No new responsibilities have been given to my Chief Press Secretary and I have no plans to change the status of the Director-General of the Central Office of Information.'[6] But Ingham had been around Whitehall too long to be defeated that easily. If he could not have the job himself, he would do the next best thing. He would have an ally appointed to it instead.

Accordingly, in September 1984, it was announced that, following Donald Grant's scheduled retirement, Neville Taylor would move from the Ministry of Defence to be the next head of the COI. Taylor, of course, was the man whom Frank Cooper had regarded as Ingham's nark at the MoD during the Falklands war. 'My appointment,' Taylor agreed later, 'may well have been partly due to the fact that he and I were known to get on.' As a further sop to Ingham, the salary of the Prime Minister's Press Secretary was increased – by nearly £3,000, to £32,350 – to match that of the COI chief. But the most significant fact was not released to the press. This was contained in a letter from Sir Robert Armstrong to Taylor setting out the terms of his employment: in future, the Director-General of the COI was required to consult the head of the Number 10 Press Office on all senior appointments.

To an outsider, it was a trivial change; to an insider, it was a significant accretion of power – which is why Ingham had fought for it. He was now well on the way to becoming what he had dismissed as malicious gossip twelve months earlier: 'a so-called "Information Overlord"'.

EIGHT

Licensed to Leak

'I'm the man who is licensed to leak . . .'

BERNARD INGHAM, SPEECH TO MARK THE FORTIETH
ANNIVERSARY OF CALDER HIGH SCHOOL, JANUARY 1990

The fountainhead of Ingham's power was his relationship with the Prime Minister, and as he approached his fifth anniversary in Number 10 that continued to run pure and strong. Few people were granted a better and more complete view of what was going on in Government than Mrs Thatcher's Chief Press Secretary. The only information kept from him was the output of the Joint Intelligence Committee and the other organizations responsible for security. 'Knowledge is power,' as Neville Taylor put it, 'especially in the information business. Because if you know what's going on, then other people have to come to you.' Ingham used this power, in part, to keep his colleagues up to the mark: 'if you're aware that Bernard is seeing all submissions going in, then you make damn sure that in your own department you find out what's going on before it gets there . . . He is very much better at keeping people on their toes than anyone else I have ever seen' – another trait he shared with the Prime Minister.

The minister responsible for co-ordinating Government presentation was the Lord President of the Council and

Leader of the House of Lords, Viscount Whitelaw. Late every Thursday morning, after the weekly Cabinet, he would wander across to Ingham's office. 'We would just have a general gossip,' recalled the amiable Whitelaw, 'about what was going on, what had happened at Cabinet, what the sort of mood was. He would see all the bare bones and I would try and give him some indication of the mood in order to help him with the tone of the briefing. I think that's the terribly difficult thing: the tone of the briefing. We also tried to foresee events, to see what we thought Government departments might do better. His political judgement was very good.'

Ingham did not attend the full Cabinet but he was often called in to the smaller – and actually more important – Cabinet committee meetings. Nominally, his advice was confined to policy presentation; actually, he helped shape decisions. The nature of his job, he once said, entailed an 'input into policy-making, as well as a communicator's output'.[1] A good example occurred at the beginning of 1984, when trade union membership was banned at the Government Communications Headquarters (GCHQ). There was an outcry at what was seen as a denial of democratic rights. Armstrong, supported by the Foreign Secretary, Sir Geoffrey Howe, negotiated a compromise: the unions could stay at GCHQ in return for a promise that they would never strike. The Prime Minister was dubious. Ingham was consulted. 'It will look like a U-turn,' he declared, simply. 'It will *be* a U-turn.'[2] Armstrong's compromise was rejected.

A few months later, Alasdair Milne, the Director-General of the BBC, was given a similar insight into Ingham's fondness for issuing off-the-cuff policy directives. He was entertaining the Chief Press Secretary to lunch at Broadcasting House and the conversation turned to the Corporation's future. 'Just take advertising on Radios One and Two,' Ingham told him, 'and don't argue!'[3]

If he spoke his mind, it was because the Prime Minister encouraged him to do so. In September 1984, at the height of the miners' strike, the editor of the *Sunday Express*, Sir John Junor, visited Mrs Thatcher in her study. Junor was an old friend, but to his surprise, Ingham was invited to sit in on the conversation. 'It was evident that Ingham was now very much part of the inner Cabinet,' he recalled. 'He intervened from time to time in our talk and it was obvious from the way the Prime Minister listened to what he had to say that she respected his judgement.'[4]

Ingham seemed to live a charmed life, for Mrs Thatcher's devastating assaults on her ministers and on other senior civil servants were legendary. These extended even to those whom she liked and promoted. 'Did you ever practise at Chancery?' she once inquired of her junior Home Office minister, David Mellor. He answered that he had not. 'I thought so,' she retorted. 'Not clever enough.' Sir Keith Joseph, leaving his office with Norman Tebbit for a meeting with her about British Leyland, was asked by his private secretary if he would be needing anything. 'Yes,' he replied. 'Ambulances for two at three.' One Cabinet Minister she sacked reputedly burst into tears; another, Lord Soames, complained after his dismissal that he would not have treated his gamekeeper 'in the way that woman treated me'. The fund of stories is endless. But not once did Mrs Thatcher extend this rough treatment to Ingham, even though he made plenty of mistakes. He was different from the others. His loyalty, unlike that of some ministers, was never in question, nor had he ever been known to make an uncomplimentary remark, even in private. Whatever he did, however maladroit, he did only for her. For that reason, if he committed an error, she would always direct her criticism at the press, holding the journalists responsible for getting it wrong; Ingham she absolved from blame.

In July 1983, he overstepped the mark by accusing

Labour's Shadow Chancellor, Peter Shore, of talking 'bunkum and balderdash' – hardly an objective dispensing of factual information about Government policy. The Prime Minister, however, thought his blunt speaking wonderful. 'Mr Ingham was fully within his instructions as my Chief Press Secretary in making these points,' she declared, 'and he found characteristically vivid and colourful phrases.'[5] Six months later she addressed the centenary dinner of the Parliamentary Lobby and went out of her way to praise Ingham: a public servant 'of whom,' she said, 'I cannot speak too highly'.[6]

At the beginning of 1985 he committed his most serious transgression to date: one which should have tested even Margaret Thatcher's high opinion of him to the limit. The issue – it was to prove a veritable running sore over the next five years – was exchange rate policy, and the differing views taken of it by the Prime Minister and her Chancellor, Nigel Lawson.

Sterling had been dropping at an accelerating rate throughout 1984, from $1.45 to just over $1.15 by the end of the year. Previously, such a fall would have sent a British Prime Minister into panic. But Mrs Thatcher was sanguine. She shared the strict monetarist view of her economic adviser, Sir Alan Walters, that the pound had to be allowed to find its own level. Government intervention – buying sterling on the foreign exchanges to prop up its value – was a relic of the bad old days of the corporate state. In Thatcherite philosophy, the market reigned supreme. This, as the New Year opened, was the message which Ingham faithfully pumped out from the Number 10 Press Office. 'Thatcher No to crisis move on the pound' was the headline in the *Sunday Times* on 6 January. The story beneath quoted Ingham ('the highest sources in Whitehall') as indicating that the Prime Minister was even prepared to contemplate the previously unthinkable: parity, with one US dollar equalling one pound.

But further down Whitehall, in the Treasury, Lawson was

beginning to change his mind. He was about to embark on the long process of apostasy which would, eventually, set him at such odds with the true believers in Downing Street that he would feel obliged to resign. He and his officials watched anxiously as, in the two or three days following the *Sunday Times* article, sterling's value continued to dribble away. On the morning of Friday 11 January, in an effort to stop the slide, and with Thatcher's full knowledge, the Bank of England raised its money market dealing rates, sending base rates up by 1 per cent.

At 2.45 that afternoon, as usual, Ingham met the Lobby correspondents of the Sunday press. What followed was highly illustrative of the risks inherent in his freewheeling role. He had not asked the Prime Minister about what he should say regarding sterling. He was unaware of the significance of the Bank of England's move a few hours beforehand. Instead, he simply launched into his normal routine, laying down the line in his customary, emphatic manner. 'You can be absolutely certain that we are not going to throw money at the pound,' the *Sunday Telegraph* recorded 'authoritative Government sources' as insisting. 'We are not going to defend a particular parity.' Intervention by the Bank of England, the 'sources' added, would be simply 'wasting Britain's substance'. The *Mail on Sunday* reported similar phrases: 'We are not throwing good money after bad.' The *Sunday Times* carried the dramatic banner headline: 'Thatcher ready to let £1 equal $1'.

In this unanimous chorus there was only one dissenting voice. As Ingham was briefing the Sunday Lobby, William Keegan, economics editor of the *Observer*, who had worked at the Bank of England for a year in the 1970s, was finishing lunch with a senior Treasury official. The Treasury man had told him a quite different story: that they had been perturbed by the previous week's *Sunday Times* article; that 'letting the pound fall to one dollar was certainly not official policy; that the Treasury and the Bank had deliberately engineered the rise in interest rates on the Friday morning. And they would do the same again, or more, on the Monday if the market was still selling sterling.' The *Observer* preferred this version of events to Ingham's. That weekend, alone in Fleet Street, it reported that the Government was planning 'a determined defence of the exchange rate.

> Ministers are now prepared to see interest rates rise at least another 1 per cent . . . Until late last week the Government had followed a hands-off policy towards sterling, accepting a steady decline in its value. Briefings to this effect from Number 10 are being blamed . . . for encouraging dealers to start selling large volumes of sterling last week.

The BBC took delivery of the early editions of the Sunday papers soon after nine o'clock on Saturday night. Which account of the Government's position was to be believed? The Chancellor and his senior officials could not be contacted. They were all away for the weekend at Chevening, the Government's country house, planning the next Budget. (In fact, at that moment, Mr Lawson was down on all fours, barking: the Treasury men were playing charades; the Chancellor was a dog.) The BBC's political correspondent rang the Number 10 Press Office for guidance. The duty officer stuck to the substance of the Ingham briefing. The *Observer*, he said, was wrong; the others were broadly right.

Next morning, the Treasury men awoke to hear the BBC announcing that the Government was prepared to let the pound fall as far as the speculators cared to push it. It was the worst possible news. The Prime Minister was soon on the telephone. So was the Governor of the Bank of England. The long-term discussion of Budget strategy had to be jettisoned in favour of a short-term scramble to shore up the pound.

Government information officers were ordered out of their beds and into Whitehall to call round financial and political journalists, urging them to ignore that morning's newspapers. The Bank had to intervene on the Hong Kong markets that night as the pound lost three cents. The next morning, Minimum Lending Rate, abandoned in 1981, was reintroduced and interest rates were hiked by 1.5 per cent to a 'crisis' rate of 12 per cent. 'I am afraid,' said Lawson in the Commons on Tuesday, in what was effectively an apology, 'that there was a feeling in the markets that the Government had lost their willingness and ability to control their affairs . . .'[7]

At a conservative estimate, the episode had cost the country £100 million in foreign reserves. It also had far-reaching political consequences. According to William Keegan: 'The searing effect of the January sterling crisis was a major influence on Lawson, who now displayed considerable interest in, and enthusiasm for, the EMS.'[8] Full entry into the European Monetary System, Lawson concluded, would lessen the speculative pressure on sterling. He was to pursue this policy, overtly and covertly, in the teeth of the Prime Minister's opposition, until his resignation in October 1989.

What, meanwhile, had happened to the author of this débâcle? The answer was: nothing. On the Monday, he was summoned to see Lawson and senior Treasury officials. But by then the Prime Minister had let it be known that no blame should attach to 'my Bernard'. Once again, she held the press, not her Press Secretary, to be at fault. The deflated Lawson could only express the hope that Ingham would guard his tongue in future.

Had the error been made by anyone else, especially a minister, she would surely have turned the flame-thrower of her wrath fully upon them. There might even have been a non-attributable briefing to indicate the degree of her fury. But Ingham was different. She went out of her way to ensure that everyone knew he was still in favour. At a party full of political journalists, held in the Commons a few days later, she insisted on parading him round, ludicrously introducing him to people he already knew: 'Have you met Bernard? Bernard's marvellous. Isn't he marvellous? He's great. He's the *greatest*.' Naturally, when word of this special attention spread around Whitehall, as she intended it would, it served only to heighten his reputation. What might have finished the career of another official became, for Ingham, a fresh demonstration of his power.

By this time Ingham was taking an increasingly conservative view of the media and society. He had even come to subscribe to that hoary right-wing theory that the decline of national standards had set in with *That Was The Week That Was* – apparently forgetful that at the time of the 1960s 'satire boom' he was himself describing the Prime Minister as 'Sir Alec Strangelove', a bomb-happy 'political fossil'. In March, two months after the sterling crisis, he addressed the International Press Institute in the spirit, he said, of a 'candid friend':

> I believe that the Watergate syndrome, combined with the broadcasters' 'confrontation' approach to interviews and the determination to take the mickey out of authority, starting with *That Was The Week That Was*, seems to require that any self-respecting reporter should knock seven bells out of symbols of authority, and especially Government. This goes beyond the normal and expected tension between Government and press. Its effect on our democracy is, in my view, corrosive . . . I can assure you that, working in the Government service, I find the reverence for fact and truth and balance more akin to that which was inculcated into me as a 16-year-old junior reporter on a West Riding weekly than I do in my close observation of quite a lot of contemporary journalism.

He accused many journalists of being conspiracy theorists, of over-simplifying, 'of laziness, laxness, or arrogance, or a combination of these'.

> Can you honestly say that British journalism, even acknowledging its right to take a particular political standpoint, strives to be fair? Of course you can't. And the reason you can't is that it doesn't strike me any more that there is a driving compulsion to be fair.

This particular point, unfortunately, was not one which he developed to its logical conclusion. For the overwhelming beneficiary of any political bias and unfairness in the British press was, of course, his own employer. In 1990, Ingham was challenged on this point by Mark Lawson in a profile in the *Independent Magazine*:

> LAWSON: When the *Sun* runs a story, as it does, which may or may not have come out of your briefings: MARVELLOUS MAGGIE SAVES THE WORLD. By the terms you've set out, that's bad journalism but, in terms of the Government, it does a lot of good . . .
>
> INGHAM: But what about the *Mirror* ignoring it totally . . . ?
>
> LAWSON: Yes, but that *Sun* story. They'd never give the other side. Is that bad journalism?
>
> INGHAM: Well, the short answer is, I don't know because I haven't got the facts . . .[9]

In truth, the self-appointed scourge of the media was always curiously selective about where he applied the lash. Most of the sins which Ingham detected in the British media – invention, distortion, misquotation, wilful refusal to check facts, persistent failure to apologize, bias in news coverage – found their ultimate refinement in the *Sun*. With a readership of over 12 million, one in four of the adult population, it was the journalistic phenomenon of the Thatcher age. Yet he never mentioned it in his strictures – presumably because it was not guilty of the only sin which really mattered: it did not believe the Government to be 'chronically up to no good'.

In November 1985, he returned to the attack, this time in a lecture to the Media Society. He confessed to a 'liking for journalists in ones or twos – as distinct from the wolf pack', but he diagnosed 'four debilitating afflictions' which had gripped the profession. These were 'the le Carré Syndrome', sufferers of which believed the Government was 'not to be trusted and conspiratorial'; the 'Conan Doyle complication' in which deduction was carried 'to such excesses that two and two became twenty-two'; 'columnar pox, a social contagion particularly affecting diarists'; and, finally, the 'Coleman or Carpenter phenomenon ... which produces in reporters an inability to report just facts; only their own commentary on those facts will do'.

As it happened, by the time he came to deliver this diagnosis, the Government was already in the foothills of a crisis which would give the le Carrés and the Conan Doyles, the pox-ridden columnists and the Colemans and Carpenters plenty more to write about.

Ingham's involvement in what became known as the Westland affair turned him into a household name. Before it, he could still plausibly insist to the Media Society: 'I am not a public figure'; after it, he was one, whether he liked it or not.

He made his first significant contribution on Wednesday 18 December 1985. On that day Mrs Thatcher had assembled her most trusted inner core of advisers, among them Whitelaw, Armstrong and the Chief Whip, John Wakeham, to discuss the developing crisis. The Defence Secretary, Michael Heseltine, was refusing to accept that Britain's sole helicopter manufacturer should be sold to the American company, Sikorsky, as the Prime Minister wished. He had assembled instead a rival bidder – a European consortium of French, German, Italian and British firms – whose claims he was pressing with near-messianic fervour.

Bismarck in his later years is said to have remarked of the Schleswig–Holstein Question of 1863 that only three men ever understood it: Lord Palmerston, and he was dead; a French professor, and he had gone mad; and he, Bismarck – and he had forgotten it. Much the same might be said of the minutiae of the Westland imbroglio. It was, in truth, a battle in which helicopters were merely the weapons. At heart, it was a contest of wills between a Prime Minister accustomed to getting her own way and an ambitious politician who had decided to face her down. Afterwards, when he was asked in private if he regretted his stand, Heseltine always shook his head. He knew, he said, the unforgiving fate which would have awaited him had he backed down: a couple of years' banishment as Northern Ireland Secretary, accompanied by a steady drip of non-attributable briefings from Number 10 about his 'lack of judgement', followed by a well-trailed return to the back-benches. He had seen the way 'they' operated. No, thank you: he preferred to go down fighting.

In the process, the Government was turned into a shambles. In public, Heseltine was repeatedly contradicting the Prime Minister's agent, the wretched Trade and Industry Secretary, Leon Brittan. In private, he was briefing friendly reporters, protesting at the cancellation of Cabinet committee meetings, accusing Armstrong of writing misleading Cabinet minutes, and – on the very afternoon that Thatcher and her advisers met – giving secret testimony about his 'European option' to the Commons Select Committee on Defence.

The Prime Minister's group discussed the problem for several hours. She wanted to send Heseltine a letter setting out strict rules about how much he could say on Westland, to which he would have to assent in writing. According to the fullest account of the affair (*Not With Honour*, by Magnus Linklater and David Leigh, published in 1986), three different drafts were prepared and discussed. Eventually, Ingham was called in and asked his opinion. For once, he counselled caution. Heseltine might use such an ultimatum as a pretext to resign. The Prime Minister already had a politically damaging reputation for high-handedness. Another dissident ex-minister on the back-benches, especially one of Heseltine's calibre, was the last thing she needed. He advised against sending any letter. Coming from anyone else, this might have sounded to the Prime Minister's ears like cowardice; from the man whose usual motto was 'screw the buggers' it carried special weight. No letter was sent. Heseltine would have to be contained by other methods. It was, with hindsight, a serious mistake.

Three days later, on Saturday 21 December, Ingham learned that both Brittan and Heseltine would be appearing on the lunchtime radio programme, *The World This Weekend* – exactly the sort of open clash the Government needed to avoid. He rang Heseltine at his home in Oxfordshire and asked him to decline the BBC's invitation. Heseltine said he would, but only if Ingham also prevented Brittan appearing. However, Brittan's contribution had been recorded already. When the Defence Secretary duly arrived at the BBC's studio in Oxford on Sunday morning, he was told that Downing Street had been putting pressure on the Corporation to drop Brittan's interview. The BBC refused. Even as Heseltine prepared to speak, another call came through from Number 10, presumably from Ingham. Heseltine declined to take it. Both interviews were broadcast.

Such incidents convinced the Prime Minister that tougher tactics were required. On Friday 3 January 1986, Heseltine inadvertently provided her with an opportunity when he wrote and allowed to be published a letter to his friends in the

European consortium. Poring over it that afternoon, Mrs Thatcher and her advisers spotted what they believed was an error. She instructed Brittan to contact the Solicitor-General, Sir Patrick Mayhew, and seek his opinion. This Brittan did the following day. Heseltine's letter had been published in that morning's *Times* and Mayhew, having studied it, agreed that at first glance part of it looked questionable. Brittan reported this view back to Number 10. Charles Powell, one of Mrs Thatcher's private secretaries, then contacted Mayhew's office and formally asked, on behalf of the Prime Minister, for the Solicitor-General to put his opinion in writing to Heseltine.

Mayhew completed his letter soon after 11.00 a.m. on Monday 6 January. It was promptly dispatched to the Ministry of Defence, with copies to Number 10 and to the DTI. They arrived at noon. Heseltine, in his words, was 'relaxed' about it. He had reason to be. Mayhew, an old friend, had warned him on Saturday night that a letter would be coming, and in the event it was hardly a damning document. Heseltine's original remarks had implied that *all* the other companies and governments involved in building a European battlefield helicopter would be concerned at a Westland link with Sikorsky; Mayhew required further evidence regarding two firms. His letter therefore concluded:

> On the basis of the information contained in the documents to which I have referred, which I emphasize are all that I have seen, the sentence in your letter to Mr Horne does in my opinion contain material inaccuracies in the respects I have mentioned, and I therefore must advise that you should write again to Mr Horne correcting the inaccuracies.

Heseltine sent the necessary extra information round to Mayhew that afternoon, and the Solicitor-General raised no further objections to the disputed sentence.

But in Number 10 and the DTI, armed with the Solicitor-General's opinion, the 'Get Heseltine' operation swung into action. Powell made one copy of Mayhew's letter and took it down to Ingham in the Press Office – an action which suggests they had already decided it was to be used publicly in some way. He then returned upstairs to take a call from his opposite number at the DTI, Brittan's Private Secretary, John Mogg. Mogg had just spoken to Brittan, who was out at lunch. He had read him the letter over the telephone. The Trade and Industry Secretary was keen to have it leaked, but only, in his words, 'subject to the agreement of Number 10'. This was a prudent precaution to take. As Brittan, an eminent QC, knew very well, advice from the Government's Law Officers was never disclosed. Besides, Mayhew's letter was marked 'Confidential' – 'unauthorized disclosure,' according to the official definition of that term, 'would be prejudicial to the interests of the nation'. Mogg therefore asked Powell if Number 10 would release it. Powell refused. The DTI would have to do its own dirty work.

The focus of activity now shifted to the office downstairs. Ingham, the Solicitor-General's letter in front of him, spoke on the telephone to Colette Bowe, Chief Information Officer at the DTI.

As it happened, there was no great love lost between the two. Bowe, a 39-year-old graduate from Liverpool, was an administrator, not a professional press officer. She pointedly did not attend Ingham's MIOs on Monday afternoons, preferring to send her deputy. She had also enjoyed a good relationship with Heseltine, working on his Merseyside task force. All these factors cast a chill over her dealings with Ingham. 'Quite apart from anything else,' recalled one senior colleague, 'there was a clash of personalities.'

There are two versions of their conversation that afternoon. One – Ingham's – is that Bowe sought his advice and he, foolishly, did not discourage her from leaking the letter. According to Hugo Young, who spoke to him in the course of writing his biography of Mrs Thatcher, Ingham (who years later still retained 'photographic recall of every twist and turn' of the affair) found only one thing with which to reproach himself: 'In the heat of the moment, he had not stated with sufficient firmness to Ms Bowe that she should have nothing to do with such an unorthodox procedure.'[10] The other version is Bowe's: that she was extremely anxious, in the wake of the prosecution of Clive Ponting, not to leak a classified letter, and had to be ordered to do so. The only point on which both agree is that Ingham, like Powell, refused to put the information out personally via Number 10.

There is no tape recording of what was said. So whom do we believe? The circumstantial evidence clearly substantiates Ms Bowe's account, for she had to be pushed and prodded into making the leak. There is no doubt that when she put down the telephone on Ingham, she was a very unhappy woman. She was sufficiently appalled at what she was being asked to do to seek professional advice. Sir Robert Armstrong subsequently confirmed that she had 'misgivings'; that she 'shared her burden'[11] with Mogg in Brittan's private office; that she wanted to follow the procedure set down for civil servants who believe they are being asked to do something 'unlawful' – that is, consult her Principal Personnel Officer and her Permanent Secretary, Sir Brian Hayes, neither of whom was in the building. Unless she underwent some miraculous change of heart while talking to Ingham, it is reasonable to suppose that she would have expressed these doubts to the *primus inter pares* of the Government Information Service. And what did he do? According to 'friends' of Ms Bowe quoted in the press at the time, he told her: 'You'll — well do what you're — well told.' Even if he did not put it in quite such crude terms, he offered naught for her comfort.

Bowe, at least, expressed some qualms; he did not. Had he done so, given her well-attested reservations, the Solicitor-General's letter would probably not have been leaked. In other words, it was in his power during that crucial telephone call to put a stop to the whole business – and he did not do it.

The conversation between Ingham and Bowe, according to Armstrong, 'was in part technical as to methods of disclosure and so on'.[12] In the event, the fortunate recipient of the scoop was none other than Ingham's trusty Lobby friend, Chris Moncrieff. 'I was in the PA room at the Commons Press Gallery,' Moncrieff remembered.

> At 2.15 p.m. a message came through from the DTI that I was to ring them. I called ... The letter was paraphrased, with just two words given in quotes ... 'material inaccuracies'. I think it was understood that this was unattributable as usual, but it was also something special. I mean, you could tell the nature of what you were getting was rather more important than the stuff Bernard gives you upstairs. It was made clear the information didn't need any checking. So I went off and put it on the tapes straightaway.[13]

Moncrieff's story, that Heseltine had been rebuked by the Government's own law officers, was running on the PA's tapes by 2.53 p.m. It came in time to make the later editions of the London *Evening Standard*. It dominated the following morning's press. 'YOU LIAR!' screamed the *Sun* (a headline for which the paper later had to apologize to Heseltine and pay damages). *The Times*, in more measured language, summed up the general tenor of Fleet Street's coverage: 'Heseltine told by Law Chief: Stick to the facts'.

The Prime Minister subsequently defended the leak on the grounds that the board of Westland was holding a press conference at four o'clock that afternoon: the directors, she claimed, needed to know the legal position regarding

Heseltine's letter. Of all the many excuses trotted out in the course of this inglorious affair, this was the most pitiful. A simple telephone call to the board would have sufficed to convey the information. The letter could have been sent round by dispatch rider. But that would not have served Number 10's purpose. The media had to be briefed as they were in order to cause the maximum amount of public damage to Heseltine's credibility. Indeed, it is a misnomer to speak of a 'leaked letter': it was not a letter but two words, taken out of context, which leaked. It was a smear.

The other question on which much ink has been expended is: how much did Margaret Thatcher know? She was in Downing Street when Mayhew's letter arrived, but Powell assured Armstrong, and Armstrong believed him, that he did not disturb her with it. Instead, he took it down to Ingham. This claim caused much merry cynicism at the time, but in retrospect it has a ring of credibility. To an unusual degree the Prime Minister was willing to leave press matters in Ingham's hands. She had commissioned the Solicitor-General's letter in the first place. She obviously hoped it would damage Heseltine. How that damage was to be inflicted was a matter for her good and faithful servants. There was thus a double layer of insulation surrounding her that Monday night. She was protected by her officials, and her officials were protected by the fact that the leak had originated in the DTI. Nobody in Number 10, it seemed, had any cause to worry.

The following morning, Ingham prepared his usual press summary and, soon after 9 a.m. went upstairs to the Prime Minister's study for the daily meeting. Naturally, his digest was dominated by the leaked law officer's advice. 'In the course of a discussion of business with members of her staff,' Armstrong later reported, 'which was not recorded and at which a considerable number of other matters were discussed, the Prime Minister was told there had been contacts between her office and the DTI. But not in any detail.'[14] The disclosure of Mayhew's confidential advice was obviously fine as far as she was concerned.

Mayhew, however, had been incensed to discover that his letter was chattering out on the club tapes less than four hours after he had written it. He wrote to Heseltine that same night to express his 'dismay' that his letter had been leaked in such a 'highly selective way'.

> Quite apart from the breach of confidentiality that is involved, the rule is very clearly established that even the fact that the Law Officers have tendered advice in a particular case may not be disclosed, let alone the contents of their advice. It is plain that in this instance, this important rule was immediately and flagrantly violated.

It is possible that Ingham had not been fully aware of the consequences of his collusion that Monday afternoon. In 1981, for example, in his private speech to the IBA, he had made it clear that he did indeed consider himself 'licensed to leak':

> I must tell you that I – and I am sure my colleagues – have never regarded the Official Secrets Act as a constraint on my operations. Indeed, I regard myself as licensed to break that law as and when I judge necessary; and I suppose it is necessary to break it every other minute of every working day, though I confess the issue is so academic that I have not bothered to seek counsel's advice.

But the Law Officers – the Solicitor-General and the Attorney-General – were in a position, and a mood, to stamp on such cavalier disregard for the rules. Bernard Ingham, the man who had applauded Sarah Tisdall's jail sentence and who had said he longed for Judge Jeffreys to try Clive Ponting, was about to feel the noose tighten around his own neck.

Mayhew had complained immediately to the Attorney-General, Sir Michael Havers. On Tuesday morning, Havers wrote to Robert Armstrong demanding a full inquiry into the leak. No action was taken. On Wednesday, Havers (in Armstrong's words) 'had some conversation with' the Cabinet Secretary about the progress of the inquiry. Again, no action was taken. Thursday was lost in the maelstrom following Heseltine's dramatic exit from the Cabinet. On Friday the 10th, Havers saw Armstrong personally and made it clear that neither he nor Mayhew was prepared to let the matter drop. Armstrong made one last attempt to dissuade him, at which point a thoroughly exasperated Havers threatened to send the police into Number 10 and the DTI. Armstrong called in Nigel Wicks, Mrs Thatcher's Principal Private Secretary, to hear this ultimatum for himself. The stonewalling could go on no longer. On Monday, a full week after the disclosure, and following three separate approaches from the Attorney-General, Mrs Thatcher gave her reluctant assent to an inquiry. Armstrong would conduct it personally. Copies of his report would go to the Prime Minister, the Attorney-General and the Director of Public Prosecutions.

Armstrong talked privately of 'unrest at the DTI'. Colette Bowe was said to be in a stage of near-mutiny. Her account of events, it was whispered, had been deposited in a bank vault. Clearly, she was not willing to be the scapegoat. Indeed, Armstrong had to ask the Attorney-General to grant her immunity from prosecution in return for her co-operation with his inquiry – something which previously had been given only to two people, one of them the Soviet agent, Sir Anthony Blunt. 'I believed I should be addressing the person who had actually passed the information,' Armstrong said later. 'It was evident that a truthful answer could be an incriminating answer . . . '[15]

Armstrong, accompanied by a Cabinet Office colleague,

interviewed Ms Bowe for forty-five minutes at the DTI. Sir Brian Hayes was present; the meeting took place in his office. She asked about the legal position. Armstrong gave her the Attorney-General's assurances. Yet even with immunity guaranteed, she stuck to her version of events: she had not wanted to do it; Ingham had told her to do it. Back in Downing Street, the Cabinet Secretary then interviewed Ingham, who arrived unaccompanied. The conversation also lasted about three-quarters of an hour. Ingham, equally, maintained his innocence. Armstrong then telephoned Bowe to confront her with this discrepancy. She would not budge. Nor would Ingham. Across this yawning chasm, even the Cabinet Secretary, with all his legendary drafting skills, could apply only the flimsiest of sticking plasters. The conversation between Bowe and Ingham, he concluded limply, was based on a 'misunderstanding'.

In all, Armstrong's inquiry consisted of brief interrogations of five officials (Ingham, Powell, Bowe, Mogg and John Michell, the official in charge of the DTI's air division), and a couple of telephone calls. It could have been wrapped up in an afternoon. Instead, it took him nine days, adding to the impression that Downing Street was in no hurry to discover the truth. The Prime Minister was handed his report on Wednesday 22 January. It had not been her intention to make it public. But Tam Dalyell, that perennial thorn in Ingham's side, had been told by two deeply disillusioned civil servants that Colette Bowe was the official who had leaked the Solicitor-General's letter. That afternoon, he 'named' her in the House of Commons. A horde of reporters immediately descended upon her. 'If you have any questions about leaks,' she told them cryptically, 'you should refer them to 10 Downing Street.' Westminster was fizzing with rumours that the Prime Minister herself would be brought down, Nixon-style, by her knowledge of her subordinates' wrongdoing. Mrs

Thatcher had no choice but to agree to make a statement on the leak the next day.

It was an immensely delicate situation. None of the officials involved would be liable to prosecution under the Official Secrets Act if the leak had been authorized by a minister. It had: by Brittan. But Brittan, his political life at stake, was insisting that he had explicitly requested the prior authority of Number 10. Naturally, the Prime Minister had to be protected from any suggestion that she had connived at the leak. On the other hand, she could hardly expect Ingham and Powell to destroy their careers by confessing they had acted without her approval.

Narrowly, the Prime Minister survived. She did so by denying prior knowledge of the leak but throwing her protective mantle, retrospectively, around the actions of her officials. Ingham and Powell, she said, had 'considered – and they were right – that I should agree with my Rt. Hon. friend the Secretary of State for Trade and Industry that the [Mayhew letter] should become public knowledge as soon as possible.' Her only regret was the method. 'Had I been consulted, I should have said that a different way must be found of making the facts known.'[16] Brittan's position was now rendered intolerable; he resigned the next day. On Monday 27 January, Conservative MPs closed ranks behind Mrs Thatcher, and she survived an emergency debate in the Commons. Her story – 'stranger than fiction,' she called it – although shaky in places, just about held together. For her, the worst was past.

For Ingham, however, the moment of maximum danger was only just approaching. With Brittan gone and the Prime Minister apparently safe, he was the next most obvious target. Only a few months earlier, he had accused journalists of falling for the 'Watergate syndrome'. Now, there were plenty who believed Westland was the British Watergate, and who wanted to cast Ingham in the role of H. R. Haldeman. The House of Commons Select Committee on Defence had set up its own inquiry into the affair. It decided to 'invite' the five key officials involved in the leak to testify. This threw the Government into a fresh panic, for it was technically within the Committee's power to summon witnesses and have them imprisoned if they refused to appear. Once again, the Prime Minister turned to Armstrong. On 4 February, flown back specially from a pre-summit meeting in Honolulu, he wrote to the Committee:

> All five of these officials gave a full account of their role in these matters to me in the course of my recent inquiry, and co-operated fully in my investigation. The PM and the Secretary of State, DTI, believe that your Committee will recognize and share their view that it would be neither fair nor reasonable to expect these officials to submit to a second round of detailed questioning, of the kind that would be involved in giving evidence to your Committee.
>
> With the PM's agreement, I am writing to you to say that, if the Committee believed it would be helpful, I should be ready to accept an invitation . . .

This offer was not as generous as it appeared. There was no means by which the Committee could make an independent appraisal of the truth. All the facts were to be filtered through Armstrong, and he had already reached his own conclusions based upon them. It was the shadow, not the substance of open government.

Realizing the danger, the Committee's deputy chairman, the Labour MP, John Gilbert, proposed that they should turn down Armstrong's offer. He was outvoted by the Conservative majority. The next day, Armstrong appeared, complete with bodyguard and red dispatch box, the key to which hung from a large chain attached to his belt. The Keeper of the

State's Secrets gave a bravura performance, turning away the wrath of the Committee with soft words which, in his mouth, never quite added up to 'giving permission': Downing Street, he averred, had given 'cover' but not 'covering authority' for the leak, a distinction which he held to be of the utmost significance. Powell and Ingham 'accepted, or they acquiesced in, or they did not object to – whatever phrase of that kind you like to use – that the DTI were going to make the disclosure'.[17] Afterwards, the Committee's bemused members agreed among themselves a compromise. They would drop their demands to see four of the officials. But they still wanted to see the Prime Minister's Chief Press Secretary.

Ingham's own mood, according to his colleagues, veered at this time between despondency and rage. He refused to talk to anyone about what had happened. 'He was going around muttering and swearing,' recalled one. 'He could not believe that he had been let down so badly by Colette Bowe.' By an exquisite stroke of bad timing, on the day that Armstrong gave his evidence to the Defence Select Committee, Ingham was due to give an evening lecture to the Worshipful Company of Stationers and Newspaper Makers, an invitation he had accepted six months earlier. He arrived at Stationers' Hall, in Ave Maria Lane in the City, to find it packed with reporters and camera crews. His response was to duck back outside and walk around in the snow until it was time for his lecture to start. Eventually, his anxious host, Ray Tindle, spotted him by the door. 'I've got him!' shouted Tindle as he steered Ingham to the podium.

There is a famous scene in *Scoop*, in which Lord Copper, at the outset of a prepared speech, suddenly realizes it to be disastrously inappropriate: glancing through it, it seems to him like 'a new form of driving test, by which the applicant for a licence sat in a stationary car while a cinema film unfolded before his eyes a nightmare drive down a road full of obstacles'. Ingham might have been forgiven similar emotions as he studied his own text – 'The Reporter: An Endangered Species' – which had been composed in calmer times. Here he was, off again, for the third time in eleven months, accusing the British media (half of which appeared to be present) of

> a cavalier approach to facts especially if inconvenient ... a readiness to make deductions which are as creative in their approach to logic as some accounting is to sound finance ... an excess of malice ... insinuation – the branding iron of contemporary journalism ...

All that most reporters really wanted was to write a story 'based on a document marked "Secret" ... The occupational hazard of the public figure today is not to be misreported; it is to be misrepresented by interpretation' – to which Sir Patrick Mayhew and Mr Michael Heseltine would no doubt have said a loud 'Hear, hear!'

'Our democracy,' he concluded, 'needs lively, determined and scrupulous reporters.'

As he stepped down from the lectern, several members of the 'endangered species' crowded round him. 'Feel better now?' asked one. 'I didn't come here to be followed around by TV cameras and journalists,' snapped Ingham. He spent the remainder of the evening, as viewers of *News at Ten* later witnessed, dodging out of sight every time a camera appeared.

The face of this supposedly anonymous civil servant was now in newspapers and on television screens across the world. If nothing else, his new-found fame suddenly meant he started hearing from people he had lost touch with decades ago:

> Like Dr Jim Wilde, the first head boy of Calder High School, in Victoria BC; School principal Sheila Lever, in Oamaru, New Zealand; peripatetic teacher Rita Cherry, last heard of in darkest Khartoum; Brian Sutcliffe, Rolls-Royce representative

in Rio; Stella Moss (and Jim Gibson) in Mississauga, Ontario ... The most touching communication I have ever received came during the Westland affair. A woman identifying herself as Betty Broadbent, who said she had taught me *Julius Caesar*, rang my wife when I was away to say that she hoped she could claim to be a part of my success. Nancy said this was the nicest thing anyone had said about me for weeks ...

'The black clouds of infamy,' he observed four years later, 'have their silver linings.'[18]

The following day, the Commons Defence Committee renewed its attempts to summon Ingham. The Committee's Conservative Chairman, Sir Humphrey Atkins, spoke to the Government Chief Whip, John Wakeham. 'Ingham won't accept an invitation,' Wakeham told him. 'However you do have the power to make Ingham come, and we won't block you.' But, he added: 'When you bring Ingham he will simply refuse to speak.'

Had the Defence Committee decided to press ahead at this point, the career of the Prime Minister's Chief Press Secretary would probably have been at an end. The House of Commons is very particular about its rights; Atkins could have appeared before it and urged a vote requiring Ingham to attend, on pain of imprisonment; the Government, according to Wakeham, would not have imposed a three-line whip to stop him; the Committee would probably have mustered a majority. Then Ingham would have appeared and, to every question, as he was entitled, refused an answer. But such a spectacle, broadcast into every home in the country, would have had a devastating effect on his reputation. 'In my present job,' Ingham was fond of saying, 'I rely on one quality: credibility.' Where would his credibility have been by the time the Committee had finished with him? If he had done nothing wrong, why did he not speak? More to the point, if the Prime Minister had done nothing wrong, why did she not encourage him to say so?

It was this latter consideration which saved him. The Conservative members of the Committee were under intense pressure from their colleagues to put an end to the Westland affair. Summoning Ingham would have guaranteed it fresh life. Atkins led the retreat. He returned from his conversation with Wakeham and made a passionate appeal. 'What are you after?' he pleaded. 'Are you just trying to have somebody destroyed?'[19] The Committee backed down, saving its face by recalling Armstrong, who had again offered to answer for the civil service.

It was over. In April, Tam Dalyell initiated a second Commons debate on Ingham: no mere Press Secretary, he insisted, but 'a man who is an adviser on central decisions of Government in Britain, and whose power has grown exponentially, along a geometric progression, with the years during which he has occupied the office'; he was, 'with the arguable exception of Sir Robert Armstrong ... the most important man making decisions in British politics'. Richard Luce, the minister responsible for the Civil Service, accused Dalyell of giving vent to 'obsessions'. Ingham was doing 'an excellent job', serving the Government 'professionally and with integrity'. The issue of Westland was 'worn to a frazzle'.[20] Whenever Thatcher was questioned about it in the future, she simply referred to the statements she had made at the time and declared that she had nothing to add.

Ingham had been lucky to survive. Just how lucky was revealed three years later, at the beginning of 1989, when Leon Brittan broke his long silence on the affair. In a television interview he stated that the leak 'was approved by Mr Charles Powell, the relevant Private Secretary at Number 10, and it was approved by Mr Bernard Ingham, the Prime Minister's Press Secretary ... there would have been no question of the leaking of that document without that express approval from Number 10.'

This was the equivalent of one of the conspirators returning to the scene of the crime and depositing the smoking gun. Had Brittan made such an allegation at the time, Armstrong's defence – that the whole affair was based on a misunderstanding between Downing Street and the DTI 'as to exactly what was sought and what was being given' – would have dropped to bits. As it was, the nearest Ingham came to an official reprimand was in the report of the Commons Defence Committee, published that summer. 'The disclosure of the Solicitor-General's letter without his permission was an improper act,' concluded the MPs. 'Yet we understand from Sir Robert Armstrong's evidence that no disciplinary action is to be taken against any of the officials concerned. We find this extraordinary.'[21]

That Ingham had done wrong, there is no question. To what extent precisely, we do not know, and probably never shall. The worst case is that he helped arrange a smear against a Government minister, then bullied a troubled colleague into breaking the Official Secrets Act with the intention of hiding behind her skirts in the event of trouble; the best is that he turned a blind eye to a notably shabby piece of political chicanery – even the Prime Minister later said she 'regretted' the way the leak was sprung.

It did Ingham damage because he had always been so pious about his own standards and those of the Government, contrasting them with the debased behaviour of the British press. If no other good came out of Westland, it did at least put a stop to Ingham's sermons on the media for the next four years. This was a special relief to those who believed that neither press nor politician was in much of a position to damn the other's morality. After Westland, political reporters could say to Ingham, rather as Michael Corleone says to the corrupt senator in *The Godfather*: 'We are both part of the same hypocrisy.'

The affair had one other significant side-effect, in that it strengthened the Prime Minister's relationship with her new Private Secretary, Charles Powell, a 44-year-old diplomat, theoretically on a short-term attachment to Number 10. Her response to the attacks on his integrity was almost maternal in its protectiveness. Powell – whose capacity for work surpassed even Ingham's – now firmly established himself as her undisputed favourite. He worked not twelve but sixteen hours a day. Strictly speaking, Powell was merely one of three civil servants in Mrs Thatcher's Private Office, working to her Principal Private Secretary, Nigel Wicks. But gradually, from assisting the Prime Minister exclusively on foreign affairs, he widened his brief to embrace matters of domestic policy. Mrs Thatcher also struck up an equally warm relationship with his Italian wife, Carla. They would gossip on the telephone. They would joke about Charles. Mrs Powell would give her advice on which clothes to buy ... These were services which Ingham could not hope to render. Gradually, almost imperceptibly, he began to be nudged out.

But all this was not to become apparent until several years after Westland. In 1986, his relationship with the Prime Minister was as strong as ever. One by one, the principal actors in the story of the leak left the stage – John Mogg was transferred out of the Secretary of State's office to other duties, Colette Bowe left the Government Information Service to work for the Independent Broadcasting Authority, Robert Armstrong retired, Leon Brittan departed for Brussels – until only the central trio was left: Bernard Ingham, Charles Powell and Margaret Thatcher. They stayed together at the heart of the Government, bound by loyalties no outsider could penetrate.

NINE

The New Machiavelli

'*From this arises the following question: whether it is better to be loved than feared, or the reverse. The answer is that one would like to be both the one and the other; but because it is difficult to combine them, it is far better to be feared than loved . . . Men worry less about doing an injury to one who makes himself loved than to one who makes himself feared.*'

NICCOLO MACHIAVELLI, *THE PRINCE*, 1541

'*We need a new version of Machiavelli's* The Prince *to explain the way in which the Lobby has been used by Number 10 . . .*'

SIR JOHN NOTT, 1987[1]

Only three people had the privilege of meeting the Lobby and briefing them about the whole range of Government activities: the Prime Minister's Press Secretary, who saw them twice a day; the Leader of the House of Lords, who saw them every Friday morning; and the Leader of the House of Commons, who saw them on Thursday afternoons.

Ingham regarded the encroachment of these two ministers on to his territory as a tiresome distraction. Their briefings were yet two more opportunities for cock-ups: two more occasions when the Government might be caught out speaking with more than one voice. He began sending along members of the Number 10 Press Office, who would sit at the back, taking notes. This served two purposes. It alerted Ingham to any deviations from the authorized version of Government policy, as emanating from Downing Street; and it deterred the ministers concerned from making disloyal remarks. Anything they said would be taken down and would, most assuredly, be used in evidence against them.

At the beginning of 1986, the Leader of the House of Lords was William Whitelaw: co-ordinator of Government present-ation, Deputy Prime Minister, and one of Mrs Thatcher's most trusted lieutenants. He might occasionally sympathize with ministerial dissidents; he might have his doubts about the Government's economic policies; but in the end he would always back the Prime Minister – a characteristic which had earned him, from some of his colleagues, the nickname 'the Devious Squire'. For Ingham, he was no problem. But Whitelaw's opposite number in the Commons, John Biffen, was a different matter.

Biffen was Thatcher's third Leader of the House since 1979. All three had posed difficulties. All three were to meet sticky ends. And all three were to have reason to blame Ingham for their misfortunes. The first, Norman St John Stevas, was sacked in 1981, and Ingham helped encourage the belief that he was dismissed for leaking details of Cabinet discussions. In Stevas's place came Francis Pym, the arch-wet whom Ingham dismissed as a notorious pessimist. When Lord Carrington resigned at the outset of the Falklands crisis, Pym had to be given the Foreign Office to balance the Cabinet. (He was to last in that position a mere fourteen months before his career, too, was terminated.) Pym's replacement as Leader of the House was John Biffen.

Biffen was no wet. He was a Thatcherite at a time when, in his words, 'Thatcher was closing grammar schools' and Ingham was writing about the wickedness of capitalism. But he had a thoughtful, original mind which made him difficult to categorize. He was, for example, the only Cabinet minister to oppose the sending of the Falklands task force and, later in the conflict, to defend the BBC against charges of 'treachery' from the Tory right – neither of which, given Ingham's gung-ho attitude, can have endeared him to the Chief Press Secretary. From the start, their relations were marked by a strictly professional coolness. 'Ours was never a relaxed and easy partnership,' said Biffen.

The Leader of the House had not been long in his new position when his staff told him that Ingham wanted to see him. 'He came over to the Commons,' recalled Biffen, 'and it was quite clear that he felt he had got a problem: that he had already had to put up with Stevas and Pym and now he had got me. He made it very clear that it was his job to present Government policy, as seen through the Prime Minister's eyes, and that the rest of us were all partially sighted. I was courteous, but made it clear I was not prepared to put up with this. From that time onwards, I felt no warmth towards him.'

Ever since Herbert Morrison first developed the practice in 1945, the Leader of the House has given his briefings at 4.30 on Thursday afternoons, after he has announced to MPs the Government's business for the coming week. Different Leaders have handled these occasions in different ways. Biffen gave careful thought to his own approach and decided that, rather than concentrate on detail, he would talk about the broad philosophical background to Government decisions. Surprisingly, the Lobby rather enjoyed these sessions. One reason was that Biffen, unlike Ingham, actually liked journalists. He was taken aback by the Yorkshireman's detestation of the Fourth Estate: 'His language was lurid. He really did treat them like shit. They were all up to no good as far as he was concerned. There wasn't one he wouldn't have suspected of being a child molester or of selling his grandmother into white slavery.' Biffen thought that such 'obvious contempt' for journalists was unwise, and that Ingham's instinctively hostile reaction to certain individuals was 'not always well-founded'.

It was slightly unfortunate, then, that in February 1983 it fell to Biffen to defend Ingham in the House of Commons against Tam Dalyell's attack. In addition to the absence of 'warmth' between him and Ingham, Dalyell was an old friend (indeed, as a student, the Labour MP had been a Tory, and Biffen had backed him, successfully, for the chairmanship of the Cambridge University Conservative Association). It was not that Biffen did not defend Ingham; he did. But somehow, compared to Dalyell's invective (a 'thug', he called Ingham, a 'truculent, arrogant bully'), his reply seemed flat and passionless. The best he could manage was 'to endorse and support what the Prime Minister said about Mr Bernard Ingham'. He even praised Dalyell for a 'fascinating' if 'controversial' speech and commended him as 'an engaging and resolute campaigner'.

On the whole, Biffen gave the impression that he regarded the affair as a slightly dotty occasion, which should not come between men of good sense. His murderous little joke about a 'rough-spoken Yorkshire Rasputin' – a description which stuck long after Dalyell's taunts had been forgotten – can hardly have endeared him to Ingham. Nor can his curiously ambivalent conclusion, that the Press Secretary should not be attacked too much because he 'may well have a future career outside the Civil Service'.[2] What species of weasel's words were these?

Biffen had been obliged to stay up all night, waiting to defend Ingham's reputation. He might have expected a note of thanks, or at least a telephone call. There was nothing. 'He felt no gratitude for what I'd done,' recalled Biffen. 'He may have thought I was too laid back in my remarks because I was an old friend of Tam.'

Nevertheless, the two managed to rub along for the next three years. Then came Westland, followed by a series of political setbacks. Unemployment began to rise again. The Cabinet was forced, under pressure from the back-benches, to drop plans to sell Land Rover to an American firm. Mrs Thatcher insisted, despite the misgivings of several ministers (including Biffen) that US planes should be allowed to bomb Libya from British bases. Her popularity hit an all-time low. Finally, on 8 May 1986, the Government had two bad by-election results. On Sunday, 11 May, Biffen gave an interview to *Weekend World* in which he boldly addressed the Prime Minister's alleged shortcomings. 'To assume that because a party has one dominant figure it thereby benefits is not necessarily true at all,' he asserted. Was he implying that Mrs Thatcher had liabilities? 'Oh yes, yes of course, that goes without saying.' He proposed that the Conservatives should fight the next election with a 'balanced ticket', giving due prominence to the more emollient aspects of Toryism – after all, 'nobody seriously supposes that the Prime Minister would be Prime Minister throughout the entire period of the next Parliament'.

Unfortunately for Biffen, that was exactly what Mrs Thatcher did 'seriously suppose'. She had a formula for these occasions. When a minister or civil servant displeased her, she would sweetly inquire of her intimates: 'Shall we withdraw our love?' That was precisely what she did. Few politicians have had Prime Ministerial affection whipped out from under them quite as quickly as John Biffen. She never said a word to him herself. On Monday morning he was given a dressing-down by Whitelaw. Then, late that afternoon, Lobby journalists began coming up to him. Had he heard what Bernard was saying about him? He had not, but the next morning it was there for all the world to read. According to the *Guardian*:

His criticism ... last night provoked a fiery counter-offensive in which he was described as a 'semi-detached member of the Government' whose views were of little consequence in its thinking ... If Mr Biffen's intention was to irritate his leader, he appears to have succeeded. The scornful tone of the responses in official quarters was unmistakable. His remarks 'did not have to be taken seriously' and he was not 'fully integrated' into the Government ...[3]

In *The Times*:

The sources said that ... Mr Biffen was a 'semi-detached' member of the Cabinet ...

In the *Financial Times*:

Mr John Biffen ... was yesterday being authoritatively described as 'a well-known semi-detached member of the Government'.

The phrase was everywhere. 'Axe threat as Biffen gets biffing' was the headline in the *Sun*:

In an unprecedented bid to discredit Mr Biffen, Downing Street sources made it clear Mrs Thatcher 'did not give two hoots' for his views.

Others close to the Premier called Mr Biffen a 'semi-detached member of the Government'.

They said Mrs Thatcher 'sometimes has to pinch herself to realise he is a member of the Government'.

Significantly, no attempt was made to deny that Mr Biffen could be the victim of her looming reshuffle.

'As far as the Premier is concerned,' reported the *Daily Mail*, 'he is in the doghouse.' In the *Daily Mirror*: 'She let it be known that in her view he is liable to think something different every week – and what he says doesn't matter anyway.'

The British press had wheeled on Biffen with the mechanized precision of a Busby Berkeley chorus line.

As with the Mona Lott episode four years earlier, what was striking was the contrast between the words used non-attributably by Ingham and those uttered publicly by Mrs Thatcher. At Prime Minister's Questions on the day the 'semi-detached' stories appeared, she told the Commons that Biffen had 'made many robust policy points on Sunday with which I wholly agree'. It was this which the errant minister found most extraordinary. She scarcely spoke to him again from that day onwards. Certainly, she never once confronted him directly about what had upset her. Instead, she had him murdered out of the corner of somebody else's mouth – quietly, in the dark, away from public gaze. He never held it against Ingham (in his lighter moments, he even acknow-ledged that 'semi-detached' was 'quite a good phrase') because he was convinced that 'Ingham had not exceeded his responsibilities: he did it because the Prime Minister wanted to make it perfectly clear she had withdrawn support from me, but couldn't yet drop me.' And so Biffen was left to twist in the wind for another year, before eventually being cut down and deposited on the back-benches two days after the 1987 General Election.

The analogy with the gibbet is not altogether misplaced. Dangling there, without the support of Number 10, Biffen was an awful warning to his colleagues of the penalty for lese-majesty. Observing the method of his dispatch, it was not surprising that many of his colleagues began inspecting the press with the care of Kremlinologists. 'They've become neurotic about it,' according to Viscount Whitelaw, 'and they all think it's Bernard all the time ... A lot of ministers feel – people who've left the Government or resigned – that before the time came for the reshuffle, Bernard had been working against them to prepare the ground for it.' Several ministers, perceiving themselves to be under threat, took their worries to Whitelaw and asked him to intercede with Ingham on their behalf. During their Thursday morning 'gossips', the Deputy Prime Minister thus found himself asking the Chief Press Officer: 'Oh, Bernard, are you sure you're right about that?' He had to be careful in his approach, for this, as he later acknowledged, was 'touchy ground even for me'.

The briefings in which ministers were mentioned tend to divide into two sorts. There were the premeditated, set-piece denigrations, of which Pym's and Biffen's were the most obvious examples. These were almost certainly performed on the Prime Minister's explicit instructions: in another of Biffen's memorable metaphors, Ingham, on these occasions, was 'the sewer rather than the sewage'.[4] Then there were the less dramatic pieces of guidance: the hints, the pauses, the raised eyebrows, the supportive remark which was conspicuous by its absence. The message was not always negative. Sometimes, he would even go out of his way to praise a minister. Kind words about John Major, for example, were commonplace when he was Chief Secretary to the Treasury. The basis for this 'mood music', by which the Lobby judged who was on his way up and who was on his way out, were the Prime Minister's own private remarks, which Ingham would slip into briefings as he saw fit.

Patrick Jenkin, dropped from the Department of the Environment in 1985, was one Cabinet Minister who complained privately to his staff about Ingham. Another was John Moore, who cautioned his aides to remember that 'Bernard's first loyalty is to the Prime Minister, not to us'. A third was the Conservative Party Chairman, Norman Tebbit. During the 'semi-detached' briefing about John Biffen, Ingham had taken the opportunity to refer to Tebbit as 'fully integrated'. Nevertheless, stories about the poor relations between the Prime Minister and her Party Chairman continued to circulate, and Tebbit became convinced Number 10 was behind them. Two months later, towards the end of July, he went stalking into Downing Street with a folder full of 'dozens' of hostile press cuttings. In his own, carefully-chosen words, they:

> must have resulted from regular press briefings by someone whose position give him credibility with the Lobby ... I realised that if Margaret had been previously unaware of the stories she would not have briefed Bernard Ingham ... to refute them; and his lack of comment must have added credibility to them.[5]

What was the truth behind this curious episode? Certainly, Margaret Thatcher was suspicious of Tebbit. She felt he had wavered over Westland and was plotting a future which did not include her. They had had a row about the US bombing of Libya. She was dubious about his managerial skills as Party Chairman. In the usual way, Ingham appears simply to have picked up these vibrations and transmitted them to the Lobby. Stephen Sherbourne, the Prime Minister's political adviser, took possession of Tebbit's cuttings file and passed on word of the Chairman's unhappiness. According to Tebbit:

> Her response next day was swift and the briefing coming out of Number 10 was that the stream of stories was baseless and the Chairman and Prime Minister were at one.[6]

He left the Government the following year.

Stevas, Pym, Heseltine, Biffen, Jenkin, Moore, Tebbit and, later, Howe ... 'We need a new edition of Machiavelli's *The Prince*,' said Sir John Nott in 1987, 'to explain the way in which the Lobby has been used by Number 10 to raise the cult of personality so far as the Prime Minister is concerned, at the expense of colleagues who have happened to disagree at the time.' Edward Heath claimed the Government 'uses the Press Office in Number 10 in a way that can be described as corrupt', going 'far beyond the achievements, even the aspirations, of any previous government'.[7] In John Biffen's view, too, Margaret Thatcher's use of the Lobby has been an essential tool of her style of statecraft:

> First of all, she wanted a good cadre of people around her, like John Hoskyns [first head of the Number 10 Policy Unit] and Alan Walters [her economic adviser], to enable her to challenge the big departments, the Foreign Office and the Treasury. But particularly she used the Number 10 Press Office with tremendous effect, to put across the line that Governments must be united and Governments are spoken for by the Prime Minister. She has centralized, presidential powers – much more presidential than anything you'll find in North America – powers which had always been there, but had simply lain dormant.

Thatcher, through Ingham, had turned the doctrine of collective responsibility inside out. In the past, the rule which Prime Ministers had insisted upon was that the Cabinet could argue strenuously in private, but that in public a united front must be presented. Mrs Thatcher used the Lobby system in precisely the opposite way: Cabinet discussions were kept to a minimum, whilst she reserved the right to make public her disagreements with her own ministers.

Thus, it was implied, Stevas was a leaker, Pym a moaner, Heseltine a liar, Biffen unreliable, Jenkin hopeless, Moore disappointing, Tebbit distrusted, Howe dispensable. And these judgements came not from the Prime Minister's personal, political agent, whispering to individual reporters; they were the official pronouncements of the Civil Service spokesman for the entire Government, in twice-daily contact with the Parliamentary Lobby. Short of marching in to Number

10, like Tebbit, there was nothing much the minister concerned could do, for, technically, the briefing never took place. Even if an aggrieved minister did confront her, she could deny any involvement. In 1981, when James Prior tackled her about these 'leaks' from Number 10, she protested her innocence.

> 'Oh no, Jim, I never leak.'
>
> 'Well, if you tell me that I must accept it, but in that case your officials and press people certainly leak for you.'
>
> 'Oh, that is quite wrong: they never know anything, so how could they leak?'

As Prior commented: 'Either she was incredibly naïve, which I have no reason to believe, or she thought I was, and I frankly doubt that. I believe she really didn't think in terms of "leaks" herself at all – if she said it, then it had to be right: how could there be any question of a leak?'[8]

The essence of the game was deniability. If Ingham's briefings had been on the record, none of these attacks on Cabinet ministers would have taken place. Even Margaret Thatcher could not have been seen openly to attack her colleagues in such a fashion: she was, after all, in the words of that increasingly threadbare maxim, only the first among equals.

The realization of what was happening prompted a degree of soul-searching among some journalists who, hitherto, had gone along with the need for a Lobby system. Were they not, in a sense, the tools by which Number 10 was extending its power? One of Ingham's favourite examples of media irresponsibility was the way in which the mere presence of television cameras could incite a riot, stimulating lawlessness 'simply by screening it night after night'.[9] Did the analogy not hold good at Westminster as well? Did the existence of the Lobby not create news which otherwise would not have happened? In that case, Lobby journalists were no better than Ingham's dangerously corrupting TV cameramen: they had ceased merely to record events and become central players. In the summer of 1986, these questions had become so insistent that Ingham found himself facing an unexpected crisis. The Lobby system, the very basis upon which his office was built, began to collapse, partly under the strain he was imposing on it.

One morning in July, at the end of one of Ingham's eleven o'clock briefings, Anthony Bevins, political correspondent of *The Times*, asked if he could have a private word with the Chief Press Secretary. Bevins was one of the most assiduous Lobby journalists, forever poring over Government documents and ministerial statements, alert for discrepancies; always first on his feet at a press conference with a hostile question. He and Ingham had had a difficult relationship. Bevins was due to leave *The Times* shortly to become political editor on the soon-to-be-launched *Independent*. Its editor, Andreas Whittam Smith, wanted to make a gesture which would signal that his paper's name really meant what it said. Could they, he asked Bevins, pull out of the Lobby? Bevins was enthusiastic and it was this decision which he was staying behind to impart to Ingham.

Ingham, Bevins recalled, was 'absolutely incensed'. He went bright red. He called the idea 'silly' and 'childish'. This only made Bevins more determined. He wrote to the editors of the *Observer* and the *Guardian*, Donald Trelford and Peter Preston, telling them of the *Independent*'s plan and asking if they would care to join a boycott of the Lobby. Both gave non-committal replies. In truth, the *Independent*'s action posed more of a problem for the *Guardian*, which was reluctant to see a rival upstaging it for the affections of progressive opinion. On 18 September, two weeks before the *Independent* was due to launch, Preston wrote to Ingham to tell him that, after the summer Parliamentary recess, his journalists would no longer be playing by the old Lobby rules:

> I have this week instructed my political staff that, when Westminster business recommences, they shall attend – as normal – your daily briefings, but that instead of employing any of the customary and increasingly threadbare circumlocutions ('Downing Street argues that . . . made clear last night', and so forth) they shall refer openly to 'a Downing Street spokesman' or 'Mrs Thatcher's spokesman' and, as relevant, quote what that spokesman says – whether it is a description of Mr Pym as 'Mona Lott' or Mr John Biffen as 'a semi-detached member of the Government'. I take your point that it would be wrong to turn you, a civil servant, into a national star turn, more ubiquitous than any of the ministers you serve: that's why I want the attribution to 'a spokesman' (whoever it is from your staff on the day) rather than a named individual – the practice we follow for other Civil Service departmental spokesmen.

To an outsider, this might appear a relatively harmless step. To Ingham, it struck at the heart of his Lobby operation and of his attempts to speak for the entire Government. He took this action by his old paper as a personal betrayal. With some *Guardian* journalists – notably the paper's political editor, Ian Aitken, whom he had known for twenty years – he severed all relations. When he learned that he and Aitken had both been invited to a mutual friend's retirement dinner, he refused to attend unless the *Guardian* man was struck off the list. His response to Preston (who had also regarded Ingham as a 'mate' in the 1960s) was acid:

> I can reply quite briefly since your letter is not for me. The Parliamentary Lobby Journalists exist as an independent body with their own constitution and rules. Under this so-called

> Lobby system, I do not invite political correspondents to briefings; they invite me. Their chairman, or acting chairman, presides and the terms under which briefings are given are covered by their rules.
>
> Consequently, if you wish to change the system you will have to find a way of addressing the Lobby ...

That was his public stance. In private, he made it clear that moves to make his comments attributable to Downing Street would take place 'over my dead body'.

The Lobby was thrown into confusion. Ingham was due to give his next off-the-record briefing on 20 October. As a stop-gap measure *Guardian* journalists were asked by their colleagues not to attend it. Two days later, a special meeting of Lobby reporters voted to hold a ballot on whether the rules governing non-attribution should be changed. If the ballot had gone against Ingham, the Lobby system, in its existing form, would have ended – and with it, quite possibly, given his outspoken opposition to change, his career as Chief Press Secretary. Instead, on 29 October, the reporters voted by a narrow margin – 67 to 55 – to keep the briefings on the same basis as before.

An inquiry was held, to which Ingham submitted evidence. Given his unremitting hostility to the Lobby over the past seven years, accompanied by his frequently expressed desire to 'screw the buggers', one might have expected him to have welcomed the chance to give up his twice-daily jousts with the media. ('I have got news for you,' he had said in his private speech to the IBA in 1981. 'I have no objection to going on the record.') But, of course, when it really came down to it, he needed them even more than they needed him. In a written submission, he described the Lobby system as something which 'within the constraints imposed by Parliament ... facilitates the flow of information and guidance'. It was common journalistic practice, he asserted, to speak to 'informants' non-attributably: 'The Government cannot accept that the Lobby should seek to treat differently collective briefings with the Chief Press Secretary.' He concluded:

> The Government considers that, properly operated according to the conventions, the Lobby system can serve a useful purpose in our democracy and for that practical reason would wish to see it continue.

When he met the inquiry's members to discuss his evidence, he characteristically went straight on to the attack, stressing his belief that the system had to be 'properly operated'. Many journalists, he claimed, no longer seemed to appreciate the rules under which he gave his briefings. In the words of the inquiry report:

> It is no longer good enough to say that everyone understands. They clearly do not. Mr Ingham told us he thought that any references to information from his briefings should be non-specific – in particular the increasingly used terms 'Downing Street spokesman' or 'Downing Street said' ... were not acceptable. In his view 'Government sources' was more accurate since he argued that he was speaking on behalf of the whole Government.

This latter point was really the crux of the matter. If Ingham spoke for the Government and not merely for the Prime Minister, then her interpretation – whether it was of policy or of colleagues – was automatically presented as the official view. Ingham could thus undermine a Cabinet minister, with or without the Prime Minister's prior knowledge, and the press would pass it on to the public as if it were the considered opinion of the entire Government. This had been the advantage of the Lobby system to Prime Ministers ever since Neville Chamberlain's time. It was this which put his collective Lobby briefings in a totally different category from the ordinary, off-the-record exchanges which are the stuff of everyday life, never mind everyday journalism.

Nevertheless – and rather surprisingly given the narrowness of the original vote – the inquiry accepted the logic of Ingham's argument: if you were going to keep the system, you had to operate it properly. And so what had begun as an attempt to make the Lobby less secretive and suggestible turned into a drive to make it more so. The report, completed in December, recommended that journalists attending Ingham's briefings should always refer to him as 'Government' or 'Whitehall sources', and that they be required to 'give a written undertaking that they are prepared to obey the rules of those meetings'. Any breaches of this 'tighter self-discipline' would lead to offenders being excluded by their colleagues from Lobby briefings.

'The *Guardian* will sign no such pledge of secrecy,' declared a leader in Ingham's old newspaper on 8 December, 'and finds it hard to believe that other newspaper editors will put their names to this voluntary endorsement of closed government.' In the event, they were not required to do so. Put to a vote in February 1987, this proposal was rejected.

When at last the smoke cleared after these months of wrangling, it was apparent that the Lobby system had been weakened badly. Nearly half its members (according to the October 29 ballot) favoured reform. Proposals designed to reimpose the old, strict discipline had failed. Two newspapers, the *Guardian* and the *Independent* (they were later to be joined by a third, the *Scotsman*), were refusing to attend Ingham's briefings. They relied instead on the substantial number of disaffected journalists still working inside the system, who were always happy to fill them in on what had been said. In their subsequent reports, the self-exiled papers, the *Independent* in particular, would sometimes take great pleasure in identifying Ingham by name. Ingham responded by making their lives as difficult as possible. 'They will not dine at this restaurant à la carte,' he was fond of insisting. If the 'buggers' refused his non-attributable guidance, they would not be given anything else, either. Even routine inquiries to the Number 10 Press Office about the Prime Minister's engagements would go unanswered.

The Prime Minister's famous trip to Moscow in March 1987 showed how political journalists now divided in Ingham's eyes: between those in the Lobby who had stayed loyal, and those outside it who could look after themselves. Downing Street had set aside twenty-two seats for reporters on the official VC-10, every one of which went to a member of the Lobby. The Number 10 Press Office refused even to help with the visas of some of those who were not in this select group. Joe Haines, by then Assistant Editor of, and columnist on, the *Daily Mirror*, had his passport returned to him and was told to do it himself. Haines telephoned Ingham. 'He said he wasn't going to help,' he recalled, 'wouldn't even tell me which hotel they were staying at, which was important to know. When I said "Why not?" he said "Because I'm in this to look after my friends". I said "You mean the Lobby?" He said "Yes".'

A few weeks before the Moscow visit, on the evening of 17 February, James Naughtie, chief political correspondent of the *Guardian*, visited Ingham at Number 10 to try to patch up relations, at least on a personal level. It was a stormy occasion. The next morning, Preston wrote again to Ingham 'to say how much I regret the individual anger, with added vituperation, that you seem continually to display towards this paper, and towards members of its staff. We have sought only to bring about some modest measure of reform in a system which we feel would benefit from it.' In his reply on 23 February, Ingham refused to respond to these points. As to the Moscow trip:

I give Lobby briefings during flights. Such briefings concern the visit itself as well as touching on matters of wider Governmental interest. You have decided, for your own reasons, that the *Guardian*'s journalists should not participate in Number 10 Lobby briefings in this country. It would be quite impracticable, in the narrow confines of the VC-10, for any *Guardian* members of the press team to absent themselves while I gave my briefings. Since you find the principle of collective Lobby briefings by Number 10 so offensive, I am sure that you would not wish to subscribe to them simply for the duration of the flight.

Ingham also turned down a plea for a seat from Anthony Bevins, asking the reporter if he proposed to hide in the VC-10's lavatory every time there was a briefing.

The treatment meted out in Moscow to Joe Haines, James Naughtie and Colin Brown of the *Independent* showed the price of antagonizing Ingham. Whilst their Lobby colleagues were whisked from the airport to the city centre in an official coach, Brown became involved in a furtive black market deal with a taxi driver 'with bald tyres'. They were put up in rooms without direct-dial telephones which made filing copy almost impossible. Ingham's morning briefings on how the visit was going were always non-attributable so Naughtie and Brown could not attend. Finally, on 1 April, when the rest of their colleagues were flown down to Tbilisi in Georgia for the last leg of the visit, there was no way they could follow. They simply gave up the chase.

That night, at 9.00 p.m., as the RAF VC-10 left Soviet airspace, a steward made his way to the press compartment in the rear of the plane bearing a silver tray and four bottles of champagne: a gift from the Prime Minister to the Lobby. The stories which had been filed to London ('SuperMag!', 'Maggiemania!'), six weeks before she called a General

Election, were a politician's dream. A 2,000-word summary of their contents had been relayed every morning from the Downing Street Press Office to the British Embassy. The drinks, it was clear, had been well-earned. When, soon after the champagne, the Prime Minister herself and her Press Secretary appeared, it was smiles all round. Ingham wore the biggest grin. He had brought off, he declared, 'the big one': one of the most successful exercises in public relations Downing Street had ever mounted. It can only have added to his pleasure that somewhere, outside in the freezing night, far below and miles behind, Joe Haines, Jim Naughtie and Colin Brown were probably still locked in a row with customs at Moscow Airport.

After the Conservatives' success in the General Election of June 1987, Ingham saw the Prime Minister and offered to resign. He had long since overtaken Harold Evans's record to became the longest-serving occupant of his office. He was fifty-five years old, nearly eight years into the job, and on to his sixth deputy. Enough time had elapsed since Westland for it not to appear that he was departing under a cloud. According to an old friend: 'He went to her and said, "Now you've won, it's a good time for a parting of the ways." But she wouldn't hear of it. He would have been happy to go.'

Like many leaders who have remained at the top for a long time, Mrs Thatcher had become peculiarly dependent upon her closest advisers. Senior civil servants, Cabinet Ministers, foreign statesmen, Leaders of the Opposition – all had changed since 1979. But Ingham, and especially Charles Powell, remained reassuringly familiar. In the words of one highly-placed official: 'She gets comfortable with the people around her and she doesn't want to change. Michel Jobert, who was President Pompidou's *chef de cabinet*, once wrote that when relations are good, there's no need to finish a sentence. So it is with Bernard.' Another intimate described Ingham as 'part of the furniture': 'This Prime Minister wants to change everything – except Number 10. It's the one thing she's very conservative about. She loves familiarity.' Maybe against his own better judgement, Ingham agreed to stay. The following year, at a Press Association lunch, Mrs Thatcher described him, with heavy emphasis, as '*indispensable*'. It appeared to be literally true.

His fame had now spread far and wide. His performances at foreign summits had made him such a star with the international press corps that they always sought out his briefings, rather as tourists to Britain might go in search of beefeaters or pearly kings. These occasions had a ritual element to them. Ingham would arrive, order all cameras and tape recorders to be switched off, then growl: 'Usual terms: British sources.' He would next proceed to belabour the other heads of government, much as his mistress was said to be doing in the conference chamber. At the European summit at Fontainebleau in 1984, he ridiculed the German chancellor, Helmut Kohl. At Milan the following year, when the leaders were having what he later called 'a real old-fashioned fall-out', he made a disastrous foray into the world of irony:

> I was asked what Mrs T thought about it all. I replied, with masterly understatement, 'Well, she's not best pleased'. A great smile of satisfaction suffused across the collective face of the media ... 'Aha,' said I, looking at the rows of smug, self-satisfied journalists in front of me, 'I know what you will be writing tomorrow. This time the Prime Minister won't just be furious; nor livid; nor even volcanic with rage. Oh no, she will be positively erupting. Krakatoan on the Richter scale.'[10]

Unfortunately for Ingham, *The Times* somehow missed the joke, and quoted 'Mr Bernard Ingham, her spokesman' as saying that the Prime Minister 'has but one emotion – fury ...

It is total volcanic eruption. Krakatoa has nothing on it.'[11] In the ensuing row, Edward Heath went on the radio to call for Ingham's dismissal (an increasingly common occurrence), while Ingham himself demanded that *The Times* print a retraction. At the foot of an article the following day, the paper faithfully reported that Ingham 'considered that both he and she had been entirely misunderstood. She was no more than vexed.' ('This episode,' said Ingham later, 'reinforced my long-standing view that nothing less becomes a press which so extols its Arthurian pursuit of the truth than its utter determination never to apologise if it can be avoided, and then only in the most illegible type available.')[12]

To the normally sedate world of international diplomacy, Ingham imported the language and tactics which had made him notorious at home. At the Commonwealth Conference in Vancouver in 1987, when Britain was alone among member nations in resisting the call for sanctions against apartheid, he rattled off figures allegedly showing that the Canadian prime minister was a hypocrite: why, Canada was actually *increasing* its trade with South Africa. The Canadian government angrily pointed out that the statistics were out of date. Other leaders professed themselves amazed at this non-attributable attack on their hosts. Bob Hawke of Australia called it 'a process of misinformation ... an abominably untrue statement, totally unfair to the Prime Minister and the people of Canada.' Robert Mugabe declared himself 'completely disillusioned and dismayed by the most dishonest way of informing the public that has been presented here this week'. Ingham ('a senior spokesman') was typically unrepentant: people might 'take some exception to the force with which we put our argument,' he said, 'but we take pride in the accuracy of our briefings'.[13] The Canadian press subsequently dubbed him 'Bernie the Bear'.

After a few years, he came rather to look forward to these

confrontations. 'I expect there'll be the usual trouble,' he said, rubbing his hands, a week before the European Council Meeting in Copenhagen in 1988. '"Blood Lake Beside Black Pudding Mountain" – that kind of thing.'

He presented to the world a curious mixture of aggression and good humour, touchiness and bad grace. In 1989, the Prime Minister flew to Paris for the annual Anglo–French summit, at the conclusion of which there was a press conference in the Elysée Palace. 'I became aware of someone in the row behind me who was muttering and fidgeting,' wrote Patrick Marnham, Paris correspondent of the *Independent*.

> An inspection by my neighbour, Edmund Fawcett of *The Economist*, revealed that this restless, rather distracting person was Mr Bernard Ingham, who seemed to be enjoying himself. Perhaps he was exhilarated by his flying visit to Paris. The last question asked at the press conference was about Camembert cheese. President Mitterand said that all Camembert was excellent and Mr Ingham, in an urgent stage whisper, replied, 'but it can poison you'. I turned to look at him again, he was grinning happily.[14]

Marnham concluded his subsequent report of the press conference with a reference to Ingham's 'unexpected little joke'. His story was published on Tuesday. On Wednesday, the *Independent* carried a letter from Ingham. 'Just for the record,' he wrote, 'I did not say camembert can poison you.' On Thursday, there was a letter from Edmund Fawcett, confirming that he had heard the same remark. On Saturday, Ingham wrote again. 'Let's stop inventing things,' he suggested. The following week, Marnham recounted this curious exchange in the *Spectator* and revealed that he had a third witness up his sleeve, 'a public official' who had been 'seated near Bernard'. Only at this point did Ingham cease his correspondence.

Of course, we were not there. We do not know. But odds of three to one suggest that Ingham did say something of the sort Marnham described. Maybe he had forgotten it. What is revealing is that he should have been so insistent he was right, so determined to have the last word, that he ended up drawing attention to something which would otherwise have passed unnoticed. He seemed to have got matters out of proportion.

Several observers put this marked and increasing sensitivity of Ingham down to the length of time he had been in Downing Street. 'If you have a close relationship with the Prime Minister,' said Joe Haines, describing his own experience at Number 10, 'you have an enormous influence, and that influence is corrupting. You don't brook argument. You've made up your mind. You're a busy man and you don't want people arguing with you. I think it's affected Bernard as it would affect most people who do that job.' There is an additional danger, peculiar to public relations, of staying in the same post too long. One head of PR for a large corporation expressed it as follows: after a couple of years, 25 per cent of the journalists he dealt with had written something so hostile he felt they had personally let him down; for Ingham, whom he knew well, he assessed that figure, after a decade, at 90 per cent. At that point, he argued, a suspicion that everyone was up to no good – a 'bunker mentality' – was the inevitable result.

'A lot of people say that I have a contempt for journalism,' Ingham told one reporter in 1987. 'I don't.'[15] But in truth, both in his private and public remarks, he expressed an almost constant contempt for the profession with which he had to deal on a daily basis. Reporters, to pick only a few of the insults he had flung at them over recent years, were smug, self-satisfied, arrogant, gossip-infected conspiracy theorists. Naturally, given his temperament, he could not keep this prejudice to himself. It kept spilling over into his work as Government spokesman.

On 6 May 1988 he met the Lobby correspondents of the Sunday press for one of his regular, Friday afternoon briefings. The row over the Thames Television documentary, *Death on the Rock* (about the SAS's killing of three unarmed IRA terrorists in Gibraltar) was at its height. Ingham had been furious about the programme, which had uncovered fresh evidence suggesting that the unarmed IRA gang had been, effectively, executed. Now he told the assembled journalists that the British media was just 'a form of institutionalized hysteria'. The following morning, the *Observer*'s political correspondent, Victor Smart, rang Ingham at home to check he had heard correctly. Ingham confirmed the words and added more: 'There is nothing wrong with the British media that a renewed respect for facts, objectivity and fairness, rather than the false gods of invention and malice, would not cure.' And that, he said, was on the record. Smart was slightly amazed. A few minutes later, he rang him back. Did he mean that those words could be attributed to him in his capacity as Chief Press Secretary? Yes, Ingham confirmed, they could.

This was a story in itself. But there was more. The press had also been told that Friday by Ingham (unattributably) that the Prime Minister felt that broadcasters should be reminded of their responsibilities; that they operated within society and were obliged to uphold its institutions, notably legal proceedings. Emanating from the Home Office that same weekend were reports that the Home Secretary would be seeking an early meeting with the BBC and the IBA. Taken together with Ingham's unprecedented action in going on the record at an off-the-record briefing, it suggested a concerted Government campaign against the media. The *Observer* reported it as such.

Ingham's remarks caused an immediate controversy.

Labour MPs denounced him as a creature of the Conservative Party. 'I was trying to start a debate,' he was reported as saying in the *Guardian* the following morning. 'It is a free society and people are entitled to write what they want, but the Government for its part is entitled to express a view on the media.' Once again, it seemed, for Ingham, 'the Government' had become interchangeable with the personal pronoun. To his chagrin, he found that more attention was being paid to his brief comments than was being given to an entire interview with Mrs Thatcher published exclusively in that morning's *Sunday Times*. He had committed the unpardonable sin of distracting attention from his employer. He threatened to have nothing more to do with Smart. With the editor of the *Observer*, after an initial, hectoring phone call the moment its first edition came out, he began a detailed correspondence about the exact context of his remarks, placing copies of his letters in the House of Commons Press Gallery.

The Sunday Lobby, in fact, was to prove a particular bane in Ingham's life. His remarks to it in January 1985 had been followed by a three cents drop in the value of sterling. His accusation about the media's 'institutionalized hysteria' had caused him problems in May 1988. That November, his handling of it was once again to land him in trouble – perhaps his most serious error of all, apart from the leaking of the Solicitor-General's letter.

I should perhaps confess here that I was a member of this subsection of the Lobby myself throughout 1987 and 1988. It was a curious business. We would gather in the entrance hall of Number 10 every Friday afternoon, just before a quarter to three. A charming lady named Rose would come and collect us. We would leave the hall, turn right and right again, and be ushered into Bernard's office. (Everyone called him Bernard.)

He would usually be settled in his mustard-coloured arm-chair, next to his desk, with his back to the window, waiting to receive us. The door to the safe in one corner of the room sometimes stood tantalizingly ajar. We would settle ourselves in chairs around the room. Rose would bring in tea – cups and saucers for the journalists, a mug for Bernard. We would begin.

It is important to appreciate that these were not 'briefings' in any formal sense. They were chats. 'What about so-and-so?' someone might begin. 'Is the Prime Minister worried?' 'Naooh,' Bernard would growl. 'Dammit, we've got more important things to bother about than that.' Across the blank notebooks, a dozen pens would begin to move. He might be gruffly monosyllabic. He might pound the arm of his chair. He might laugh – a noisy, gurgling chuckle, marginally more disconcerting even than his barks of disapproval. 'What about the Exchange Rate Mechanism?' a reporter might ask. 'Who cares about that?' 'Well, Geoffrey Howe made a speech –' 'I can assure you they are not discussing the Exchange Rate Mechanism in the Two Ferrets at Hebden Bridge.' His language was a strange, old-fashioned blend of the colloquial and the formal: 'You may come again, if I may say so.' His oaths were also slightly antique: 'By Jove! ... Dammit! ... Bunkum and balderdash!' Sometimes, if the spirit moved him, he would launch into a five- or six-minute monologue, laced with his own, homespun philosophy: 'One of the troubles with people today, if I may say so ...' Gradually, the pens would cease to move. He was off.

It was often impossible, in this torrent of Yorkshire grit, to work out which were Ingham's opinions and which were Mrs Thatcher's. This enabled him to plant stories which were neither true nor false, but inhabited some grey area in between. For example, when Bernard had a rant about the hypocrisy of highly-paid National Health Service consultants protesting about NHS cuts, several papers carried stories along the lines of 'Maggie to Move Against "Greedy" Doctors'. She never did; probably she never had any intention of doing so; but the headline served as a useful reminder to the British Medical Association that it should watch its step. (In the summer of 1989, he hinted that the Prime Minister was unhappy about the large salary increase awarded to Lord King by British Airways: King subsequently inquired anxiously of her if this was true; she placed her hands on his shoulders, looked him in the eye and told him not to be 'silly'.) Nobody complained about this bizarre style of news dissemination, for the very good reason that it often provided good copy. The point about Bernard was that he was so aggressively opinionated, there was always the chance he would say something usable. God, how our hearts would slip into our boots on those Friday afternoons when we walked in to find he was not there and his deputy, the lugubrious Mr Perks, was sitting in his chair.

The potential for error, for misinterpretation, for reading too much into too little or of missing something altogether, was obviously immense. One of the strangest aspects of Ingham's fulminations against the media was his repeated condemnation of speculation and the press's reliance on the words 'may' and 'could':

The average newspaper, shorn of all stories carrying these invaluable technical aids – invaluable because they at once permit the wire of possibility to be stretched to its twanging limit without actually breaking the journalist's protection – would look like a moth-eaten rag ... these words 'may' and 'could' are also symptomatic of a journalism which manufactures news in a different way – by interpretation and comment. It is now often far more difficult for the reader of the average newspaper to determine what was actually said or done than it is to discover the reporter's interpretation of what was said or done.[16]

But this, as Donald Maitland concluded twenty years ago, is precisely what the Lobby system is all about. Nods and winks, kite-flying and speculation are the stock in trade of a system which is non-attributable. Ingham seemed to want to have it both ways. When the headline was wrong and did not suit his purposes ('Thatcher ready to let £1 equal $1'), he complained; when it was wrong but did suit him ('Maggie to Move Against "Greedy" Doctors') he said nothing.

Over the past few years, the Sunday Lobby has proved a particularly tricky device to handle. There is less political news around at the weekend. Consequently, the journalists who attend briefings, Ingham's or anyone else's, are always keen to find something – and if they find it, their papers are likely to give it greater prominence than it might have enjoyed had it emerged mid-week. For the person giving the briefing, this presents both a tremendous opportunity and a terrible danger. On Friday 4 November 1988, Nigel Lawson met the Sunday press in Number 11 Downing Street to offer non-attributable 'guidance' on his Autumn Statement. The result was an expensive disaster for the Treasury. Virtually every Sunday paper came away with the same impression and ran the same story: that the Government was considering means-testing benefits for the elderly. Mr Lawson gave an interview the following Monday, admitting the existence of the briefing and denouncing the reporters as liars. He was then challenged to produce the tape recording which his press officer had been seen making at the time. The Treasury, to its great embarrassment, reported that the tape was missing. Mr Lawson's explanation for the misunderstanding was that when he talked about 'targeting', he had actually meant extra benefits, not fewer. Without the tape, the only way he could convince

Parliament he was telling the truth was to put his money where his mouth had been. The cost to the Exchequer was estimated at some £200 million.

Ingham could be forgiven for deriving a certain grim satisfaction from this particular incident. He had been abroad with the Prime Minister at the time of Lawson's briefing. No blame attached to him. Indeed, the incident proved his point: if the Treasury, like the Foreign Office, insisted on appointing ordinary civil servants to run their press relations, there was bound to be a cock-up. Now Lawson, the man who had reprimanded him over his sterling briefing in 1985, had had a briefing blow up in his face. When the battered Sunday political correspondents trooped into Downing Street the following week, Ingham merely shook his head and grinned: 'Don't come looking to me for sympathy.'

The Friday after that, 18 November, I was away on holiday and missed Ingham's briefing. On the Sunday morning I glanced at the *Observer*'s front page on a Paris news stand. The headline was 'Thatcher: No, Your Majesty', over a report stating that the Prime Minister would not let the Queen visit Russia. A good story. I looked at the *Sunday Times*: 'Queen can't go to Russia – Thatcher'. I rifled through the stack of British papers. 'Queen to be told: don't visit Russia' (the *Sunday Telegraph*); 'Queen told to call off Russia visit' (the *Mail on Sunday*); 'NIET Snub Russia, Maggie Will urge Queen' (the *Sunday Mirror*). All were quoting 'Government sources'. All had the same tale to tell. There could be no doubt as to its origin. *Now* what was Bernard up to?

Relations between Buckingham Palace and 10 Downing Street are sensitive at the best of times, but they had been particularly delicate during Margaret Thatcher's premiership. As long ago as 1982 there had been authoritative reports that the two women did not get on and that the Queen 'dreaded' her weekly audiences with Mrs Thatcher.[17] In 1986, a Buckingham Palace press officer had given a briefing to the *Sunday Times* in which he spoke of the Queen's worries about the handling of the miners' strike and her 'misgivings' over the bombing of Libya. The monarch was said to be 'very much to the left on social issues' and concerned that the Thatcher Government was 'not caring enough'. There were clear disagreements between them over sanctions and the role of the Commonwealth. All in all: a minefield.

In response, the Prime Minister brought to her dealings with the Sovereign an almost oriental formality and discretion. Nobody curtsied lower or more deferentially. She made a point of turning up at the Palace for her weekly audience fifteen minutes early. With her inner circle, she might pass a comment or two on a minor royal, 'but when it comes to the Queen,' said an intimate, 'not a whisper'.

As it happened, by the middle of November, a new 'Queen versus Thatcher' story was already beginning to circulate in Westminster. On the 11th, the Queen had attended a dinner hosted by the Speaker of the House of Commons. Labour had just lost the Glasgow Govan by-election to the Scottish Nationalists. Her Majesty put this down to the voters' poverty. 'They have got nothing,' she is supposed to have remarked, adding, somewhat Antoinettishly, 'I know, because I have sailed *Britannia* there.'

The *Sunday Express* was preparing to run this story as an 'exclusive' when Ingham met the Sunday Lobby on the 18th. The Govan by-election was not mentioned. Instead, the journalists had a different question about the Queen, based on reports coming out of Moscow: given the new spirit of *glasnost* and *perestroika*, would she soon be paying a state visit to the Soviet Union?

Ingham did not say 'no', but he launched into a long monologue about the difficulties a visit would pose which left the reporters in no doubt about Downing Street's position. 'It came pouring out, with very little prompting from us,' one journalist recalled. 'All this stuff about the murder of the Tsar, cousin of the Royal Family, and so on. He was clearly getting over a view he wanted got over.' Ingham talked of the 'butchering' of the Romanovs, of how 'constitutionalists' might be offended by a visit, of the dangers of seeming to 'reward' the Soviet regime with a stamp of royal approval before it had made sufficient concessions on disarmament and human rights ... Ingham's answer filled six pages in one reporter's notebook. They all knew, even as they were taking it down, that this had the makings of another row. 'Here we go again,' whispered one Lobby veteran.

What followed, from Mrs Thatcher's point of view, could scarcely have been worse. Advice tendered by the Prime Minister to the Sovereign is highly confidential. Yet here it was, plastered all over the press. Worse, the stories appeared to confirm the damaging rumours that the Prime Minister saw herself as superior to the Queen, treating her as a glorified roving ambassador to be dispatched hither and thither as she saw fit.

The briefing burst that weekend over a bewildered Foreign Office and Buckingham Palace. An FO official claimed that, 'from a political point of view, there would be quite a lot of merit in a royal trip'.[18] One of the Queen's press officers believed 'the historic problem of the murder ... would not necessarily stand in the way of a visit'.[19]

Ingham was in trouble. On Monday, lest anyone was in any doubt, the non-Lobby papers named him as the source of the stories. On Tuesday, from his vantage point in the Commons Press Gallery, he watched the Prime Minister uncharacteristically thrown off balance by an intervention from the Labour MP Dennis Skinner who demanded to know why she was 'stopping the Queen from going to Russia'. Mrs

Thatcher, obviously flustered, replied (in the royal plural) that 'we do not discuss this matter. The matter has not been addressed in any way at all.'[20] The Labour benches dissolved into disbelieving laughter. Neil Kinnock demanded to know how she could reconcile this assertion with Ingham's briefing. Three senior Labour Privy Councillors and twenty-seven MPs put down an Early Day Motion demanding a statement.

That night, in the words of the Court Circular, Mrs Thatcher 'had an audience of Her Majesty'. Most unusually, Buckingham Palace discreetly let it be known that the Prime Minister had apologized for the briefing. The *Daily Telegraph* carried an editorial entitled 'Damaging Gaffe' about the regrettable breach of confidentiality: 'for an official to commit such a breach was an impertinence . . . A bad day's work.'[21]

We do not know what transpired between Mrs Thatcher and her Chief Press Secretary, but we can guess. To his colleagues, he appeared terribly low. There were rumours in Fleet Street that he was about to resign. He rang the organizer of the Sunday Lobby to complain that his identity as the source had been leaked. 'I feel very fed up,' he said. When the political correspondents arrived for their briefing that Friday, he could barely bring himself to say a word. 'I am not prepared to speculate to this Lobby in the future,' he declared. The reporters were back on the pavement within fifteen minutes.

However aggrieved Ingham might have felt, he had nobody to blame but himself. He had seen some official correspondence, or heard the Prime Minister talk, or both, and decided, probably on his own initiative, to pre-empt any invitation from the Soviet government. It was, to say the least, a hamfisted way to send a message to the Russians. Ingham had always claimed he was no Machiavelli. Incidents of this sort certainly went a long way towards acquitting him of that charge.

But if his enemies within the Government and outside it thought this marked the beginning of the end for Ingham, they reckoned without the Prime Minister. It was like the sterling disaster of 1985; just as Mrs Thatcher went out of her way to demonstrate her loyalty to him then, so she did now. Ingham was about to confound his critics and bounce back with greater power than ever.

TEN

Minister of Information

'There may be many complaints levelled, justifiably or unjustifiably, against the Government Information Service; but one there is not: party political partiality. Our independence, our ability to transcend party . . . is one of the peculiar strengths of our system.'

BERNARD INGHAM, ADDRESS TO THE IBA, 1981

'A code of ethics is essential . . . to protect those members who are expected to expound untruths on behalf of the Government, produce dodgy material or leak documents in the Government interest.'

MEMBER OF THE GOVERNMENT INFORMATION SERVICE, SPEECH TO THE CONFERENCE OF THE INSTITUTE OF PROFESSIONAL CIVIL SERVANTS, 1988

In February 1988 the new Secretary to the Cabinet and Head of the Home Civil Service, Sir Robin Butler, received a disturbing letter from Ingham's old friend and colleague, the Director-General of the COI, Neville Taylor.

For forty years, the COI had been responsible for all Government advertising. But in 1987, thanks chiefly to pressure from Lord Young, Whitehall departments (to use their euphemism) had been 'untied'. They were now free to hire private companies to handle their publicity and marketing. Taylor had watched with mounting unease as the Government's spending on advertising and promotion had proceeded to triple. Much of this expenditure was devoted to persuading the public to buy shares in the old nationalized industries. Most of the rest went into campaigns. Some of these, like the health warnings about Aids, were straightforward public information. Some, however, seemed slightly more dubious, both politically and in terms of value for money.

For example, as Secretary of State for Trade and Industry, Lord Young had called in the design consultancy Wolff Olins to give the DTI a new logo. It was now, apparently, the 'Department for Enterprise'. There was also Young's 'Enterprise Initiative' (cost: £7 million), ostensibly launched to remind companies about various aid schemes, but with the obvious additional message that this was a Government for free enterprise. Other, equally questionable 'initiatives' were being planned by other, equally ambitious ministers, who realized they, too, could spend millions promoting their achievements to the electorate. Suddenly, for advertising agencies, PR consultants and marketing firms, the once notoriously parsimonious Whitehall beckoned like a second Klondyke. By 1988 it was outspending even such industrial giants as Unilever.

Taylor put up with it for a year. Eventually, tired of being told to stop interfering, he took his concerns direct to the Cabinet Office. He threatened resignation. He demanded a full-scale inquiry into what he saw as both a waste and an abuse of taxpayers' money. Butler agreed. This review was about to begin when, in March, Taylor had a serious heart attack. Ingham – who had supported his stand, on the grounds that here were more bloody amateurs interfering in the professionals' business – sent him a large bunch of flowers in hospital with the message 'Love from Bernard'.

Gradually, it became apparent that Taylor, who was lucky to survive, would not be returning to his old post. As a consequence, the review subtly broadened in scope to consider the whole future of the COI. On 28 July, the Cabinet Office circulated a letter on the future of Government publicity which clearly had been drawn up in consultation with Ingham. This effectively reduced the COI to little more than a services agency. Henceforth, the Treasury would be the final arbiter on matters relating to value for money; the Cabinet Office ultimately would rule on the 'propriety' of individual campaigns. But for all practical purposes, in the words of the letter:

> The principal source of advice to Ministers and Heads of Department in this field is the Departmental Head of Information. Heads of Department should ensure that the Head of Information always has sufficient opportunity to advise on proposals for paid publicity . . .[1]

The Heads of Information, of course, reported through the MIO to Ingham.

All that was necessary now was to dispose of the last important outpost of the ailing Taylor's empire. That happened six months later. On 9 February 1989, eleven weeks after the controversy over the Queen's visit to Moscow, it was formally announced that Ingham was to be made Head of Profession for all Government Information Officers.

The evolution of bureaucracies is dry stuff. It excites the interest of historians rather than journalists. So perhaps it is not surprising that the news of Ingham's promotion produced not a ripple in Parliament. The press barely mentioned it. Yet it was much more significant than most of the episodes which had caused so many storms. What had happened was without precedent. Ingham now had four separate functions. He was the Prime Minister's personal media adviser. He was the non-attributable spokesman for the entire Government. He had responsibility for the 'recruitment, training and career development' of 1,200 information officers. He co-ordinated an advertising and publicity budget of some £168 million. In any other country he would have been given the proper title: Minister of Information. The appointment also represented a further, significant centralization of power in the hands of the Prime Minister: unlike the Director-General of the COI, Ingham, through the Head of the Home Civil Service, was responsible to her alone. In 1983, Mrs Thatcher had told David Owen: 'I do not have and have never had any intention or plan to centralize control of Government Information in 10 Downing Street, and I have no plans to extend the responsibilities of my Chief Press Secretary.' Now she had done both.

It had happened through a combination of Ingham's ambition and poor Neville Taylor's ailing heart. First, Ingham had utilized his chairmanship of the MIO, neglected by his predecessors, to 'co-ordinate' Government information. Then, when his attempt to widen his role was blocked, he had ensured that the COI's Director-Generalship was given to an ally. The status of his own post as Downing Street Press Secretary had been raised, along with his salary; his right to advise on appointments formalized. Finally, when the chance came for the COI to be broken up, he had made sure he was there to pick up the important pieces. Power had come to him, in part, simply because he had been around so long.

One did not have to be one of Ingham's despised conspiracy theorists to see the implications of this. Under the rules of the Civil Service, restated by Sir Robert Armstrong in 1985, officials owe their allegiance 'first and foremost' to the minister for whom they work. But information officers have a dual loyalty. Their careers were now to a large extent determined by the Prime Minister's Press Secretary. What did they do if their minister wished to go one way and Number 10 another? And when they were called in to advise their ministers, whose advice was it that they were passing on: their own, or the line laid down by Ingham at the MIO? Ingham, in Neville Taylor's words, had an 'open line' into every department, down which he could both speak – and listen:

> The Press Secretary at Number 10 can find out what is planned to be said – action, proposals, policies and so on – every day and umpteen times during the day merely by picking up the phone and saying 'Neville, what's your Secretary of State up to?' Perhaps no formal paper has gone anywhere. The Prime Minister is unlikely to pick up the phone. The Private Secretary's a bit wary about it because it's a more formal channel. The better the contact between the Press Secretary and the Heads of Information, the better informed Number 10 is.

By 1989, at least one Cabinet Minister was telling his special adviser not to talk too openly in front of the Department's Chief Information Officer: the person concerned had once been Ingham's deputy at Number 10. Indeed, it has become difficult to find a departmental head of information who has not worked for Ingham at some stage. His contacts are equally good further down the chain of command. By the end of 1985, he could boast that fifty Whitehall press officers had served at Number 10 on a six-week or two-month attachment. By the end of 1990, that figure had risen to almost 100. His judgements of people, in Taylor's opinion, tended to be 'a bit quirky':

> Whereas most of us come to a view over a long period of time, balancing one thing against another, Bernard's views on most things are both extreme and simplistic. All his geese are swans. People are either 'no bloody good' or 'possibly alright' or 'brilliant'. Everybody fits into one of three categories. All the

people who have ever worked for him, whom he selected, are marvellous – not one single failure among them. People who haven't worked for him, it's: 'Never heard of him. If they're any good, why didn't they come to Number 10?'

This raises longer-term questions. No Chief Press Secretary has ever stayed on at Number 10 beyond the term of the Prime Minister they served; rarely is there even a transition period. They leave Downing Street on the same day as their employers. For that reason, none of Ingham's predecessors had even sought, let alone been offered, the post of Head of the Government Information Service: first, they recognized they were not in a position to take a detached, long-term view of the profession; secondly, they were, by the nature of their work, seen as the partisan agents of a particular Prime Minister.

These reservations applied to Ingham with peculiar force. Few Press Secretaries had been as closely identified with their Prime Ministers as he had with Thatcher. An incoming Labour government might be forgiven for regarding an information service recruited by him as stuffed with like-minded people. In 1987, for example, one of Ingham's assistants, Christine Wall, had gone directly from Downing Street to work full-time for Conservative Central Office; another member of the Government Information Service, Alex Pagett, had moved across to work for the Scottish Tory Party.

In the past, this would not have mattered. But now, because of the virtual destruction of the COI, a new government would be in a position to act on any suspicions. A precedent had been established, of control from Number 10. In 1974, Joe Haines's first action on re-entering Downing Street had been to purge the Press Office of anyone whose loyalty he suspected. A future Joe Haines would inherit responsibility for the careers of more than 1,000 men and women across

Whitehall. The purge could grow in proportion. Sir Robin Butler, custodian of the flame of Civil Service neutrality, was well aware of the danger, discussed it with ministers, and floated the idea that Ingham should give up the Chief Press Secretary's job to concentrate on being Head of Profession. The Prime Minister would not hear of it.

Ingham regarded such fears as so much twaddle. Two months after his appointment, in April 1989, he received a letter from the information officers' trade union, the Institute of Professional Civil Servants (IPCS). This enclosed a draft 'code of ethics', drawn up after their last conference had heard first-hand reports of life inside the GIS. Peter Cook, a press officer at the Department of Employment, claimed that he and his colleagues had been 'put under increasing pressure from ministers to work on projects which at best can be described as favourably disposed towards Government policies and at worst blatantly party political'. They had been required to write 'articles of a party political nature on behalf of their ministers for insertion in the press', and he gave examples of dubious campaigns, such as Action for Jobs 'which said little about the Department of Employment's services but much about the Conservative Party's views on unemployment and the unemployed'. Peter Dupont, an official at the COI, had called for a code of ethics 'to protect those members who are expected to expound untruths on behalf of the Government, produce dodgy material or leak documents in the Government's interest'.

The IPCS's suggested guidelines were fairly innocuous: for example, that it was 'the responsibility of Information Officers in the Government Service to describe and explain Government policies; it is not their function to justify or defend them'; that 'Information Officers in Government Service should avoid identification with the political philosophy of any particular administration' and that 'Information

Officers in Government Service shall not distort or suppress information for reasons of political expediency, advertising or sponsorship.' The wording was based on evidence from Lord Bancroft, former Head of the Home Civil Service, to the House of Commons Treasury Select Committee.

Ingham, however, seemed to take it as a personal affront. He sent a copy of the code with a covering note to Robin Butler. 'I propose to give the letter short shrift,' he wrote. 'It is outrageous that the IPCS gave the letter to the media – the Press Association, I understand – even before I had the opportunity to consider it. I think I should make it clear I do not intend to conduct business with them on this basis.' He wrote back to the union refusing even to discuss it. This remained his public stance on the issue. When, in his new role as Head of Profession, he held a recruitment seminar at a hotel in York, he discovered that the proceedings had been gate-crashed by a reporter and photographer from the *Mail on Sunday*, wearing buttonholes and posing as wedding guests. 'Bugger off!' he yelled at them. 'And if you want it on the record: Sod off!'[2]

How did he find the time? That was what his current and former colleagues found so puzzling. In the words of one retired senior civil servant: 'Here we are, in the middle of this supposedly wonderful managerial revolution in Whitehall, and what do we do? We put in charge of 1,200 people, overseeing the expenditure of millions of pounds, a part-time itinerant spokesman . . . '

Certainly, Ingham did not neglect the traditional aspects of his work. One minute he was busying himself with the appointment of the new Director of Public Affairs at the Metropolitan Police, the next he was telling the Lobby that the reports that Kenneth Baker was to be appointed Conservative Party Chairman were 'fevered speculation'. He was closely involved in setting the scene for Mrs Thatcher's 1989 Cabinet reshuffle. The Prime Minister was determined to shift Sir Geoffrey Howe from the Foreign Office and Ingham discreetly prepared the ground. When, in July, the BBC's *Nine o'Clock News* carried a report that Howe and Nigel Lawson would not be moved, he was on the telephone within five minutes, demanding to know of the Corporation's political editor, John Cole, whether he had a better reading of the Prime Minister's mind than her Chief Press Secretary.

Despite such indications, Howe failed to spot the scaffold which was being erected for him. On 24 July, the Prime Minister summoned him to Number 10 and offered him the Home Secretaryship. He refused and, after consulting with his friends, came up with a veritable shopping list of demands as the price of his departure from the Foreign Office: Leader of the House of Commons, Lord President of the Council, the chairmanship of various Cabinet committees, a house in the country, and – crucially – the title of Deputy Prime Minister. Only on these terms would he remain in the Government. He had too strong a following in the party to be sacked outright. Mrs Thatcher, reluctantly, gave him what he wanted. Her technique, as usual, when confronted by such disloyalty, was to pay lip service to the proprieties in public and unleash Ingham in private. The following day, Howe was blackjacked at the eleven o'clock Lobby briefing. The title of Deputy Prime Minister, previously awarded to Lord Whitelaw in recognition of his special role in the Government, had, Ingham asserted 'no significance'. It did not mean automatically that Howe would be sent for by the Queen in the event of Mrs Thatcher's political or bodily demise. It did not mean he would be in charge at home when the Prime Minister was abroad: given the effectiveness of modern communications, she would remain in control at all times.

Constitutionally and technically, this was no doubt correct.

But it was also clearly intended as a signal that Mrs Thatcher had given Howe nothing of substance. Once again, the press reports the next day left nobody in any doubt that Ingham was the source of this 'guidance'. 'Government sources,' reported *The Times*, 'emphasized that the title of Deputy Prime Minister is a "courtesy".' The *Daily Telegraph* used the same phrase:

> While Sir Geoffrey was insisting that he would continue to have an important influence on Government policies at home and abroad, those close to Mrs Thatcher were describing the role of Deputy Prime Minister as a 'courtesy title' with no constitutional status.

The *Daily Mail* was more blunt:

> Whitehall sources firmly refused yesterday to confirm the claim that Sir Geoffrey had been offered the Home Office. Meanwhile, his new role has already been downgraded by Downing Street. It was suggested that the titles he has acquired are constitutional fiction – and in any case the Prime Minister does not think they matter.

This was a brutal way to treat the Cabinet's most senior member, and Howe never really recovered from it: he resigned fifteen months later with his authority in tatters. David Howell described Ingham's briefing as 'nauseating and intolerable.'[3] That was the general feeling. When Howe made his first appearance as Leader of the House, he was greeted by more than a minute of cheering from the Tory benches – an unprecedented display of support, and a clear signal to Thatcher and Ingham.

The Prime Minister, characteristically, took no notice. When, on 25 October, Nigel Lawson told her of his dramatic decision to resign as Chancellor of the Exchequer, she did not even bother to let Howe, her supposed 'deputy', know what was happening. The only advisers she consulted were Charles Powell and Bernard Ingham. Many in her own party were now frankly critical of her obvious reliance on these two unelected officials. She was said to be isolated in Number 10. Her judgement was going. She treated her colleagues with contempt. 'One way to restore confidence in Cabinet government,' proclaimed Sir Barney Hayhoe, a former minister, 'would be to have Bernard Ingham and Charles Powell moved to quieter pastures before the end of this year. Such a signal would be welcomed by her ministerial colleagues as well as by back-bench members.'[4] Lord Hailsham, the former Lord Chancellor, went further. Ingham, he said, had been used 'unscrupulously on occasions' to undermine ministers. 'This is dishonourable conduct towards colleagues.' (Later, questioned about Hailsham's remark in the Commons, the Prime Minister declared herself 'very surprised that he made it. It is totally untrue.')[5]

In the wake of his departure from the Treasury, Mr Lawson, too, grumbled to his friends about Ingham's behaviour. That November, he bumped into a prominent left-wing columnist in the cloakroom of the Savoy and told him that if he wanted a good topic, he should write about 'the use of black propaganda by Number 10'. Whether he meant the Press Office or some other persons, he did not say.

What did Ingham care? His position went from strength to strength. In November 1989, he was promoted to Deputy Secretary, the third highest rank in the Civil Service. In February 1990, he unleashed another of his tirades against the media, the first since that memorable night in Stationers' Hall at the height of the Westland crisis. 'I sometimes compare press officers to riflemen on the Somme,' he told a Press Gallery luncheon, 'mowing down wave upon wave of distortion and taking out rank upon rank of supposition, deduction and gossip, while laying down a barrage of facts behind which something approximating to the truth might advance.' He trotted out his familiar compendium of journalists' diseases – the Le Carré syndrome, the Conan Doyle complication, the Coleman/Carpenter phenomenon – and something he called 'separatitis':

> its symptoms are an insistent, and some would say unreasoning assumption of rights to the exclusion of all responsibilities. An unshakeable belief in the media's entitlement to lead a privileged existence which sets its practitioners apart from, and above, the ordinary mortals on whom they depend for their livelihood, protection and security. A conviction that whatever they do is sanctified by the blessed state of freedom which they enjoy.

'Somehow, dammit, we rub along,' he concluded. 'But I think it would help at times if some of you weren't so blessed precious.'[6] Afterwards, he agreed to grant the BBC his first radio interview. The following morning, the nation awoke to hear, for the first time, the gravelly tones of the Prime Minister's Chief Press Secretary talking about 'the conspiracy theory which, I think, motivates journalism as a craft'. The interview included this memorable exchange:

> INTERVIEWER: And the electronic media?
> INGHAM: Oh, you've got to accept your share of the blame, too.
> INTERVIEWER: What's the electronic media's share of the blame? Where are we guilty?
> INGHAM: Well, you suffer from the diseases of journalists. Dammit, you're journalists aren't you?
> INTERVIEWER: You don't feel, then, that the electronic news medium in Britain is trying to maintain an independent report of what is happening in Britain?

INGHAM: I think it *thinks* it's trying to maintain that.

INTERVIEWER: What of the view, though, the other side of this, that journalists might believe the Government *is* up to something, that it –

INGHAM: Well, you're now proving my point.

INTERVIEWER: Even by asking the question?

INGHAM: Yes.[7]

'Bernard's behaving like a second-term president,' said one of Mrs Thatcher's former advisers who heard the broadcast. Ingham had achieved all he wanted. He was going to say what he liked. He had nothing to lose.

Outspokenness in public was matched by an equally combative style in Whitehall, where he patrolled the walls of his newly-built empire, alert to any potential encroachment. He always kept one eye open for Tim Bell, the self-advertising advertising executive and Prime Ministerial favourite. Bell had advised the National Coal Board on public relations during the miners' strike of 1984, and Ingham had been infuriated by the abrupt dismissal of his friend, Geoff Kirk, who had been handling the industry's press relations since Ingham's days on the *Yorkshire Post*.[8] The following year, Lord Young had wanted to dispense with his information officer at the Employment Department. 'But she had been recommended by Bernard Ingham,' recalled Young, 'who had always been very helpful to me. I had no wish to upset him.'[9] Bell had come up with the solution: an employee of his named Howell James, who had handled PR for Capital Radio and TV-am, became Young's 'Special Adviser'. In 1987, Young had taken another Bell man, Peter Luff, to do the same job at the DTI. Now, in 1990, with the Government experiencing 'presentational difficulties', who should step forward to assist but the ever-present, ever-helpful Mr Bell.

He suggested to Kenneth Baker that certain key ministers

should employ outside public relations advisers to improve their 'media profiles'. He volunteered himself to take on the challenging task of improving the image of the Home Secretary, David Waddington. Ingham read of the scheme in the *Independent on Sunday* on 29 April. He had wrecked it within thirty-six hours. On Monday afternoon he sent a memorandum to all Heads of Information in Whitehall, gleefully describing what he had done. It provided a telling glimpse of Ingham in action, and of his power to call even Cabinet ministers to heel:

> As Head of the Government Information Service, I telephoned Mr Kenneth Baker, Chancellor of the Duchy of Lancaster, this morning about the reported appointment of Public Relations Minders to three Cabinet Ministers: Home Secretary – Tim Bell; Kenneth Clarke [Health Secretary] – John Banks; John MacGregor [Education Secretary] – Robin Wight.
>
> I said I was doing so in response to serious concern which had been expressed to me by Heads of Information, especially as there seemed to be the possibility of further appointments.
>
> I said we needed to deal with this issue immediately in order to prevent damage to the GIS. The announcement of the appointments, made without any consultation with the Heads of Information concerned, was seen as a grave reflection on the competence of the GIS – indeed as an insult to it.
>
> The GIS had and, I was sure, would continue to do its level best for the government of the day.
>
> But it was inevitably getting a lot of flak these days and this kind of episode would be damaging of its morale unless there was proper consultation and explanation.
>
> It was absolutely essential that Ministers and Messers Bell, Banks and Wight handled the GIS with kid gloves, given the circumstances of their appointment.
>
> Mr Baker regretted the publicity and said no announcement

had been made. It had leaked out . . . He was sorry if it was felt the appointments, and the manner in which the appointments had become public, reflected on the competence of the GIS. That had not been the intention and it did not reflect the view in which the GIS was held.

I said that we needed to dispel that impression immediately. I asked him to make it clear to all inquirers – and to the GIS – that these were party appointments and did not and were not intended to reflect upon the competence and abilities of the GIS. Mr Baker agreed to do this.

I strongly urge you to communicate these sentiments to your Permanent Secretaries and to deploy them as necessary with your Ministers.[10]

No more was heard of Mr Baker's scheme. Ingham's memo was published in the following week's *Mail on Sunday*. No leak inquiry was established.

Despite Ingham's new executive powers, business proceeded with the Lobby as before. On 27 June he was reported to have 'erupted in fury' at the four o'clock meeting. He was being asked repeatedly if the Government proposed to apologize to Parliament for having misled it over the sale of Rover to British Aerospace, when he suddenly snapped that he was 'not going to put up with any more of this'. But wasn't it a legitimate matter of public interest? Ingham's reply was emphatic: 'I am not going to grovel before this Lobby!'[11]

Exactly one month later, on 27 July, he met the Sunday Lobby and delivered an unattributable karate chop to the unsuspecting neck of Sir Alan Walters, the man whose back-stairs influence had precipitated the resignation of Nigel Law-son. Sir Alan had published a book, *Sterling in Danger*, attacking the Exchange Rate Mechanism of the European Monetary System. Rather embarrassingly, it had been revealed recently that he was still seeing Mrs Thatcher.

Pressed in the Commons, she had described him as 'a family friend'. But the reporters were left in no doubt that he, too, had now fallen from grace. 'Downing Street hits out at Walters,' said the *Observer*, on 29 July, quoting 'one Downing Street insider' as remarking: 'Alan Walters plays no part here. He can canvass his own views . . . It is all out of the text books. It hasn't been tested.' In the *Sunday Correspondent*, 'a source close to the Prime Minister' called Walters's ideas 'half baked'. 'Walters frozen out by cool Thatcher,' reported the *Sunday Times*, quoting 'senior sources'. In the *Sunday Telegraph* it was 'Cabinet snubs Walters over Europe'; in the *Mail on Sunday*, 'No 10 snub for "friend" Walters' ('Downing Street sources pointedly said Mrs Thatcher had not seen [him] for well over two months . . .').

First Lawson, now Walters: if there was 'black propaganda' from Number 10, it had at least been distributed with an even hand.

That summer, Ingham celebrated his fifty-eighth birthday. It was clear that he would stay with Mrs Thatcher as long as she needed him. He was due to retire in two years' time, at the age of sixty. If she went before then, he admitted openly, he would go, too. Otherwise, his retirement date looked like being conveniently close to the next General Election. His name had been connected with a few jobs outside – editor of the *Yorkshire Post*, head of public relations at the Prudential, a chair in Government Communications at Newcastle University, funded by his old friends in British Nuclear Fuels – but they never amounted to much more than gossip. He talked of writing a book, and several publishers came to see him at Number 10. Lord Weidenfeld was said to be hawking the serialization rights around Fleet Street. But unfortunately, as he made clear to his disappointed visitors, he had kept no diary and claimed to have no intention of writing a kiss-and-tell autobiography. 'It will be an exposition of the job for my successors,' he insisted, 'not a memoir.' Visions of a six-figure advance, which he could have commanded with ease, apparently held no attractions for him – or at least they didn't, until he was actually confronted by them the following year.

In fact, the belief in Westminster by the summer of 1990 was that he was no longer as close to Mrs Thatcher as he had been. It was the view of several witnesses, who were in a position to know, that there had been a decided shift in the balance of power in Number 10. One very highly-placed official, who saw the Prime Minister and her Press Secretary almost every day for some years, believed that gradually, from the mid-1980s, he came to lose his unique place in her affections:

> She certainly trusted him, but she didn't always share with him what she was thinking. I wouldn't have said – although she had a great respect for him – I wouldn't have said he had a relationship with her like that she had with Charles Powell. Powell came to establish a close bond with her, and that changes the relative influence of the others ... Subsequent Principal Private Secretaries have found [Powell] a difficult colleague to cope with. It's a very over-protective relationship.

Influence, as courtiers have found since at least the days of the Pharaohs, is proportionate to access. Ingham's access to Thatcher was great, but it was as nothing compared to that enjoyed by her Private Secretary. Although Powell got off to a slow start when he joined the Prime Minister's staff in 1984, it was no exaggeration, six years later, to say that he saw more of her than any other person, including her husband. He saw her throughout the day in Downing Street. He saw her at night at official receptions and banquets. He attended every talk she had with every visiting foreign leader. He accompanied her on every tour abroad. He and his wife saw the Thatchers socially. They even spent Christmas Day with them at Chequers.

The Inghams were simply not in this league. It was the *Guardian* all over again, with the Jenkins/Powell figure up in the officers' mess and Bernard slaving away below with the poor bloody infantry. A telling demonstration of their relative status was provided in June 1988, when Ronald Reagan paid his farewell visit as President to see Mrs Thatcher. The Powells joined the Reagans, the Thatchers, the Geoffrey Howes and the George Schultzes for the intimate candle-lit dinner; Ingham was left outside to hand out details of the menu to the press.

Powell also established his own links with journalists, separate from Ingham's. On one famous occasion he dined with Conrad Black, owner of the *Daily Telegraph*, and was rumoured to have discussed the political reliability of the paper's editor, Max Hastings. This was trespassing on to the Chief Press Secretary's closely-guarded turf and, not surprisingly, jealousies stirred. What was once a most powerful axis – for a while, the nearest Britain had to a genuine Deputy Prime Minister – was eventually replaced by a well-attested, unmistakable, mutual *froideur*. Such are the squabbles of good and faithful servants.

Crowned with Glory

*'This business of communication is fraught with peril. It is a
wonder I survive. Perhaps I won't . . .'*

BERNARD INGHAM, SPEECH TO CALDER HIGH SCHOOL,
JANUARY 1990

At the beginning of October 1989, the Hebden Lodge Hotel, a
modest establishment on the busy main road of Hebden
Bridge, had a sudden influx of guests from London. There
were so many Heads of Information from Whitehall under
one roof, the manager could have been forgiven for thinking
he had a convention on his hands. In one room were Bernard
and Nancy Ingham; in another, Neville Gaffyn, former Head
of Information at the Department of Education, and his wife,
Jean Caines, Chief Information Officer at the Environment
Department; a third room was occupied by Romola Christo-
pherson, in charge of media relations at the Department of
Health. Eventually, some thirty Government press officers,
many of them clutching mobile telephones, including Brian
Mower and Jim Coe from the Home Office and the Ministry
of Agriculture, were to be seen swarming around the town.
All were friends of Ingham. All had worked for him at
Number 10. All had come north to celebrate his tenth anni-
versary as Chief Press Secretary.

It was a cross between a pilgrimage and a works outing. They ate half a celebratory cake (Ingham had shared the other half with the Prime Minister and her staff in Downing Street earlier in the week). They piled into cars and drove down the narrow lanes to Derek Ingham's farm. They clambered up to a local beauty spot high above the town. 'I hope,' declared Ingham, 'I am not the first and last Chief Press Secretary to conduct his entire world media operation by yuppie phone from the cloud-enveloped balcony of Stoodley Pike.'[1] They saw Nutclough Mill where Ingham's father used to work, now restored by a heritage preservation group and kept as a living museum; the Ebenezer Chapel, where Ingham started out as a journalist, now an antiques centre; and Garnet's beloved Co-operative Society, now converted into a three-star hotel, specializing in parties from America. Gone were the smoking chimneys, the warehouses, the grimy slums. Hebden Bridge, with its pizzerias and its Tourist Information Centre, had changed over the past twenty years nearly as much as its most famous son.

The visit was a remarkable demonstration, both of Ingham's personal hold over the Government Information Service, and of his pride in his old home town. The political correspondents would have loved to have covered it, but they missed it – their attention was concentrated across the Pennines, in Blackpool, where the Conservatives were holding their annual party conference. Ingham, professional to the last, made sure the story went as an exclusive to the *Hebden Bridge Times*. 'Not all his colleagues could attend,' reported his old paper, 'and those overseas sent goodwill messages.' So did Margaret Thatcher.

In retrospect, that tenth anniversary year was the high point for both of them. Before it, Westland apart, their run of successes was extraordinary; after it, the failures multiplied, until eventually the errors and misjudgements made by the

Prime Minister conspired to drag both of them down. First, the economy – the revitalization of which was supposed to be the jewel in the Thatcherite crown – began to go badly wrong. Then, in the spring, the introduction of the poll tax led to a haemorrhaging in support for the Government that was unprecedented in modern political history. In March 1990, the Conservatives lost the Mid-Staffordshire by-election in the biggest swing since 1933. Nationally, Gallup gave Labour its largest-ever lead – 24.5 per cent – and reported that Thatcher was the most unpopular Prime Minister since polling began. 'When things were going well, I used to feel like the goal-keeper for Liverpool,' Ingham is reported to have lamented privately around this time. 'Now I feel like the goalie for Halifax Town.'

If Labour had scored a crushing victory in the local elections that May, Mrs Thatcher might well have faced a full-scale Cabinet revolt over the poll tax, obliging her to resign in the summer. Instead, although Labour won an extra 300 seats, the Conservatives held on to their 'showpiece' London boroughs of Wandsworth and Westminster. Temporarily, at least, the crisis was past, and it was with more than the usual relief that the Government whips greeted the Parliamentary recess that summer. When, a few days later, Iraq invaded Kuwait, the Prime Minister's position appeared impregnable. How could there be a challenge to her leadership when the country was close to war? Her opponents in the Tory Party were despondent. Even she could not blow it now.

But, once again, Margaret Thatcher was to surprise everyone. At the European Community heads of government meeting in Rome, with Ingham at her side, she made her most vigorous attack to date on the whole concept of economic and monetary union. 'No, no, no,' she shouted in the House of Commons on her return. It was a fatal miscalculation. Two days later, aghast at this latest display of anti-Europeanism,

Sir Geoffrey Howe resigned. On 13 November 1990, he made perhaps the most devastating resignation speech in Parliamentary history: carried live on television, with Tory MPs behind him wincing and Mrs Thatcher before him visibly paling, he effectively called for her dismissal. Michael Heseltine announced the following day that he would at last make his long-awaited challenge for the leadership.

It would be absurd to blame Margaret Thatcher's political demise on Bernard Ingham. He was not the cause of the terminal malady. He was, however, one of its symptoms. Like her, he had been around perhaps a couple of years too long. Like her, there was a general feeling that he had grown too big for his boots. And, like her, he seemed to have lost touch with the world beyond the bunker of 10 Downing Street. In retrospect it is clear that his treatment of Sir Geoffrey Howe, in July 1989, was one hostile briefing too many. Howe never really recovered from Ingham's brutal dismissal of his title of Deputy Prime Minister as a mere 'courtesy'. His vengeful resignation, in turn, cleared the way for another man who had experienced Ingham's way of doing business, Michael Heseltine. And Heseltine's leadership campaign was supported, overtly and covertly, by several ex-ministers who nursed grievances of their own against the mighty Chief Press Secretary, among them Nigel Lawson. For Thatcher and Ingham, November 1990 unfolded like a kind of horror film. It was the revenge of the unburied dead.

In the course of the leadership campaign, even some of the Prime Minister's staunchest supporters urged her, as part of the price of restoring confidence in her premiership, to dispense with Ingham's services. 'Mrs Thatcher's exotic triumvirate of Charles Powell, Bernard Ingham and Sir Robin Butler could do with a change,' declared a leader in *The Times* on 20 November. The *Spectator* (edited by Lawson's son, Dominic) was even more emphatic. 'She cannot brook opposition,' the magazine asserted on 17 November; 'in particular she allows Mr Bernard Ingham to rubbish Cabinet colleagues in a way that can be described at best as divisive and at worst as grossly disloyal.' The magazine called upon her to 'appoint a Press Secretary capable of putting the civil back into service'.

But by then it was too late. On Tuesday 20 November, Thatcher and Ingham were in the British Embassy in Paris when the result of the Tory leadership ballot came in, shortly after 6.00 pm. Heseltine had won the support of 152 Tory MPs – two-fifths of those eligible to vote. These, plus the sixteen abstentions, were enough to force a second ballot. It was a shattering blow. Thatcher nevertheless strode down the embassy steps to declare her intention of fighting on. Millions of viewers watching the scene live on television saw Ingham, looking like a granite-jawed bouncer at some northern night club, elbowing journalists aside, demanding: 'Where's the microphone?'

The next day, the Prime Ministerial party returned gloomily to London. Ingham issued one of the last, shortest and (as it turned out) least accurate of the hundreds of press releases he had put out on his mistress's behalf. It consisted of seven words, uttered by Thatcher on the steps of Downing Street. 'I fight on,' it declared. 'I fight to win.' It was hollow bravado. That night, one by one, members of the Cabinet trooped in to see her. Their message was blunt: she could not win a second ballot. Ingham later recounted to a group of businessmen and journalists how he had looked in to see her at 8.45 pm, before leaving Downing Street for home. The Prime Minister, he said, was in tears. 'It's all drifting away,' she told him. His reply – 'Chin up, cheer up, *we're* all behind you anyway' – only produced more tears. He knew then that it was all over. The following morning, he was instructed to release the news of her resignation. Five days later, the leadership of the Conservative Party was won by John Major.

It had long been believed in Whitehall that both Ingham and Charles Powell were too closely identified with Thatcher to serve any other Prime Minister. In the event, Powell stayed on, while Ingham was removed with almost unseemly speed. Major's first appointment, literally, on the night he became leader, was a new Chief Press Secretary: Gus O'Donnell, a 38-year-old economist who had been Major's media adviser at the Treasury. The following week, the last vestiges of Ingham's empire were demolished when the Director-General of the COI was once again made Head of the Government Information Service.

Ingham, effectively unemployed for the first time in seventeen years, at once retreated into purdah in Purley. Within days he was hard at work on his memoirs – a book he had vowed never to write, but for which, on condition that he revealed what it was really like to work with Mrs Thatcher, he was paid more than £100,000. It was provisionally, and wholly characteristically, entitled *Kill the Messenger*. He was offered, and accepted, a knighthood in the Resignation Honours List. There was even, when Albion's identity became known, talk of his writing a new column: not in the *Leeds Weekly Citizen* but in the *Daily Express*.

Four weeks after The Fall, shortly before Christmas 1990, Ingham broke off briefly from his literary activities to give an interview to the Halifax *Evening Courier*. It showed that whatever else had changed, he had not:

> You can't do the job I did without picking up enemies, especially when I refused to take some journalists at their own excessive valuation. It's a good Hebden Bridge trait not to be over-impressed with people and some of those journalists thought they were too damned clever, a load of 'snobocrats' who really resented a lad like me getting the job ... Blaming

me [for Mrs Thatcher's downfall] is just pent-up resentment, jealousy and nastiness overflowing from people who have achieved nothing in their lives apart from making snide comments about those who have. I just have to rest my case on my reputation and I think that's pretty secure.

Looking back, he could think of only three mistakes he had made in eleven years: 'I regret calling John Biffen and Francis Pym names and I wish I had been clearer in my decision not to leak documents during the Westland affair.'[2] (In an interview in the *Mail on Sunday*, he actually claimed that he had been 'trying to defend Pym and Biffen' when he made his famous remarks.[3])

He was asked about his political views. What about Albion? Had he not once loathed the Tory Party? 'I don't think I loathed it,' he replied. 'I just didn't like what it represented. It stood for privilege and I think Mrs Thatcher has changed all that.' He went on:

I'd prefer not to say who I voted for in the eighties. Suffice to say that in my time I've voted for all three parties, nationally and locally. That shows what a free thinker I am.

I think it would be fair to call me a failed politician. I can't think of anything which would have given me more satisfaction than representing my own people.

I don't feel that I have sold out on any political principles. But I plead guilty to total and absolute loyalty to Mrs Thatcher. I'm a supporter of her, not the Tory Party, and the two shouldn't necessarily be equated. After all, they got rid of her.

The country was enormously blessed that at last we had a PM who knew her own mind and cared for the north.

Even in retirement, he continued to serve Margaret Thatcher. He called her 'Prime Minister emeritus'. More than two months after leaving Downing Street, he was still fielding requests for interviews with her, referring to her as 'the PM'.

It was to her that he owed his success. That is not to decry his own achievement. It was his ambition, his determination and his relentless hard work which had lifted him out of Hebden Bridge in the first place, taken him via Halifax and Leeds to London, through Fleet Street and Whitehall to Number 10. He had not buried his talents in the back garden; he had taken them out into the world.

But the unprecedented power and influence which he amassed during his years in Downing Street were entirely due to her. A decade earlier they had struck an unspoken bargain. He gave her most of his waking hours, and his unstinting loyalty. In return, she gave him a free hand with the media, her complete support and an occasional blind eye. The result has been unique in British political history. One day, no doubt, some historian will write an authoritative account of Margaret Thatcher's statecraft: of how she centralized power in Number 10, turning the Cabinet, in the words of one former minister, into a 'rubber stamp', by taking decisions in ad hoc committees with like-minded colleagues; of how she exploited the fact that she had to answer for the entire Government at Prime Minister's Questions to enable her to immerse herself in every department's affairs; of her adroit manipulation of the powers of patronage vested in her office, promoting and ennobling to keep her party loyal.

Her use of the Press Office and the Lobby system fell under the same category: chopping ministers off at the knees, whilst publicly appearing to give them her support; having her own passions and prejudices aired in the media as if they were Government policy, even if there was a majority in Cabinet against them; sometimes distancing herself from her own administration when it suited her to do so. As Mrs Thatcher pushed the powers of her office to the limit, so, in her shadow and in her service, Mr Ingham did the same with his. 'Future Prime Ministers,' according to Sir John Nott, 'have a lot to learn from it all.'[4]

On 9 November 1989, one year before he left office, Ingham attended a memorial service for the former political editor of the *Daily Mirror*, Victor Knight.

Assembled in the journalists' church of St Bride's on Fleet Street were many men whose paths had crossed his over the years: James Callaghan, who had come to speak for Douglas Houghton at the Sowerby by-election when Ingham was a sixteen-year-old junior reporter; Joe Haines, whom he had first met as an industrial correspondent; Edward Heath, upon whom he had poured such scorn in the *Leeds Weekly Citizen* and who had lately denounced the operations of the Number 10 Press Office as 'corrupt'; William Whitelaw, who had briefed Ingham after Cabinet meetings and who had seen those same operations at first hand; and Francis Pym, whom Ingham had dismissed as Mona Lott.

Heath, Whitelaw and Pym sat together – the Old Guard of a Tory Party whose day had passed. Haines watched them from the pew opposite, and was surprised, 'on this solemn occasion', to see Heath suddenly begin to laugh, the shoulders giving their familiar heave. He passed his order of service to Whitelaw, pointing to something. Whitelaw looked at it, then his face, too, broke into smiles. They let Pym in on the joke. It was extraordinary.

Ingham had been asked to give a reading from the Book of Proverbs, and it was only as the Hallelujah Chorus came to an end, and the Chief Press Secretary stepped into the pulpit, that Haines realized the source of their amusement. The text he was to read was printed on the service sheet. 'Get wisdom, get understanding,' began Ingham. 'Forget it not, neither decline from the words of my mouth.' And then he went on:

Forsake her not, and she shall preserve thee: love her and she
   shall keep thee.
Wisdom is the principal thing. Therefore get wisdom, and with
   all thy getting, get understanding.
Exalt her, and she shall promote thee: she shall bring thee to
   honour when thou dost embrace her.
She shall give to thine head a garland of grace; a crown of
   glory shall she deliver to thee.

Heath and Whitelaw were like schoolboys trying to suppress
a fit of the giggles at morning assembly. Ingham, 'even redder
in the face than usual', made his way back to his pew. Afterwards, Haines tried to find him, but he had already slipped
away through the throng of journalists and politicians and
was lost in the crowd on the busy London street.

APPENDIX

Prime Ministers' Press Secretaries

RAMSAY MACDONALD (1929–35)
STANLEY BALDWIN (1935–7)
NEVILLE CHAMBERLAIN (1937–40)

George Steward (1929–1940)
Official, Foreign Office News Department; appointed Press Relations Officer, 10 Downing Street, 1929; Chief Press Liaison Officer of Her Majesty's Government, 1937.

WINSTON CHURCHILL (1940–5)

No press adviser appointed.

CLEMENT ATTLEE (1945–51)

Francis Williams (1945–7)
Editor, *Daily Herald*, 1936–40; Controller of News and Censorship, Ministry of Information, 1941–5; appointed Adviser on Public Relations to the Prime Minister in 1945.

Philip Jordan (1947–51)
Journalist; civil servant; died in office.

Reginald Bacon (1951)
Journalist; Treasury civil servant.

WINSTON CHURCHILL (1951–5)

Thomas Fife Clarke (1952–5)
Lobby correspondent, Westminster press local newspapers; Principal Press Officer, Ministry of Health, 1939–49; Controller, Home Publicity, COI, 1949–52; appointed Adviser on Government Public Relations and Adviser on Public Relations to the Prime Minister, May 1952.

ANTHONY EDEN (1955–7)

William Clark (1955–6)
Diplomatic correspondent, *Observer*; resigned in November 1956 over his opposition to Eden's Suez policy.

HAROLD MACMILLAN (1957–63)

Harold Evans (1957–63)
Local newspaper reporter, 1930–9; Ministry of Information, 1942–5; Public Relations Officer, Colonial Office, 1945–57; appointed Public Relations Adviser to the Prime Minister, 1957.

ALEC DOUGLAS-HOME (1963–4)

John Groves (1964)
Lobby correspondent, Press Association and *The Times*, 1947–58; Head of Press Section, HM Treasury, 1958–62; Deputy Public Relations Adviser to the Prime Minister, 1962–4; Acting Adviser, 1964.

HAROLD WILSON (1964–70)

Trevor Lloyd-Hughes (1964–9)
Political correspondent, *Liverpool Daily Post*, 1951–64; appointed Press Secretary to the Prime Minister, 1964.

Joe Haines (1969–70)
Political correspondent, *Scottish Daily Mail*, 1960–4, the *Sun*, 1964–8; Deputy Press Secretary to the Prime Minister, Jan–June 1969; Chief Press Secretary, 1969. (Subsequently, Chief Press Secretary to the Leader of the Opposition, 1970–4.)

EDWARD HEATH (1970–4)

Donald Maitland (1970–3)
Diplomat. Head of News Department, Foreign Office, 1965–7; Principal Private Secretary to Foreign Secretary, 1967–9; Ambassador to Libya, 1969–70; appointed Chief Press Secretary, 10 Downing Street, 1970.

Robin Haydon (1973–4)
Diplomat. Head of Foreign Office News Department, 1967–71; High Commissioner, Malawi, 1971–3; Chief Press Secretary, 10 Downing Street, 1973.

HAROLD WILSON (1974–6)

Joe Haines (1974-6)

JAMES CALLAGHAN (1976–9)

Tom McCaffrey (1976–9)
Civil servant. Chief Information Officer, Home Office, 1966–71; Press Secretary, 10 Downing Street, 1971–2; Director of Information, Home Office, 1972–4; Head of News Department, Foreign Office, 1974–6; appointed Chief Press Secretary to the Prime Minister, 1976.

MARGARET THATCHER (1979–1990)

Henry James (1979)
Civil servant. Various posts in Government Information Service, including: Chief Information Officer, Ministry of Housing and Local Govt., 1969–70; Director of Information, Department of Environment, 1971–4; Director-General of the COI, 1974–8. Chief Press Secretary to the Prime Minister, May–Oct 1979.

Bernard Ingham (1979–1990)

JOHN MAJOR (1990–)

Gus O'Donnell (1990–)

PREFACE: 'Albion'

1 *Leeds Weekly Citizen*, 11 June 1965.
2 Ibid, 28 February 1964.
3 All references are drawn from the *Leeds Weekly Citizen*: to Heath, 11 February 1966; to Maudling, 24 July 1964 and 16 April 1965; to Hailsham, 25 December 1964; and to Powell, 20 January, 1967. ('I have given Powell the facts,' wrote Ingham on 27 January 1967. 'God alone can give him understanding. And it will be an all-forgiving deity that perseveres in that daunting task.')
4 Ibid: to house, 22 April 1966; to eleven-plus, 25 June 1965; to unions, 10 June 1966; to full employment, 13 March 1964; to socialism, 10 April 1964; to 'serfs', 5 June 1964; to 'fellow slaves', 25 September 1964; to the 'Golden Calf', 10 July 1964; to Mammon, 15 January 1965.
5 Ibid: to the Tory press, 21 August 1964; to a Labour press, 16 October 1964.
6 Ibid, 29 July 1966.

ONE: Dear Bernard

1 Quoted in Hugo Young, *One of Us* (Macmillan, 1989), p. 166.
2 Interview in the Halifax *Courier*, 20 July 1989.
3 Interview in *The Thatcher Decade: The Most Important Man*; BBC Radio 4, 18 April 1989.
4 Craig Brown, *A Year Inside* (Times Books, 1989), p. 124; Ingham speech to Calder High School, 13 January 1990.
5 The visitor, John Junor, recounts the episode in his autobiography, *Listening to the Midnight Tram* (Chapman, 1990), p. 309.
6 'She is not a relaxed person . . .': interview in the *Sunday Express*,

1 October 1989; 'an instinctive rapport . . .': interview in the *Sunday Telegraph*, 6 February 1983.

7 Speech to the Guild of Newspaper Editors, May 1983.

8 Interview in the *Sunday Express*, 1 October 1989.

TWO: Hebden Bridge

1 *Leeds Weekly Citizen*, 14 October 1966.

2 Ibid, 11 February 1966.

3 Ibid, 25 June 1965.

4 Speech to Calder High School, 13 January 1990.

5 *Hebden Bridge Times*, 5 December 1947.

6 Speech to Calder High School, 13 January 1990.

7 Speech at the opening of the Labour Party Christmas Fair; quoted in the *Hebden Bridge Times*, 13 December 1957. The fair was opened by 'Mr Peter Shore, BA, prospective Labour candidate for Halifax . . .'

8 *Hebden Bridge Times*, 27 April 1951.

9 Ibid, 20 May 1957.

10 Speech to the Worshipful Company of Stationers and Newspaper Makers, 5 February 1986.

11 Speech to the Guild of British Newspaper Editors, May 1983.

12 Speech to Calder High School, 13 January 1990.

13 Speech, 5 February 1986.

THREE: Reporter

1 *Hebden Bridge Times*, 9 November 1956.

2 Ibid, 21 February 1958.

3 Speech to Calder High School, 13 January 1990.

4 *Guardian*, 8 January 1963.

5 Ibid, 29 July 1963.

6 Ibid, 23 January 1964.

7 City of Leeds Labour Party papers deposited at the West Yorkshire Archive Service, Leeds; Box 41 'Nomination Papers'.

8 *Guardian*, 2 October 1963.

9 *Leeds Weekly Citizen*, 5 June 1964.

10 Ibid, 10 April and 7 August 1964.

11 Ibid, 9 October 1964.
12 Interview in the *Sunday Express*, 1 October 1989.
13 *Leeds Weekly Citizen*, 21 May 1965.
14 Speech to the Guild of British Newspaper Editors, May 1983.
15 *Leeds Weekly Citizen*, 21 December 1965.
16 Ibid, 4 February 1966.
17 Ibid, 28 January 1966 and 16 April 1965.
18 Ibid, 5 March 1966.
19 Ibid, 20 May 1966.
20 Ibid, 3 December 1965.
21 Ibid, 8 July 1966.
22 Ibid, 14 October 1966.
23 Ibid, 8 July 1966 and 3 March 1967.
24 Speech to the Worshipful Company of Stationers and
    Newspaper Makers, 5 February 1986.
25 Speech to the Guild of British Newspaper Editors, May 1983.

FOUR: Press Officer

 1 Tony Benn, *Against the Tide: Diaries 1973–76* (Hutchinson,
    1989), p. 452.
 2 Interview in the *Sunday Telegraph*, 6 February 1983.
 3 Ibid.
 4 *Leeds Weekly Citizen*, 17 February 1967.
 5 Clive Jenkins, *All Against the Collar* (London, 1990), p. 88.
 6 Barbara Castle, *The Castle Diaries 1964–70* (Weidenfeld and
    Nicolson, 1984), p. 443.
 7 Harold Evans, *Downing Street Diary* (Hodder and Stoughton,
    1981), p. 26.
 8 *Leeds Weekly Citizen*, 17 December 1965.
 9 Ibid, 4 June 1965.
10 Ibid, 11 March 1966.
11 Speech to the Guild of British Newspaper Editors, May 1983.
12 Lord Carrington, *Reflect on Things Past* (Collins, 1988),
    p. 262.
13 Quoted in Robert Jenkins, *Tony Benn: A Political Biography*
    (Writers and Readers, 1980), p. 227.

14 Antony Part, *The Making of a Mandarin* (André Deutsch, 1990), p. 172.
15 Tony Benn, op. cit., pp. 412–13.
16 *Guardian*, 3 July 1975.
17 Tony Benn, op. cit., p. 414.
18 Ibid, p. 416.
19 Ibid, p. 452.
20 *The Thatcher Decade: The Most Important Man*, BBC Radio 4, 18 April 1989.
21 Tony Benn, op. cit., p. 460.
22 Ibid, p. 463.
23 Ibid, pp. 463–4.
24 Ibid, p. 560.
25 Tony Benn, *Conflicts of Interest: Diaries 1977–80* (Weidenfeld and Nicolson, 1990), pp. 23–4.
26 Ibid, p. 257.
27 Ibid, p. 289.
28 Speech, 5 February 1986.

FIVE: Prime Minister's Press Secretary

1 Interview with the author.
2 Speech to the Media Society, November 1985.
3 Ibid.
4 Quoted in Richard Cockett, *Twilight of Truth* (Weidenfeld and Nicolson, 1989), p. 5.
5 Ibid, p. 6.
6 Ibid, p. 15.
7 William Clark, *From Three Worlds* (Sidgwick and Jackson, 1986), p. 163.
8 Ibid, p. 196.
9 Ibid, p. 209.
10 James Margach, *The Abuse of Power* (W. H. Allen, 1978), p. 118.
11 Harold Evans, *Downing Street Diary*, p. 28.
12 Marcia Williams, *Inside Number 10* (Weidenfeld and Nicolson, 1972), pp. 53–4.

13 Written evidence to the Lobby's inquiry into its own future,
    1986.
14 Quoted in Denis Healey, *The Time of My Life* (Michael Joseph,
    1989), p. 298.
15 'The Lobby Correspondent's Role', *Listener*, 21 January 1965.
16 Marcia Falkender, *Downing Street in Perspective* (Weidenfeld
    and Nicolson, 1983), p. 98.
17 Written evidence to the Lobby inquiry, 1986.
18 James Callaghan, *Time and Chance* (Collins, 1987), p. 407.
19 Written evidence to the Lobby inquiry, 1986.

SIX: The Yorkshire Rasputin

 1 Hansard, 7 February 1983.
 2 Speech to an IBA seminar, 28 October 1981.
 3 Ibid.
 4 Ibid.
 5 Andrew Thomson, *Margaret Thatcher: The Woman Within* (W.
    H. Allen, 1989), p. 226.
 6 Speech to the Media Society, November 1985.
 7 Jim Prior, *A Balance of Power* (Hamish Hamilton, 1986),
    p. 135.
 8 Ibid, p. 163.
 9 Hugo Young, op. cit., p. 229.
10 Prior, op. cit., p. 135.
11 Thomson, op. cit., p. 224.
12 Quoted in Thomson, p. 222.
13 Harold Evans, op. cit., p. 22.
14 Barbara Castle, op. cit., p. 631.
15 Hansard, 2 February 1982.
16 Quoted in *The Times*, 5 January 1988.
17 Norman St John Stevas, *The Two Cities* (Faber and Faber,
    1984), p. 83.
18 *Leeds Weekly Citizen*, 10 March 1967.
19 Evidence to the House of Commons Defence Committee, 9
    November 1982, para. 1718.
20 Quoted in Robert Harris, *Gotcha!* (Faber and Faber, 1983),

p. 23.

21 Ibid, p. 116.

22 Quoted in Derrick Mercer and others, *The Fog of War* (William Heinemann, 1987), p. 50.

23 Ibid, p. 161.

24 Evidence to the Commons Defence Committee, op. cit., para. 1724.

25 Harris, op. cit., p. 116.

26 *The Thatcher Decade: The Most Important Man*, BBC Radio 4, 18 April 1989.

27 Mercer, op. cit., p. 53.

28 Harris, op, cit., p. 118.

29 Ibid, p. 118.

30 Quoted in Hansard, 28 April 1986.

31 Quoted in Michael Cockerell and others, *Sources Close to the Prime Minister* (Macmillan, 1984), p. 74.

32 Interview in the *Sunday Telegraph*, 6 February 1983.

33 Quoted in Cockerell, op. cit., p. 181.

34 Roy Hattersley, *Press Gang* (Robson Books, 1983), p. 28.

35 Hansard, 7 February 1983.

SEVEN: Conducting the Orchestra

1 Tony Benn, *Conflicts of Interest: Diaries 1977–80*, pp. 368–9.

2 IBA seminar, 28 October 1981.

3 *Guardian*, 7 July 1980.

4 Quoted in Cockerell, op. cit., p. 49.

5 *The Times*, 7 September 1983.

6 Hansard, 31 October 1983.

EIGHT: Licensed to Leak

1 IBA seminar, 28 October 1981.

2 Hugo Young, op. cit., p. 356.

3 Alasdair Milne, *DG: The Memoirs of a British Broadcaster* (Hodder and Stoughton, 1988), p. 164.

4 John Junor, op. cit., p. 309.

5 Quoted in *The Times*, 6 August 1983.

6 Quoted in Cockerell, op. cit., p. 232.
7 Hansard, 15 January 1985.
8 William Keegan, *Mr Lawson's Gamble* (Hodder and Stoughton, 1989), p. 156.
9 *Independent Magazine*, 24 February 1990.
10 Hugo Young, op. cit., p. 443.
11 Fourth Report from the House of Commons Defence Committee, Session 1985–6, paragraph 174.
12 Defence Committee, op. cit., Armstrong's evidence, paragraph 1289.
13 Magnus Linklater and David Leigh, *Not With Honour* (Sphere, 1986), pp. 137–8.
14 Defence Committee, op. cit., paragraph 184.
15 Ibid, paragraph 193.
16 Hansard, 22 January 1986.
17 Defence Committee, op. cit., Armstrong's evidence, paragraph 1297.
18 Speech to Calder High School, 13 January 1990.
19 Linklater and Leigh, op. cit., p. 202.
20 Hansard, 28 April 1986.
21 Defence Committee, op. cit., paragraph 213.

NINE: The New Machiavelli

1 Interview with the author for *Panorama: Thatcher's 3000 Days*, transmitted on 5 January 1988.
2 Hansard, 7 February 1983.
3 *Guardian*, 13 May 1986.
4 Interview with BBC television's *On the Record* programme; the BBC declined to transmit the remark.
5 Norman Tebbit, *Upwardly Mobile* (Weidenfeld and Nicolson, 1988), p. 250.
6 Ibid.
7 Hansard, 2 February 1989.
8 Prior, op. cit., p. 134.
9 Speech to IBA seminar, 28 October 1981.
10 Speech to Calder High School, 13 January 1990.

11 *The Times*, 1 July 1985.
12 Speech to the Media Society, November 1985.
13 Quoted in the *Sunday Telegraph*, 18 October 1987.
14 *Spectator*, 11 March 1989.
15 Interview in the *Sunday Telegraph*, 31 May 1987.
16 Speech to the Worshipful Company of Stationers and Newspaper Makers, 5 February 1986.
17 Anthony Sampson, *The Changing Anatomy of Britain* (Hodder and Stoughton, 1982), p. 6.
18 Quoted in the *Observer*, 20 November 1988.
19 Quoted in the *Sunday Telegraph*, 20 November 1988.
20 Hansard, 22 November 1988.
21 *Daily Telegraph*, 24 November 1988.

TEN: Minister of Information

1 Quoted in National Audit Office report, Publicity Services for Government Departments (HMSO, 1 December 1989), p. 54.
2 Profile of Ingham in the *Sunday Times*, 7 May 1989.
3 Quoted in the *Daily Mail*, 27 July 1989.
4 Quoted in the *Independent*, 28 October 1989.
5 Hansard, Prime Minister's Questions, 31 October 1989.
6 Speech published in the *Sunday Times*, 11 February 1990.
7 BBC Radio 4 *Today* programme, 8 February 1990.
8 Sunday Times Insight Team, *Strike* (André Deutsch, 1985), p. 198.
9 Lord Young, *The Enterprise Years* (Headline, 1990), p. 143.
10 *Mail on Sunday*, 6 May 1990.
11 *Private Eye*, 6 July 1990.

CONCLUSION: Crowned With Glory

1 Speech to Calder High School, 13 January 1990.
2 *Halifax Evening Courier*, 24 December 1990.
3 *Mail on Sunday*, 2 December 1990.
4 *Panorama*, op. cit., 5 January 1988.

INDEX